HEROES

HEROES

U.S. MARINE CORPS
MEDAL OF HONOR WINNERS

MARC CERASINI

BERKLEY BOOKS, NEW YORK

B

A Berkley Book
Published by The Berkley Publishing Group
A division of Penguin Putnam Inc.
375 Hudson Street
New York, New York 10014

Copyright © 2002 by Martin H. Greenberg
Book design by Tiffany Kukec
Interior photos courtesy Official U.S. Marine Corps Photos,
via National Archives and Records Administration Collection

ISBN 0-425-18159-6

CONTENTS

PART FOUR
COLD WAR IN KOREA

PART FIVE
THE MARINES IN VIETNAM

FOREWORD

H EROES—a must-read for all Marines. The history of our glorious Corps from its inception through Vietnam, highlighting significant battles in which Marines and corpsmen distinguished themselves in combat and performed "above and beyond" the call of duty, actions that earned them the Medal of Honor. *Heroes* is an easy read, chronicling the growing pains experienced by the Marine Corps, and the attempt to do away with the Corps after several conflicts. It pays tribute to the professionalism and success of the true combat warriors who, through their drive, determination, and loyalty to Corps and country, made our Corps what it is today, and would make any Marine proud to share the title Marine with the giants of the Corps.

As a recipient of the Medal of Honor, I read with much interest the exploits of the Marines and Corpsmen who earned the Medal of Honor, men whom I've been associated with for thirty-five years. I never really knew what acts they performed that resulted in their being given our nation's highest award for valor in combat. Because when we're all together, we don't talk about war and the pain of combat, we don't look back, because we realize we can't change what is in the past. We look forward and discuss the future, because we can all influence tomorrow.

Heroes underscores the fact that those who have received the Medal of Honor are ordinary men. From every part of the country, every ethnic group, every religion, every creed and color. They were men who didn't want war, but who put their lives on hold, answered the call to arms, served our country with distinction, and did what needed to be done.

As the proud history of the United States Marine Corps is chronicled by recognizing the few combat warriors who were awarded the Medal of Honor, *Heroes* in fact recognizes and pays tribute to all those who have earned the title Marine, and fought as a member of a team to always accomplish their mission.

Those of us who wear the Medal of Honor don't consider ourselves heroes. We do, however, wear the medal with pride, as it honors those gallant warriors who fought by our side in defense of freedom, in defense of the American ideal. We are but caretakers of the medal for those great corpsmen and Marines we were fortunate to serve with. It recognizes their gallantry as much as the gallantry of those who received it.

—Colonel H. C. "Barney" Barnum USMC (Ret.),
past president, Congressional Medal of Honor Society
and Vietnam Medal of Honor recipient

THE CORPS

∎

T HE men and women of the United States Marine Corps are a special breed. Neither sailor nor soldier, Marines are amphibians—equally at home on land and at sea. Born before our nation, but without a distinctive mission, the Marine Corps has learned to take what they are given and make it their own. Often under-manned and ill-equipped, too often dispatched to perform nonmilitary, police, or political roles or thrust into military adventures that lack a clear goal, the Corps has learned to improvise, adapt, and overcome.

The Marine Corps has its own traditions and esprit de corps. From the green uniforms Marines wear to the ceremonial Mameluke swords they carry, their customs and culture are different from any other armed service in the world. The same can be said of the remarkable men and women who serve in the ranks. The fighting tradition of these "few good men" spans 225 years. The Marine Corps is older than these United States, and every fresh-faced Marine recruit sent to Parris Island or San Diego knows it. New recruits are steeped in the Corps history, traditions, and philosophies from the moment they step off that bus in the dark of night and begin boot camp training. The Corps' future leaders—those young officers educated at the Basic School at Quantico—also know the value of tradition and history, and they are taught the customs of the Corps even as they learn how to lead men into battle.

Marines have been called upon to defend America's interests on hundreds of occasions, in places mostly forgotten by all but historians. They have fought our nation's battles aboard ship, on far-flung beaches and shores, in jungles and deserts, and, when necessary, on our own hallowed ground.

As an arm of American expansion—or American "imperialism"—the fighting soldiers of the Marine Corps have been both our nation's representatives and its "big stick." During their long and glorious history, Marines have been hailed as heroes or vilified as interventionists, imperialists, and warmongers. "From the Halls of Montezuma to the shores of Tripoli," the citizens of many nations first encountered the growing power and influence of the United States of America through these green-clad ambassadors.

From their first beachhead assault on New Providence Island in the Bahamas in 1775, to the smoldering deserts of Iraq in 1992, to Somalia, and on to Bosnia, the Marine Corps has evolved to meet changing roles. From a ragtag group of revolutionaries firing from the masts of ships, the Corps has transformed itself into the most elite fighting force on earth. They accomplished this feat by constantly redefining their mission, their training, and their tactics, and by attracting—or sometimes conscripting—the finest military talent into their ranks.

By and large, modern Americans think of the Marine Corps with a mixture of awe and respect—respect for their rich history, the heroism of the men who served, and the price those men paid in blood. Today, a Marine earns our instant respect.

But this was not always the case.

There is a story about the early Corps that Marines like to tell—though the telling is no doubt laced with a sense of irony. It is a story that speaks volumes about the esteem in which the Corps was held by politicians and the other branches of the United States military.

After the Revolutionary War, so the story goes, the nation went about the task of downsizing its military forces. After months of negotiation between the Army and the Navy over how the remaining resources should be divided, all that was left was a pack of mules and two battalions of Marines. The Army and Navy commanders agreed to decide this final matter with the toss of a coin.

The Army commander won. He took the mules.

Though almost an orphan, from these humble beginnings would rise the Marine Corps we know today. A Corps of men—fighting men—men who are willing to lay down their lives for their country and for their fellow soldiers. We call men like these heroes.

This book is about heroes, the Marines who, through courage above and beyond the call of duty, have earned the Medal of Honor. Of course, there were Marine Corps heroes long before the first Medal of Honor was minted, and it would not be proper to exclude them simply because they did not earn a medal. So we must take our cue from the Marine Corps motto—*Semper Fidelis*—and be "always faithful" to the men who have given so much, expecting so little in return.

So this is really the story of *all* Marine Corps heroes, from every conflict the United States has participated in, from the Revolutionary War, to Vietnam, and beyond.

It is these heroes to whom this book is dedicated.

PART ONE

HUMBLE BEGINNINGS

"[I go] where the sound of thunder is . . ."

—Lieutenant General Alfred M. Gray, U.S. Marine Corps

CHAPTER ONE

THE CONTINENTAL MARINES: A TRADITION IS BORN

■

1775–1783

O LDER than the nation it helps to defend, the United States Marine Corps can trace its roots all the way back to the Revolutionary War.

In the autumn of 1775, Philadelphia was the center of a seething political rebellion that would change the world forever. Burdened by taxation dictated by a tyrannical autocracy in Britain, the American colonies declared their independence. But things were not going well for these new "Americans." Boston was occupied by the British, and without this vital New England port, the outside world was cut off from the seething center of the American rebellion. At the same time British soldiers and war materials were flowing into America. The British were better organized and better equipped than their colonial counterparts. They were also veterans who had fought against the best armies Europe had to offer.

Meanwhile, George Washington's beleaguered Continental Army had yet to win a victory—or even muster enough volunteers to fill its ranks. Worse, the Continental Army was always strapped for muskets, cannon, powder, shot and shell—not to mention food and adequate clothing.

Victory seemed impossible. Yet the longing for freedom had not been diminished. Meeting in Philadelphia, the Second Continental Congress went about the serious business of creating a nation and establishing the first representational democracy in history.

So it was that by the close 1775, the people of Philadelphia had become accustomed to innumerable displays of patriotic fervor. Daily, in taverns, inns, and on street corners, passionate orators harangued anyone who would listen with visions of a brilliant democratic future for mankind based on the rule of reason. Pamphleteers walked those crowded streets too, sharing their revolutionary ideas and not always agreeing. Philadelphia seethed with so much political activity that a detachment of soldiers, marching through the narrow streets beating snare drums, playing fifes, and waving banners seemed not all unusual.

But one particular unit, dispatched on a chill, blustery morning in late November, was charged with a historic mission. Organized by a fervent revolutionary named Samuel Nicholas, these soldiers were marching to enlist volunteers for a new service to be called the Continental Marines.

Benjamin Franklin, on a walk through the city, briefly encountered these fighting men. Writing of the incident, Franklin noted that their drums were emblazoned with a coiled rattlesnake and the phrase DON'T TREAD ON ME.

The first steps to create an American Marine Corps actually began a few weeks earlier. On November 10, 1775, the Continental Congress resolved that two battalions of American Marines "be inlisted and commissioned to serve for and during the present war between Great Britain and the colonies." This date stands today as the traditional birthday of the United States Marine Corps. A few weeks later, on November 28, John Hancock, the president of the Second Continental Congress, placed his signature on papers that commissioned Captain Samuel Nicholas the very first Marine Corps officer.

Nicholas, barely thirty, was a native Philadelphian, a Quaker, an innkeeper, and a blacksmith's son. He was known more for his love of fox hunting and fishing than any maritime skills he may have possessed. And Quakers—even those raised in sophisticated Philadelphia—did not generally hold military ambitions. Most were pacifists.

Captain Samuel Nicholas was a patriotic man. Whatever his qualms about war, he took his duties as a Marine quite seriously and was determined to raise his quota of Marines. He immediately dispatched fife and drum corps through the streets of Philadelphia to recruit volunteers.

Legend has it that these first recruits later gathered at Peg Mullan's Beef-Steak House on the corner of King Street and Tun Alley—Tun's Tavern. But Marine Corps historian Edwin Simmons argues that the real recruiting rendezvous was more likely a tavern called the Conestoga Waggon on Market Street. The Waggon was owned by members of Nicholas's family and he probably had free rein of the premises.

Unfortunately, Captain Nicholas managed to raise only five companies of Marines by December. Most volunteers were from Pennsylvania, but a third of them—nearly a hundred men—came down from Rhode Island. Early the next year, Rhode Island native William Jones began a second recruitment drive with an ad he placed in the *Providence Gazette*. Jones asked for "a few good Men" to volunteer for "a short Cruize"—thus creating a Marine Corps recruitment slogan that has endured for two centuries.

By the end of January 1776, Captain Samuel Nicholas commanded five companies—about three hundred Marines. While he was out recruiting them, the Continental Navy was busy trying to assemble a squadron of ships for their first naval action. In this era of wood and sail, before the invention of steam engines or iron hulls, Marines and warships traveled together. Generally the sailors did the work and Marines preserved shipboard discipline and did much of the fighting.

The Continental Marines were modeled after their British counterparts, the Royal Marines. Both Corps shared many of the same traditions and performed the same duties. The Royal Marines had served with pride for over a century before the American Revolution. British Marines not only preserved order and discipline aboard ship, they also gave their vessel a *national* character. Like the Navy officers in command, the British Marines wore uniforms. The sailors of this period did not. In fact, many sailors serving aboard British warships were foreign-born, and most were pressed unwillingly into service by "press gangs" who roamed coastal towns, dragging young men off to sea. Unfortunately, when guns were fired and men began to die, these reluctant sailors proved unreliable. Marines were required at each cannon to maintain ship's discipline and keep the sailors at their posts. British Marines also climbed the mast, to perch among the sails and fire their muskets at the officers and sailors on the deck of an enemy ship, often the prelude to boarding her.

During the Revolutionary War, most American sailors were volunteers—there were no press gangs in the Colonies. America was a coastal nation and there were adequate numbers of able-bodied and experienced seamen to be found. Though colonial sailors lacked combat experience, they could generally be relied upon in a fight. But American Marines were still required to carry muskets and grenades to the "fighting tops" where they raked the decks of enemy ships with a deadly fire.

THE FIRST AMPHIBIOUS LANDINGS

Commodore Esek Hopkins, one of the Rhode Island volunteers, had spent forty years at sea. Blustery and profane, he led a hard and adventurous life. A longtime merchant sea captain and former privateer during the French and Indian War, Hopkins brought much-needed organizational skills, military experience, and eight ships with him when he jointed the Continental Navy. Like the rest of the fledgling fleet, most of Hopkins's vessels were converted merchantmen, ranging from the twenty-four-gun, 450-ton *Alfred* to the tiny six-gun *Fly*.

Commodore Hopkins was given full command of these refitted vessels on December 3, 1775. He was also given command of Captain Nicholas and a Marine squadron. Nicholas served aboard Hopkins's flagship *Alfred* as senior Marine Corps officer. Captain Dudley Saltonstall of Connecticut was commissioned as *Alfred*'s captain, but he deferred all major decisions to the more experienced and higher-ranked Hopkins. Altogether Commodore Hopkins commanded 1,500 men, including 300 Continental Marines.

In early February, Hopkins went to war. His original mission was to clear the Chesapeake and the waters off the Carolinas of all British warships—an impossible task with a mere eight vessels. But Commodore Hopkins's orders were flexible, and he was also ordered to "follow such Courses as your best Judgement shall suggest." Hopkins devised a daring scheme to carry America's war for independence into enemy territory. Part of his plan involved the first amphibious landing made by American Marines on a hostile shore. It happened in the Bahamas.

On March 1, 1776, Hopkins's fleet assembled off Great Abaco Island to attack

New Providence, a rich British crown colony with a sizable population of British soldiers, planters, merchants, and bureaucrats. A landing party of Marines and sailors was formed to attack the stone strongpoints on the island, Fort Nassau and Fort Montagu. The original plan called for the capture of the town of Nassau and the British ships moored at her docks. Unfortunately, the American fleet had been spotted by vigilant British sailors the day before and the element of surprise was lost. Commodore Hopkins revised the mission, focusing instead on the capture of 600 barrels of gunpowder the British Navy had stored on the island. On the sunny Sunday afternoon of March 3, 1776, American Marines rowed ashore on whaleboats in plain sight of the enemy. Miraculously, no one seemed to notice. The Marines' landing on the beach was unopposed, so the troops assembled and moved inland toward the first fort.

Twenty-eight-year-old Lieutenant John Trevett, the oldest son of a seafaring family in Rhode Island, led one contingent of Marines. Captain Nicholas led the other. When the invaders were finally spotted as they marched to Fort Montagu, the British governor sent out an emissary under a flag of truce to learn the Americans' intentions. Captain Nicholas explained that his Marines were there for the military stores, and meant the town and its inhabitants no harm. The emissary withdrew, and the pitifully few defenders at Fort Montagu fired two or three shots at the Americans to satisfy honor. Then they spiked their cannons and abandoned the ramparts. The Marines kicked in the gates and occupied the fort as the British fled out the back door.

Unfortunately, it didn't take long to turn this triumph into an embarrassing defeat. Because it was late afternoon, Captain Nicholas decided to spend the night at Fort Montagu before mounting an attack on the second fort. This blunder gave the British enough time to load the bulk of the gunpowder aboard a waiting warship. And because Commodore Hopkins failed to use one of his ships to blockade the harbor, this British vessel escaped on the first tide with the precious cargo of gunpowder in its hold.

At daybreak Monday, March 4, Captain Nicholas marched his men into the town of Nassau and demanded the keys to the second fort, which were duly handed over. The Marines took possession of Fort Nassau without firing a shot, but inside they found only twenty-four casks of powder—not the hundreds they had been expecting. They *did* capture forty-six cannons and a brace of smaller guns, but the richest cargo had eluded them. On the voyage home, Hopkins's fleet met the British warship *Glasgow*. During the ensuing ninety-minute sea battle, eleven Americans were killed, four of them Marines. Four Brits were killed, and the *Glasgow* was so badly damaged it had to limp to Newport for repairs.

When Hopkins's Gunpowder Expedition returned to Philadelphia, they were greeted as heroes. But the euphoria lasted until a board of inquiry was convened. Hopkins's superiors soon demanded to know why the commodore failed to capture the gunpowder. His answers did not satisfy them and Hopkins was dismissed from military service. Despite a fine performance by the Continental Marines, the board had few kind words to say about Captain Nicholas or the men under his command.

On January 27, 1778, Captain John Trevett returned to New Providence Island. His objective was the capture a British brig *Mary* that was docked at Fort Nassau.

▪ **The Fighting Leatherneck**

Marine drill instructors have been telling recruits for two centuries that green was chosen as the color for the Marine Corps uniform because green is the traditional color worn by riflemen. Though this legend is quite inspirational, it is probably false. According to Marine Corps General Edwin Howard Simmons "green seems to have been chosen simply because green cloth was plentiful in Philadelphia." This is likely true, because the Continental Marines were not riflemen. They carried muskets—British-built Tower muskets early in the war, and French-built Charleville muskets later on.

During the Revolutionary War, a local Pennsylvania militia group called the Associators wore green uniforms. Perhaps their attire was also an inspiration for the Marine Corps' color choice. As part of their uniforms, the Associators sported a black leather stock around their necks. This stiff, uncomfortable stock was adopted as part of the first Continental Marine uniform as well. Worn by enlisted men and officers, this accoutrement may have served a useful purpose. Some believe it was there to protect a man's throat from a cutlass slash; others think the stock was used to keep the soldier's head erect during parades and long marches. This hot, uncomfortable stock remained a part of the Marine Corps uniform for a century, and inspired one of the Marine Corps best-known and most enduring nicknames—Leathernecks.

The *Mary* was a prize in itself, but there were also rumors that American prisoners were being held in the town. It was after midnight when Trevett and twenty-six Marines rowed ashore. This time the element of surprise was with the Americans and they stunned the troops guarding the fort with a swift, silent, deadly assault.

When dawn arrived, the people of Nassau were unaware they had been invaded until Trevett and his men turned the fort's cannons toward the city streets and raised the American flag. Panic swept the island and Fort Montagu fell in short order. The Marines captured the *Mary* without firing a shot and released thirty American sailors and civilians who had been captured months before. The Marines sailed away aboard the *Mary* with the rescued Americans and a hold stuffed with British gunpowder.

Captain Trevett returned home a hero and served with distinction throughout the Revolutionary War and beyond. He would lose his right eye during a sea battle in 1780, but continued to serve the cause of freedom despite this injury. First and foremost, the invasion of New Providence Island was a victory for the Marine Corps. Though the first amphibious landing in the Bahamas was deemed a waste of time, this second landing was a rousing success.

DEFEAT AT FORT GEORGE

After the failure of the Gunpowder Expedition and his commander's dismissal from the Navy, Captain Samuel Nicholas was surprised to learn he had been promoted to major—the highest rank any Marine would attain during the War for Independence. His new assignment was to recruit four more companies. The drive began in Philadelphia, where innkeeper Peg Mullen's young son Robert was given a captain's commission in one of the new companies. This time Mullen's Tun Tavern in Philadelphia really *was* used as the Marines' rendezvous—earning its rightful place in the history of the Corps.

Now Continental Marines were issued regulation uniforms—green coats with white facings, a round hat with the left brim pinned to the crown with a cockade. As the War for Independence progressed, green-clad Continental Marines would fight at George Washington's side at the Battle of Trenton and on the western frontier. They would be dispatched on a campaign to control the Mississippi River, where they would raid British homes, bases, and other property along its muddy shores. In duels on the high seas, in battles along the river, and in the bloody fight for control of the Great Lakes, Marines would fill the ranks of boarding parties used to capture enemy vessels and fire their muskets from the fighting tops. On land, Marines would serve as artillerymen, as sentinels, and as fast-attack, hit-and-run raiders. But over the course of the War for Independence, the Marines would conduct only one more amphibious landing. Tragically, the battle to capture Fort George was an unmitigated disaster.

In spring of 1779, the British were threatening to invade the American colonies from across the border in Canada. A British force moving south from Halifax, Nova Scotia, began construction of a new strong point. Fort George was near the mouth of the Penobscot River, in an area that is now part of Maine. The fortress was built to protect Loyalists in New England from colonial aggression and to provide a staging area for further military incursions into American territory. The Continental Congress immediately dispatched three Navy warships with orders to capture Fort George. This force included 300 Marines under the command of Captain John Welsh, a volunteer officer added to the muster during the second round of recruitment.

On July 16, British and American warships clashed off the coast of Maine. After a two-hour battle, the British were forced to retreat up the Penobscot. Some of the land-based fortifications the British had occupied—specifically Fort Nautilus Island near the entrance to the harbor and Fort George on the main land—were suddenly vulnerable. Captain Welsh and his Continental Marines quickly departed the sloop *Providence* and landed on Nautilus Island. They routed the Royal Marines, then made preparations to drive the British forces out of Fort George.

At dawn on July 28, the Marines and soldiers of the Massachusetts Militia assaulted the partially constructed British fort from two fronts. The Massachusetts Militia took the left approach over land. The Marines rowed from Nautilus Island and came ashore on the right flank—to face an almost vertical climb to the enemy-held fortifications above them. For what must have seemed like an eternity the Marines—without rope or tackle—slowly crawled up the rocky face of the cliffs under the blazing guns of more than 300 British regulars. The closer the Americans got to the fort, the more accurate the British fire became. Captain Welsh and eight other Marines were killed outright. But amazingly, some of Americans actually reached the top of the walls and onto the battlements, where they clashed hand to hand with the British.

When the Massachusetts Militia failed to capture their end of the fort, the Marines had no choice but to retreat. Brigadier General Solomon Lovell, commander of the Massachusetts Militia, continued his halfhearted siege of Fort George for three bloody weeks, giving the British enough time to dispatch a fleet from New York harbor to rout the Americans.

Like the British fleet they had defeated, the American warships were forced to retreat up the Penobscot River. All but three American vessels were destroyed, the rest captured. The Americans were forced to melt into the Maine wilderness, where they evaded enemy forces and hostile Indians as they made their way back to friendly territory in New England. Fort George remained in British hands for the duration of the Revolutionary War.

The attack was such an unmitigated disaster that the Marines would not attempt another amphibious invasion until the Mexican War fifty years later. But despite the tragic outcome at Fort George, the officers and enlisted men of the Continental Marines had performed courageously. They had faced enemy fire during an amphibious landing for the first time, had made a near-impossible climb into the teeth of British guns, and took and held the battlements until their position became untenable and they were compelled to retreat by circumstances beyond their control.

THE MARINES INVADE GREAT BRITAIN

Marines played a vital part in the many duels fought in European waters by Captain John Paul Jones, the first great naval hero in American history. On April 22, Jones sailed his ship *Ranger* across the North Atlantic to Great Britain and anchored at Whitehaven, on the Irish Sea. At midnight, Jones led a raiding party ashore. The force consisted of two fifteen-man boats packed with sailors and armed Continental Marines.

Captain Jones commanded one boat, Marine Lieutenant Samuel Wallingford the other. They rowed for three hours in near-total darkness and rough seas until they reached the British shore. The Americans easily took both defensive batteries at Whitehaven and captured the soldiers stationed there. Their plan was to set fire to the British ships in the harbor, but the trip across the choppy seas had extinguished their torches. Undeterred, Jones boldly entered a public house, obtained another torch, and set fire to the largest British vessel in the harbor. As the ship began to burn, one of Jones's prisoners—an Irishman serving with British regulars—broke away from the American sailors guarding him and began banging on the doors of the village, warning the townsfolk that Yankee pirates had arrived. At daylight, a group of armed townsfolk filled the street. Captain Jones held off the mob with a pistol while he and his men made their escape.

That same morning, Jones staged a second raid on the estate of the Earl of Selkirk on St. Mary's Isle. He hoped to take the earl hostage—a pawn to be used for prisoner exchange. Pretending to be a Royal Navy press gang, Jones discovered from the estate's gardener that the earl had gone to take the waters at Buxton. Undeterred, Captain Jones gave his men permission to enter the manor and grab the earl's silver. Sailing master David Callam and Marine Lieutenant Wallingford entered the manor house with small detachment, interrupting the countess at breakfast. The Americans grabbed the silver along with the tea settings and returned to the *Ranger*. The Countess of Selkirk later wrote that Jones's sailing master had "a vile blackguard look," but the other soldier was "a civil young man in a green uniform." Her shocking tale of a personal brush with piracy became the major topic of conversation among the upper classes for the rest of the social season.

▪ *French-Irish Marines and American Blood*

Perhaps the oddest collection of Marines who ever served in the Revolutionary War fought alongside John Paul Jones aboard the *Bonhomme Richard* during what was to be the commodore's final battle. Jones commanded a squadron of five warships, all with a complement of Marines aboard. But the largest detachment was found on Jones's own flagship.

Commanded by Lieutenant Edward Stack—an officer in the Irish Regiment of the French Army on paid "leave" with the Americans to help fight the British—the 137 Marines aboard the *Bonhomme Richard* were all Irish-born, British-hating members of the French Marine Corps.

Uniformed in red and white instead of traditional green, Stack and his men were nevertheless commissioned as American Marines for the duration of the war. Though there were always many foreign-born recruits in the American Marine Corps, Lieutenant Stack and his French-Irish Marines were truly unique in the annals of war.

Commanding the second-largest vessel in Jones's fleet—a warship called the *Alliance*—was Captain Pierre Landais, the only Frenchman to be given charge of a Continental Navy vessel during this conflict. Unfortunately, Captain Landais's performance was less than stellar.

On the afternoon of September 23, 1779, Commodore Jones and his squadron met a convoy of forty-one British merchant vessels and warships in the North Sea, escorted by a brand-new fifty-gun frigate, *Serapis,* and a twenty-gun sloop of war, *Countess of Scarborough.* When the British spotted the Americans bearing down on them, the merchant ships fled. Then the *Countess of Scarborough* engaged the American ship *Pallas* while the *Bonhomme Richard* sailed for the larger warship *Serapis.* Captain Landais kept the *Alliance* out of range of British cannon, leaving the *Bonhomme Richard* to fight the British warship solo.

During the battle, Marine Lieutenant Richard Dale commanded the guns while Marine Lieutenant James O'Kelly and twenty Marines were stationed on the poop deck. In the fighting tops, Lieutenant Stack led four sailors and fifteen French-Irish Marine sharpshooters in clearing *Serapis*'s tops of Royal Marines then raking her decks with gunfire. Jones quickly moved into range and fired a broadside into *Serapis.* The British returned fire, and

within an hour most of Jones's twelve-pound guns were blown out of action. But Stack's Marines had managed to clear the *Serapis*'s tops and decks—which were now slick with blood and littered with British corpses.

Jones had his ship lashed to the British vessel and the two warships repeatedly fired into each other while their crews battled on the decks. Stack and his Marines swung into the *Serapis*'s rigging, even as the *Bonhomme Richard* was pierced by cannon fire. Jones's flagship reeled under the British guns and was in danger of sinking. But Stack's Marines held their ground in the *Serapis*'s rigging as both ships began to burn. The surviving British tried to board the American flagship, but were repelled by deadly musket fire from Stack's Marines firing down at the British from their own mast. When the British captain appeared on deck with a flag of truce and demanded that the Americans surrender, Commodore Jones answered with one of the most famous quotes in naval history: "I have not yet begun to fight!"

The rate of fire increased on both sides. The *Bonhomme Richard,* burning and listing, was down to just three guns. It was then that the Marines turned the tide of battle. Remaining on the *Serapis*'s rigging as the two ships continued to burn, Stack and his Marines mowed down any British sailor or Royal Marine who emerged from the hold. Finally an American sailor dropped a grenade into an open hatch and detonated the gunpowder stored in the *Serapis*'s belly. Twenty British sailors died as the *Serapis* reeled from secondary blasts that ripped apart her hull. Suddenly the *Alliance* appeared. Captain Landais ordered three broadsides to be fired, even though the American and British warships were still lashed together. *Alliance*'s guns did as much damage to the *Bonhomme Richard* as they did to the *Serapis,* killing Lieutenant O'Kelly where he stood.

Finally the *Serapis* struck her colors and surrendered. But it was too late to save the *Bonhomme Richard.* Still afire, with five feet of seawater in her hold, she sank on the morning of April 25 long after the crew abandoned her. The American flag was still flying above her deck as she slipped beneath the waves. But despite the dubious performance of the *Alliance* and her French commander, Commodore John Paul Jones had won the single greatest sea battle of the Revolutionary War. He could not have done it without the help of the French-Irish Marines, the most diverse and peculiar Marines who ever fought in an American war.

A day later Jones and his men got into an hour-long battle with the British sloop of war *Drake*. The British lost twenty-five men, including their captain—who was killed by a Continental Marine sharpshooter firing from the "fighting tops." Captain Jones made his escape from British waters and sailed in triumph back to America, where John Paul Jones bought up the countess's silver at auction and had it shipped it back to her, along with a personal letter of apology. He did not tell the countess that Marine Lieutenant Wallingford—the "civil young man in a green uniform"—had been killed by a British Marine in the bloody duel with the *Drake*.

THE END OF THE CONTINENTAL MARINES

The 1780 defense of Charleston, South Carolina, was the last battle fought by the Continental Marines in the War for Independence. It ended in defeat when British forces captured the city. Eighteen months later the British forces under General Cornwallis surrendered. On November 31, 1782, the Treaty of Paris was signed, ending hostilities between Great Britain and her former colony.

Because the Founding Fathers had good reason to fear a standing army under the command of a tyrant—be he king, prime minister, or president—they decided to disband all but a token military force when the War for Independence ended. While it was deemed prudent to keep a tiny Army, the Continental Congress voted not to retain any ships of the line or armed frigates. Without ships, America didn't need Marines, and the last officer was discharged in September 1783. It looked as if the glorious history of the Marine Corps was over almost before it had a chance to begin.

CHAPTER TWO

"ANOTHER SHABBY SET OF ANIMALS"

▪

1794–1814

WITHIN a decade after the last Continental Marine was released from duty, the American people discovered that a nation without a military was an easy prey for tyrants. That lesson was taught at the hands of pirates and kidnappers on the opposite side of the world. Trouble began when Algerian corsairs who plied the waters off the coast of Africa began to prey on American shipping. Piracy threatened free trade and the economic health of the young nation, so something had to be done. But the United States had no Army, no Navy, nor a Marine Corps to protect the lives and property of her citizens.

The Naval Act of 1794 was meant to correct this deficiency. But the law had been controversial from the moment it was proposed. Some considered it an act of aggression and resisted the formation of an organized militia. Others wondered how they could afford a large Navy without imposing burdensome taxation—which had caused the American Revolution in the first place. In the end, reason prevailed, the funds were found, and the act approved.

Hardly the starting gun that set off a burgeoning arms race, the Naval Act of 1794 authorized the construction of a mere six frigates—none of them the large, heavily armed "ships of the line" the European powers deployed for "defense." Six sleek new frigates, all with fewer than fifty guns, were deemed sufficient to revitalize the United States Navy and defend America's interests. But before those ships could be constructed, the United States was forced by circumstance to sign a treaty with the Moroccan pirates, who had seized a number of unescorted American merchant ships, taken American citizens hostage, and were threatening to sell them into slavery. The terms of this humiliating treaty cost the United States government over a million dol-

---

▪ Hand-Me-Down Blues

When the United States Marine Corps was established on July 11, 1798, they were given blue uniforms. Little did they know that they were actually hand-me-downs left over from "Mad Anthony" Wayne's legion. Wayne, a Revolutionary War veteran, led a two-year campaign against a coalition of Native American tribes that ended in the 1794 victory at the Battle of Fallen Timbers in Ohio. Four years later uniforms left over from Wayne's campaign turned up in a government warehouse. Marines were issued these uniforms, which historians believe was the origin of the Corps "dress blues."

This act of governmental financial prudence may have begun another, less glorious Marine Corps tradition. Because Marines are an expeditionary force meant to be followed by reinforcements, they have never really had an infrastructure of their own. Marines have always shared their vehicles, weapons, supplies, and technologies with the other armed services. In the best of times, that meant that the Corps got the same top-of-the-line material the other armed services were issued. In the worst of times, it meant that the Corps has had to make do with outmoded weapons and material no longer needed by the other services.

In the short war in Korea in 1871, Marines discovered that the "barbarians and bandits" they fought were equipped with better weapons than their own. That didn't prevent them from winning the fight, but it sure hurt their sense of pride. Nearly a century later, during World War II, the Marines who landed on Guadalcanal were carrying the same ancient rifles their fathers carried at Belleau Wood twenty-five years before. The Japanese defenders on the island outnumbered them, and were well entrenched. Yet the Marines prevailed, because victory at Guadalcanal—as in the victory against the Tiger Hunters of Korea—was not achieved through the quality of the Marine Corps firepower, but because of their tenacious fighting spirit.

---

lars in ransom and bribes, but American shipping was safe from further aggression for a time.

The ink was not even dry on the treaty with the Algerian pirates when the French began to harass American shipping. In an eighteen-month period between July 1796 and December 1797, more than 300 American merchant vessels were captured or looted by French warships. Since the end of the Revolutionary War, America's warm relationship with France had cooled considerably. The tyranny of Maximilien Robespierre and the bloody Reign of Terror that followed the French Revolution troubled many intellectuals in America. Now France's insistence that the United States help them wage continuous war on the British further dimmed America's enthusiasm for her onetime ally. The American people believed they were heeding George Washington's warning against getting involved in "foreign entanglements." But after the assistance they had provided during the War for Independence, the French regarded America's neutrality as a betrayal.

Though the Naval Act had been controversial, by the time the first ships were ready to sail, the slogan "Millions for defense, but not one cent for tribute!" drowned out the voices of the timid. Now that America had a Navy, it needed shipboard Marines to keep ship's discipline, so on July 11, 1798, an act of Congress resolved that "there shall be raised a battalion, to be called the Marine Corps."

President John Adams appointed William Ward Burrows, a stocky middle-aged lawyer from South Carolina to head this Corps. New Marine recruits were issued blue uniforms with red facings and a round hat edged in yellow—the beginning of the Marine Corps' traditional "dress blues."

In 1798, Philadelphia was still the nation's capital, so it was there that Commandant Burrows established Marine Corps headquarters. The office of the Marine Corps would remain in Philadelphia until 1800, when headquarters were transported to "Eighth Street and I" in Washington, D.C.

Soon a detachment of Marines was assigned to each of the Navy's vessels. These Marines were a coarse, rowdy, and sometimes combative lot. Culled from the streets of the major seaport cities or recruited from the wilderness frontier, the first United States Marines were a tough and unsentimental, hard-drinking and hard-fighting lot. In this respect, they were much like the sailors of this period. But most Marines weren't sailors, they were dockworkers, backwoodsmen, failed settlers, hunters and trappers—landlubbers with few maritime skills. But these rustics were among the best marksmen in the world.

CAPTAIN DANIEL CARMICK'S "ANIMALS"

Captain Daniel Carmick was a young man from Philadelphia who served as one of the Corps first commissioned officers. An urbane, educated man born in one of America's most sophisticated cities, Carmick was not sure what to make of the rough lot he was assigned to command. After he reviewed his fifty-man detachment—the Marines aboard the frigate U.S.S. *Constitution*—Captain Carmick wrote in a letter to Commandant Burrows: "I think it is not possible to produce such another shabby set of animals." They weren't pretty, but Carmick soon learned that this "shabby set of animals" could fight. The new Marine Corps would draw first blood in the Caribbean.

During the troubles with the French, the United States government decided to help the former slaves of Haiti overthrow their French oppressors. The Haitians were led by a black physician, general, and former slave named François-Dominique Toussaint-Louverture. General Louverture had already expelled most of the French and Spanish forces from the island of Hispaniola—which was roughly divided into two nations, Haiti and the Dominican Republic. But several coastal ports and fortified towns were still controlled by Europeans, and the general had not been able to dislodge these old-world powers from his shores.

When the U.S.S. *Constitution* arrived in the Caribbean, Navy Captain Silas Talbot's orders were to offer practical help to the Haitians and obstruct further French incursions into the region. In 1800, a Marine landing party from the *Constitution* came ashore at the seaport town of Puerto Plata on the northern edge of the Dominican Republic. Led by Captain Carmick, these Marines immediately captured the *Sandwich,* a British sloop taken by the French and converted into a privateer. Then the Marines waded through neck-deep water to capture the French gun emplacement on the other side of town. They swiftly overran the surprised garrison, chased the soldiers away, and spiked the cannon. Mission accomplished, Captain Carmick and his men quickly refitted the *Sandwich* and sailed away with a store of sugarcane and coffee in her hold. Writing about this incident later, Carmick altered his opinion of his Marines: "The men went on board like devils," he proclaimed with pride.

After this daring raid, tensions increased between France and the United States.

But before a state of war could be declared, Napoleon Bonaparte seized power in France. Fortunately, his plan for European domination did not include a simmering, undeclared war with the United States. Negotiations began almost immediately, and peace between the two nations was restored. Continued talks with the French would result in the largest real estate deal in history—the Louisiana Purchase.

THE BARBARY PIRATES

Algiers, Morocco, Tripoli, and Tunis were predatory political entities that survived by pirating American and European shipping. The corsairs they produced had been a thorn in everyone's side since the pirate leader Barbarossa seized Algiers in 1510 and established an outlaw state. For centuries, the Barbary pirates had restricted their activities to the Mediterranean Sea. But a treaty signed by Great Britain and Portugal in 1793 gave Algerian warships free rein to attack ships on the Atlantic Ocean—so long as they left British and Portuguese vessels unmolested. The Algerians stepped up their piratical activities after this agreement was signed, capturing hundreds of American merchant ships and selling their crews and passengers into slavery.

By 1803, the United States government had finally had enough. President Thomas Jefferson stretched his executive authority to the limit, dispatching America's brand-new fleet of warships to the Mediterranean in a "show of force." This was as far as the president could risk going without creating a constitutional crisis or asking Congress to declare war, but he wanted to go further. For several weeks, the United States Navy paraded her ships off the coast of North Africa, hoping to intimidate the pirates. When the fleet departed, the *Philadelphia,* commanded by Captain William Bainbridge, was left behind to blockade the port city of Tripoli.

Yusef Karamanli, the Pasha of Tripoli, had actually declared war on the United States in May 1804. It was a ploy to extort money from the government in Washington, and his pirates had been particularly aggressive in attacking American ships since that declaration was made. The blockade by the thirty-six-gun frigate *Philadelphia* effectively stopped Tripolitan piracy, but only until disaster struck. On October 31, as the *Philadelphia* was chasing down a pirate ship, it ran aground on an uncharted sand reef off the coast, within sight of Tripoli. Helpless, the American frigate was quickly surrounded by Tripolitan gunboats. The pirates had been waiting for the chance to rid themselves of the Americans. Now they smelled blood.

For the next four hours, gunboats fired round after round at the stranded American frigate—often at point-blank range. Captain Bainbridge did everything he could to lighten the ship—including pitching the cannons overboard—but they could not float the ship free of the reef. Miraculously, no crewmen had yet been killed, so Bainbridge struck his colors and surrendered. He and his crew of 300 men—including 43 Marines—were paraded through the city in chains. They would languish in a Tripolitan prison for the next year and a half. After the battle, the pirates freed the *Philadelphia* from the reef and berthed her under the protective guns of the stone fortress at Tripoli Harbor.

▪ *The Pirates of Tripoli*

Tripoli is now the capital city of Libya, but in 1551, this port in Northern Africa was part of the Ottoman Empire and a pirate stronghold. Governed by powerful *beys*—warlords—who commanded large tribal armies or naval forces, Tripoli concentrated its military might on the coast, allowing the interior of the country to be ruled by nomadic tribes. In 1711, Ahmed Karamanli, a cavalry commander of mixed Turkish and Tripolitan blood, seized power. The Ottoman sultan was forced by circumstances to recognize Ahmed's rule, and the Karamanli family dominated Tripoli's government until 1835.

Tripolitan pirates operated in the Mediterranean, off the coast of Italy. They preyed on Venetian and Sicilian merchant shipping. But during the seventeenth century, the Tripolitan pirates became embroiled in a larger conflict involving Great Britain, France, and the Netherlands, against the more powerful pirate havens at Algiers and Tunisia. Several treaties with European powers, and a few visits by French and British warships, tamed Tripolitan pirate activities for over a century. But in 1754, Ali Karamanli became pasha and increased piratical activities across the board. He treated corsair captains as national heroes, and encouraged aggression against nations that refused to pay him an annual tribute in gold. The Napoleonic Wars further reduced Britain and France's vigilance, and the pirates of Tripoli became more bold. But because they still feared the naval powers of Europe, this new breed of pirate only preyed on ships from smaller nations—including vessels flying the flag of the newly established United States of America.

Encouraged by his initial success, Yusef Karamanli declared war on the United States in 1801. This was the beginning of his downfall, and the Barbary War that followed broke the back of the Karamanli regime. During the brief war with the United States, most of Tripoli's piratical fleet was destroyed and its ports were effectively blockaded. The European nations stopped paying their annual tribute, and the pasha's government soon went bankrupt. To maintain order, Yusef Karamanli was forced to borrow heavily from English and French banks. Finally, his government could not repay its debts and collapsed. The Ottoman sultan stepped in and removed the Karamanli family from power and placed their own ruler on the throne.

Though Libya became an independent nation in 1951, the government in Tripoli did not reemerge on the global stage until the 1960s, when rich oil reserves were discovered in the deserts of the country. Under the current regime of Muammar al-Qaddafi, Libya has become a major sponsor of international terrorism. The current anti-Western, anti-American regime in Libya is not so very different from those old-fashioned pirates who plied the waters off the shores of Tripoli two centuries ago.

In America, a public outcry ensued, so Jefferson dispatched the entire fleet to the Mediterranean—including 400 of the Corps' 500 Marines. Captain Edward Preble commanded the American fleet, and decided to destroy the *Philadelphia* before the enemy had a chance to use her. United States Navy Lieutenant Stephen Decatur conceived a plan of action. Decatur, who was born in a log cabin in Maryland and joined the Navy at a young age, would become one of the Navy's first heroes. He was promoted to captain when he was just twenty-five and would become a commodore, only to die in an 1820 duel fought against a man named James Barron, whom he helped to court-martial in 1808. But at the time of the Tripoli campaign, Decatur was a dashing young lieutenant with fire in his belly and a bold scheme to rescue the American hostages. He would lead a force of seventy-five men—including eight Marines—on a daring nighttime raid of Tripoli's harbor. The attack was launched at sundown. Decatur and his men sneaked into the harbor on rowboats and captured a ketch, which they renamed *Intrepid*. Then they cautiously approached the *Philadelphia,* still docked near the fortress, pretending to be a friendly vessel. Once aboard the captured warship, the Americans struck. In a savage half-hour battle, Decatur and his men killed or captured all the pirates aboard the *Philadelphia* and set the ship afire. They escaped in the *Intrepid* while the frigate burned, without suffering a single casualty.

News of this swift and decisive action was greeted with joy all over America. Even Admiral Horatio Nelson, the Englishman who would defeat Bonaparte's Navy on the high seas, was impressed. He called Decatur's operation "the most bold and daring act of its age." But an even more bold and daring campaign against the Pasha of Tripoli was yet to come.

THE DIPLOMAT AND THE MARINE

American Navy ships bombarded the city of Tripoli five times between August 3 and September 2, 1804, without success, so they tried sending in a floating bomb. On the night of September 3, the *Intrepid* was loaded with black powder and sent toward Tripoli's harbor. Unfortunately, the boat exploded prematurely, killing all sixteen Americans on board.

The Navy concluded that Tripoli would not fall from a naval bombardment alone—there would have to be an attack from land to ensure victory. In 1804, a lettered diplomat, Dartmouth graduate, Arabic scholar, and former U.S. Army captain named William Eaton arrived in the region with a secret plan to unseat Pasha Yusef Karamanli and replace him with a ruler more friendly to America. Karamanli had taken control of Tripoli by killing one of his brothers and sending another brother into exile. The key to Eaton's plan was locating exiled brother Hamet and convincing him to join an American-sponsored rebellion.

With a detachment of Marines, Eaton sailed up the Nile in search of Hamet Karamanli. After looking for several weeks, he succeeded; Hamet was living in the desert surrounded by a protective force of hundreds of Mameluke warriors. A powerful and influential Islamic warrior people descended from slaves, the Mamelukes and their *beys* (warlords) more or less controlled Egypt until Napoleon Bonaparte defeated them in the Battle of the Pyramids in 1798. To escape the French, tribes of Mamelukes melted into the African desert or up the Nile to carve several tiny kingdoms of their own. It was to one of these kingdoms that Hamet had fled after being exiled.

Eaton and Hamet hammered out a final agreement. Then Hamet turned around and convinced the Mamelukes to join the rebellion. Weeks later Hamet Karamanli and his Mamelukes returned to Egypt under the flag of the United States of America and under the protection of the Marines.

Over the next few months, a ragtag army was assembled in Alexandria. This force—composed of several hundred Mamelukes, thirty-five Greek mercenaries, a small group of European soldiers of fortune, a hundred camel drivers, and an eighteen-man detachment of United States Marines commanded by Lieutenant Presley Neville O'Bannon—set out to attack the Tripolitan fortress at the town of Derna on the African coast.

Unfortunately, Derna, a tiny seaside village in what is now modern Libya, was separated from Eaton's expedition by the Libyan desert—over six hundred miles of scorched, waterless hell. Unperturbed, this army of 500 men and a hundred camels began the trek across the desert on March 8, 1805. Crossing the desert would be a difficult feat for the mechanized armies of German General Erwin Rommel in World War II. It was nearly impossible to contemplate such a crossing in 1805. But Eaton and O'Bannon were convinced they could pull it off. Eaton's improbable expedition had seven weeks to reach its destination, and there was trouble from the start. The Christian and Muslim factions fought incessantly. Soon blood feuds developed and there were duels, thefts, and even murders—not to mention an attempted mutiny that was quelled only by force. When the Arab warriors threatened to abandon the expedition altogether, Lieutenant O'Bannon and seven other Marines took control of the food supply. They soon cowed the Arab mutineers, but had to watch their backs for the rest of the trek.

On April 25, the weary expedition reached the outskirts of Derna and camped on a hilltop overlooking the town and the sea beyond. At dawn, Eaton sent a flag of truce to the governor of the city, demanding the surrender of the garrison. But the governor was confident. He had a superior force of 800 bloodthirsty soldiers ready to repel the invaders. His reply to Eaton was simple: "My head or yours!"

Twenty-four hours later the governor of Derna awoke to a nasty surprise. The bulk of the American fleet had appeared off his coast and warships were in the harbor, firing on the city. Without any form of long-distance communications to coordinate an attack from land and sea, even the concept of a naval bombardment was risky. But Eaton's timing had been perfect: his expedition was just where it was supposed to be when it was supposed to be there. Now, as the Tripolitans concentrated on the American frigates in the harbor, Eaton, O'Bannon, and the Marines attacked from land.

Lieutenant O'Bannon led the afternoon assault on the Tripolitans' exposed flank. He used all eight of his Marines, along with the Greek mercenaries, one cannon, and an artillery crew, and a few Arabs. The closer the Americans got to the walls, the more punishment they took. There was little protective cover for O'Bannon's men, so, as the Marines approached the fort, they faced relentless gunfire. Soon O'Bannon's force was pinned down, unable to advance or retreat. William Eaton rushed into the fray with his reserves—Mamelukes, mostly—giving the Marines an opportunity to regroup and formulate a new strategy.

Captain O'Bannon decided on a second charge—this time with bayonet. As musket balls whizzed past their heads, he led his Marines crashing through the ruins of the heavy wooden gate, which had been shattered by his lone cannon. Suddenly the Marines found themselves in the middle of the hostile fort. So many shots were directed at them that, by one account, some of the pirates were cut down by their own crossfire. Almost immediately several of the Greeks fell, and William Eaton was shot through the wrist. Marine Private John Whitten was killed outright. Private Edward Steward died later of his wounds. A third Marine went down, wounded and out of the battle.

But O'Bannon would not give up. He and his men cut and slashed their way through the fort with sword and bayonet. When bayonets broke and cutlasses shattered, the Marines used their muskets as clubs to beat the life out of the persistent enemy. The furious speed of the assault gave the surprised defenders no time to reload their muskets, and the Marines and their allies showed the pirates no quarter. At 3:30 on that bloodstained afternoon, Lieutenant Presley Neville O'Bannon climbed the ramparts of the smoldering fortress and became the first Marine to raise the American flag over conquered territory in the eastern hemisphere. As a result of the valiant effort of O'Bannon and his Marines, a New World army had defeated a hostile force in the old world.

This stunning and unexpectedly swift victory brought Eaton and O'Bannon a host of new problems. Eaton had to persuade Hamet's "allies" to use restraint when dealing with the conquered people of Derna. His plan called for Hamet Karamanli to be perceived as a liberator, not a tyrant like his brother. But the Mamelukes had a propensity to loot the people they conquered, and it took all of Eaton's diplomatic skills to maintain control of his allies.

Lieutenant O'Bannon, meanwhile, had prisoners to deal with, wounded to ship out, and Marines to resupply. And he was well aware that the pasha would not take a foreign invasion lightly. O'Bannon hastily organized a defense of the captured city by repairing the gate, gathering stores, guarding the wells, and taking fresh ammunition off the Navy ships. As predicted, within days of the fall of Derna, the pasha dispatched an army from Tripoli with orders to retake the town.

On May 13, the pasha's army attacked. In a fierce six-hour battle, the Tripolitan forces were thrown back repeatedly, with heavy casualties. They soon ceased their frontal assaults and adopted hit-and-run tactics, and the next several weeks were filled with attacks, counterattacks, and skirmishes with the pasha's men. The Marines fought constantly, manning the walls and battling side by side with the Mamelukes against the pasha's forces.

Hamet Karamanli finally managed to defeat his brother's army on June 10. It was a glorious victory. But soon—too soon—it turned bittersweet. The very next day, the U.S.S. *Constitution* arrived in Tripoli's harbor with appalling news. Even as the battle for Derna was being waged, American diplomats had made peace with Yusef Karamanli. President Jefferson, impatient with the eighteen-month standoff, had authorized a new representative to sign yet another onerous treaty. This one included a $60,000 ransom for the return of the sailors and Marines captured off the *Philadelphia*. Of course, the prisoners had already been freed by the Marines on June 3, so the treaty signed on the tenth—the same day the pasha's forces were crushed by his brother's Mamelukes—was meaningless. But Eaton found he could not honor his word to Hamet, as the American government paid the ransom before they learned the American hostages had been liberated. It was a dishonorable end to a well-planned and well-fought campaign. The Marines who participated in this struggle felt betrayed by their government. So did a lot of people back home. President Jefferson's popularity took a nosedive.

Hamet Karamanli, who expected to take control of Tripoli, was bought off with American dollars. William Eaton and Lieutenant Presley O'Bannon returned home to be hailed as heroes. According to legend, Hamet Karamanli presented Lieutenant O'Bannon with a jewel-encrusted sword to honor the Marine officer's service. It is said that this sword became the model for the "Mameluke sword" Marine Corps officers still carry today. Upon his return to America, the state of Virginia also presented

O'Bannon—a Blue Ridge Mountain boy—with a ceremonial gold sword to honor his glorious victory in Tripoli. But despite these honors, the Marine Corps was far less gracious to the hero of Tripoli. They neither promoted O'Bannon nor honored this fine officer with a brevet—an honorary promotion.

In 1807, Presley O'Bannon resigned his commission and moved to Kentucky. He married and settled down in Logan County, where he died in obscurity. In 1920, O'Bannon's grave was moved to Frankfort, the state capital, where he was reburied with honors.

Though the war fought on "the Shores of Tripoli" ended without victory, it would be forever celebrated in lyrics of the Marine Corps anthem. But no matter the outcome, the Corps had drawn first blood in a conflict on the other side of the world, and had conducted themselves with honor, skill, and bravery. More importantly, the officers and men who fought in the Tripoli campaign gained valuable experience that would serve them well in the larger conflict to come. Once again, that conflict would be with Great Britain.

THE WAR OF 1812

The protracted war with Napoleon bled Great Britain dry of men and war material. Impressing sailors from ships on the high seas was the primary means of recruitment used by the Royal Navy, and despite the terms of the Treaty of Paris, the British still regarded Americans as subjects of the Crown. When James Madison assumed the office of the president in 1812, the number of impressed American sailors had exceeded 6,000. There were more Americans in the Royal Navy than there were in the U.S. Navy.

Something had to be done to remedy this intolerable situation, so Madison asked Congress to declare war. They did so, on June 18, 1812.

But the United States was ill-prepared for a second war with Great Britain. The Navy had no large ships of the line, and only three frigates with more than forty guns, while the British had over 200 ships of the line and 300 fast frigates. And the British had been fighting the French for years—effectively providing on-the-job training for an entire new generation of Royal Navy officers and British Marines.

The Americans, however, had three things going for them. Their Navy and Marine Corps had also been tested in battle and both services had a core of officers with combat experience. The Americans also had a technological advantage—their frigates were newer, faster, more maneuverable, and more tenacious than their British counterparts. And America had the United States Marines—quite simply the finest military marksmen in the world.

When William Burrows retired as commandant of the Corps in 1804, President Jefferson replaced him with Lieutenant Colonel Franklin Wharton. It was a choice based on seniority not competence. Wharton's tenure would be marked by several great victories, and by shocking personal disgrace.

The first Marines to see action in the War of 1812 were the fifty-man detachment aboard the U.S.S. *Constitution*. On August 19, a windy, overcast day with heavy seas,

▪ Weapons of the Marine Corps

During the Revolutionary War, the American Marines were armed with the same French and British muskets everyone else used, though they converted these weapons for use aboard ship. "Sea service" muskets were shorter—to fit in tight shipboard spaces—and had brass fittings and tin-plated barrels to resist saltwater corrosion. Near the close of the Civil War, the Marine Corps embraced the hand-cranked, multibarreled Gatling gun before anyone else, though this weapon was not in general use until the 1870s.

In the 1880s, the Marine Corps also began to use smokeless gunpowder, which enabled the firing of smaller-caliber bullets at much higher velocities and greater ranges, without smoke to reveal the shooter's position to the enemy. And the Corps was the first military service to adopt the Winchester-Lee "straight-pull" five-shot rifles and the Colt-Browning machine gun in 1895.

In 1900 the formidable Krag-Jorgensen rifle replaced the Winchester-Lee, and it was during this period that the Marine Corps began to stress marksmanship skills over all other types of training. In 1912, the Springfield M-1903 .30-caliber rifle replaced the Krag, and in 1916, the Lewis light machine gun—which was rejected by the Army—became a permanent part of the Marine Corps' arsenal. The Lewis could still be found on the battlefields of World War II—which was ironic, considering that it did not see much action during the First World War. When the Marines joined the American Expeditionary Force to fight the Germans, they had to put aside their weapons of choice in favor of those used by the rest of the Allied Armies. So it was that the Lewis was replaced by the Hotchkiss heavy machine gun and the Chauchat light machine gun. After the armistice, these inferior weapons were set aside in favor of the Lewis machine gun, and the new Browning M-1917 heavy machine gun. The Marines also adopted the M-1918 Browning automatic rifle. The BAR would continue to be utilized by the Corps through the Pacific war and the Korean conflict of the 1950s.

The Marines adopted the Thompson submachine gun in the 1920s. The "Tommy" gun was light and easy to carry, but hardly accurate beyond 100 meters. During the Second World War, the Marines used the M-1903 Springfield rifle. In time, the Springfield would be replaced by the eight-shot Garand M-1 rifle. This semiautomatic weapon would be used until the 1960s, when it was replaced by the M-14 and M-16 rifles.

---

the *Constitution* opened fire on the British frigate *Guerriere* 750 miles off the coast of Boston. After many salvos were fired, the ships came in to close contact. Marine Lieutenant William S. Bush leapt onto the rail, turned to Captain Isaac Hull, and cried, "Shall I board her, sir?" A moment later he was shot dead by a British Marine.

The *Constitution* pressed the attack while American Marines cleared the enemy decks with accurate and deadly fire from the fighting tops. Gut-shot, with her masts blown away, the *Guerriere* burned and sank. For the first time in history, an American vessel had vanquished a British warship on the high seas. It was unthinkable to the British—until it happened.

Next came the duel between the American sloop *Wasp* and the British brig *Frolic* off the coast of Bermuda. Again the battle was fought in rough seas, and again the victory went to the Americans. United States sailors and Marines swiftly boarded the British ship and captured all hands. Though the *Wasp* was subsequently ambushed and recaptured by the British warship *Poictiers,* the Royal Navy had nevertheless been handed another stinging defeat. Four months later the *Constitution* met the *Java* off the coast of Brazil. American Marines once again provided unwavering fire, and the slaughter on the British decks was horrendous. Before long the *Java*'s decks were slippery with blood, its hold choked with the wounded and dying. The captain struck the flag and surrendered to the Americans. The editorial pages of the London *Times,* which had initially sneered when the upstart Americans declared war, were now singing a different tune. GOOD GOD! CAN SUCH THINGS BE? a headline inquired.

There was no American victory on June 1, 1813, when the *Chesapeake* met the *Shannon* near the mouth of Boston Harbor. After a running duel, British Marines boarded the *Chesapeake*. Captain James Lawrence—who had been with Stephen Decatur when he burned the *Philadelphia* in Tripoli—was mortally wounded and carried belowdecks. His final command: "Don't give up the ship!" Though the sailors panicked, the Marines heeded their captain's dying plea. The British cut down the Marines almost to the last man and captured the *Chesapeake*. It was America's first defeat in this struggle.

One reason the United States declared war on Britain was because the U.S. government had designs on Canada. But when an invasion attempt failed, the tide of war shifted against the United States. With the war against Napoleon over, the British could focus their full attention on the conflict in America. The Duke of Wellington's army of 30,000 soldiers was shipped to Canada and deployed in the Hudson Valley. The British intended to cut the American continent in two, a scheme that had failed during the Revolutionary War. This time the strategy almost worked.

DISGRACE

The United States found itself between a rock and a hard place. The duke's army was coming down from Canada, and on August 19, a second British force landed unopposed in Benedict, Maryland, perilously close to Washington. The defense of the nation's capital was the responsibility of Brigadier General Henry Winder. But his army was a paper tiger—mostly untrained militia and a few green recruits. Nor was Washington a fortified city. There were no ramparts, no cannons, no defenses ringing the town.

But there was still reason to hope. On August 22, Captain Samuel Miller arrived on the scene with 110 Marines. Along with Joshua Barney, a tough Navy veteran of the Revolutionary War, these Marines would stage a defense that delayed the British from entering the city, buying the government and the inhabitants of Washington precious time to escape.

As the British forces began their forty-plus-mile march to Washington in the blistering heat, Winder established a defensive line in Bladensburg, Maryland, just four miles northeast of the capital. Barney's men were clustered in the center, while Captain Miller's Marines took position on a hill slightly behind the defensive line to protect the flanks in case the defenders broke. The British marched up the road to Washington in hundred-degree heat, chafing in their wool uniforms. But as they tried to cross the only bridge over the eastern branch of the Potomac, Barney's experienced naval gunners cut them to pieces with cannon mounted behind their hastily erected defensive walls.

The British pulled back, then moved to the left to flank the Americans. It was there that they clashed with Miller's Marines. Initially, the British troops were stung by uncannily accurate musket fire from an unseen enemy. Then the American forces countercharged with bayonets and cutlasses. The charge was so daring and unexpected that it turned back two British regiments.

Though the Marines fought well, most of the regular troops defending the main line were outgunned, inexperienced, and just plain frightened. They broke and ran, leaving Barney's sailors and Miller's Marines to cover their retreat. The Marines fought on, but when Barney had his horse shot out from under him, and Captain Miller fell "in a shower of musket-balls" the British forces overwhelmed the Americans. Fifty-four-year-old Joshua Barney and young Captain Miller—who was wounded and helpless—were both captured. As night fell, the British marched unopposed into Washington. President Madison, his cabinet, and most high-ranking government officials had already fled. So did Franklin Wharton, the commandant of the Marine Corps. As the British approached and his Marines took their stand at Bladensburg, Wharton snatched the payroll and traveled by buggy and boat to Frederick, Maryland, with the Corps' paymaster. His ignominious retreat disgraced the Marine Corps.

For the next two days, the British rampaged through the capital, burning, killing, and looting. The Gallatin House was stormed and destroyed when snipers hiding inside of it fired on the British. The Capitol building was set ablaze, and the two British commanders—Major General Robert Ross of the Army and Rear Admiral George Cockburn of the Royal Navy—marched on the White House and personally put the structure to the torch. Cockburn even burned the offices of Washington's newspapers, making sure that all the letter *C*s were destroyed so Americans "could not print scandals" about him. For the British this was sweet revenge for their defeat at Yorktown. Curiously, during the two-day rampage through the city, the Marine barracks and its commandant's house remained untouched. Legend has it that these were spared to honor the spirited defense mounted by Miller and his tiny force of Marines. Whatever the reason, the Corps headquarters at Eighth and "Eye" still stand today as the Marine Corps oldest post.

When the British turned their attentions toward Maryland again, 8,000 Americans showed up outside Baltimore to help in the city's defense. Major General Ross and his British troops met stiff resistance fourteen miles outside of Baltimore. Their advance was checked, and Ross, a decorated veteran of Britain's war against Napoleon, was killed.

A British night attack on Baltimore's Fort McHenry came on September 13, followed by a naval bombardment. But at dawn—as young Francis Scott Key later wrote in his lyrics to our national anthem—the fort was unconquered: "Our flag was still there . . ." The attack on Maryland floundering, the British returned to their ships and sailed for Jamaica.

Perhaps the most glorious battle fought by the Marine Corps in the War of 1812 occurred after the Treaty of Ghent that ended hostilities was signed on Christmas Eve, 1814. Though this second war with Britain was effectively over, in an era without mass communications it took almost six weeks for word of a peace deal to reach America. A lot of blood was shed in those weeks. In January 1815, Lord Wellington's brother-in-law, British Major General Sir Edward Parkenham, led a force of 9,000 men, many of them veterans of the Battle of Bladensburg, on a march to take New Orleans.

Captain Daniel Carmick, the young Philadelphian who led the capture of the *Sandwich* in Puerto Plata, was in New Orleans too. Carmick's 300 Marines joined a horde of frontiersmen, a bevy of Southern gentlemen, a ragtag Creole Army, numberless and undisciplined militiamen, and a gang of Jean Laffite's swamp pirates and smugglers to defend the mouth of the Mississippi River. This polyglot force was led by the gaunt, mercurial military genius, Andrew Jackson. Jackson, a major general in the Army who would later become president of the United States, rode into New Orleans with a meager force too small to defend the city. There was talk of surrender. But when the British showed up on their doorstep, the citizens of New Orleans rallied behind General Jackson to defend their city and their way of life.

By December 23, the British were just nine miles from New Orleans, so Jackson moved his forces in front of the approaching British. On the twenty-eighth, the two armies clashed. After stiff fighting, the British were beaten back. Daniel Carmick, leading a counterattack, was wounded in the head by shrapnel—perhaps from a Congreve rocket. Though Carmick's injuries were severe, he did not die from them until almost two years later. It was a sad and pitiful end to the brave and noble Marine from Philadelphia.

More running battles were fought in the next few days. Finally, the Americans, ensconced behind a defensive line built of cotton bales along the shallow depression of the Rodriquez Canal—flanked on one side by a cypress swamp, the Mississippi River on the other—waited for the final assault they knew would come. The British attacked on January 8.

The British Army, which had defeated Napoleon's forces in battlefields all across Europe, were overconfident on this day. They boldly marched toward the canal, across open ground veiled only by a thick fog. When they were within range of the American defenses, the fog suddenly lifted and the British troops were exposed. Without cover, they marched right into the teeth of American muskets, and artillery manned with deadly accuracy by Laffite's battle-hardened pirates.

Hours later, despite repeated British attacks, the American line held, its defenders hardly bloodied. The British had not fared so well. Their commander was dead, hit three times by musket fire. So were 700 of Parkenham's best soldiers. In all, the British suffered 2,100 casualties. The American defenders suffered seventy casualties—but only eight Americans were actually killed in the battle. It is difficult to imagine a more lopsided victory.

On January 18, a truce was called and prisoners were exchanged. Then the British returned to their ships. On February 11, word reached New York that the War of 1812 was officially over. The bloody Battle for New Orleans, and several major and minor duels on the high seas, need never have been fought. After the war, General Sir Edward Parkenham returned to his estate in Ireland—his corpse sealed in a cask of rum. In his after action report, Andrew Jackson praised the Marines who stood with him in that battle. Though the United States had no official military decorations, Congress passed a resolution stating "that Congress entertains a high sense of the valor and good conduct of Major Daniel Carmick, of the officers, and noncommissioned officers, and Marines under his command."

Men like Presley O'Bannon, Daniel Carmick, Lieutenant William S. Bush, and Captain Samuel Miller are among the Marine Corps' first heroes. And there were many others, such as Marine Lieutenant John Brooks, son of the governor of Massachusetts, who served under Oliver Hazard Perry and distinguished himself in the battle for control of Lake Erie. Or Lieutenant Levi Twiggs, who fought the British in New York Harbor and died in battle—still a Marine—thirty years later during the war with Mexico. Or Captain Archibald Henderson, who served aboard the U.S.S. *Constitution* and would become a most respected commandant of the Marine Corps. From its inception, the Marine Corps was adept at molding men into heroes, and there was further glory to come.

JOHN MARSHALL GAMBLE GOES TO SEA

Lieutenant John Marshall Gamble was the first Marine to see action on the Pacific Ocean, and the only Marine in the history of the early Corps to command his own ship. When the American frigate *Essex,* under Captain David Porter, sailed around Cape Horn, Gamble commanded the thirty Marines aboard. Barely nineteen, with black hair and piercing eyes, Gamble had received his commission at seventeen. His father was an officer during the American Revolution and his three brothers would all die in battle. For Gamble, service to country was a family tradition.

Captain Porter left the United States without fanfare, his mission to harass British shipping, primarily the English whaling fleet. The *Essex* reached Pacific waters in early March. Over the coming months, Porter's men would capture a number of British vessels and convert them for their own use. In May, they captured the whaling ship *Greenwich,* which was armed with ten cannons. Though he was not a sailor, Porter put Lieutenant Gamble in command of the *Greenwich.* Gamble proved himself on July 12 when the *Essex* and *Greenwich* took on three British warships—including the finest ship in the region, the fourteen-gun *Seringapatam.* From the deck of the *Essex,* Porter watched as his Marine commander raked the *Seringapatam* with cannon fire. Finally, the American Marines boarded the British ship and its crew surrendered. Though Gamble was wounded, he had won the day.

Captain Porter continued his campaign against the British off the shores of South America, until the *Essex* was captured after a furious struggle against superior odds. Captain Porter and some of his sailors later escaped on the *Essex,* and eluding the British, reached safe harbor. Meanwhile, Lieutenant Gamble had established a base on Marquesas Island. But when Captain Porter failed to return on schedule, Gamble's crew of foreign-born sailors mutinied. The lieutenant and the Marines with him were taken prisoner by the mutineers. Gamble himself was shot in the foot.

The mutineers raised the British flag with a cheer, and sailed away with the Marines chained in their hold. But when the mutineers saw the sails of the *Greenwich* on the horizon—now commanded by Captain Porter and flying the American flag— Gamble convinced them to free the Marines. The mutineers placed the men in a leaky boat without supplies. They could no longer see the *Greenwich,* so Gamble and his men rowed for hours until they again reached Marquesas Island. As they gathered provisions and made ready to sail away, hostile natives attacked the Marines on the beach and some of Gamble's men were slaughtered.

On May 9, Gamble and his few remaining Marines sailed aboard the *Hammond,* a small British ship they had captured months before. The lieutenant had no compass, no maps, no cannon, and only a few rounds of ammunition for his muskets. The *Hammond* ran with the trade winds for two weeks until it reached Hawaii. The Marines took in more supplies, rested, and set sail for home. Gamble was captured when the *Hammond* was boarded by the British two weeks later. He and his men were kept in the hold until the British warship reached Rio de Janeiro, where the captain learned that the War of 1812 was over and released the surviving Marines.

His health ruined, Lieutenant Gamble sailed for New York City. The Corps greeted him as a returning hero and he was given a commission, but he never fully recovered from his ordeal. He died in Brooklyn on September 11, 1836, at the age of forty-six.

CHAPTER THREE

Riots, Pirates, Adventures in California, and a War with Mexico

■

1815–1847

THE Marine Corps had been scandalized by the disreputable behavior of its commandant during the siege on Washington. Franklin Wharton's cowardly retreat offended the honor of the brave men who remained behind to fight. Archibald Henderson, a Marine who had served with distinction, held his own beliefs about how the Corps should be led. After the War of 1812, he convened a court-martial of Commandant Wharton. Unfortunately, the Senate refused to hear evidence against the accused and President Monroe accepted the Senate's decision "with regret." Wharton was acquitted.

Despite the disdain many Marine Corps officers had for Wharton, the old man remained in his post until his death in 1818. Brevet Major Anthony Gale was named to replace him, principally because of the same worn-out seniority system that produced Wharton. Born in Ireland, Gale was commissioned in 1798. A year later he killed Lieutenant Allen McKenzie of the Navy in a duel. Gale didn't get along with Wharton either, and was exiled to a post in New Orleans. There he began drinking, and in time exhibited the first signs of alcoholism. It wasn't long before Commandant Gale was brought up on charges, which included public drunkenness and frequenting houses of ill repute. Lacking Wharton's political connections, he was found guilty of all charges and dismissed from duty. He would be the only Marine Corps commandant to suffer such an ignominious fate.

Archibald Henderson succeeded Gale as commandant of the Corps. A vigorous Colchester, Virginia, gentleman born in 1783, he had a distinguished service history, including a tour of duty aboard the U.S.S. *Constitution* during the War of 1812. Henderson would become one of the Corps' great leaders. During his thirty-seven-year tenure as commandant, the Marine Corps would assume a wider role in the nation's destiny. Henderson's vigorous, intelligent, and forceful stewardship would restore honor and self-esteem to the Marines.

Commandant Henderson's first mission was to attract new volunteers. When he took command, the Marines had fewer than a thousand officers and men. Henderson aggressively recruited more soldiers, and established a training school for officers at the Marine Corps headquarters in Washington—the origin of the Basic School where Marine Corps officers are trained today. Commandant Henderson also shifted the leadership roles and command responsibilities inside the Corps. He introduced the unique practice of making the NCOs—noncommissioned officers—the heart and soul of the Marines. It was—and still is—a revolutionary practice. In the modern Corps, it is the noncommissioned officers who mentor the new recruits, who instill in them the values and traditions of the Marine Corps. No matter the rank he may attain, a Marine Corps officer will *always* look to his NCO when he needs sound advice. Under combat, when units become fragmented and the pool of officers is rapidly diminished, the Marines remain a formidable and cohesive fighting force because of this "democratic" command structure. In a pinch, any Marine, down to a lowly private, can assume command responsibilities because the Corps instills leadership skills *at every level.*

During the Henderson era the Marines would be called upon to serve their country in several dramatic incidents, often at the urging of their energetic and determined commandant. As the nation grew, so did the role of the United States Marine Corps. In the coming decades, the Marines would boldly carry the flag to the four corners of the earth. On several occasions they would be asked to stop trouble brewing right here at home.

In March 1824, Robert Wainwright led a Marine detachment from the Boston Navy Yard to quell a riot at the state prison. Boston authorities were ill-equipped to deal with the situation when a large group of prisoners seized a portion of the prison. They asked the federal government for help. But when the Marines arrived, the locals, fearing a massacre, requested that Wainwright and his thirty Marines fire muskets filled with powder—but no musket balls—at the prisoners to "frighten and dispirit them."

Sensibly, Wainwright refused. Instead, he marched his detachment right through the prison gates and into the inmates' dining room. As the rioters looked on, Wainwright ordered his men to form a defensive line, muskets at the ready. Then Wainwright addressed the rioters, informing them that they had three minutes to go back to their cells. When the prisoners refused, he had his men load their weapons and take careful aim at the prisoners.

Wainwright checked his pocket watch and reminded the rioters that they had less than three minutes to disperse before his men opened fire. It was a bold and risky strategy. The Marines were outnumbered, and the survivors of the first volley could easily have overwhelmed and slaughtered the Marines. But the prospect of certain death broke the rioters' spirit and they retreated to their cells. Order was restored.

News of this brash act of heroism spread across the country, and increased America's respect and admiration for the Marine Corps. This incident was described in *McGuffey's Readers,* from which generations of schoolchildren first learned of the

Marine Corps. There is no telling how many of those young boys, enthralled by this stirring tale of courage under fire, grew up to become Marines.

It wasn't long before Marines were needed again on the other side of the world. On February 4, 1832, the frigate *Potomac* landed at Quallah Battoo, on the island of Sumatra. Aboard was a detachment of Marines, there to avenge an insult to American honor and the murder of its citizens. Eleven months before, in 1831, a merchant ship out of Salem, Massachusetts, had landed in Sumatra. While the crew were trading with the islanders, a warlike band of raiders rushed out of the jungle and brutally murdered three American sailors. The raiders turned out to be Sumatran pirates led by the corrupt local rajah. After suffering the indignities of Tripolitan corsairs, French privateers, and British press gangs, the United States was in no mood to take this new affront lightly.

As the Pacific sun rose hot and bright on the morning of February 8, Brevet Captain Alvin Edson and Marine Lieutenant George H. Terrett led a landing party of 300 sailors, backed by a core of battle-ready Marines. The force immediately attacked a brigand fort near the gates of Quallah Battoo. Then the Americans marched through the center of town toward the main fortress, where the Rajah of Sumatra had taken refuge with most of his brigands when the Americans landed four days before. Captain Edson divided his meager forces, dispatching the sailors to attack the rajah's main fort while he and his smaller force of Marines stormed a second walled stronghold behind the town. The Marines quickly subdued this second fortress, killing everyone who did not flee or surrender. With the two smaller strong points captured, Edson reunited his forces and attacked the rajah's main fortress with added gusto.

After two hours of ferocious fighting, there was a sudden explosion that all but leveled the rajah's main building and knocked a few Marines off their feet—the ammunition stores inside the fort had been hit by a stray musket ball. The destruction of the ammunition stores ended the siege with an impressive display of sound and fury. The brigands fell back, to regroup in the jungle. Two Marines had been killed in the initial assault and Edson was wounded. It was time for an organized withdrawal. The Marines provided accurate and deadly musket fire to cover the sailors' retreat. When the sailors were out of range of the enemy's muskets, the Marines boarded the landing boats and rowed back to the *Potomac*. The town of Quallah Battoo had been burned to ashes, the rajah's fortress leveled, and his brigands slaughtered. The Marine Corps brought American power to the shores of the Pacific for the first time.

In the spring of 1836, Commandant Henderson led a force of Marines to Columbus, Georgia, to counter an uprising by American Indians opposed to resettlement in the wilderness beyond the Mississippi. President Andrew Jackson, who had moved to disband the Corps just two years before, now utilized their battle-ready skills to reinforce the U.S. Army. The Army at this time numbered fewer than 4,000 men, huge in comparison to the Marine Corps but inadequate for the task that lay ahead. Most of its forces were scattered in a hundred towns and forts, protecting settlements and guarding the border against incursions by outlaws and smugglers. It was next to impossible for the Army to muster enough men and material to fight a war *and* patrol the nation's expanding frontier. Marines were required to fill the gap.

Commandant Henderson was instrumental in getting the Marines involved in this

■ *Osceola and the Seminole Wars*

Historians tend to divide the Seminole Wars into three parts. The first stage began in 1817 when European settlers skirmished with Native American tribes on the Florida border. This phase of the conflict ended a year later, when General Andrew Jackson led the Army to Florida, destroyed several Native American settlements, executed two British traders accused of encouraging Seminole resistance, and took Pensacola away from the Spanish in May 1818.

The second stage, which began in 1835, is the most infamous. As white settlers moved from the north, the Native American population was forced farther and farther south, into disease-ridden swampland unfit for farming. In 1823, the Seminoles officially ceded most of their tribal land to the United States government. In a second treaty, signed at Paynes Landing in 1832, the Seminoles were required to relocate west of the Mississippi River within three years. Enter Osceola, a half-English, half-Seminole leader born near the Chattahoochee River in Georgia. His mother, the daughter of a Creek chief, took him to live in Florida when he was very young. It was there that Osceola became an influential leader, heading the opposition to cession of tribal lands to the United States.

In 1835, Osceola was imprisoned by United States authorities for resisting migration. He was released a few months later and immediately began armed resistance to the government in Washington. It was during this phase of the conflict that Archibald Henderson and his Marines entered the war. After Osceola was captured again, he was imprisoned at St. Augustine, and at Fort Moultrie, South Carolina, where he died in 1838.

The third and final stage of the Seminole conflict began in 1855. When most Seminoles surrendered in 1842, a few hundred renegades fled deep into the Everglades. These warriors and their descendants began to raid white settlements until they were put down in 1858. After 1859, about half the remaining Seminoles submitted to forced resettlement and moved west. The rest stayed in Florida, and their descendants did not sign a peace treaty with the United States until 1935.

fight. But if he was expecting glory, he was disappointed, for what the Marines got was a protracted, unpopular, undeclared war in the jungles of Florida—a grueling guerrilla campaign not unlike the Vietnam conflict 130 years later.

In 1836, Commandant Henderson marched his men to Fort Brooke. There, the Marines were complemented by regular Army troops and 750 Native American volunteers, most culled from the just-defeated Creek Nation. Used mostly as scouts, these Native American troops wore white turbans to distinguish them from the enemy in close combat. It was the first time Marine Corps officers commanded "native" troops in the field. Over the coming decades this practice would become more common. The Marines, led by their Creek scouts, staged repeated raids deep into the Great Wahoo Swamp. But the Seminoles, led by a charismatic, half-English, half-Creek war chief named Osceola, fought a successful guerrilla campaign. Outnumbered and outgunned, the guerrillas fired from concealment and melted into the jungle when confronted by an organized force. Marine Lieutenant Andrew Ross, leading a detachment of Creeks against the Seminoles, was the first casualty of this campaign. Shot from concealment by a Seminole sniper, Ross was the first Marine to be killed in action since the War of 1812. Over the next five years, dozens of Marines, Army regulars, Creek scouts, and civilians who got in the way would die, along with countless Seminole tribesmen.

In January of the following year, a detachment of the famed "Horse Marines" clashed with a large force of Indians while on patrol in the wilderness. The results were inconclusive. Five days later Commandant Henderson himself led the Marines into the Great Cypress Swamp to find and destroy several Seminole settlements. When his Creek advance scouts located the enemy, Henderson attacked. The Marines and the Seminoles clashed on opposite banks of a shallow river. For fifteen minutes, the Marines fired their muskets across the muddy waters of the Hatchee-Lustee River, trading shots with the Seminoles. Their accurate fire stunned the enemy, who had been surprised in the open. Inevitably, the Seminole line broke. As they fled, the Marines charged into the swift currents of the river in hot pursuit. Exposed, the Marines made better targets. One was killed and three wounded in the crossing. On the opposite shore, Henderson regrouped and pursued the Seminoles through the thick cypress jungle. The guerrillas made repeated stands to cover their retreat, splitting up their forces each time to elude pursuit. Eventually, they scattered into the swamp and escaped.

The battle on the Hatchee-Lustee was the largest of the Seminole War. But the only enemy dead found after the battle were two escaped slaves and one Seminole warrior. Days later Henderson met with the Seminole chiefs under a flag of truce, and a peace treaty was hammered out. The chiefs agreed to relocate to what is now Arkansas, and news of a peace deal was sent to Washington. Henderson was promoted, along with some of his officers. It looked as if the war was over, but it wasn't.

In a night raid at Tampa Bay, Osceola's forces surprised the Marine detachment guarding the Seminole warriors who were camped there, awaiting resettlement. Osceola captured the chiefs who had signed the peace treaty, and convinced 700 men to join him in a new struggle. This second stage of the Seminole War would last five years. Even the 1837 capture of Osceola—who agreed to parley with the Marines under a flag of truce and was betrayed and imprisoned—failed to end the long, savage conflict.

Army General Zachary Taylor took to the field in the autumn of 1837, and on Christmas Day, he commanded American forces at Lake Okeechobee during the last battle of the war. Again the Indians vanished into the swamp when the tide of battle turned against them. Taylor was unable to defeat the Seminoles and the war proceeded. In 1839, two more companies of Marines were dispatched to the Florida wilderness. Led by First Lieutenant George H. Terrett, who had fought the pirates at Quallah Battoo, these companies made hundreds of sorties into the Everglades. They inflicted casualties and suffered them, but over the next three years the Marines failed to subdue their tenacious enemy. In the end, the Seminoles were never conquered.

This phase of the Seminole Wars officially ended in July 1842. Public opinion had turned against the conflict, and when the fugitive Native Americans ceased to raid white homesteads and settlements, there was little reason to continue to pursue them as they retreated ever deeper into the vast Everglades. During the Seminole Wars, hundreds of Marines saw action and nineteen of them died, but the actual number of casualties was much higher. By the close of the conflict, a total of 1,466 men of the Army and 61 Marines perished, almost all from tropical disease.

No one bothered to count the Seminole dead.

In 1840, while the Seminole War raged on in Florida, thirty-three Marines led by a tough staff sergeant accompanied United States Navy Lieutenant Charles Wilkes on a four-year voyage of discovery. A hundred years before Marines shed their blood on these remote Pacific islands during World War II, the Wilkes Expedition surveyed and mapped Tarawa, Wake Atoll, and Makin Atoll. Some of Wilkes's charts would actually be used in planning the invasion of those Japanese-held islands a century later. Besides surveying over 200 Pacific landmasses, the Wilkes Expedition sailed to the Antarctic region, fought murderous native tribes in the Gilbert Islands, visited Manila, Singapore, rounded the Cape of Good Hope, and returned to New York City over four years later.

ARCHIBALD GILLESPIE'S CALIFORNIA DREAM

Two military campaigns that helped to expand the size and power of the United States also occurred during this period, and the Marines were active participants in both. The conquest of California was a magnificent military and political accomplishment, and the success of this venture was due in no small part to the heroic efforts of a single United States Marine.

In late October 1845, an afternoon meeting between George Bancroft, the newly appointed secretary of the Navy, and a thirty-three-year old Marine Corps first lieutenant named Archibald H. Gillespie was held in Bancroft's spartan office. Secretary Bancroft grilled Gillespie about his proficiency in Spanish, his fitness for duty on the frontier, and his overall initiative. Satisfied by his answers, the secretary explained that he would be assigned to carry political dispatches to several posts in the West.

When President James K. Polk took office he wished to expand the nation's borders. His gaze turned to the West. Polk's plan was to stretch the influence of the United States "from sea to shining sea" and have strategic seaports and naval bases on both coasts. On July 4, Texas had been admitted to the Union after declaring independence from Mexico; why not extend the Texas border all the way to the Pacific Ocean? To pull it off, President Polk knew he would have to dislodge the Mexicans, who held sway over most of the Pacific coast from the Baja Peninsula to the tiny bay town of Yerba Buena—now called San Francisco. Locked in a perpetual state of political unrest, Mexico's territories in the Far West were ripe for picking. All that was needed was the political will, and a few good men.

On Thursday night October 30, in a secret White House meeting, President Polk sat down with Lieutenant Gillespie. During the conference, Gillespie was handed confidential communiqués to deliver to the consul in Monterey, Thomas O. Larkin; to Commodore John D. Sloat with his fleet off the coast of Mexico; and to Army Lieutenant John C. Frémont. Frémont was somewhere out there—nobody was quite sure where—mapping the Far West with the Army's Topographical Corps. Disguised as a whiskey salesman, Gillespie sailed to Vera Cruz, traveled across land to Mexico City, and finally reached Monterey in April 1846, where he delivered the dispatches to Consul Larkin. Still in disguise, Gillespie proceeded north until he caught up with Frémont, who was encamped on the shore of Klamath Lake in present-day Oregon. After a late-night Indian raid that killed three of Frémont's men, Frémont and Gillespie, with a group of frontiersmen in buckskins, rode into California to meet with the 800 or 900 American citizens who lived there. In San Francisco Bay, Gillespie obtained a keg of powder and percussion caps enough to make 9,000 bullets from a U.S. Navy warship, even as Frémont rode to Sonoma, north of San Francisco.

On June 15, California was declared a republic when the "Bear Flag" was raised over Sonoma. Frémont assumed control of the "village republic's" meager military forces. Gillespie, as executive officer, set about training and supplying the irregulars, who came to be called the California Battalion of Mounted Riflemen. On July 7, Commodore Sloat received word that a state of war existed between Mexico and the United States. Following President Polk's instructions, delivered to him by Gillespie, Sloat "invaded" California. Without firing a shot, Captain William Mervine of the United States Navy raised the Stars and Stripes over the customhouse in Monterey, and the West Coast's first Marine Corps post was established.

Soon Commodore Robert F. Stockton assumed overall command in the Far West as the conflict shifted to San Diego. Stockton sent several battalions south to isolate a force of Mexican regulars operating near Los Angeles. The Stars and Stripes were raised over San Diego on July 30 and Marines entered the sleepy little coastal town of Los Angeles on August 12. As Stockton's forces moved southward, Lieutenant Gillespie remained behind with a token force to hold San Diego. When the bulk of the American military sailed to Acapulco to march on Mexico City, Gillespie was named commandant of the Southern District—comprising of all of the California coast—and moved his command to Los Angeles. Almost immediately, anti-American feelings rose and Gillespie's detachment was attacked by angry Californians. After a three-day siege of his headquarters, Gillespie moved his men to a fortified hilltop. It was a stronger position, but there was no water. Outgunned and outnumbered, he was forced to withdraw or be defeated. He marched out of town with full military honors, secretly vowing to return. Except for a tiny force still holding San Diego, the invasion of Southern California was a bust.

But Gillespie was undeterred. He contacted the Navy, and on October 7 a force of Marines attempted to recapture Los Angeles. This attack was a disaster, and the Marines and sailors were forced to retreat to their ships and flee the region.

Good news came a few weeks later. Colonel Stephen Kearny's "Army of the West"—fewer than 120 road-weary dragoons guided by legendary scout Kit Carson—had reached California after a grueling trek across deserts, over mountains, and through the wilderness. Gillespie and his own tiny force turned out to meet them. So did the Mexican Army. At San Pasqual, they attacked the Americans. In a furious battle that was mostly fought with Mexican lances and American swords because bad weather had dampened the ammunition on both sides, the Army of the West was defeated. Kearny was pierced three times by lances, and Gillespie was also stabbed before the Mexican force withdrew to regroup. Kearny lost nineteen men, a sixth of his force. Now his Army of the West was surrounded by a force of Mexican soldiers and California irregulars. Kit Carson slipped through the enemy lines in the night and rode for help. Only the timely arrival of a Marine Corps detachment dispatched by Stockton saved Lieutenant Gillespie, Colonel Kearny, and the Army of the West from total annihilation.

Another force, this time led by Commodore Stockton, again tried to take Los Angeles. They marched from San Diego and met the Mexicans on the bluffs behind the San Gabriel River. As the attack commenced, the Americans waded into the river and charged as Mexican horsemen flanked their position on both sides. The Marines and sailors, assigned to guard the outer perimeter, drove the Mexicans back after a protracted struggle. When the Americans who forded the river under heavy fire finally reached the bluffs, the battle was over. One American was killed and six were wounded. The Mexican forces withdrew to La Mesa, where they took their last stand. It took three separate charges by Gillespie's Marines to drive them off, and Gillespie himself was wounded yet again. But in the end, the Marines captured Los Angeles. By the afternoon of January 10, the American flag flew over the City of Angels. California officially belonged to the United States of America.

President Polk's vision of a nation that stretched from ocean to ocean had been realized. This victory was due in no small part to the fierce determination of the soldiers, scouts, frontiersmen, and irregulars commanded by Kearny and Frémont, to the wise leadership of Commodore Stockton, and most especially to the resourcefulness and tenacity of Lieutenant Archibald Gillespie, a Marine who just wouldn't give up.

THE HALLS OF MONTEZUMA

In Mexico, the fighting men of the Marine Corps were poised to add another stanza to their stirring anthem. After General Zachary Taylor avenged the slaughter at the Alamo by defeating Antonio López de Santa Anna's army at the battles of Palo Alto and Resaca de la Palma, he crossed the Rio Grande River into Mexico on May 18. He planned to fight his way to Mexico City and occupy the capital. Unfortunately, General Taylor had underestimated the resistance he would face from an aroused populace.

Meanwhile, Commodore David Conner's Gulf Coast Squadron was tasked with blockading Mexican Gulf ports while supporting Taylor's army as it slowly moved through Mexico. The 200 Marines of the Gulf Coast Squadron were combined into a provisional battalion under the command of Captain Alvin Edson, the veteran of Quallah Battoo. This was the first time the Marines were assembled from their scattered posts aboard Navy ships and allowed to fight as a unified force, but there were other Marine Corps firsts during the coming conflict. When General Taylor's campaign through the heart of Mexico became stalled, he realized there was no way he could fight his way down to Mexico City in a timely fashion. Instead, he put 12,000 soldiers aboard seventy ships and sent them down to the port city of Veracruz. They landed in force on the hostile shore in March 9, 1847—the first D day in American history. It was a race against time for the United States military. Yellow fever was a deadly, mosquito-borne killer, and the fever season on the Yucatán Peninsula was fast approaching. Because the disease was somewhat limited to the jungles along the coast, Major General Winfield Scott, the head of the U.S. Army, wished to move inland before it decimated his soldiers.

On the sweltering morning of March 9, troops began climbing off Navy warships to board the specially designed "surf boats"—American flat-bottomed landing craft built specifically for amphibious operations. Unlike the disastrous attack on Fort George fifty years before, the Marines now possessed proper equipment for their amphibious landing at Veracruz. At six in the afternoon, warships began to pound the landing area with shot and shell as the first landing parties rowed quickly toward shore. As the first surf boats reached Collado Beach, Captain Edson took the lead. But when he charged ashore, Edson discovered the beach was empty. The defenders had fled behind the walls that surrounded the city of Veracruz. Over the course of that long, muggy night, all 12,000 American soldiers came ashore guided in by signal fires set by Edson's Marines. It was a perfectly executed amphibious landing, the first in U.S. Marine Corps history. After the landing, Commodore Matthew Perry took command of the Gulf Coast Squadron. Over the next ten weeks, he would seize the coastal towns of Alvarado, Tuxpan, and San Juan Bautista with slashing amphibious assaults using Marines, sailors, and the nimble surf boats. The seeds of the Marine Corps amphibious campaigns during the Second World War were sown in this conflict with Mexico.

After surrounding Veracruz with trenches and fortifications, Taylor's army laid siege to the city. On March 29, the Mexican forces marched out and surrendered. The conquest of Veracruz was a rousing success. The most important port in Mexico had been captured, and a large force of Mexican regulars had surrendered—at the cost of only nineteen American lives. The occupation of Veracruz broke the back of Mexican resistance and turned the tide of the war.

Scott and his army beat a second Mexican force sent against them at Cerro Gordo on April 18, then camped at the little town of Puebla for the hottest weeks of the long summer. Because the enlistment period of most of his volunteer soldiers was running out, General Scott requested more men for the next phase of his campaign—the attack on Mexico City. President Polk sent him six companies of Marines, commanded by Lieutenant Colonel Samuel E. Watson and Major Levi Twiggs, both veterans of the War of 1812. Despite their battle-hardened leadership, these new Marines were mostly untested recruits; the best and most experienced Marines were already serving with the fleet. Though competent commanders, both were men of advanced years who stuck to tried-and-true tactics, eschewing bold action. Both Watson and Twiggs would die in the fight to come, but the Marines who arrived with them were poised for glory.

As summer progressed, Winfield Scott marched his army out of Puebla and onward to Mexico City. There were 30,000 Mexican regulars between his army and Scott's objective. Nevertheless, Scott's army reached the outskirts of the capital by mid-August. After several skirmishes, Santa Anna asked for an armistice and a ceasefire was honored for two weeks.

On September 7, the Americans launched an offensive against Molino del Rey, an old mill on the outskirts of Mexico City. Casualties were so horrendous—over 700 men had fallen by the end of the first day—that reinforcements were needed. Scott ordered that the Marines led by Brigadier General John A. Quitmen be committed to the battle. The general needed to clear the Mexican defenders off the Hill at Chapultepec. The Hill was 200 feet high, surrounded by high, thick stone walls, and topped by a fortress that served as a military school. From their vantage point, the defenders on Chapultepec could lay heavy fire on any American attack across either of the two causeways that led into the heart of Mexico City. To take the capital, Scott's men would have to cross one or both of these causeways and charge through the gates of Belén and San Cosme—both guarded by fortified blockhouses.

At eight o'clock on the morning of September 13, 1847, Quitman, his regulars, and the Marines cautiously approached the southern wall of Chapultepec under daunting fire from the defenders. Major Twiggs, leading a storming party, was shot and killed almost immediately. While the Army led a diversionary attack on the western face of the Hill, the Marines struggled up the south face, fighting individual hand-to-hand duels with nests of defenders. Americans from both sides of the hill reached the castle after prolonged fighting. Once there, they shot and clubbed the last of the Mexican defenders to death. By 9:30 on that bloody morning, the flag of the United States of America flew over the Hill at Chapultepec.

Then Marine Captain George Terrett led a force in pursuit of the retreating Mexicans. With him was Second Lieutenant Charles A. Henderson, son of Commandant Archibald Henderson. The Marines raced down the road that led into the city under heavy fire, assisted by a small force of Army regulars led by a young lieutenant named Ulysses S. Grant. They fought their way across the San Cosme causeway until they reached the blockhouse. When the recall sounded, Captain Terrett went back to report. First Lieutenant John D. Simms and Second Lieutenant Henderson remained behind, where they led a force of twenty-five Marines in the opposite direction—right up to the stout wooden gate. A frontal assault was deemed impossible because of heavy fire, so Simms split his tiny force and attacked from the left. Four of his men died in the first moments of their assault. Henderson, wounded and limping, led the suicidal frontal assault. Together with Simms and his men, Henderson's Marines managed to seize the gate. For the next fifteen minutes, they withstood incessant Mexican counterattacks. In all, six Marines died and Lieutenant Henderson was wounded, but the Americans had their foot in the door.

When the Mexican forces on Chapultepec were finally routed, the gates at Belén and San Cosme were overwhelmed and captured. As darkness fell, American soldiers held the causeways and the blockhouses beyond. They waited for the sun to come up to enter the city.

The final assault was mounted at dawn on September 14. But when the American soldiers rushed through the gates and seized the Grand Plaza, they discovered that Mexico City had been left undefended. Santa Anna and his men had slipped away during the night. Quitman and the Marines under his command took possession of the National Palace—where, in the time of the Aztecs, the Halls of Montezuma once stood. Scott named General Quitman governor of the conquered city and he and his men went to work. It took another day and a half to clear the last resistance and halt the looting. When it was over, the United States had conquered Mexico. America's expansion to the Pacific Ocean was complete.

In mid-November, Lieutenant Colonel Watson, who acted indecisively in the battle for Mexico City, became ill and died—the last casualty of the Mexican War. By 1848, the two battalions of Marines had returned home from south of the border. The rest were dispersed to their old posts aboard the Navy's warships. But a new generation of Marines and their commanders had been tested in battle. They had learned the arts of war and of amphibious assault and fought together as a cohesive unit. In the coming years, these Marines would bring this knowledge and experience to their next conflict—a tragic and senseless civil war that threatened to rip the fragile Union asunder.

PART TWO

"THIS UNFORTUNATE CONFLICT..."

"Let us have faith that right makes might, and in that faith let us to the end dare to do our duty as we understand it . . ."
—Abraham Lincoln, 1860

CHAPTER FOUR

HARPERS FERRY, THE CIVIL WAR, AND THE MEDAL OF HONOR

■

1848–1865

I N the fifty years following the Mexican War, the Marine Corps represented America's interest on a half-dozen foreign fronts. They showed the flag in Buenos Aires (1852), Nicaragua (1853), Uruguay and Paraguay (1855), the Fiji Islands (1855–1858), and Panama (1856). In brief skirmishes or under heavy fire, whenever a crisis erupted in one of the far-flung corners of the world, the Marines were sent to protect American life and property.

The Pacific Rim would become the domain of the Marine Corps in the coming century. Six Marines, battle-ready at their posts, were among the officers aboard Commodore Matthew Perry's flagship when his fleet of Navy warships steamed into Tokyo Bay on July 8, 1853. Tokyo was off-limits to all foreigners. Before portly, pugnacious Perry ignored the rules, no other nation had dared venture beyond the port city of Nagasaki, the Europeans' center of trade in "the Japans." But Americans were all but excluded from trading in Nagasaki by the Dutch, who controlled the city and saw no reason to let another foreign power threaten their monopoly.

Commodore Perry felt that if the Dutch were going to be stubborn, then he would carry the America's flag to Tokyo himself—whether the Japanese emperor or his *shogun* (or warlord) liked it or not. Perry had his orders, signed by President Millard Fillmore himself. He was to *personally* deliver the president's greeting to "suitably high-ranking" Japanese officials. Initially the Japanese demanded that Perry and his men depart. But Perry refused, insisting he be permitted to deliver a message from his president to the emperor himself, or a high-ranking representative of the emperor's government. Perry made it a point of honor to deliver his letter to the highest official he could possibly reach, and his perseverance paid off. After long negotiations, the commodore and some of his men were permitted to come ashore. When Perry finally reached dry land, the second American to follow him onto Japanese soil was Major Jacob Zeilin, a future commandant of the Marine Corps.

The Japanese had constructed a building solely for this historic meeting. A hundred U.S. Marines, resplendent in their uniforms, lined the route to the meeting hall. In a short ceremony Perry delivered the president's greetings, then departed with the promise he would return next spring to negotiate a treaty between Japan and the United States.

During his second visit, sixty Marines were sent ashore at Shanghai, China, to protect the lives and property of British and American citizens during the bloody T'ai P'ing Rebellion. As this revolution against foreign influence in China spread, the Manchu emperor sent Chinese troops to attack European trading settlements on April 4, 1854. With the help of British sailors and Royal Marines, the U.S. Marines pushed the Manchu's army out of all foreign settlements by force of arms.

Two years later, more trouble erupted in China. On November 16, 1856, a United States warship was fired upon. The cannon fire came from one of the forts that guarded Canton Harbor. The Navy fired back, bombarding all four Chinese forts in the vicinity. Then fifty Marines, under the command of John D. Simms, went ashore with 300 sailors. In three days they captured the four forts, routing over a thousand Chinese soldiers in the process. In desperate, hand-to-hand combat, the Marines led the hard-fighting sailors to victory.

Over the next hundred years and beyond, Marines would be dispatched to the Pacific Rim to fight the Chinese, the Japanese, the Koreans, and the Vietnamese. Though they didn't always win, the Marines always fought with courage and determination.

TENSION MOUNTS AT HOME

During the municipal elections of 1857, the tiny Washington police force was having a difficult time quelling civil unrest surrounding the polling places. The violence, perpetrated by roving gangs of various political factions, were preventing honest citizens from exercising their constitutional right to vote. Indeed, tempers flared all over the United States during that election, for the nation was in the midst of a struggle for its future and its soul.

The issue was slavery. In the agricultural South, slavery was an institution that enabled farmers to produce abundant crops and raw materials cheaply and with a measure of efficiency. But to the industrial North, which relied on cheap immigrant laborers to man its furnaces and factories, slavery was an abomination to be abolished as soon as possible. There was no compromise between these differing viewpoints, and with time this issue moved westward. As more territories petitioned for statehood, the existence of slavery became more and more problematic. Would slavery grow and spread with the nation or would it be limited to the South? This question was tearing the Union apart.

The federal city of Washington was a flash point in the debate. As Election Day wore on, the violence escalated beyond the control of the municipal police force. Finally, the mayor closed the polls and called out the Marines, the only sizable federal militia within Washington city limits. At noon on June 1, 1857, two companies left the Marine barracks and marched through the chaotic streets of Washington to the steps of city hall. Commodore Henderson, now seventy-four years old and head of the Marines for the last thirty-five years, marched with them.

When the Marines turned onto Pennsylvania Avenue, they found themselves staring into the muzzle of a cannon. A gang of roving toughs had snatched a brass signal cannon and dragged it up Pennsylvania Avenue to the corner of seventh and K streets. When the Marines came upon them, the mob was in the process of gathering powder to load the weapon.

Henderson, armed with only an umbrella, charged ahead of his men to make sure the cannon was not turned against the Marines. He demanded that the mob disperse immediately. Shots were fired—most of them at the bearded, white-haired commandant who continued to rage at the mob. When he saw his commandant in danger, Brevet Major Jacob Zeilin sent a platoon forward to attack the crowd and rescue him. They were immediately driven back by the mob. The cannon made the mob bold and bloodthirsty and some of the rioters were armed.

One Marine was shot in the face; many others were injured by paving stones torn up and thrown by the crowd. But after a bout of chaotic hand-to-hand fighting, the Marines managed to wrest the cannon away from the rioters and haul it off. As the mob surged forward to reclaim their prize, the Marines fired. The rioters quickly retreated out of range, dragging their wounded with them. Commandant Henderson pushed his way through a crowd of spectators to stand between the Marines and the rioters. In a booming voice, he demanded a halt to the shooting. At that moment, he was fired upon from point-blank range.

Miraculously, the rioter missed. A Marine sergeant wounded the would-be assassin and Commandant Henderson finished off the man by beating him to the ground. The Marines pressed forward and dragged the perpetrator off to jail. There were more shots and more rocks thrown. Another Marine was hit. Finally, as the soldiers formed an orderly skirmish line and loaded their muskets for a second volley, the crowd dispersed. The Marines then spread throughout the city. Within a few hours, the riot ended. But the tensions that caused the unrest still simmered.

Eighteen months after the Washington riot, Colonel Archibald Henderson died at his home. His tenure as commandant brought glory to the Marines, and his passing left them no successor. The end of the Henderson era marked the beginning of perilous times for the Marine Corps and for the United States. The new commandant of the Corps was Colonel John Harris. Like Henderson, he was a veteran of the War of 1812. Sixty-one years old when he assumed command, he was not a man to make demands or spend time dreaming up new duties for his Marines. He was content with the way things were. But America was changing, and even as Harris assumed command, trouble was brewing in the wilderness of Kansas, in the Carolinas, and in Virginia.

WITH THE MARINES AT HARPERS FERRY

The fighting skills of the Marine detachment in Washington were needed just two short years after they quelled the Election Day riots. This time they were called upon to rescue the victims of Americans' very first encounter with political terrorism. The enemy the Marines fought at Harpers Ferry was a group of political fanatics convinced they were waging a just war. These violent radicals were nurtured and financed by unyielding abolitionists in New England and inflamed by rabid pro-slavery adherents in the South. In the coming battle there could be no winners.

On Sunday morning, October 16, 1859, a bearded man calling himself Isaac Smith rode into the small town of Harpers Ferry in Virginia (now West Virginia) where the Potomac meets the Shenandoah River. "Smith" was actually the butchering abolitionist leader John Brown—"Old Brown of Osawatoomie"—who had come down from his stronghold in the mountains leading a pack of armed men, white and black.

Wanted for the murders of five pro-slavery adherents in Pottawatomie Creek, Kansas, Brown had led a decade-long struggle against the forces of slavery. Of late he had taken his fight westward, where new states were entering the union. Brown wanted to ensure that these states did not permit slavery. Southern expansionists saw things differently, and viewed slavery as a states' rights issue and an issue of property not morality.

John Brown began his struggle through peaceful means. In the beginning he taught blacks to read, ministered to the sick, and arranged asylum for escaped slaves. But in later years he had become more zealous, and his struggle had turned violent. Helped by abolitionists in the northeastern states who eagerly funneled money to his cause, Brown conceived a bold plan to free all the slaves in America by forming his own army of liberation. As the first step in this campaign, he and his men seized the federal arsenal at Harpers Ferry, which also housed a gun factory. They were seeking weapons to arm their followers.

Shortly after riding into Harpers Ferry, Brown and his gang, which included his two sons, swept into the arsenal, shot some federal troopers, and took the rest of the garrison and several civilians hostage. Unfortunately for Brown, an aroused group of local militiamen quickly surrounded the buildings where he and the hostages were holed up. Under sustained gunfire, which killed a number of Brown's raiders, the abolitionist leader moved the hostages into a stout brick building that housed two fire engines, and dug in for a long siege. Outside, the inexperienced militiamen waited impatiently for leadership before mounting a rescue attempt.

The Marine barracks in Washington was alerted the next morning. Information about the attack, sent by telegraph, was still sketchy, but it was clear that a military force was needed. Eighty-five Marines assembled at the navy yard. Led by First Lieutenant Israel Greene, they wore their dress uniforms. These new, navy-blue suits recently replaced the old gray uniforms with scarlet facings to symbolize the blood Marines had spilled at Chapultepec. Greene's Marines looked smart, martial, and impressive in their dress blues with white belts and facings. But the lieutenant's choice of attire would have dire historical consequences.

Even as the Marines marched to the railyard with orders to report to the senior U.S. Army officer in the field at Harpers Ferry, that officer was being dispatched by the secretary of war. Army Lieutenant Colonel Robert E. Lee, a hero of the Mexican War now on leave from active duty in Texas, was ordered to lead the Marines in putting down the insurrection. Lee's friend, confidant, and aide J.E.B. Stuart volunteered to join him in the rescue attempt. They took the train to Harpers Ferry, meeting up with the Marines at ten o'clock that night. Since Lee was confident that Brown could not escape, his chief concern became the safety of the hostages. He assigned Greene and his Marines the task of taking Brown and his outlaws down—with sword and bayonet so as not to harm an innocent with a stray musket ball.

Early the next morning J.E.B. Stuart approached the firehouse under a flag of truce and demanded that Brown lay down his weapons, turn the hostages loose, and surrender. Brown refused, which was Stuart's cue to wave his famous plumed hat—the signal to start the attack. Lieutenant Greene and thirteen Marines rushed forward in two columns to divide the abolitionists' fire. They immediately began battering at the thick, reinforced door of the small brick building. It took a few minutes—and the imaginative use of a ladder in place of a battering ram—but the door came down. Greene, sword drawn, was the first man through the gap. The two Marines behind him were both hit by musket fire. Private Luke Quinn was gut-shot and mortally wounded.

As Brown and his surviving raiders tried to reload, the Marines overwhelmed them. Greene raised his ceremonial sword—which went well with his dress blues but was much less serviceable than a cutlass forged for combat—and slashed the unsharpened blade across the back of John Brown's neck. The blow knocked Brown to the floor but did not kill him. Greene's second thrust became tangled in Brown's thick leather harness. The ceremonial sword bent double and failed to pierce the man's body. Brown, who should have died from Greene's slashing and stabbing attack, lived long enough to stand trial and hang for his crimes, and to become a living symbol, then a martyr for the abolitionists' cause. Brown's trial and execution only served to heighten political tensions and hasten the coming of the American Civil War.

Historians regard Brown's raid at Harpers Ferry as the first volley fired in the Civil War. If that is so, then the first uniformed fatality of this tragic and costly conflict was Irish-born Luke Quinn, the young United States Marine shot and killed that fateful day.

ILL-PREPARED FOR WAR

When the Civil War erupted, the Marine Corps was not prepared. The decades of peace that followed the Mexican War had diminished the Corps numbers, and as its leader, Commandant Harris lacked the vision to forge a new role for the Marines.

Even worse, when the conflict began in 1861, the Marines—composed of fewer than 2,000 officers and men—lost over half its captains and two-thirds of its lieutenants in a single week. All resigned to take commissions with the Confederacy. Among these "turncoats" were some of the Corps' finest leaders: George H. Terrett, the hero of Mexico City; John D. Simms, who took the Barrier Forts; three of Commandant Henderson's four sons; even Lieutenant Israel Greene, the hero of Harpers Ferry. All these fine officers resigned their commissions to lend their support to Southern rights.

The Army and Navy suffered hundreds of similar defections; West Point graduates on active duty in the Army were especially prone to defect. States' rights meant more to these soldiers than the integrity of the Union, and men like J. E. B. Stuart and Robert E. Lee "went South." Lee would ultimately lead the Confederate forces in the field as commander in chief. J. E. B. Stuart would become a martyred hero to the Southern cause. But the Marine Corps, simply because it was the smallest military force in the Union, was more decimated by these mass defections than the other services. Fortunately, the enlisted Marines, mostly recruited from the industrial Northeast, remained loyal to the Union cause. Irish and German immigrants mostly, they had little incentive to join the Confederacy. But even with a core of loyal enlisted men filling their ranks, when Marines marched out of Washington to fight in the first battle of the Civil War, they could field only thirteen officers and 336 men.

The American Civil War marked the dawn of modern warfare. Over the course of the next four years, every branch of the United States armed services would find its evolution accelerated by the first military confrontation of the industrial age. The United States Navy would move from sail to steam, from wooden ships to ironclad. Both the U.S. and Confederate Navy would experiment with torpedoes, armored turrets, submarines, and graduated gunsights. The Army would replace muskets with reliable repeating rifles, smoothbore cannons with rifled barrels, pistols with revolvers, and roaming armies that lived off the land with tactical organization and advanced battlefield logistics. The Army would also experiment with a deadly new innovation—the rapid-fire Gatling gun, a forerunner of the modern machine gun. The Union Army would even attempt aerial observation using manned hot air balloons.

But none of these advances in weapons and strategies would affect the Marine Corps. Even though its ranks would swell to nearly 4,000 men during the War Between the States, its tactics and its role would remain virtually unchanged because the Marine Corps' leadership was old, stale, and lacked vision. The Marine Corps unwillingness to adapt to the requirements of modern warfare would threaten its very existence when the Civil War was finally over. "On the whole," says Marine Corps historian J. Robert Moskin, "it was not to be a time of distinction for the Corps."

As the war progressed, a handful of bold Marines would fight with courage and distinction, and would bring honor to the Corps—but not until the fourth and final year of the conflict. In the very first action of the war, the Marines' performance under fire was less than exemplary.

As the armies of the Union and Confederacy marched to Virginia, the public's perception was that the war would be short and relatively bloodless. Everyone assumed that the Union had the advantage because of its vast industrial might. When war was declared, there was not a single cannon foundry, munitions factory, or large shipbuilding facility in the South. The North seemed to hold all the cards. But inside the military services there was a growing realization that despite their industrial output, the North was no more prepared for war than the South. The Union armies were in disarray as a result of mass defections and generally poor leadership in the higher ranks. Their weapons, while plentiful, were outmoded. So were their tactics for waging war. Though this last charge could be leveled at both sides, the dearth of leadership in the Union forces would prove disastrous in the first years of the war.

THE FIRST BATTLE OF MANASSAS

On Sunday morning, July 21, 1861, the armies of the North and South clashed for the first time in the rolling hills of Virginia. Hundreds of ordinary citizens, thrilled by the chance to witness such a spectacle, made a day of it. They streamed out of Washington on foot and in carriages to watch the battle. Many brought their families or packed a picnic lunch.

That morning, the Marines, led by Major John G. Reynolds, advanced with Army regulars and Captain Charles Griffin's "West Point Battery" of six cannon. They were supposed to circle the Confederates' left flank and take the enemy by surprise. But as they forded a stream, called Bull Run Creek, they came under heavy and sustained fire from Confederate forces. The Marines pushed the enemy back until they found themselves in the swirling center of the battle, defending a prominent residence called Henry Hill House. They could push no farther because the First Virginia Brigade, commanded by Brigadier General Thomas J. "Stonewall" Jackson stood its ground and refused to budge.

The Army and Marine units traded shots with the First Virginia until a second group of infantrymen in blue uniforms emerged from a nearby line of trees. The Union soldiers thought they were reinforced, until the new arrivals leveled their muskets and fired at them. The Union troops had fallen victim to the 33rd Virginia, a regiment too proud of their original blue uniforms to adopt Confederate gray. As the 33rd raked the Marines and Army units with deadly fire, the Union line wavered.

The battle continued until late afternoon, when J. E. B. Stuart ordered a Confederate charge. All along the battle lines, the Union forces began to collapse. Three times during the Confederate assault, the Marines fell back, but rallied each time. But when the entire Union line broke, the Marines joined in the retreat. The withdrawal to Washington was orderly and disciplined, until the Confederates shelled the only bridge leading back to the city. Then it became a rout. Mobs of soldiers, weapons cast aside, streamed into the federal city. Their unruly presence caused civil unrest and frightened a populace already convinced the Rebels would take Washington.

There was no federal army to protect the capital, but fortunately for the Union, the Confederate forces were so badly battered they could not press their attack. Had the Confederate Army occupied Washington, the United States might have ceased to exist after 1861.

Two weeks later, when Marines saw action again, the outcome was very different.

They, along with U.S. Navy officers and sailors reinforced by an Army unit, seized two forts at Hatteras Islet on the North Carolina coast. Six hundred rebel prisoners were captured in what amounted to a surprise attack. There was not one Union casualty.

Two separate military actions with two wildly different outcomes. This trend would continue for the rest of this war. Because the bulk of the Corps' troops were posted aboard Navy ships, the Marines almost never fought as a cohesive unit. When they did, they discharged their duties with skill and bravery and usually emerged victorious. The Civil War Marine Corps did most of their work enforcing the blockade against Southern ports or fighting on the nation's waterways. It was during the sustained campaign against Confederate ports and shipping that the Marines truly distinguished themselves. Two battles in particular would illustrate the Corps' limited but vital role in the Civil War and demonstrate the valor and determination of the men who fought and died to preserve the Union.

THE BATTLE OF DREWRY'S BLUFF

Two months to the day after the indecisive duel between the ironclads *Monitor* and *Virginia* (formerly the *Merrimack*) off Hampton Roads, Virginia, the Confederate Army retreated from Norfolk and burned the navy yards—destroying the *Virginia* in its berth to prevent the damaged ironclad from being captured. Her guns had already been stripped and placed on the high cliffs of Drewry's Bluff to defend the city Richmond. It was a sad ending to this once-noble warship.

On the morning of May 9, 1862, just off Norfolk's shore, the *Monitor* joined the attack on Norfolk. With her was another Union ironclad, the U.S.S. *Galena*. Constructed along more traditional lines than the *Monitor,* the *Galena* was simply a draft-hulled steam frigate with interlocking armor plates welded over its original wooden frame. *Galena*'s armor was much thinner than the steel sheets used to protected the Confederate ironclad *Virginia,* and this flaw in her design would prove disastrous.

While 200 Marines led by Captain Charles G. McCawley took possession of the Norfolk Navy Yard, the *Monitor,* the *Galena,* and the lightly armored floating battery *Naugatuck* steamed up the James River in front of the Union fleet. They were dispatched to bombard Richmond—the first step in seizing the Confederate city.

Early on the morning of May 15, the ironclads encountered a battalion of Confederate Marines waiting behind the half-completed fortifications at Drewry's Bluff, just eight miles downriver from Richmond. These Confederates Marines were led by one of the heroes of Mexico City, Captain John D. Simms, and were armed with a battery of cannons placed on the bluff under the supervision of General Robert E. Lee himself. With these Confederate Marines was a detachment of sailors off the *Virginia,* who were manning the guns stripped from the burned ironclad's hold. After fighting the *Monitor* to a draw, these men were itching to settle the score against a Union ironclad—*any* Union ironclad. What happened to the U.S.S. *Galena* on that sunny spring morning was the South's revenge for the loss of the *Virginia* and the fall of Norfolk.

As the Union ships moved into position, a single cannon shot echoed across the river and shattered the morning stillness. The Union shell burst over the fortifications on Drewry's Bluff, heralding the commencement of hostilities. The Confederate guns returned fire, their cannons aimed at the *Monitor*. Once again Confederate cannonballs bounced off the *Monitor's* thick steel armor. The ironclad moved closer to the shore and blasted away at the Confederate fortifications from a distance of less than 800 yards. During this exchange, the *Monitor* took repeated hits from cannon and musket fire but was never damaged. The Union ironclad finally withdrew because her guns could not elevate high enough to hit the heaviest enemy fortifications on top of the bluff. It was then that the U.S.S. *Galena* valiantly entered the fray to cover the *Monitor's* retreat and take her turn at leveling the enemy fortifications.

Over the course of the next hour, the *Galena* took the worst of it from the Confederate guns, which fired on her with deadly accuracy. The ironclad reeled under twenty-eight hits, all of them damaging. Eighteen times the enemy cannon shells punched through the interlocking steel plates. Each penetration sent hot cannon fragments ripping through the bodies of the huddled Union crew. The *Naugatuck* came to the defense of her sister ship, but after sustained fire the Perrott gun on her deck burst. Defenseless, the *Naugatuck* was struck repeatedly and floundered, her crew slaughtered.

On the *Galena's* shattered and exposed deck, the after battery crew was completely obliterated by a ten-inch Confederate shell. The explosion left the deck strewn with debris and the dead. Corporal John F. Mackie gathered a team of twelve sailors to clear away the casualties and wreckage and get the battery's gun up and running again. Confederate fire continued until the *Galena's* decks ran red with blood. As dead and dying sailors piled up where they fell, as the wounded filled *Galena's* hold, as her crew panicked from repeated hits, twenty-seven-year-old Corporal Mackie from New York City refused to give up. He rallied the faltering crew and remained at the gun battery, returning fire as the stricken ship limped out of range of the enemy's guns. Thirteen sailors aboard the *Galena* died that morning, eleven others were wounded. As the crippled ironclad steamed back down the James River, the Confederates defenders, especially the sailors off the *Virginia,* cheered. At last they could claim victory against a Union ironclad.

One year and two months later, on July 17, 1863, aboard the U.S.S. *Seminole* off the coast of Texas, Corporal John F. Mackie became the first United States Marine to receive the Medal of Honor. The award was presented by order of President Abraham Lincoln himself. The desk-bound—some would say hidebound—commandant of the Marines had failed to acknowledge Mackie's courage.

Born on October 1, 1835, in New York City, Mackie would remain a Marine for several years after the end of hostilities. He eventually rose to the rank of orderly sergeant. After his stint in the Corps, he received a pension and returned to civilian life. John Mackie, the first Marine ever to be awarded the Medal of Honor, died on June 18, 1910, and is buried in Drexel Hill, Pennsylvania. But this was not the end of his story. One final honor remained for the first Marine Corps Medal of Honor recipient. On the morning of May 17, 2000, a dedication service for an interpretive marker honoring Corporal John F. Mackie was held in the National Battlefield Park in Virginia. The marker was placed on Drewry's Bluff, overlooking the James River, on the exact spot where the Confederate Marines who fired upon the *Galena* stood on that other, far less tranquil morning in May.

THE MEDAL OF HONOR

Prior to the Civil War, American military leaders disagreed over the wisdom of awarding medals of valor. Some felt it made sense to copy this ancient tradition, which dated back to the warriors of ancient Greece and Rome. But others felt that because America was the first true democracy in human history, the United States should dispense with such "European"-style honors.

But during the Mexican War of 1847, so many men distinguished themselves that Congress scrambled for a way to honor them. They created the Certificate of Merit and bestowed it on a number of soldiers who fought at Chapultepec. Men from the Army, the Navy, and the Marines received this honor. But there were drawbacks to awarding a certificate. For one thing, a piece of paper was not something that the honoree could display on his dress uniform.

When the Civil War began, a bill was introduced in the Senate to "promote the efficiency of the Navy." President Abraham Lincoln approved it on December 21, 1861, and the Navy Medal of Honor was born. Senator Henry Wilson of Massachusetts introduced a bill for an Army Medal of Honor in the following year and Lincoln signed it into law. Though the Army and Navy medals differ in appearance, the overall requirements were and still are the same. The Medal of Honor was the only medal awarded for bravery in battle during the Civil War, which explains why so many of them were handed out during this conflict. It still remains the highest military award for bravery that can be bestowed on any individual in the United States of America.

The deeds of the person considered for this honor must be proved by uncontestable evidence of at least two eyewitnesses. It must be so outstanding that it clearly distinguishes his gallantry beyond the call of duty from lesser forms of bravery. It must involve the risk of his life and it must be a deed that, if he had not done it, would not have subjected him to any justified criticism. The Medal of Honor is presented "in the name of the Congress of the United States," and for this reason has sometimes been called the Congressional Medal of Honor.

During the first decades the Medal of Honor was awarded, warfare was fought very differently. Honor and respect for flags and regimental banners was deemed important and any soldier who captured an enemy flag or rescued his own flag or the flag of his unit from "dishonor" in combat could be counted on to win a Medal of Honor. There were even incidents of entire units receiving the Medal of Honor simply for volunteering to remain in uniform! Since the end of the Civil War, the requirements for the nation's highest military honor have become much more stringent. Far fewer Medals of Honor have been awarded in subsequent conflicts, and some awarded during the Civil War are no longer recognized.

The first six men to be awarded the medal earned it in a raid known as the Great Locomotive Chase. During the Civil War, scores of Union soldiers and sailors would be so honored. Eighteen United States Marines received the Medal of Honor for action in the Civil War. During this period about half the winners were foreign-born—roughly the composition of the Corps itself. Enlisted men and noncommissioned officers received the vast majority of the Medals of Honor awarded. Officers continued to be awarded for gallantry through brevet—honorary—promotions.

THE DESTRUCTION OF THE MISSISSIPPI

Marines distinguished themselves in the long and bloody campaign to close the Gulf ports to the Confederacy, capture New Orleans, and control the Mississippi River. On March 7, 1862, the U.S.S. *Hartford*, the flagship of the West Gulf Blockading Squadron commanded by Admiral David G. Farragut, arrived at the mouth of the Mississippi. After a violent exchange of fire with the defending forts—which cost the Union over 200 casualties in less than an hour—Farragut sent a Navy officer ashore at New Orleans, backed by twenty Marines. The officer demanded the city's surrender while the Marines held off an angry mob of locals swarming at the docks. The city fathers rejected the terms of surrender, so the delegates rushed back to the protection of the Marines. Captain John L. Broome, who commanded the Marine detachment, seized the initiative—along with the New Orleans Customs House and City Hall. With their major government institutions in enemy hands, the city fathers surrendered.

Admiral Farragut followed this victory with two sorties up the Mississippi River to study Confederate defenses. On the night of March 14, 1863, his fleet felt the sting of cannon as his ships sailed within range of the Confederate defenders at Port Hudson. In the confusion, the steam side-wheeler *Mississippi* ran aground. Lieutenant George Dewey, the *Mississippi*'s commander, was ordered to destroy his ship to prevent its capture. But over sixty of Dewey's men were already casualties—it would be difficult to get the wounded men onto the boats and away under sustained gunfire. Dewey gathered his crew on deck and ordered them to check the fallen to see if any still lived. They found a few survivors, and even discovered the cabin boy alive and unharmed, buried under a pile of corpses. Dewey had the boats lowered on the side facing away from the Confederate cannon, and began their escape. It took time, but under relentless fire from the fort, the crew abandoned the *Mississippi* except for one man. Marine Sergeant Pinkerton Ross Vaughn remained aboard to set fire to the stricken warship. He accomplished this feat at great personal risk, and without a means of escape.

As pieces of flaming sail and broken mast rained down around him, Sergeant Vaughn dived into the muddy river. In minutes he was retrieved by a lifeboat. But the *Mississippi*, still burning, floated free of the sandbar and drifted unmanned, endangering the other Union ships on the river. The wreck finally piled up on the shore of Profit's Island and exploded in what one observer called "the grandest display of fireworks I have ever witnessed, and the costliest."

Sergeant Pinkerton Vaughn was born in 1839 in Chester, Pennsylvania, and was twenty-four years old at the time of the Battle of Port Hudson. He received the Medal of Honor for his courageous actions aboard the stricken *Mississippi* and continued to serve in the Marine Corps until his death in August 22, 1866, just eighteen months after the Civil War ended.

THE BATTLE OF MOBILE BAY

After Admiral Farragut battled the guns at Port Hudson, he sailed the fleet to Mobile, Alabama, and attacked the city on August 5, 1864. Mobile was the last open port of the Confederacy, and desperately needed supplies would be cut off if the city fell. The Confederate Army and Navy staged a valiant defense but were outnumbered and outgunned. Despite waters filled with almost 200 enemy "torpedoes"—what we now call mines—the Union fleet moved into the bay and bombarded the coastal portions of the city. What followed was probably the most decisive naval battle of the Civil War, a battle that severed the Confederacy's final lifeline.

To enter Mobile Bay, the Union ships—including Admiral Farragut's flagship the U.S.S. *Hartford*, the *Brooklyn*, the *Metacomet*, the *Monongahela*, the *Ossippee*, the *Richmond*, the *Lakawanna*, and the *Oneida*—had to sail between two heavily fortified defensive batteries at Fort Gaines and Fort Morgan. It was a deadly gauntlet. If the guns didn't get the ships, the hundreds of floating mines surely would. Four Union ironclads led the assault as the frigates, lashed together in pairs, followed closely behind. On both sides of the attackers were the forts, in the center of the bay a massive minefield. The Union was about to pay a heavy price for attempting to capture Mobile.

The battle began at 6:30 in the morning when the Confederates at Fort Morgan fired their cannons at the Union fleet. As Farragut's frigates ran the passage, they rained heavy fire down on the forts. But the Confederates had been preparing long and hard for such an assault. With cannonballs heated to red-hot temperatures in the forts' furnaces, the Rebel cannon fire ripped through the wooden hulls of the Union ships, setting them ablaze.

The U.S.S. *Brooklyn*, along with the *Hartford* and *Metacomet*—which were lashed together—took some of the worst damage. According to one witness, the Confederate fire was "mowing down men, deluging the decks with blood and scattering mangled fragments of humanity so thickly that it was difficult to stand on the [*Hartford*'s] deck."

The U.S.S. *Brooklyn* slowed down to keep from overtaking the sluggish Union ironclads when suddenly a muffled blast was heard. The stern of the ironclad *Tecumseh*—which had been struck by at least one mine—rose out of the water, its screw still spinning. Then, unbelievably quickly, it disappeared beneath the waves, taking a hundred of her crew with her. The *Brooklyn* faltered, right in front of Fort Morgan's guns. Over the next few minutes the Union steamship would take most of its fifty-nine hits, thirty-nine of them to the hull.

The defenders smelled blood and increased their rate of fire, changing over from cannonball to grapeshot—which raked the decks of the Union ships with blasts of clustered, fist-sized missiles that tore through flesh and splintered bone. Then the

Hartford took a second round of hits. Men were falling too quickly for the surgeons belowdecks to tend them. A shell took off a gunner's head, then a sailor's legs. When the legless man threw up his arms in agony, they were shot away too. Farragut, who had himself hauled up to the fighting tops by rope so he could see the battle, realized that the ships behind him were taking the same punishment as his flagship. With cannon on both sides and mines ahead, the admiral acted boldly.

"Damn the torpedoes! Full speed ahead," he commanded.

The first pairs of Union ships steamed through the withering fire and through the minefield—miraculously, they never took a hit—to cross the bay to a safe position out of range of the Confederate guns. Suddenly another ironclad, this one belonging to the Confederates, steamed into the fray. It was the C.S.S *Tennessee,* commanded by Admiral Franklin Buchanan, prewar head of Annapolis. Behind the *Tennessee* came three smaller Southern gunboats, the *Sema, Gaines,* and *Morgan.*

Farragut charged them, his Union ships *Brooklyn* and *Richmond* steaming in right behind the *Hartford.* The Confederate *Tennessee* tried to ram and sink the Union flagship, but the *Hartford* nimbly escaped the lumbering iron giant. The Confederate gunboats *Sema, Gaines,* and *Morgan* were taken out in short order by accurate Union fire—here the superiority of the Union rifled cannon barrels over the Confederate smoothbores was proved beyond a shadow of a doubt.

The *Tennessee*—her sister ships out of the battle—was supported only by the guns of Fort Gaines. The courageous Confederate sailors engaged up to seven ships at once, but they could not hope to prevail. With her stack so riddled with holes that the interior of the *Tennessee* filled with choking smoke from her boiler, and her commander wounded twice, the Confederate ironclad withdrew. The *Tennessee*'s crew surrendered two hours later.

Only Fort Gaines was left to defend Mobile Bay. It held for two days, garrisoned by Confederate veterans of the Battle of Shiloh and green recruits from the Pelham Military Academy, some as young as thirteen years old. Finally, with all but one of her guns destroyed, Fort Gaines surrendered to Union forces on August 8. The last open Southern port—the Confederates' only lifeline for supplies from overseas—had fallen. The Union lost 172 men. More than half the fatalities were from the crew of the sunken *Tecumseh.*

Aboard two Union frigates, Marine sharpshooters had distinguished themselves with conduct above and beyond the call of duty. Only eighteen Marines would be awarded the Medal of Honor during the Civil War. Half earned their medals at the Battle of Mobile Bay. From the U.S.S. *Oneida,* Sergeant James S. Roantree—born in Dublin, Ireland, in 1835—was presented with the Medal of Honor for bravery under fire in the battle against the Confederate ironclad *Tennessee.* Despite the death of countless gunners and the destruction of the ship's boilers—which scalded sailors with deadly steam when they exploded—Sergeant Roantree performed his duties with skill and courage. Roantree, who entered service in New York City, rose to the rank of first sergeant. He died in Boston in 1873.

From the U.S.S. *Galena*—where John F. Mackie, the first Marine to win the Medal of Honor had fought—Irish-born Quartermaster Edward S. Martin earned the nation's highest honor. Edward Martin helped lead the stricken *Oneida,* which had her steering rudder shot away, past the enemy forts and into the safety of the bay. Edward Martin returned to New York City a local hero. He died in Brooklyn in 1901.

Aboard the U.S.S. *Richmond,* another Irishman, Sergeant James Martin of Derry, received the Medal of Honor for refusing to abandon the gun under his command despite heavy fire. James Martin also survived the war to die in Philadelphia in 1895. Also aboard the *Richmond* was Sergeant Andrew Miller, a German-born Marine who entered service at the Marine Corps barracks in Washington. Miller received his Medal of Honor for refusing to abandon his gun, and for bravery in facing the fire from Fort Morgan. Born in 1836, Miller left the Corps after the Civil War, moved westward, and vanished from the pages of history.

One of the "old men" at the Battle of Mobile Bay was also aboard the U.S.S. *Richmond.* Orderly Sergeant David Sprowle of Lisbon, New York, was fifty-two years old when he received the Medal of Honor for directing "a division of great guns" and remaining at his post for the duration of the two-hour battle.

Aboard the U.S.S. *Brooklyn,* two Marine Corps sergeants distinguished themselves. Sergeant Michael Hudson of County Sligo, Ireland, received the Medal of Honor for using his gun "with skill and courage." He survived the war and moved to Michigan in the general exodus west that followed the conflict. He died at the end of December 1891, at the age of fifty-seven. Sergeant J. Henry Denig of York, Pennsylvania, also received the Medal of Honor for bravery under fire. He vanished from history after the war ended.

Also aboard the U.S.S. *Brooklyn,* Corporal Willard Moon Smith and Corporal Miles M. Oviatt, both originally from Cattaraugus County, New York, received Medals of Honor for stalwartly manning their guns with skill and courage under extreme danger. Corporal Smith returned to his home in Olean, New York, after the war but later moved to Buffalo. Smith died in Brooklyn in 1918 and is buried in Buffalo.

Corporal Miles Oviatt's story is unique in that he left a long account of his life and times aboard the two ships he served on during the Civil War. This diary, edited by Oviatt's great-granddaughter, was published in 1998. *A Civil War Marine at Sea* offers a rich personal history of the period and a peek into the daily life of a Civil War recruit assigned to shipboard duties in the Marine Corps.

Miles Oviatt was born in Cattaraugus County, New York, on December 1, 1840. His father, Thomas, started out as a river rafter who worked for a local lumber company. His job was moving logs along the waterways, as far as Warren, Pennsylvania, and Cincinnati, Ohio. After his marriage to Lydia Jane Rice, Thomas quit his rafting job and purchased a farm tract near Olean, New York, in order to provide a stable life for his family. Miles was the second child born to the couple and the first son. His older sister was born in 1838, his younger brother in 1845.

Life was pleasant in the rural area around Olean until the late 1840s and 1850s when secessionist tensions began to sweep the land. But politics held little interest for Miles, who desired only to break away from his family and make a life for himself. Though his older sister and younger brother remained on the family farm, the 1860 census lists Miles Oviatt's occupation as tinsmith's apprentice and had him living in a hotel on Union Street. When the Civil War erupted in April 1861, Miles's uncle Luther V. Oviatt and his son Thomas—both enthusiastic Unionists—volunteered for service. Luther joined the 14th Pennsylvania in October. A year later he died in Maryland of severe diarrhea. His son Thomas served with the Pennsylvania Militia Infantry and later with the 144th Pennsylvania.

Miles and his best friend, Willard Moon Smith, along with comrades George H. Banfield and George W. Kelsey, left Olean for New York City, where they volunteered for the Marine Corps. They were all young—Miles was just nineteen—and caught up in war fever. It must have seemed a grand adventure to leave their small town for the bigger world.

According to his enlistment papers, Miles Oviatt was five feet eleven and a half inches tall, with blue eyes and brown hair. These documents also list his civilian occupation as clerk, which indicates that he had tried another profession either before or after becoming an apprentice metalworker. Miles soon came to regret his hasty decision to enlist when he discovered that life in the Marines was not what he had expected, but he was young and learned to make the most of his impulsive decision. In time he came to love the Marine Corps. Miles Oviatt sent home painted picture postcards of the ships he was posted on, and would eventually return to active duty in the military long after the Civil War ended.

Miles Oviatt was posted aboard the U.S.S. *Vanderbilt,* where he served until March 1864. During this period, the *Vanderbilt* cruised in the South Atlantic on the prowl for Confederate blockade runners. Oviatt was promoted to corporal on his first voyage. But when the *Vanderbilt* docked at the Brooklyn Navy Yards, he was immediately hospitalized for a severe cold—perhaps pneumonia. He was down for some time and the *Vanderbilt* sailed off without him. On April 14, Oviatt was formally transferred to the U.S.S. *Brooklyn*—probably through the contrivance of his friend Willard Smith, who was also posted aboard. The Union forces had just taken Port Hudson and opened the Mississippi, and the *Brooklyn* was about to join Admiral Farragut's fleet in the campaign to capture Mobile. On Friday, August 5, the *Brooklyn* joined her sister ships at the Battle of Mobile Bay.

Oviatt's diaries offer a detailed eyewitness account of the battle, as he saw it from the deck of his beleaguered frigate. He tells of the attack by the C.S.S. *Tennessee,* referring to the Confederate ironclad as "The Ram." He writes eloquently about the fate of some of the other Union ships, but glosses over his own contribution to the battle—declaring modestly that "we fired at the enemy" or "our guns fired upon The Ram." Oviatt makes no mention of the terrible carnage he must have witnessed on the decks of the *Brooklyn,* nor does he state whether he was close to any of the casualties.

After recounting the dramatic moment when The Ram struck her white flag and surrendered, Miles Oviatt simply states that "our loss was 14 killed & 30 to 40 wounded." He mentions that "The Brooklyn was struck 59 times, 39 to her hull, 4 in the M. [main] Mast, rest in her rigging" and speaks with pride about the surrender of Fort Gaines. "We took 850 Prisoners, 50 or 60 guns & ammunition, & 6 Mos. provisions for the garrison."

On August 26, the U.S.S. *Brooklyn,* crippled from the fight, struck her anchor and made for Pensacola Harbor, where she waited in anchor to sail back to Boston for repairs. Oviatt mentions in passing that he was promoted to sergeant on September 1. While he was in Pensacola, news reached the crew of the *Brooklyn* that the C.S.S. *Alabama* had been taken by the Union ship *Kearsarge* off the coast of France. That daring Confederate warship had long been a thorn in the side of the Union fleet, and the crew of the *Brooklyn,* along with every other ship in the United States Navy, had hunted for her. Oviatt greeted the news of the Rebel ship's demise with joy.

When the *Brooklyn* was repaired sufficiently to resume her sea duties, she participated in the Battle of Fort Fisher. Oviatt was there and provides another rich account of the chaotic struggle. The *Brooklyn* returned to Hampton Roads in January 1865. Sergeant Oviatt was reassigned to the Marine barracks in Brooklyn, New York, then to the Barracks in Washington, D.C., where he was presented with the Medal of Honor.

Finally, First Sergeant Miles Oviatt was posted aboard a third ship, but he never assumed his duties. It was during this period that he was hospitalized again—this time for severe head pain and chronic diarrhea. His original term of service nearly over, Oviatt was honorably discharged in August 1866 and returned to Olean, New York, and his former trade as a metalworker. On July 19, 1868, Miles Oviatt married Lucetta Alzina Crandall, twenty-one. By 1875, they had established a house in Pleasant Valley, and Frances Emily Oviatt—their first and only child—was born on November 26, 1876.

In 1876, Civil War General Philip Sheridan was commander of the Army, fighting Indians on the plains of the West. Bored with small-town life, Miles Oviatt enlisted in the Pleasant Valley Cavalry, hoping to enter the fray. But while he was training and drilling his men, Oviatt was taken ill. After what must have been a quick decline, he died at the age of thirty-nine on November 1, 1880—the cause of death listed as "Congestion of Brain and Inflammation of Lungs due to Exposure." Miles Oviatt is buried in Pleasant Valley Cemetery, just north of Olean. In 1989, the United States government placed a bronze marker on his grave to commemorate his actions at the Battle of Mobile Bay.

Curiously, no contemporaries in the town of Olean seemed to have been aware of Miles Oviatt's war record—or the fact that he was awarded the nation's highest honor for bravery. The local history of the town does not mention Miles Oviatt's record, though it extensively tracked the military careers of other Civil War veterans from the region. When Oviatt died, the obituary in the Olean paper was short and made no mention of his four-year service with the Marine Corps or his Medal of Honor. Only his service with the Pleasant Valley Calvary was cited.

An even greater mystery was uncovered in the 1990s when Mary Livingston, Miles Oviatt's great-granddaughter, set out to find out all she could about her illustrious ancestor and discovered that Olean's nineteenth-century newspaper files were complete—except for the years 1861 through 1865! This strange omission has never been explained, and no one today knows if Miles Oviatt and Willard Moon Smith's exploits aboard the U.S.S. *Brooklyn* were ever reported to the people in their own hometown.

Willard Smith—Miles's friend and fellow Medal of Honor recipient—moved to Buffalo shortly after the Civil War ended. No letters or correspondence between these men has survived. Ten years after Miles Oviatt's death, his widow remarried.

His only daughter, Frances, grew up to become an influential businesswoman, owning a partnership in the W. H. Mandeville Insurance Company. Frances was appointed a delegate by New York Governor Franklin D. Roosevelt to the Conference of the National Tax Association in 1929 and 1930. Only with the publication of Miles M. Oviatt's diary in 1998 was the story of this forgotten Civil War hero and Medal of Honor recipient revealed.

THE WAR ENDS

On May 12, 1864, Colonel John Harris, the commandant of the Marine Corps, died in Washington just eight days before his seventy-fourth birthday. Because so many military traditions were shattered during the Civil War, Secretary of the Navy Gideon Welles broke another—he ignored the seniority system, retired several officers, and reached over the heads of others to select Major Jacob Zeilin, Jr., as the new commandant. An experienced Marine with a distinguished war record, Major Zeilin had quelled the Election Day riot in Washington and marched into Tokyo with Commodore Perry. Zeilin, now fifty-seven, would become the first Marine to attain general officer rank. Of German extraction, Zeilin looked like a dour Pennsylvania Dutch farmer. But he was energetic for his advanced age, and his promotion would prove to be a boon for the Corps.

The sad fact was that the once-dashing Harris had never been a competent commandant. In his mid-sixties when he took the job, he resisted the innovations in warfare that evolved during the Civil War. He never pushed for a mobile, amphibious Marine Corps capable of landing and holding a hostile beachhead—yet those were precisely the skills and tactics often required during the siege of Southern ports in the river campaign. Harris insisted on continuing the outmoded tradition of posting tiny groups of Marines on Navy ships for boarding parties or for shooting the enemy from the fighting tops. But in the new age of steam, screw, and paddle wheel, boarding parties and fighting tops were becoming things of the past.

Under Harris's stale leadership, the Corps' scattered units came together only three times to attempt an amphibious landing on a hostile shore. All three actions ended in disaster.

Early in the war, Major John G. Reynolds, who had been unjustly criticized for "holding back" at Chapultepec, assembled a large force of Marines to begin an amphibious campaign in South Carolina. Reynolds intended to land his troops near a Southern port and march on its defenses while using his warship for a naval bombardment. It was a sound strategy, but Reynolds's luck was all bad. His troopship floundered in a storm off the coast of Cape Hatteras and sank. Most of his men survived, but lost their entire complement of weapons and equipment.

On September 8, 1863, Captain Charles McCawley, another veteran of Chapultepec, led a landing party of Marines in an attempt to retake Fort Sumter, the first Union post to fall to the Confederacy. Since its loss, the strong point had become a powerful symbol for both sides. The Union was desperate to recapture it.

Captain McCawley's attack was staged from thirty-five rowboats, carrying 500

Marines and sailors. The plan called for the boats to come toward the fort from many directions. Almost from the start, the complex, unrehearsed action crumbled. Darkness and a stiff head wind served to separate the "fleet." Then the sounds of their oarlocks alerted the Confederate guards, who began to fire on the approaching boats. Finally, two small enemy gunboats appeared—they had been lying in wait at the rear of the fort to be used to fend off just this kind of attack.

The gunboats, as well as the cannons from the fort, blew up several Union boats, drowning the men aboard. As cannonballs ripped across the bows of the remaining rowboats, the Marines kept their heads low and pushed on through water that was thick with debris and floating corpses. The few who managed to make a landing scrambled up the rock-strewn shore to find the paths leading up to the ramparts blocked by tons of masonry. They also faced heavy and accurate fire from sentries who had been drilled in defensive tactics. The battle lasted for an hour, becoming more savage as it went on. The Confederates rained bricks, rocks, and explosive grenades down on the Union attackers. A few Marines got within reach of the Confederates, to stab at them with bayonets—it was all they had, as their ammunition was damp and useless or had been spent. Finally, McCawley called for a general retreat. The attackers boarded the surviving boats, leaving a third of their force behind. Over 150 soldiers were killed, captured, or drowned.

The third and final time the Marine Corps attempted an amphibious landing was at Fort Fisher in North Carolina. On January 15, 1865, Captain Lucian Dawson and 500 Marines were supposed to provide covering fire for a landing party of 1,600 sailors assigned to capture Fort Fisher in a direct attack with pistols and cutlasses. From the start, this "buccaneer" attack was doomed. The sailors, overconfident and too eager, refused to wait for the Marines to take up firing positions. Instead, they charged right into the teeth of the fort's considerable defenses. Confederate marksmen cut the sailors down from the safety of the parapets. The slaughter was doubly tragic because the Marines and sailors were involved in what amounted to a diversionary tactic. The *real* attack was taking place on the northern palisades, where Major General Alfred Terry's U.S. Army infantrymen easily took the walls even as sailors and Marines died by the hundreds on the other side of the fort.

Though Fort Fisher fell, so many Marines and sailors died needlessly that the concept of amphibious assaults was dealt another stinging setback. More tragic was the fact that Jacob Zeilin was commandant of the Marines during the battles of Mobile Bay and Fort Fisher. He was itching to change the role and tactics of the Marine Corps and saw amphibious assault as the way to go. But in the face of the tragic failures off Cape Hatteras, at Fort Sumter, and at Fort Fisher, he could never again make a case for future training in amphibious tactics. It would be another fifty years before the Marines even attempted it again.

A small bit of history was made at Fort Fisher when Marine Private Henry Wasmuth gave his life to save an eighteen-year-old Navy officer, Acting Ensign Robly D. Evans. Evans would become Admiral "Fighting Bob" Evans in the years ahead. Decades after his heroic self-sacrifice, a World War II destroyer would be named in honor of Henry Wasmuth.

On April 8, 1865—Palm Sunday—Robert E. Lee surrendered his Confederate forces at Appomattox, a tiny town in northern Virginia. The Civil War was over, but one more casualty was yet to fall. On Good Friday, while Abraham Lincoln attended a play at the Ford Theater in Washington, John Wilkes Booth, acclaimed thespian and Southern sympathizer, shot him in the back of the head. Colonel Zeilin was one of the pallbearers at the state funeral to honor this national martyr. In all, over a half-million Americans perished in the Civil War, which remains America's costliest conflict.

CHAPTER FIVE

AMERICAN EMPIRE

■

1866–1898

A FTER the Civil War, there were renewed attempts to downsize the Marine Corps or abolish it altogether. In 1866, a committee was formed to assess the value of an independent Marine Corps. In its final report, issued in February 1867, the committee concluded that "its organization as a separate Corps be preserved and strengthened." So the Marine Corps was saved from extinction. One question remained. What exactly was a "separate Corps" supposed to do? Marines were still posted aboard United States Navy warships, and they continued their role of defending American interests abroad in a series of quick, decisive military interventions on foreign soil.

Yet this was also a time of waning strength, shrinking ranks, and an aging officer corps. The need for a fully amphibious expeditionary force had not yet been established to anyone's satisfaction, so the Marines made assaults on occupied beachheads with a minimum of training or special equipment. This was a tremendous leap backward. During the War of 1812, the Marines had had specialized surf boats for beach assault. Sixty years later it was as if they'd forgotten all they had learned. Though Commandant Zeilin did not possess the vision to create an amphibious expeditionary force, he did take significant steps to improve the quality of the Corps.

In 1867, the Marines adopted the new system of infantry tactics developed and codified by General Emory Upton of the United States Army. Thanks to General Upton's diligent efforts, everything that an officer commanding men in the field needed to know was reduced to a pocket-size blue book that became a military bible. Commandant Zeilin also instituted changes in uniform and traditions that endure to this day. In 1869, the Marines adopted the modern dress uniform—a blue-black shell jacket and trousers with plenty of gold braid. In November 1868, the Marine Corps emblem in its present form was adopted. Imitating the Royal Marines, this emblem would feature a fouled anchor, a central globe depicting the western hemisphere (the Royal Marines' insignia sports the *eastern* hemisphere), and an American bald eagle clutching a furled ribbon on top.

This was also the period when the Marine Corps march, "Semper Fidelis," and "The Marine Corps Hymn" first began to be heard, though the origins of the latter are murky. Tradition says that a Marine on duty in Mexico in 1847 wrote the original words of the hymn to go with the music of the gendarmes' song in the operetta *Geneviève de Brabant* by Jacques Offenbach. If so, this Marine obviously had trouble finding a rhyme for "Montezuma" and reversed the order of events to "From the Halls of Montezuma to the Shores of Tripoli."

In the wake of the Civil War, the Marines intervened three times in China—in 1866, in 1894, and in 1895. They were also called upon to fight four times in Nicaragua and once in Korea, Uruguay, Mexico, and Panama. The Marines fought three times in Hawaii—in 1874, 1889, and 1893; in Egypt, in Haiti twice—1888 and 1891; and in Samoa, Argentina, in Chile and Colombia. Marines helped rescue the Greeley Arctic Expedition and halted the slaughter of seals in the Bering Sea.

Marines also served at home, quelling riots or aiding American citizens during various disasters. In 1866, they helped the victims of a fire that destroyed Portland, Maine. Two catastrophic fires also occurred in Boston in 1872 and 1873, and Marines were needed to prevent looting and help restore civil services. In 1870, Marines from the Brooklyn Navy Yard closed illegal stills in New York City. In the summer of 1877, Marines were asked to quell various disturbances during prolonged and bitter labor riots in Baltimore, Philadelphia, and other cities along the East Coast.

THE WEEKEND WAR

In the 1800s, Korea was known in the American press as "Corea, the Hermit Kingdom," or "The Land of the Morning Calm." That calm was shattered on June 11, 1871, when a United States Navy "flotilla" of five outmoded warships and an improvised landing force of rowboats packed with Marines and sailors attacked the Korean forts on the Salee (Han) River.

After the Civil War, American merchants were determined to open Korea to trade and American missionaries were anxious to save the heathens of Asia and enlarge their flocks. But forces inside the country were resolved to resist any foreign influence. The worst of the trouble occurred in 1870–1871, when the crew of an American freighter was massacred and two American gunboats fired upon. Both incidents took place along the Salee River, where a network of Korean forts was strategically placed on Kanghwado Island to guard the approaches to Seoul, Korea's capital. These forts had already been used to repel Western invaders, when French warships tried to visit Korea uninvited just five years before.

The Asiatic Squadron, based in Japan and commanded by Rear Admiral John Rodgers, was ordered to sail immediately Seoul. Rodgers was to deliver Frederick F. Low, a representative of the United States government, to Korea to discuss the dangerous political situation and attempt to negotiate a treaty of "commerce and friendship." After preliminary contact was made, American naval vessels were fired upon on May 30 as they began to move upriver toward Seoul. On the thirty-first, Admiral Rodgers dispatched a survey party in a small boat to go ashore and study the Korean defenses. They were also attacked and two sailors were badly wounded. Admiral Rodgers, who had been given full decision-making powers, put aside his peace mission and a bold battle plan was formulated—a plan that resulted in the first large-scale American amphibious landing in Asia. The landing party consisted of 542 U.S. Navy "bluejackets" and 109 Marines manning twenty-two rowboats. Also squeezed onto those boats were seven light howitzers, ammunition, and gun crews.

The objective was the fort on Kanghwado Island. There was actually a network of forts, each under the control of a separate commander, but all of them ultimately commanded by Korean General O Yu-jun—who may or may not have been acting under orders from his superiors when he fired at American ships. Among General Yu-jun's soldiers were the most feared troops in the Korean Army—the elite "Tiger Hunters." Born and bred in the Yalu River region, each member of this fierce fighting force had to kill a tiger single-handedly as a rite of passage. Like the samurai of Japan, the Tiger Hunters adhered to a strict code of conduct and were sworn to fight to the death. Tiger Hunters held all "shorthairs"—Westerners—in contempt. Wild rumors had circulated through the American fleet about these white-clad Korean troops. Many sailors and Marines believed the Tiger Hunters had mutilated, skinned, cut up, and pickled or crucified their enemies—including the crew of the American frigate. These stories, as wild as they were untrue, served to stiffen the enlisted men's resolve.

On the morning of June 11, the five Civil War–era sailing ships of Admiral Rodgers's fleet, led by the forty-four-gun flagship *Colorado,* cautiously moved into the range of the Korean cannon. They were fired upon by shore batteries, then from the parapets. The Korean cannons were old and inaccurate, but there were over 400 of them and the fleet sustained a few damaging hits. The ships had to be wary of the bogs and shallows that surrounded the island. The Navy had no accurate charts, so the warships were constantly in danger of running aground.

The landing parties, cobbled together from all the ships in the fleet, had rowed ashore under cover of darkness the night before. When they arrived on Kanghwado Island, the Americans found themselves mired in swampy mudflats. "Sinking up to their thighs, losing shoes, socks, leggings, and in some instances a part of their pants," wrote one participant. But by morning they had reached their objective. The Marines were the first troops to move toward the forts. They were commanded by Marine Captain McLane Tilton, and most were battle-hardened veterans of the Civil War who had seen action during the Confederate blockade and the river campaigns.

When the duel between the Navy ships and the cannons on the Korean ramparts began at dawn, Captain Tilton noted that the Koreans were using antique smoothbore cannon instead of more accurate artillery. Two years before, back in Washington, D.C., Captain Tilton had been an influential member of the naval board that in 1869 adopted the Remington .50-caliber "Rolling-Block" breechloader for use by the Navy and Marine Corps. These guns were far more accurate than any weapon in America's military arsenal in this period. Compared with the pre–Civil War muzzle-loading rifles the Navy and Marines carried into battle this day, the Remingtons had a phenomenal rate of fire. But these new Remingtons weren't ready for delivery when the Asiatic fleet departed for the Far East in 1870, so the sailors and Marines were attacking the Korean forts armed with what Captain Tilton contemptuously called "Civil War Muzzle-Fuzzels."

The combined Navy and Marine forces easily took the first two fortifications but ran into trouble when they arrived at the base of the third fort, called the Citadel. The core of General O Yu-jun's Tiger Hunters was inside that massive fortification, which dominated a 150-foot conical hill. Captain Tilton would later write that "the topography of the country [was] indescribable, resembling a sort of chopped sea, of immense hills and deep ravines laying in every conceivable position." But Tilton had more to worry about than geography. There were 3,000 Korean soldiers behind those walls, and as his men moved forward, they faced heavy fire. Though the first volleys were wildly inaccurate, Captain Tilton's worst fears were realized—these Koreans were armed with better rifles than his Marines.

As the Marines approached the walls, one officer reported that "the air seemed literally alive with whistling projectiles." Those projectiles were mostly fired by Koreans, who had repeating rifles. Despite the rapid fire, a small group of Americans managed to scale the ramparts. Lieutenant Hugh W. McKee was the first over the wall. He was shot, then mortally wounded by a spear thrust from an aggressive Tiger Hunter. Several Marines, including Irish-born Private John Coleman, rushed forward and spirited their commander behind the lines. But they were too late to save McKee, the highest-ranking casualty of this Weekend War. Behind the luckless Marine lieutenant came Navy Lieutenant Commander Winfield S. Schley, who battled the Koreans at close range with pistol and cutlass. He survived this action to become an admiral in the Spanish-American War.

As more Marines poured over the wall and into the fort, the defenders filled the air with their eerie battle cry. The Korean battle chants sent a shiver of fear through the Americans, who were already rattled by grim tales of Eastern torture and butchery. "It was like nothing human," wrote one bluejacket. The chants "rang in our ears longer than the terrible clashing of bayonet, cutlass and spear." While the Marines and bluejackets fought on the ramparts, Rear Admiral Rodgers's fleet fired repeated broadsides into the fortress. The naval bombardment divided the defenders' attention long enough for the American landing parties to capture the walls of the Citadel.

Meanwhile, aboard the *Colorado* and the American gunships *Monocacy* and *Palos,* spotters and gun crews bravely remained at their posts as hundreds of Korean cannons returned fire, splintering masts, cracking decks, and tearing flesh with antique cannonballs. Several of the brave seamen later received the Navy's Medal of Honor.

After firing the first few volleys, the Marines relied on their bayonets to clear the fort, and by the time the first Americans reached the top of the ramparts, the fighting was hand to hand. Captain Tilton slashed at Koreans with his cutlass and dispatched a few with his Remington pistol. In his after-action report, Rear Admiral Rodgers praised the Marines' marksmanship, but the truth of it was they hardly had a chance to shine. Their rifles took so long to load it was more prudent to go hand to hand as fast as possible rather than stand around trying to reload under sustained fire from repeating rifles. That said, Captain Tilton and his men were very lucky that day. Though the Koreans had superior weapons, they were poor marksmen. It was only in hand-to-hand combat that the Korean elite were truly effective—but not as effective as the Marines.

At the end of a fierce thirty-minute battle, over 200 Korean soldiers were dead. The brisk naval bombardment had obliterated another hundred. When the Citadel was about to fall, the remaining Tiger Hunters pulled back from the fight and threw themselves off the parapets. According to their code, it was better to drown in the river far below than surrender. Others, including General O Yu-jun, cut their own throats rather than be captured by the reviled shorthairs. The only Korean prisoners taken that day were so severely wounded that they could not drag themselves to the edge of the parapet. Frederick F. Low later reported that "the Koreans fought with desperation, rarely equaled and never excelled by any people."

After the battle, Captain Tilton—wary of claiming credit for killing Korean soldiers who chose suicide over dishonor—disputed the official U.S. Navy count of enemy casualties. But no matter how you look at it, it was a lopsided victory. The American forces suffered only four dead—Lieutenant McKee and Private Dennis Hanrahan of the Marine Corps; Seaman Seth Allen and Seaman Patrick Murphy of the Navy—and another ten wounded. A wounded Marine later died of fever. In all, 481 Korean cannon were captured, along with a number of impressive Korean battle standards, and the Marines relieved the fallen Koreans of their superior rifles.

Six Marines and nine sailors received the Medal of Honor for bravery during the Weekend War in Korea. Because the Medal of Honor was still the only award the United States bestowed for courage above and beyond the call of duty, it was rather freely given in the aftermath of this short and bloody campaign. But the capture of the Salee River forts was still an impressive feat. The sailors and Marines had defeated an elite fighting force in hand-to-hand combat and paved the way to opening Korea for Western commerce.

The most celebrated enlisted man to take part in the Weekend War in Korea was thirty-two-year-old Private James Dougherty, who personally killed a Korean commander on the ramparts in full view of his fellow soldiers. Private Dougherty was counted as one of the wounded that day, though he recovered enough to return to active duty several weeks after the battle. Born in Langhash, Ireland, Dougherty entered service in Pennsylvania. After retiring from the Marine Corps, he settled in Brooklyn and died at the age of sixty-two. Another Irishman honored for his actions that day was twenty-four-year-old Private John Coleman, who was born in County Cork. During the initial attack, Coleman was instrumental in attempting to save the life of his wounded commander, Lieutenant McKee. He snatched the officer out of harm's way and carried him to safety.

A third Irish-born Marine distinguished himself on the ramparts of the Citadel. Private Michael McNamara was just thirty when he scaled the walls and snatched a matchlock out of an enemy soldier's grip before the Korean could fire. McNamara held his advanced position on the wall under sustained fire until more Marines could relieve him.

Private Michael Owens, born in New York City, was the most severely wounded of all the honorees. He suffered multiple stab wounds during hand-to-hand fighting with the Tiger Hunters. He recovered sufficiently to receive his Medal of Honor with the other recipients in the ceremony held on February 8, 1872. Owens left the Marine Corps when he returned to the United States. He died on December 8, 1890.

Private Hugh Purvis was born and raised in Pennsylvania. He was twenty-five at the time of this action and received the Medal of Honor for being the first to scale the walls and maintaining his position until he could be joined by others. He also captured one of the impressive Korean battle standards that the American forces brought home with them. He was posted at the Washington barracks, then at Annapolis, where he died in 1922. Corporal Charles Brown was the highest-ranking member of the Marine Corps to be honored in this campaign. He was born in New York City, but his age at the time of the battle is not known. We do know that he enlisted in the Marine Corps in Hong Kong, which indicates he may have been a merchant seaman long before joining the military. During the attack on the largest fort, Brown captured a Korean battle standard.

Private Hugh Purvis

In the United States the only reminder of this forgotten conflict is a plaque in the chapel of the United States Naval Academy at Annapolis, dedicated to the memory of Lieutenant Hugh W. McKee, the first man over the parapet of the Citadel. But in Korea, it is a very different story. On Kanghwado Island, which lies just seventy-five miles from the demilitarized zone that U.S. soldiers and South Korean regulars have guarded since the 1950s, the original earthworks and the shore batteries with their ancient cannons have been preserved. Korean history texts refer to this battle as the "Foreign Disturbance of 1871," and monuments were erected to honor General O Yu-jun and his Tiger Hunters. The inscription on one of these monuments reads: "Western barbarians invade our land. If we do not fight we must then appease them. To urge appeasement is to betray the nation."

MORE CHANGES

On November 1, 1876, Brigadier General Zeilin retired after forty-five years of service. President Ulysses S. Grant appointed Colonel Charles Grymes McCawley to replace him as commandant. McCawley was born in Philadelphia and was the son of a Marine Corps captain. When he was twenty he was commissioned and fought at the walls of Chapultepec. During the Civil War, he was a commander at the failed attack on Fort Sumter.

In 1871, as the Marines were riding a wave of renewed popularity for conquering the Korean forts, Colonel McCawley was summoned to Washington by Commandant Zeilin and informed he would be the next commandant. McCawley set to work immediately, firing off a number of directives and memos in preparation for his promotion. He concentrated on implementing higher enlistment standards, improved training for enlisted men and officers alike, enforcement of uniform regulations, and fast-track promotion of competent officers. Until McCawley's tenure, Marine Corps officers had been drawn from civilian life by direct appointment. But in 1882, McCawley managed to get several graduates of the Naval Academy assigned to the Corps. Under his tenure, from 1883 to 1897, all fifty new Marine Corps officers were graduates of the Naval Academy. Called the "Famous Fifty," five of these graduates would become commandant, thirteen would rise to general, and fifteen others would make it to the rank of colonel. Commandant McCawley also attempted to remedy the supply problems the Corps faced. He succeeded in establishing a clothing factory to manufacture uniforms in Philadelphia, and this factory would supply the Marine Corps until the Vietnam era.

In 1880, Commandant McCawley appointed John Philip Sousa the new conductor of the Marine Corps Band. The son of Antonio Sousa, a carpenter and sometime band member at the Marine Corps barracks in Washington, John Philip Sousa enlisted as a Marine Corps "music boy" on June 9, 1868, when he was thirteen years old. When he was twenty-one, his enlistment ended and he became a violinist in theater orchestras in and around Washington. His life changed in 1880 when the conductor of the Marine Band was dismissed as "unfit for the Service." With some prodding by father Antonio, Commandant McCawley appointed John leader of the band. Over the next twenty years, Sousa composed dozens of world-famous marches, including "Washington Post March" (1889), "King Cotton" (1897), and his most popular tune, "The Stars and Stripes Forever" (1897). Most of his early works were composed for the Marines. One of his marches—"Semper Fidelis," written in 1888— would leave a lasting mark on the United States Marine Corps. In 1891, Sousa took the band on a whirlwind tour that made them and their illustrious conductor internationally famous.

In the decade between 1872 and 1882, most of the Marine Corps battles were fought internally. Commandant McCawley continued his restructuring of the officer corps while improving training tactics overall. The Marine Corps got a new rifle—the Springfield .45-70 single-shot breechloader—and there were refinements to the regulation uniform. The peace ended in 1882, when Marines were needed to show the flag

▪ *Of Marines and Mottoes*

Of John Philip Sousa's stirring marches, none is more famous than "Semper Fidelis"—Latin for "always faithful." This music still stands as the only congressionally authorized march for use by a branch of the armed services. "Semper Fidelis" is played at Marine Corps reviews and parades to this day. The term *Semper Fidelis* had been adopted as the Marine Corps motto by Commandant McCawley in 1883, which no doubt inspired Sousa to compose his march. But this was not the first motto considered or tried by the Marines. Tentative mottoes, like *Fortitudine*, had been tested without success. "A Few Good Men" worked better as a recruitment slogan than a motto. And "First to Fight" didn't come into vogue until World War I.

In their quest for an enduring motto, the Marines even tried borrowing one from the Royal Marines, whose motto in 1876 was *Per Mare, Per Terram*—sometimes used in its English form, "By Sea and by Land." Even the motto *Semper Fidelis* is not unique; it is shared with the Devonshire Regiment in Great Britain.

Once *Semper Fidelis* was established, this motto was put on the ribbon placed in the eagle's beak on the Marine Corps emblem, where it exists today. The motto also thrives as the cry "Semper Fi!" a sometimes patriotic, sometimes irreverent greeting from one Marine to another.

in Africa. When the combined British and French protectorate of the Khedive was threatened by a nationalist uprising, the British fleet sailed into battle. So did the paltry fleet of three warships that composed the United States European Squadron. On July 11, the British bombarded the Egyptian positions. On the fourteenth, Marines under the command of Captain Henry Clay Cochrane landed on Egyptian soil. Eighteen years before setting foot in Africa, Cochrane had ridden the train to Gettysburg with Abraham Lincoln and watched as the president delivered the Gettysburg Address. Unfortunately for the Marines, by the time the Americans arrived, there were already 4,000 British troops ashore.

The French would provide the impetus for the Marine Corps' next adventure. After successfully completing the Suez Canal, French engineers planned to construct a canal that cut through the Isthmus of Panama. It was a brilliant scheme, but this Franco-Panamanian engineering project was doomed from the start. In time, the French would abandon the project, but not before they lost an estimated 30,000 workers to disease and native uprisings. The Panama Canal would not see the light of day until the United States stepped in during the administration of Teddy Roosevelt, exterminated the mosquitoes that carried yellow fever, and completed the job with a few thousand losses of their own. But this did not happen until the early part of the twentieth century. Back in 1884, the French were still struggling to build the canal despite harassment by Panamanian insurgents. They relied on the Colombian Army to protect them until Colombia was suddenly forced to withdraw its troops to fight insurgents at home.

On January 18, 1885, the U.S.S. *Alliance,* a rebuilt wooden gunboat, arrived on the Atlantic Ocean side of Panama to deliver a Marine detachment to protect the property and lives of those working for the American-owned Panama Railroad. Before the end of March, the revolution had spread and a "loose coalition" of rebel factions was in control of most of the rail lines along with the cities of Panama and Colón. The fighting in Colón was still raging when the U.S.S *Galena*—the Civil War–era ironclad that fought in the Battle of Mobile Bay—arrived. A Marine detachment under Second Lieutenant Charles A. Doyen rowed ashore by night, guided by the fires burning in the city. More Marines landed with the Gulf Coast Squadron in March, and by April 3, the railroad and the city of Panama were in Marine Corps hands again. By April 13, the Colombian Army was back and the Marines returned home. This swift in-and-out victory would establish a pattern for Marine Corps interventions in the Caribbean and Central America that continues to this day.

"The Marines have landed and have the situation well in hand." So wrote war correspondent and novelist Richard Harding Davis, one of the best-known journalists of his generation. Davis, a war correspondent in every conflict from the Greco-Turkish War to World War I, would find many occasions to use this phrase as the nineteenth century drew to a close.

A NEW COMMANDANT AND ANOTHER WAR

On February 1, 1872, Marine Corporal James A. Stewart dived off the deck of the U.S.S. *Plymouth* and into the busy waters of France's Villefranche Harbor, risking his life to rescue a drowning midshipman named Osterhaus. Moments later an exhausted Stewart and a dazed midshipman were pulled out of the water, safe and sound. James Stewart, born in Pennsylvania in 1839 and raised in Philadelphia, would be the only Marine Corps Medal of Honor recipient for the next sixteen years.

Colonel McCawley retired at the end of January 1891. Despite his best efforts to motivate the Corps, recruitment was down and promotions were slow. The best officers graduating from the Naval Academy in Annapolis naturally preferred to pursue a career in the Navy. Colonel Charles Heywood, the new commandant, immediately instituted a fitness policy and promotion examinations to rid the Corps of deadwood—mostly unfit or elderly officers left over from the Civil War. One of his appointees was Captain Daniel Pratt Mannix, who commanded the Washington barracks. Mannix was instrumental in changing the role of the Marine Corps for the new century—a century of iron ships, coal power, and revolving armored turrets that had little use for shipboard Marines. To bring the Corps up to speed on new weapons and technology, Captain Mannix established a School of Application at its Washington headquarters. This training school, with a course of study for both officers and enlisted men, taught the Marines such rudimentary skills as operating the new Colt-Browning M-1895 6mm machine gun and the Hotchkiss 37mm gun. Captain Mannix's standard text was "the little blue book"—General Upton's *Tactics*. Though the older officers were skeptical of such academic pursuits, the fresh graduates from the Naval Academy relished the opportunity for some hands-on experience. Captain Mannix was able to attract a core of new officers that would take the Marine Corps into the twentieth century. By 1900, there was a marked improvement in Marine Corps training. Uniform adaptations and the shift to the single-shot Springfield Model 1884 caliber .45-70 with a folding sight further prepared the Marines for the multiple conflicts looming on the horizon.

On Inauguration Day, 1897, as outgoing President Grover Cleveland rode from the Capitol with President Elect William McKinley, Cleveland said, "I am deeply sorry, Mr. President, to pass on to you a war with Spain. It will come within two years. Nothing can stop it." This remark would prove optimistic. War erupted less than eleven months later.

When McKinley became president, Cuba was in the midst of yet another revolution. Unlike those in the other Spanish colonies that had achieved independence from Europe, the elite class in Cuba had been frightened by the bloody Haitian slave revolts and relied on the presence of Spanish troops to maintain order. In the 1870s, there were almost a half-million slaves in Cuba, all harvesting and processing sugar. Slavery did not end on the island until the 1880s, but by then sugar prices had fallen worldwide and the country was in social, political, and economic chaos. Many Cubans looked to the United States for support, and some even advocated statehood. But independent-minded Cubans wanted no foreign presence, and they were the majority.

When the Cuban Revolutionary Movement moved to open revolt against colonial rule on February 10, 1895, the government in Spain immediately dispatched 200,000 troops under the command of Captain General Valeriano Weyler—known as "The Butcher"—to put the rebellion down. The carnage that followed Weyler's arrival on Cuban shores parallels the Holocaust of the 1940s. Cuban political activists, revolutionaries, and the poor were uprooted from their homes and villages and sent to so-called reconcentration camps. Many died of starvation, disease, or exposure on long forced marches, and when the survivors finally arrived at the camps, the treatment they received was inhuman. Thousands of Cubans perished in these camps and more would die as Weyler's men ravaged the countryside in search of "enemies." The American press covered the Spanish atrocities with sensational and not always factual exposés that created sympathy for Cuban independence. Public outcry became so intense that by 1891, President McKinley was forced to act. He decided on a half-hearted measure that was more show that substance. Instead of openly supporting the Cuban cause with the full force of the United States military, he sought to intimidate General Weyler and the Spanish government by sending a newly christened American warship, the U.S.S. *Maine,* to Havana Harbor to "show the colors." This action would have tragic consequences.

When the *Maine* steamed into the harbor on January 25, 1898, the Spanish government's reception was cool and formal. For three weeks this formidable steel warship—the pride of the new, modern Navy—sat at anchor. The *Maine* was scheduled to depart for Mardi Gras in New Orleans on February 17, but at 9:40 P.M. on the night of the fifteenth, it was shaken by two explosions—a small blast followed by a much more powerful detonation. Captain Charles Sigsbee was in his cabin, drafting a letter to his wife, when he felt the blasts. He rose and rushed out into the smoke-filled passageway. A Marine orderly ran up to him.

"Sir!" Private William F. Anthony cried, saluting crisply. "I beg to report that the captain's ship is sinking."

Despite the smoke, Captain Sigsbee made his way belowdecks to assess the situation, which was dire. The entire bow of the ship was blown off and seawater was gushing into the hull faster than the pumps could flush it out. Topside, the fires began to eat away at the stories of ammunition. They soon exploded, sending fireballs into the sky and threatening to bring down the ceiling on top of Captain Sigsbee.

First Lieutenant Albertus W. Catlin, commander of the Marine detachment aboard the *Maine,* was also in his cabin at the time of the blast. He stumbled through dark, choking passages, filled with heat, smoke, and panicked sailors, to the deck, where the crew was futilely attempting to put out fires and free the lifeboats. Within minutes, the *Maine* sank, taking 232 seamen and twenty-eight Marines down with her. While the cause of the blast was and still is unknown, the American press quickly reached its own conclusion. REMEMBER THE *MAINE*! the headlines screamed. Soon a vast majority of the American people were clamoring for war. President McKinley was again forced to act. Three days after the destruction of the *Maine,* Congress declared war on Spain.

THE SPANISH-AMERICAN WAR

The war with Spain would be fought on two fronts. In the Caribbean on the island of Cuba and in the Pacific Rim in the humid jungles of the Philippines. On April 27, 1898, Commandant Heywood ordered a Marine battalion to be assembled. Five days later they sailed from the Brooklyn Navy Yard for Key West, Florida, in a converted banana boat, the U.S.S. *Panther.* The commander of this operation was Marine Lieutenant Colonel Robert W. Huntington, who had been with John Reynolds during the humiliating Union rout at the First Battle of Manassas. Even as these Marines steamed southward, another battle was brewing half a world away. Commodore George Dewey steamed out of Hong Kong on April 24. On the night of April 30, his fleet secretly entered Manila Bay. At dawn, they fired on the large but outmoded Spanish fleet waiting at anchor off Sangley Point. Commodore Dewey, scanning the array of Spanish vessels, turned to his executive officer and issued his famous order: "You may fire when you are ready, Gridley."

For the next two hours the U.S. Navy ships decimated the Spanish fleet. The Americans broke for breakfast, then returned to Manila Bay to finish the job. At the end of the battle seven Spanish ships were sunk and three land batteries were destroyed. Nearly 400 Spanish troops were killed, and Commodore Dewey had two officers injured slightly. On May 3, First Lieutenant Dion Williams took a detachment of Marines ashore and occupied the Spanish arsenal and the docks of the Cavite Naval Station. There were still 13,000 Spanish troops inside the city of Manila and Lieutenant Williams and his paltry force of Marines were ordered to hold their ground until the United States Army could arrive.

The Battle of Manila Bay was an amazing naval victory that left governments around the world stunned. The United States became a major naval power in the Pacific literally overnight. Meanwhile, in the Caribbean, Rear Admiral William T. Sampson had bottled up the Spanish fleet in Santiago de Cuba. But there was one problem—Sampson was forced to stagger his ships, sending some of them back to Florida for coal and resupply. The secretary of the navy made a suggestion: "Can you not take possession of Guantánamo, occupy as a coaling station?"

Rear Admiral Sampson's reply was short and to the point: "Yes. Send me Huntington's Marine battalion." On June 7, the U.S.S. *Panther* steamed out of Key West, even as the U.S.S. *Marblehead* began a naval bombardment of Guantánamo. Several of Sampson's Navy officers were sent ashore to reconnoiter. On the tenth, the Marines landed inside Guantánamo Bay. Though there were over 9,000 Spanish troops between Guantánamo and Santiago forty miles away, the Marines met no resistance. Four Marine companies pitched their tents on a hill above Fisherman's Point.

Late that night, the Spaniards struck, killing two privates on sentry duty. Two companies of Marines pursued the raiders but lost them. Over the next few nights, the Spanish attacked repeatedly, killing the Marines in two and threes, until Lieutenant Colonel Huntington counterattacked on June 14 with two companies of Marines and sixty Cuban guerrillas. Because Guantánamo was arid, Huntington came to the logical con-

Sergeant Major John H. Quick

clusion that his Marines and the attacking Spaniards both needed water to conduct operations. But the only available source was Cuzco Well, six miles east of Guantánamo. Huntington decided to capture that well and drive off any Spanish troops guarding it. His plan involved the U.S.S. *Dolphin*, which was to provide naval support. After a difficult march, Huntington's Marines—commanded by Captain George Fielding Elliott and accompanied by Cuban guerrillas—attacked six companies of the Sixth Barcelona Regiment defending Cuzco Well. As the two armies exchanged fire, the *Dolphin* began its bombardment.

Without adequate communications there were bound to be mistakes. When the men aboard the *Dolphin* discharged their cannons at the Spaniards, they didn't realize that the Marines were in their line of fire. Shells began dropping into the Marine lines, sending hot shrapnel through the underbrush and into the flesh and bone of the Americans huddled there. Sergeant John Henry Quick, a tall, soft-spoken redhead from Charleston, West Virginia, leapt to his feet and scrambled up a low hill. Ignoring heavy Spanish rifle fire directed at him, Quick improvised a signal flag from a blue, polka-dot handkerchief. Then he stood up, turned his back on the enemy, and began to wave semaphore messages to the crew of the *Dolphin*.

While the Spanish concentrated their fire on the lone figure on the hill, the *Dolphin*'s crew translated Quick's message and shifted their bombardment to the Spanish positions. As shells began to rain down on the enemy, Quick took up his rifle and returned fire at those who shot at him. After the Marines regrouped, Captain Elliott divided his force and flanked the enemy. The Americans charged, and hand-to-hand fighting in the thick jungle around the well became intense. Within minutes of the final Marine assault, the Spanish retreated. The Marines took possession of Cuzco Well.

Captain Elliott, a future commandant of the Marine Corps, reported six Marines killed and sixteen wounded. But the real story was that Elliott and his Marines had managed to rout a force three times their size. For his bold actions during the fighting, John Henry Quick was nominated for a Medal of Honor by his grateful commander. To receive the Medal of Honor it is necessary to have an eyewitness attest to the soldier's act of courage. In this respect Sergeant Quick was fortunate indeed, for watching his brave action from the safety of the underbrush was renowned journalist, war correspondent, and novelist Stephen Crane, author of the Civil War classic *The Red Badge of Courage*. Crane, who had accompanied the Marines to Cuzco Well, marveled at Sergeant Quick's tranquillity under fire.

"I watched his face, and it was as grave and serene as that of a man writing in his own library . . . He stood there amid . . . the crack of rifles, and the whistling snarl of the bullets and wig-wagged whatever he had to wig-wag without heeding anything but his business. There was not a single trace of nervousness or haste . . . I saw Quick betray only one sign of emotion. As he swung his clumsy flag to and fro, an end of it once caught on a cactus pillar, and he looked sharply over his shoulder to see what had it. He gave the flag an impatient jerk. He looked annoyed."

Stephen Crane's chronicle of Sergeant Quick's actions at Guantánamo was carried in newspapers all over the United States and Quick became a national hero. He was presented with the Medal of Honor on December 13, 1898. Quick was later promoted to sergeant major and remained a Marine for many years. We shall hear of him again.

Overshadowed by Quick's instant notoriety, Private John Fitzgerald of Limerick, Ireland, also earned the Medal of Honor at Cuzco Well, for conspicuous bravery during vicious hand-to-hand combat with Spanish regulars. Fitzgerald rose to the rank of gunnery sergeant and retired to Brooklyn, New York, where he died in 1948.

In all, fifteen Marines received the Medal of Honor for bravery during the brief war with Spain. With the exception of John Quick and John Fitzgerald, these men were all shipboard Marines, posted aboard the U.S.S. *Brooklyn,* the U.S.S. *Nashville,* or the U.S.S. *Marblehead.* Most received the Medal of Honor for their participation in the hazardous U.S. Navy action to cut the communications cable at Cienfuegos, Cuba. These recipients include Canadian-born Private Daniel J. Campbell; Jersey City's Private Oscar Wadsworth Field; Private Joseph John Franklin of Buffalo, New York; Irish-born Private Philip Gaughan; Private Frank Hill of Connecticut; Private Michael Kearney, born in County Cork, Ireland, who would rise to the rank of captain; Private Hermann Wilhelm Kuchneister, born in Hamburg, Germany; Private James Meredith (real name Patrick F. Ford) of Omaha, Nebraska; German-born Carpenter's Mate William Meyer; Private Parker Pomeroy of North Carolina; Private Edward Sullivan of Cork, Ireland; Finland-born Chief Carpenter's Mate Axel Sundquist; and Private Walter Scott West of Bradford, New York.

After Cuzco Well was captured, there was no more fighting at Guantánamo and the land-based Marines were pretty much left out of the war. But on July 3, the Spanish Navy moved out of Santiago de Cuba to face the U.S. Navy's fleet. Commodore Winfield Scott Schley's five American battleships attacked immediately and every Spanish ship was either sunk or surrendered. Philadelphia-born Marine Private Harry MacNeal, posted aboard the U.S.S. *Brooklyn,* received a Medal of Honor for bravery under fire.

The war with Spain ended on August 12. The next day the United States Army entered the city of Manila in the Philippines. They brought twenty-nine-year-old, half-Chinese, half-Tagalog rebel leader Emilio Aguinaldo with them. On June 12, Aguinaldo declared himself president of an independent Philippines. When he entered Manila, Aguinaldo fully expected the government to be handed over to him. Instead, he and his rebel army were ordered out of the city by American authorities—setting the stage for the Philippine Insurrection.

The actual hostilities began on February 4, 1899, with an abortive rebel attack on Manila. On March 9, Commodore Dewey called in the Marines. The first battalion of Marines under the command of Colonel Percival C. Pope arrived on May 23. A second battalion led by Lieutenant Colonel George Elliott of Cuzco Well fame arrived in September. The war in the Philippines had begun.

CHAPTER SIX

FROM THE PHILIPPINES TO CHINA AND BACK AGAIN: PACIFIC ADVENTURES

■

1899–1917

A S the twentieth century dawned and America was battling Filipino insurgents in the Pacific, the sleeping giant that was China was beginning to stir. In the northern provinces, a xenophobic uprising against foreign influence had erupted and was spreading fast. Western merchants and missionaries were being slaughtered along with Chinese Christians and anyone doing business with foreigners. This violent political and cultural movement was insidious, spreading all the way to Peking and endangering the lives of American merchants, ministers, and ambassadors quartered in the Chinese capital. The situation was so dire that United States military forces were dispatched to help protect American lives and property. Suddenly the United States found itself embroiled in two major conflicts at the same time—one of their own making in the Philippines, and another brewing on mainland China.

The American people had learned to accept strife. The nation had been in a constant state of war more or less since its inception. Beyond the Revolutionary War, the war in Tripoli, the War of 1812, the Civil War, and the dozens of tiny conflicts all over the globe, the European descendants on the American continent had engaged in a ceaseless campaign against the indigenous peoples. But involvement in two simultaneous conflicts fought in distant *foreign* lands was a new experience. Unfortunately, quick and painless victories in the recent past had made the Americans cocky, and the nation was still floating on a tidal wave of enthusiastic support for the concept of Manifest Destiny. The United States was young, vital, and flexing its muscles all over the world. Americans were eager to enter the international political arena and were reluctant to stay out of a fight. The United States had just expelled Spain from the western hemisphere. Now it was ready to strut with renewed confidence onto the world stage.

As the nineteenth century closed, the campaign against the Filipino insurgents became more intense. Clashes that began in the winter months stretched into the summer rainy season. Soon fighting was constant, and the Army was bogged down and overextended. More troops were needed, so Commodore Dewey called for a Marine battalion to reinforce the Cavite Naval Station in March 1899. Two hundred and sixty Marines arrived on May 23 under the command of Colonel Percival C. Pope. A second battalion under Major George Elliott of the Battle at Cuzco Well arrived in late September. This piecemeal but steady buildup of forces would appear ominous to any student of our war in Vietnam. Even before these battalions arrived, Marines had been bloodied in the Philippines in ferocious clashes with insurgents in March and April 1899. While jungle-fighting beside their comrades in the United States Army, twenty-three-year-old Private Joseph H. Leonard and thirty-three-year-old Private Howard Buckley, both of New York, along with Irish-born Corporal Thomas Francis Prendergast, demonstrated "distinguished conduct in the presence of the enemy in battle, while with the 8th Army Corps," becoming the first Marines to receive the Medal of Honor in the Philippine Insurrection.

Novaleta, a fortified town near the Marine staging area at Cavite, had long been controlled by Aguinaldo's rebels. Clashes were frequent and harassment from this enemy bastion became a thorn in the side of the Americans. In concert with a large United States Army force, Elliott's Marines attacked the fortified walls of the town on October 8, 1899. Elliott split his force of 375 Marines into two columns. Each group sloshed through swampland and rice paddies until the soldiers converged near the walls of the town. After cannon fire from the gunboat *Petrel* pounded the Filipino positions, the insurgents were routed by a Marine-led frontal assault. Novaleta was taken, at a cost of three Marines killed and ten wounded. Despite this defeat, the insurgents became increasingly belligerent and a third battalion of Marines under Major Littleton W. Tazewell "Tony" Waller arrived in mid-December. Waller would become one of the Corps' brightest stars in the coming years.

In many ways, the Philippine Insurrection foreshadowed the conflict in Vietnam a half century later—a bloody, grinding, protracted jungle war against an invisible army of guerrillas that grew incrementally until it flew out of control. Like Vietnam, the war in the Philippines became increasingly unpopular with the American people as it dragged on. During the insurrection, the largest force of Marines ever assembled would take to the field, foreshadowing the role of the Marine Corps in the twentieth century. No longer would Marines fight in limited numbers aboard U.S. Navy warships. From this point on, the Marines would go to war as a unified force, no different from the United States Army—except for their added expeditionary role of storming and holding hostile beachheads, a skill the Army would not even begin to master until the Second World War.

After their initial success at reinforcing Cavite Naval Station, the Marines secured the area around strategic Subic Bay. But just when they were beginning to gain momentum in the Philippines, the main bulk of the Marine Corps forces were uprooted and sent half a world away—to fight a new war on the Chinese mainland.

THE BOXER REBELLION

At the close of the nineteenth century, the European powers had annexed and occupied huge regions of China, carving the mainland into vast areas of "economic domination." The United States, a relative newcomer, was a bit more restrained in its imperialist fervor, maintaining what Secretary of State John Hay called an "open-door policy" with the Chinese government. America desired trade and the guaranteed safety of its merchants and missionaries in the region, but nothing more. But when the I Ho Ch'uan—the Society of "Righteous and Harmonious Fists," or simply "Boxers"—began to hold sway over the populace in the northwestern provinces, the situation turned violent. Begun as a political movement to expel all foreign influence from Chinese soil, the Boxers gained a large following.

Floods and a devastating drought in China added to the social chaos and brought in thousands of farmers to swell the Boxers' rank. Boxer activity rapidly spread beyond the northwest provinces into some of the major cities, which were soon filled with screaming mobs, egged on by "Yao rebels," who believed they had been made invulnerable by sorcery and rituals of incantation. Those mobs attacked Western-built rail lines, churches, and foreign settlements. The Boxers were publicly opposed but secretly supported by Tz'u-hsi, the dowager empress of the Manchu dynasty and the absolute ruler of China. This treachery on the part of the Chinese government infuriated the Western powers and forced them to act on their own against the Boxers.

Because of their anti-Christian leanings, the Boxers initially targeted European and American missionaries and their Chinese-born followers. Thousands of Christians were murdered in the remotest provinces. Sometimes the empress dowager and her authorities acted to save the Western missionaries, but mostly they stood by and did nothing, allowing the slaughter to continue for almost two years. The attacks spread to Western-run railroad lines and businesses, and soon all foreign economic activity ground to a halt. Finally, in May 1900, thousands of screaming Boxers converged on Peking, terrifying the 500 permanent foreigners living in the Legation quarter and the thousands of Western missionaries and merchants who had already flocked to the capital from the outer provinces for protection. Eight nations had headquarters in the Legation quarter—the United States, France, Germany, Austria, Great Britain, Italy, Japan, and Russia. All had economic interests in China and were unwilling to be expelled by a native uprising no matter how large or how popular.

The U.S.S. *Newark,* the first ship flying the United States flag to arrive in China, reached Taku Bar on the Yellow Sea on May 27. On the twenty-eighth the U.S.S. *Oregon* steamed into port. Both ships anchored just forty miles downriver from the trade city of Tientsin and prepared to board a train to travel there, then on to Peking. But the Boxers burned several railroad stations on the Belgian-built line and rail travel to Peking became impossible, so the Marines decided to travel by river instead. On May 29, fifty Marines under the command of Marine Captain John "Handsome Jack" Myers set off for the Legation quarter in Peking, dragging a wheeled Colt "Potato-Digger" machine gun behind them. They were followed by sixty sailors, four naval officers, and a second machine gun. Traveling in tightly packed Chinese junks towed by a commandeered steam tug, the Marines reached the Legation quarter at eleven o'clock at night. They were greeted warmly by a European brass band and a cocktail party.

Among the foreigners holed up in Tientsin was twenty-five-year-old mining engineer and future president of the United States Herbert Hoover. Hoover marveled at the calm displayed by these Marines as they entered the city. According to him, they responded to the stirring music performed by the European brass band by playing a song of their own—"There'll Be a Hot Time in the Old Town Tonight."

The Chinese authorities at Tientsin balked at getting a train prepared to take the Marines to Peking. As soldiers from other nations joined the Americans, the British made it clear that if the Chinese stationmaster didn't deliver a train, they would hang him. A train was produced and the polyglot soldiers from eight nations boarded it. When the train chugged into Peking many hours later, the Marines were met by representatives of the various foreign legations and by thousands of Chinese, who maintained a threatening silence as they watched the Marines debark. "The dense mass which thronged either side of the roadway seemed more ominous than a demonstration of hostility would have been," Captain John T. Myers wrote. Within hours, Myers's Marines were exchanging fire with the Boxers.

Boxers in full ceremonial garb were now moving freely through the streets of Peking, stirring up antiforeign sentiment and attacking any Westerner not protected by the walls of the legation. Each day hundreds of Westerners arrived at the legation's main gate, clamoring for sanctuary. Hundreds of Chinese Christians, some of them wounded or horribly burned, also begged to enter. The walled Legation quarter, which covered less than three-quarters of a mile square, was soon crammed with 3,000 frightened people and 2,500 armed troops. There was little water and less food. Worst of all, the legation was defended by an inadequate military force that was isolated and short of weapons, ammunition, and supplies.

THE SEYMOUR EXPEDITION

By June 6, the Boxers had severed all railroad lines to Tientsin and Peking was cut off as well. Vice Admiral Sir Edward Seymour of the British Royal Navy assembled a multinational force to march on Peking and relieve the troops and civilians trapped there. This expedition would experience some of the heaviest fighting and suffer the worst casualty rate of any Western combat force during this uprising.

On June 10, Seymour's expedition departed Tientsin with U.S. Navy Captain Bowman H. McCalla of the U.S.S. *Newark* as second-in-command. The goal was to reach Peking, ninety miles away. With McCalla were sixty Navy bluejackets and two squads of Marines. As the expedition proceeded along five commandeered trains, the troops attempted to repair the rail line and partially burned bridges. The task proved daunting. In all, there were 2,129 men, but only one of them—a U.S. Navy sailor—knew how to set out a fishplate and spike down a rail. Everyone else had to be taught. The work went slowly and the expedition moved at a snail's pace.

Harried by thousands of Boxers, now joined by Imperial Chinese regulars who were openly fighting the foreigners, the Seymour Expedition was stopped—literally—in its tracks at An Ping on June 18. The steel rails had been torn up and carried away and the bridges ahead of them burned. The expedition had a simple choice—retreat or annihilation. Now burdened with a hundred wounded, the soldiers abandoned the trains at a wrecked bridge and retreated toward Tientsin. From June 18 to 22, 1900, Seymour and McCalla and their multinational forces battled thousands of red-scarved Boxers. They retreated slowly and even rescued a few civilians. They also managed to kill hundreds of Boxers. But soon, with over 200 wounded to care for, the expedition could neither retreat nor advance. In desperation, the American Marines—along with the Royal Marines and some German regulars—stormed the fortified Chinese arsenal at Hsi-ku just six miles outside of Tientsin. They annihilated the troops guarding the ammunition stores and brought the bulk of the expedition to the arsenal. There they remained, with ample food, modern weapons, and medical supplies taken from the enemy, until they were rescued three weeks later.

Of Captain McCalla's force of 112 sailors and Marines, 32 of them were killed or wounded on the long trek, and McCalla had been wounded three times. By percentage, this small American contingent sustained almost twice as many casualties as any other nation's force during this failed relief effort, because the U.S. Marines were always on point.

A second relief attempt—this one mounted by Marine Major Littleton "Tony" Waller—left Taku on an old train the morning of June 19. These Marines were augmented by 450 white-clad, leather-booted Russian soldiers. Waller's expedition was stopped by a blown bridge just twelve miles out of Tientsin. Across the chasm the railroad bridge once spanned were thousands of Imperial Chinese soldiers and hordes of angry Boxers. The expeditionary force decided to press on.

That night, Marines and Russians moved in darkness, creeping across the valley without being noticed. But as the sun rose they found themselves trapped by Boxers on one side and Chinese troops on the other—they had inadvertently entered a deep pocket in the enemy ranks. Now they were almost surrounded. The Russians bolted the way they came, leaving the Americans to battle their way out. Major Waller led his men to safety with three dead and nine wounded. During the fierce fight, it was discovered that one wounded Marine had been inadvertently left behind.

A rear guard consisting of Lieutenants Smedley Butler and A. B. Harding and four enlisted Marines went back to recover the wounded man. Under continual Chinese fire, running from attacks by cavalry and artillery, the six Marines carried their wounded comrade seven miles without a stretcher. Two of the enlisted rescuers were themselves wounded, but everyone made it to safety. Lieutenants Butler and Harding both received brevet promotions for gallantry. The four enlisted Marines each received the Medal of Honor for bravery under fire—the first Marines to earn this distinction in the China Campaign. Before the rebellion ended, thirty-three United States Marines would be so honored.

Major Waller and his Marines, after battling all night with no sleep and only hardtack to eat, eventually stumbled upon Captain McCalla's troops and the remnants of Seymour's expedition still holed up in the Hsi-ku arsenal. Captain McCalla, feverish and suffering from the wounds sustained during the failed relief mission, turned his command over to Major Waller. On June 25, the men at the arsenal were finally relieved by an international force. Major Waller burned the Hsi-ku arsenal to the ground and marched his Marines back to Tientsin, bringing out almost 300 wounded from the aborted Seymour Expedition with him.

Waller's Marines were barely rested before their pugnacious commander sent them into harm's way again. On June 27, Russian soldiers, British sailors, and United States Marines led by Major Waller attacked the Tientsin East Arsenal, which held some 7,000 Boxers and much of the munitions used against the legation. In stiff fighting, the multinational force charged the walls, and within an hour the arsenal was captured and the Boxers stationed there killed or routed.

A STATE OF WAR

On June 18, foreign ministers in Peking received word from the empress and the Chinese government that a state of war would soon be in effect. The Chinese were angered by a daring raid by foreign powers that had captured the Taku forts the night before. The Westerners trapped inside the legation were given twenty-four hours to leave Peking—but were guaranteed safe passage only to Tientsin. The foreign delegation declined the offer, so the dowager empress issued a declaration of war that included praise for "the brave followers of the Boxers." On June 20, Boxer rebels and Chinese regulars began a two-month siege of the city—the infamous "Fifty-five Days at Peking." From the first day the fighting was intense and the Chinese kept the legation under almost constant bombardment.

The Legation quarter was cut from east to west by a wide boulevard called Legation Street, and from north to south by a canal. At the southwest corner was the American Legation, protected by the Marines. This part of the compound was backed up against the Tartar Wall—a stone structure sixty feet high and almost forty feet wide that faced east, toward Hata Men Gate. The Marines under Captain John T. Myers constructed a wooden and wire barricade on top of this wall. The British Legation, where the women and children were housed, was at the northwest corner, as far away from the fighting as possible and far from the worst of the daily shelling. All during the siege, the Marines held their ground on the Tartar Wall. They never turned their back on the enemy or gave an inch of ground for more than the few minutes it took to regroup and counterattack. Outside the walls, the Chinese had ringed the legation with barricades of their own. By now there were an estimated 50,000 Boxers in Peking, and an Imperial Chinese Army force of indeterminate number. From the safety of their hastily erected positions they fired into the legation with cannon, and on exposed troops manning the ramparts with small arms.

On June 23, the Chinese set fire to Hanlin Yuan Academy just outside the British Legation, hoping the fire would rip through the foreign residences. Marines—U.S. and Royal—streamed outside the legation's walls to drive the Boxers off with bayonets. Then they battled the fire. On the twenty-fourth the Boxers attacked the British compound and were driven off. On June 27, the Chinese made a tactical error—they attacked Captain Myers's position in broad daylight. The Marines, using a Colt machine gun, cut the attackers to pieces without suffering a single casualty.

Weary of losing Marines in ones and twos, Captain Myers sent out a single brave Marine to reconnoiter the Chinese fortifications in preparation for an attack. On the night of June 28, Private Richard Quinn crawled on his hands and knees to the enemy position and scoped out its defenses. He returned hours later, his knees scraped and bloody, and delivered a detailed report. After that, the Marines were able to deliver more stinging rifle and sniper attacks, though the return fire from the Chinese positions continued unabated.

On July 1, the Chinese shelled the German positions inside the legation until the German force broke, leaving Myers and his men exposed. The Marines fell back for a moment, then—with the help of the British—they regrouped and took back the Tartar Wall and the Germans' abandoned positions. On July 2, the Boxers moved a fifteen-foot siege tower up to the Marines' position on the Tartar Wall. Under covering fire from snipers atop the tower, the Chinese managed to move most of their barricades on the south face of the legation dangerously close to the Marines manning the ramparts. Chinese fire was suddenly more accurate, and something had to be done about it.

At two o'clock the next morning, Captain Myers led his Marines on a daring attack against these fortifications. The assault, staged during a torrential rainstorm, caught the Chinese by surprise. In brutal fighting, often hand to hand, two Marine privates were killed and Captain Myers was wounded in the calf when he tripped over a Chinese spear in the darkness. Boxers spied the hobbled Myers and tried to grab him. Several Marines rushed forward and spirited their captain to safety, stabbing at the enemy with bayonets as they withdrew. The night attack continued—illuminated only by the incessant flashes of gunfire and lightning—until the Chinese fell back to their former positions, leaving over thirty dead behind. By morning, the Marines—minus two slain the night before—had resumed their position on the ramparts. The artillery barrage and sniper fire from the Chinese barricades continued, but it was a lot less accurate than before. Myers's wound became infected, and weakened by typhoid fever, he was forced to turn his command over to Captain Newt H. Hall.

By July 3, the situation was becoming desperate. Over a quarter of the international troops guarding the legation compound had already fallen. Many of the wounded suffered from infection and disease was beginning to spread through the besieged area. Food, water, some types of ammunition, and all medical supplies were in short supply. The Marines took stock of their situation and fought on.

Fortunately, the Chinese became more cautious after the attack that drove them back from the Tartar Wall. There was a general lull in the fighting until July 13, when Imperial Chinese regulars and a mob of Boxers mounted one of their largest assaults of the campaign. The Japanese detachment was driven back by a determined Chinese attack. The British were hard-pressed and in danger of losing the buildings harboring the women and children. Fighting was so intense that it looked as if the Chinese would finally prevail. But the United States Marines and a determined force of German Army regulars refused to retreat. As the Marines fought from the ramparts, ignoring the deadly fire coming at them from three directions, the Germans mounted an aggressive bayonet counterattack that pushed the Chinese back and cleared a portion of Legation Street. So many soldiers were killed or wounded in this assault that the Legation's walls were under-manned for the next several days. It was a dangerous situation and two nights later the Chinese exploited this weakness.

On July 15, a lone Marine from Glen Cove, Long Island, New York, volunteered to man an advanced position on the wall for the night. He was armed with a rifle, a few bul-lets, and a regulation bayonet. Under cover of darkness, the Chinese attacked in force, con-centrating their fire on the Marine's position. Despite intense fire, Private Daniel Joseph Daly refused to relinquish his post. He stood on top of the ramparts and fired down at his attackers, holding them off long enough for Captain Hall to bring up reinforcements and turn back the assault. For this gallant action Private Dan Daly—who was only twenty-five years old at the time—was awarded the first of two Medals of Honor he was to receive during his long and distinguished career in the Marine Corps. Daly's was one of the most visible acts of heroism during this blood-stained campaign, so a legend was born. A former New York City newsboy who enlisted in the Marines to find adventure, Daly would go on to win his second Medal of Honor in Haiti and further distinguish himself in the trenches of World War I.

Sergeant Dan Daly

THE SIEGE OF TIENTSIN AND THE END OF THE BOXER REBELLION

On July 16, an uneasy truce was declared by the Chinese government. Unknown to the multinational defenders at the legation, there was a reason for this cease-fire. By the middle of July, the foreign forces assembled outside Tientsin numbered nearly 6,000 troops, half of them British or American. So many foreign armies were con-verging on Peking that the empress realized her country was facing annihilation.

On July 13, an international coalition attacked Tientsin, which had two fortified stone walls, an outer wall and an inner palisade. Between those two walls were miles of rice paddies, salt mounts, mud, manure piles, sewage canals, and Chinese graves. The day was hot and suffocating—nearly 105 degrees—but that did not deter the United States Marines who spearheaded the attack. Young Herbert Hoover accompanied the American forces as a kind of unofficial guide. The Marines got behind the first wall with relative ease, but the land between the outer and inner walls became a hotly contested battleground very quickly. Lieutenant Smedley Butler later wrote: "We charged over the mud walls. We struggled through this filthy swamp, with bullets splashing and whining around us. The low mud walls of the rice paddies provided some slight protection. We crouched behind them, firing furiously . . ."

Butler's company and some Welsh Fusiliers reached the interior stone wall after much struggle. Then Butler was wounded, shot through the leg. Sustained by brandy from a British officer's canteen and aided by Sergeant Clarence Edwin Sutton and First Lieutenant Leonard, who was minutes away from being gravely wounded himself—he later lost an arm—Butler made it back to the field hospital. He was out of this battle for good, though he would live to fight again. Sergeant Sutton received the Medal of Honor for assisting his wounded commander. Despite an aggressive opening attack, the first day of the assault ended in a draw. As the day waned, and after the coalition forces ran out of ammunition, they withdrew to the outer walls for the night. Twenty-one Marines had fallen, including Colonel Liscum of the Ninth Infantry, who was killed carrying the regimental colors.

Before dawn of the next day, the Japanese forces staged a daring night attack that blew open the main gate to the city. Tientsin was now defenseless. By daybreak, the entire international force was inside the city. There was looting, but the well-disciplined Marines focused on seizing the vault of the Chinese state commissioner's building, where $800,000 worth of silver bullion was buried under the ruins. Though the soldiers of other nations were subsequently cited for looting and other misdeeds, the United States Marines were never charged with any wrongdoing.

When Tientsin fell, the dowager empress lost her nerve and declared a truce. In a surprising turnaround, Imperial Chinese soldiers withdrew from the Legation quarter and the military assault ended. But the foreign soldiers and civilians were still trapped inside the compound by thousands of Boxers.

Fortunately, relief was on the way.

On August 3, the 18,600-strong international liberation army set out for Peking. There were two concentrations of Boxers between the allies and the city, but they were easily defeated despite the terrible heat and a lack of water. On August 13, the liberation force arrived at the outskirts of the city. When the defenders inside the legation heard the sound of machine guns, they knew relief was close. The battle raged on the walls of Peking all the next day, but by the fifteenth, Peking was at the mercy of the military force besieging its walls. The legation was relieved the following day.

Political considerations initially delayed the allied troops' triumphant entry into China's capital. All during China's 2,000 year history, no foreign power had ever violated the walls of Peking. It was decided that a token force made up of elements of all the nations involved in the siege should march from one end of the Forbidden City to the other in a ceremonial show of strength. This was done on August 28. As the last troops passed the north gate, a twenty-one gun salute proclaimed the fall of the Forbidden City and the final liberation of the Legation quarter. There were sporadic outbreaks of violence in remote parts of China, but it was left to the German military to deal with them. In September, the Boxer Protocol, a formal peace treaty between the Chinese government and the West, was signed, ending all hostilities.

Of the fifty-six Marines who served in China during the Boxer Rebellion, seventeen of them were casualties—nearly one in three. During the siege, many Marines distinguished themselves by meritorious conduct under fire. The well-publicized courage of Daniel Daly was heralded throughout the world. But other Marines performed with equal heroism under extreme conditions during the legation's defense.

Private Harry Fisher of McKeesport, Pennsylvania, was killed on July 16, 1900, by a Chinese bullet while helping Marines erect a barricade on the Tartar Wall under heavy fire. When the siege was lifted his body was returned to his family in Pittsburgh and Private Fisher was buried with honor at Versailles Cemetery in McKeesport. On the first anniversary of his death, his family was presented with the Medal of Honor. Fisher's story is typical of the character and bravery of many members of the Marine Corps in this era.

Harry Fisher was the first Marine to be awarded the Medal of Honor posthumously, "for distinguished conduct in the presence of the enemy at the Battle of Peking." According to official government files, Fisher had enlisted in the Marine Corps for a five-year stint on May 19, 1899, at Marine barracks in Washington, D.C. According to his enlistment papers, he was a brakeman from Pennsylvania with no prior military service.

This was not true.

"Fisher"—whose real name was Franklin J. Phillips—was actually a former private in Company M, First U.S. Army Infantry. During his second enlistment in the Army, he had deserted from Camp A. G. Forse in Huntsville, Alabama, on December 17, 1898. He contracted malaria while serving in Cuba and deserted when he was denied a sick furlough. He made his way home to Pennsylvania for treatment by his family, and when he recovered, he telegraphed the adjutant general in Washington and asked to be reinstated. But his old unit had already returned to Cuba and the adjutant general's office issued Special Order No. 63 on March 17, 1899, ordering that Private Franklin J. Phillips be "discharged without honor from the service of the United States . . . by reason of desertion." Phillips joined the Marine Corps two months later and served honorably under the name Harry Fisher until he was killed in action in China. In a letter dated May 6, 1901, Phillips's mother, Mrs. W. C. Means, wrote Brigadier General Charles Heywood, then commandant of the Marine Corps, requesting that the Corps' rolls be changed to reflect his true name. That request was denied.

In 1988, after repeated requests from two congressmen in Pennsylvania, commandant of the Marine Corps General Alfred Gray directed that Harry Fisher's records be changed to reflect his true name. But there was a complication. In 1985, a cargo vessel was christened the MV *Private Harry Fisher*. In 1988, to reflect the change in the governmental records, the maritime prepositioning ship was renamed the MV *Private Franklin J. Phillips*. This vessel, one of thirteen ships of the Maritime Sealift Command, was specifically designed for transporting Marine Corps supplies and equipment in time of crisis. It is still in service today.

Private Erwin Jay Boydston, who replaced Private Phillips on the Tartar Wall, received the Medal of Honor for courage under fire as he helped to erect barricades. Boydston, from Deer Creek, Colorado, was twenty-five years old at the time of the action. He left the Marine Corps after the Boxer Rebellion and settled in Hawaii. He passed away May 19, 1957.

Another Marine at the barricades was Private William M. "Charlie" Horton of Chicago. He received the Medal of Honor on January 5, 1902, for distinguished conduct in defense of the legation. Horton would rise to the rank of sergeant, retire, and move to Seattle, Washington, where he died in 1969 at the age of ninety. Also on the barricades was Private Albert Moore of Merced County, California. Moore, who was nearly forty at the time, was a former first sergeant with the United States Army, his highest rank. Moore died in Port Mason, California, in 1916.

Private Oscar Jefferson Upham of Toledo, Ohio, received the Medal of Honor for erecting and manning the barricades under intense fire. He died in Guthrie, Oklahoma, in 1949. John Alphonsus Murphy, an eighteen-year-old drummer in the Marine Corps, received the Medal of Honor for action inside the legation. He returned to New York City after his term of service expired and died there in 1935. Another New Yorker, Private William Henry Murray, also earned the Medal of Honor during the defense of the legation.

Private Herbert Irving Preston of Union County, New Jersey, received the Medal of Honor for "meritorious conduct" during the siege. Private William Louis Carr of Essex County, Massachusetts, received a Medal of Honor for courage displayed throughout the siege. Carr was wounded at Peking but would remain a Marine for most of his life, to rise to the rank of corporal. He died in Sandusky, Ohio, on April 14, 1921, at the age of forty-three and is buried at the Ohio Veterans Home Cemetery.

Many other Marines were awarded the Medal of Honor for consistent courage throughout the siege at Peking. Among them were Private William F. Zion of Knightstown, Indiana; Private Frank Albert Young of Milwaukee; Private France Silva of Heywood, California; Scottish-born Sergeant Edward Alexander Walker; Private David John Scannell of Boston; Private Martin Hunt of County Mayo, Ireland; and Corporal John Olof Dahlgren of Kahliwar, Sweden.

For a daring small-boat raid in conducted during the battle for Peking against several buildings that housed Chinese snipers on June 20, 1900, three Marines received the Medal of Honor. One of them was Private James Burnes of Worchester, Massachusetts. Burnes entered Marine Corps service in California and was thirty at the time of his heroic action. He left the Corps at the end of his enlistment and vanished from history. Corporal Edwin Nelson Appleton of Brooklyn, New York, was another. Under heavy fire, he rowed across a canal and helped to destroy several structures. Appleton died in 1937 and is buried in Greenwood Cemetery, Brooklyn. The third Marine to receive a Medal of Honor for this action was Private Henry William Heisch. Born in Latendorf, Germany, Heisch entered service in California, where he died in 1941.

Many of the honorees in this campaign received their Medals of Honor for action during the protracted struggle to relieve the legation. In alphabetical order they are: Sergeant John Mapes Adams of Massachusetts; Corporal Harry Chapman Adriance of Oswego, New York; Private Albert Ralph Campbell of Williamsport, Pennsylvania; Private James Cooney of Limerick, Ireland; Sergeant Alexander Foley of Heckerville, Pennsylvania, who died in Puerto Rico in 1910; Private Charles Robert Francis of Bucks County, Pennsylvania; Private Louis Rene Gaienne of St. Louis; Private Thomas Wilbur Kates of Shelby Center, New York; Private Clarence Edward Mathias of Royalton, Pennsylvania; Private Harry Westley Orndoff of Sandusky, Ohio; Corporal Ruben Jasper Phillips of San Luis Obispo County, California; and Scottish-born Gunnery Sergeant Peter Stewart.

With a peace treaty signed in September, the campaign in China was officially over. It was time for the U.S. Marines to return to the Philippines and finish the job they'd started.

"CIVILIZE THEM WITH A KRAG!"

On September 28, the Navy ordered the First Marine Regiment to return to Cavite Naval Base in the Philippine Islands. The regiment marched out of Peking in early October and sailed from Taku. When they landed, they were organized into a brigade—two regiments of two battalions each—with a total strength of 1,678. It was the largest organized force of Marines to take to the field in the Corps long history. The First Regiment was sent to Olongapo, the Second Regiment stayed at Cavite.

On the main island of Luzon, order had been restored. The predominantly Christian Tagalog people had accepted American occupation, but on the southern islands the Moros, who were predominantly Muslim, continued to cause trouble. In March 1901, the United States Army's VII Corps captured rebel leader Emilio Aguinaldo. Soon the insurrection died down and an uneasy peace resulted. But a new local leader quickly arose, a man who called himself Brigadier General Vincente Lukban. General Lukban would score a decisive victory against the American forces—a victory that would result in the death of countless Filipinos and the subjugation of his people.

The tentative peace was shattered on September 28, 1901, when Company C of the U.S. Army's Ninth Infantry, stationed on the southeastern island of Samar near the barrio town of Balangiga, was caught by surprise by a mass attack of rebels. The officer in charge of this detachment was a supporter of President McKinley's "benevolent assimilation" program. Out of political concerns he had allowed a number of women into Balangiga without searching them. The women were in the barrio town on the pretext of burying their children, who had died of cholera. But these women were really men in disguise—Moros insurgents—and their children's coffins were filled with weapons, not corpses. When the Americans sat down to breakfast, the rebels struck. Forty-seven American soldiers were hacked to pieces by bolos. The dead were further mutilated where they lay. Heads were cut off and burned. The commander had his ring finger bitten off. Skulls were split, genitals mutilated, eyes gouged out.

▪ Weapons of the Filipino Insurrection

The Marines sent to the Philippines were armed with one of the better handheld weapons of the period, the Krag-Jorgensen Model 1898 .30-caliber rifle. Though not perfect, the "Krag" was a useful tool of war. It had more stopping power than the Navy-issue Lee "Straight-Pull" 6mm rifle, which the Marines had been using since the Spanish-American War. The Krag was also used by the Army, so ammunition was always in plentiful supply.

The Krag-Jorgensen had other advantages. It used smokeless powder, which made Marine sharpshooters difficult to spot even after they fired. And the weapon became something of a public relations tool too. The Krag-Jorgensen gave rise to the Marine Corps' battle cry, "Civilize 'em with a Krag!"—a soldier's defiant response to the antiwar press back home. The Krag came with three bayonets—one knife-edged and straight; one curved like a bowie knife, but fragile; a third fashioned after the Filipino *bolo* but not nearly as good. In fact, none of these blades would prove satisfactory. But it was the heavy weight and low muzzle velocity that would be the Krag's undoing. Dragging the long, heavy rifle through the jungle was tiresome and the low muzzle velocity meant that bullets bounced off foliage. Four years after the Philippine Insurrection, the Marine Corps would adopt the Springfield "03" rifle. The Springfield would be with them in the trenches of World War I and at Guadalcanal in World War II.

The Filipino insurgents used many weapons and carried rifles of various types, most left over from the Spanish occupation. Some were armed with old muskets or single-shot rifles. Later many Filipinos would possess rifles taken from fallen American soldiers. Insurgents also carried a variety of handheld weapons. They favored the *bolo*—a long-shanked, swordlike machete that was vicious in close combat. The rebels also carried straight *Balisong* knives and a longer, heavier edged knife called a *punal*. Many Filipinos were also trained in the use of the *escrima* stick—a long pole utilized in Filipino martial arts.

During the insurrection, the rebels employed various terror weapons. Ditches filled with spikes and topped with foliage, poison darts, poison-tipped or manure-tipped spears, trip ropes, hangmen's snares, and formidable cannons called *lantacas*—constructed of fire-hardened bamboo filled with powder and nails, bolts, or shards of glass—were all employed against American troops. These terror weapons would also be used by the Viet Cong during the Vietnam War sixty years later. The caves on the Sohoton River, where the Moros made their last stand, were defended by a complex network of these defenses. Fortunately, Major Waller's Marines made it past these devilish traps and into the heart of the rebel stronghold without falling prey to these guerrilla-style terror weapons.

Thirty-six U.S. Army survivors fled by boat and reported the slaughter to their commanders. Editorial writers in the United States compared the massacre to General Custer's defeat at Little Big Horn. The viciousness of the assault was widely publicized, and the Filipinos lost any sympathy they may have had in the United States. Some newspapers decried Army General Arthur MacArthur for misleading the public into believing that the war was over.

Theodore Roosevelt, who assumed the presidency after McKinley's murder, was unsympathetic to the notion of benevolent assimilation. He ordered that "most stern measures to pacify Samar" should be undertaken. The Marines, who had fought side by side with the Ninth Infantry during the Boxer Rebellion, petitioned for the right to seek out those responsible and exact vengeance. Major Littleton Tazewell Waller—short, portly, and belligerent—was sent off to pacify Samar. Waller's orders, handed down from Army Brigadier General Jacob "Hell-Roaring Jake" Smith, were clear: "Make Samar a howling wilderness . . . I want no prisoners. I wish you to burn and kill. The more you burn and kill, the better it will please me. I want all persons killed who are capable of bearing arms in actual hostilities against the United States." Revenge was the order of the day, and Major Waller delivered.

Three hundred Marines were going up against an estimated 3,000 Moros, but the odds—ten to one—didn't bother Major Waller. For the next five months, Marines tore through Samar. Villages were burned, food supplies destroyed, pack animals were slaughtered, and according to some sources, thousands of Filipinos died in countless atrocities. By one account, the population of the Philippines declined from 312,192 to 257,715. Others suggest that only 8,000 civilians and rebels were killed by the Marines. Whatever the numbers, the Marines' campaign against the insurgents was effective. The Moros were in full retreat by November.

Back home the war was unpopular. Though the Marines were denounced in the American press, the troops in the Philippines refused to bow to public pressure. "Civilize them with a Krag!" became the Marine Corps battle cry as

Captain Hiram I. Bearss

they continued their pacification campaign against the native population. The Moros withdrew in disarray, retreating to a forest stronghold in the cliffs above the Sohoton River. Built in heavily fortified caves over 200 feet above the jungle floor, the stronghold seemed impenetrable. The jungles around it were so thick not even the Spaniards, who first colonized the Philippines, penetrated the region. Undeterred by these seemingly insurmountable difficulties, Major Waller staged a bold attack against the Moros on November 17. In one of the most dramatic and effective military actions of the twentieth century, Waller's Marines defeated the Moros, pacified the Philippines, and exacted revenge for the butchered Americans in a single, decisive action.

The three-pronged Marine assault on the cliffs above the Sohoton was risky, complex, and brilliant. Major Waller split his forces into three columns; one he led himself, another was led by Captain Hiram Iddings Bearss, the third by Captain David Dixon Porter. The insurgents were encamped in defensive positions high above the jungle floor, in a honeycomb of caves running through a high cliff of volcanic ash. Waller's column used pole boats to move upriver while two columns of riflemen, led by Porter and Bearss, were dropped off and vanished into the forest at different points along the shore. These Marines moved under cover of night through the trackless jungle until they linked up on the opposite side of the Sohoton River from the rebel stronghold.

The guerrillas had prepared a variety of defenses. Nets full or boulders—called *bejucos*—were placed high on the cliff face, ready to rain death onto the attackers.

Sergeant Major John H. Quick

Fire-hardened bamboo cannons were packed with black powder and lead bolts and aimed at any trail an opposing force might use. There were Moros sentries placed at various points and torches constantly illuminated the jungle floor. But the Marines had impressive weapons of their own. Captain Bearss's column dragged a wheeled Colt-Browning M-1895 6mm machine gun through the jungle. And the Marines had their trusty Krag-Jorgensens, a heavy rifle that a Marine sharpshooter could wield with deadly effect.

Within sight of the rebel compound, Gunnery Sergeant John Quick—the Marine Corps signalman who had become a hero at the Battle for the Cuzco Well—opened up on the Moros with his machine gun. It was early evening and the large groups of Moros relaxing outside the caves and on the jungle floor were taken by surprise. Accurate, short bursts from Quick's Potato-Digger cut them down. When the insurgents tried to return fire, the riflemen on the other side of the river opened up. Soon dead Filipinos were plunging off the cliffs to the jungle floor far below. They fell "like the leaves of autumn," according to one Marine.

Under covering fire, Corporal Robert Leckie swam across the surging waters, captured a native boat, and pushed it back across to his comrades. Moros repeatedly tried to kill him, but every time one of them stuck his head out to aim, a Marine sniper shot it off. When it was in range, Marines surged aboard Corporal Leckie's boat and crossed to the enemy side. More vessels were captured and soon boatloads of Marines were crossing the river under intense fire. The Moros tried to mount a counterattack as the Marines rowed across the water. That's when Major Waller's column arrived on the pole boats. A fieldpiece barked from the deck of Waller's craft and stopped the Moros in their tracks.

Finally, the Marines reached the base of the cliff, disarmed some of the booby traps, skirted the poison-tipped spears and the deadly spike pits that awaited them, and with Captain Bearss and Captain Porter in the lead, they climbed bamboo and rope ladders to the caves above. The hand-to-hand fighting through torch-lit caverns and across swaying bamboo bridges was treacherous. When the Marines ran out of ammunition, they used bayonets. When their bayonets broke, they snatched weapons from the dead. It was a bloody day's work. Waller and his men expected no quarter and gave none—not one rebel survived. When the Marines were finished, so was the rebellion in Samar.

Captain Hiram Bearss and Captain David Porter both received Medals of Honor for their actions at the Battle of Sohoton River. Bearss, who was Waller's second-in-command, would remain in the Marine Corps and rise to the rank of brigadier general. He waited a long time to receive his Medal of Honor, but his courage was finally celebrated in a White House ceremony on April 5, 1934, just four years before his death. Captain Porter, who was born in Washington, D.C., would also wait over thirty years before his courage was recognized. Porter would rise to the rank of major general. Franklin D. Roosevelt awarded him the Medal of Honor in the same White House ceremony that honored Hiram Bearss.

But before they left the Pacific Rim, Captain Porter and Captain Bearss would join Major Waller and Medal of Honor recipient John Quick on one final adventure in the Philippine jungle—an adventure that nearly killed them all.

THE HELL OF SAMAR

Three weeks after his victory at the Battle of Sohoton River, Major "Tony" Waller led his Marines into the jungles of Samar to survey the region for a telegraph line. It was a disastrous, ill-conceived mission that was doomed. Following vague and contradictory orders from General Smith, Waller set out with an expedition to find an old Spanish trail across the island, a legendary jungle path that the Army had failed to locate under optimum conditions. December was the beginning of the rainy season and the weather—along with everything else in the jungle—was unpredictable. Waller's expedition consisted of five officers, fifty Marines, two native guides, and thirty Filipino bearers. They departed Lanang on December 27, 1901, and planned to hike about fifty miles. But their maps proved useless in the jungle and Waller was forced to rely on his Filipino guides.

Trouble began with the arrival of the incessant daily rains, during which trails were swept away, hills became waterfalls, trees fell, paths were blocked, and landmarks obliterated. In minutes the monsoon rain could turn a gentle stream into a muddy creek, a creek into a surging river, a river into a raging force of destruction. The guides turned mutinous. Rations ran short, and fever ripped through the ranks. Major Waller decided to divide the expedition. He and the strongest men would push on to the village of Basey to get help, while the main force—commanded by Captain David Porter with Hiram Bearss as second—would follow as best they could. But after a few days, many of Porter's Marines became sick and could not be moved. Porter made the same decision his commander had made and split his force. He and the strongest Marines turned back to Lanang, leaving thirty sick Marines and some bearers behind, under the command of First Lieutenant Alexander S. Williams. Porter and his men reached Lanang on January 11.

Major Waller and his column had made fairly good time too. They had stumbled out of the jungle at Basey on January 6. But Waller hardly rested before plunging back in to search for the rest of his men. He combed the jungle for nine days, never realizing that Captain Porter's column had turned around and headed back to Lanang. Meanwhile, Lieutenant Williams—still lost in the jungle with thirty helpless Marines—

was attacked by the Filipinos in his party. His life was only saved when his feverish men stumbled to their feet and beat off the Filipinos with sticks. Lieutenant Williams and his command were finally rescued by Army searchers on January 17. Ten Marines were lost in this expedition. Most died of fever.

Major Waller had long suspected that Filipino treachery was involved in the destruction of his expedition. From his hospital bed he ordered a court-martial and had eleven of the Filipino guides and bearers shot in the public plaza at Basey—earning the title of "The Butcher of Samar" from a hostile American press. When he and the Marines recovered enough to travel, they returned to Cavite Naval Station. Waller may have anticipated a heroes' welcome for his successful campaign at the Sohoton River. Instead, he was court-martialed by the U.S. Army on March 17. He was acquitted of murder and the whole case was ultimately thrown out on a legal technicality. But the shadow of this debacle hung over Major Waller for the rest of his career, and though he was twice nominated for the job, Tony Waller never became commandant of the Marine Corps because of lingering doubts about his exploits at Samar.

INTERNATIONAL ADVENTURES

Before, during, and after their actions in the Philippines, Marines were dispatched to quell unrest in several Caribbean nations and one Pacific island. On April 1, 1899, Marines from the U.S.S. *Philadelphia* went ashore in Samoa in a combined landing party with Royal Marines from two British ships. They were there to intervene in an argument between two tribal leaders over the succession of the Samoan throne. The Marines were ambushed, burned a village or two, then retreated. Three Marines—Bruno Albert Forsterer, a German-born sergeant; British-born Private Henry Lewis Hulbert; and Private Michael Joseph McNally of New York City—received the Medal of Honor for this brief campaign. Henry L. Hulbert would rise to the rank of lieutenant and die in combat near Mont Blanc, France, during World War I.

Closer to home, the Spanish-American War and the presidency of Theodore Roosevelt revived American interests in a canal across the Isthmus of Panama. The property of the defunct French Panama Company, which had failed to construct a canal due to the ravages of yellow fever, had been acquired by the United States government for a paltry $40 million. But the Colombian government was the actual proprietor of the isthmus, and the United States had to negotiate with it before they could begin work. The government in Cartagena demanded $25 million in exchange for U.S. sovereignty over a ten-mile-wide strip across the isthmus. President Roosevelt offered them $10 million. When the Colombian government failed to act, the United States government used a bloodless coup in Panama as an excuse to invade Central America. The Marines landed at Colón on the Atlantic side of the isthmus with orders to tame the Colombian garrison stationed there. Major John A. Lejeune's Marines easily convinced the Colombians to depart and Theodore Roosevelt recognized the independence of the new Republic of Panama. Work on the canal commenced. The Marines stayed in Panama until 1914.

On January 3, 1904, a Marine detachment landed in the Dominican Republic to defend American interests. Two days later 300 Marines arrived in Seoul, Korea, to protect Americans there from the ravages of the Russo-Japanese War. In 1906, Marines were sent to Cuba to guard American-owned railroads and sugar plantations. In 1909, Major Smedley Butler and his battalion landed at Corinto on the west coast of Nicaragua to depose dictator José Santos Zelaya and replace him with General Juan J. Estrada, who was friendly to the United States. With the help of Butler's Marines, José Santos Zelaya was driven into exile and Estrada marched triumphantly into Managua in 1910.

VERACRUZ

In 1914, Mexico was in chaos. President Francisco Madero had been assassinated and General Victoriano Huerta made himself dictator-president. Huerta was no friend to the United States, and actively petitioned for European help against his belligerent neighbor. Germany was more than happy to expand its influence into the western hemisphere and sent arms and military advisers to Mexico. This made the American government uneasy, but there was nothing they could do unless provoked.

On April 9, 1914, the paymaster from the United States warship *Dolphin* went ashore in Mexico to purchase gasoline. He and several sailors were arrested by the authorities at Tampico. Though these men were quickly released with an apology from Presidente Huerta himself, Admiral Henry T. Mayo, commander of the U.S. Navy fleet off the Mexican coast, was not satisfied. He demanded a twenty-one gun salute to the American flag in addition to the apology. Huerta balked at the request, and the Navy used his reticence as an excuse to blockade Mexico's Gulf ports.

Tensions in Mexico escalated a few weeks later when Washington learned of the imminent delivery of more German arms and munitions to the Mexican government. President Woodrow Wilson dispatched the brand-new Marine Advance Base Force south of the border to stop further European encroachment. The Advance Base Force was an innovation developed by Major Henry C. Haines. With Marines no longer posted on Navy vessels, a new role had to be found for the Corps. An Advance Base Force seemed to be the answer. This force was established to capture and hold a hostile beach, construct a forward naval base, and defend that base if necessary. Exercises off Newport, Rhode Island, and around Nantucket, followed by a regimental-sized landing exercise on the island of Culebra, east of Puerto Rico, demonstrated the effectiveness of Haines's training and tactics. And even critics of the Marine Corps agreed that having a small expeditionary force at hand for deployment in trouble spots was a wise use of military resources. The first real test of the Advance Base Force would come in the conflict with Mexico.

Colonel John Archer Lejeune, a Cajun from Louisiana, was in temporary command of the Advance Base Force poised for deployment in New Orleans and Pensacola, Florida. Lejeune, a graduate of the Naval Academy at Annapolis and a veteran of the Spanish-American War, was ordered by President Wilson to "take Veracruz at once." But it was the Second Marine Regiment, commanded by Lieutenant

Colonel Wendell C. "Buck" Neville, who landed first. Neville's men arrived in Veracruz on the morning of April 21. Initially there was no resistance and the Marines were able to capture the cable station and power plant. But by noon an intense firefight had developed at the railyards. Soon resistance from Mexican regulars, military cadets, and armed citizens became quite fierce.

Lieutenant Colonel Neville was on the ground and in the thick of the fighting from the start. Born in Portsmouth, Virginia, he would receive the Medal of Honor for his actions at Veracruz. All during the fight, he stood at various "points of great danger," and according to his citation, "upon his courage and skill depended, in great measure, success or failure." Neville rose to the rank of major general and died in 1930.

The fighting continued, increasing in intensity, all through the night. Morning heralded the arrival of the Marine Advance Base Force, and the action became even hotter. Soon the Marines were fighting in the streets, house to house and hand to hand. Both sides resorted to picks, shovels, knives, and bayonets in combat that cost the Mexicans hundreds of lives. In streets choked with powder smoke and the haze from burning buildings, bullets flew in every direction. Street fighting is the most dangerous and difficult type of combat. Each building, each room, has to be pacified. In Veracruz, the heavy style of Spanish architecture made things even more difficult. Snipers had places to hide and stout walls to protect them. Casualties on both sides were heavy.

As Mexican regulars arrived to reinforce those already fighting, these troops refused to abandon their packs, bedrolls, and field gear. Heavily laden with useless equipment and marching in columns, these regulars were ill-prepared for street-to-street warfare. The Marines, fortified with fresh troops of their own, cut the Mexican soldiers to pieces. Moving quickly, through windows and houses, across roofs, over, around, and sometimes through thick stone walls, the Marines pushed back the Mexicans alley by alley, street by street, building by building. After two and a half days of intense fighting that ended on the evening of April 24, Veracruz was pacified. Hundreds of Mexican casualties lay in the streets. American losses stood at about 135. Nineteen Marines were dead. With 7,000 U.S. Marines and sailors on the ground or coming ashore—and the United States Army on the way—Presidente Huerta found it prudent to sue for peace. In the face of Washington's resistance to his administration, he was exiled in July. The brief, violent campaign in Veracruz was over.

Nine Marines earned the Medal of Honor in this battle. One of the four highest-ranking recipients, along with Lieutenant Colonel Neville, was Major Randolph Carter Berkeley, an officer of the Advance Base Force. Virginia-born Berkeley was cited for his "cool judgement and courage, and his skill in handling his men in encountering and overcoming the machine gun and rifle fire down Cinco de Mayo and parallel streets." A lifelong Marine, Berkeley rose to the rank of major general before his mandatory retirement. He died in 1960 and is buried in Arlington National Cemetery.

The second officer to receive the Medal of Honor was Major Smedley Darlington Butler, a veteran of the attack on Tientsin. Born in West Chester, Pennsylvania, he was a battalion commander during the Mexican Campaign. When informed of his

Major Smedley D. Butler

Colonel Albertus W. Catlin

nomination, Butler humbly refused his Medal of Honor. But his commanders insisted he accept and eventually they prevailed. Less than a year after the battle for Veracruz, Major Butler would receive a second Medal of Honor for his actions in Haiti.

Major Albertus Wright Catlin of Gowanda, New York, was cited for "distinguished conduct in battle." He would rise to brigadier general, and fight in France during World War I. Major George Croghan Reid of Lorain, Ohio, was cited, along with Major Berkeley, for courage during the fighting along Cinco de Mayo and its side streets. A career officer, Reid would rise to the rank of brigadier general before his death in 1961.

Captain Jesse Farley Dyer of St. Paul, Minnesota, was a company commander in Mexico and received the Medal of Honor for "leading his men with skill and courage." He would rise to the rank of brigadier general before his death in 1955. Captain Eli Thompson Fryer of Mercer County, New Jersey, received the Medal of Honor for "distinguished conduct in battle." He became a brigadier general between the First and Second World Wars, retired after the Pacific Campaign of the 1940s, and passed away on June 6, 1963.

Captain Walter Newell Hill, was "in both days' fighting at the head of his company" during the battle for Veracruz. He received the Medal of Honor in December 1915. Born in Massachusetts, Hill rose to the rank of brigadier general and retired after the Second World War. He died in 1955. Captain John Arthur Hughes of New York City received the Medal of Honor for courage and coolness during the chaotic fighting. He rose to the rank of colonel and fought in the bloodiest campaign in Marine Corps history, the Battle of Belleau Wood.

During the Civil War and the conflicts that followed, enlisted men and noncommissioned officers were the sole recipients of the Medal of Honor. Commissioned officers were usually rewarded for conspicuous courage by brevet promotions. But by the time of the Battle of Veracruz, that practice was reversed—not one enlisted man or NCO was awarded the Medal of Honor. Every single recipient was a member of the officer corps. This pattern reflects the rising esteem in which the Medal of Honor was held.

THE HAITIAN CAMPAIGN

It was not a military crisis, but economic collapse that precipitated United States' intervention in Haiti in 1915. When Haiti's banks failed the year before, European and American financial institutions were stunned. Haiti owed millions in loans to foreign investors and American banks. Germany, France, Great Britain, and the United States all had good reason to put troops ashore. The United States offered the Haitian government a bailout deal, but the Haitians refused to accept the terms. In December 1914, a Marine detachment went ashore at Port-au-Prince to seize the last $500,000 stored in Haiti's treasury vaults.

A March 1915 coup put Vilbrun Guillaume Sam in power, but his government was torn asunder by internal strife. Facing chaos, President Sam slaughtered 167 political prisoners and hid from his own people in the French Legation. A mob stormed the building and the French turned Sam out. The mob tore him to pieces and literally devoured his heart.

To keep order Rear Admiral William B. Caperton landed a regiment of Marines under the command of Captain George Van Orden. They entered Port-au-Prince under heavy sniper fire, restored a semblance of order, and stopped the slaughter. On August 4, a more permanent force of Marines landed, under the command of Colonel Eli K. Cole. A larger force arrived on the fifteenth, this one commanded by Colonel Tony Waller—the infamous "Butcher of Samar." Waller had 2,000 Marines at his disposal and he moved quickly. His men captured ten customhouses and garrisoned in all the important towns. Waller went north to Cap Haitien, where the chaos seemed to originate. He brought the First Battalion with him, and Major Smedley Butler as backup commander.

The rebels in the north—called Cacos after a bright, scarlet-plumbed Caribbean bird—wore red armbands, bandannas, or scarves as a mark of identification. The Cacos were led by General Rameau, and his men had been harassing the Marine garrison based at Gonaives. Major Smedley Butler, leading a force of Marines, stormed into the mountains and caught General Rameau and his men on September 18. Butler literally yanked the Haitian general off his horse as Lieutenant Alexander A. Vandergrift subdued and hog-tied the insurgent leader. They dragged General Rameau back to Port-au-Prince in chains and the Cacos uprising in the north ended.

Then Major Butler and forty mounted Marines went after a large Caco stronghold

Sergeant Dan Daly

Captain William P. Upshur

called Fort Dipitie, deep in the mountains in the region near Fort Capois. After dark on October 24, while the Americans were crossing a river, they were ambushed by Cacos firing from the jungle. The Cacos fired from three sides—they could hardly miss. Twelve packhorses were killed, including the one carrying the patrol's only machine gun and ammunition. Weighted down, the dead animal sank like a stone. The rest of the pack train was scattered as the Marines fled for cover.

Gunnery Sergeant Dan Daly—already a Medal of Honor recipient for action during the Boxer Rebellion—volunteered to sneak back and recover the gun. Despite hundreds of Cacos who roamed the area—and several dozen who took potshots at him—he managed to reach the river, dive for the gun, cut it loose from the dead horse, and haul it back to the patrol, which was pinned down in a deep ravine. Sergeant Daly received a second Medal of Honor for his bold action.

Captain William Peterkin Upshur also earned a Medal of Honor. Despite heavy fire, he and his men remained in position near the walls of the Cacos stronghold, waiting for Daly to return with the machine gun. Upshur's Marines faced incessant gunfire—but only returned it when the Cacos dared to approach. When Daly returned near daybreak, Captain Upshur and Major Butler organized their men, divided them into three columns, and fought their way out of the ravine by counterattacking in three different directions against overwhelming odds. With fire support from the machine gun, the Marines ambushed their ambushers. The Cacos scattered, and seventy-five of them died. One Marine was wounded. Upshur, a graduate of the United States Naval Academy, was born in Richmond, Virginia. He remained in the

First Lieutenant Edward A. Ostermann

Marine Corps and rose to the rank of major general. He died in Sitka, Alaska, in 1943.

Accompanying Butler and Upshur on this patrol was First Lieutenant Edward Albert Ostermann of Columbus, Ohio. He led one of the three columns in the decisive counterattack that broke the back of the ambush. A career officer, Ostermann rose to the rank of major general and died in Fairfax, Virginia, in 1969.

When Butler returned to Port-au-Prince, Major Waller gave him five companies of Marines and sent him off to clean out Fort Capois once and for all. In a lightning attack on November 5, Butler captured the fort without incurring casualties. The last of the Cacos, led by General Josefette, were driven to the ruins of an eighteenth-century French fort eight miles south of Grande Rivière. Fort Rivière was built on top of a 4,000-foot mountain called Montagne Noire and was thought to be impregnable. With three companies of Marines and a company of sailors wearing Marine Corps uniforms, Butler marched to the fort and engineered a nighttime assault.

The Marines began their climb on the night of November 17. Smedley Butler led the column and arrived at the foot of the wall with two lieutenants and twenty-four Marines at his side. At 7:30 in the morning, he blew the whistle and the attack was on. Some of the Cacos tried to hold the walls, but Marine marksmen cut them down with their Benet rifles. In the final charge, across naked ground with little cover, the Marines located an open sewage drain, four feet high and three feet wide, they thought was unguarded. But when they peered inside, Caco bullets streaked out at them. The insurgents were alerted and the element of surprise was lost.

"Hell!" Sergeant Ross Lindsey Iams exclaimed. "I'm going through."

The tunnel was so tight that only one man could enter at a time. With bullets whizzing past him through the narrow space, Sergeant Iams flattened himself against the wall and crawled into the opening with Butler's orderly Private Samuel Gross—real name Samuel Marguiles—right behind him. Butler entered third, and the rest of his column followed.

On the other side of the drain, Sergeant Iams found several Cacos waiting for him. The sergeant fired first, taking the head off one Haitian. Then Iams, Gross, Butler, and the rest streamed into the Cacos stronghold. An unruly hand-to-hand struggle ensued. The Cacos were armed with swords, rocks, and clubs—called *coco-*

macaques—along with an ax or two. The Marines had their rifles, a few Benet automatics, and their bayonets. The Cacos broke first. Most hopped the wall and vanished into the wilderness. General Josefette's body was found later. He was dressed in a frock coat, his top hat lying nearby.

Major Smedley D. Butler, who had tried to refuse his first Medal of Honor for action in Veracruz, received a second for the battle at Fort Rivière. He and Sergeant Dan Daly are the only Marines to ever receive the Medal of Honor for two separate actions. Sergeant Iams and Private Gross were both awarded the Medal of Honor. In all, six Marines received the medal for action during the Haitian Campaign.

In Port-au-Prince, a new government friendly to the United States had been installed. They agreed to the creation of a Haitian constabulary officered by Americans to keep the peace. The first commandant of the Gendarmerie d'Haïti was Smedley Butler, who was promoted to lieutenant colonel. The gendarmes were native Haitians from the urban areas. They were given surplus Marine uniforms, Krags, and drilled in English. With the help of the Marines, these gendarmes kept the peace for a generation. Alongside the Marines and a corps of engineers, they built roads, telegraph systems, began a postal network that still delivers mail today, improved water supplies and general sanitation in the urban areas, and built and staffed schools open to all Haitians.

THE FIRST DOMINICAN CAMPAIGN

Even as the conflict ended in Haiti, trouble began across the border in the tiny nation of Santo Domingo. Like Haiti, Santo Domingo was indebted to a number of European nations, and during its first economic crisis, some of those governments threatened intervention. In 1906, the Dominican government signed a fifty-year treaty with the United States that gave Washington sovereignty in exchange for debt relief. Both before and after that treaty was signed, small detachments of Marines had paid the Dominicans a "visit." But when all-out civil war exploded in 1916, a much larger force was needed to restore order.

On May 5, 1916, Captain Frederic M. Wise steamed over from Port-au-Prince, skirted the Dominican's capital city, and moved to Fort Geronimo, an American installation just outside Santo Domingo. With him were two companies of Marines. They were joined in short order by Major Newt Hall—a veteran of Peking—and more troops. The American force promptly attacked Santo Domingo, the oldest European city in the New World. Captain Wise would later write that it was much like Veracruz—but without the shooting. It was an easy march to the heart of the city. There was no enemy to fight.

On May 26, Captain Wise boarded the U.S.S. *Panther* and steamed over to the northwest corner of the island nation. He landed at Monte Cristi and ran smack into a force of over a 150 rebels. He and his men cut them down with raking fire from a single Colt-Browning machine gun. A Marine landing at Puerto Plata on June 1 did not go as well. The Marines faced stiff resistance and accurate rifle fire. It took them several hours to push the rebels out of the city and into the surrounding hills. Finally, on June 18, the Fourth Marine Regiment—a thousand Marines commanded by Joseph Pendleton—landed at Monte Cristi. Leaving a fourth of his men behind to garrison the city, Pendleton started down the road toward Santiago de los Caballeros. Between the Marines and their goal was a place called Las Trencheras, a ridgeline crossing the main road at right angles. It was here that Dominican insurgents had defeated the Spanish in 1864.

"Uncle Joe" Pendleton knew that the rebels were waiting for him, so instead of charging down the road, he lined up his artillery and pounded the ridge, followed by effective machine-gun fire. By June 27, the rebels were in tatters and the Marines finished them off with a bayonet charge that cleared the ridgelines. The rebels counterattacked after midnight—some say they were under the mistaken notion that machine guns wouldn't function at night. But the machine guns worked just fine and the rebels were repulsed.

On July 3, the rebels struck again, this time on the road to Guayacanas in a position similar to the ridgeline at Las Trencheras. Pendleton began with artillery, but the fire was less effective this time. When Marines moved into position to set up a machine-gun enfilade, the rebels returned fire from hidden trenches. It became a running fight, with Marines moving parallel to the rebel entrenchment, both sides firing furiously and mostly ineffectually. What the Marines needed was more firepower. They got that—and more.

Corporal Joseph Anthony Glowin, a twenty-four-year-old Marine from Detroit, rushed forward under continuous fire, dragging his machine gun. When he got close, he dropped behind a log that was partially blocking the road and fired into the enemy trenches. His first burst cut several rebels down, but the log didn't provide much cover and Glowin was crouching in plain sight of the Dominicans. They fired at him from several directions until the log he was hiding behind became splintered with lead. Finally Glowin was struck by a grazing shot that threw him sideways. He staggered up, bleeding, and began to fire again. His comrades noted that he never lost control. Despite his wounds, his shots were fired in measured, quick bursts that usually found their mark. When a second bullet struck him, Corporal Glowin spun around and slumped over his gun.

First Sergeant Roswell Winans of Brookville, Indiana, staggered forward, burdened with his own Colt-Browning machine gun. Without bothering to seek cover, he dropped to his knees and opened fire. Under cover of the sergeant's machine gun, Marines rushed forward and dragged Glowin to safety.

Many of the Dominicans had moved to the far end of a long irregular trench—away from Glowin's gun—only to find themselves exposed to fire from Winans's Potato-Digger. Though outgunned, the rebels returned brisk fire. The shooting was so concentrated that seven Marines were wounded and one killed within a twenty-foot radius of Sergeant Winans. But despite his exposed position, Winans never wavered. He continued to fire into the trenches, cutting down the huddled Dominicans and forcing the survivors into a panicked retreat. Miraculously, the thirty-year-old career officer was only slightly wounded. For their courageous actions at Guayacanas, both

Corporal Joseph Glowin and First Sergeant Roswell Winans received the Medal of Honor on November 2, 1916.

One other Marine would earn this distinction in the first Dominican Campaign. On November 29, 1916, twenty-nine-year-old First Lieutenant Ernest Calvin Williams—who usually commanded 125 Marines—rushed the gate of the Fortaleza, a Dominican stronghold at San Francisco de Macoris, leading a meager force of twelve. The situation was desperate. A local government official had threatened to free a hundred captured rebels and common criminals held in the Fortaleza's jail. First Lieutenant Williams got wind of the situation. With a dozen men, including a few members of the division band, he hurried to the prison.

His squad was spotted and the Dominicans on the wall opened fire. Eight of the twelve Marines were cut

Captain Roswell Winans

down, but the lieutenant pressed on. As the rebels were closing the gate, he slammed his shoulder against the door and wedged his body in the gap. A rebel rushed up, fired, and missed. Williams pointed his pistol at the man and pulled the trigger. Nothing happened—the gun had jammed. Just then the division's drummer jumped in front of the lieutenant and snatched a rifle away from a startled Dominican. The four surviving Marines surged forward, pushed the gate open, and blasted away at the massed defenders. Two Dominicans fell. The rest scattered. The Marines seized the fort and secured the prisoners. First Lieutenant Ernest Williams received a Medal of Honor on April 27, 1917. He remained in the Marine Corps and rose to the rank of lieutenant colonel. He passed away in 1940 near his birthplace in Broadwell, Illinois.

On the very same day that Lieutenant Williams performed his heroic actions, Rear Admiral Harry S. Knapp became the military governor of the Dominican Republic. The Marines would occupy this Caribbean nation for the next eight years, where they trained a police force modeled after the one in Haiti. The Guardia Nacional Dominicana was activated on April 7, 1917.

CHAPTER SEVEN

"FIRST TO FIGHT!":
THE MARINES IN WORLD WAR I

■

1914–1918

WORLD War I—the "war to end all wars"—erupted in August 1914. Over the next four years the bloodiest, costliest conflict in human history was fought on the fields of Belgium and France—a holocaust of such ferocity and magnitude that it could not even be imagined prior to its coming. For the first time in human history, all the invention and innovation of the industrial age were brought to bear for a single purpose—the annihilation of the enemy. Whole nations mobilized for a war that was brought closer to home by forced conscription, the telephone, the telegraph, the motion picture, and the airplane.

While the nations of the old world tore one another to pieces on the Western Front, using the most efficient weapons that technology could develop and industry produce, the United States remained aloof. America was busy with tiny conflicts in Haiti and the Dominican Republic. To most of its citizens, the war in Europe seemed far away and of little concern to them. What little the public knew of the slaughter horrified them. But there were those in Woodrow Wilson's administration, including the mild-mannered college professor turned president himself, who believed that the United States could not stand by idly while the nations of Europe waged war. Wilson looked at the carnage on the Western Front with dread and hoped the catastrophic cost of the war would bring the Europeans to their senses. His second-term slogan was "He kept us out of war!"—though Wilson would later claim that he was never for neutrality.

Despite the country's isolationist leanings, the U.S. military had already begun a minor buildup. Even then, when the United States finally entered the war on April 7, 1917, our military was unprepared. There were not enough men in uniform to wage war. The United States Army, with 135,000 men in garrisons scattered all over the world, was a puny joke compared to the titans beating each other senseless across the

Atlantic. American soldiers were grouped together in units no larger than a regiment. None were trained, organized, or equipped to fight a modern war. Some recruits in the U.S. Army had never even fired a gun. More ominous was that while America was fast becoming the richest and most productive economy on earth, it had no industrial infrastructure for the production of war materials. The few hundred machine guns, cannons, and airplanes produced by the tiny American munitions factories would not supply the European Front for a day. Initially at least, U.S. troops would rely on weapons produced by their allies. Despite the government's mandate for total industrial mobilization, no American-built weapons reached the front for six months.

There was an irony here. While the United States could not *produce* war materials in any great numbers, American technology and invention dominated the European battlefield. During the Great War, the machine gun, the tank, the submarine, and the airplane came into their own. These were all American inventions. It was the Confederate Navy that introduced the combat submarine, the C.S.S. *Hunley*. Now the German Navy ruled the sea with their U-boats. Two American bicycle makers gave the world powered flight. But it was Dutchman Anthony Fokker who built the first warplanes for the German Army. It was an American inventor named Hiram Maxim who demonstrated the first automatic machine gun in 1884, a gun that used the force of the recoil to operate the cartridge-ejection system. Now there were dozens of machine guns in use on the Western Front, all based on Maxim's original patents.

Machine guns were the first innovation of this war. Massed infantry attacks faltered against entrenched machine guns. The casualties were horrendous. In the French military, the Hotchkiss machine gun was developed using Maxim's patents. Its inventor was Benjamin B. Hotchkiss, an American imported to France from the Colt factory. In England, the Lewis gun, light enough to be mounted on an airplane, was developed by Isaac Newton Lewis, an American graduate of West Point. His machine gun helped turn the airplane into a tool of war.

Firepower—an American concept—ruled the battlefields of Europe, and the Marine Corps appreciated firepower more than any other branch of service. The Corps stressed skill with weapons, and their training produced the best marksmen in the world. The Marines also pioneered the use of machine guns. In this regard, they were more prepared for modern warfare than America's other armed services.

Even with the underpreparedness of its military, however, the United States had one vital commodity the Europeans lacked, and that was manpower. After four years of unrelenting war, Europe had been bled dry. Hundreds of thousands of young men had been wasted. The British, the Belgians, and especially the French needed an infusion of fresh troops to prevail. The Europeans would provide the guns, the bayonets, the tanks, and the airplanes. America provided the muscle, the sweat, and the blood.

"FIRST TO FIGHT"

By 1917 the war in Europe had bogged down to a tense and unbreakable stalemate. Enemies faced one another along a 400-mile killing field that ran like a festering wound through the heart of Belgium and France. Artillery and machine-gun fire raked the front daily, shattering men and equipment in astronomical numbers. Troops on both sides were mired in defensive positions. Armies traded tons of munitions and a sea of blood for a few meters of battlefield that they lost the next day.

No military services were prepared for such a war, but Marines suffered the most. Trench warfare was the opposite of what they were trained for. A ravaged terrain of tangled barbed wire, foxholes, shifting battle lines, and incessant artillery barrages was not conducive to covert operations, slashing attacks, or fast raids—tactics the Marines had successfully employed for fifty years. On the Western Front, the element of surprise was nonexistent. War was waged with enormous bombardments followed by large-formation assaults across a shell-torn landscape. These massed attacks were mounted against entrenched machine guns through clouds of lethal poison gas. The Marines had not fought in large units since the Civil War. Though they were the best marksmen in the world, how many well-placed shots could be fired by a man huddled at the bottom of a muddy trench, half choked by poison gas and blinded by his gas mask?

Despite these obstacles, the Marine Corps would perform miracles on the battlefields of the Western Front. Their courageous actions in Europe would eclipse all of their previous accomplishments. The Marines would pay a enormous price for such glory.

In 1917, there were 22,000 Marines bearing arms. Before the end of the year, that number would double, and the 40,000 men the Corps would eventually send overseas were among the best-trained forces at the front. But despite the Corps' brash new slogan—"First to Fight!"—none of the other branches of the armed services wanted the Marines in Europe, least of all the Army. When the American Expeditionary Force was formed and its troops prepared to sail for Europe, U.S. Army General John J. Pershing tried hard to exclude the Marines. The Army was still smarting from their humiliation at Veracruz, when the Marines finished the war for them. The friction between the Army and the Marine Corps would intensify as the war progressed.

Though the Marines could put an effective brigade of infantry marksmen and expert machine gunners at Pershing's disposal, the general felt that supplying the Marines with their unique uniforms, weapons, and ammunition would become a logistical nightmare, so a compromise was reached—the Marines would trade their green uniforms for Army-issue olive drab and would forgo their beloved Lewis guns for heavy French Chauchats. And they would accept anonymity. Only a service patch would distinguish the Leathernecks from the other American doughboys. Even then, the first Marines to reach Europe were assigned unglamorous duties at ports and supply depots. It would take months of political maneuvering in Washington and inside Pershing's general staff before the first Marine units were dispatched to the front. To make matters worse, a muddled command structure whose members were working at cross purposes with one another hampered efficient action. The French wanted the American troops to arrive in Europe raw, to be trained by French Army veterans in the "art" of trench warfare. After that, the American divisions would be broken into small units that would reinforce decimated French Army divisions. The British had a similar plan.

General Pershing resisted these schemes, believing that victory would not come by teaching Americans to fight like Europeans, who had already been fighting for four years and had accomplished nothing. Pershing believed that mobility and offense, not immobility and defense, were the keys to victory. In his eyes, the French and British Armies were already defeated. Years of static trench warfare had stripped their soldiers of the will to fight and the grit to prevail. Pershing planned to field a brand-new Army in Europe—an *American* Army—with fresh troops, fresh ideas, a fighting spirit, and the will to win. That Army, the general insisted, must be commanded by American officers, not the British or French commanders who had wasted four years and millions of lives in futile conflict.

Major Smedley D. Butler

In the end, the British and French prevailed. Though Americans went to war at division strength, they were scattered among dozens of previously defeated French and British units with the taste of defeat in their mouths.

During the summer and fall of 1917, the armed services mobilized, aided by a brand-new concept—forced conscription. Despite the patriotic fever that was sweeping the land, there were not enough volunteers to fill the ranks. The only way to field sufficient numbers of American servicemen was to draft them.

But the Marines remained primarily a volunteer outfit. Their exuberant slogan attracted 20,000 fresh-faced recruits, many with romantic notions about war and glory. Most of them had never fired a weapon. Unlike previous generations of Marines, who were recruited from the docks or the mean streets of American's urban areas, these new volunteers were solid members of the middle class. Most were educated and some were highly educated. This new breed of recruit would transform the Corps before the first Marine even set foot in Europe.

Only one out of five men in the first Marine divisions to arrive in France was a veteran. These men had fought in a half-dozen conflicts, ranging from the jungles of the Philippines to the walls of Peking. Members of this "Old Breed" included Medal of Honor recipients Dan Daly and John Quick as well as seasoned commanders like Colonel Albertus Catlin, Smedley Butler, and Captain John Blanchard. Suddenly these veterans shared the stage with a brash new breed of volunteer—men like twenty-two-year-old Lieutenant John Overton, a member of the Yale University track team and holder of the world's indoor record for the mile. Upper-middle-class young

Colonel Albertus W. Catlin

men like Overton would fight shoulder to shoulder with the Old Breed, learning their ways and the traditions of the Marine Corps.

Sixty percent of the Marines who fought in the First World War were college graduates or had attended college. Many hailed from the best Ivy League institutions. These men selflessly postponed their education to do their patriotic duty, and though the new recruits were very different from the salty, tattooed, blasphemously profane veterans of the Corps' previous wars, a year on the battlefields of Europe would weld the two types of men into a well-honed fighting machine unmatched in all the world.

Before the American troops were deemed ready, they had to undergo additional training by French and British instructors. Americans would have to "unlearn" all their "bad habits" before they could be dispatched to the front. It was an unpleasant education for the Marines, who believed that hiding in a foxhole was insane, cowardly, and unthinkable. After U.S. troops learned the rudiments of trench warfare from their European instructors, General Pershing insisted that these same troops be retrained in the traditional tactics of the United States Army to keep their "fighting spirits" up. This further delayed frontline deployment, and neither course of training proved to be adequate. But morale remained high.

The Yanks were coming, and they were ready for a fight!

THE ENEMY

There is a prevailing myth that Germany was, for all practical purposes, defeated before the first American troops arrived on the battlefields in 1918. Its allies—Italy, Austria-Hungary, Turkey—had already been crushed or were on the verge of defeat by 1917. But tales of food riots in Berlin, mutinous frontline troops, and catastrophic production and logistical problems are simply untrue. Though Germany was suffering a major manpower shortage, the German military was in a better strategic shape than the Allied powers because they had been granted a reprieve of sorts.

By the end of 1917, Germany's fiercest foe had dropped out of the the war. Russia was in the throes of the revolution that gave birth to the Soviet Union. With the czar's armies out of the fight, more than a million German soldiers and thousands of guns could be moved against the French, the British, and the Americans. German industry continued to churn out more and better weapons, and while no German city had suffered an attack, the Germans had mounted nighttime bombing raids over London and Paris. General Erich Ludendorff, commander in chief of the Imperial German Army, planned a series of offensives to crush the Allies completely in the spring of 1918. His attack was scheduled to take place *before* American troops could enter the war in significant numbers. Ludendorff would commit all of his reserves and the entire resources of Germany to this make-or-break effort. If the offensive failed, the war would spiral out of control or become locked in a new stalemate, but Ludendorff was confident he could capture Paris before the Americans set foot on the battlefield. His plan nearly succeeded. It was thwarted only by the determined effort of a handful of United States Marines who just happened to be at the right place at the right time. That place was Belleau Wood.

THE GERMAN OFFENSIVE BEGINS

Ludendorff wanted to split the British and French forces in half, then destroy them separately. The British were first on his list because they were busily conducting an offensive war while the French were willing to sit in their trenches and wait for the Germans to come to them. He devised a sweeping new battle tactic for his offensive. His finest officers would lead the assault with cadres of highly trained advance troops attacking by *infiltration* rather than in massed formations that were vulnerable to machine guns and artillery. These highly trained advance troops were called *Sturmtruppen*—storm troopers. Mobilization was the key to their success. Armed with rifles, grenades, and light machine guns, these storm troopers were supposed to punch a hole through the Allies' lines, disorganizing defense efforts and crushing the enemy before reinforcements could arrive.

Storm troopers were urged to bypass pockets of resistance, leaving them to be neutralized by close support units made up of heavy machine guns, trench mortars, flamethrowers, mobile artillery, and tanks. These units followed the infiltrators, eliminating the last vestiges of resistance. Twenty years later, with the addition of dive-bombers and armored spearheads, Ludendorff's visionary tactic would become *blitzkrieg*—the "lightning war" that helped Adolf Hitler conquer Poland, Belgium, Holland, France, and Scandinavia.

But Hitler's armies were trained in *blitzkrieg* tactics from the start. Ludendorff's forces had conducted a defensive war for four years. They would have to learn to fight offensively. Ludendorff established special warfare schools that stressed small-unit initiative, attack by infiltration, and hand-to-hand combat. It took months and the training was accomplished in absolute secrecy, but when the storm troopers were unleashed, it came as a complete surprise to the Allies.

By the spring of 1918, the new German Army was ready to move. At 4:00 A.M. on the foggy morning of March 21, they unleashed the most powerful concentration of artillery fire the world had ever seen. Along a forty-mile front, 6,000 German guns fired high-explosive and poison-gas shells to soften up the enemy positions, disrupt communications, shatter the command structure, and demoralize the defenders. For five hours guns rained death upon the French and British lines. At 9:30 A.M., German mortars took the forward trenches under direct fire while German engineers eliminated the tangles of barbed wire in No-Man's-Land with explosive charges. At 9:40, the German assault groups went over the top.

The Allies, who were still waiting for a massed attack, were taken by surprise when the first shock troops hit them. The storm troopers attacked with grenades, machine guns, and flamethrowers. Before they knew what was happening, the Germans were among them, blasting through their trenches and gunning down soldiers too surprised to react. Often the first inkling French or British units had that they were under attack was when grenades exploded in their midst. By then it was too late. French and British communications were disrupted. No one knew who held what and runners sent to regimental headquarters for instructions often found that German shock troops had already captured their command posts. Officers at the front found themselves surrounded and leaderless. They received meaningless, contradictory orders or no orders at all. Entire divisions ceased to exist.

By March 23, Ludendorff implemented the second phase of his offensive. Secret German artillery emplacements seventy-five miles from Paris began to bombard the French capital with high explosives, even as the Allied lines continued to buckle in the face of relentless attacks. In four days of constant forward momentum, the German Army had advanced fourteen miles—an astounding rate. Previously, victory had been measured in yards. Now almost nothing stood between Paris and the German Army. But logistical problems forced Ludendorff to halt his offensive and establish a new front. This unexpected delay bought the Allies precious time to reorganize and reinforce. But reinforce with what?

On March 25, General Pershing offered the French a few American divisions for temporary use. Pershing was unshakable in his belief that the Americans should fight as a unit. But the situation at the front was so dire that he agreed to a limited American deployment to soothe French fears of a total defeat. The American divisions were dispatched to the front in early April—just in time for General Ludendorff's second offensive. During this initial deployment, the Yanks got their first taste of trench warfare. They performed well under fire, but not spectacularly.

The new German offensive hit the Allies between Soissons and Reims on May 27, 1918. Again the high command was taken by surprise. With ease the Germans captured Soissons and reached the north bank of the Marne River at Château-Thierry, forty miles from Paris. This caused some quick changes in the Allied high command. French General Ferdinand Foch was named commander in chief of all Allied Armies in France. General Pershing was forced to abandon his dream of an American Army, and reluctantly agreed to deploy his Second and Third Divisions to halt the German advance. On May 31, the Third United States Division—comprised mostly of U.S. Army regulars—managed to temporarily halt the German advance at Château-Thierry. Undaunted, the Germans twisted to the right, moving toward the town of Vaux and a kidney-shaped hunting preserve for the French upper class called Belleau Wood, a tranquil forest on the north side of the Marne. If the Germans crossed the river, nothing could prevent them from taking Paris.

▪ *The Horrors of Trench Warfare*

In September 1914, in the wake of the Battle of the Marne, the German Army retreated to the River Aisne. General Von Falkenhayn ordered his troops to hold their ground against the French and British at any cost, and instructed his men to dig deep trenches that would provide protection from the advancing enemy. Trenches had been used effectively during the American Civil War but had fallen out of fashion. The German high command doubted that trenches could hold back a determined enemy for long, but they were out of options. To their surprise, when the British and French Armies hit the trenches, their offensive evaporated. When the Allies realized they could not penetrate the trench line, they dug trenches of their own. In a few months trenches had spread from the North Sea to the Swiss frontier.

Soon the front lines of both sides were composed of a series of forward trenches, support trenches, advanced trenches, observation posts, parapets, and machine-gun nests. Between the two lines lay No-Man's-Land—a desolate killing field of barbed wire and shell holes where the enemy lurked as far away as a half mile or as close as twenty yards. Trenches were about seven feet deep and six feet wide. There were three or four parallel rows of trenches, which formed the defensive line. The front trench, which looked out over No-Man's-Land, was called the firing trench or parapet. The top two or three feet of the parapet was composed of a thick pile of sandbags meant to absorb bullets and shell fragments. It was impossible to see over such high walls, so a two- or three-foot wooden ledge was constructed, usually from scrap wood. This ledge ran all along the floor of the forward trenches and was called a fire step.

The second trench ran directly behind the parapet. Called the cover trench, it provided a reserve position in case the parapet was overrun. Off-duty troops lived in the third line of trenches, called support trenches. These were usually lined with dugouts, where the men slept and took refuge during artillery barrages. Communication ditches connected the trenches and were used by runners to carry orders to and from headquarters, to deliver food and ammunition, and to move troops in and out of the forward trenches.

Life inside those trenches was appalling. The Allies, forced to dig in lowlands because the Germans held the high ground, suffered most. Their trenches were dug at or slightly above sea level. As soon as the soldiers shoveled down a few feet, they hit water. When it rained the trenches would fill. Sometimes Allied soldiers slogged through knee-deep muck. The only way to escape the flood was to get out of the trench—and expose yourself to enemy artillery, snipers, gas, grenades, and machine guns.

Trench warfare involved a never-ending struggle against three enemies—Germans, moisture, and vermin. Food preparation was impossible, so the British employed 300,000 field-workers behind the lines to cook and supply food. Hot meals were carried in large metal pots called dixies that were suspended between two poles and carried through the communication trenches to the forward positions. Under artillery fire, such supply could take many hours. Seldom did a hot meal actually arrive hot. Bread took up to a week to reach the front and was always stale. Often it contained added protein in the form of roaches and other vermin that had infested the flour before baking. Under optimum conditions, dixies were packed in straw and delivered by *camions* or horse-drawn supply wagons. This system resulted in more regular deliveries and more palatable food, but was the exception rather than the rule.

By the winter of 1916, even these amenities were in short supply. At the beginning of the war, British troops were supplied with ten ounces of meat and eight ounces of vegetables a day. By 1916, the ration had been cut to six ounces of meat—and much of that was bully beef canned in Madagascar, which had such an unpleasant taste soldiers took to calling it "monkey meat." Other canned items included a concoction called Maconochie—sliced turnips and carrots in a thin broth. It was edible if heated, thick with congealed grease and unpalatable if consumed cold. Later in the war troops not at the front would see meat only nine days out of every month. Frontline troops were allotted higher rations of protein, but flour was in such short supply that bread was made with dried ground turnips. Foraging was common, and Allied soldiers felt free to take whatever they could appropriate from the enemy or the civilian population. The Allies took great pains to hide their food shortages from the enemy.

When the Americans arrived, the French diet caused additional problems. Twice a day French soldiers were provided *vin rouge* or *vin blanc*—red or white wine. Most young American boys had never been exposed to so much alcohol and drunkenness became common—even among the ranks of the well-disciplined Marines. American soldiers were known to get falling-down drunk. During the winter, a number of American soldiers passed out in a drunken stupor and died of exposure.

Other than alcohol there were few diversions. The men sang, swore, played cards, wrote letters home, and smoked. They also had to deal with a most irritating and constant companion. Body lice— "cooties" the Americans called them—were omnipresent. The soldiers lived in such close quarters and under such unsanitary conditions that the vermin spread like wildfire through the ranks. The lice, according to one British soldier, were "pale fawn in colour . . . and left blotchy red bite marks all over the body." They also created a stale, sour smell that added to the general misery level. Various methods were employed to kill the lice, but none was effective. Among the Germans, a heated metal can was an effective way of dispatching body lice. Soldiers would pull the insects from their hair and clothing and toss them into the can, where they vanished in a sizzle and a puff of smoke. The British preferred a lighted candle, but the skill of burning the lice without burning one's skin or clothes had to be learned.

Body lice was more than a nuisance—they carried disease, the most formidable of which was pyrexia or trench fever. The first symptoms were shooting pains in the extremities followed by a high fever and delirium. Although trench fever seldom killed its victims, it did stop soldiers from fighting until the illness ran its course, which took a week to ten days. When possible, the Allies arranged for their soldiers to take baths in huge vats of near-boiling water while their uniforms were being put through delousing machines. The machines killed the lice but left a fair number of eggs in the clothing. Within hours of delousing, a soldier's body temperature hatched the next generation of lice and the scratching began anew.

Another unwelcome pest were rats—millions of them. "Fat black bastards" one Marine called them. Men killed in battle were buried where they fell. If a trench caved in or new trenches needed to be dug, the activity unearthed large numbers of decomposing bodies buried just under the surface. These corpses attracted rats. A pair of rats can produce over 800 offspring in a year, so the trenches were swarming with them. Some of these rats were exceedingly large. These the soldiers called trench rats. "They were so big they would eat a wounded man if he couldn't defend himself," wrote one British officer.

Trench rats were fearless. They would steal food from the pockets of sleeping men and swarm through the trenches during an artillery barrage. Two or three rats would always be found on a dead body—they ate the eyes first, then burrowed their way into the body cavity to munch on the soft organs. One British soldier described finding a group of enemy dead while on patrol: "I saw some rats running from under the dead men's greatcoats, enormous rats, fat with human flesh. My heart pounded as we edged towards one of the bodies. His helmet had rolled off. The man displayed a grimacing face stripped of flesh; the skull bare, the eyes devoured and from the yawning mouth leapt a rat."

Dysentery, trench mouth, and trench foot were among the unpleasant maladies men in the trenches were prone to contract. Outbreaks of dysentery were caused by bad water or rotten food. Despite the rain that filled the trenches and the mud the soldiers slogged through, clean potable water was a problem. Fresh water, like hot meals, was brought from the rear. Like the food supplies, its delivery was irregular and uncertain. Front-line troops often ran out, especially after a long artillery barrage. In desperation they would drink the filthy water that collected in shell holes, water infected with disease and bacteria from rats, feces, and rotting corpses. Without proper sanitation facilities the dysentery spread through the feces, which was mixed in the mud the soldiers slogged through on a daily basis.

Trench mouth, or Vincent's disease, is an infection of the mouth that results in open sores on the mucous membranes of the tongue, lips, mouth, and throat. Like dysentery, it is caused by foul, unsanitary conditions.

In the trenches men lived in waterlogged ditches, unable to remove their wet socks and boots for days on end. Trench foot, an infection caused by cold, wet, and unsanitary conditions, was endemic in the early stages of the war. Almost every soldier on the front suffered from this affliction in the first year. His feet would gradually go numb and the skin would turn red or blue. If untreated, trench foot led to gangrene, which led to amputation. Over 20,000 British soldiers were felled by trench foot in 1914–1915, but by the end of 1915, the British and French found ways to combat the disease. Each soldier carried three pairs of socks, and changed them twice a day. A special area was set up in the trenches that allowed the men to dry their feet and cover them with whale oil, which repelled water. A battalion at the front would use ten gallons of whale oil every day.

The horrors of trench warfare have left an indelible impression on the popular imagination for the past ninety years, and the tactical stalemate that evolved from this ill-advised defensive policy has influenced military strategists ever since. Never again would great armies face each other from trenches or earthworks dug into the ground. Mobility would be the key to victory in all future conflicts. This is the one lesson—learned at great cost during the First World War—that seemed to stick.

BOIS DE BELLEAU

Just before General Ludendorff launched the third wave of his offensive, Marine Corps General Charles Doyen had to be relieved of duty in France because of a terminal illness. Brigadier General John Lejeune was assigned to replace him. But Lejeune was still in Washington. Until he could reach Europe, General Pershing made his own chief of staff, Brigadier General James Harbord, temporary commander of the Marine Corps divisions. A National Guard Cavalry officer recalled to active duty for the war, Harbord must have been intimidated by the caliber of men he was to command. His two regimental commanders, Colonel Catlin and Colonel Neville, were hard-edged veterans and Medal of Honor recipients. More discouraging was the fact that when Pershing handed Harbord this duty, he did it with a warning.

"Young man, I'm giving you the best brigade in France. If anything goes wrong, I'll know who to blame."

With an unfamiliar commander in the field, ammunition and equipment in short supply, and grenades unattainable, the Marines moved to the front. On May 30 the Second Division—which included the bulk of the Marines in France—were dispatched to join French General Joseph Degoutte's Sixth Army in desperate fighting along the Marne River. The Marines were needed to reinforce the shaky French lines that had nearly disintegrated in the face of Ludendorff's shock troops. At holding stations around Verdun, the Marines were roused from their tents at dawn and hastily assembled. Through the fog scores of *camions* lumbered slowly onto the scene. The *camions*—canvas-covered French trucks with rumbling engines, solid rubber tires, and seats on either side of the rear carriage—delivered the Marines to the front after hours of bumpy traveling across shell-pitted roads. The trip was hot and uncomfortable. Dust from the roadway seeped between the canvas flaps, powdering the Marines. The trek was also painfully slow, as the Paris-Metz Highway—the only passable road to or from the French capital—was choked with refugees fleeing the German advance. Not since the first months of the war had the enemy been so close to victory, and the bombardment of the French capital by Ludendorff's artillery was having its desired effect. Parisians were in a panic. Most were preparing to abandon the besieged capital—including the government itself. Near Château-Thierry, the Marines finally debarked from their vehicles, stiff-legged and sore from hours sitting on hard wooden seats. As they stretched, patted the dust off their uniforms, scratched at "cooties," cursed the war, the heat, and the enemy, or spit, smoked, and gobbled down cold tins of "monkey meat," few of these Marines could know they were about to make history.

On June 1, Château-Thierry fell despite the timely arrival of American reinforcements. The Germans had also captured several villages along the Marne, including Vaux, Bouresches, Lucy, and Torcy. As a result of the usual supply problems, the Germans had to slow their advance and dig in. It was during the lull that the veteran 461st German Infantry Regiment, reinforced with Maxim machine guns and hand grenades, first occupied the game preserve at Belleau Wood. Panicked French troops who were supposed to reconnoiter the forest for the advancing Americans had retreated instead. No one on the Allies' side knew that the woods were held by the enemy.

That night the Germans knocked a hole through the lines just left of where the Marines had dug in. French troops, staggering through the American lines, were the first indication that there was trouble ahead. Major Julius S. Turill's First Battalion of the Fifth Marines rushed his men forward in a nighttime forced march to plug the gap created by the retreating French. By dawn, Turrill's Marines were in place. When General Harbord learned of the French rout, he dispatched more troops to the area until an entire twelve-mile stretch of the front lines facing Belleau Wood was defended solely by United States Marines. It was a very *thin* line, and the Marines were still short of ammunition, grenades, food, and water.

The landscape was sparsely wooded with fields of grain waving above low rolling hills and an occasional copse of trees to break the monotony. It was a vulnerable position—there was not much cover and no high ground in friendly hands. Before noon, German artillery began to rain down on the Americans. The Marines were ordered to "hold where they stand." Most of them had long before discarded the shovels they had been issued—they saw no need for them. There were enough trenches in France, and they were there to fight, not dig. Now, under a torrent of artillery, the Marines used bayonets, utensils from their mess kits, and their bare hands to claw shallow holes in the ground. These holes were not as deep as a trench, nor were they interconnected. But a man could lie prone in them and fire at the enemy. Someone in the American division dubbed these individual ditches "foxholes" and the name stuck. That same night the Germans reinforced their own positions. They held higher ground and could clearly see the Marine Corps positions across an expanse of farmland. The Germans occupied ground between Triangle Farm and the village of Lucy. They also owned the highest piece of real estate in the region—Hill 142—which they defended with troops armed with machine guns and trench mortars.

On the afternoon of June 3, the Germans, with shock troops in the lead, moved toward the American lines. The day was hot and the advance troops slowly crept through the tall, rippling fields of wheat, crouching but in good formation. At this point the German high command did not know that the troops they were facing were Americans. They believed that the French had reinforced the forward positions with their own troops. But the Germans may have gotten an inkling that something was different when the soldiers on point began to die from uncannily accurate rifle fire while they were still hundreds of yards from the enemy positions. Sometimes a man would fall before his comrades heard the crack of the rifle shot that killed him. Marksmanship of this quality was not something they'd seen from the French before.

As the Germans raced forward through wheat fields, the Americans opened up with everything they had. The noise was deafening as the first wave of German troops were cut to pieces. The survivors went to ground and attempted to defend themselves. Their fire was sporadic and moderately effective. Stalks of wheat were mowed down by machine guns and rifle fire that slaughtered the Germans where they stood, lay, or knelt. A few officers rose to rally their men and were shot where they stood.

In the first minutes, First Lieutenant Lemuel C. Shepherd was struck in the neck by a German machine-gun bullet. He spun to the dirt. Surprised to be alive, Shepherd bandaged himself with the help of a private, then went back into action. Throughout the day, he refused medical care and urged his men to fight, a fine example to the rest of the Marines on the front. The shock troops that Ludendorff had pinned his faith on didn't get close enough to inflict much damage on the Marines. Instead, they broke like waves against a beach. The defeated survivors fled back through the grain fields to the safety of the tree line. Their losses were horrendous. Over a two-mile area, hundreds of the Kaiser's finest lay strewn among the trampled wheat.

Miraculously the thin wall of Marines had held their ground. But the Americans, suffering casualties and chronically short of supplies, were in no position to exploit their victory by staging a counterattack. There were not enough of them left. And the French were still disorganized, demoralized, and in retreat. One French major ordered Marine Captain Lloyd Williams to withdraw his men before they were slaughtered. Williams stared at the man in disbelief, then cried: "Retreat, hell! We just got here."

It was a bold statement, and there was no guarantee the Marines could back it up. Fortunately, the Germans were so battered that they rested for two entire days, making only halfhearted assaults designed to probe the Allies' positions more than break them. Each time the Germans advanced, they were thrown back by the Marines. Artillery fire from both sides increased and Germans and Americans fell prey to shrapnel. Soon an uneasy truce was instituted by both sides so that the wounded could be taken from the field. It was shattered when an eagle-eyed Marine spotted Germans carrying a stretcher with a Maxim machine gun on it moving dangerously close to the American positions. Soon corpsmen tending the wounded became fair game, and many died trying to rescue their comrades.

Over the next two days the Marines were reinforced by the 167th French Division. There were now two American battalions at the front and a third in reserve. Allied high command knew that all of the American units would be required in the struggle to come. In his memoirs, published after the war, Albertus Catlin wrote that "[we] now stood facing the dark, sullen mystery of Belleau Wood." With what the Allies felt were superior numbers, it was the Americans' turn to advance. Little did they know that General Ludendorff had also ordered a major offensive for that same day. German intelligence had finally determined that they were facing the first Americans to arrive at the front. The news had an electrifying effect on the high command. General Ludendorff's fear had been that the Americans would field a well-equipped army to overwhelm his own battle-weary forces. But if Germany struck first, they might inflict so many casualties that President Wilson would withdraw from the war.

Ludendorff commanded that "American units appearing on the front should be hit particularly hard."

So as the Allies were preparing their own attack, the Germans were reinforcing Belleau Wood in an effort to punish the Americans. Two titanic forces were about to clash, and the future of the Marine Corps and the fate of France hung on the outcome.

JUNE 6, 1918—PASSING OF THE OLD BREED

The Allied plan called for the 167th French Division to attack the German front while the United States Marines took Hill 142, the vital tactical position that overlooked much of the battlefield. From that hill German gunners threatened the Allies' flank. It was imperative that Hill 142 be neutralized. According to the unrealistically optimistic plan, after Hill 142 was captured, the Marines were to continue their advance. By afternoon they were expected to take the ridge overlooking the towns of Torcy and Belleau, then the town of Bouresches itself. The Marines were to finish the day by capturing the hunting reserve called Belleau Wood.

Needless to say, things did not go according to plan.

The problem was that the Marines took French reports that Belleau Wood was free of enemy forces at face value and did not send in scouts of their own. No one suspected that an entire German infantry regiment—complete with interlocking machine-gun nests and predetermined artillery coverage—had been waiting among those trees for two days. It was a deadly trap and the Marines were set to walk right into it. Behind those woods lurked more Germans. Belleau Wood—a square-mile game preserve thick with trees, vegetation, and tumbled boulders—was no longer a small obstacle blocking the German advance to Paris. In the mind of the German high command, Belleau Wood had become a symbolic battleground where the future of the European war would be decided once and for all.

At 3:45 A.M. on the morning of June 6, the first Marines crawled out of their trenches and melted into the morning mist. Most were exhausted, as a continuous German artillery barrage had allowed for little sleep. Many had spent the better part of the night foraging for food. No meals had reached the extreme front lines in many days, and even the unpopular tins of Madagascar monkey meat the Marines brought with them had been consumed. Now the Marines moved cautiously from their defensive positions in the early morning darkness. The weather had been intolerably hot, but today the Marines advanced through a chill, clinging, knee-deep ground fog.

The First Battalion, Fifth Marines, were the first to make for the German positions. They burst from their foxholes and quick-marched through trim fields of grain toward Hill 142 in four waves, their lines neatly dressed—just as their drill instructors had taught them. Unfortunately, those tactics had not been employed since 1915 because they had proved disastrous against fixed machine guns. Tragically, no one had seen fit to inform the French instructors of this fact, and they continued to drill the Americans in this long-discredited tactic. The Marines had to cross half a mile of ground, some of it uphill, before they reached the enemy trenches. Despite the fog, the Germans spotted them, but waited until the Americans were in range before they fired their machine guns. In the first few bursts, the Marines in the first ranks fell. Some of them were literally cut in half by German bullets. A deadly rain of trench mortars followed on the heels of the machine guns. Explosions sprouted in the middle of the ranks, churning up the soil and blasting Marines to bits.

The Germans reaped a deadly harvest that morning. The entire first wave of Marines was annihilated. The survivors went to ground among the dead. As hot lead shredded their comrades, the Marines crawled forward on their bellies into the teeth of disciplined machine-gun fire. One Marine recalled the sickening thumps he heard as bullets struck the men around him. Within seconds, a hundred Marines were dead or wounded. First Sergeant "Beau" Hunter—one of the old veterans who trained and inspired

Sergeant Ernest A. Janson

his young recruits—was shot to death in the first minutes of the assault. Before this day was over, he would find himself among distinguished company.

It is a credit to the bravery of the Marines that they doggedly pressed forward, crawling on their hands and knees through the wheat to get a shot at the enemy. Short of grenades, they had to move within bayonet range to take out the German positions. Marine Gunner Henry L. Hulbert, who had received the Medal of Honor in Samoa as a private in 1899, relentlessly pressed his men forward. This Yorkshire-born Marine, now fifty-one, pushed his command until they reached their first objective. Hulbert was cited for personal bravery during this action, but would fall four months later at Blanc Mont while reorganizing his men to halt a German counterattack.

Though their initial assault had been stopped in its tracks, the Marines surrounded Hill 142 and reached the first line of German defenses by late morning. By noon they had captured the hill in brutal hand-to-hand combat under the blazing sun. Gaining the high ground cost over 400 American casualties. American and German dead where sprawled everywhere. In the steadily rising temperatures, the flies feeding on the corpses and the choking smell of death became all-pervasive.

When the Marines were on the verge of taking the hill, the Germans staged a final counterattack. Grenades began to explode among them. During this counterattack, Gunnery Sergeant Ernest A. Janson of the 49th Company spotted a dozen German shock troops crawling unseen toward his company's position, armed with automatic rifles and grenades—which they were preparing to hurl at the Americans. Sergeant Janson called out a warning to his commander even as he plunged his bayonet into the heart of the German on point. Yanking his blade free, Janson leapt over the corpse and thrust his bayonet into the throat of a second enemy soldier. This bold charge surprised and unnerved the remaining shock troopers. They retreated, leaving their machine guns behind. Thirty-nine-year-old Ernest A. Janson—who served under the name Charles Hoffman—was a career Marine from New York City. His swift and decisive action that day saved his company from certain death. For his bravery Sergeant Janson received both the Army and Navy Medals of Honor. He was the first Marine to earn the Medal of Honor during the First World War and is among the few recipients who received two medals from two different branches of the armed services for the same action. Janson survived the war to retire in the 1930s. He passed away in New York City in 1940.

During the initial assault on Hill 142, some of the Marines had become confused and overshot their mark. They bypassed their target and reached the town of Torcy, where they found the Germans waiting for them. After a fierce exchange of fire, only three Marines survived long enough to actually enter the village. When they discovered Germans in large numbers holding the town, they dispatched one of their number, a wounded man, to the rear to bring back reinforcements. While he was gone, the Germans attacked. Both Marines fought stubbornly and hard. But facing overwhelming odds, they perished waiting for support that would never come.

There was no time to mourn fallen comrades. Over the next several hours the Marines advanced en masse toward their next objectives—Belleau Wood and the towns beyond. They moved through the fields in the same formation, their lines neatly dressed—a perfect target. As they approached the woods, the Marines trampled a field of bloodred poppies. When the Germans cut loose, the first wave of Marines dropped, wounded or dead. The vulnerable formation the French had taught them was excellent—for a turkey shoot, with Marines playing the role of turkey. The Americans were cut to pieces by interlocking German machine gun fire. As before, the survivors hit the dirt and crawled into the dubious protection of the grain fields or into the dense foliage of Belleau Wood. Again the Marines wormed their way through mud and between rocks, dodging German lead as they pushed deeper into the forest.

Many Marines went to ground and stayed there. Most of their officers were down, and the few who survived the initial fusillade were ripped to pieces by massed machine-gun fire as they vainly tried to rally their men. Soon the American advance degenerated into small pockets of resistance. Command structure ceased to exist. Fortunately, each Marine had been trained to seize the initiative in a pinch, and many did. Some improvised a cunning strategy to reach the German emplacements. A first group would pop out of hiding and blast away at the Germans, providing cover fire for a second group, who rushed forward, hopefully gaining a few precious feet. When the second group went to ground, they would provide covering fire for the first group, who would leapfrog ahead of them and repeat the process. The Marines kept this up until they overran the enemy or were slaughtered.

While this strategy was effective, it cost many lives. The Germans were entrenched, and they had plenty of ammunition and the advantage of interlocking fields of fire—which meant that no one could advance without some enemy shooter getting a bead on him. The woods were crawling with enemy sharpshooters, and barbed wire lurked among the dense foliage to trip up any American assault. Without grenades, it seemed impossible to overrun the entrenched Germans. The Marines tried anyway.

Near the edge of Belleau Wood *Chicago Tribune* war correspondent Floyd Gibbons had crossed No-Man's-Land in the second wave. Now he was pinned down with a few desperate, wounded Marines, surrounded by ranks of American dead. Gibbons could hear the thud of machine-gun bullets striking the men hugging the dirt around him, along with their agonized cries. He had been hit by a glancing blow to the arm, and with Marines dying all around him, the reporter was sure he'd filed his last dispatch. The Marines Gibbons had accompanied were mostly new recruits facing the enemy for the first time. Now they were too terrified to advance or retreat as German machine-gun fire was picking them off, one or two at a time.

Then a shadow fell over him. Gibbons watched in awe as a figure lifted a Springfield above his head in a bold gesture of defiance. It was Gunnery Sergeant Dan Daly—double Medal of Honor recipient and hero of the Boxer Rebellion. Gibbons reported what he saw later: "The sergeant swung his bayoneted rifle over his head with a forward sweep, yelling at his men, 'Come on, you sons-of-bitches, do you want to live forever?' "

This battle cry, uttered by one of the Corps' esteemed Old Breed, awakened the paralyzed Marines. With a roar they leapt out of cover and followed their sergeant through the shattered stalks of wheat into the teeth of the enemy guns. With pistols and bayonets, they slaughtered the Germans. Floyd Gibbons struggled to his feet and tried to follow. A moment later he saw Major Benjamin Berry spin and fall as he was struck in the forearm. Gibbons moved to help the wounded officer, only to have three German bullets rip through him—one taking out his left eye. Gibbons's wounds would have dire historic consequences. Before he was struck, the reporter had filed a dispatch that stated that he was "with the Marines" at Belleau Wood. Later, when he failed to return from the front, it was assumed he was dead, and his final dispatch passed the censors unedited.

When Gibbons's report appeared in the American newspapers, it made it look as if the Marine Corps had done all the fighting and saved Paris single-handedly. The U.S. Army command was deeply offended—after all, soldiers of the Army were fighting and dying in France too. Why should the Marines get all the glory? This unfortunate incident so poisoned relations between the Army and the Marine Corps that when World War II broke out, Marines were denied a role in the European theater and did all their fighting in the Pacific. A few days later, Floyd Gibbons turned up at an Allied field hospital, wounded and permanently blind in one eye. He never intended his report to cause so much trouble, but the damage had already been done.

Inside the tree line, the battle for Belleau Wood rolled on. Second Lieutenant Louis F. Timmerman, Jr., led his platoon straight through the mile-wide wood. When he came out on the other side, his men became the target of German fire from all sides. The Marines dashed back into the woods, captured two machine-gun nests, and tried to mount a second charge. They were decimated. Lieutenant Timmerman was shot in the face, and he and a few survivors staggered back into the woods to reclaim the enemy emplacement they had previously abandoned, even as more dazed American stragglers began to arrive. Soon Timmerman had forty men under his command. They fought to hold this position far from their comrades.

At six o'clock in the afternoon of June 6, the Marines had a toehold in Belleau Wood but were nowhere near achieving their objective of securing the forest. One Marine unit led by a Tennessee law-school graduate named Lieutenant Clifton B. Cates had even punched through the German defenses and was converging on the town. When Cates was knocked down by a German bullet, he patched himself up and moved on. The tall, thin, soft-spoken lieutenant quick-marched his Marines to the edge of Bouresches and took up position there. He held the edge of town, but like Timmerman, he was cut off from the rest of the American forces. Over the next few hours there would be no rest for Timmerman or Cates. Both would battle enemy probes and counterattacks while attempting to hold their tenuous positions, awaiting Allied reinforcements that might never arrive.

Erroneous reports reached headquarters that Cates had captured *all* of Bouresches (he held only the outskirts). Reports also indicated that ammunition was in short supply (it wasn't). But how could Cates and his boys get resupplied when they were surrounded by Germans? High command sadly wrote Cates and his unit off. They would have to fend for themselves until help arrived. So, as night began to fall, most Marines huddled just inside the tree line of the game preserve, enduring artillery barrages and enemy probes. Behind them the fields were littered with American dead—1,087 of them, every one a Marine. Several companies were now led by NCOs—they'd lost their commanders.

June 6, 1918, was the bloodiest day in the 143-year history of the United States Marine Corps. More Marines died on that single day than in every other battle Marines fought *combined*. As staggering as the death toll was, it was only part of the story. Invaluable veterans had fallen. Men like Beau Hunter, killed taking Hill 142, or Colonel Albertus Catlin, shot in the lung as he approached Belleau Wood. By evening, there were precious few members of the Old Breed standing. Some had been wounded and lay in field hospitals. Most were dead. It would be up to the new recruits—the New Breed—to shoulder the heavy burden of Marine Corps honor and tradition. Luckily, these men had the finest instructors in the world. In the days ahead, they would not fail their nation or the Corps.

The Allied commanders had no real notion of where they stood or what was going on. Many units had failed to take their first or second objective, and the Americans were nowhere near securing Belleau Wood. After nightfall, when high command received the news that Lieutenant Cates was alive and holed up in Bouresches, details were sketchy. Working under the mistaken notion that Cates needed ammunition, forty-eight-year-old Sergeant Major John Quick—hero of Cuzco Well and Sohoton Cliff—commandeered a battered Ford Model I truck from the headquarters staff and loaded it with ammo and a supply of grenades that had just reached the front. At midnight, June 7, Quick and Lieutenant William Moore, a young Princeton University track and football star, set off for Bouresches across bumpy, shell-torn roads right through the middle of No-Man's-Land. Framed against the horizon by flashes of artillery, the truck made a perfect target for gunners on both sides.

Quick drove without lights, so the Germans fired flares to illuminate the jagged landscape of No-Man's-Land. At the sound of the flare, Quick would swing off the road, stop dead, and wait until the wavering light faded—his eyes shut to preserve night vision. When darkness returned he drove on. Bullets struck their vehicle, poking holes in the canvas, shattering the windshield, and gouging out chunks of rubber from the solid tires. The pockmarked road was slick, and once they skidded in the mud and broke a wheel. A hasty repair, accomplished in near-total darkness, enabled them to continue their hazardous trek. Both Marines expected to die at any moment. A white-hot bullet could ignite the truck's deadly cargo and end their lives in a fiery blast. To their astonishment, Quick and Moore made it to the outskirts of Bouresches before dawn. Lieutenant Cates was grateful for the supplies, but was more excited about the arrival of two more soldiers to help him hold the town. German reinforcements occupied the train station and railyard and were constantly harassing Cates's position. Quick and Moore concluded it was safer to stay in the embattled town than to drive the trashed Ford back to headquarters. For their actions that night, and their subsequent bravery in the capture of Bouresches, Quick and Moore earned the Distinguished Service Cross and the Navy Cross.

During the night, the Germans mounted counterattacks in a futile attempt to drive the Marines out of Belleau Wood. In the confusion and turmoil of night fighting, the Marines sometimes fired on their own. So did the enemy. The Marines tenaciously held their ground at the fringes of the forest, and by the morning of June 7, they reorganized and began to move deeper into the game preserve. The shelling continued all that day, snapping trees and tangling barbed wire. Men were felled by splintered wood, blown from trees by artillery fire. When the Marines attempted to mount a large-scale assault, they were pushed back by sustained machine-gun fire even more intense than the previous day. The German defenses were just too strong, and the enemy was being resupplied. Outgunned, the Marines reverted to their previous tactics, mounting small-unit attacks that slowly but steadily gained ground and smothered the German positions one by one.

The German Army was widely recognized as the premier close-combat fighters in the world. But at Belleau Wood the Leathernecks proved themselves an equal. After years of fighting in No-Man's-Land, the Germans had grown too dependent on their Maxims and grenades. But the battle waged over the coming days would be decided by courage and bayonets, not grenades or machine guns. Utilizing the improvised tactics they'd devised the day before, the Marines slowly overcame the enemy's fixed positions. Once they got within hand-to-hand combat range, the contest was over. The Marines slaughtered the Germans with blasts from their Springfields, Chauchats, or a quick bayonet thrust.

But approaching the German machine-gun nests cost them dearly. Without grenades, the first Marine to reach the German emplacements had to grab the hot barrel of the chattering Maxim and wrest it from the gunner's grasp or thrust it aside in order to allow his comrades the opportunity to pour into the emplacement after him. This reckless tactic cost more than one Marine his hand, his arm, or his life.

As the battle dragged on, separate Marine divisions continued to fight without regard to the orders issued by high command, which was distant and out of touch with the shifting situation on the battlefield. There was so much chaos that previous objectives were forgotten. Units became lost in the smoke and confusion. There were no landmarks—just trees, boulders and paths, and the chatter of German guns. It was easy to become disoriented. Lieutenant Colonel Fritz Wise led his battalion through the blasted landscape for five days without any communication with high command. He and his men pressed on, uncertain of who was on their flanks—other Americans, the French, or the enemy—or if they were moving in the right direction. Even the sun and stars could not help as they fought through smoke, clouds of poison gas, and heavy fog under a dark canopy of trees.

On June 9, a French artillery barrage devastated Belleau Wood. In the space of an hour the once-pristine hunting preserve became a gauntlet of shattered trees, churned earth, and smoke and fire. Over it all hung the pervasive stench of death. The battle was a stalemate. The Allies had underestimated the strength of the German positions and the German high command had underrated the determination of the American Marines. Communication breakdowns continued to plague both sides, but was particularly bad among the American forces. On June 11, Wise finally made contact with his superiors. They ordered him to attack the center of the woods. But Wise's units were understrength and exhausted from days of continuous fighting. The thirty-nine-year-old career officer from New York and veteran of China and the Philippines had lost 30 percent of his command. How was he was supposed to mount a large-scale assault without reinforcements? Wise questioned the wisdom of his orders even as he tried to carry them out. Before sunrise, his battered battalion moved through the freshly plowed wheat fields under the protection of a thick morning fog. Again the Germans were waiting. Marines began to die almost as soon as they showed their faces. Lloyd Williams—another member of the Old Breed—was wounded in the morning and died late that night. Wise's battalion was nearly decimated.

"The only thing that drove those Marines through those woods in the face of such resistance as they met was their individual, elemental guts, plus the hardening of the training through which they had gone," Wise reported.

During the advance, his men had moved very much off target. Instead of probing deeper into the featureless woods, they had moved directly across the narrow waist—Wise's left-flank companies ended up where his right flank should have been. Wise was unaware of this mistake and reported that his objectives had been taken. By seven o'clock that night, the Allied high command announced to the world that the northern edge of Belleau Wood had been captured. They were wrong.

By the afternoon of June 12, it appeared that the Marines were going to prevail—at least it did to high command. That situation changed dramatically in the early morning hours of the thirteenth. General Ludendorff, concerned about the Allied advances, ordered a massive counteroffensive concentrating on Belleau Wood and the towns around it. Reinforced with fresh troops, the Germans bombarded the fragile American lines with an artillery barrage and saturated Bouresches with mustard gas. On the streets Marines fell choking, their eyes smarting and their flesh burning. For those most exposed, it was just the beginning of their torment.

■ *Poison Gas*

Poison gases had been tested for a long time before World War I broke out, but the great powers were reluctant to use it. Gas was hard to control—an errant wind could carry the vapors back to one's own troops—and many officers considered it to be a savage, cruel, and uncivilized weapon. The French were the first to open Pandora's box when they fired tear gas at the Germans during the first months of the conflict. In October 1914, the German Army responded by firing shrapnel shells packed with steel balls that had been treated with a chemical irritant.

In April 1915, the Germans used chlorine-gas cylinders against the French at the Battle of Ypres. French soldiers reported seeing yellow-green clouds drifting toward their trenches and detected a distinctive smell like a mixture of pineapple and pepper. When the gas reached the trenches, the soldiers began to complain of pains in the chest and a burning sensation in the throat. Chlorine gas destroyed the respiratory organs of its victims, and this led to slow death by asphyxiation. Like other gas weapons it was important to have the right weather conditions before an attack. In 1916, poison-gas shells were invented, making the gas somewhat more controllable. Artillery could send shells filled with poison for many miles, to drop down on enemy troops far behind the front lines. Later in the war chlorine was replaced by phosgene, which is much more deadly. Only a small amount was needed to make it impossible for the enemy to keep fighting. Phosgene killed its victim within forty-eight hours. Advancing armies also utilized a mixture of chlorine and phosgene called "white star."

By 1917, the German Army was using yperite, dubbed mustard gas by frontline troops, the most lethal of all the poisonous chemicals used in the First World War. It was nearly odorless and took twelve hours to take effect. Yperite was so powerful that only a small amount had to be added to high-explosive shells to be effective. Once in the soil of No-Man's-Land, the toxin remained active for several weeks. Mustard gas blistered and burned the skin. Soon the victim began to vomit as the gas caused internal and external bleeding and attacked the bronchial tubes, stripping off the mucous membranes. The pain was so extreme that victims had to be strapped to their beds until they perished.

During a gas attack, the toxic cloud hugged the ground like a fog. It filled the trenches and forced soldiers to withdraw or perish. The only defense against poison gas was the gas mask, but at best the masks were inefficient. The first gas masks in the war were issued to British troops in May 1915. They were made from canvas and filled with cotton pads soaked in urine. It was discovered that the ammonia in the urine would neutralized the chlorine. Handkerchiefs soaked in human urine and flannel body belts dampened with a solution of bicarbonate of soda were also tried.

By late 1915, frontline soldiers were given "efficient" gas masks and antiasphyxiation respirators. Both the British and French had their own types of gas masks, but neither provided sufficient protection from all toxins. When the United States Marines went into battle in 1918, they carried both French and British gas masks. Weighing between six and eight pounds, these masks were slung around a man's neck at all times.

Engaging the enemy while wearing a gas mask proved to be the most difficult feat of all. Colonel Albertus Catlin described the experience: "[The mask was] a hot and stifling thing [that] seemed to impede the faculties. The wearer takes in the air through his mouth, after it has been sucked through the purifying chemicals. His nose is not trusted and is clamped shut. Imagine yourself fighting with a clothespin on your nose and a bag over your mouth and you may be able to get some notion of what a gas mask is like."

DEVIL DOGS!

German soldiers were perplexed and demoralized. Why were these Americans so stubborn? Didn't they know when they were beaten? Apparently not, for everywhere the Americans struck, they prevailed—at tremendous cost to both sides. One German private, who had lost three-fourths of his company to tenacious Marine attacks, wrote in a letter home: "We have Americans opposite us who are terribly reckless fellows."

So reckless that legend has it that the enemy took to calling them *Teufelshunde:* Devil Dogs.

The Germans established a new line in front of Lieutenant Colonel Fritz Wise's beleaguered forces, then reinforced it with hundreds of fresh troops. Wise had already lost half of his division. When combat engineers arrived in the night, he put them on the front. Then Wise waited for the assault he knew would come. On the morning of June 13, as the Germans cautiously approached the American lines, they began to fall to American sniper fire. Resistance intensified and soon the Germans withdrew. As they moved to the rear, American field artillery went into action. High-explosive shells plunged down onto the dwindling German ranks. In less than an hour the back of the German counterattack was broken.

General Pershing and his staff had already announced to the world that Belleau Wood had been taken. Now the Americans had to capture it before the error was discovered. Under a prevailing misconception that German defenses would be light, high command again ordered Wise to push forward. Reluctantly, the lieutenant colonel followed orders. His Marines were promised a high-explosive artillery barrage to soften up enemy defenses, but when the shells came, they were off the mark and left the defenders untouched. German artillery responded in kind—supplementing high explosives with mustard gas. The gas swirled ankle-deep around the Marines, seeping through clothes and under gas masks to burn skin, eyes, mouth, and throat. During the fighting, the masks became stifling, but to remove them was certain death.

When the artillery ended and the gas dispersed, the Marines burst from their foxholes and charged the German lines on schedule. They hit the enemy with everything they had, using rifles, bayonets, pistols, trench knives, shovels, and even their bare hands in the most savage attack of the campaign. One unit watched in horror as their commander, Captain John Francis Burns, was killed by German artillery. They rushed across No-Man's-Land, leapt into the German trenches, and quite literally ripped enemy soldiers limb from limb. The rage and frustration that had been building for weeks was finally unleashed. Savagery of this kind occurred all along the front. Lieutenant Colonel Fritz Wise later wrote of the brutality he witnessed that day: "The Marines took [all of a German machine-gun nest] prisoner. No one was killed. And that minute another German machine gun opened up on their flank. They left their prisoners, charged the second gun and captured it . . . And that minute the captured gun crew they had left behind opened fire on them again. [The Marines] couldn't play back and forth like this all day. They bayoneted every man of that second German gun crew, went back and captured the first gun all over again, and bayoneted every man of that crew before they went on."

But brutality was not always the order of the day. There were accounts of courage and self-sacrifice as well. On Wise's flank, Private Aloysius Leitner, who had been wounded in the initial assault, continued to fight. He went on to capture six German machine guns and several prisoners before he collapsed and died from loss of blood. His actions saved countless lives, and his comrades stood by his side as he breathed his last. Aloysius Leitner was posthumously awarded the Army Distinguished Service Cross and the Navy Cross.

During the intense enemy bombardment, Gunnery Sergeant Fred William Stockham of the Second Division—one of the Old Breed—noticed that a soldier in his command had had his gas mask shot away. Wounded and in agony, seventeen-year-old Private Barrett Mattingly of Missouri was facing certain death. With no regard for personal safety, Stockham gave his own gas mask to the private. The sergeant continued to direct the evacuation of casualties until he was overcome by gas and collapsed. Stockham died in a field hospital a week later from the grisly effects of mustard-gas exposure. Thirty-seven years old at the time of this courageous action, Stockham was a tough career Marine. Though he had entered service in New York City, he was born in Detroit, Michigan. After his death, Stockham was awarded the Medal of Honor. His remains were interred at the Hollywood Cemetery in Union, New Jersey. There is an American Legion Post in St. Louis, Missouri—Private Mattingly's hometown—named in Stockham's honor.

Captain Roswell Winans

Major John "Johnny the Hard" Hughes lost over 450 men to poison gas. Choking and half blind, his Marines leapt from their trenches and met the enemy hand to hand. When it was over, Hughes, his lungs burning and his eyes swollen shut from the effects of the gas, lost none of his bravery. His message to high command read: "Have had a terrific bombardment and attack . . . everything is OK . . . Can't you get hot coffee to me?"

GAINING GROUND

On the morning of June 15, Captain Roswell Winans—who had earned the Medal of Honor as an enlisted man in the Dominican Republic—led his men in the capture of the western edge of Belleau Wood. They met less than effective enemy resistance, and it seemed that the battle for Belleau Wood was winding down. In two weeks of combat, the Marine Brigade had suffered more than 50 percent casualties. Sixty officers and over 2,000 enlisted men were dead. During the lull in fighting, the exhausted veterans were sent behind the lines to recuperate. Meanwhile, a fresh German battalion moved into the woods to reinforce their battered comrades.

While the American Fourth Marines—bearded, exhausted, and filthy—rested among the haystacks of a French farm, the Germans moved into the northern edge of Belleau Wood in strength. The Allied Seventh Infantry—French and American units who were untested in battle—failed to press the Germans effectively and had to be withdrawn in the face of the enemy advance. The veterans were brought back to Belleau Wood to finish the job they'd started. The American attack on June 23 cost the Marines over 130 casualties. It was a halfhearted effort and failed to dislodge the enemy. On June 24, accurate artillery fire pummeled the German emplacements. The barrage was followed by a Marine Corps attack on the afternoon of the twenty-fifth. The men who moved into the woods found the enemy emplacements blasted into oblivion. But the Germans still resisted the American advance with snipers and grenades, and Marines again died in significant numbers.

Finally, the Germans pulled back to the Belleau-Torcy road on the northern end of the woods. They were running out of replacements and the will to fight. This is illustrated by the experience of Marine Private Henry P. Lenert. A runner for his battalion, Lenert stumbled into a trench filled with Germans. Instead of being shot, he was approached by a captain who spoke perfect English. The officer asked if there were more Americans behind him. The quick-thinking Marine replied that the Sixth Marines were ready to pass through the area at dawn. Then the captain asked Private Lenert to lead him and his eighty-two-man command back to Allied brigade headquarters to surrender.

On June 26—twenty days after the first Marine stormed into Belleau Wood—Major Maurice Shearer of the Fifth Marines wiped out the final German emplacement. The wood belonged to the Marine Corps, but it was a bitter victory. They had suffered over 5,000 casualties—more than half the entire brigade. Whole rifle companies had ceased to exist; others were so devastated they were no longer combat-effective. The grateful French handed out hundreds of medals and citations and renamed Belleau the Bois de la Brigade de Marine in honor of their victory. Along with the U.S. Army's victories at Cantigny and Vaux, the battle for Belleau Wood demonstrated that the American military could prevail on the modern battlefield. The campaign provided the Marines with invaluable combat experience and was a proving ground for the next generation. Four veterans of Belleau Wood—Neville, Holcomb, Cates, and Shepherd—would all be named commandant in the decades ahead.

But the Marines suffered one critical defeat at Belleau Wood. They lost the goodwill of the Army because of the erroneous story filed by Floyd Gibbons, which had made it appear as if the Marines saved Paris single-handedly—an insult to the thousands of Army regulars who fought and died defending the French capital at Vaux, Château-Thierry, Cantigny, and elsewhere. The results of this error were tragic and unfair. Though the Marines were hailed as conquering heroes back home, their comrades-in-arms in Europe despised them as glory hounds. This rift between the Army and the Marines still exists today.

SOSSIONS

On the July 4, 1918, Parisians mounted a huge celebration to mark America's Independence Day and honor the men of the Allied Expeditionary Force. Marines who faced bullets and shrapnel at Belleau Wood now marched through a shower of

▪ *Canvas Falcons: Marines in the Air*

Early in the war, the "aeroplane" was used for battlefield observation, artillery spotting, and intelligence gathering. But when guns were added, the airplane was transformed into a formidable weapon. Soon the era of the fighter plane and the fighter pilot was born. By the end of 1914, the skies were filled with dueling airplanes struggling for control of the high ground.

The pioneers who hurled their fragile aircraft against the enemy without benefit of radio or parachute gained mythological status in the public's imagination. In the modern era of total war, the fighter pilot was seen as a romantic throwback—a contemporary knight fighting with honor and without regard to personal safety. Tales of chivalry in the air, often exaggerated, were comforting in the midst of the savagery of modern war and added to the aviator's mystique.

Soon the popular press on both sides of the conflict praised the pilots' exploits and the military reaped the propaganda benefit such publicity had on the war effort. High command began calling a pilot who downed five or more enemy planes an "ace." Over time these aces of World War I achieved maximum celebrity, were showered with medals and gifts, and hailed as conquering heroes by an adoring public. Kings, queens, and princes greeted them as equals, and young women swooned in their presence. We still recall their names and celebrate the legendary exploits of men like Manfred von Richthofen, Germany's "Red Baron," who downed eighty enemy planes; Max Immelmann, who created the air maneuver that bears his name; Billy Bishop, Britain's greatest ace, who took to the skies because he hated the mud of the trenches; and Eddie Rickenbacker, the highest-scoring American pilot of the war.

But despite all the acclaim and the glory showered on these so-called knights of the air, the Marine Corps had a different view of the airplane's role in combat. Since its inception in 1912, the officers of the Marine Corps Aviation service believed the airplane should be used as a ground-support weapon, not a platform for personal glory.

When the United States entered the war, Marine Corps Aviation consisted of six officers, one warrant officer, and forty-odd enlisted men. The Corps amphibious mandate was achieved through an equal division of forces—three land-based aircraft and two seaplanes. This meager unit was headquartered at the Marine Aeronautical Station at Pensacola, Florida, under the command of Captain Alfred Cunningham. After hostilities were declared, the unit was transferred to the Philadelphia Navy Yard, where a hangar was built on the shore of the river. The structure boasted modern aircraft facilities and access for both land-based aircraft and seaplanes.

But by the middle of 1917, the bulk of Cunningham's air forces were transferred again—the land-based aircraft were moved to Mineola, Long Island, and the seaplanes to the Azores, where they flew hundreds of antisubmarine patrols and bombed German submarine pens. Eventually, Captain Cunningham convinced his superiors that Marine Corps aviators should fight in the skies over Europe. Four squadrons were moved to Europe and incorporated into the Navy Northern Bombing Group based near Calais. These squadrons—A, B, C, and D—were formed on July 30, 1918, and composed the First Marine Aviation Force in Europe. Placed under the command of Captain Cunningham, they were scheduled to receive the first seventy-two British-designed De Havilland DH-4s to roll off the assembly lines in America.

But when the DH-4s finally arrived, they were so badly assembled by the American manufacturer that the entire lot had to be stripped down and rebuilt. Pilots testing these reconditioned aircraft faced an onerous task, and there were several crashes due to faulty engines or wing, wire, or strut failure. The DH-4 was far from a perfect aircraft under optimum conditions. Its fuel tank was situated between the pilot and the rear gunner's compartment and was lightly armored. A few well-placed incendiary shells would cause the aircraft to erupt into a ball of burning debris—hence its ominous nickname, "The Flaming Coffin." Other Marines flew with Royal Air Force Squadrons 217 and 218. In the volatile De Havilland bomber they attacked strategic targets in Belgium and France. A few Marines were lucky enough to be assigned to RAF Squadron 213, where they learned to fly one of the premier fighter aircraft of the First World War, the Sopwith Camel.

In the last phase of the war, Marine Corps aviators flying American-built DH-4s bombed artillery emplacements, supply convoys, airfields, and vital railheads. Their ranks swelled to 200 officers and a thousand enlisted men. In all, Marines flew sixty bombing missions over Europe alongside their counterparts from England and France. Only fourteen missions were carried out exclusively by the Marine Corps.

Occasionally the Marines faced German fighters on these bombing runs. Piloting a DH-4, Lieutenant Everett Brewer and Gunnery Sergeant Harry Wersheimer shot down the first enemy aircraft claimed by Marines on September 28, 1918, in a dogfight over Belgium. Both Marines were severely wounded in the encounter. In all, Marines were credited with downing a dozen German aircraft. They gained valuable experience in these missions. After the war, these officers returned to their stateside postings with a new respect for airpower. Some went on to pioneer the innovative tactics used in air combat and ground-support operations during the Second World War and beyond.

Though Marines generally scorned the glory and the peril of dogfighting in favor of missions in support of ground units, a few made their reputations in air combat, and two of them earned the Medal of Honor. On October 14, 1918, Squadron C of the First Marine Aviation Force participated in a bombing mission against the Thielt railway junction in Belgium. This railhead was an important target—the Germans were moving men and matériel through this junction on a daily basis.

A formation of eight USMC DH-4s took off after sunup. The heavily laden planes lumbered through the grass and into the air. Hundreds of pounds of bombs lined the undersides of their wings. The DH-4s were painted an overall brown with gunmetal-gray engine cowlings and exhaust pipes and a red, white, and blue tail fin. Each had the Marine Corps emblem emblazoned on the fuselage. On the first pass, the DH-4s slowed to about ninety-five miles per hour and released their payload as antiaircraft fire rose up to greet them. Most of the bombs missed their targets, though the explosions managed to ignite a few large fires on the ground. The DH-4s swung around to finish their raid with a strafing run, but smoke rising from the destruction disoriented the pilots and the formation broke apart. Suddenly a dozen German warplanes dived out of the sun, Spandau machine guns chattering. The assault panicked the pilots and further scattered the ragged formation.

The attackers were flying Fokker D-VIIs—arguably the finest all-around fighter to see action in the First World War. The D-VII incorporated many new innovations, including a reliable, sturdy engine. One model was powered by a 165-horsepower Mercedes, another by a 185 horsepower BMW engine. A biplane, the D-VII was angular but sleek, with thick cantilever wings. The wings were canvas over a frame with steel tubing for struts. The D-VII's control wires

Second Lieutenant Ralph Talbot

were embedded inside the wings, which reduced drag and increased the aircraft's agility. Though not spectacularly fast—its maximum speed was only 116 miles per hour—the D-VII was easy to fly and maneuverable at high altitudes. The DH-4s, with a maximum speed near 140 miles per hour, were faster than the Fokkers, but were still hopelessly outmatched by the nimble German fighters.

As the Americans scattered, several Fokkers concentrated on a single DH-4. The pilot was Second Lieutenant Ralph Talbot of South Weymouth, Massachusetts, with Gunnery Sergeant Robert G. Robinson of Wayne, Michigan, in the observer's cockpit. As the Fokkers circled for the kill, Sergeant Robinson fired burst after burst with his rear-mounted machine gun. A gifted marksman, he struck a Fokker just as it was taking up position on their tail. The D-VII stalled, then exploded. As the burning debris plunged to earth, a second and third German fighter closed on the Marines.

Bullets ripped through the De Havilland's fuselage, barely missing the vulnerable fuel tank. Robinson's elbow was shattered, rendering his arm useless. He staggered, then returned fire. Almost immediately his machine gun jammed. As another Fokker positioned itself on the DH-4's tail, Robinson managed to clear his weapon with his one good hand and fire another burst. He missed the Fokker but convinced the German to break off.

Lieutenant Talbot performed a series of wild maneuvers in an effort to dodge the torrent of enemy bullets hurled at him. In the rear cockpit, Sergeant Robinson's luck ran out. With wounds to his arm, stomach, and hip, he collapsed. Lieutenant Talbot could not shake the Fokkers. He had no defense without his tail gunner, but instead of retreating, he spun his aircraft around and attacked. Forward machine gun blazing, Talbot managed to shoot down a second D-VII and kill the surprised pilot. Then bullets ripped into his engine, causing it to sputter. Talbot broke off his attack and dived for the ground. The slower Fokkers couldn't keep up with him. When he finally leveled off, Talbot was flying less than fifty feet above the ground and directly over the German trenches. Small-arms fire arched up at him, striking the wings, fuselage, and even the struts—but miraculously missing Talbot and Robinson. The DH-4 raced over the enemy's lines, turned around, and headed back toward home. Once again ground troops fired but failed to shoot it down. Lieutenant Talbot nursed his faltering aircraft until he spotted an Allied field hospital. He landed in a nearby field and found medical help for his wounded observer. With Sergeant Robinson in the doctors' hands, Talbot returned to his DH-4. Within a few hours, he managed to make preliminary repairs and take off again. The lieutenant flew the crippled DH-4 back to his aerodrome to file a report.

Lieutenant Talbot, the son of an upper-class New England family who had just completed his freshman year at Yale when he joined the Corps, was immediately returned to active duty. Eleven days later, while he was performing an engine test on one of the rebuilt DH-4s delivered from America, his plane crashed on takeoff. The fuel tank exploded on impact and Talbot burned to death. He was twenty-three years old. Second Lieutenant Colgate W. Darden, Jr., Talbot's observer on this doomed mission, was thrown clear before the plane exploded. Darden was wounded but survived the war; he would later became a governor of Virginia.

Gunnery Sergeant Robert Guy Robinson—who was twenty-three at the time of his Medal of Honor citation—recuperated in a field hospital and later in a facility near Paris. The war was over before he could recover enough to return to duty. He continued his career in the Marine Corps and rose to the rank of first lieutenant. Robert Guy Robinson passed away on October 5, 1974, in Maryland and was buried with honors at Arlington National Cemetery in Virginia.

Marine Aviation forces suffered forty-seven casualties in the First World War—three died in action or of wounds, three were wounded and unable to return to duty, and sixteen died of influenza. By the time of the armistice, there were 2,462 officers and enlisted men in the Marine Corps Aviation Forces.

---

confetti and flower petals to the cheers of all Parisians. Some Americans encountered lost comrades on the packed streets of the French capital. Lieutenant Lemuel Shepherd—who had been wounded late in the battle for Belleau Wood and refused to be evacuated unless the medics took his little dog, Kiki, with them—stood watching on crutches while the Yanks passed in review. When Shepherd saw the remnants of his old unit, he limped into the ranks and joined them, Kiki trotting by his side.

But the mood of celebration was short-lived. The Allies planned a major offensive on the Western Front for July 18 and furloughs were cut short. The Marines were dispatched to booster the French's 10th Army in the area around Soissons. Once again they found themselves packed into *camions* on a bumpy ride to the trenches. This time the Marines had some interesting help. The First Moroccan Division would fight side by side with them in the battle ahead. The Germans hated these North African troops. Among the Moroccans was a large contingent of fanatical Muslims who believed that every infidel they killed paved their way to paradise. Though Muslims were fair marksmen, they favored dispatching the enemy in close combat with handheld weapons—like the long knives they regularly employed to disembowel

German soldiers. Evidence of the First Moroccans' grim handiwork had been discovered before, usually when the Germans dispatched patrols to search for missing units. Bloody rumors about "mad African savages" were spreading through the Kaiser's ranks almost as quickly as the tales of the ferocious American Devil Dogs.

But as the AEF made ready for the scheduled offensive on the eighteenth, General Ludendorff beat them to the punch by launching the final German offensive of the war. The German offensive line stretched from the Argonne Front to the Marne. After a massive artillery bombardment all along the front, the Germans rose from their trenches on the morning of July 15. They hit the Allied lines at a hundred points, disrupting communications and scattering the defenders. The Allies were caught in the middle of making plans for their own offensive and units were in various states of readiness.

On the rainy night of July 17, the Marine brigade slogged through the mud to a staging point near the Forest of Retz. It was so dark, and the maze of trees so confusing, that the Marines marched in singlefile, each man clinging to the pack of the man in front of him. At 4:35 A.M., the Americans formed an assault line in the woods, fixed bayonets, and launched their counteroffensive even as the Germans let loose with everything they had. By nightfall the Americans had stopped the Germans. A fast-moving detachment of Marines had even captured the village of Vierzy.

The battle for Vierzy was particularly brutal. Lieutenant John "Johnny" Overton, Yale track star and one of the Corps' college-educated New Breed, was leading a probe on an entrenched enemy position when they were fired upon. Private First Class Carl Brannen, a new replacement fresh from the States, offered a firsthand account of what happened next: "Lt. Overton [was] walking backward and trying to shout something back to us . . . The din and roar was so terrific that I didn't have any idea what he was saying, but interpreted it from his expression to be some words of encouragement. He was soon down, killed . . . all the men around me were shot down."

Lieutenant Overton died trying to relay commands to his troops. Battlefield communications were a chronic problem. Without field telephones—the lines were usually cut in the first minutes of the battle—runners had to be dispatched to carry orders from the headquarters to the front. They suffered under horrifying conditions—artillery fire rained down all around them, machine guns blazed with constant fire, and snipers made it a sport to kill Allied message runners on sight. Lieutenant Overton was one of the best—crossing open ground countless times that day in an effort to keep the lines of communication open.

For two days the Marines advanced, until they ran into a sizable German counterattack on July 18. Casualties quickly exceeded those suffered at Belleau Wood. Over 2,000 Marines were killed or wounded, but despite these heavy losses, things were going better for the Americans than for the enemy. While Germany was nearly drained of manpower, over a million Yanks had poured into Europe. Even supply problems had eased somewhat. More importantly, the Marines now engaged on the front lines were led by a core of men who were blooded and battle-hardened. They knew the enemy. They had beaten him soundly at Belleau Wood. And in the savage fight for Vierzy, these Marines never lost their indomitable fighting spirit.

When the 96th Company was halted by stubborn German resistance, Lieutenant Clifton B. Cates—the only officer in his company who was still standing—sent this immortal dispatch to his commanders in the rear: "I have only two men out of my company and 20 out of some other company. We need support, but it is almost suicide to try to get it here as we are swept by machine gun fire and [a] constant barrage is on us. I have no one on my left and only a few on my right. I will hold."

Lieutenant Cates did not inform his superiors that he was fighting on despite a festering shrapnel wound to his leg, or the embarrassing fact that his pants had been shredded in the explosion that injured him. Now Cates was limping around giving commands with a blanket wrapped around his waist and a pistol in his hand. But he held, until a large Allied force relieved him and swept the Germans from the field.

Major Louis B. Cukela

The Marines' fighting spirit was also demonstrated by two foreign-born sergeants distinguished in the fight to take Vierzy. On the morning of July 18, during the advance through the Forest of Retz, the 66th Company of the Fifth Marines found their way blocked by a German emplacement. On point was Sergeant Louis B. Cukela, an immigrant from Spalato, Yugoslavia, who was leading a platoon. Cukela spoke English with a slight Serbian accent that sometimes amused his men, though they had a healthy respect and admiration for their no-nonsense sergeant. When Cukela realized his platoon was pinned down and on the verge of being annihilated, the thirty-year-old sergeant crawled out to the flank of the enemy under heavy fire. He carefully circled behind the German strong point until he was behind it. Then he rushed the machine gun nest. His unexpected appearance shocked the defenders. Before they could react, Cukela was among them. The first German fell when the sergeant's bayonet tore out his throat. A second was stunned by the butt of the Cukela's rifle. The others were killed or fled. Hurling captured hand grenades, Cukela blasted his way through the rest of the strong point, destroying two Maxim machine guns. Sergeant Cukela single-handedly neutralized a dozen enemy troops and led four prisoners back to headquarters for interrogation. Sergeant Louis Cukela received both the Army and Navy Medals of Honor for his actions. He remained in the Corps and rose through the ranks. Major Louis B. Cukela (ret.) died in Bethesda, Maryland, in 1956 and is buried in Arlington National Cemetery in Arlington, Virginia.

Near Vierzy on that same July day, Austrian-born Sergeant Matej Kocak, also of the 66th Company, went forward to scout alone, unprotected by covering fire. He was hunting for a hidden German machine-gun nest that had slowed down the 66th's advance and killed several of his men. He found the enemy in short order, but they spotted his advance and opened fire. Instead of retreating, Kocak rose from cover and attacked the German emplacement. He scattered the crew and captured the position. When a second machine gun fired on him, Sergeant Kocak crawled into a nearby ditch and found himself sharing it with a group of Moroccans who had become separated from their company. Sergeant Kocak rallied the Moroccans and led them in an attack on the second emplacement. They slaughtered the crew and captured two machine guns, which were later turned on the enemy. Kocak's and Cukela's reckless actions revealed the existence of a "secret society" that thrived among the Marines of the 66th. This group—called "The Solo Club"—was a loose affiliation of battle-hardened veterans who had performed a special rite of passage. To become a member a Marine had to destroy or capture a German machine gun nest "solo." Sergeant Matej Kocak received both the Army and Navy Medals of Honor, but did not survive the war. At the age of thirty-six, he was killed in action on October 4, 1918, at the battle for Blanc Mont Ridge. Sergeant Kocak is buried in the Meuse Argonne Cemetery in France.

French tanks entered the fray in support of the Marines. Under a scorching July sun, the Allies continued their advance toward Soissons. They were finally stopped less than a mile from the Mauberge Highway, their original objective. The lead battalions had suffered over 50 percent casualties. With supplies slow, water scarce, and the chain of command fractured, the exhausted survivors had no choice but to dig in. The Marines had fought well and the enemy had been repulsed. But General Ludendorff was not yet ready to concede defeat. He still had more than a million armed men at his disposal, so the war would continue.

ST.-MIHIEL AND BLANC MONT RIDGE

Seven weeks of peace followed Soissons. Between July 25 and September 12, 1918, there were only fifteen casualties in the Marine Brigade. During this lull, the Allies trained for the next fight. During this climactic phase of the war, General Pershing finally got his wish—he was given the opportunity to field an all-American force and mount an American-led offensive against the Germans. When they saw combat again, the Yanks would fight as part of the United States First Army in Europe. The Allies had chosen their next target—St.-Mihiel—and were determined to dislodge the occupation force from the fortress city of Metz on the Moselle River. This sector had been quiet since the German push that captured the region two years before. In the northwest, mixed French and American divisions pounded away at the enemy, keeping the Germans preoccupied until the new offensive could be launched. By early August, the French and American divisions held a reinforced defensive line that ran from Soissons to Reims.

For Germany, August 8 was a "black day." The surprise British offensive tore a hole in the Imperial Army's defenses and cost the lives of some of their best divisions. This attack was so effective that it convinced Kaiser Wilheim that it was time for Germany to sue for peace. But because of internal dissension, the German leader failed to make a determined effort to bring about a diplomatic settlement, so the war continued. The French were not inclined to sit back and wait for a treaty. French Army General Ferdinand Foch decided to mount an offensive in the area of St.-Mihiel, where the Germans still occupied a bulge in the Allied lines. This was the last salient point still in dispute.

This attack was the U.S. First Army's baptism of fire. Among the Allied commanders, only General Pershing was convinced that the Americans were capable of executing a successful military campaign on their own. In the end, six French divisions and over 400 French tanks were added to the U.S. forces for support, but the offensive at St.-Mihiel would be carried out primarily by nineteen American divisions and over a thousand airplanes commanded by U.S. Army Colonel William "Billy" Mitchell, a pioneer proponent of airpower. As usual, the Americans would bear the brunt of the fighting. But this time they would be led into battle by their own countrymen. Marine Corps General John Lejeune finally arrived from the United States to take over command of all Marines in Europe. St.-Mihiel would be his first campaign as overseas commander.

The Germans were aware that St.-Mihiel was the target of this new offensive, so they began pulling back even before the fighting began. But the first units had barely began to withdraw when, beginning at around 1:00 A.M. on September 12, a four-hour bombardment by 3,000 Allied guns rained down on their position. At dawn the Americans moved. Resistance was slight and mostly ineffectual. The combined force of U.S. Army regulars and U.S. Marines overran the forward German defensive positions by the second day and captured over 15,000 prisoners. But because the enemy were already in retreat, most slipped through Pershing's grip.

Eventually, the American advance threatened the Hindenburg Line, at the French-German border. This heavily defended position was the line of defense for the German homeland. The German Army mounted repeated counterattacks from their strong positions along the line. Though these assaults failed to drive the Americans back, the offensive ran out of steam. Four days of constant fighting had exhausted the troops and depleted their supplies. The First Army's advance was halted by logistical problems, not by the enemy. Among the Americans, casualties were light—132 dead and 500 wounded. German high command expected the Allies to move on and seize Metz. They were surprised when the Allies concentrated instead on the Meuse-Argonne region, where the First Army troops were fighting hard. The Germans had constructed elaborate defensive positions in the area, including artillery, concrete emplacements, and interlocking machine-gun grids. They also controlled the high ground on two sides—the bluffs east of the Meuse and the autumn-brown, tree-covered Argonne hills to the west. Although the Americans outnumbered the enemy eight-to-one, the Germans made good use of their artillery, their deep defenses, and the rough terrain that favored them. They refused to retreat farther for fear of opening their homeland to assault, so the American troops ended up bloodying themselves again and again in determined but fruitless attacks against a well-entrenched army. A thousand men fell, but the First Army kept up the pressure.

On the clear, frigid night of October 1–2, the Marines occupied a section of the front north of Somme-Py, where the French advance had been effectively halted. It was a desolate, war-torn landscape—chalk white, scarred by trenches, tangled with barbed wire, and pocked with thousands of shell holes. The high steeples of the churches in Reims were just visible in the haze. That morning the guns were silent and the men could smell the fresh breezes from the north—chill winds with the first hint of winter.

At 5:50 A.M. on the foggy morning of October 3, the Marines and their French allies attacked the German positions on Blanc Mont Ridge. Capturing Blanc Mont— "White Mountain"—was the key to victory in this sector. If the German Army retained control of this strategic high ground, which they had occupied and reinforced since 1914, the entire momentum of the war could shift in their favor. After a short but murderous five-minute artillery bombardment by 200 guns, the Americans moved out of their positions and charged the first line of German fortifications.

In the early hours of this assault, two Marines of the 78th Company, both enlisted men, performed acts of bravery that earned them the Medal of Honor. One was Private John J. Kelly, an abrasive Irish-American bullyboy from the mean streets of Chicago. Private Kelly was what's known in military circles as a hardcase. He was insubordinate, disobedient, and defiant—"every first sergeant's nightmare," according to Marine Corps historian Colonel Joseph H. Alexander. In boot camp, Kelly barely avoided being brought up on charges. In combat, he became a one-man army. His moves were aggressive and bold, and Kelly had taken the initiative in several engagements prior to Blanc Mont Ridge.

On this day, operating solo, Private Kelly moved ahead of his unit in the first minutes of the attack. He raced through the American artillery barrage "yelling like an Indian," according to one eyewitness. He reached the enemy's forward position and immediately came under fire. He wasted a German machine-gun nest with a well-placed hand grenade, shot a German officer at point-blank range with his pistol, and frightened eight other defenders so badly that they dropped their weapons and surrendered. As Kelly led his prisoners through the American lines, he winked and called out to his comrades in the 78th: "Just what I told you I'd do!"

Having already won the Distinguished Service Cross during the destruction of an enemy strong point at Soissons, Private Kelly would be awarded both the Army and Marine Corps Medals of Honor for this action. He was presented with these medals in 1919 by General "Black Jack" Pershing himself. Kelly, who remained disrespectful of military discipline, left the Corps after his term of service ended. He passed away on November 20, 1957, in Florida, and his remains were returned to Illinois for burial at All Saints Cemetery in Des Plaines.

On that same bloody day, Corporal John H. Pruitt of Fayetteville, Arkansas, also distinguished himself. As his unit advanced toward the German emplacements, Pruitt watched as his point men were cut down by accurate German machine-gun fire from two entrenched positions. Rather than see more men die, the corporal sent his unit to the rear, then rose from cover and attacked the two emplacements by himself. He single-handedly destroyed the machine-gun nests and killed both enemy gunners, but he wasn't finished yet. Pruitt proceeded to leap into a trench full of Germans, waving his bayonet wildly and shouting at the forty soldiers cowering there to surrender—and they did!

After the corporal marched his prisoners to American lines, he returned to battle. Pruitt continued to snipe at the enemy. Several times he had to rally his men to stand against enemy counterattacks. As the day waned, a German artillery barrage sent the Americans to ground. A well-placed round exploded among the Marines and Corporal Pruitt was mortally wounded. He died the next day—October 4, his twenty-second birthday. John Pruitt's remains were returned to the United States, where they were buried with honors at Arlington

Corporal John H. Pruitt

National Cemetery. Corporal Pruitt was awarded both the Army and Navy Medals of Honor posthumously.

The fighting at Blanc Mont Ridge was fierce from the moment the two armies clashed. But the combat was especially brutal on the western slope, where the Germans refused to give up an inch of territory. Enemy machine-gun fire swept the valley and cleared the reverse slope of Americans. When the sun set, the Germans still held the mountain. The Marines, reeling from exhaustion, dug in for the night. From their foxholes they gazed with bleary eyes at the heavily defended enemy emplacements and knew that the next day would be even worse.

October 4 stands today as one of the bloodiest days in Marine Corps history. At dawn, while the Marines were advancing toward the village of St.-Étienne, the German Army launched a determined counterattack that disrupted the American assault and pounded the Marines particularly hard. By midmorning the Marines had withered under sustained fire from three directions and the fiercest artillery bombardment experienced by any American unit in the First World War. All along the front, Americans were slaughtered by fast-moving shock troops in an attack that represented Germany's last gasp. In one battalion a thousand Marines surged forward through the smoke, artillery fire, and a storm of bullets in a futile assault against an entrenched enemy. Nine hundred men fell and the Americans failed even to dent the German defenses. Every inch of territory the American troops captured was bought with blood.

Sergeant Dan Daly

Despite all their efforts, the Imperial German Army failed. Blanc Mont Ridge was captured on October 5 with heavy losses on both sides. With their high ground lost, the German Army began its final retreat, unaware that their Kaiser had sent a cable to U.S. President Wilson asking for an armistice. But despite this diplomatic opening, the slaughter continued unabated. Over the next four days, the fighting would be particularly fierce around St.-Étienne. The Marines suffered more than 2,500 casualties, and one company lost 90 percent of its strength. The Germans staged devastating night attacks in an effort to dislodge the Marines from their defensive positions.

In the struggle for St.-Étienne, the Corps suffered a stinging loss. First Sergeant Dan Daly—the hero of Belleau Wood, two-time Medal of Honor recipient for actions in Peking and Haiti, and valued member of the Corps' Old Breed—was severely wounded and had to be evacuated. Daly was a one-man army, a hero whose exploits inspired other heroes. "The most astounding Marine of all time," according to Marine Corps Commander John Lejeune, who had intimate knowledge of Sergeant Daly's exploits. "The fightin'est Marine I ever knew," declared Major Smedley Darlington Butler—an extraordinary nod from one fighting man to another.

Daniel Joseph Daly was born on November 11, 1873, in Glen Cove, Long Island, but much of his early life was spent hustling for work on the mean streets of New York City. His first job came when he was nine. Daly worked as a newsboy in New York City's Park Row section. He had other odd jobs growing up, but no civilian pursuit could satisfy his curiosity and thirst for adventure, so he enlisted in the Marine Corps during the Spanish-American War—too late to see action. His baptism of fire would come in the defense of the Legation quarter in Peking, where he earned his first Medal of Honor. Daly later fought in Haiti and became the only enlisted Marine in history to earn the Medal of Honor for two separate actions. During his distinguished career, Dan Daly was also awarded the Navy Cross and Army Distinguished Service Cross for heroism at Belleau Wood. It was at Belleau Wood where Daly uttered the immortal cry: "Come on, you sons of bitches, do you want to live forever?" At least that's what war correspondent Floyd Gibbons reported in his dispatches and in his rousing memoirs published after the war, *And They Thought We Wouldn't Fight*. But Daly himself disputed Gibbons's version of this famous quote, and insisted that what he really cried out was an exasperated plea to get his men moving: "For Christ's sake, men—COME ON! Do you want to live forever?"

Whatever the actual cry, Daly's reputation grew to near-mythic proportions after the story reached America. According to an anecdote told by historian Frank Janual in an article for *Over There!*, a young Marine, fresh to the shores of Europe, when told that Dan Daly would be his sergeant cried out: "My God! Do you mean he's real? I thought he was somebody the Marines made up—like Paul Bunyan."

Indeed, Dan Daly may have been bigger than Paul Bunyan—he was cool in the face of danger, brave to a fault, a tough, fair, and inspiring leader, and a living symbol of the fighting spirit of the Marines Corps. Yet Daly was also humble and seemed bemused by his legendary status, and he was modest about his astounding feats of courage. Yet Daly's Distinguished Service Cross, awarded for his actions in the First World War, began as a recommendation for an unprecedented *third* Medal of Honor. The citation was downgraded by high command because they believed that no one should have three awards—an opinion that Daly himself subscribed to. His Distinguished Service Cross was actually the result of two actions. At Belleau Wood, he risked his life by putting out an ammunition-dump fire, then captured a machine-gun nest single-handedly. There is no mention of his immortal rallying cry in the official citation. When Daly was wounded at St.-Étienne, an era came to an end. The last of the Old Breed had fallen. Daly could no longer remain on active duty and was shipped back to the United States on March 24, 1919, along with the first 600 Marines to be discharged from service in Europe.

When he returned to Long Island, a reporter asked Citizen Daly how he had earned his medals. His reply was rich with homespun humor: "I was out there pickin' pansies for my gal in Brooklyn one day," he said to the reporter, explaining that a car full of "brass hats" suddenly drove up and "pinned a medal on me."

Back in Glen Cove, Dan Daly became a homegrown hero. A precious few Marines die at home in their beds, but Daniel Joseph Daly was one of them. He passed away in Glendale, New York, on April 27, 1937, surrounded by his large and loving family. He was sixty-three. Daly was buried with honors in Cypress Hills National Cemetery in Brooklyn.

MEUSE-ARGONNE: THE FINAL BATTLE

The Meuse-Argonne Campaign began as an attempt to drive a wedge through a two-mile section of the Hindenburg Line and fill the gap with American soldiers. But the First Army in Europe faced two German divisions—one of them the Bavarian 15th Division, which the Marines had fought on Blanc Mont Ridge. Supported by artillery and a division of tanks, the offensive began on the morning of November 1, 1918, with the Marine Brigade in the forefront. By dusk the Americans had advanced seven miles into German territory and captured nearly 2,000 enemy soldiers.

At the Meuse River, the Germans took a stand. Fighting was fierce and the stubborn resistance the Americans faced surprised them. All over the front the Imperial German Army was in retreat, but not the troops facing the Americans. Here the enemy mounted stiff resistance against the First Army.

It wasn't until November 4 that the Americans probed the banks of the Meuse, searching for a suitable crossing point. The Germans had destroyed the bridges during their retreat, but the Marines, with help from U.S. Army engineering units, eventually crossed the river on November 10, 1918, the 143rd birthday of the Corps.

On the opposite shore, the Germans had the advantage. They held the high ground and were well entrenched. But the Americans mounted assault after assault. Compounding the misery was the fact that an armistice that would end hostilities was about to be signed and everyone knew it. To the doughboys on the front, this final assault was deemed futile, and there was much anger and bitterness directed at the Allied commanders. But the orders for the attack came from General Foch himself. So after a brief assault on the morning of November 11, 1918, the armistice went into effect. After four years and three months of the most intense warfare the world had ever known, it was quiet on the Western Front. The First World War was over.

In all, 32,000 Marines fought in France. Though a relatively small number, it was a huge effort on the part of the Marine Corps, which had seldom fielded more than a division in any conflict before this one. The Corps swelled to seven times its original size in 1917–1918. At the close of the conflict, over 79,000 men served in the Marine Corps. For the first time in its history, the Marine Corps established a reserve force. By war's end, there were 7,500 men in the Reserves, ready to fight if needed. The Women's Marine Corps was also established. Opha Johnson, who enlisted in August 1918, was its first volunteer. Marine Corps Aviation was born during this period as Marines fought in the skies for the first time.

In World War I, the Marines had 9,000 wounded and 3,300 killed. They impressed their allies and the enemy with their tenacity and fighting spirit, and their exploits, as filtered through newspaper accounts, books, plays, and movies, would inspire the next generation of volunteers. But perhaps the greatest compliment came from U.S. Army General S.L.A. Marshall, who stated that the Marines who fought in Europe were "without doubt the most aggressive body of diehards on the Western Front."

CHAPTER EIGHT

THE BANANA WARS

■

1919–1939

T HE Treaty of Versailles that effectively ended hostilities in Europe sowed the seeds of future conflict. Cooperation among the Western nations seemed to end with the war, and instead of fostering goodwill, the Treaty angered and embittered the defeated nations and made the victors appear arrogant and vindictive. France's vengeful attitude toward its former enemies and the ruinous reparations they imposed on Germany and Austria caused social upheaval and paved the way for Adolf Hitler's rise to power in the 1920s.

President Woodrow Wilson's solution to growing international pressures was the League of Nations, a political body that would moderate disputes through diplomacy. But this early prototype of the United Nations was doomed when the U.S. Congress failed to ratify its treaty or join the organization. Without America as a participating member, the power, prestige, and effectiveness of the League was greatly reduced. In the Pacific Rim, political decisions made after the war also set the stage for future conflict. In 1919, the League of Nations mandated that all Pacific Islands once held by Germany should be handed over to the Japanese as a reward for their "help" during hostilities. With the sweep of a pen, the Marshall Islands, the Marianas, the Carolines, and the Palaus were given over to Japanese control. In the next two decades, the Japanese militarized these islands along with Saipan, Tinian, and Rota. Japanese expansion in the Pacific would soon clash with American interests in the region, leading to all-out war in 1941. Americans would die by the thousands in hard-fought campaigns to neutralize or capture these fortified Japanese strongholds.

There *were* those who warned against Japanese militarism before and after the First World War. The Corps' own visionary prophet was Lieutenant Colonel Earl H. "Pete" Ellis. On the civilian side, it was author and adventurer Jack London, who witnessed Japanese militarization long before anyone in the diplomatic corps took notice. Both men traveled extensively and both wrote of their concerns. Colonel Ellis was especially vocal, and he was also the exception. Few in the high command had time to ponder the possibilities of a future war in the Pacific. They had more immediate concerns. Peacetime politicians were scoring points with their constituencies by promising to downsize the military. Some even spoke of doing away with the Marine Corps altogether. Prosperity was the order of the day. Few politicians wanted to "squander" valuable resources on useless and outmoded institutions like the Marine Corps. Wasn't the First World War supposed to be "the war to end all wars"? They asked. Why, then, did the United States need armed forces at all?

As naive as this statement sounds today, it was the prevailing opinion in the post–World War I era. In the decades following the war, every branch of the military experienced downsizing. Without a unique role in national defense, the Marine Corps was more vulnerable than the other services. Though the Leathernecks returned from the First World War as conquering heroes, their lack of a distinctive mission—one that would not compete with the U.S. Army's role—threatened the Marine Corps existence. Two visionary Marines stemmed this rising tide of antimilitary feeling and preserved the Corps' integrity for future generations. One was Lieutenant Colonel Ellis, who uncannily predicted the fury of the coming Pacific war and proposed a strategy to deal with the Japanese. The other was the future commandant of the Marine Corps, John Lejeune, who brought Ellis's plans to fruition.

Colonel Ellis served in France as part of the Fourth Marine Brigade. After the war he joined the Marine Corps general staff and in 1921 he wrote his groundbreaking study, *Operation Plan 712: Advanced Base Operations in Micronesia, 1921.* "It will be necessary for us to project our fleet and landing forces across the Pacific and wage war in Japanese waters," Ellis predicted. In just two decades his prophecy would become reality. After publishing his study, he took a leave of absence to travel through the Central Pacific region on a fact-finding mission. He visited many island chains and gathered valuable intelligence about Japanese military activities. Lieutenant Colonel Ellis would have been an invaluable asset in the Second World War, but fate—or perhaps the Japanese—had other plans for him. During a visit to the Japanese-controlled Palau Islands, he died under mysterious circumstances. He may have been poisoned by his Japanese hosts, or he may have died of natural causes; some believe it may have been acute alcoholism. The truth will never be known, but whatever the cause of his demise, Lieutenant Colonel Ellis's ideas would change the course of the Corps' evolution in the twentieth century.

John Lejeune, the Cajun Leatherneck who was appointed commandant in June 1920, was impressed with Ellis's work. An energetic leader with strong opinions and a clear vision of how the Corps should operate, Lejeune would transform the mission and the culture of the Marine Corps during his nine-year tenure by stressing the importance of amphibious operations and hands-on combat experience. After months of fighting on the Western Front, many officers in the Corps had learned to think like Army men. Under Commandant Lejeune, the Marines returned to their naval roots. "A mobile Marine Corps force adequate to conduct offensive land operations against hostile Naval bases" was Commandant Lejeune's vision. He convinced Congress and the Navy to go along with this plan, and in the winter of 1923–1924, combined units of the Marine Corps and the United States Navy conducted experimental fleet-landing exercises in the Caribbean. Though the results were less than spectacular, the Marines managed to learn a thing or two about amphibious operations.

Despite Commandant Lejeune's best efforts, the Corps was ultimately downsized, retaining less than a third of its peak strength of 75,000 men during the First World War. The numbers were reduced so drastically that Lejeune never again had enough troops to conduct amphibious landing exercises. But he did manage to retain a core of officers who participated in these maneuvers, and he always made sure his Marines gained valuable combat experience whenever the opportunity arose. During the 1920s, these opportunities arose often, and Lejeune willingly dispatched his Marines to every hot spot where America's interests, lives, or property were threatened.

The hottest spots in the 1920s were Haiti and the Dominican Republic in the Caribbean and Nicaragua in Central America. The United States had already intervened in each place, fighting a series of "Banana Wars" before the First World War erupted. A permanent Marine Corps detachment had been stationed in Haiti since its occupation began in 1915. Now, with the ink hardly dry on the Treaty of Versailles, more Marine Corps "advisers" were dispatched to Port-au-Prince to preserve order and protect American interests in the Republic of Haiti.

The twenty-three-year-long military campaign in Haiti would be the Marine Corps' longest and least successful military operation. It began with the American occupation in 1915 and did not end until President Franklin D. Roosevelt ordered the Marines out of the country in 1937. Before World War I, fighting men like Sergeant Dan Daly became heroes by participating in small, hit-and-run operations against the Cacos, as the Haitian bandits—or revolutionaries, depending on your political point of view—were called. The war in Europe had interrupted these operations, but the Marines returned in strength soon after the war in Europe ended.

Before he was dispatched to the trenches, Smedley Butler helped establish the Gendarmerie d'Haïti, a native police force officered and trained by U.S. Marines. The gendarmes were created to keep the peace, but despite their good works, they were universally hated by Haitians. Anti-American feelings were running high because of the criminal antics of a number of corrupt American officials and an edict that forced able-bodied Haitians to work without compensation. The workers were needed to help the Gendarmerie and American occupation force construct roads, bridges, sewage systems, and schools. Though these public works greatly improved conditions, the resentment over forced labor laws far outweighed any positive results. Haiti *was* a nation of former slaves and the Corps' forced labor policies were, at the very least, insensitive to the feelings of the people.

The chaos began during a crisis in the Haitian National Assembly. Future U.S. President Franklin Roosevelt had drafted a new constitution for the Haitian people, one that gave renewed legality to the American occupation. But the assembly refused to ratify Roosevelt's constitution and moved to draft their own—a document that was far less friendly to the occupation forces. The situation came to a head on June 19, 1917, when Smedley Butler and a squad of Marines stormed into the National

Assembly chambers and dissolved the institution. This rash and highly criticized action destabilized the Haitian government and precipitated a new era of guerrilla warfare in the countryside. The violence erupted on October 11, 1917.

Haitians objecting to the forced labor laws attacked the home of Captain John L. Doxey, who commanded the Gendarmerie in the Hinche district of central Haiti. The gendarmes easily defeated the attackers, killed the Caco leader, and captured his lieutenant. Implicated during the subsequent trial were three brothers named Peralte. Two were captured and tried, the third escaped. Only one, Charlemagne, was found guilty of revolutionary activity; he was sentenced to five years' hard labor. Despite his European education, Charlemagne was put to work sweeping the streets of Cap Haitien, a humiliating task that further inflamed his revolutionary fervor. In September 1918, he fled to the mountains to establish makeshift headquarters. He quickly attracted thousands of followers. His ultimate goal was to drive the Americans out, but Peralte's more immediate concerns were feeding and equipping his growing Caco army, so he set out on a campaign to supply his rebels.

Peralte proved to be a formidable resistance leader and an accomplished jungle fighter. His men ambushed supply convoys and heavily armed Gendarmerie detachments, murdered Haitians they considered collaborators, burned Gendarmerie headquarters in several northern districts, and seized food, supplies, and American weapons. Soon the Marines were waging twenty firefights a month against Peralte's Cacos and the rebellion was spreading. Peralte enlisted another Caco leader named Benoit Batraville. Soon these chiefs divided Haiti between themselves— Batraville controlled the Cacos in central Haiti, Peralte commanded the rebels in the north. The Cacos gained momentum and popular support as months of guerrilla activity dragged on.

November 10, 1918, was the Corps' 143rd birthday and the date of the final assault against the Germans along the Meuse River. On that same day Marine First Sergeant Patrick F. Kelly, a lieutenant in the Gendarmerie, led a detachment against the Cacos in the Hinche District of Haiti. The hour-long battle that followed was the first decisive action of the new campaign. During Kelly's offensive, thirty-five rebels were killed before the Cacos were driven out of the district and back to the hills. Sergeant Kelly became a hero to the gendarmes under his command. Later on, Kelly, now promoted to captain, was saved from certain death when he and his men were ambushed by Cacos. One of Kelly's gendarmes selflessly threw himself in front of an assassin's bullets. The native gendarme lost an arm and a leg in the attack, but become a hero in his own right.

The violence continued until, on March 21, 1919, Marine Sergeant Nicholas B. Moskoff and five of his gendarmes were ambushed by a large force of Cacos. Moskoff was mortally wounded with a bullet to the spine. His men, all native Haitians, carried their injured commander to safety as they fought a two-hour retreating action to escape the enemy. During the attack, Moskoff's second-in-command was wounded. The gendarmes watched in horror as the Cacos decapitated him. Sergeant Moskoff made it to a field hospital but later died of his injuries.

The situation in Haiti was deteriorating and the Marines reacted by sending in an entire brigade, commanded by Brigadier General Albertus W. Catlin, twice-wounded

Colonel Albertus W. Catlin

Colonel Herman H. Hanneken

hero of the Battle of Belleau Wood. The Fourth Marine Air Squadron was also dispatched to the country, where thirteen rickety aircraft—outmoded Jn-4 "Jenny" biplanes—would first experiment with low-level glide-bombing tactics. This was the beginning of modern air-ground operations pioneered by Marine Corps aviators like Lieutenant Lawson H. M. Sanderson. The irony was that while the United States Navy ignored Sanderson's experiments, both Hitler's Luftwaffe and the Imperial Japanese Navy would utilize many of Sanderson's strategies during the *blitzkrieg* and the subsequent attack on Pearl Harbor.

The Marines discovered that Peralte was receiving supplies and help from people in Port-au-Prince, the Haitian capital. On October 7, he openly attacked the capital city, perhaps counting on a popular uprising to oust the Americans. Although the Cacos were finally driven off by the gendarmes, the attack was so bold that headquarters was becoming alarmed. It was hard to know who was a friend and who was an enemy—a disagreeable situation that would arise a half century later during the war in Vietnam. Though the Marines sent large numbers of men into the hills to capture the rebel leader, it wasn't the military that defeated Peralte. The Caco leader was stopped in one of the first covert operations ever mounted by the Marine Corps. The scheme was the brainchild of twenty-six-year-old Sergeant Herman H. Hanneken, a St. Louis native then serving as a captain in the gendarmerie.

Hanneken was a contradictory figure; tall, blond, and powerfully built, he studied to become a Roman Catholic priest before moving west to lead a rough-and-tumble life as a cowboy. A few years after quitting the seminary, he enlisted in the Marine

Corps and soon joined the detachment in Haiti. Sergeant Hanneken got along with the men under his command—so much so that he convinced two loyal Haitian civilians and a gendarme to work undercover for him. A wealthy Haitian businessman named Jean B. Conze risked his life repeatedly during this covert operation, gathering intelligence among the Cacos and delivering the information to Hanneken on a regular basis.

The plan to catch Peralte was simple. First, Hanneken's double agents publicly denounced the United States occupation and established themselves as Caco chiefs near the town of Fort Capois. Within a few weeks these operatives attracted a number of followers and were soon visited by emissaries representing Charlemagne Peralte himself. Hanneken and the Marines under his command staged several mock raids on the "Cacos" operating on the outskirts of Fort Capois—and one time the sergeant even wore his arm in a sling while he walked through the town, feigning a battlefield wound. A few weeks later Hanneken sent a portion of his Gendarmerie force marching back to Cap Haitien while quietly spreading the rumor that the Americans feared a Caco attack in their "weakened" state.

Finally, Jean Conze, still posing as a Caco, convinced Peralte to attack the Marine garrison at Grande Rivière du Nord. Peralte arrived at Fort Capois on Sunday, October 26, 1919, with a thousand men to plan an assault scheduled for Friday, October 31. It was determined that Peralte would wait at Mazare, a thirty-minute march from the scene of the attack. If the assault went well, he would march triumphantly to the American base at Grande Rivière du Nord to proclaim victory.

The Marines prepared for this assault by secretly reinforcing the garrison with troops and machine guns. Then they lay in wait for the Caco attack. Meanwhile, Sergeant Hanneken and fellow Missourian Corporal William R. Button had their faces and arms blackened so they could pass for Haitians. Then they led twenty well-armed gendarmes disguised in dirty, ragged civilian clothes to Mazare to locate Charlemagne Peralte. But the Caco leader had had second thoughts. Instead of showing up at Mazare, Peralte decided to wait out the battle on a hill between Fort Capois and Grande Rivière. After the battle Jean Conze was supposed to send word to Peralte—the code for victory was "General Jean." Hanneken and Button decided they would carry the "victorious" news to Peralte personally. With their gendarme "deserter" Jean Edmond François, the two marines hiked for three hours, passing through several rebel roadblocks designed to protect the Caco leader from just such acts of duplicity. But Jean François was a trusted figure and helped clear the way for the two Americans, whose disguises would not stand up to close scrutiny. Hanneken was armed with two .45-caliber revolvers, but Corporal Button carried a Browning automatic rifle, an obvious Marine Corps weapon. At the fifth outpost the Americans were stopped by suspicious sentries. Corporal Button's BAR had attracted undue attention, but François smoothed over the trouble by insisting that Button had taken the weapon from a dead *blanc* and wished to present it to Peralte personally. The ploy worked and the group was allowed to pass.

At last the Marines slipped through the final sentry post and moved toward a small force camping in the hills. Hanneken and Button immediately recognized Charlemagne Peralte as they entered the rebel camp. The Caco leader was standing over a campfire, speaking to a woman. Jean François dropped behind the two Marines to cover their backs as Hanneken and Button moved within range of the rebel leader. At fifteen feet Sergeant Hanneken shot the Caco leader twice in the chest with a .45 as Button opened fire with his Browning, cutting down Peralte's bodyguards. Within a few minutes, Corporal Button and Jean François cleared the area while Hanneken grabbed Peralte's corpse. At the sound of gunfire the rest of the gendarmes moved swiftly into the camp, killing any Cacos still standing. Then Hanneken and his men established defensive positions to ward off a possible counterattack while they waited for daybreak.

At dawn they slung the corpse of Charlemagne Peralte over the back of a mule and left the camp. Fending off repeated attacks, the detachment returned to Grande Rivière du Nord, where the Marines waiting in ambush had thrown back the Caco assault and killed forty rebels. Next morning, Sergeant Hanneken led a second assault against the Cacos, killing more and driving the rest into the hills. Charlemagne Peralte was laid to rest in a block of cement—a precaution to prevent anyone digging up the rebel leader's corpse and reviving it as a zombie. This notion is not as ridiculous as it sounds. While few believed that Haitian shamans had the power to revive the dead, a resurrection ploy staged by the Cacos could easily inflame the populace to a new level of violence.

Today, Hanneken and Button's actions would merit international condemnation, a congressional investigation, and perhaps a court-martial. But things were different in the 1920s and Sergeant Hanneken and Corporal Button were both awarded the Medal of Honor for the heroism, skill, and initiative they displayed in the destruction of the Haitian leadership. Hanneken became a feared figure after the facts of Peralte's assassination became known. Over 300 Cacos surrendered to the sergeant in the weeks following Peralte's death, and in April, Sergeant Hanneken killed a second powerful leader during a surprise attack on the man's camp. For this second action Sergeant Hanneken was presented the Navy Cross.

This was only the beginning of Herman Hanneken's illustrious military career. He was commissioned in 1920, fought in the Second Nicaraguan Campaign and in the Pacific theater in World War II—where he earned the respect of his men and the nickname "Hard Head Hanneken." He retired from the Marine Corps in the late 1960s with the rank of brigadier general and moved to La Jolla, California, where he passed away on August 23, 1986, at the age of ninety-three. He was given a hero's burial at Fort Rosencrans National Cemetery in San Diego, California.

Corporal William Robert Button was not so fortunate. The young Marine from St. Louis contracted malaria and died of fever at Cap Haitien on April 15, 1921—nine months after he was presented his Medal of Honor by Commandant John Lejeune in a Washington, D.C., ceremony. Button was only twenty-five years old at the time of his death.

After the defeat of Charlemagne Peralte, the rebellion in the north sputtered and died. But in central Haiti, Benoit Batraville kept the pressure on the Americans— raiding towns, stealing military supplies, killing gendarmes, and beheading Marine Sergeant Lawrence Muth, a personal friend of Lieutenant Colonel Lewis "Chesty" Puller, Marine Corps legend of World War II and Korea. During the campaign against

▪ Pioneering Air-Ground Operations in Haiti

Lieutenant Lawson Sanderson commanded the Marine Corps Aviation detachment in Haiti and was a pioneer advocate of coordinated air-ground operations. The bombing and ground-support tactics he developed during the Haitian Campaign would be adopted by every military in the industrialized world in the decades to come. Sanderson believed that the traditional approach to aerial bombing was inherently flawed and that the horizontal, high-altitude attack was the reason the Marines had fared so poorly on their bombing runs over Europe during World War I. Wind drift, antiaircraft fire, smoke, and inadequate bombsights made pinpoint targeting impossible.

Sanderson searched for a new tactic to improve bombing accuracy. Through experimentation he discovered that he could hit his target with bombs by pushing an aircraft "over to a steep dive of 45 degrees, aiming the nose at the target, and releasing the bomb from about 250 feet." Today we call this tactic dive-bombing.

In Germany, officers charged with the responsibility of rebuilding the Luftwaffe after the Germany's defeat in the First World War were so impressed by Sanderson's innovation that they designed the Stuka dive-bomber to perform just such tricky aerial maneuvers. (Biplanes, because of the drag from the wires, struts, and fixed landing gear, could easily perform steep dives, but monoplanes like the Stuka had to be built with dive brakes to slow their descent.) The Stuka, used in conjunction with tanks and massed ground assaults, would become the backbone of Adolf Hitler's *blitzkrieg*. The dive-bomber, along with the tactics pioneered by Marine Lieutenant Lawson Sanderson—helped Hitler conquer Europe in 1939–1940.

During the Haitian conflict, Lieutenant Sanderson employed coordinated air-ground tactics in the fierce campaign against Benoit Batraville's Cacos. Rebels found themselves trapped in the crossfire between attacking ground troops and strafing aircraft. These tactics were further improved during the Second Nicaraguan Campaign, when accurate dive-bombing methods were tried for the first time. When air-ground radio communications were added to the mix during the Second World War, bombing and strafing accuracy improved even more. Through his pioneering efforts, Lawson Sanderson proved that airplanes could be utilized in direct support of ground forces, giving rise to the unique cooperation between Marine Corps airpower and ground units that persists to this day.

Batraville, Marine Corps Aviation units were employed to track rebel movements and support ground troops. Lieutenant Sanderson, who commanded the fliers in Haiti, even employed early dive-bombing tactics to harass the Cacos.

But the Marines couldn't seem to reach the heart of the rebellion—Benoit Batraville himself. That changed on May 18, 1920, when thirty Marines led by Captain Jesse L. Perkins attacked Batraville's main rebel camp. Sergeant William F. Passmore spotted the Caco leader as he tried to flee the battlefield. Dropping to one knee, Passmore fired, killing Batraville. When the corpse was examined, it was discovered that the rifle the rebel leader carried had once belonged to Sergeant Dan Daly, who lost it in a Haitian ambush before the First World War—the very ambush that earned him his second Medal of Honor. A revolver tucked in Batraville's belt had been issued to Sergeant Muth. It was later discovered that Benoit Batraville had personally cut out Muth's heart and eaten it, along with the man's liver.

With the deaths of Charlemagne Peralte and Benoit Batraville, the Haitian uprising ceased to exist and order was duly restored. But the Marines would remain active in Haiti for eighteen more years. They built roads and bridges, trained members of the Gendarmerie, organized a postal system, and built and taught in schools. Though they never won the "hearts and minds" of the populace, the United States Marines in Haiti did manage to impose social order and improve the standard of living for generations of Haitians.

THE SECOND NICARAGUAN CAMPAIGN

One of the most remarkable feats in the annals of Marine Corps Aviation occurred in January 1928 during a protracted campaign against rebels in Nicaragua. Trouble had begun nearly twenty years before, in 1909, with the execution of two idealistic United States citizens who joined forces with a revolutionary group attempting to overthrow the dictatorship of President José Zelaya. The U.S. government broke off relations with Managua and sent in the Marines to aid the rebels, led by the charismatic Adolfo Díaz. With the help of the Navy and Marine Corps, Díaz eventually seized power and negotiated a treaty of friendship with the United States.

By 1910, U.S. forces had departed from Nicaragua, but 2,000 Marines were sent back two years later to shore up the Díaz government, which was under pressure from a brand-new crop of left-wing revolutionaries. By the close of 1912, the United States was in control of Nicaragua's export trade through its customhouse, and a Marine Corps detachment was permanently installed to keep order in Managua, the capital city. By 1925, U.S. President Calvin Coolidge was ready to pull the Marines out of the country altogether, but a new round of unrest changed his mind. Secretary of State Frank Kellogg justified this third intervention by claiming that Communist rebels were trying to establish a foothold in the western hemisphere. But the rebels causing trouble weren't Communists—they were cranky and idealistic leftists trying to oust the aging Adolfo Díaz, whom they saw as a corrupt puppet of the United States. Díaz was resisting the totalitarian rule of General Emiliano Chamorro Vargas, who had declared himself president in a coup that sent his political rivals fleeing into exile.

Washington spurned the rebels and sided with America's old ally, Adolfo Díaz. Lawyer, statesman, and diplomat Henry L. Stinson was sent to Managua to negotiate a settlement and help establish the Guardia Nacional, a Nicaraguan national guard patterned after the gendarmes of Haiti. The Guardia would be recruited, trained, and officered by Marines.

But the Guardia Nacional would not be operational for many months, and immediate action was required to stem the rising tide of anti-American sentiment, which was spreading beyond Nicaragua's borders to other Latin American countries. The Mexican government became involved, insisting that exiled leader Juan Sacasa, who was hiding somewhere in Guatemala, was really the legitimate president of Nicaragua. With the help of the Mexican Army and the Guatemalans, Sacasa would return to his native land to make trouble for the Americans. With a rebel army led by José María Moncado controlling much of eastern Nicaragua, it seemed inevitable that Moncado and Sacasa would join forces against the Marines.

This happened in December 1926. For the next few weeks the revolutionaries rampaged along the Mosquito Coast, raiding American fruit plantations, railroad supply depots, lumber companies, and mining facilities. Finally, at Puerto Cabeza, a U.S. citizen was killed and the Marines were ordered ashore in force to establish "neutral" areas of protection for American citizens. As Moncado's army moved toward Managua, the Marines, under the command of Lieutenant Colonel James J. Meade, assumed responsibility for the defense of the capital. Brigadier General

Logan Feland arrived on March 7 with the Marine Corps Fifth Regiment and took command of all 2,000 Marines in Nicaragua.

Marine Observation Squadron One, under the general command of Major Ross E. Rowell, arrived at the end of February with six vintage, reconditioned De Havilland bombers left over from the First World War. "Rusty" Rowell was a forty-two-year-old Iowan who commanded fewer than a hundred officers and men. Yet despite his tiny force, Rowell and his pilots would make history in Nicaragua. They would be the first Marines to utilize air-to-ground communications and move troops and supplies by air into a combat zone. Rowell's aviators would also improve upon the dive-bombing tactics developed in Haiti and would be the first to dive-bomb an enemy.

In Managua, Henry Stinson was able to negotiate a settlement that all of the rebel factions signed—with the exception of one group. Two hundred revolutionaries commanded by fiery leader Augusto C. Sandino stubbornly vowed to continue the fight until all U.S. forces were withdrawn.

Sandino was a worth adversary. A slender, frail intellectual, he was a fervent nationalist who wanted Nicaragua to determine its own destiny. Moderately educated, the young rebel worked in the Mexican oil fields and marched alongside revolutionary Pancho Villa before he returned to his native land and joined the uprising against the American occupation forces.

Clashes between Sandino's revolutionaries and the Marines began almost immediately. They were small and sporadic until the early-morning hours of May 16, 1927, when a large group of rebels attacked the town of La Paz Centro, where there was a Marine garrison. Its commanding officer, Captain Richard B. Buchanan, led his troops in a counterattack. But the rebels were waiting in ambush for the Americans, and Captain Buchanan and Private Marvin A. Jackson were both killed before the rebels retreated back to the hills. Soon the Marines were howling for revenge, but Sandino and his men had already melted into the countryside, where the populace protected them. Traveling at night, Sandino led his army northward to the Honduran border, a sparsely populated region dotted with coffee plantations and mining operations.

A Marine garrison commanded by Captain Gilbert D. Hatfield followed the rebels with a detachment from the Guardia Nacional in tow. Hatfield established a base at Ocotal, the provincial capital and a town sympathetic to Sandino and his cause. On the night of July 15, Sandino's forces, numbering about 500 men, began to infiltrate Ocotal. At 1:15 A.M., a sentry at the thick-walled Spanish house where the Marines were billeted saw shadows moving in the street and fired a warning shot. This vigilant sentry probably saved his garrison from annihilation.

The element of surprise lost, Sandino's men emerged from the shadows and surrounded the house. Inside, thirty Marines of Captain Hatfield's command were now effectively trapped. Though the forty-eight-man Guardia detachment housed in a building across the street was able to support the Marines with rifle fire, without tactical training and automatic weapons they were unable to mount a counterattack to break the rebel siege. Three times Sandino's men charged the house. Three times the Marines beat them back, inflicting heavy casualties on the rebel forces. After two hours, there was a lull as both sides waited for dawn. At sunup the Marines could see dead rebels lying in the streets and hoped that the enemy had finally withdrawn. But by midmorning Sandino's forces attacked again, and a spokesman for the rebels demanded that the Marines surrender. Captain Hatfield, calling from a window of the bullet-scarred house, explained that Marines were not taught how to surrender, so he and his men had no choice but to fight on. This reply amused Hatfield's Marines and confounded the rebels—didn't these Americans know when they were beaten? Actually the Marines knew something the rebels didn't. They knew help was on the way.

Later that morning two of Major Rowell's De Havillands flew over the town. Anticipating the arrival of this routine air patrol, the Marines used aerial signal panels—white cloth sheets used to spell out messages to low-flying aircraft—to request relief. After the pilots read the message, they used hand signals to formulate a plan. One airplane proceeded to strafe the enemy while the second—flown by Lieutenant Hayne D. Boyden—circled the town to reconnoiter enemy positions and gauge rebel strength. The Sandinos were stunned by the arrival of the patrol and the unexpected air attack that followed. They fled into surrounding buildings, leaving their dead behind.

Meanwhile, Lieutenant Boyden landed his De Havilland on the outskirts of Ocotal and learned from a peasant that the Marines were surrounded. Boyden flew back to Managua to report while Polish-born Chief Marine Gunner Michael Wodarczyk—nicknamed the "Polish Warhorse" by his squadron mates—continued to strafe the rebels with his DH-4's forward machine gun. Finally, low on fuel and out of ammo, Wodarczyk was forced to break off the attack and return to his base in Managua, 110 miles away. When Sandino's men saw the aircraft depart, they felt safe enough to prepare a final assault against the Marine compound. It took several hours for the rebels to position their forces, but just as they were moving toward the besieged garrison, five DH-4s dived out of the afternoon sky. At 3:35 P.M., the first dive-bombing mission in military history began.

One by one, the De Havilland biplanes dipped into a steep dive from an altitude of 1,500 feet. At about 300 feet—and sometimes much lower—the airplanes released their seventeen- and twenty-five-pound bombs and pulled up. During the vertical descent, the forward machine guns blazed, cutting down rebels trapped in the open streets. After the drop, the rear gunner fired on the rebels as the DH-4 streaked back into the sky. The rebels who were caught in the open, and many who took shelter in the surrounding buildings, were slaughtered by this highly effective attack. "The ground was strewn with the dead and dying," wrote Marine Corps historian William L. Roper. "Houses, in which [the rebels] had taken refuge were demolished. Groups were in stampede."

Things only got worse for Sandino's forces as the day wore on. After the bombing run, the rebels mistakenly clustered in groups to fire at the airplanes, making themselves easy targets. The pilots continually strafed the streets, cutting down rebels and driving the citizens of Ocotal out of their city. During the forty-five-minute attack, over 4,000 rounds of ammunition were expended and twenty-seven bombs were dropped. Over a hundred Sandino rebels were killed. Many more were wounded and escaped. When their ammunition was spent, the warplanes headed for home. Along the way they flew into a thunderstorm, ran out of gas, and were forced to make emergency landings at the village of León. But despite this complication, the first dive-bombing mission in history was a rousing success.

Emboldened by air support, Captain Hatfield rallied his Marines and cleaned out the rest of Ocotal. Fifty-six rebel corpses were recovered from the streets, more from shattered buildings. The Marines lost seven men—six wounded and one killed. For the rebels, the battle at Ocotal was a rout. Major Rowell was awarded the first Distinguished Flying Cross ever earned by a Marine. Before this attack, Augusto Sandino had scoffed at the effectiveness of military aircraft. He was quoted in *The New York Times* as telling his men that airplanes "only made noise." If this was true, the Marines in Nicaragua made a noise loud enough to be heard around the world. Air-combat tactics were forever transformed by the actions of Rowell and his airborne Marines on this hot afternoon in July 1927. After his stinging defeat at Ocotal, Sandino was forced to curtail rebel activities. He could no longer move forces in daylight or mount an attack against a fortified position without being spotted from the air. The uprising was pretty much over. Augusto Sandino just didn't know it yet.

The rebels, in full retreat, struck the village of Telpaneca east of Ocotal. They killed two Marines and raided the town before moving to a rugged mountain stronghold called El Chipote. It was the start of the rainy season, so Sandino figured he would be safe for the time being. He did not take into account America's resolve, or the increasingly sophisticated tactics of the Marine Observation Squadron. Marine aviators constantly patrolled the mountains, trying to locate Sandino's hidden fortress. The Marines also brought in brand-new Fokker trimotor transports to supply the infantrymen scouring the mountains on horseback. These planes hauled everything from food to ammunition to mules to tobacco to the soldiers' pay.

On October 8, 1927, the rebels managed to shoot down one of two low-flying De Havilland airplanes patrolling around Quilali. Gunner Wodarczyk, at the controls of a second De Havilland, saw his comrades crash and burn. He was not sure if there was survivors. Wodarczyk flew back to his base to report the loss and mount a rescue attempt. Miraculously, the two Marine aviators *had* survived the crash and fled the scene in an effort to elude the rebels. Second Lieutenant Earl A. Thomas and Sergeant Frank E. Dowdell had taken refuge in a cave when the rebels captured them. They were never seen again.

Meanwhile, mounted Marines and members of the Guardia had been dispatched from Ocotal to rescue the downed pilots. Led by First Lieutenant George J. O'Shea, this party was ambushed near the crash site and barely escaped with their lives. They had to fight their way back down the mountain, losing both horses and supplies—but at least there were no additional casualties. The pursuit of Sandino and his rebels continued despite the loss of two airmen. The Americans knew they had to drive the rebels out of El Chipote—but first they would have to locate the secret stronghold.

On November 23, 1927, Marine aircraft pinpointed the location of the rebels. After that, weather permitting, the Marines made daily bombing runs on El Chipote. After a few weeks, the old De Havillands were replaced by newer Vought Corsairs and Curtiss Falcons—two rugged biplanes with much greater bomb-carrying capabilities. With an infusion of new equipment, the campaign against the rebel base at El Chipote intensified.

On January 14, 1928, the largest bombing mission yet staged dropped eighteen seventeen-pound bombs, four fifty-pound demolition bombs, and an additional eighteen white phosphorus hand grenades on El Chipote. The stronghold was wrecked and 1,500 rebels finally abandoned it in February. Unfortunately, Sandino's men escaped into the countryside before U.S. ground forces could engage them. In truth, these ground forces—made up of 140 Marines led by Captain Richard Livingston—had problems of their own. On the last day of December 1927, they had left Ocotal for El Chipote but were ambushed by the rebels a mile south of Quilali, a village precariously poised on the edge of a tall cliff. In a ninety-minute fight, five Marines were killed and twenty-three of them, including Livingston himself, were wounded.

A second force of Guardia members was dispatched to rescue Livingston's men but were ambushed as they approached Quilali from the north. Dynamite bombs and machine-gun fire killed First Sergeant Thomas G. Bruce, who won the Navy Cross at the battle for Ocotal. A Guardia sergeant named Policarpo Gutiérrez lost his arm recovering Bruce's body. The men, encircled by rebels, finally charged up Las Cruces Hill and took the crest, where they dug in and waited for help. After Marine Corps warplanes strafed the enemy, a rifle platoon rushed out of Quilali and pushed on to relieve the Marines on the hill. This combined force spent the night on Las Cruces, then broke and ran for the town at dawn. They reached Quilali by midmorning and found Captain Livingston and thirty other wounded Marines in desperate need of medical attention. With two detachment of Marines now in Quilali, Sandino's forces laid siege to the town. The Americans and their Guardia allies were effectively trapped. They were also low on ammunition, food, and water. Only a miracle could save them.

Enter First Lieutenant Christian F. Schilt, a tall, gangly thirty-two-year-old former racing pilot from Olney, Illinois. Schilt—who loved fast airplanes and danger—volunteered to fly in supplies and bring out the wounded despite the fact that the town had no airfield. Schilt claimed he could land his plane in the middle of main street. At Quilali, the Marines got word of the proposed evacuation and received their instructions through notes dropped from low-flying aircraft. They set to work leveling the buildings on either side of the main street, transforming the boulevard into an instant landing strip. But the strip was perilously short and ended with a 200-foot drop over a steep cliff, and the Vought O2U-1 Corsair biplane Schilt would be flying had no landing brakes. As soon as the wheel touched the ground Marines were told to rush forward and grab the wings before the rolling aircraft plunged over the cliff. To keep the aircraft's weight down, Schilt removed the machine guns and left his parachute behind.

As Lieutenant Schilt made his first approach, rebels emerged from cover and fired volley after volley at his airplane. Dodging bullets, Schilt had to stall the engine and literally drop the plane the final ten feet to the ground. The Corsair landed with a bump and bounced several times before the Marines jumped onto the wings to slow it down. It finally rolled to a halt less than forty feet from the edge of the cliff. Under constant fire the Marines unloaded their supplies and strapped those most seriously

First Lieutenant Christian F. Schilt

wounded onto the wings—one on each side to balance the aircraft. When Schilt took off again, his overburdened aircraft plunged over the edge of the precipice and dropped from sight before rising again and lumbering home.

From January 6 to January 8, 1928, Lieutenant Schilt made ten daring landings at Quilali, each time under enemy fire. He brought in 1,400 pounds of supplies and evacuated eighteen of the most grievously wounded Marines. Every trip was fraught with danger. On his eighth landing Schilt wrecked his tail skid and later took off without it. On his ninth landing the center struts bent under the shock of the bumpy descent onto the street. But the bold aviator pressed on until the town was finally relieved by ground troops. Schilt saved the lives of at least three Marines, whose wounds were so severe they would not have survived without immediate care. In the early-morning hours of January 10, a large force entered Quilali and drove the rebels off. The trapped Marines were finally rescued.

For his courage, First Lieutenant Christian Franklin Schilt received the Medal of Honor, presented to him by President Calvin Coolidge in a ceremony on the White House lawn. The following year, Schilt and aviator Charles A. Lindbergh worked out air routes over Nicaragua for Pan American Airways. Despite his newfound fame, Lieutenant Schilt remained a Marine, serving with the occupation forces in Nicaragua until the United States withdrew in 1933. During the Second World War, he rose to the rank of general. He retired from active duty due to ill health in the 1970s and passed away in Norfolk, Virginia, on January 8, 1987. He is buried at Arlington National Cemetery.

The Second Nicaraguan Campaign would drag on for another five years. Though the Marines never defeated the rebels in a decisive, face-to-face battle, their harassing tactics eventually forced Augusto Sandino to flee the country. Political unrest continued in Nicaragua, but the Marines increased the size and power of the Guardia until the native force could stand on their own against the rebels. It was the Guardia that finally ended the activities of the revolutionaries. After inviting the rebels to talks in Managua and guaranteeing the rebel leader's personal safety, members of the Guardia ambushed and assassinated Augusto Sandino. It was an ignominious end to a competent and accomplished revolutionary, but Sandino's legacy would endure to the 1970s, when the Sandinistas, Communist rebels named in honor of Augusto Sandino, seized power in Nicaragua. These Communists were

First Lieutenant Christian F. Schilt

later ousted in free elections held in the 1980s but remained a thorn in America's side until their defeat.

The Marines who served in the Second Nicaraguan Campaign performed their duties under grueling conditions—weathering anti-American sentiments, three separate Guardia mutinies, election-day chaos, an earthquake that all but leveled the capital city of Managua, and near-constant rebel assaults. Legendary warriors like Captain Merritt A. Edson, First Lieutenant Evans F. Carlson, First Lieutenant Lewis B. "Chesty" Puller, and First Lieutenant Herman H. Hanneken would experience their first taste of jungle fighting in Nicaragua. This harsh and difficult on-the-job education would pay off in the global conflict to come.

▪ *Marine Corps Heroism Outside of Combat*

During the interim between the First and Second World Wars, two Marines received the Medal of Honor for courage and distinguished conduct—but not in combat. On the morning of February 11, 1921, twenty-three-year-old Private Albert Joseph Smith was on sentry duty at Gate No. 1 of the naval air station at Pensacola, Florida, right outside of the Marine barracks. At about 7:30 in the morning, Smith heard the sputtering of an aircraft engine. He looked up in time to watch a seaplane plunge out of the sky. The airplane slammed into the ground and broke apart. Within seconds the gas tank exploded, engulfing the aircraft in flames. Despite the danger, Private Smith climbed onto the burning wreckage to search for survivors. He found U.S. Navy Machinist Mate Second Class Plen M. Phelps pinned beneath the flaming debris. Despite suffering burns on his hands, arms, neck, and head, Smith dragged Phelps out of the wreckage to safety.

In October of that same year, while serving in the Dominican Republic, Private Smith was awarded the Medal of Honor for his act of selfless bravery by Brigadier General Henry Lee. A native of Calumet, Michigan, Smith eventually rose to the rank of sergeant. He passed away in Detroit, Michigan, in 1973.

On April 24, 1932, South Carolina native Corporal Donald Leroy Truesdell was the second-in-command of a Guardia patrol along the Coco River in Nicaragua. Truesdell was looking for armed bandits who had struck near the village of Constancia. His men had exchanged rifle fire with the bandits earlier that day and were following their trail to the river. One member of the patrol failed to properly secure his weapon and a rifle grenade fell from its carrier and struck a rock, igniting the detonator. With two or three seconds before the explosion, the patrol dived for cover. Truesdell, standing a few yards away, could have sought cover too. Instead, he grabbed the grenade and attempted to toss it away from the patrol.

The grenade exploded in his right hand, blowing it off and inflicting wounds on his head, neck, and body. The young corporal bore the brunt of the explosive force, saving his commanding officer as well as the lives of his comrades. He miraculously survived his wounds to receive the Medal of Honor. Donald Leroy Truesdell passed away in 1993.

PART THREE

THE CORPS COMES OF AGE: WORLD WAR II

"For us who were there, or whose friends were there, Guadalcanal is not a name but an emotion . . ."

—Samuel Eliot Morison, *The Struggle for Guadalcanal*

"God favors the bold and the strong of heart . . ."

—Medal of Honor recipient Major General Alexander Vandegrift in an address to his Marines before the siege of Guadalcanal

"Victory was inevitable. The only question was the price we would have to pay for it."

—Medal of Honor recipient Lieutenant Colonel David Shoup on Tarawa

"Everything about Peleliu left a bad taste in your mouth."

—an anonymous Marine during Operation Stalemate, the invasion of Peleliu, 1945

"Here lie officers and men. Negroes and whites, rich men and poor—together. Here are Protestants, Catholics, and Jews—together . . . No prejudices. No hatred. Theirs is the highest and purest democracy."

—from a eulogy for the dead at Iwo Jima by Chaplain Roland B. Gittelsohn, March 14, 1945

CHAPTER NINE

THE PACIFIC WAR BEGINS:
PEARL HARBOR, MIDWAY, GUADALCANAL

■

1941–1943

T HE December sun was a bright yellow ball in a sky that was cloudless and blue. At dawn the bugler blew reveille, the officers of the watch made their rounds, and the color guard raised the flag. But the United States military base at Pearl Harbor was slow to rise. It was Sunday and few duties had been scheduled. Though the bulk of the Pacific fleet was moored in the harbor, as it was nearly every weekend, the atmosphere was relaxed. It would not stay that way for long.

Political tensions had been running high in the Pacific for many months. A violent decade of military adventures in China that began with the Japanese invasion in 1931 had made the Western democracies uneasy. Though the United States was not at war with Japan, many believed a conflict was inevitable. A war had been raging in Europe since September 1939, and it was only a matter of time before America would be pulled into it. As a security precaution, extraordinary measures had been taken to guard the installation at Pearl Harbor. By order of the joint Army and Navy commanders, all aircraft had been moved out of their hangars to the center of the airfields, where MPs armed with .45s guarded them against saboteurs. Hawaii had a large Asian population; up to 150,000 people on the main island were of Japanese descent. Sabotage was a very real threat and military intelligence wondered how many agents might have already infiltrated the Asian community and were waiting to strike.

The aircraft carrier *Enterprise* had been dispatched from Pearl to Wake Island, loaded with a cargo of fighter airplanes for the Marines stationed there. Wake was poorly manned and needed fighter aircraft to boost its defenses. Like the *Lexington,* which was delivering Marine Corps aircraft to Midway Island, the *Enterprise* was not moored at Pearl on this particular Sunday. Two of America's other frontline carriers, the *Hornet* and the *Yorktown,* were on duty with the Atlantic fleet and the *Saratoga* was being refitted in San Diego. This happy accident would spare the carriers from destruction.

In an isolated section of Oahu, the U.S. Army hurried to establish a radar system. The experimental radar was meant to provide Pearl Harbor with advanced warning against the approach of hostile aircraft. Unfortunately, no one considered the need for someone at headquarters to alert in the event that the technicians manning the radar station actually detected something. When they spotted suspicious blips on their screens, the technicians reported it to a junior officer and were told to ignore the signal. They were informed that it was just a scheduled flight of B-17s.

Other precautions were ignored. There was no ammunition near the antiaircraft guns despite regulations to the contrary. Aircraft spotters were not positioned on the beaches or peaks around the base despite the fact that Pearl Harbor was supposed to be in a high state of readiness; the U.S. Army chief of staff had issued a warning on November 27, and on the twenty-eighth, the chief of naval operations informed Admiral Husband Kimmel that Pearl Harbor was a possible target of Japanese aggression. A follow-up alert had even been issued on Saturday and a written version was dispatched to Pearl by telegram because atmospherics had been so bad that no secure radio communications between the island and the mainland could be established. The letter arrived on the commander's desk on Sunday morning—in the middle of the Japanese attack.

DAY OF INFAMY

At Ewa Mooring Mast Field, Marine Captain Leonard Ashwell strolled out of the mess hall at 7:54 A.M. on Sunday, December 7, 1941, and heard the rumble of aircraft engines. He looked to the northern sky and spotted an orderly formation of Japanese torpedo bombers flying eastward. Seconds later twenty-one Zero fighters—the premier combat aircraft of the Japanese military—streaked over the mountains and dived on the airfield. As Captain Ashwell raced to the guardhouse to sound the alert, the Zeros opened fire on the sleeping base. Racing across the airfield at an altitude of twenty feet, the fighters strafed the aircraft of Marine Air Group 21. The planes were parked wing to wing in the middle of the field and guarded by MPs, as per General Short's antisabotage directive. In pass after pass, the Zeros shattered the undefended ranks of American warplanes.

The Marines did what they could to defend their base. There were no antiaircraft guns, so sergeants doled out rifles and handguns while troops hurriedly established makeshift defensive positions and returned fire. While Marines armed with rifles and machine guns shot at the Zeros, ground crews and pilots tried desperately to get a few airplanes into the sky. In desperation, some opened fire on the Japanese with machine guns ripped from wrecked American fighters. By 8:05 A.M. the first wave of the surprise attack was over. Thirty minutes later the Japanese returned with "Val" dive-bombers. This time they concentrated on the buildings, the hastily erected hospital tents set up to deal with the wounded from the first attack, and personnel on the ground who were mounting a vigorous defense.

Sergeant Emil F. Peters and Private William C. Turner dived for cover inside the cockpit of a parked bomber. As they loaded the rear machine gun, one Japanese pilot after another strafed their airplane. Sergeant Peters aimed the rear gun at an approaching enemy bomber and returned fire. Bullets tore through the engine block of the Val and the warplane staggered, burst into flames, and plunged into the tarmac. Enraged by the loss of their comrade, the other pilots concentrated their fire on the American plane, shredding the fuselage and wings. Sergeant Peters and Private Turner were both wounded. During a lull in the attack, the Marines were dragged from the shattered plane. Peters survived, but Private Turner succumbed to his injuries.

At the Marine barracks near the harbor, Major Harold Roberts, acting commander of the Third Defense Battalion, managed to deploy antiaircraft guns at strategic locations around the parade ground. Without voice or radio communications, he established an improvised early-warning system. He sent spotters into the center of the field accompanied by musicians from the battalion band. When the spotters saw enemy aircraft, the musicians used their instruments to provide azimuth indicators—one blast for north, two for east, three for south, and four for west. Using this code, the Marines were able to down several Japanese warplanes.

At 9:45, the surprise attack was over. The results of the two-hour bombardment were devastating. In the harbor four battleships of the Pacific fleet lay shattered, burned, or sunk. Four others, along with three cruisers, were heavily damaged; 2,280 soldiers, sailors, and Marines were dead and 1,109 were wounded. Untold numbers of sailors and Marines were trapped belowdeck in capsized warships like the *Arizona,* to perish from their wounds or from suffocation, in utter darkness, and without hope of rescue. At Ewa Field, four Marines were killed and thirteen wounded in the strafing attack. All forty-seven Marine Corps warplanes at Ewa were destroyed. None got off the ground.

The commanders at Pearl Harbor had grievously underestimated the resolve and ingenuity of the Imperial Japanese Navy. But the attack was not an unequivocal success. The Japanese committed several tactical blunders that would come back to haunt them as the war progressed. The attack failed to sink even one U.S. carrier—yet the aircraft carrier posed the greatest threat to Japanese hegemony in the Pacific. Carriers could ferry aircraft to within striking range of any Japanese-held island, or even, in the case of the Doolittle Raid, to the Japanese mainland. With carriers the United States Navy could still put up a vigorous fight. The Japanese also erred when they concentrated their dive-bomber attacks on the American warships and ignored the vital harbor installations and the equally important fuel-storage depots. Replacing the ships was far easier than rebuilding the base or pumping oil to replace the bounty stored at Pearl.

To be fair, Admiral Chuichi Nagumo, commander of the Japanese forces that struck Pearl, had planned to hit the land installations in the third wave. But when he learned that no carriers were present, he canceled this phase of the plan and withdrew, fearing the Americans were lying in wait for his fleet somewhere between the

Hawaiian Islands and Japanese waters. Because Admiral Nagumo had no way of knowing that the American carriers were too far out of range to mount a counterattack, his fear was justified. But because the dry docks and tank farms were spared, Pearl Harbor would continue to service and supply American ships and their allies throughout the war. Though the attack was a triumph, it was not the final, decisive victory the Japanese had hoped for. The United States Navy survived to fight another day. In the coming months, the Japanese would pin their hopes of victory on a final decisive naval battle against the United States Navy—a battle that never materialized.

THE MARINES ON DECEMBER 7

Yoshio Shiga was one of 600 Japanese airmen who participated in the attack on Pearl Harbor and one of several dozen pilots who strafed Ewa Field. During a low-level pass in his Zero fighter, he spotted a lone Marine standing near the shattered wreckage of an airplane. He circled the field, then dived at the man. Though the Zero's machine guns were blazing, the Marine refused to budge as bullets pitted the tarmac around him. To the Japanese pilot's surprise the American raised his pistol and returned fire! "The bravest American I ever encountered," Shiga said later.

There was no shortage of courage on that terrible day, and the duel between Japanese and American forces on December 7 did not end with the surprise attack on Pearl Harbor. That same morning—December 8 on China's side of the International Date Line—the U.S. Marine garrison in Chinwangtao was surrounded by Japanese soldiers. The twenty-two Marines in this village east of Tientsin were preparing to abandon their post when Japanese marines—the fierce *rikusentai*—rushed their compound. The Americans were outmatched, outflanked, and outgunned—and ready to fight to the death. Led by Chief Marine Gunner William F. "Ironman" Lee, a hard-bitten veteran of the Nicaraguan Campaign, the Marines established defensive positions and stared at their counterparts over the barrels of their rifles. It was a stalemate—neither side was willing to fire the first shot.

The Japanese had reason to fear Lee. A crack shot and expert at small arms and hand-to-hand combat, he was also a skilled knife fighter. He earned two Navy Crosses and the nickname "Ironman" in Nicaragua, where he fought alongside legendary Marine Lewis "Chesty" Puller, but it was in the Pacific where he would really earn the moniker. Second Lieutenant Richard M. Huizenga, the Marines' commander, had been caught outside the compound when it was encircled. Under a flag of truce, Huizenga was given permission to enter the garrison. After a long talk with Lee and the others, the lieutenant convinced them to surrender. Death might have been preferable, for Huizenga had unwittingly consigned his Marines to years of hellish captivity inside a prisoner-of-war camp.

"Ironman" Lee endured forty-four months as a Japanese prisoner of war. He was beaten, starved, burned by cigarettes, and repeatedly threatened with execution. Despite this torment, he survived. After the war, he held various positions with the Marines in Quantico, Virginia, and retired at the rank of colonel in 1950. William F.

Lee died at the age of ninety-eight on December 27, 1998, near his home in Ferry Farms, Virginia. He was married twice and widowed once and left behind four daughters and three stepsons, along with eleven grandchildren and two great-grandchildren.

While the Japanese were busy in China, another engagement was about to occur off Midway Island. In order to strike at Pearl Harbor, the Japanese Navy had sent six aircraft carriers and their destroyer escorts to a position 230 miles north of Hawaii, within aircraft range of the American base. The Japanese had launched 360 warplanes just after daybreak, even as Japanese diplomats were preparing to deliver their declaration of hostilities in Washington, D.C. Japanese losses in the attack were minimal—five midget submarines with nine crewmen and twenty-nine planes with fifty-five airmen lost—but after Vice Admiral Nagumo, wanting to put as much ocean

First Lieutenant George H. Cannon

between his ships and the Americans as possible, made the decision to cut and run rather than send a third wave to hit Pearl's harbor installations, the Japanese fleet had to pass Midway Island, which was occupied by American troops, guns, and aircraft. Nagumo dispatched his destroyers in a preemptive strike on Midway before the Americans could move against his forces.

News of the attack at Pearl Harbor had reached Midway, along with a warning of possible Japanese aggression. The Americans scrambled their defenses and hunkered down to wait. Late on the night of December 7, Japanese warships began shelling Midway. During a twenty-three-minute engagement, Japanese ships came so close to Midway that Marines raked the decks of their destroyers with machine guns. The meager facilities on Midway were shattered by naval guns and four Marines were killed, nineteen injured. In the middle of the attack a well-aimed artillery shell blasted through the air vent of Midway Island's main communications center, to explode deep in the bowels of the reinforced concrete structure. The center had a large staff and was commanded by twenty-six-year-old First Lieutenant George Ham Cannon. Cannon was a long way from St. Louis, Missouri, where he had grown up, but the Midwesterner was all Marine, as he would prove on this day.

Nearly deaf and wounded from the initial blast, Lieutenant Cannon refused to evacuate until the other wounded were rescued. Bleeding from a score of shrapnel wounds, he repeatedly refused medical attention while directing the recovery effort, even as the Japanese bombardment continued. Only when the danger to his men had passed did the lieutenant surrender his command. But it was too late to save the young officer's life. Cannon died from loss of blood a few minutes after arriving at an aid station. First Lieutenant George Ham Cannon, who received a hero's burial at the National Memorial Cemetery of the Pacific in Honolulu, Hawaii, was the first Marine to receive the Medal of Honor in World War II. Before the end of the bloodiest and costliest conflict in human history, eighty-one Marines would be so honored.

THE SIEGE OF WAKE ISLAND

In the aftermath of their attack on Pearl Harbor, the Japanese moved to consolidate their victory by snatching territories away from the United States, Great Britain, the Netherlands, and France. Democracies like Australia and New Zealand were threatened with invasion and Americans feared that the Japanese were preparing to invade the Hawaiian Islands. But the Japanese had other plans. They turned their attention to the Philippines, to China, and to Guam. They also had designs on a tiny atoll in the middle of the Pacific Ocean, a strategic location still occupied by a skeleton force of Marines and Marine Corps aviators that was called Wake Island.

But because of its location, less than a thousand miles south of Tokyo, Guam had to be taken first. The islands surrounding it were already in Japanese hands and had been since 1914. But Guam, the largest island of the Marianas chain, belonged to the United States since 1895. On December 8, the Japanese landed a force of 6,000 troops on the island. Only about 150 U.S. Marines were stationed there, along with 600 Navy personnel and a few native Chamorro militiamen. These troops had no artillery and only few machine guns. They mounted a stubborn resistance anyway, killing ten before they were overwhelmed and captured. It would be two and a half years before the United States Marines returned to Guam.

Twenty-four hours after Guam fell—at 5:00 A.M. on December 11—Japanese warships began a naval bombardment of Wake Island. The Americans knew they were coming: they had spotted enemy ships the night before illuminated by the brilliant light of a half-moon. Now Marine Corps gunners manning three- and five-inch coastal artillery hunkered down and waited until the enemy got within point-blank range before returning fire. When the Americans cut loose, the Japanese light cruiser *Yubari* was struck three times and hurriedly withdrew, trailing columns of black smoke and fire. When the *Yubari* turned tail and ran, the American gun crews got so excited they stopped firing and began to cheer.

"Knock it off, you bastards," Platoon Sergeant Henry A. Bedell barked. "What d'ya think this is, a ball game?"

The men returned to work and struck three more Japanese ships while coastal gunners on the other side of the atoll, at a point called Wilkes Island, used five-inch guns to sink the Japanese destroyer *Hayate*. Stung by this unexpectedly stubborn resistance and the loss of two ships, the Japanese fleet steamed out of range. The coastal batteries on Wake Island had successfully driven off an invasion force—a feat that would never be repeated by either side during the rest of the Pacific War.

As the Japanese ships passed out of range of the coastal batteries, the pilots took to the air. Led by Major Paul A. Putnam of Washington, Iowa, four Grumman F4F-3 Wildcats of Marine Fighting Squadron 211 attacked the retreating ships. Despite a wall of Japanese antiaircraft and machine-gun fire, the Wildcats made several low-level strafing passes, then dropped hundred-pound bombs on the enemy task force. Thirty-six-year-old Captain Henry Talmage Elrod of Thomasville, Georgia, swooped over the deck of the Japanese destroyer *Kisaragi* and dropped every one of his hundred-pound bombs. The magazine exploded, and within moments the *Kisaragi* broke apart and sank. There were no survivors.

The Americans had mounted a stiff resistance at Wake Island. Two enemy ships had been sent to the bottom and 500 sailors went down with them. The Americans also shot down three Japanese bombers and damaged four more. Though it was a minor victory, Americans on the home front welcomed the positive news. But courage and tenacity would not be enough to keep Wake Island in American hands. The island lay along Japanese supply routes and was the perfect place for an airfield, and the Japanese were determined to capture the island at any cost. For two weeks they attacked the atoll daily with long-range bombers flown from land bases in the Gilbert Islands. Without bomb shelters or underground tunnels, the Americans on Wake had nowhere to hide. Bombs shattered their facilities and wrecked the Wildcat fighters one or two at a time. The Marines cannibalized parts from damaged planes to keep the few that survived in the air, but every day they had less to work with, and the enemy kept on coming.

The U.S. Navy made plans for a relief mission to secure Wake Island. On Saturday, December 20, 1941, a U.S. Navy PBY "Catalina" seaplane landed off Wake, bringing the beleaguered garrison word of this effort. When the PBY took off next morning, the Marines on Wake believed their salvation was at hand. They were wrong.

Just two hours after the Catalina flew away, the skies above the island were filled with Japanese carrier-based dive-bombers—the first wave in a new enemy offensive. By December 22, only two Wildcats could still fly. With Captain Herbert C. Freuler and Second Lieutenant Carl R. Davidson at the controls, these warplanes rose into the skies to confront the enemy. The American aviators attacked an overwhelming force—thirty-three Japanese dive-bombers and a dozen Zero fighters were poised to strike the island. Davidson was downed as he rushed for the bombers. Freuler shot down two Zeros before he crash-landed his battered Wildcat back on Wake. After this battle, there were no planes left to defend the American atoll. The U.S. Navy relief expedition was still 600 miles away when the Japanese landed in force on the afternoon of December 23. A hundred Japanese troops hit nearly Wilkes Island while a thousand *rikusentai* came ashore on Wake. The atoll was defended by fewer than ninety Marines armed with a single coastal gun, some rifles, and a smattering of machine guns.

Major Putnam, Captain Elrod, and the few survivors of Marine Fighting Squadron 211 joined the ground troops in the final assault. They fired artillery shells at the Japanese landing craft until there was no more ammunition. The airmen fought off several hundred Japanese *rikusentai* for six hours until all but one of them was killed. Among the dead was Hank Elrod, the second Marine and the first Marine Corps aviator to earn the Medal of Honor during World War II.

▪ *Rikusentai: The Special Naval Landing Force*

Before the 1920s, when the Japanese Navy needed infantry to defend coastal positions or quell unrest, they simply armed their sailors and sent them ashore. The United States did the same thing when there were no Marines available. But this practice can be costly and dangerous; sailors must be trained in infantry tactics, and ships are more vulnerable and less efficient when sailors are stripped from the crew and sent ashore to keep the peace.

So the Japanese Navy established a permanent amphibious corps called the Special Naval Landing Forces, or *rikusentai*—their equivalent of the Marine Corps. Though the *rikusentai* made their first appearance in 1885, it was not until the 1920s that this force came into its own. Recruiters traditionally chose young men of exceptional fitness and initiative, though as the Second World War progressed, the quality and training of the SNLF troops declined steadily. The SNLF used the same equipment, weapons, and uniforms as the Japanese Army with a single exception—the *rikusentai* had an anchor insignia on their helmets to symbolize their amphibious mission.

At the beginning of the war, the *rikusentai* spear-headed the amphibious landings in China, Java, Rabaul, and the Solomon Islands, but they were neither as numerous nor as formidable as their American counterparts. While the Marine Corps could boast a hundred, battalion-sized combat units at the height of the Pacific War, the Japanese possessed fewer than three dozen *rikusentai* battalions—about 50,000 men. The SNLF are usually found in garrison strength on small islands, or aboard warships. They also participated in the defense of the Japanese homeland.

Over the course of the war, the *rikusentai* and the Marines Corps clashed several times. They fought first at Guam and Wake in December 1941, with the Japanese victorious in both campaigns. But as the war progressed, the SNLF would suffer many defeats at the hands of the United States Marine Corps. *Rikusentai* fought to the last man in their doomed defense of Tulagi and Gavutu, and at Tarawa, where these Japanese marines inflicted the heaviest one-day casualty rate the Marine Corps ever suffered.

The *rikusentai* fought their last battle on Okinawa, where they inflicted 1,600 American casualties in a pitched, ten-day battle. Okinawa was considered part of the Japanese home islands, and the 5,000 *rikusentai* died to a man defending their divine emperor and the Japanese people from foreign invasion.

Thirty-six-year-old Hank Elrod of Turner County, Georgia, fought daily aerial duels between December 8 and 20, when the beleaguered base at Wake finally exhausted its supply of operational aircraft. Though he was a pilot, Elrod took up a rifle and joined the infantrymen in the final defense of the American island. He died fighting hand to hand just two days before Christmas 1941. After the war, his remains were moved to Arlington National Cemetery, where he was buried with honor.

The Japanese captured 1,600 prisoners on Wake—1,146 civilians and 470 officers and enlisted men. On January 12, the prisoners were shipped to a prison camp in Shanghai. To the end they hoped for a rescue, but the U.S. Navy ultimately had to abandon their efforts. En route to the POW camp the prisoners were beaten and starved. Two sergeants from the 211 Squadron and three sailors were beheaded by their captors. Over the next several weeks, small isolated American garrisons in China, on Guam, and at countless smaller Pacific specks found themselves isolated and trapped in the middle of hostile territory. The Japanese had been handed the Marshalls, the Marianas, the Carolines, and the Palaus after World War I in "grateful acknowledgement" for their "assistance" in defeating the Kaiser's forces. After Pearl Harbor, they went on to capture the Pacific islands they did not already possess, and there was nothing the United States could do about it.

THE PHILIPPINES FALL

Only a handful of Marines fought in the doomed five-month defense of the Philippine Islands, which was primarily a U.S. Army campaign. It was a hopeless cause, but the Americans fought on, giving up ground every day until Manila fell. On March 12, 1942, President Roosevelt ordered Army General Douglas MacArthur to leave Corregidor for Australia. MacArthur unwillingly left half of his command behind but vowed to rescue them. Few survived until the general's triumphant return to the Philippines in 1944.

When MacArthur departed, he left a detachment of Marines in Luzon. They fought on until the crumbling American-Filipino line broke on April 3. Bataan fell six days later, and over a hundred Marines were among the 75,000 Americans and Filipinos who trekked northward to the Japanese POW camps during the infamous Bataan Death March. During the march and the subsequent internment, many died of neglect, disease, and starvation.

In time, only the small island of Corregidor remained in Allied hands. It would fall after a twenty-seven-day siege, when Marine Colonel Samuel Howard was forced to surrender his surviving forces. While his regimental colors burned and his Marines dashed their weapons against the rocks, Colonel Howard moaned quietly: "My God. And I had to be the first Marine officer ever to surrender a regiment." Of the 1,282 Marines who surrendered, only 239 would survive four horrendous years of imprisonment.

The Pacific War was five months old and the U.S. military had already relinquished more of its former territories than at any other time in the nation's history. Now only the garrison on Midway Island stood between the Imperial Japanese Navy and the West Coast of the United States.

THE BATTLE FOR MIDWAY

The Japanese planned to invade Midway in late April 1942. Because it was considered the northernmost island in the Hawaiian chain, its strategic importance and symbolic value were immense. The Japanese attack was meant to smash what remained of the U.S. Navy—including the American carriers—and extend Japan's hegemony by over a thousand miles. The actual capture of Midway Island was of secondary importance to the goal of destroying the remnant of the American Pacific fleet in a final, decisive naval battle. The tiny atoll would feel the brunt of early fighting, only to be ignored later, as American and Japanese carrier-based fighters, dive-bombers, and torpedo planes dueled in the skies over the two fleets.

The Midway Campaign was the brainchild of Admiral Isoroku Yamamoto, the military genius who masterminded the attack on Pearl Harbor. But this time things would not go so well for the Japanese. On the morning of June 4, the Japanese carrier *Akagi* launched 108 planes for an attack on Midway. Alerted by radar while the enemy were still 90 miles away, the warplanes of Marine Fighter Squadron 221 and Marine Bombing Squadron 241 took off to intercept the attackers. The American force was composed of inexperienced pilots flying twenty-seven aged and obsolete Vindicator dive-bombers and twenty-six ancient Brewster Buffalos, with a smattering of the newer, but still outclassed Grumman Wildcat fighters. The untested Americans were quickly slaughtered by the experienced Japanese airmen at the controls of their formidable Zero fighters. Despite heavy losses, the dive-bombers led by Major Lofton R. Henderson pressed on to attack the *Akagi*. For these pilots, it would be their first taste of combat. For most, it would also be their last.

One of the aviators under Henderson's command was twenty-four-year-old Captain Richard Eugene Fleming of St. Paul, Minnesota. Fleming enlisted in the Marine Corps Reserves in 1939 and immediately applied for flight training. He earned his wings on November 13, 1940, and was sent to Pearl Harbor. He survived the surprise attack on December 7, 1941, but was frustrated by his inability to get into the air. Captain Fleming was dispatched to Midway, where his squadron spent the next six months patrolling the ocean around the island without contact with the enemy.

When the dive-bombers attacked the *Akagi*, they did so without fighter protection—a recipe for disaster. Antiaircraft fire was intense as the Vindicators dived for the carrier. Within seconds, Major Henderson's aircraft was engulfed in a fireball. But Fleming pressed his attack even though his plane was struck 179 times—Fleming's gunner later told his squadron mates that the noise was like "a bucket of bolts" being thrown into the propeller. Without adequate bombsights the Vindicators missed their target. But the air attack forced Vice Admiral Nagumo to order a second assault on Midway. In all, fifteen Marine Corps bombers went down in flames. The American fighters that charged the Japanese formation failed to stop enemy aircraft from attacking Midway, but they did disrupt the attack. When the enemy arrived over the atoll, antiaircraft gunners sent several Japanese dive-bombers and fighters spinning into the ocean. The ground fire was so intense that most Japanese bombers missed their targets.

"There is need for a second attack wave," a flight officer radioed back to Nagumo. But the unexpected attack from Midway's bomber group had already convinced the vice admiral of the need for a second strike. Nagumo's decision to mount one would spell doom for the Japanese carriers. While they were refueling and rearming their warplanes, 200 American dive-bombers launched from U.S. carriers appeared in the skies over the Japanese fleet. The Japanese carriers—their flight decks crowded with a lethal mixture of live bombs, torpedoes, aviation fuel, and live ammunition—were sitting ducks. When the smoke cleared, four Japanese carriers had been annihilated, with their planes and crews lost.

On June 5, a Japanese counterattack crippled the U.S. carrier *Yorktown;* an enemy submarine would finish her off the next day. But as the duel of the carriers continued, Marine aviators flying off Midway Island harried Japanese shipping with repeated air attacks. Many of these aviators paid the ultimate price. That same morning, after less than four hours sleep, Captain Fleming led six Vindicators on a dive-bombing attack against the crippled Japanese cruiser *Mikuma*. Antiaircraft fire rose from the warship's deck, riddling the American planes. Most were downed before they got within range of the enemy, but Captain Fleming managed to get closer.

While tracers arched into the air around him, he aimed the nose of his dive-bomber at the *Mikuma*'s deck, and ignoring the unrelenting fire, pressed his attack. His bomber was soon riddled with holes, its engine sputtering. With no hope of escape and his gunner already dead, Fleming slammed his Vindicator into the cruiser's after-gun turret, setting fire to the starboard engine room. Trailing smoke, the *Mikuma* retreated out to sea. Though Captain Fleming failed to sink the Japanese warship, his suicidal attack slowed the cruiser enough for a second dive-bomber assault to finish her off the next day. Richard Eugene Fleming was the forty-ninth Marine to die in the Battle of Midway and the last. By June 10, the campaign was over and the United States Navy was the victor. Captain Fleming was awarded a posthumous Medal of Honor for his courage and self-sacrifice.

General Alexander A. Vandegrift

A week after the Battle of Midway, the First Marine Division arrived in New Zealand with Major General Alexander Vandegrift, a veteran of Veracruz, as its commander. Vandegrift knew that that his Marines were not ready to face the Japanese and had been hoping for six months to train them before their first campaign. He was shocked to learn that his Marines were expected to execute the first American amphibious assault of the Pacific War within six weeks. The target was an island in the Solomons that Vandegrift had never heard of before—a place called Guadalcanal.

But before that invasion, the Marine Corps wanted to test the mettle of one of their most eclectic units—the Second Raider Battalion, affectionately known as Carlson's Raiders. Evans Carlson was a pipe-smoking, forty-six-year-old career officer on the slow track to retirement when he was selected to lead the Raiders—a special elite unit that was the brainchild of Secretary of the Navy Frank Knox. Carlson had a can-do attitude and transformed his recruits into something like the elite fighting force they were meant to be in just nine months. The Raiders were handpicked Marines who could hike fifty miles a day, live off the land, fight with all manner of projectile weapons, with knives, and hand to hand. Two battalions were created. Lieutenant Colonel Merritt A. Edson, a hero of Nicaragua, led the First Raider Battalion, organized on the East Coast, while Colonel Carlson commanded the Second, organized on the West Coast. Utilizing commando tactics gleaned from the British, the Raiders were trained in guerrilla warfare. They learned how to mount quick, hit-and-run assaults and secret reconnaissance runs to spearhead amphibious assaults. One of the Raiders' biggest boosters was President Roosevelt. Captain James Roosevelt, the president's son, was among the ranks of the "Gung-Ho Boys" of Carlson's Raiders.

While half the Raiders were dispatched to reinforce Midway the other half mounted a raid on Makin Island. Touted as a way to distract the Japanese from the planned landings on Guadalcanal, Carlson's Raid was a first attempt to assert American military power after the demoralizing defeat at Pearl Harbor. Like the Doolittle Raid, in which long-range U.S. bombers hit targets in downtown Tokyo, the Carlson Raid lacked strategic value but had a positive effect on American morale.

On August 9, 1942, just two days after the Marines hit Guadalcanal, the submarines *Nautilus* and *Argonaut* sailed from Pearl Harbor on a secret mission. The boats were packed with A and B Companies of the Second Raider Battalion—220 men, their weapons and equipment. On Makin Island, the Japanese had established a seaplane base that could be used to reconnoiter U.S. Navy surface movement. Intelligence estimated that there were only forty-five Japanese defenders on the island—there were actually over a hundred—and believed the mission would be a "cakewalk" for the specially trained Raiders. On the moonless night of August 17, the Raiders blackened their faces and boarded rubber boats. Paddling for over an hour, they reached the eastern shore of Butaritari, the largest island in the Makin chain. The boats landed in three different locations. Things went as scheduled until one of the Raiders accidentally discharged his Browning automatic rifle, alerting the Japanese.

Enemy troops swarmed out of their huts and manned machine-gun nests scattered around the perimeter of the Japanese air base. Snipers climbed coconut palms and trained their weapons on the Americans. While A Company crossed the island and headed for the enemy, Colonel Carlson had the *Nautilus* fire their deck gun, wrecking shore batteries and damaging two enemy ships moored in the harbor. The Japanese responded with a *banzai* charge.

Armed with a shotgun for close fighting, twenty-seven-year-old Sergeant Clyde A. Thomason of Atlanta, Georgia, decimated the enemy assault before a sniper firing from the trees killed him. Thomason, a Marine Corps reservist, was calm during the fighting. At one point he walked up to a hut hiding a Japanese sniper, kicked in the door, and dispatched the man with his pistol. Sergeant Clyde Thomason became the first enlisted Marine to earn the Medal of Honor in World War II. It was awarded posthumously.

The Marines advanced into the teeth of machine guns, snipers, and blasts from a Japanese flamethrower. Finally, Carlson sent B Company into the fight, committing nearly all of his reserves. At noon the Japanese dispatched a bomber to strafe the Marines even as two enemy floatplanes packed with reinforcements landed nearby. The Marines, firing from the shore, destroyed the new arrivals and the seaplanes stationed on the island. Then they retreated north, to draw the Japanese out of their defensive perimeter. The plan worked. When the Marines pulled out, the Japanese pursued them. An enemy bomber unleashed its payload where the Marines had been hiding, annihilating the Japanese troops who were pursuing them.

Carlson and his men tried to escape the island, but less than half their force made it to the beach. Paddling against the powerful tide, the American boats capsized or were swamped. Of the original force of 220, fewer than 150 remained, and 8 of them were severely wounded. Cowering on the beach throughout a rainy night, the Marines fought off repeated enemy incursions. Arkansas-born Private Jesse Hawkins was shot twice, but still managed to drive off a determined Japanese assault on his position. At dawn James Roosevelt, Carlson's executive officer, came ashore with five boats and evacuated half the Raiders before enemy planes strafed the beach. The seventy Raiders still stuck on Makin, along with Captain Roosevelt, turned around to attack the Japanese base again. To their surprise, they couldn't find the enemy. The Raiders marched all the way back to the main Japanese installation only to find it abandoned. The Marines destroyed the base, stole several Japanese boats; and rowed back to the submarine. In all, ninety Japanese soldiers were killed and the air base was permanently damaged. It was discovered later—through talks with the local natives—that in addition to the twenty-one Marines who were killed, nine others had been left behind. They were captured and moved to Kawjalein, where they were beheaded on October 16. This atrocity was not avenged until after the war, when the Japanese admiral who ordered the executions was hanged.

Despite this unpleasant postscript, Carlson's Raid on Makin Island was touted as a success, and the men who participated in it were highly decorated. Along with Thomason's Medal of Honor, fourteen participants were presented with the Navy Cross. More importantly, the American public woke up to banner headlines about a U.S. victory in the Pacific—a rare event in 1942. If nothing else, Carlson's Raid was a major propaganda coup.

GUADALCANAL

There was almost no information on Guadalcanal available to Vandegrift's staff as they planned their invasion. There were no maps or reliable information about tides and water depths around the island. Staff members knew that Guadalcanal was covered in jungle, that it lay in the southern Solomons just north of the Coral Sea off Australia, and that the main island had three island neighbors. The largest was Florida Island, the others were called Savo and Tulagi. Savo was useless as a base. A tiny island dominated by a single mountain peak, it had no beach.

Tulagi was more hospitable. It lay just nineteen miles across Sealark Channel from Guadalcanal and the Japanese had already established a seaplane base there. That base made the Americans nervous. From Tulagi, Japanese planes could threaten the American invasion fleet. Compared to Guadalcanal, Tulagi was positively civilized. It had been occupied by the British before the Japanese came, and was the seat of the Anglican bishopric in the Solomon Islands. Tulagi boasted a cricket field, a British residency, and magnificent anchorage in its tiny harbor. The Japanese had dug in at Tulagi, with most of their defenses concentrated in the southeastern tip of the island. They lurked in hillside caves and in volcanic fissures, ready to fight repel an invasion.

Guadalcanal was reinforced as well. The Japanese had a large force posted there, though no one was sure what they were doing or how many troops actually defended the island. Guadalcanal was not hospitable. The island was slashed by three parallel rivers: the deep and rapid Tenaru, the shallow and slow Lunga, and the Matanikau.

There were countless other waterways—more in the rainy season, when much of the jungle was flooded. No one was quite sure where the Marines could make a safe crossing, as the nature of each river depended on the intensity of the near-constant tropical rains. When the weather was dry, the rivers were manageable. When it rained, they became raging rapids.

Aircraft from the U.S.S. *Yorktown* had been dispatched in May to photograph Guadalcanal, Tulagi, and Savo in preparation for the invasion, but those pictures went to the bottom of the Pacific on June 6, when the *Yorktown* was sunk by Japanese submarines. Military planners were compelled to turn to other, less reliable sources for information. American officers were dispatched to New Zealand and Australia to interview former Guadalcanal residents—natives, missionaries, planters, traders, and the colonial officials who fled the island before the Japanese occupation. They also studied an acclaimed science-fiction story published in *Cosmopolitan* magazine in October 1918. "The Red One" was one of author Jack London's last works of fiction. An adventurer and sailor, London visited Guadalcanal in 1907 along with many Pacific islands during a twenty-seven-month voyage through the Pacific. He wrote of his experiences in *The Voyage of the Snark*. London also wrote several editorials warning the American public about Japanese expansion in the region. Unfortunately, the accuracy of London's story was suspect; the author spelled the name of the island "Guadalcanar"—an error that has been corrected in subsequent editions—and provided few geographic details beyond pulp-magazine-like descriptions of the jungle and the native population. More intelligence was needed.

A quick, dangerous, American flyover of the Solomons revealed that the Japanese were carving a large airstrip out of the jungles on Guadalcanal. Japanese bombers flying from a permanent base in the Solomons could strike U.S. supply ships steaming through the region, so the timetable for the invasion—code-named Operation Watchtower—was stepped up. The Marines sailed for New Zealand from California and Hawaii, packed like sardines in cramped cargo ships. Life aboard troop transport ships was tedious and uncomfortable. Most troop holds were below the waterline, where five levels of hammocklike bunks were slung from the bulkheads, a few inches of space between each level. The close air reeked of unwashed bodies, tobacco smoke, gun oil, and the constant stench of diesel fuel. As the ships moved to more tropical waters, life belowdeck became insufferably hot. The troops were permitted saltwater showers, which made their bodies feel sticky and unclean even after a thorough washing. Boredom was a constant companion during the days or weeks it took to cross the ocean. Amusement could be found in the fresh air on deck, but after lights-out, everyone headed below, where they could visit the chaplain, play cards, shoot craps, or write letters home.

Chow on these ships was generally bad, but a tradition evolved during the Pacific Campaign; on the morning of an invasion, the Marines dined on a sumptuous feast of steak and eggs accompanied by a shot of whiskey. Unfortunately, too many Marines suffered from preinvasion jitters to enjoy this rare and special treat. Daily food service on board ship was another matter—dehydrated eggs and potatoes, Spam, cheese, beans, and sliced white bread were staples.

When the Marines arrived at Wellington Harbor on July 11, 1942, they faced a new challenge. Self-serving labor unions in New Zealand refused to help the American troops unload and reload their ships in time for the scheduled invasion. Marines were forced to perform this exhausting work themselves, toiling twenty-four hours a day, seven days a week, in driving rains that ruined perishable supplies that had been carefully ferried across the Pacific. Though the loading operation was accomplished in good order, this time could have been better spent in drills and training. But the ordeal provided the American troops with their first taste of the kind of place they were bound for. Guadalcanal was one of the wettest places on earth—a jagged volcanic island steaming with jungle rot and suffocating tropical heat.

Though beautiful to view from the ocean, with her towering central mountain, white sand beaches, and verdant trees, Guadalcanal was a hellish place up close. Its jungles were filled scum-crusted lagoons, rivers teaming with hungry crocodiles, spiders as big as a man's hand, fire ants whose bite burned, tree leeches that dropped onto necks and down shirts, finger-sized wasps, clouds of malaria-infected mosquitoes at night, and swarms of disease-ridden fleas by day—not to mention several varieties of poisonous spiders, insects, and snakes. Wounds tended to fester in Guadalcanal's climate. Heat exhaustion was common, and despite the rain, finding fresh water was a chronic problem.

Military intelligence estimated that there were fewer than 2,000 Japanese troops on Guadalcanal and 1,500 on Tulagi. The invasion plan called for five simultaneous landings, with Group X-Ray—the First and Fifth Marines led by General Vandegrift—hitting the beach near Lunga Point, where the Japanese airstrip was being constructed. The Marines' primary goal was to seize and hold that airfield at any cost. Other units would hit the north side of the island while Lieutenant Colonel Merritt A. Edson's Marines captured nearby Tulagi. Edson, nicknamed "Red Mike" because his thinning red hair, would make a name for himself and his glorious Raiders during the campaign to capture Guadalcanal. Major Robert H. Williams was to land his First Parachute Battalion on Gavutu-Tanambogo—with landing craft, not parachutes—while the First Battalion, Second Marines, secured Florida Island.

The Marines participating in this invasion were a mixture of old veterans and new recruits, men born in the American heartland mingling with those from a nautical background. In other words, these recruits were the same sort of men the Marines Corps had attracted since its inception. Though their backgrounds differed, they shared many common virtues—cunning, courage, tenacity, and initiative among them. They also shared the rich traditions and fighting spirit of the Marine Corps.

Major Samuel B. Griffith III, who led elements of the First Raider Battalion—dubbed "Edson's Raiders"—onto the beach, wrote of the Marines under his command: "They were a motley bunch. Hundreds were young recruits only recently out of boot training at Parris Island. Others were older . . . the professionals, the 'Old Breed' of the United States Marines. Many had fought the 'Cacos' in Haiti, 'bandidos' in Nicaragua." Among their ranks were "French, English, Italian, and American soldiers and sailors [from] every bar in Shanghai, Manila, Tsingtao, Tientsin, and Peking . . . They were inveterate and accomplished scroungers [who] cursed with wonderful fluency and never went to chapel . . . [These men] knew their weapons and they knew their tactics. They knew they were tough and they knew they were good."

▪ Small Arms of the Pacific Theater

By the beginning of the Second World War, the Marine Corps had evolved into a small, efficient armed service that was often dispatched to fight against a much larger force. For that reason, they relied on superior firepower and marksmanship skills. But because the Marine Corps was also the unwanted stepchild of the American military, they often had to make do with equipment cast aside by the other services.

The Pacific War was an infantry war, with most of the fighting carried out on the beaches, in the jungles, and on rugged mountaintops. Under these conditions troops had to depend on their personal weapons. Most of the troops fighting in the Pacific utilized a combination of First World War—era and newer types of small arms. Early on, the Marines were generally equipped with Springfield bolt-action rifles in use since 1903, and adopted the Thompson submachine gun in the 1920s. The "Tommy" gun was light and easy to carry, but inaccurate beyond 100 meters. That really didn't matter because the Marines had very few of them. In the main, the men who stormed Guadalcanal were armed with the bolt-action Springfield, and a smattering of BARs. Later in the war—in time for Iwo Jima and Okinawa—the Springfield as replaced by the eight-shot Garand M-1 rifle, which would be used until the 1960s.

The Japanese Army had used the Type 38 "Arisaka" rifle since 1905. A bolt-action weapon more suitable to the First World War than the Second, the Type 38 was a sturdy, simple rifle that fired a 6.5-caliber bullet. Though it had less stopping power than the American 7.62-caliber rifles, a 6.5 shell tumbles and breaks apart after impact, causing terrible wounds.

Because the Japanese stressed "fighting spirit" over innovations in technology, the Imperial Army fought World War II with essentially the same small arms that they marched into Manchuria with two decades before. The average Japanese recruit was the son of a rural farmer, dragged from his home by the need for ever-larger armies to hold conquered territory. These recruits were rigorously trained in hand-to-hand combat, knife and bayonet fighting, stealth and camouflage tactics, and endurance. They were also instilled with a fighting spirit that compelled them to accept death before capture. Marksmanship skills were not overly stressed.

Each Arisaka rifle had the symbol of a chrysanthemum stamped on its barrel, which told the recruit that his weapon was a gift from the emperor—essentially a gift

from heaven. As the war progressed, the Type 38 was replaced by the Type 99, which fired a 7.62-caliber bullet. This rifle had more stopping power but was often made of inferior metal, and many shattered with heavy use.

Since the days of the samurai, the Japanese warrior has revered the blade, so bayonets were issued to every soldier. But an Arisaka was already fifty inches long; add a fifteen-inch bayonet and you have a rifle that is longer than the man who carries it is tall! The Arisaka was so long that Japanese soldiers were trained to fire it from a squatting or kneeling position. Another drawback was a dustcover that was standard. It made a sharp noise that gave away a soldier's position, so experienced soldiers quickly discarded them. The Japanese also carried the Type 44 carbine, a 1911 cavalry weapon with an unusual feature—a permanently fixed, fold-up bayonet. The Type 44 fired the same bullets as the Arisaka but was shorter and less unwieldy.

Both sides had sniper variations. The Japanese used the Type 38 equipped with telescopic sights. The Marines employed a special M-1903 Springfield with a telescopic sight. But unlike the Americans, who had Thompsons and the M-3 "grease gun," the Imperial Army had no submachine guns in general use during the Pacific War.

Japanese officers carried the Type 14 pistol, a puny handgun next to the American Colt .45. A semiautomatic with an easy trigger pull, the Type 14 was not much respected. It tended to jam, and the trigger guard was so small a man wearing gloves could not fire it. Imperial Japanese Army officers purchased their own handguns, and many set aside national pride to buy European models like the German Luger.

Japanese officers also carried samurai swords, issued to them by the Army or Navy. These swords were not as aesthetically pleasing or as rugged as the traditional samurai sword of a bygone era, but their symbolic value to their owners was immeasurable.

As the Pacific War dragged on, American weapons were improved and became more plentiful, while Japanese weapons declined in both quality and quantity. In the last years of the war, Japanese handguns and rifles were made from metal forged in backyard furnaces. These weapons were unreliable at best, and often more dangerous to their owners than they were to the enemy. While the Japanese retained their much-valued fighting spirit throughout the Pacific War, their technology and manufacturing abilities could not keep up with the furious pace of the conflict.

These Marines would perform near-impossible feats of toughness and endurance in the coming battle. The campaign to take Guadalcanal was supposed to last five or six days—two weeks at most. Instead, it dragged on for six grueling months, with the Marines on point for four of them. The task force left New Zealand for Fiji, where they were to conduct a sort of dress rehearsal of the invasion on July 28. The maneuvers went badly and Vandegrift knew his Marines were not ready, but time was running out.

The Marines departed Fiji on July 31. Bad weather kept Japanese reconnaissance planes based on Rabaul and Tulagi grounded, so the American fleet had not been spotted as they approached the Solomons. On the night of August 6, the landing force was moored just west of Guadalcanal and was still undetected by the enemy. The Marines slept in their chain link hammocks wearing utility packs, their rifles oiled, loaded, and at the ready. They were awakened at 4:00 A.M. and fed a breakfast of beans and tepid black coffee—preinvasion steak and eggs was not yet a tradition. At 6:13 A.M., the heavy cruiser Quincy opened fire on the Japanese shore batteries. From all indications the enemy had been taken by surprise and the enemy guns were quickly silenced. The battle for Guadalcanal had begun.

THE LANDING

At dawn on an overcast Friday morning, the first Marines climbed down cargo nets into the thirty-six-foot Higgins boats that would take them to Tulagi or Guadalcanal. At 9:13, the first units landed at Red Beach, a black sand shoreline east of the Tenaru River on Guadalcanal. There was no resistance beyond a midday air attack. By nightfall, 11,000 Marines and most of their supplies were ashore. Two veterans of the war in France—Colonel LeRoy S. Hunt and Colonel Clifton B. Cates—led their Marines in the capture of the Japanese airstrip early on the first day. Resistance was light; the Japanese fled inland to await a Japanese Navy counterattack they were sure would come.

At Florida Island, the Marines didn't have to fire a shot. A detachment of Edson's Raiders led by Major Griffith secured the island, then waded across the narrow channel to Tulagi's Blue Beach. Some were cut by the sharp coral under the surface of the channel, but the Marines entered the jungle, crossed Tulagi's central ridge, and moved south along the far shore in an effort to flank the Japanese. Things did not go as easily for two other detachments of Edson's Raiders.

The fighting on Tulagi was the fiercest. The Japanese decided to defend their seaplane base. A Company, led by Captain Lewis W. Walt, and C Company, commanded by Major Kenneth D. Bailey, faced stiff resistance around Tulagi's Hill 281. The Japanese were dug into coral caves, with snipers perched near tall coconut palms, concealed in the roots and among the tall branches, waiting patiently until the Marines passed their positions before opening up on the American's unprotected flank. The Marines were forced to take cover in a deep ravine, where they were effectively pinned down by fire coming from all sides.

Hidden in a cave near the base of Hill 281 was a Japanese machine-gun nest. The Marines led by Major Bailey—a strapping, six-foot three-inch former University of

Illinois football player—drew heavy fire from this emplacement. The impatient Bailey grabbed a BAR and cleaned out the cave himself. But there were more enemy emplacements, in caves and among the rocks. It took the Marines an hour to climb the hill on their bellies, under merciless fire, before they could charge the enemy. Meanwhile, other Marines crossed the British-built cricket field that lay cradled between two low, green hills—both fortified by enemy gun emplacements. These Marines, suddenly surrounded by enemy guns, had no choice but to go to ground as the sun set. The first *banzai* charge came that night.

The Japanese were adept at nighttime operations. They relied on camouflage and deception to defeat their enemies and drilled their armies at night to improve their performance. But a *banzai* charge is more of an expression of hopelessness than a sound military tactic. When the Japanese staged a *banzai* assault, they were signaling that they knew they were doomed but refused to go down without a fight. The Japanese soldier accepted death as his patriotic duty. The *banzai* charge was a logical extension of this devotion.

On that first night the Marines were hidden in hastily dug foxholes in pitch darkness. They could hear the enemy assembling in the jungle beyond their field of vision and knew an attack was imminent. Occasionally a Japanese officer would shout insults in fractured English meant to freeze the blood of the Marines. "Death for the emperor!" was popular. Cries of "American dogs die!" and "Japanese boy drink American boy's blood!" could be heard as well. The Americans could also hear the enemy approach. Just before the assault began, the Japanese fired into the air in an effort to stimulate nervous return fire and get the Americans to expose their positions. Then a horde of blood-mad Japanese soldiers burst from the jungle and charged the American lines. Howling officers led the assault, waving their long *katana*—samurai swords—as they ran into the teeth of the American guns. The Marines patiently held their fire, waiting for the enemy to get closer. Soon grenades spiraled through the air to explode among the Japanese, even as the enemy, in twos and threes, tried to close on the Marines with bayonets and knives. The fighting became hand to hand, and within a few minutes the Marines drove the Japanese back into the jungle. More assaults would follow. Over the course of the long first night, the Japanese staged five separate *banzai* charges. Each time they were pushed back with grenades, rifles, mortars, and in hand-to-hand combat.

Private Edward H. Ahrens was attacked by a horde of Japanese. Shot twice in the chest and bayoneted three times, the young Marine took thirteen Japanese soldiers down with him. He died with the dawn, telling his commanding officer that "they tried to come over me last night, but I don't think they made it." When dawn finally came, the Marines on Tulagi were exhausted. The fighting had been hard, the night sleepless. Now they were expected to push forward. With the sun came elements of the Second Marines. They used dynamite to blow Japanese-occupied caves before moving in to clean out the area. By sunset of the second day—Saturday, August 8, 1942—the island of Tulagi was secure. Two hundred Japanese soldiers were killed and Major Edson had earned his second Navy Cross—fourteen years after winning his first at Coco River.

GAVUTU-TANAMBOGO

Off the coast of Florida Island lay the tiny isles of Gavutu-Tanambogo. It was here that the Marines experienced their first real amphibious assault of the war, an attack from the sea against heavily defended beaches. Though a carrier aircraft attack had destroyed the Japanese base and naval artillery pounded the island, the enemy was huddled in reinforced coral caves and virtually untouched when the landing boats appeared on the horizon.

At noon on the first day, the First Parachute Battalion hit the beach at Gavutu in three waves—to be halted by an impenetrable wall of concentrated machine-gun and rifle fire. The first wave was decimated on the beach. The second and third waves were pinned down on the shoreline and could not advance. After a few hours, one in ten Marines that came ashore at Gavutu became a casualty and the enemy was still pouring it on.

On Tanambogo, the story was much the same. The first wave of Americans hit the beach and was slaughtered. By Friday night the Marines had to withdraw to the shoreline. On Saturday they returned—this time supported by two tanks. The first tank was destroyed immediately, its crew killed as they fled the wreckage. The second tank proceeded inland with sixty Marines following in close support. All that night the fighting was heavy, but by Sunday afternoon the tiny islands of Gavutu-Tanambogo were in Marine Corps hands. The Americans lost 108 men, the Japanese over 1,500. All during these assaults, the Japanese threw bombers, dive-bombers, and torpedo planes against the U.S. fleet. Though the Americans downed thirty enemy aircraft, they also suffered serious hits. Fearing a mass attack, the Navy withdrew the fleet twelve hours sooner than they had said they would.

General Vandegrift was alarmed. Without the support of carrier-based aircraft and naval guns, he feared his Marines would be stranded and slaughtered on Guadalcanal. Even as the Navy was retreating, the Japanese Eighth Fleet moved into Sealark Channel. At 1:30 A.M., the enemy attacked the Allied fleet. In the brief but deadly encounter, three U.S. cruisers and an Australian cruiser were sunk. In the pitch-black, shark-infested waters, over a thousand Americans and 300 Australians lost their lives.

The Battle of Savo Island—or the Battle of the Sitting Ducks, as some Americans dubbed it—stands today as one of the worst defeats ever suffered by the United States Navy. But at least the Japanese left the transport ships alone as they concentrated on the warships. The freighters continued to unload their cargo of military supplies off Lunga Point, where the precious ammunition, food, and war matériel lay exposed to enemy attack on the white sand beach. Even worse, 1,400 Marines never made it ashore; they remained stuck aboard the ships that hastily withdrew.

With U.S. naval support gone, the Japanese controlled the air and sea around the Solomon Islands. On Guadalcanal, on Florida Island, on Tulagi, and on Gavutu-Tanambogo, 16,000 United States Marines were trapped with a thirty-seven-day supply of food and a meager four days' worth of ammunition. The bulldozers and other heavy equipment they were counting on to expand the captured air base had never even made it to shore. The survival of these Marines now depended on that airfield.

Holding it became General Vandegrift's number-one priority. He dispatched several units to make the airfield operational with the equipment on hand—mostly material captured from the enemy.

General Vandegrift expected the Japanese to return in force and make an amphibious landing of their own. Instead the enemy relied on naval bombardments and air attacks to decimate the American forces. Japanese warships sailed up "The Slot," as the Marines renamed Sealark Channel, and shelled the beach at will. Dive-bombers—nicknamed "Washing Machine Charlie"—harassed the Marines by night, making sleep impossible. Though the air base was ready by August 12, no aircraft were yet available to land there. Finally, on August 15, four supply planes touched down. The aircraft were chock-full of aviation fuel, ammunition, supplies, and a Seabee unit. On August 20, thirty-one warplanes of Marine Aircraft Group 223 arrived from the escort carrier *Long Island*. The as-yet-unnamed American air base—the sole supply link for the Marines trapped on Guadalcanal—was operational. On August 16, Major John L. Smith, commander of VMF-223, scored his first kill. From now on, a steady stream of Army, Navy, and Marine Corps aircraft would deliver crucial supplies to the beleaguered Marines.

THE BATTLE OF THE TENARU RIVER

The first crucial contest for Guadalcanal began on the night of August 18, when a thousand Japanese regulars landed twenty-two miles east of Lunga Point and another 500 *rikusentai* came ashore just west of the Marines' perimeter. Early the next morning a Marine patrol commanded by Captain Charles Brush encountered an enemy unit. In an hour-long clash, the Americans killed thirty-one Japanese soldiers. Then Captain Brush and his men hurried back to camp, dragging their wounded and leaving behind three dead Marines, to warn General Vandegrift that the enemy had landed on Guadalcanal in force.

With the Americans alerted to their presence, Colonel Kiyono Ichiki, commander of the Japanese landing force, decided to attack the airfield immediately. It took two days for him to move his men into position, but at 3:10 A.M. on August 21, a large Japanese force came screaming out of the jungle toward the American defensive positions around the field. The Japanese crossed the sluggish, scum-crusted Ilu River—which Marine Corps maps mistakenly identified as the Tenaru River. With fixed bayonets the Japanese surged over the barbed-wire fence, only to be cut to pieces in a hail of bullets.

West of the river it was a different story. There the Marines were pushed back by the determined and suicidal charge that broke through their perimeter. Illuminated by moonlight, the battle was fought with knives, shovels, rifle butts, and samurai swords. The Japanese waded through the ocean surf to the mouth of the Ilu in an attempt to flank the American positions. This was a critical error that cost them their only chance at victory. Along the shoreline the Americans had established heavily armed defensive positions to repel an expected amphibious landing. These artillery pieces and the machine guns were turned on the advancing Japanese with devastating results.

At dawn the morning sun revealed a sandy stretch of beach littered with corpses. More enemy dead were found floating in the murky Ilu, half-eaten by crocodiles.

At 7:00 A.M., elements of the First Battalion moved upstream to flank the enemy. This move compelled the Japanese to concentrate their forces on the eastern bank of the Ilu. They counterattacked with bayonets in an attempt to escape the Marines who had hemmed them in. They were strafed by Marine aviators flying from the air base, and at 3:00 P.M., American tanks overran the Japanese positions and chased the few survivors into the open, where they were cut down by Marine Corps riflemen. By five o'clock that afternoon; the Battle of the Tenaru (Ilu) River was over. Eight hundred Japanese were dead. The rest fled into the jungle to perish from disease or starvation. Dishonored by his defeat, Colonel Kiyono Ichiki committed *seppuku*—ritual suicide—to avoid capture.

THE CACTUS AIR FORCE

One of the most enduring legends of the campaign for Guadalcanal is the story of the "Cactus Air Force," the name given to the conglomeration of U.S. Army, Navy, and Marine Corps aviators who flew from the beleaguered airfield during the six-month campaign to secure the Solomon Islands. The Cactus Air Force engaged the enemy almost daily, without reinforcements and with little sleep. They lived under deplorable conditions, and helped secure victory despite chronic shortages of warplanes, aircraft parts, ammunition, fuel, bombs, ground crews, and adequate food.

When General Vandegrift rose on the morning of August 9 to find his support ships gone, what began as Operation Watchtower became "Operation Shoestring." Critical supplies were dangerously low and the matériel he had expected the Navy to deliver had sailed off into the sunset with the fleet. General Vandegrift had 16,000 Marines on the island with enough food to last a month and sufficient ammunition to last for four or five days of heavy fighting. Many critical supplies were still aboard the Navy ships—including earthmoving equipment, high explosives, and the engineers needed to expand and maintain the captured air base. Suddenly this half-completed airfield was the only link to the outside world.

Instead of pushing inland to engage the Japanese, Vandegrift decided to concentrate his forces in and around the vital air base. He reinforced the perimeter even as support troops began expanding the landing strip with tools and vehicles captured from the enemy. With limited food on the island, the general was forced to reduce rations and use the foul foodstuffs the Marines had captured from the Japanese and had been prepared to discard only a few days before. Soon the main meal of the day was composed of Spam and dehydrated potatoes, which formed something like a hash that was usually served cold. Breakfast featured the wormy rice and dried fish the Marines discovered when they captured the base, chased down with scalding coffee. Soon the hungry soldiers had a new nickname for Guadalcanal—"Starvation Island."

General Vandegrift established a perimeter of antiaircraft guns around the airstrip. These guns intimidated the Japanese warplanes that assaulted the island daily. The lumbering "Betty" bombers had to fly a little higher to avoid the guns, which made their bombing runs much less accurate. All the while Vandegrift's engineers toiled night and day to make the 1,000-foot grass airstrip designed for fighters and scout planes into a 2,600-foot airfield suitable for all types of military aircraft— including large transport planes.

The general followed a long-standing but unwritten law of the Marine Corps— when in a jam, rely on the ingenuity and grit of the NCOs under your command. Vandegrift's noncommissioned officers performed miracles on Guadalcanal. One NCO realized that a forest of tall palms prevented anything but fighters from landing on the short airstrip. Using captured Japanese explosives, he deforested the land around the base in just two days. Other NCOs foraged for food, adapted the Japanese machine shop and hangars for American use, established lookout points, and constructed a functional kitchen with fifty-five-gallon metal drums for ovens.

When the first wave of Marine Corps aviators touched down on August 20, they were greeted by General Archer Vandegrift himself. "I was close to tears and I was not alone. When the first SBD taxied up and this handsome and dashing aviator jumped to the ground, 'Thank God you have come,' I told him." Within twelve hours these aviators helped to finish off the last elements of Kiyono Ichiki's doomed landing force with repeated strafing runs. After that short and bloody clash, the pilots begged General Vandegrift to allow them to name the base "before some rear-echelon staff pogue gets the notion." In a simple flag-raising ceremony, the base became Henderson Field in honor of Lofton Henderson, the Marine aviator who had sacrificed his life at the Battle of Midway.

The crude airstrip lacked revetments, taxiways, drainage ditches, and radar—the pilots relied on spotters scattered in the surrounding islands for early warnings of enemy air attack. But when the Marines finished construction, Henderson Field would have operational hangars, a working machine shop, and a large communications station. There was even a control tower built by the Japanese that resembled a pagoda. Though the Marines on "Starvation Island" lacked food, the clever NCOs managed to get the ice plant up and running again, so the water they drank was cool and refreshing.

Less than two weeks after the Marines hit the beaches, two squadrons were permanently stationed at Henderson Field—Captain John Lucien Smith's F4F-4 Wildcat fighters and Major Richard Mangrum's squadron of Douglas SBD-3 Dauntless dive-bombers. The designated radio call sign for Guadalcanal was "Cactus" and this led the airmen to dub their command the Cactus Air Force.

On August 21, 1942, the aviators of the Cactus Air Force intercepted a Japanese bomber force flying out of Rabaul, New Britain, to bomb Guadalcanal. Captain Smith and four Wildcats attacked thirteen Japanese Zeros head-on. Up to now the Japanese Zero fighters had been considered invincible, and the Grumman Wildcats seldom fared well against them. But this time out, all four American planes survived, though one was so badly damaged it crashed in a dead-stick landing back at Henderson Field. Later that same week Captain Marion Carl shot down two Bettys and his second Zero (his first was shot down over Midway). Captain Carl and Captain Smith became friendly rivals in the weeks ahead, vying to become the island's "Top Gun."

On September 3, the aviators met their new commanding officer, who flew in on the very first transport plane to land on the island. Roy Geiger was a flying general. At fifty-seven, Geiger was a big, burly, white-haired veteran who had flown combat missions over France during the First World War. He believed in airpower, but he was also a Marine and a student of ground warfare. On Guadalcanal, General Geiger regularly visited the front lines to better coordinate the actions of air and ground units. Within weeks the Marines were referring to him as "The Old Man"—not because he was the oldest Marine on the island, but because he intimidated them all. A pilot felt more gut-wrenching torment when summoned to Geiger's personal roost in the Pagoda than he ever experienced from the queasy, chronic stomach disorder the men called jungle nausea.

Geiger made a vivid and lasting impression during an incident on September 22, three weeks after he arrived. One of the pilots ordered on a bombing mission complained that the runway was too pocked by shell holes to take off safely—especially with a thousand-pound bomb strapped to the aircraft's underbelly. Angry, Geiger waddled onto the field, squeezed his prodigious bulk into the Dauntless dive-bomber's cockpit, and flew the mission himself. The grumbling Marine was mortified, and General Geiger enjoyed the rare pleasure of dropping a thousand-pounder on the enemy.

The pilots in the Cactus Air Force were all in their early twenties, with the exception of "Indian Joe" Bauer, who was thirty-four. Young or old, after a few weeks of combat, they acquired the same flinty gaze. The pilots all wore faded khaki shirts, identical blue baseball caps with the bill shading their eyes, and regulation leather shoulder holsters with automatic pistols. "The Cactus Air Force . . . looked so much alike on the ground . . . that it was not surprising to see them fighting like wing-joined twins in the skies," wrote historian Robert Leckie. That teamwork was the secret of their success. Geiger's pilots never jumped into a solo dogfight with a Zero. Solo duels worked against the lumbering, fix-wheeled Val dive-bombers or the cigar-shaped Betty bombers—which literally burned like a cigar when hit. But the Zero was too agile and fast for the sluggish and clumsy Wildcat to take on alone. But *two* Wildcats, working as a team, could take on three, four, or even five Zeros and down them all—as often happened over Guadalcanal.

With time and experience, the Americans learned to exploit the Wildcat's strengths while taking advantage of the Zero's weaknesses. The Wildcat outgunned the Japanese fighter and had more armor—it could take plenty of punishment. The Zero paid a price for its speed and agility—it had no armor, and the lack of a self-sealing gas tank made it terribly vulnerable to incendiary bullets. Between the end of August and early November 1942, members of the Cactus Air Force would bring glory to the nation they served, and five of them would earn the Medal of Honor.

By the end of August, the Cactus Air Force grew to include fourteen Bell P-400 Airacobra fighter-bombers from the Army Air Force and nineteen Wildcats from VMF-224, under the command of Major Robert E. Galer. The P-400 was a cheap, underpowered version of the P-39 manufactured for export to poorer countries. The Soviets were sent hundreds of them to use against the Nazis, but the Airacobra probably did more to help Luftwaffe pilots run up impressive tallies than it did to save Mother Russia. Slow and sluggish, the Airacobra was useless in a dogfight but performed well as a ground-attack plane. In the Pacific, it was used on scouting missions and to strafe Japanese shipping. The pilots on Guadalcanal had a running joke that compared the Airacobra to another outmoded American fighter, the Curtiss P-40 Tomahawk.

"What is a P-400?" the joke began.

"It's a P-40 with a Zero on its tail!"

By September 10, only three Airacobras remained operational, and Marine aviator Marion Carl was among the missing pilots shot down flying one. In mid-September, twenty-four more Wildcats arrived to reinforce Henderson Field—just in time to take part in the Battle for Bloody Ridge. By mid-October, the pilots in the Cactus Air Force, had shot down 224 Japanese planes. Nineteen victories belonged to Captain Smith, the highest-scoring American airman so far in the war. Captain Marion Carl, Smith's rival, unexpectedly returned to the squadron, alive and well, after being missing for a week. He had bailed out of his burning P-400 and spent five days among the natives before making his way back to Henderson. He was distressed to learn that Smith had pulled ahead of him in victories and begged his commander to ground Smith for a week so he could catch up. In all, seven of the pilots who came to Guadalcanal on August 7 left the island an ace. Six others who arrived that day were killed and six were wounded and had to be evacuated. Of the dive-bomber squadron only Lieutenant Colonel Mangrum, the commander, left the island unscathed. The rest were killed or wounded.

Conditions at Henderson were always dangerous. Every day, as the American planes took off or landed, they were fired upon by Japanese troops lurking in the jungle around the base. Fuel had to be hand-pumped from fifty-five-gallon drums delivered by transport planes. Though there were plenty of bombs, there were no bomb hoists—each 500-pounder had to be wrestled from the ground and attached to a dive-bomber by hand. Malaria, dengue fever, beriberi, and dysentery were rife. No man could avoid duty unless he was so sick he couldn't move. Generally the medics required a man to have a 102-degree fever before he was excused from duty.

The living conditions were abominable. The pilots were billeted in mud-floored tents that flooded in heavy rains. Their living area was inside a copse of coconut palms dubbed "Mosquito Grove" for obvious reasons. The latrine was a long trench with an insect-ridden log for a seat. The shower was the cool waters of the Lunga River—but only when it was safe to approach the water without being shot by a Japanese sniper. Like clockwork, Japanese bombers would appear at noon over the base, their bombs chewing up the field and destroying airplanes, equipment, ammunition, and fuel stores. Coastal watchers provided some advanced warning, and the P-400s often scrambled to meet the enemy as they approached. These warplanes took off in clouds of dust on sunny days, and in sucking mud when it rained. The field was constantly in disrepair from daily bombings, and pilots had to avoid the worst shell holes on takeoff and landing. Over time, the field would be covered by steel mesh, which was sometimes blasted into twisted metal by enemy bombs.

There was a problem with the radios. The men on the ground could hear the transmissions of the pilots in the air, but the tower could not talk to the pilots because of interference from nearby islands. Those who remained behind listened helplessly to the frenzied communications among the pilots fighting in the air. After each engage-ment, the ground crews would count the survivors as they landed. An ambulance stood ready for those who crashed upon landing or were wounded. The pilots who returned unscathed climbed aboard a rickety jeep that carried them to a debriefing, while the ground crews patched up and serviced their warplanes for the next action. On bad days the medics worked feverishly to save the wounded. Entertainment came from smoking captured Japanese cigarettes, playing cards, or listening to the radio—which usually meant the propaganda broadcasts of Tokyo Rose, which mixed music with propaganda and misinformation. Even this peaceful interlude was interrupted by nightly air attacks from two hated enemies—"Washing Machine Charlie" and "Louis the Louse," the nicknames given to the Japanese pilots who attacked their base every night. These raids made an unbroken night's sleep impossible.

Between October 13 and November 14, the Japanese pulled out all the stops to destroy the American air base. Japanese artillery was smuggled onto the island at night, and shells began to rain down on the Americans twenty-four hours a day, while Japanese warships steamed close enough to launch naval bombardments. By the morning of October 14, the base was shattered and the pagodalike tower destroyed. That night the Japanese heavy cruisers *Chokai* and *Kinugasa* pelted the field with 700 eight-inch rounds. At dawn Japanese transport ships offloaded an invasion force at Tassafaronga, just ten miles from the Lunga River. On the night of October 16, the cruisers *Myoko* and *Maya* came through the Slot and shelled the base. Over forty air-craft at Henderson Field were lost. At dawn, just as a swarm of Aichi D4YI Val dive-bombers plunged out of the blue sky to finish off the air base, nineteen Wildcat fighters from VMF-212 arrived on the scene and scattered the Japanese formation. But the Japanese continued to land more men and matériel on Guadalcanal under cover of darkness. Dubbed the "Tokyo Express" by U.S. high command, these enemy supply ships arrived every night to deliver fresh troops to be hurled at the belea-guered Americans on the other side of the island.

November 13, 1942, was the turning point for the Cactus Air Force. Two Japan-ese battleships and fifteen other warships steamed down the Slot to smash the Amer-icans once and for all. But this time the United States Navy was alerted to their approach and ambushed the enemy fleet. The Japanese battleship *Hiei* was hit eighty-five times during the three-day naval battle for Guadalcanal. It was floating dead in the water by the end of the clash, and aircraft from the Cactus Air Force finished her off the next day. "It should be recorded that the first battleship to be sunk by Ameri-cans in the Second World War was sunk because of a handful of Marine and Navy aircraft," the official report stated.

On November 14, the Japanese made their final run on the airfield, attacking with a combined cruiser and transport ship force commanded by Vice Admiral Gunichi Mikawa. The Japanese ships were attacked by every single warplane from Henderson along with carrier aircraft from the U.S.S. *Enterprise*—and were decimated. Two Japanese cruisers and seven troop transports were sunk. Only 4,000 of the 10,000 Japanese Army troops aboard the doomed ships managed to swim ashore. So many ships were sunk in the Slot that it soon gained a new nickname—"Iron Bottom Sound."

▪ Warplanes of the Pacific Theater

At the outbreak of the Second World War, the premier fighter in the Pacific was the Mitsubishi A6M Zero-Sen fighter—code-named "Zeke" by American intelligence but called simply the Zero by the men who flew against them. For the Japanese, the Zero was more than an airplane, it was a visible symbol of their national will. Like the Spitfire for the British and the Messerschmidt Bf-109 for the Germans, the Zero mirrored the progress of the war in the minds of the Japanese people.

In the beginning, the Zero was the most formidable warplane in the skies. But by the end of hostilities, it was outgunned, outnumbered, and outmoded by the warplanes churned out by America's arsenal of democracy. That was because the basic design of the Zero did not change throughout the war. By 1945, the design of the newest American fighter aircraft exploited four years of technological evolution and battlefield innovation—changes Japanese aircraft engineers chose to ignore. Yet in the early days of the war, the Zero possessed almost mystical powers in the minds of Allied pilots. Far more maneuverable than any other aircraft on the front, it was quick and nimble in a dogfight. It could climb to 13,000 feet in a little over four minutes and had exceptional range due to its light design and relatively small engine. It was important for Japanese and American warplanes to be carrier-capable. With a wingspan of thirty-six feet and a length of twenty-nine feet, the Zero was compact enough to fit inside the bowels of a Japanese aircraft carrier or on its packed deck. Later models came with folding wings to make them even smaller. At 340 miles per hour, the Zero began the war as the fastest plane in the air. But with only two 20mm cannons and three machine guns, even the technically inferior Grumman Wildcats the Americans flew possessed more firepower. Of course the Zero's strength didn't come from its firepower, but from its speed and agility.

There were drawbacks to the Zero's design, though they weren't apparent until months into the war. For one thing, its speed came at a price—a total lack of armor. While the Wildcat and even the Airacobra could take plenty of punishment, the Zero was frail. It lacked self-sealing gas tanks, so a few well-placed rounds could transform the warplane into a gasoline-fed fireball.

One secret of the Zero's early invincibility in the Pacific theater was the relative experience of the pilots who flew it. Japanese airmen had been fighting for nearly a decade before they went to war against the United States. Their weapons, tactics, and martial spirit had been tested in the fire of battle. With the exception of isolated units like the American Volunteer Group—better known as the Flying Tigers—few American pilots possessed combat experience or adequate combat training when the United States entered the war. In contrast, the first wave of Japanese pilots who flew the Zero—whether in the Imperial Army or the Imperial Navy—were among the best-trained military aviators of the twentieth century.

In *Samurai!*, the autobiography of Japan's most celebrated ace, Saburo Sakai vividly described the grueling regimen of training he received as a cadet: "One of the more unpleasant of the obstacle courses was a high iron pole which we were required to climb. At the top of the pole, we were to suspend ourselves by one hand only. Any cadet who failed to support his weight for less than ten minutes received a swift kick in the rear and was sent scurrying up the pole again . . . Every enlisted man . . . was required to be able to swim. There were a good number of students who came from the mountain regions and had never done any swimming . . . The training solution was simple. The cadets were trussed up with rope around their waists and tossed into the ocean, where they swam—or sank."

Sakai states that later in the war the pilots who graduated from flight school were inferior to those who had washed out in his day. Japan's voracious need for manpower had cut the once-rigorous training schedules in half, then half again, until the pilots arriving at the front were barely competent. And Japanese pilots never learned teamwork. While their American counterparts were using two Wildcats to shoot down five or six Zeros, Japanese pilots only fought solo.

When the Japanese attacked Pearl Harbor, they did it with a frontline warplane developed for the sole purpose of dive-bombing the enemy. The Aichi D3A "Val" was one of the earliest dive-bombers to enter mass production. Like Germany's Ju-87 Stuka, the Val had fixed landing gear, which caused drag and made the plane slow. But the Val had a sturdy airframe that outperformed the Zero's and its appearance in the sky over an Allied target was cause for alarm. By January 1943, the Val was totally outmoded, but in the first two years of the war this aircraft sank more

Allied fighting ships than any other single type of Axis aircraft.

The G4M "Betty" was the heaviest Japanese bomber of the war. Its range was phenomenal but came at great expense—its lack of armor meant no protection for the crew. A cigar-shaped, twin-engine bomber, the Betty could carry three tons of aviation fuel and 2,200 pounds of bombs. But without self-sealing gas tanks, it was prone to explode after a few hits. Though unpopular with its crews, the Betty was used heavily during the first years of the war, especially in the skies over Guadalcanal.

The United States began the war with an arsenal of outmoded fighter aircraft, including the Brewster Buffalo, the P-39 Airacobra, and the P-40 Warhawk. But one aircraft manufacturer had developed an effective fighter for the United States Navy. The Grumman Ironworks created the sturdy F4F Wildcat in the 1930s as the Navy's second monoplane, after the disappointing Buffalo. The Wildcat went into production right before the outbreak of hostilities.

The Wildcat was an ugly aircraft with the tenacity of a belligerent pitbull. The pilots loved her because the rugged, indestructible warplane could take punishment and dish it out. Though it was slower and more sluggish than the Japanese Zero, the pilots who flew the Wildcat developed innovative tactics to utilize its assets and compensate for its flaws. The Wildcat outgunned just about every other Japanese warplane—its six 12.7mm machine guns made wrecks out of many enemy planes. The Wildcat flew off the decks of aircraft carriers, or from mud airstrips built around land bases. Used exclusively by the Navy and Marine Corps, it never saw action in the European theater. Pilot Joe Foss, who flew the F4F out of Guadalcanal, summed up the aircraft's virtues in a single sentence: "That's the ugly sonofabitch that brought me home . . ."

The Grumman F6F Hellcat was called "The Aluminum Tank" by the airmen who flew it. With six .50-caliber Browning machine guns, it could produce a hail of fire that few enemy aircraft could survive. Japanese pilots viewed the Hellcat with the awe and respect that Allied pilots initially gave to the Zero. Like the Wildcat, the Hellcat could take punishment and pilots joked about returning from battle with "holes where the airplane used to be." One Hellcat that had been burning for a hundred miles still made a successful carrier landing. Like the Wildcat, the Hellcat flew from carriers and land bases but saw no action in the European theater.

The gull-winged, single-engine Vought F4U Corsair was the finest U.S. Navy fighter of the Second World War. It could outfight, outclimb, and outrun any other aircraft in the Pacific theater. Designed by engineers at the United Aircraft Corporation, the parent company of Vought-Sikorsky, the Corsair entered service in 1940, but not in sufficient numbers to see action until 1943. The idea behind the plane was to merge the smallest, cleanest airframe with the biggest engine and lots of guns—the Corsair featured six .50-caliber Colt-Browning M-2 machine guns and some models were equipped with four 20mm cannons instead. The aviators of Pappy Boyington's "Black Sheep Squadron" carved out a legend for themselves flying the Corsair.

Though there were initial difficulties in early carrier tests—the Corsair's engine had a tendency to stall at slow speeds, which made carrier landings dicey—these obstacles were soon overcome and for the next fourteen years the Corsair remained the United States Navy's premier frontline fighter. The Corsair saw combat in World War II, the Korean War, and Vietnam before it was retired from active duty in the early 1960s.

The United States began the war at a disadvantage but worked to improve its weapons and tactics. By the end of hostilities, America's military was unmatched on the battlefield and its industrial output was the envy of the world.

After the failed attacks of October/November, the Japanese gave up trying to recapture Henderson Field, but the fighting in the skies and waters around Guadalcanal never ceased. Between August 1941 and January 1943, the Cactus Air Force suffered heavy losses: 148 aircraft were shot down and 94 airmen were killed. In addition to these staggering totals, 43 warplanes were destroyed on the ground by artillery or air attack. Estimated Japanese losses are as high as 900 aircraft and 2,400 men. In the months ahead, more pilots would arrive at Henderson Field to join the Cactus Air Force as its legend continued to grow.

HEROES OF THE CACTUS AIR FORCE

JOHN L. SMITH

Captain John L. Smith was twenty-seven years old when he landed his Grumman F4F-4 Wildcat on Guadalcanal. Born in Lexington, Oklahoma, he had joined the Corps in 1936 after graduating from the University of Oklahoma. Fascinated by airplanes, he applied for flight training after two years in artillery. Smith flew dive-bombers first, but anxious to see action, he transferred to a fighter wing that was on its way to Wake Island. When the island fell to the Japanese, his squadron was diverted to Midway, where Smith logged plenty of flight time and developed some innovative fighter tactics he would soon employ over Guadalcanal. His superiors took notice of his initiative and Smith was promoted to captain and given his own command, VMF-223.

Strikingly handsome, with dark hair and eyes and a razor-thin nose, "Smitty" proved to be a moody and demanding officer. He pushed his men hard and washed out those that didn't measure up to his exacting standards. Smith believed that the only way to counter the technically superior Japanese fighter aircraft and the enemy's more experienced pilots was through rigorous training and repeated drills. When VMF-223 was ordered to Guadalcanal, Smith was still dissatisfied with the performance of some of his men and hastily arranged a swap—eight of his pilots for eight pilots with more combat experience from another squadron.

Captain Smith led his squadron into combat the day after they arrived on Guadalcanal, and by the end of the week he had downed five enemy aircraft, making him Guadalcanal's first ace. Before his arrival at Henderson Field, the Zero fighter and the reborn samurai at its controls were considered invincible. Captain Smith's success went a long way in proving to the Marines that the Zero was vulnerable and the men who flew it human.

On a single day—August 30, 1942—Smitty added four enemy airplanes to his total. As six Zeros dived down on a flight of U.S. Army P-40s, he and his wingman followed the enemy planes down at a speed of 300 miles per hour. Lining up behind four Zeros, Smith ordered his men to pick a target and never let it go. Then he pressed the trigger on his control stick. The Wildcat's six machine guns spoke and the Zero filling his windscreen exploded into an orange fireball. Then Smith dived under the belly of a second Zero and fired. The Japanese fighter broke apart—so close to Smith's aircraft that chunks of metal bounced off his canopy. As his Wildcat flew into a billowing cloud, Smith's radio crackled to life. "Bandits ahead!" his wingman warned.

A dark silhouette appeared in the clouds. Smith fingered the trigger, waiting to confirm the identity of the other plane before he fired. When he could just make out the red ball painted on the fuselage, Smith cut loose and a third Zero spun into the ocean. Still lost in the mist, Smith searched for a way clear or for a glimpse of his wingman. He spotted two Zeros flying below him, low over the jungle. He sent one crashing into the trees, but the second Zero eluded him. When Smith landed back at Henderson, the ground crew was waiting for him.

"How many?" someone cried over the rumble of the Wildcat's engine. Smith smiled and held up four fingers. The ground crew cheered.

By the time Smith was rotated off Guadalcanal in mid-October, he was the Marine Corps' leading ace, with nineteen kills to his credit. He also received a promotion, so it was *Major* John L. Smith who arrived in the States, where he participated in a nationwide War Bond–selling tour. His movie-star good looks were a draw for the ladies and got Smith's photo on the cover of *Life* magazine. Soon he was receiving sacks of fan mail. Major Smith met with President Roosevelt on February 24, 1943, and was presented with the Medal of Honor. He begged to be allowed to return to combat, but was told by his commanding officers that before he could do that he would have to train "150 more John Smiths." Though he eventually returned

Major John L. Smith

to a frontline unit in the Philippines, Major Smith never saw combat again. An uncompromising commander burning with energy and imagination, he was no doubt the role model for John Wayne's portrayal of "Major Dan Kirby," leader of "VMF-247" in the 1951 RKO war epic *Flying Leathernecks*. Like his big-screen counterpart, Smith was meticulous and exacting, virtues that no doubt made him a superb combat flight instructor. He remained in the Corps after the war, serving in staff positions before retiring as a full colonel in 1961. He joined an aerospace firm and worked as an executive for nine years before he was laid off during an economic downturn. Despondent over the loss of his job, John Lucien Smith, the first Marine Corps ace of the Second World War, took his own life on June 9, 1972. He was fifty-eight. ▪

"INDIAN JOE" BAUER

Lieutenant Colonel Harold William Bauer was possibly the finest fighter pilot of his era. Skipper of VMF-212, he acquired the nickname "Indian Joe" at the Naval Academy at Annapolis because of his high cheekbones and darkly handsome features. A big, burly man, Bauer played football at the Academy and was quarterback in 1930.

Bauer spent seven years in Marine Corps Aviation before the outbreak of the war. His pilots called him "The Coach" because he ran his squad like a football team. At thirty-four, Bauer was older than most of the pilots serving in the Solomon Islands, and his men looked up to him. They respected his sound judgment and the effectiveness of his battle tactics.

Lieutenant Colonel Harold W. Bauer

Before it was sent to Guadalcanal, Bauer's squadron flew out of Efate. In that time, Bauer made a few visits to Guadalcanal and fought side by side with the pilots of VMF-223 and Marion Carl, their leading ace. Bauer and Carl had developed a not-so-friendly rivalry when they served together in San Diego before the war. Any lingering ill-feelings were repaired after the two aviators staged a mock dogfight somewhere over the South Pacific, after which Carl and Bauer became respectful comrades-in-arms if not bosom buddies.

Indian Joe Bauer's finest hour came on October 3, 1942. While on a patrol with Marion Carl, he shot down four Zeros with four well-aimed bursts. He fired so quickly that five out of six machine guns on his Wildcat jammed. As he returned to base, Bauer noticed a Zero shooting at an American pilot who had bailed out and now hung helplessly under his parachute. Enraged, he turned around and charged the Zero, downing it with a few bursts from the one machine gun that still functioned. Low on fuel and with all of his guns now out of action, Bauer ignored the danger to himself and remained in the area, flying circles around the American pilot until a U.S. Navy destroyer pulled the man out of the ocean.

When the Japanese made their push against Gaudalcanal in mid-October 1942, Bauer and his command were sent to the island to reinforce the Cactus Air Force. The squadron took off at dawn, October 17, on the long flight to Henderson Field. Their appearance in the skies over Guadalcanal was both dramatic and timely. As they approached the island, Indian Joe spotted two dozen Val dive-bombers preparing to make a bombing run on the airfield. Henderson Field was already in shambles from days and nights of artillery and naval bombardment and the Vals were there to obliterate the last vestiges of the American base. Because they were low on fuel, Bauer ordered his men to land at Henderson. Then he jumped the enemy bombers in a brazen solo attack. Though critically low on fuel himself, Bauer managed to scatter the Japanese formation and shot four of them down. As the Vals fled, Bauer's engine sputtered, its fuel exhausted. The Wildcat's engine cut out as the pilot's wheels touched ground. For this impressive action, Lieutenant Colonel Bauer received the Medal of Honor.

"The Coach" was an aggressive, fearless pilot with an utter disdain for the enemy. He was older and more experienced than many of his colleagues, some of whom had logged barely thirty hours in the cockpit before being shipped off to Guadalcanal. Like Captain Smith, Bauer was born in America's heartland. He hailed from a Kansas town called Woodruff, in the middle of rich farm country between Prairie City and Harlan County Lake. Before his fortuitous arrival over Henderson Field on that October morning, Bauer had downed five enemy planes, all in fearless attacks against superior numbers. His aggressive, solo assault against more than twenty Vals over Henderson Field did not surprise the men who knew him.

Less than a month after this engagement, Lieutenant Colonel Bauer was involved in one of the most savage air attacks of the Pacific theater. On November 12, the Japanese sent the battleships *Hiei* and *Kirishima,* the cruiser *Nagara,* and fourteen destroyers through the Slot in an effort to snatch Guadalcanal from the Americans. The United States Navy either drove off or annihilated the ships in what Fleet Admiral Ernest J. King called "the fiercest naval battle ever fought." But then a second armada of eleven Japanese transport ships packed with 12,000 enemy troops landed on the western coast of Guadalcanal. Escorting these supply ships was the destroyer *Hoyashio,* under the command of Tadashi Yamamoto. Shortly before noon on the fourteenth, Yamamoto received word that the American airfield had been destroyed and there were no enemy surface ships in the region. That was good news, if inaccurate, and the Japanese commander gazed out at the vulnerable transport ships with trepidation. He knew it would be at least six hours before the troops completed their landing. What if American ships were to arrive? Or worse, American planes? Commander Yamamoto's worst fears were soon realized.

After days of enemy shelling, there were only fourteen operational Wildcats left on Guadalcanal, along with a handful of Dauntless dive-bombers. The Americans knew the Japanese were landing on the opposite coast, and that the Marines fighting on the ground would have to kill every Japanese soldier who came ashore if they were to secure the island. Bauer took off in a Wildcat, alongside his best friend, Joe Foss, and two wingmen. A flight of Dauntless dive-bombers accompanied them. Their mission was to stop the enemy force on the beach before they melted into the jungle.

When Commander Yamamoto heard the sound of engines, he looked up to see American dive-bombers dropping on his transports. They were followed by Wildcats on a strafing run, guns chattering. Several transports were destroyed by bombs. Others were strafed by the Wildcats. The Japanese troops were crowded on decks, preparing to board landing boats, when the Americans warplanes arrived. Soon the Cactus Air Force pilots were joined by carrier planes off the *Enterprise* and by aircraft from remote land bases like Efate. For several hours the American planes raked the Japanese ships, sinking many and setting others ablaze. The water around the burning ships was bloody. Corpses blown overboard bobbed on the waves, to be torn apart by hungry sharks. The absolute butchery of this operation was evident to the American pilots, but they continued to slaughter the helpless Japanese. Though they realized that it was better these soldiers die now, before they had a chance to engage the hard-pressed U.S. Marines clinging to the opposite side of the island, that understanding was scant comfort to the men who pulled the trigger. Aircrews seldom see the appalling result of their attacks, but here the devastation wrought by the American warplanes was clearly visible, and it took its toll on the aggressors. Battle-hardened Navy and Marine Corps aviators vomited over their control panels. If they flew too low, the Americans could actually hear the screams of the dying over the roar of their engines. Six thousand Japanese were torn to pieces by bullets or plunged burning from the decks of capsized ships. Many drowned, trapped below the bulkheads of sinking transports. Explosions tossed shattered bodies into the air. Sharks circled the crippled ships, waiting to devour the dead and dying.

At four o'clock in the afternoon—four hours into the relentless air assault—Bauer and Foss's Wildcats were ambushed by two Japanese Zeros. Lieutenant Colonel Bauer spun around and immediately fired on his attacker. The Zero vanished in a fireball, but Bauer's Wildcat was also hit. The pilot either bailed out or ditched, for when he was spotted again by Joe Foss he was already in the water. Indian Joe was alive, unwounded, and seemed to be swimming toward the shore wearing his bright yellow life jacket, so there was immediate danger of drowning. As Foss wiggled his wing, Bauer signaled him to go home. Low on fuel, Foss obeyed, but returned less than two hours later aboard a Catalina seaplane. It was so dark that the rescue team could find no trace of Bauer, so they returned to the area the next morning and resumed the search.

Lieutenant Colonel Harold Bauer was never found. Eventually he was declared missing in action and his ultimate fate is still a mystery. Indian Joe was mourned by his squadron mates and by his friend Joe Foss. The tragic loss was compounded by the fact that he vanished just six days before his thirty-fifth birthday. When he disappeared Indian Joe had eleven Japanese planes to his credit—six of them were shot down over Guadalcanal. This feat is all the more remarkable because Bauer flew only four combat missions with the Cactus Air Force. He was such an exceptional airman that, had he lived, Indian Joe Bauer's score might have exceeded that of the Marine Corps' greatest ace of the Second World War—Major Gregory "Pappy" Boyington of the Black Sheep Squadron.

There is no gravestone to mark Harold Bauer's final resting place, but his name is inscribed on the Wall of the Missing at American Battle Monuments Commission (ABMC) Manila Cemetery in the Philippines, a fitting tribute to this bold warrior of the skies.

JOE FOSS'S FLYING CIRCUS

Joseph Jacob Foss was born on April 17, 1915, at his family's farm near Sioux Falls, South Dakota. His family was poor and worked long hours to wrestle a livelihood out of the arid land. The Foss homestead was primitive, with no running water and no electricity installed as late as 1945. At fifteen, Joe saw his first airplane when the Marine Corps staged a local air show. Three years later he paid five dollars for his first ride in one.

In 1933, when Joe was just sixteen, his father was killed in a car accident. After that, Joe had to provide most of the family's income and he worked hard to earn it. At six feet and 175 pounds, Foss could find plenty of work—but only of the most back-breaking sort. By high school, he found a better job working at a local filling station, where he pumped gas and learned the rudimentary skills of a mechanic. He begged his mother to allow him to quit school and work full-time to support the family, but Mrs. Foss forbade it; she wanted her sons to have an education.

By 1937, Joe was earning enough money to take flying lessons and attend the University of South Dakota. When he graduated he already had his pilot's license. In 1940, he enlisted in the Marine Corps and earned his wings in March 1941. Foss taught flight school in Pensacola, then shipped out for Guadalcanal in August 1942. He had to battle his superiors to see action. When the war broke out he was assigned to aerial photographers' school. When Joe protested, he was told that at twenty-seven, he was too old to be a fighter pilot. Foss managed to get hold of a Wildcat and

Joe J. Foss

logged 150 flight hours in his spare time. Suddenly he was the most experienced pilot in the Pacific theater and was handed the command of VMF-121. On October 9, 1942, Joe catapulted off the deck of the escort carrier *Copahee*—his only carrier mission. He and his squadron landed at Henderson Field, where they were greeted with the news that this "cow pasture" was now their home base. Joe would lead a flight of two four-plane divisions, known as "Foss's Flying Circus." He would go on to shoot down sixty Japanese planes. Five members of the Flying Circus would become aces. Two would perish.

Joe Foss downed his first Zero four days after he arrived on Guadalcanal, but it was a humbling experience. He was caught flat-footed by a Zero that came out of nowhere. Fortunately, the Japanese pilot overshot Joe's Wildcat and flew right into his sights. Foss pressed the trigger by instinct and destroyed the enemy plane. Three more Zeros attacked him moments later, and he barely managed to get back to Henderson in one piece. In his debriefing, Foss realized exactly what he had done wrong.

"You can call me Swivel-Neck Joe from now on," he told his comrades. After that, Foss kept his eyes open and his head swiveling, and no Japanese pilot ever got the drop on him again. Foss borrowed the tactics of Indian Joe Bauer, learning to get so close to the enemy that he couldn't miss. This philosophy paid off the next day, when Joe shot the wing off a Zero that was chewing up the tail of another Wildcat. By October 25, he had achieved fourteen victories in thirteen days. He had also been shot up twice and wounded in the head.

On November 7, Joe's Wildcat was shot up yet again. But this time his plane was too damaged to make it back to Henderson and he was forced to ditch in the ocean near Malaita Island. He nearly drowned when his parachute harness became entangled as he tried to escape the sinking Wildcat. He actually went down with his airplane, and was gulping salt water when he finally freed himself and swam to the surface. Foss managed to inflate his Mae West but had no strength to swim against the current. He decided to float on his back, awaiting rescue. Then he saw shark fins cutting the water. Airmen were issued pouches of chlorine powder, which was supposed to repel sharks. Foss opened one and sprinkled it into the water and the shark fled. At dusk he was found by local natives and brought to Malaita's Catholic mission, which was staffed by two nuns who had lived on that tiny island for forty years. They fed him steak and eggs, and Foss relished the feast after the inadequate fare on Guadalcanal. A PBY Catalina landed and "rescued" Joe Foss the next day.

On November 9, Admiral "Bull" Halsey pinned the Distinguished Flying Cross on Foss and two other pilots, but the rest of the month did not go well for the Flying Circus. On the fourteenth, Joe's best friend, Indian Joe Bauer, was lost at sea. Soon after, Foss was diagnosed with malaria and had to be evacuated. He would not return to active duty for six long weeks. On January 15, 1943, he shot down three more enemy planes for a total of twenty-six. Now his official tally matched that of America's greatest ace—World War I pilot Eddie Rickenbacker. On January 25, Joe Foss flew his final combat mission. A few months later he was ordered to Washington, D.C., then toured the country, where he visited factories, sold War Bonds, and gave talks.

In May 1943, President Franklin Delano Roosevelt presented Foss with the Medal of Honor for outstanding heroism above and beyond the call of duty. When he returned to active duty, it was as a flight instructor at the Santa Barbara Marine Corps air station. After the war, Foss was commissioned in the South Dakota Air National Guard. Then he turned to politics and was elected to the South Dakota House of Representatives. After briefly returning to active duty during the Korean War, Foss became a brigadier in the South Dakota Air National Guard, but in 1954, he returned to politics. Foss was elected governor of South Dakota in a landslide and later became the first commissioner of the American Football League, a position he held until the American and National Football Leagues merged in 1966. In the late 1980s, Foss was elected president of the National Rifle Association, and in 1991, he coedited the best-selling book *Top Guns: Americas Fighter Aces Tell Their Stories* with Matthew Brennan.

OTHER DISTINGUISHED AVIATORS

Another Medal of Honor recipient who fought in the skies over Guadalcanal was Major Robert Edward Galer, commander of VMF-224. Galer, of Seattle, Washington, arrived on the island in mid-August 1942 to reinforce Major Smith's command. In the next two weeks, he shot down four Japanese planes, was shot down himself, parachuted into the water, and swam to shore to fly again. Before fighting in the

Solomons ended, Galer shot down thirteen Japanese airplanes—eleven of them in his first thirty days of combat.

At twenty-nine, Major Galer was a gifted and experienced airmen. He would have scored higher in the Pacific theater but for some unfortunate luck— he was shot out of the skies three times, which may account for his relatively low score compared with the other airman of the Cactus Air Force. Galer survived the war, remained a Marine, and rose to the rank of brigadier general. He was awarded the Medal of Honor by Franklin Delano Roosevelt in a White House ceremony on March 24, 1943, during which he was cited for his "gallant fighting spirit."

Twenty-two-year-old First Lieutenant James Elm Swett of VMF-221 was another ace-in-waiting when he arrived at Guadalcanal. He showed up in time for the second phase of the campaign.

Major Robert E. Galer

Like Galer, Swett was a Seattle native, though he entered service at San Mateo, California. As part of the Marine Air Group 12, First Marine Air Wing, he managed to shoot down seven Japanese dive-bombers on his first combat mission before being jumped by a swarm of enemy planes and shot down himself. When Lieutenant Swett arrived in the spring of 1943, Guadalcanal was no longer considered the front lines. He was twenty-two and eager to see action. Though he flew the Grumman Wildcat on raids against Japanese bases farther up the Solomon Island chain, he had never fought a dogfight. Things changed on April 7, when Admiral Yamamoto ordered a major Japanese strike against Guadalcanal—involving over 400 warplanes from both the Japanese Army and Navy air forces in the region.

Lieutenant Swett just happened to be flying a standard defensive dawn patrol with three other Wildcats when the Japanese arrived near the end of his mission. The lieutenant had actually touched down back at Guadalcanal when the word of an imminent attack came. He was ordered back into the sky without a refuel and sent to Tulagi Harbor to protect the supply ships from Japanese bombers. At 17,000 feet, Swett spotted twenty Vals heading right for his flight of four Wildcats. When the Vals turned on their wings and dived at the helpless American ships, Swett attacked. But Zeros suddenly appeared behind the Vals and it became a race. Would the fighters hit Swett's Wildcats before the wildcats could shoot down the Vals?

Focusing on the target ahead, Swett closed to within 300 yards of a Val and opened fire. The plane began to smoke, then twisted out of control and plunged into the harbor. As bombs began to drop on the ships, Swett hit a second Val—which

First Lieutenant James E. Swett

exploded instantly. A third plunged into the ocean trailing smoke, and Lieutenant Swett began to doubt his sanity—before today he had never dueled in the air. Now he was almost an ace!

Following a fourth bomber as it closed on the ships, Swett fired repeated bursts into the Val without bringing it down. Mindful of the Zeros waiting to pounce on him from above, Swett pulled up. But suddenly his fighter was rocked by a powerful blast. As he struggled with the controls, Swett noticed that a ragged hole had appeared in his left wing—he had been struck by American antiaircraft fire. He concluded that things were too hot at sea level and began to climb. He flew into a cloud bank, then veered around and dived, aiming for a second wave of Val dive-bombers making a run on the ships. Swett got so close to a Val that the Japanese plane filled his windscreen. Only then did he open fire. The antiaircraft damage to his left wing had frozen the guns, but the right wing guns still functioned. Pieces of metal flew away from the Japanese warplane and pinged off of his cowling as the burning Val arched into the ocean. His fifth victory quickly followed the fourth and First Lieutenant James Swett became an ace—in a battle that lasted mere minutes. Swett had more ammunition and his aircraft was in fair shape, so he decided to fight on. He downed two more Vals in swift succession, and got on the tail of another.

Suddenly glass splinters pelted him and he felt a blast of cold air. His canopy had been shattered by the rear gunner on one of the dive-bombers! Swett squinted against the wind and opened fire. He struck the Val but his guns cut out after a few seconds—Swett was out of ammo. Then a loud thump warned him that his fighter had taken another hit. The plane began to shimmy in the air and Swett knew the damage was severe. As he flew back to Henderson, Swett's oil pressure gauge went to zero and his engine cut out. He decided to ditch in the ocean near Florida Island. At 500 feet, American antiaircraft guns on the coast opened up on him. Swett ignored the fire and jettisoned his canopy. As his plane hit the ocean, he smashed his face against the control panel and broke his nose. Bleeding, he struggled to free himself from the shattered cockpit as the Wildcat sank beneath the waves. From the water, Swett fired his .45 into the air to attract attention and was rescued by a picket boat. Army intelligence was skeptical about Swett's account of downing seven kills in a single mission, but after interviews with witnesses, he was credited with all of the victories. For this action Lieutenant Swett was awarded the Medal of Honor, presented to him by Major General Ralph Mitchell while Swett was serving in the New Hebrides.

Flying an F4U Corsair later in the war, Lieutenant Swett scored eight more victories for a total of fifteen. He also participated in the dramatic rescue effort after the aircraft carrier *Bunker Hill* was set ablaze by a *kamikaze* attack in 1945. When the war ended, James Elm Swett—who had attended San Mateo College prior to the outbreak of the Pacific conflict—worked as a manufacturer's rep for his family business and remained in the Marine Corps Reserve, where he eventually rose to the rank of colonel. Today Swett is enjoying his retirement. He lives in Trinity Center, California, and says he "has nothing to do but boating, swimming, hunting and fishing, and enjoying life with his marvelous wife and visits with his sons, daughters, and six grandchildren."

Like Lieutenant Swett, First Lieutenant Jefferson Joseph DeBlanc of VMF-112 earned the Medal of Honor for breaking up a large formation of Japanese attack planes and downing several of them in a single mission. It was on the last day of January 1943 when DeBlanc, as the flight leader of a section of six fighters, was escorting a large formation of American dive-bombers and torpedo planes off Kolombangara Island in the Solomons. His force encountered a large number of Zero fighters protecting a half-dozen Japanese surface vessels. DeBlanc charged the Zeros and scattered the formation. Despite heavy damage to his aircraft, he managed to run off some Japanese floatplanes that also attacked the American warplanes.

DeBlanc shot down two Zeros before he was downed himself. He parachuted out of his burning Wildcat over enemy-held Kolombangara Island at a perilously low altitude, landing in some trees almost before his parachute fully deployed. Luckily, a coast watcher found him and hid him from Japanese patrols. Two weeks later the man traded DeBlanc back to the Marines for a sack of rice. In 1946, Jefferson DeBlanc, now a colonel, was presented with the Medal of Honor by President Harry S. Truman in a White House ceremony. He retired from the Corps in 1972 with a doctorate in education. DeBlanc taught mathematics, physics, computer science, and other subjects in his hometown of St. Martinville, Louisiana, and is now semiretired.

The aviators of the Cactus Air Force helped turn the tide of the Pacific War. At the controls of their stubby, rugged Wildcats these men hurled themselves against a seasoned and superior enemy, fighting and dying under deplorable conditions. General Merrill "Bill" Twining, operations officer of the First Marine Division on Guadalcanal, expressed his admiration for these brave aviators: "[The Cactus Air Force] transformed our miserable little strip into an unsinkable aircraft carrier. Their deeds are legendary."

EDSON'S RAIDERS

As the Cactus Air Force battled in the skies around Guadalcanal, Marine Corps rifle and infantrymen continually battled the Japanese on the perimeter of Henderson Field, on the banks of the rivers, and in the jungle.

After the bloody, two-day Battle of the Tenaru River, Colonel Ichiki's ground troops were virtually annihilated. The Japanese commander burned his regimental colors and shot himself in disgrace. Ichiki had underestimated the strength and determination of the Marines who defended the air base. General Kiyotake Kawaguchi, the next officer dispatched to Guadalcanal to take back the island, would make the same mistake. Kawaguchi was the leader of the 36th Infantry Brigade, which had seen action in the jungles of Borneo and were considered an elite combat unit. Kawaguchi's 5,000 troops assembled and boarded transport ships hours after receiving orders. They sailed from Truk in the western Carolinas and on the night of August 31 landed in Guadalcanal, where they linked up with a few hundred demoralized men from Colonel Ichiki's shattered command.

Kawaguchi had the manpower to push the Americans off the island, but he made a strategic blunder. Instead of concentrating his forces at a single point on the perimeter of the air base, where he might have punched through and overwhelmed the field, Kawaguchi decided to divide his army into three groups, each with its own objective. The general would lead 3,000 men against the southern perimeter of the field, where the Marines were most vulnerable. Kawaguchi wanted the Americans to defend against multiple attacks with meager troops—a wise strategy on paper.

Unfortunately, the success of the Japanese general's plan hinged on a simultaneous, three-pronged assault against the American base. But with the three Japanese units out of touch with one another as they moved through the jungle, such timing was nearly impossible. Almost immediately the rugged terrain began to wreak havoc with Kawaguchi's timetable. Marching through the thick rain forests at night was difficult and units became disoriented, divided, and blocked. Within hours of separating, all three elements were behind schedule. As the days dragged on, the Japanese forces became more confused and mired in the vast tropical forest. They were compelled to discard their heaviest equipment—artillery pieces and machine guns they would need when they finally clashed with the Marines.

More surprising, considering that the 36th were seasoned jungle fighters, the Japanese advance was very noisy. Marine patrols heard the enemy in the jungle and knew they were coming long before they arrived. What Vandegrift and his officers didn't know was precisely where the Japanese would strike, or when. Vandegrift sensed that the weakest link in the chain of defenses that protected Henderson Field was on the southern perimeter, so he placed one of his most trusted officers to command that crucial position.

Lieutenant Colonel Merritt "Red Mike" Edson was a steady hand to his men. Already in his mid-forties when the war broke out, he pushed the much younger men under his command to the physical limit. He commanded the First Raider Battalion and the First Parachute Battalion in this phase of the defense of Henderson Field. Frustrated because they lacked intelligence on enemy strengths, Edson led 700 men—many of them weakened from constant battle, a near-starvation diet, and bouts with malaria—on an amphibious reconnaissance raid on the Japanese-held village of Tasimboko. As the Raiders stormed the hamlet, the token Japanese force that guarded the town and the supplies stored there fled into the jungle. Edson's Raiders burned the supplies, stole what they could salvage, and threw the enemy's guns into the sea. Edson managed to snag a Japanese general's white dress uniform and later displayed it with pride to General Vandegrift. Edson estimated that there were between 4,000 and 5,000 enemy troops on the island, all brought in on the last two days of August, via the "Tokyo Express." Documents captured in the raid indicated that the Japanese were interested in attacking from high ground, specifically an unnamed ridge that ran south from the airfield.

The Battle of Bloody Ridge—"Edson's Ridge"—began at 10:00 P.M. on Saturday, September 12, 1942, when over 3,000 Japanese surged forward to hit the southward perimeter of Henderson Field, a weak defensive line that stretched four miles. This position was guarded by scattered outposts—there were not enough men to fill the ranks—and Edson's Raiders held the very center of the thin line. Because Edson knew the Japanese wanted the ridge, he walked the ground that morning while his Marines took up positions along that same long, *kunai*-grass covered slope. It was the

Lieutenant Colonel Merritt A. Edson

best high ground in the area—keeping it in American hands was the Marines' objective. The entire southwest perimeter was guarded by fewer than 800 battle-weary Americans. After the Japanese hit on the twelfth Major Edson's forces counterattacked at dawn on the thirteenth, hoping to drive the enemy back into the jungle. When he realized his Marines were outnumbered, Edson pulled back to even higher ground and ordered his men to dig in. There was fighting all along Edson's Ridge that night, even as Henderson Field was hard hit by air raids and naval bombardment.

At 9:00 P.M. on Sunday night, September 13 after a lull in the fighting, the ragged sound of a badly tuned airplane engine was heard in the darkening skies. "Washing Machine Charlie" dipped low over Edson's troops, wagged his wing, and dropped a green flare. A moment later Japanese destroyers firing from Sealark Channel rained destruction down on the American base. Then a Japanese officer fired a red rocket from somewhere in the jungle and two battalions of Japanese infantry, screaming "Gas! Gas! Gas!" burst out of the night and charged the ridge. Machine guns cut down the enemy, who waded through the tall stalks of swishing *kunai* to attack the American position. The Marines heard the blood-mad howls, then the agonized screams of the dying as grenades exploded in the midst of the Japanese.

Lieutenant Colonel Edson's command, made up of mixed elements of parachutists and raiders, were the last hope America had of keeping a toehold in the Pacific Rim. If they lost the ridge, then Henderson Field would fall. If Henderson was lost, then the war in the Pacific might well be lost too. Edson's men knew the stakes were high and vowed to fight to the death.

Thousands of Japanese regulars surged out of the jungle, shouting and shooting. The Marines fired back, aiming carefully—ammunition was precious—even as enemy mortar shells rained down on them and a naval bombardment ravaged the airfield to their rear. The noise was unimaginable. Death was all around. There was no avenue of escape beyond death itself. Soon Edson's left flank wavered from the impact of the first wave of enemy soldiers. The Marines rallied and beat back the Japanese at the point of their bayonets, then with grenades. The lines became blurred and the fighting dissolved into individual contests—hand-to-hand and face-to-face. American Marines and Japanese soldiers massacred the enemy as they looked him in the eye. The night was illuminated by blinding flashes from a hundred explosions, by blue-white tracer rounds, and thousands of muzzle blasts from rifles, BARs, and machine guns. The Marines who faced these elite jungle fighters were not green recruits. The Raiders had trained hard under Red Mike and were veterans of night jungle fights on Tulagi, where they battled the *rikusentai* toe-to-toe. The Marine parachutists were tough too. They had survived the rigors of airborne assault school and were familiar with infiltration and commando tactics. This contest was a battle of equals for perhaps the first time in the Pacific War. The Japanese were surprised to discover that the Americans were nothing like the lackadaisical Chinese armies they had defeated in countless battles over the last decade. These Americans were willing to fight and die and stubbornly refused to retreat. All during the clash, Major Edson fought on the front lines, performing the duties of a platoon sergeant rather than a general officer. He pushed, threatened, and cajoled his men to fight as hard as they could under the most perilous circumstances. Over the course of the next two days and nights, the fighting along Bloody Ridge was intense, chaotic, and unrelenting. Edson's steady hand and reassuring presence did much to boost the flagging spirits of his Marines.

Three times Kawaguchi's forces came over the ridge on that first night. Three times Edson's Raiders drove them back into the rippling waves of long grass. Finally, at about 3:00 A.M., the Japanese attack petered out. Edson informed General Vandegrift that he could hold his position but needed reinforcements. As the sun rose, Edson rallied his exhausted men and reorganized their defenses. He tightened the line and reinforced it with elements of the Fifth. He also cooperated with Marine Corps artillery teams and registered some key points along the ridge. When the Japanese returned, American 75mm howitzers would already be aimed at the heart of their forces. The Japanese had learned to fear the artillery. The American Marines were able to place fire where it was needed, and seemed to have more artillery as the campaign progressed.

At 6:30 that evening, Kawaguchi's main force charged the Marines in the most formidable assault so far. The Japanese came in waves that broke over the American lines, battering the Marines and threatening to drown them in a sea of enemy troops. Marines fell, shot dead, stabbed by bayonet or sword, or blown to pieces by Japanese grenades. The enemy fell upon the ridge with renewed fury, bayonets forward. They clawed their way up the slope, eager to get at the Marines. Soon the first enemy soldiers reached the top and were among the Americans. At many points along the perimeter the fighting was hand to hand. Edson pushed his men, moving back and forth behind the lines to direct fire and guide artillery. At one point a Japanese soldier leapt into Edson's command post and charged the American with his bayonet. A Marine named Sheffield Banta pulled out his pistol and shot him dead.

This incident was repeated on the east perimeter, where the attack came in relentless waves that threatened to overwhelm the Americans. One Japanese officer leapt into the American command trench and spotted Captain Robert Putnam, helpless with a radio in his hands. The Japanese officer raised his samurai sword to decapitate Putnam when a shot rang out. Sixteen-year-old Marine Corps Private Marion Peregrine had killed the man, saving his commander's life.

At the top of Bloody Ridge with Edson was Major Kenneth Dillon Bailey, who commanded one of the most exposed and threatened companies on the perimeter. Bailey directed his riflemen to fire on enemy concentrations while drawing fire himself in an effort to ferret out hidden snipers. Both Edson and Bailey struggled to keep their men focused, to fill the gaps created by fallen Marines, and to direct the artillery. Both officers organized quick counterattacks when possible, in futile attempts to push the Japanese into the jungle. Fearing annihilation, Vandegrift committed his reserves to the battle—leaving the airfield defenseless. If Edson's men broke, there would be no stopping the enemy from recapturing Guadalcanal.

But Edson's men refused to quit. They fought to the limits of human endurance and beyond. American artillery barrages rained down on the Japanese positions all through the night, devastating Kawaguchi's 36th. The deafened, disoriented Japanese who managed to reach the ridge were greeted by seasoned Marines thirsty for blood. By dawn, General Kawaguchi had lost half of his attack force. The general mounted two subsequent attacks—both were short and desperate actions—but failed to penetrate the thin line of weary defenders. By afternoon the surviving enemy troops had pulled back into the jungle to regroup. The Japanese counteroffensive was broken, and Edson's Raiders still clung to the ridge with bloodstained hands.

For commanding the successful defense of Henderson Field, Lieutenant Colonel Merritt A. Edson and Major Kenneth Dillon Bailey of Pawnee, Oklahoma, both received the Medal of Honor. Major Bailey's award was posthumous. The thirty-one-year-old officer was killed by a burst from a Japanese machine gun while leading an assault less than two weeks after the battle for Bloody Ridge. Merritt Austin Edson had a long and distinguished career in the Marine Corps before he ever heard of Guadalcanal. Born in Rutland, Vermont, he entered service in his twenties. As a thirty-year-old captain, he served in Nicaragua during the campaign against Augusto Sandino's rebel army. Edson developed a bold strategy to rout the rebels, and to implement it he led five Marines up the Coco River in a flat-bottomed boat powered by a motor snatched from a Ford Model T. Edson's unit penetrated 300 miles into rebel territory in three weeks, and returned with invaluable intelligence information about the enemy.

Later Captain Edson devised a strategy to trap a sizable rebel force at the junction of the Coco and Huaspac rivers. With thirty-two Marines he moved into position and established an ambush. When the rebels didn't show, Edson pushed up his men through the jungle to a rebel camp at Bocay. Living off bananas, beans, beef, fruit, and "monkey meat," the Marines reached Bocay and found the rebels had already gone. A third expedition was more successful. Edson left Bocay with twenty-one of his thirty-two-man force and proceeded up river. He and his men lived off the land while skirmishing against roving rebel bands. The fighting intensified and Edson knew he was getting close to a rebel settlement. When a Marine Corps airplane dropped supplies, the pilot spotted an enemy camp and passed along the information. Edson struck immediately. In a swift firefight ten rebels were killed. Edson lost one Marine, with four wounded. For this action, Merritt Edson was awarded his first Navy Cross.

At Guadalcanal, Edson would continue to defend the perimeter until the island was secure. After the Second World War, he became embroiled in a political dispute over the future of the Marine Corps as an independent branch of the military. Though a leading candidate for commandant, Edson resigned his commission. He was recalled to active duty during the Korean conflict and rose to the rank of major general, but returned to civilian life shortly thereafter. On August 14, 1955, he was found dead in his garage, killed by carbon monoxide poisoning. "Red Mike" Edson was fifty-eight years old.

STRIKE AND COUNTERSTRIKE

After the battle for Bloody Ridge on September 18, the Seventh Marines arrived with 4,300 fresh troops, plenty of ammunition, tons of rations, and even a few tanks. Getting these men to Guadalcanal was costly—the aircraft carrier *Wasp* was struck by torpedoes and sunk and the battleship *North Carolina* was heavily damaged. But now General Vandegrift had almost 20,000 troops at his command. It was time to push the Japanese off Guadalcanal once and for all.

The Seventh was led by legendary Marine Lieutenant Colonel Lewis B. "Chesty" Puller. Like "Hard Head" Hanneken—the fabled Marine who killed rebel leader Charlemagne Peralte in Haiti and now commanded a battalion on Guadalcanal— Puller was a "Banana Warrior" who participated in the Corps military actions in the Caribbean. At forty-four, he was a short, tough, profane commander who enlisted in the Corps during the First World War, after a brief stint at the Virginia Military Institute. Puller was commissioned during the war, but was discharged in the downsizing of the Marine Corps following the armistice. He reenlisted as a private and served in Haiti, Nicaragua, and China. He attended university, was recommissioned, and decorated several times before arriving in the Solomons. "Chesty" Puller earned his third Navy Cross fighting for the airfield on Guadalcanal and would become the most decorated Marine in the long history of the Corps.

Puller personally led his command into the jungles of Guadalcanal on September 23, 1942. The Seventh was made up of young recruits, many just out of boot camp. As the only man in the battalion with real combat experience, he had to lead his raw Marines into their first battle. After a mauling that cost his forces seven men, Puller pressed westward toward the Matanikau River. Late afternoon on the twenty-sixth, he was ambushed by Japanese mortar and machine-gun fire. Casualties were heavy and Edson was dispatched to relieve Puller of his command.

With Edson in charge and Puller as his executive officer, an assault was planned for the next day. But that night the Japanese moved to higher ground, and when the Marines attacked at dawn, they were ready for them. The Americans were mauled and Major Kenneth Dillon Bailey, who had earned the Medal of Honor at Bloody Ridge, was killed. While these Marines engaged the Japanese on land, a second detachment circled the Japanese position in Higgins boats and landed behind the enemy. This force met with initial success, but was soon cut off and trapped between two large Japanese contingents. During the withdrawal of the wounded by landing boats, Douglas A. Munro placed his vessel between the evacuating Marines and the Japanese attackers and was killed protecting the lives of the evacuees. Munro became the only Coast Guardsman to receive the Medal of Honor.

Puller and Edson's offensive was a disastrous failure. One hundred and seventy Marines had been killed or wounded and the Japanese remained on the island in force. Two weeks later a second American offensive would also end in failure. The situation was in danger of evolving into a military stalemate—and with the Tokyo Express delivering enemy troops, ammunition, and weapons every night, a stalemate would ultimately result in the defeat of the United States Marines.

On October 13, 3,000 more Marines arrived. But the following day the Japanese also landed 3,000 troops on the opposite side of the island—this time in broad daylight. Among the Japanese forces was the elite Sendai Division, seasoned jungle fighters who achieved victory every time they faced an enemy. Stunned by this bold tactical move, General Vandegrift angrily demanded that the United States Navy take control of the sea around Guadalcanal. Meanwhile, on the sixteenth, a large Japanese force reinforced by armor set out on an eight-day march through the jungle to strike at the airfield. Vandegrift was unaware that such a force even existed. Fortunately, the Marines on the front lines were vigilant. When this force struck on the twenty-third, they were pummeled by American artillery and machine guns. It turned out that Vandegrift had long expected an attack from the west and had reinforced his defenses on that portion of the perimeter. The secret enemy force had attacked from that direction and just happened to hit the area where the Americans were strongest. In the melee that followed, twelve Japanese tanks were lost and hundreds of infantrymen were slaughtered by an effective American counterattack. When the sun rose in the morning, the sandbar where the engagement took place was covered with shattered trees, burned-out tanks, Japanese corpses, clouds of insects, and dozens of crocodiles— sluggish and bloated from feasting on the dead.

This failed attack did not spell the end of Japanese aggression, for the Sendai Division had secretly moved into position for their own assault on Henderson Field. The Sendai arrived outside the base perimeter under cover of darkness on Saturday evening, October 23, at about 9:30 P.M. Two hours before this attack, at sunset, Platoon Sergeant Mitchell Paige led his men on a quick march to their assigned position on an isolated part of Edson Ridge, on the left flank of the Matanikau River. The platoon reached their position in near-total darkness; the night was moonless and overcast, with a storm rumbling in the distance. Sergeant Paige got on his knees and felt around with his hands until he found a good spot to place his pair of machine guns. Then he ordered his men to set up the weapons while he felt his way around the perimeter, trying to get the lay of the land. The platoon was situated on top of a ridge made of sheets of shale, mud, and twisted tree trunks. The machine gun nests they were establishing were on high ground, overlooking the jungle and a string of barbed wire that marked the beginning of the American defenses. Paige's men assembled their weapons in silence, never quite sure what lurked in the shadows nearby.

With work completed, Paige realized that no one had arrived with dinner despite a promise that rations would follow them up the ridge. The sergeant thought about sending one of his men back to retrieve some chow. But after due consideration he decided to keep his platoon intact. Paige and his men shared a can of Spam, and did not feel the need to gripe about the lack of food. Gnawing hunger was a common thing on Starvation Island, and though things had improved in recent weeks, the Marines were used to living, working, and fighting with an unpleasant feeling of emptiness in the pits of their stomachs.

After dinner, it began to rain. Soon the rain was falling in sheets. The Marines huddled in their ponchos, covering their machine guns with tarps and cradling their rifles close to keep them dry. A little after midnight, they heard the sound of gunfire over the noise of the storm. Something was happening, but not close to Paige and his men, so they hunkered down and waited for the war to come to them.

A Sendai attack had hit Chesty Puller's position after midnight. They burst from the dark, dripping jungle and rushed the Marines on Edson's Ridge. The Japanese concentrated their forces at a point left of Sergeant Paige's position, where another Marine Corps NCO—Sergeant John "Manila John" Basilone—had positioned his own platoon. The enemy, wearing mushroom-shaped helmets and khaki uniforms, charged the Marines in the pouring rain. The ground was slick, the night overcast, and visibility was spotty through the rain. The Marines were huddled in muddy, half-flooded foxholes dug on the top of a slope. Their position was defended by a perimeter fence of tangled barbed wire, with a barren killing ground between the wire and the foxholes. The Marines were armed with machine guns, rifles, mortars, and plenty of grenades.

The first wave of Sendai threw themselves over the barbed wire, to let their comrades run across their backs and over the fence. Howling troops seemed to come from every direction at once, and the fight quickly became as chaotic as it was fierce. The black night was illuminated by muzzle fire and the brilliant flashes of exploding grenades and mortar shells. For some of the old vets it was World War I all over again, with thousands of screaming soldiers charging into merciless machine-gun fire that cut them down en masse. Dozens of Japanese fell in the first moments of the attack. But still they came, clustering at the barbed wire, where they were snagged, shot, or blown to bits.

Suddenly there was a powerful explosion at the fence—the Japanese had blown a gap in the wire and the Sendai were surging through the opening and up the slope. Shouting in triumph, Colonel Masajiro Furumiya, leader of the Japanese 29th Regiment and a hero of the Sendai Division, led his color company through the gap. The Americans trained their BARs and machine guns at the opening and massacred the Japanese as they tried to surge through it. Now Colonel Furumiya and his company were cut off from their main force—trapped between the barbed wire and the

Marines firing from foxholes. Aiming their machine guns at Furumiya and his men, the platoon commanded by Sergeant John Basilone opened fire. The Japanese soldiers were concentrated around the wire when the first burst hit them. Most fell dead. Others spun away with multiple wounds. A few clawed their way into the mud and waited for death to claim them. Sendai corpses quickly filled the gap while more enemy soldiers climbed over the grisly mound of bodies to reach the Marines.

After fifteen minutes of constant fighting, Basilone's platoon was almost out of ammunition. Manila John yanked off his boots to avoid losing them in the sucking mud he was about to slog through. Then, shirtless and soaking wet, he burst from his foxhole and ran to the rear to collect more ammo. While Basilone was gone, his platoon tried to hold the enemy off with rifles and grenades. The situation was perilous.

Gunnery Sergeant John Basilone

Without machine guns the Marines knew they could be overrun at any moment.

On their right Japanese troops had already annihilated an American machine-gun nest, bayoneted two Marines to death, and chased the rest off. The Japanese struggled with the unfamiliar American machine guns for a few minutes, then trained them on Basilone's Marines. Fortunately, both guns jammed and the Japanese abandoned the position and moved to the rear. Colonel Furumiya and the shattered remnants of his color guard would wander through the American perimeter for five days before trying to escape on November 1. All of his men were killed or captured, and Furumiya, after burying his regimental colors, took his own life. The Marines found his corpse the next day, along with a diary that outlined his activities during this second attack on Edson's Ridge and its aftermath.

When Sergeant Basilone had returned on the night of battle, swathed in heavy belts of ammunition, a runner burst out of the night with a warning: "They've got the guys on the right!"

Basilone, still carrying the ammo, immediately veered down the path to the right. In the darkness he stumbled into a private named Evans, one of the survivors from the overrun position. At eighteen years old, Evans was nicknamed "Chicken" by his fellow Marines. Now the teenager, pumped with adrenaline, was firing his rifle at the invisible enemy while screaming at the top of his lungs. "Come on, you yellow bastards! Come and get me!"

Basilone grabbed the young man's arm and pushed him back toward his own platoon. Then the sergeant ran forward and leapt into the foxhole that had been overrun and abandoned, and discovered the two machine guns that the Japanese had jammed. Instead of trying to clear them in total darkness, he ran back to his position to retrieve one of his own guns.

Back at his own foxhole, Basilone draped the heavy machine guns over his back and barked orders to the rest of his platoon. Half were to follow him back to the first position, the others were ordered to stay where they were and hold off the Japanese. He tossed his men a couple belts of ammo and took off for the foxhole on his right. When Basilone reached a bend in the trail, he ran into six Japanese soldiers who had slipped through the gap and were heading to the rear. From behind their sergeant, Basilone's men cut the startled Japanese soldiers down before they could fire a shot. When he reached the foxhole, his men set up the new machine gun while Manila John worked to clear the guns that were already there. All the while Japanese troops were streaming through the gap in the barbed wire. This time it was the Japanese Ninth Company that hit Basilone's men. Firing all three machine guns, Manila John's Marines slaughtered the entire company. For a few seconds the gap was clear. Then another Sendai horde raced out of the night to attack the Marines.

It was a long night, during which Sergeant Basilone kept the pressure on the enemy. As the Japanese rushed out of the darkness, wave after wave was cut down. For nearly an hour Basilone and his platoon held off repeated assaults. When a direct attack against the Marines was no longer possible, Japanese infiltrators began to circle Basilone's foxhole, crawling on their bellies to get a shot at the Americans. Ever vigilant, Sergeant Basilone and his men coolly dispatched the intruders with pistols and bayonets. Finally, by the light of intermittent shell flashes, the Marines could see that the Japanese had withdrawn. At about 2:00 A.M., the torrential downpour slowed to a steady rain that washed away the mud and the blood. At 2:30, the fighting around Basilone's position ceased.

Now things were getting hot for Sergeant Paige and his Marines. At 2:00 A.M., they heard the sound of furious gunfire. The noise came from their right. Already on edge from the fighting they'd heard earlier, the Marines were instantly alert. Paige crawled forward to the edge of the ridge and peered into the darkness below his position. He heard men whispering, not in English. Sergeant Paige slipped a grenade from his belt. His men, hearing the sound, pulled out grenades too. On cue, Paige and his platoon dropped hand grenades into the jungle below. There were many flashes. The sharp sound of the blasts were mixed with the cries of the wounded and the dying. The Marines manned their guns, ready for an all-out assault. None came.

At dawn, the Japanese withdrew. As the sun rose hot and bright, the Marines along Chesty Puller's line could see the horrendous damage they had inflicted. Hundreds of enemy soldiers lay torn and lifeless under clouds of buzzing insects. The earth was churned from artillery and mortar shells, and bushes, tree stumps, and even the shredded clothing on dead soldiers smoldered under the tropical sun. The jungle vegetation was ripped asunder, and snagged corpses dangled from the twisted barbed-wire fence. On the perimeter a young Marine pulled the helmet off his head with a shaky hand. Squinting into the morning sun, he wiped the dirt and sweat off his brow, lowered his head, and said a silent prayer. The Marine had just remembered that today was Sunday.

DUGOUT SUNDAY

Sunday, October 25, 1942, was the first pleasant weather day in a week. But things were anything but pleasant for the Marines on Guadalcanal. All during that bloody Sunday, the Japanese attacked Henderson Field from the sea, from the air, and through the jungle. At 10:00 A.M., the *Akatsuki, Ikazuchi,* and *Shiratsuyo* steamed into Iron Bottom Sound, guns blazing. They obliterated the shore batteries and sank most of the harbor craft. At 2:30, Japanese carrier planes arrived to bomb the airfield and support facilities. The enemy believed that Henderson Field had been knocked out. In a sense, they were right. The torrential rain the night before had turned the airstrip into a muddy swamp. But by noon General Geiger's determined ground crews had cleared the field and the hot tropical sun dried out the mud. The Cactus Air Force leapt into the sky and took on the Japanese bombers. In all, twenty-six Japanese planes were shot down by Wildcats and by American antiaircraft fire. At sunset Henderson Field was still in American hands.

The day had been long, hot, and miserable for the Sendai Division as well. When they regrouped in the jungle after the night assault, their officers discovered that casualties had been heavier than first suspected. These troops had no idea where they were on the maps, or in relation to the other units. Dire rumors spread through the Japanese ranks like wildfire. They were trapped. They were surrounded. More Americans were landing. None of these stories as true, but after their defeat the night before, the Sendai were demoralized enough to believe the worst. Now, as they tried to keep dry in the sopping jungle, as they rested, tended the wounded, or devoured their meager rations, the troops were informed that they would be attacking the Americans again that night.

The Sendai assembled at 11:00 P.M. at a position in the jungle near Puller's defensive line. Their officers loudly addressed the troops, whipping them into a fighting frenzy. Soon the Japanese were chanting, "U.S. Marine, you going to die tonight. U.S. Marine, you going to die tonight . . ."

The Marines could hear the cries and unleashed their mortars. Shells began to close on the Japanese position, and when the enemy charged, artillery rained down on them. At two in the morning, the human wave hit the ridge where Sergeant Paige was positioned with his platoon. Paige warned his men to use only grenades; he did not want the Japanese to see their muzzle flashes in the darkness.

"Don't let 'em spot the guns. Fire only when you have to."

The Marines rolled the grenades down the steep slope into the charging Sendai. The night was illuminated by explosions. Shrapnel whizzed through the air, cutting leaves and thunking into the trunks of jungle trees. The enemy's battle cries had turned to death shrieks, then to moans of agony and despair. But the brave men of the Sendai Division continued the charge. They got so close to the American positions

Sergeant Mitchell Paige

that the Marines were taken by surprise. They fired a short burst, then the Japanese were swarming over them. The fighting was hand to hand after that, and Paige recalled seeing one of his men lose a leg to a Japanese officer's sword before the man broke the neck of the officer with his other foot. A third wave raced out of the jungle, toward the ridge. The Marines could hear their bloodthirsty cries over the noise of battle: *"Banzai! Banzai! Banzai!"*

There was more killing and more dying and then suddenly the Japanese were gone—dead or retreating down the slope. Paige's platoon had beaten back the first wave, but there was no time to celebrate their victory. As the sergeant raced to clear a jammed gun, a shot fired from the forest shattered the weapon—and he felt a burning sting race from his fingers to his forearm. Surprised, Paige looked up to find that the second wave had arrived.

The fight lasted all night, but the Japanese never managed to penetrate Puller's lines. At dawn Paige was still firing a machine gun at the shattered remnants of the once-cherished Sendai Division. In the growing light, the sergeant spotted an abandoned American machine gun. There were dead Marines around the weapon and it was unattended—but not for long. Several Japanese infiltrators were crawling on their bellies toward the weapon. If they made it, the Japanese could turn the machine gun on his Marines. Paige leapt to his feet and raced across open ground toward the weapon.

As several Japanese soldiers rose to stop him, Paige dived for the trigger. The sergeant fired a burst of lead that cut the Japanese to pieces. Bullets started striking the ground around him and Paige knew he was not safe yet. Japanese troops were rushing out of the bushes all around him. Three Marines ran to aid the officer, carrying more ammunition. One went down with a bullet to the belly, a second from a groin shot. The last Marine was shot in the neck. Gushing blood, Paige ordered the wounded man back.

Then, dragging the heavy machine gun, he crawled back and forth along the perimeter. He fired a burst at the enemy, then moved on before they had the chance to shoot back. Hanging over the edge of the ridge, Paige spotted a Japanese officer in the tall grass. He shot the man, disemboweling him with a single burst. As more Japanese rose from behind the tall *kunai* grass, Mitchell Paige gunned them down. Then, still lugging the gun, the hot barrel burning his hands, he rose from cover.

"Let's go!" Paige yelled to his men as he hefted the machine gun and moved forward.

His platoon followed, screaming a rebel yell all the way. The Marines fired from the hip as they ran, cutting down the surprised Japanese, who popped out of the grass or from behind trees. Within minutes, there was no sign of the enemy. The ridge, and the grassy field below, were clear of all but the dead.

Platoon Sergeant Mitchell Paige was awarded the Medal of Honor for his bravery in the defense of Henderson Field. Born in Charlaroi, a little industrial town outside of Pittsburgh, Pennsylvania, he had enlisted in the Marine Corps out of patriotic spirit, and remained a Marine throughout the war and after its conclusion, to rise to the rank of colonel. At his presentation ceremony in Balcombe, Australia, it was General Vandegrift who awarded this fighting NCO his medal. Today, Mitchell Paige lives in LaQuinta, California.

Another NCO who won the Medal of Honor that day was Sergeant John "Manila John" Basilone. Sergeant Basilone was only two years older than Mitchell Paige, but he had led a very different life. Born in Buffalo, New York, he grew up in Raritan, New Jersey. As one of ten children in a poor Italian-American family, John was forced by economic necessity to drop out of the local Catholic school at fifteen so he could help support his family. His father was a tailor and John worked as a laundry-truck driver.

But in 1934, in the depths of the Great Depression, John was laid off. He had two choices—hang out with the troublemakers on the street or find another job. When no work was forthcoming, John enlisted in the Army. He was sent to the Philippines and fell in love with Manila. At that time the city was a rough seaport with an unsavory reputation. But Basilone felt at home. He drank in the bars along Dewey Boulevard and flirted with the pretty Filipino girls. When his stint in the military ended, he was discharged and got a job in a Raritan chemical factory. Three years later, bored with civilian life, Basilone enlisted in the Marine Corps. Benefiting from his previous military experience, he rose through the ranks. It was his wild tales about nightlife in the Philippines earned him the nickname Manila John.

Basilone arrived on Guadalcanal with Chesty Puller's First Battalion, Seventh Marines, and earned his Medal of Honor in the same battle as Mitchell Paige. Basilone was promoted to gunnery sergeant—it is said that the Marines offered him a lieutenant's stripe but he turned it down—and was sent back to the States to recuperate. He was treated like royalty in Raritan, where the town turned out for "Basilone Day." Tobacco heiress Doris Duke threw a high-society ball in his honor. Then the handsome sergeant traveled the country selling War Bonds. During this tour, Basilone met a young Marine sergeant named Lena Riggi. It was love at first sight, and in July 1944, they were married.

But John Basilone was itching to get back into action and the Marine Corps finally sent him back to the Pacific. In late 1944, he joined the Fifth Marines, who were assembling in Hawaii for a secret operation. On February 19, 1945, Gunnery Sergeant John Basilone was among the first wave to hit the beach at Iwo Jima. When his Marines were pinned down, Basilone took on a Japanese pillbox and wiped it out.

Suddenly a mortar shell landed at his feet. There was an blinding flash and Manila John Basilone was dead. His heroism at Iwo Jima earned him a posthumous Navy Cross, which was presented to his widow.

Almost forgotten in the Guadalcanal Campaign were the gallant actions of Corporal Anthony Casamento, a twenty-year-old section leader on Puller's defensive line. On November 1, 1942, Corporal Casamento advanced with a small detachment of Marines. While moving along a ridgeline, lugging a machine gun and plenty of ammunition to provide covering fire for two flanking units, the corporal and his men were attacked by a superior force of Japanese infantrymen. All of the Marines around Casamento were either killed or wounded, and Casamento was hit three times. Despite his injuries, he rushed the Japanese and wiped them out, then tackled a machine-gun nest the enemy was establishing to ambush the advancing American forces. After capturing the position, Corporal Casamento set up his gun and remained there throughout the night.

In total darkness, Casamento repulsed multiple attacks while doing his best to tend to the wounded. The corporal vigilantly provided cover fire for the Marines on his flank until he was found early in the morning among his dead and wounded comrades. In all, twenty-nine Marines from his unit were killed, but the stubborn corporal refused to give up. Tony Casamento, from New York City, was evacuated with the wounded.

Casamento, who left the Marine Corps in the late 1940s to settle in Long Island, New York, waited thirty-eight years for his courage to be recognized. Two survivors from his unit eventually came forward and documented his heroism, and on September 12, 1980, President Jimmy Carter presented him with the Marine Corps Medal of Honor. Casamento passed away less than seven years later, on July 18, 1987, and is buried at Long Island National Cemetery in Farmingdale, New York.

THE ARMY TAKES OVER

After the climactic battle of October 24–26, 1942, the Marines' fight on Guadalcanal was over. The Sendai Division, minus 3,000 casualties, retreated back into the jungle. The Marines and their Army reinforcements lost less than a tenth of that number and were ready for more action. During the final battle, the Marines were impressed with the performance of the Army's new M-1 Garand. It packed a punch and had a clip of eight rounds that fired semiautomatically—a real improvement over their five-round, bolt-action Springfields. Soon the Marines would have M-1s of their own.

On December 9, after four months of constant combat, after a half-dozen major battles on land, sea, and air, the Marines stood down. General Vandegrift relinquished his command to General Alexander Patch of the United States Army. Patch's GIs would fight for another two months before Guadalcanal was secure and before the Tokyo Express spirited away the last demoralized elements of the Japanese troops who tasted defeat at the battle for Guadalcanal.

On the day he surrendered his command, General Vandegrift visited a cemetery in the jungle, a place the Marines called Flanders Field. There were 1,200 graves in that cemetery—all of them men who had fallen on Guadalcanal under Vandegrift's command. In all, 2,100 Americans had been killed in the campaign. Another 700 suffered from a plethora of jungle diseases, the most common being malaria. An unknowable number were traumatized by the ordeal in ways that would not manifest themselves for years or even decades. The Presidential Unit Citation that the Marines were presented was scant comfort to the emaciated and dog-tired survivors of Guadalcanal, but at least they were alive and on their way to Australia for an extended period of rest and relaxation. They had earned it. For four months, they had faced the best the Japanese hurled at them, and had prevailed.

The Americans learned an important lesson at the battle for Guadalcanal. They learned that the Japanese were tough, clever, stubborn warriors—but they were not the invincible gods of war many thought they were. Guadalcanal was the first battle in human history that was waged on land, on the sea, and in the air. The campaign had consisted of four series of battles: air combats in defense of the air base; ground fighting on the island; carrier battles in the general vicinity; and surface naval battles in the waters near the island. But in truth, Guadalcanal was far more complex than that, a series of distinct clashes, each with a name and a date: the Landing, the Battle for Tulagi, Gavutu-Tanambogo (August 7–8); the Battle of Savo Island (August 9); the Battle of the Tenaru (August 21–22); the Battle of the Eastern Solomons (August 24–25); Edson's Ridge (September 12–14); the Air Campaign (August 12–January 31); the Battle of Cape Esperance (October 11); the Battle of Henderson Field (October 24–25); the Battle of Santa Cruz Islands (October 24); the Naval Battle of Guadalcanal (November 12–15); and the Battle of Tassafaronga (November 30). All of these clashes were crammed together around an island in the South Pacific that would be forgotten today if not for the prodigious amounts of blood shed over it in the middle of the last century.

"God favors the bold and the strong of heart," Major General Alexander Vandegrift told his Marines on the eve of the invasion of Guadalcanal. Some divine providence must certainly have favored the Marines. Despite horrendous odds, these bold warriors gained a foothold on Guadalcanal, captured the Japanese airfield, and made it their own, stood their ground against every division the Japanese threw at them, and transformed the Solomons into an American base. Under the brilliant leadership of General Alexander Vandegrift, the Marines carved out a legend on Guadalcanal—a legend etched in mud and blood on a field of jungle green. One of the last of their number to be decorated was General Vandegrift himself, who was awarded the Medal of Honor for his "tenacity, courage and resourcefulness" during the campaign for Guadalcanal.

Novelist James Michener wrote of the veterans of Guadalcanal in the years following the war. His words have new meaning today, as the ranks of those young men who fought tyranny during the Second World War dwindle with each passing day: "They, like their victories, will be remembered as long as our generation lives. After that, like the men of the Confederacy, they will become strangers. Longer and longer shadows will obscure them, until their Guadalcanal sounds distant on the ear like Shiloh and Valley Forge."

CHAPTER TEN

BLOODY BEACHEADS:
BOUGAINVILLE, TARAWA, THE MARSHALLS,
THE MARIANAS

■

1943–1944

A FTER four harrowing months, the Marine Corps successfully completed its first operation of the Pacific War. But the momentous clash at Guadalcanal was just the beginning of a series of hard-fought amphibious landings and bloody ground campaigns they would conduct over the next four years. There were still dozens of Japanese outposts in the Pacific. One way or another they had to be neutralized. Some could be isolated and starved out. Others had to be taken by force.

In the aftermath of its defeat at Guadalcanal, the Japanese military was demoralized. They had sacrificed too much, only to be defeated in the end. Following their victory at Pearl Harbor, the Japanese had suffered two major setbacks at the hands of the American military. After Midway and Guadalcanal, they would begin to adopt a defensive posture for the first time since the start of their aggressive expansion a decade before. But the Japanese still possessed a fierce fighting spirit and the war was not over yet.

One region of Japanese dominance was Rabaul, a small settlement at the northern end of New Britain Island in the Bismarck Archipelago. Rabaul was located on the opposite end of a long chain of Pacific islands that ended with Guadalcanal. The settlement had a natural harbor but few modern facilities when the Japanese took the island from the Australians in January 1942. In time the Japanese built Rabaul into their largest base south of Truk, with four paved airstrips, hundreds of aircraft, and 100,000 troops. All Japanese operations in the Solomons were supported by Rabaul.

Early in the war the Allies developed Operation Cartwheel, a planned invasion of Rabaul. But the realization that an invasion would pit a vulnerable landing force against 100,000 armed defenders and half the Japanese Navy gave the Joint Chiefs pause. Operation Cartwheel was abandoned and the Allies decided to invade the ring of Japanese-held islands *around* Rabaul, hopping from one to the next, isolating the main base and its personnel. With supply convoys blocked and friendly airfields farther and farther away, Rabaul would wither on the vine. Bougainville was the first objective in this island hopping campaign. It was an ideal location to stage bombing raids on Rabaul and already had a small airfield.

On paper the attack appeared simple, but Bougainville would prove to be a challenge for the Marines. The island was defended by 36,000 Japanese troops under Lieutenant General Haruyoshi Hyakutake, who had been defeated at Guadalcanal and was desperate to redeem himself. The Marines were still understrength, underequipped, and suffering from the staggering losses sustained in the campaign for the Solomons. But the Joint Chiefs expected miracles and the Marines were ordered to conduct three major amphibious landings in twelve months. It was a herculean task and the Third Marine Division was handed the job in late 1943. Commanded by Major General Allen H. Turnage, a veteran of World War I, Haiti, and China, the Third Marine Division was scheduled to hit Bougainville before year's end—another rushed offensive. Along with the Second and Third Raider Battalions and the Ninth Marine Division, the Third would land at Cape Torokina on the clear, bright morning of November 1, 1943.

Landing simultaneously on twelve beaches stretching from the port of Torokina northward, the Marines planned to surround and overwhelm any pockets of resistance that survived the naval bombardment. Unfortunately, they received little in the way of help from the Navy. Four destroyers were dispatched to pepper the beaches, but they fired salvo after salvo into the water around the Marines' landing craft instead. Their marksmanship skills were so bad that the Japanese defenses were untouched as the American boats made their approach. Fortunately, Marine Corps air support was more accurate and American dive-bombers managed to cover the main landings.

The Ninth Marines bore the brunt of the misery during the landing, losing eighty-six landing craft to rough seas and friendly fire. But once they were on the beach, it was the First Battalion, Third Marines, who faced the heaviest resistance—the beach they hit was defended by eighteen concrete pillboxes and a 75mm gun protected by a casement constructed of coconut logs and sandbags. That Japanese gun managed to sink four landing craft and damage ten others before the boats reached the shore.

There were the usual difficulties associated with amphibious landings, but most of the boats made it to shore. Marine Private Peter Bowman described the disembarkation procedure, which began when the bow of the landing craft hit the sand and the ramp dropped: "Men on the right hand side of the landing craft disembark over the front corner of the ramp and step off to the right oblique, while those on the opposite side move similarly to the left. The coxswain keeps the engines turning in order to prevent the boat turning sideways . . . Draw in your breath. Hold your piece at high port. . . . Churn through the foam. Don't try to run or the drag of the waves will upset your balance. Proceed diagonally through the swirling surf with feet wide apart."

But for the First Battalion, things did not go as planned. The 75mm Japanese fieldpiece fired into an American boat as the ramps opened, annihilating the Marines

Sergeant Robert A. Owens

inside before they could disembark. Heavy machine-gun and rifle fire from pillboxes pinned dozens of units on the beach. One of the first Marines to struggle ashore was Sergeant Robert A. Owens of Greenville, South Carolina. Owens lay in the wet sand, watching in horror as the Japanese 75mm gun fired on the approaching boats. Posting four Marines to pin down the bunkers protecting the casement, Owens slowly crawled on his belly toward the cannon. When he got close enough to see the fire port, he jumped to his feet and charged the emplacement. He was hit repeatedly by Japanese riflemen as he rushed the emplacement, but Owens pushed on. He leapt through the gun port, shot the gunner dead, and wounded the loader. The rest of the gun crew rushed out of the rear of the casement, where they were cut down by Marine riflemen.

As his men rushed to aid him, Sergeant Owens sank to the sand, where he succumbed to his wounds. The twenty-three-year-old Marine's ultimate sacrifice cleared the beach of its most formidable obstacle, and the landing on Cape Torokina was completed in short order. For his courageous action, Sergeant Robert Allen Owens received a posthumous Medal of Honor. He is buried at ABMC Cemetery in Manila, Philippine Islands.

Before Bougainville was secure, two other Marines would earn the Medal of Honor. On November 7, six days after the landing, the Marines on the perimeter spotted Japanese barges coming ashore west of their position. The main bulk of this enemy counterattack concentrated on an area held by the Third Battalion, Ninth Marines. The Japanese assault was driven back, and the survivors retreated into the jungle, where they occupied foxholes the Marines had abandoned a few days before. The Japanese dug in, threatening the American advance. Under the command of Lieutenant Orville Freeman, the Marines established rearguard ambush sites to cut down the enemy if they moved from their foxholes. Then, for the next thirty hours, Freeman fought to recapture the Marines' former position. He prevailed, but lost one soldier and was wounded himself. General Turnage, fearing a flanking action, sent in the First Battalion, Third Marines. They charged into a tangle of jungle vines, massive trees, and entangling bush with less than five yards of visibility on any side. Crashing through the brush, the Marines shot at anything that moved, even as concealed machine guns cut them down. Using grenades, the Marines tried to dislodge the invisible enemy.

Sergeant Herbert Thomas, a twenty-five-year-old Marine from Columbus, Ohio, had already taken out two machine-gun nests when he stumbled upon a third. Thomas hurled a missile at the Japanese emplacement but it became entangled in some overhead lianas and dropped back down among the sergeant's squad. Thomas threw his body over the grenade and was killed instantly, a self-sacrifice that earned him a posthumous Medal of Honor. Minutes after Thomas perished, a Marine Corps tank led an assault that annihilated the enemy troops in the area.

Two days later Private First Class Henry Gurke of Neche, North Dakota, was pinned down in a two-man foxhole with a machine gunner. As the Japanese surged forward to capture their position, they hurled grenades at the Marines. When a grenade landed in the foxhole next to Gurke, he dropped his rifle and dived on it, smothering the blast and saving the life of the machine gunner, who poured continuous streams of lead at the enemy. Eventually the relentless fire from this machine gun forced the Japanese to retreat. Private Gurke, who had just turned twenty-one on November 6, perished from the blast. For this ultimate sacrifice Private Henry Gurke received a posthumous Medal of Honor.

In December, the Marines on Bougainville were relieved by two U.S. Army divisions. Few of the 14,000 Marines who fought on the island would miss the "tropical paradise" where "the oppressive heat, the continuous rain, the knee-deep mud, the dark overgrown tangled forest with the nauseous smell of the black earth and rotting vegetation, all combined to make this one of the most physically miserable operations that our troops were engaged in." So said an artillery officer from the Twelfth Marines, and a corporal from that same outfit concurred: "What we ought to do when the war is over is to give Bougainville to the Japs—and make 'em live on that damned place forever." In all, 432 Marines were killed and 1,418 were wounded. Though the island was secure and the air base operational when the Marines departed, the Japanese never completely relinquished it. There were still enemy troops fighting on Bougainville when the war ended.

THE COMING OF THE CORSAIR

The gull-winged Vought F4U Corsair arrived in the Pacific in February 1943. Ideal for ground-support missions in the Pacific theater, it was a fast and agile fighter too. Larger, faster, and more powerful than the Wildcat it replaced and the Zero it battled, the Corsair had a top speed of 410 miles per hour and could climb to 3,000 feet in under a minute. The Japanese met the Corsair over Bougainville on February 14. Within a few months, the Corsair gained near-total mastery of the air. Japanese pilots referred to the American warplane as "The Bent-Wing Devil," while their compatriots on the ground at Okinawa and the Philippines called them "The Whistling Death."

Though the Wildcat and the Hellcat both raised holy hell in dogfights against the nimble Zero, it was the Corsair that turned the tide of the air war in the Pacific. In the hands of an experienced pilot, the Corsair became a killing machine. In dogfights over Rabaul, a new generation of Marine Corps aces were born. First Lieutenant Kenneth Ambrose Walsh became the Corps' first Corsair ace on May 13, 1943, when

First Lieutenant Kenneth A. Walsh

he shot down his fourth, fifth, and sixth Zeros in a single furious morning. Twenty-seven years old, Lieutenant Walsh hailed from the mean streets of Brooklyn, New York. He entered service as a teenager and volunteered for Marine Corps Aviation right after basic training. He received his wings as a private in 1937.

In the Pacific theater, Walsh became flight leader of VMF-124. He proved to be a fearless and determined warrior and a fine leader and continued to rack up enemy kills. On August 15, 1943, Lieutenant Walsh performed one of the two most daring feats of his military career. Determined to thwart an enemy bomber attack against Allied ground forces and shipping at Vella Lavella in the Solomon Islands, he dived his Corsair wing into an enemy bomber formation that outnumbered his own flight six to one. Despite repeated hits, Walsh pressed the attack, circling the enemy formation over and over again, looking for openings. By the end of the engagement, he had shot down two Val dive-bombers and a Zero.

Two weeks later, on August 30, Walsh was flying escort when he developed engine trouble. He managed to land his crippled Corsair on Munda and replaced it with another aircraft. On his way to rejoin his flight, he spotted fifty Zeros attacking a force of U.S. Army Air Force B-24 bombers flying over Bougainville. Walsh immediately jumped the fighters. In a swirling, frenzied dogfight, the lieutenant shot down four Zeros before cannon fire wrecked his aircraft and he was forced to ditch in the ocean. Walsh survived many hours at sea to returned to duty. In all, he shot down twenty-one Japanese warplanes.

On February 8, 1944, First Lieutenant Kenneth Ambrose Walsh was presented with the Medal of Honor by President Franklin Delano Roosevelt in a White House ceremony.

Lieutenant Kenneth Walsh was the *first* Corsair ace, but First Lieutenant Robert Murray "Butcher Bob" Hanson was the *greatest*. In a few short weeks of intense combat, Hanson achieved an incredible twenty-five kills at the controls of his F4U— twenty of those victories came in a six-day period. Hanson's abilities were so superior to his fellow pilots' that he shined like a beacon in their eyes. His rise was so meteoric that his men had begun calling him Butcher Bob only days before he was killed. His death was doubly tragic—coming hours before his twenty-fourth birthday and days before he was scheduled to be rotated back to the States.

Hanson was born in Lucknow, India, the son of missionary parents. A stocky, powerfully built lad, he became the heavyweight wrestling champion of the United Provinces at the age of eighteen. After high school, he returned to the United States to complete his education. He matriculated at Hamline University in St. Paul, Minnesota, where he continued his varsity wrestling career.

Hanson was a superb gunner who never lost his sharpshooter's eye. On his very first combat mission—with a unit nicknamed "The Swashbucklers"—Bob Hanson not only shot down his first enemy plane, he also saved the life of wingman Stanley T. Synar, who was wounded in the attack. Hanson did not escape unscathed; his Corsair was badly shot up, with a Japanese 20mm round exploding between his wing guns. After two victories with the Swashbucklers, Hanson had a first tour with VMF-215. But it was during his second tour that he became what historian Bruce Gamble called "a holy terror." Hanson was credited with five kills—all fighters—on January 14, 1944. Then the young lieutenant went on to ring up fifteen more victories by the end of the month—racking up an incredible twenty planes in a seventeen-day killing spree. But Hanson's fleeting career ended on February 3. While he was diving to strafe an essentially worthless ground target, antiaircraft fire struck his Corsair and sent it crashing into the earth. His mother was later presented with his posthumous Medal of Honor.

"Butcher Bob" Hanson shared many traits with another famed Marine Corps aviator, Gregory "Pappy" Boyington. Both spent time in India, both were collegiate wrestlers, both flew with VMF-214—though not at the same time—both became Corsair aces in a single day, and both received the Medal of Honor. Hanson's luck ran out and he was killed by enemy fire. Boyington was shot down too, but survived the war to become a controversial figure.

THE BLACK SHEEP SQUADRON

Only a handful of squadrons in the annals of air combat have achieved a permanent place in history and in the popular imagination. In World War I, Baron Manfred von Richthofen, known throughout the world as the Red Baron, formed his legendary Flying Circus. Between the wars, an eclectic group of American expatriates called the Flying Tigers carved out a legend for themselves in the skies over China. These maverick pilots defended China as soldiers-for-hire before hostilities between the United States and Japan were declared. The adventurers who flew with the Tigers were often eccentric and unpredictable. After the war, several of them would return to the United States and form the notorious Hell's Angels motorcycle gang.

During World War II, two legendary squadrons of Marine aviators battled in the Pacific theater—the Cactus Air Force and Major Gregory "Pappy" Boyington's cadre of contentious misfits and malcontents known as the Black Sheep Squadron. The Black Sheep's legendary status is due in no small part to the charisma and showmanship of its commander. Today, sixty years after the events occurred, it is difficult to separate the legends of the Black Sheep Squadron and its flamboyant commander from the reality. Much of Boyington's formidable reputation springs from his 1958 autobiographical history of his squadron. *Baa Baa Black Sheep,* which is still in print

Colonel Gregory Boyington

after forty-five years, has been hailed by admirers as a harrowing re-creation of the war from the view of a Corsair pilot and a prisoner of war, and dismissed by critics as grandiose and self-serving—despite Boyington's efforts to minimize his own heroic stature in the book and in interviews conducted throughout his life.

Gregory Boyington was born in Coeur d'Alene, Idaho, on December 4, 1912. His father was a dentist, his mother a music teacher. Boyington grew up in Idaho and in Tacoma, Washington. Enamored with flying from an early age, he majored in aeronautical engineering at the University of Washington and graduated in 1934. A natural athlete, he was a collegiate wrestler and swimmer. He joined the Army to fly with the Air Corps, but was commissioned with the coastal artillery corps instead. Big guns were not to his liking and Boyington arranged for a transfer to the Marine Corps in 1935. On March 11, 1937, he earned his wings and was assigned to the Second Marine Air Group and later to the elite Marine Corps exhibition flying team. In 1941, when he was a flight instructor at the naval air station at Pensacola, Florida, Boyington resigned his commission to take a "civilian job" with the Central Aircraft Manufacturing Company. CAMCO was no ordinary corporation. Central Aircraft Manufacturing was the cover name for a covert operation charged with recruiting pilots to fight the Japanese in the skies over China and Burma. The volunteers became the legendary Flying Tigers—soldiers of fortune who were paid a bounty for every Japanese aircraft they downed. Though their actions were not officially condoned, the U.S. government turned a blind eye to the recruitment activities of CAMCO while disavowing the exploits of its pilots. Gregory Boyington spent nearly a year with the Flying Tigers and logged over 300 combat hours in an outmoded P-40. He shot down six Japanese planes before the Tigers were disbanded in July 1942.

When his stint with the Flying Tigers ended, Boyington requested reinstatement in the Marine Corps. But in the words of historian Edward F. Murphy, Boyington was *"persona non grata* for leaving the country in a 'time of national emergency.'" Stunned by this setback, he got a miserable job parking cars in a Seattle, Washington, garage. After three months of mind-numbing menial labor, Boyington fired off a desperate telegram to the secretary of the navy and was finally reinstated. After some retraining, he was dispatched to Guadalcanal, and by September he was given his own command—VMF-214. He proceeded to recruit the brightest and most talented pilots, though they were not always the most disciplined or respectful officers. Some were just plain trouble. But in thirty days he whipped this band of "misfits and misanthropes" into shape. His squadron soon had an appropriate nickname, the Black Sheep Squadron.

Legend has it that his men referred to Boyington as Pappy because he was over thirty—ancient in the profession of combat aviation. There is little doubt that the young lieutenants he commanded felt that he was something of a relic. But to his squadron mates Boyington was "Greg" or "Gramps" and sometimes "Grandpappy." The first mention of the name Pappy came in a *Time* magazine article dated January 10, 1945, eighteen months after Boyington vanished over the Pacific. Contemporary press accounts failed to mention that Boyington was a profane, hard-drinking, combative, and contentious Marine who was not popular with his commanders or his peers. But the effectiveness of Boyington's training and the combat tactics he developed for the Corsair were never in doubt. After he was shot down, his executive officer assembled a report entitled "The Combat Strategy and Tactics of Major Gregory Boyington, USMCR." Within weeks of its publication, the report was distributed throughout naval and Marine fighter forces and became required reading.

By September 1943, Boyington had completed the Black Sheep's training and the squadron was sent to the Russell Islands to protect U.S. long-range bombers hitting targets deep in Japanese territory. The squadron flew its first combat mission on September 16 in support of a formation of American bombers sent to attack the Japanese air base at Bougainville. As the warplanes began their bombing run, a flight of forty Japanese Zeros plunged out of the clouds. A Zero raced at Boyington's Corsair and wagged its wings. Boyington squeezed the trigger, but had forgotten to arm his guns, so nothing happened. He remedied the situation and shot the Zero down—his first victory as a Black Sheep. Moments later he made a second kill.

Suddenly Boyington found himself alone over enemy territory. As he turned to race for home, he spotted a Zero flying low and slow over the ocean. He dived to make a kill but realized too late that he had flown into a trap. As he raised his nose, he spotted a second Zero diving out of the clouds, right for him. He sent it smoking into the water, and low on fuel, he made a fourth kill on the way home. Boyington decided he couldn't make it back to the Russell Islands, so he detoured to Munda air base, which was closer. On the way he spotted a smoking Corsair with a Zero chewing up its tail. He attacked as the Zero stood on its tail to face him. A quick burst from his six .50-caliber machine guns and the Japanese warplane exploded.

In addition to Boyington's impressive score of five, his squadron had downed ten more planes on their very first mission and the legend of the Black Sheep Squadron was born. Over the course of a month, Boyington would shoot down fourteen more Japanese warplanes, and on December 23, 1943, he and the Black Sheep would down twelve enemy planes on a single mission—four of those kills were made by "Gramps." Up to then Joe Foss had been the leading Marine Corps ace of the war. But his record of twenty-six kills was in jeopardy. Boyington already scored twenty-four—and counting.

But Boyington's luck suddenly seemed to run out. On a mission four days later, he'd just downed his twenty-fifth plane when his Corsair was hit. Oil spewed from its engine, coating the windscreen with an impenetrable black film. Boyington was forced to return to Torokina Airfield, where bad weather grounded him for the next seven days. During this time on the ground, the American press got wind of Boyington's combat record. War correspondents swarmed to Bougainville, all wanting to be the first to report that Joe Foss's record had been broken. The pressure was on "Grandpappy," and even his squadron mates were eager to see their commanding officer tie with the legendary Foss. As Boyington's fame grew, the enemy also became aware of his exploits. The Japanese first encountered him during the Black Sheep's trademark "fighter sweeps" of their airfields. Boyington and his wingman would make a low strafing run against a Japanese air base. During the attack, Boyington would tune his radio to the Japanese frequency and challenge the enemy pilots to come up and fight him. In time he became a marked man and Japanese pilots sought out his Corsair during dogfights.

After eight days—days in which the pressure on Boyington to beat his rival's record became almost intolerable—the weather broke. On January 3, 1944, Boyington led a flight of forty-eight Corsairs on a mission over Rabaul. His wingman that day was Captain George Ashmun, who understood the strain his commander was under. "Shoot all you want, Gramps," Ashmun told him. "All I'll do is keep 'em off your tail."

When the Americans were over Rabaul, sixty Japanese fighters rose to greet them. The Black Sheep heard their commander's voice, tense with emotion, crackling over the radio. "Let's get the bastards!"

When the Corsairs and Zeros mixed it up, Boyington made the first kill. "I poured a long burst into the first enemy plane," he wrote in his memoirs. "I saw the pilot catapult out and the plane itself break into fire."

Now he was tied with Joe Foss, but that was the last thing on Boyington's mind. The engagement had become a free-for-all. The Japanese seemed more determined than usual. To avoid the swirling melee, Boyington and Ashmun climbed until twenty Japanese fighters surrounded them. The Zeros circled, waiting for an opening. The Corsairs swooped in and out, Boyington and Ashmun watching their own back and each other. They fired when they could, until Ashmun spotted an opening and fired a quick burst. A Zero exploded and cartwheeled into the ocean. Boyington fired on a second fighter and scored kill number twenty-seven.

He was now the leading ace in the Pacific theater, but there was no time to celebrate—Boyington spotted his wingman going down. Ashmun's Corsair was scorched by hot oil, the engine smoking. A dozen Zeros where chewing up his tail. Boyington turned on his wing and dived. As he approached the melee, he fired indiscriminately, hoping to break up the swarm of Zeros swirling around Ashmun's damaged Corsair. But suddenly his wingman's plane shuddered, struck the waves, and broke apart.

Enraged, Boyington aimed at the Zero that had downed his wingman and pressed the trigger. The Japanese plane disintegrated, its debris scattering over Ashmun's watery grave. It was Boyington's twenty-eighth and last kill. More Zeros closed in on his tail. He pushed the throttle forward, racing over the water at 350 miles an hour, the belly of his Corsair less than a hundred feet above the waves. Tracers whizzed around him and the Corsair lurched as shells struck its tail and fuselage. Finally,

Japanese bullets stitched a line along its right wing. There was an explosion, and Boyington was scorched by a hot yellow flash as the main gas tank blew. He popped the canopy and hurled himself from the burning warplane. His parachute had barely opened before he struck the waves.

Stunned by the impact, Boyington watched the debris from his Corsair sink. Then he spotted four Zeros diving for him. The Japanese opened fire, churning up the water around him until they ran out of ammo and flew away. Boyington dived repeatedly under the waves to avoid the stream of bullets. At one point he felt a sting and knew they had gotten him.

When the sky was finally clear of enemy aircraft, Boyington inflated his rubber life raft and climbed aboard. He was bleeding from a half-dozen superficial and not so superficial wounds. A chunk of his scalp hung down over his eye. One ear was ripped loose and he had a gash in his thigh the size of his fist. His left ankle had been shattered by a Japanese bullet and he was seeping blood from several coin-sized shrapnel wounds. He bound up his injuries as best he could and waited for shock to set in.

For eight hours, Boyington floated in the raft, hovering near death. Then the ocean around him began to swirl as a submarine surfaced right next to his boat. A Japanese submarine. Within another eight hours, Boyington found himself a prisoner at the Japanese stronghold at Rabaul. He was beaten and tortured for several weeks, the brutality gaining in intensity when the Japanese realized whom they had captured. He was America's preeminent ace—and their helpless prisoner. Boyington's tormentors would vent their rage on him for six weeks. Nearly every day he was brutalized in some barbaric manner—blindfolded and beaten, burned with cigarette butts, kicked, punched, slapped, utterly humiliated. Boyington was finally moved to Truk, then on to a camp on the Japanese mainland. He ended up at Ofuna, a brutal prisoner of war camp outside of Yokohama. He languished there for twenty months, until the Japanese surrendered in 1945. After being liberated, and after a stay in a hospital, Colonel Gregory Boyington was sent home. He was awarded the Navy Cross for downing three planes on his last mission. Then, on October 5, 1945, Colonel Gregory "Pappy" Boyington was presented with the Medal of Honor by President Harry Truman in a Rose Garden ceremony. He ended the war as the greatest Marine Corps ace, beating Joe Foss's record and everyone else's too.

It should have been a happy ending to a story of incredible heroism, but Boyington's troubles were just beginning. After the war, his life spiraled out of control. Drinking, three bad marriages, tax trouble, and business failures dogged him. When he finally set down his memoirs, it was late in the game and publishers were dubious about the success of yet another tired war story. They needn't have worried. *Baa Baa Black Sheep* has gone through two dozen editions and has never gone out of print.

In 1976, Boyington was again thrust into the public eye when his book was turned into an NBC television series called *Baa Baa Black Sheep* by producer Stephen Cannell and actor Robert Conrad. Fresh from his success on *The Wild Wild West,* Conrad played Pappy in this weekly, hour-long drama that was a fictional account of the Black Sheep's exploits. The credits included "Colonel Gregory

'Pappy' Boyington, USMC (ret.)" as "adviser." *Baa Baa Black Sheep* was pulled after one season, revamped, and returned as *Black Sheep Squadron* for the 1977–1978 season, after which it was canceled for good—though the show can still be seen in syndication.

Boyington's final years were spent in Fresno, California, with his fourth wife. He became a landscape painter, and sometimes painted battle scenes that were avidly sought by collectors. Gregory Boyington passed away on January 11, 1988, at the age of seventy-five.

ASSAULT ON THE GILBERT ISLANDS

After Bougainville, the Japanese high command assumed that their enemy would rest until early 1944, then begin a campaign directly against their main base at Rabaul. They were wrong.

While the Marines were fighting for possession of Guadalcanal, Cape Glouchester, and Bougainville, Admiral Chester Nimitz was creating a brand-new navy out of the ashes of Pearl Harbor. And not just a *new* navy but a new *type* of navy—one capable of semi-independent action, with carrier planes providing cover for an armada of warships and support vessels. This force was designed to reach deep into enemy territory, capturing and holding islands in its wake, claiming mastery over more and more territory until it threatened the Japanese mainland. Nimitz was ready to turn his *Essex*-class carriers and their escorts loose on the high seas. Behind them would follow the first large-scale, self-sustaining amphibious assault force in history—troop ships, supply ships, light carriers, fuel ships—everything needed to land, capture, and hold the islands of the Pacific. This modern amphibious task force would be accompanied by old battleships like the *Maryland,* which had been heavily damaged at Pearl Harbor but were now repaired and refitted. These refurbished warships were too slow to keep up with the speedy new carriers but could be used to support amphibious landings. During the invasion of Tarawa, these aging battleships would be sent to hammer the island in advance of the landings.

In 1943, the U.S. Joint Chiefs were dreaming up a new plan of action for the Central Pacific. They thought it advantageous to attack the Marshall Islands. From there, the Army Air Force could strike at the very heart of Japanese-controlled territory with long range bombers. But Admiral Nimitz rejected the idea and insisted that the Gilbert Islands be attacked first. The Marshalls were out of range of air reconnaissance, but the Gilberts could be reached by long-range photographic reconnaissance flights. Without adequate intelligence, Admiral Nimitz refused to risk any of his new amphibious task force in a risky campaign for the Marshalls.

Nimitz believed that the Gilbert Islands were well situated to support further incursion into Japanese territory and were a natural stepping-stone to the Marshalls. With an air base on one of the Gilbert Islands, the United States could command a big chunk of the sky over the Central Pacific. In late September, the Joint Chiefs ordered Nimitz to take the Gilbert Islands in the next six weeks. Once again the Marines scrambled to prepare for a new amphibious assault. The Tarawa chain was chosen for the first incursion into the Gilberts, and the Marines planned to strike at the largest island of the group, a hunk of coral reef, sand, rock, and palm trees called Betio.

Major General Julian Smith, commander of the Second Marine Division, would lead the attack. A soft-spoken Marine who lacked charisma, Smith would prove to be a superb combat leader. For his executive officer, Smith picked Colonel Merritt "Red Mike" Edson, fresh from his victories on Tulagi and Guadalcanal. But Smith's amphibious planner was a newcomer. Lieutenant Colonel David M. Shoup was from a farming family. Born in Battleground, Indiana, on December 30, 1904, he left the family homestead to earn a degree in mathematics at DePauw University in 1936. During his studies, Shoup took an ROTC commission as a second lieutenant in the Marine Corps. As a young Marine, he spent years performing duties in foreign lands and serving aboard ship. Before Tarawa, he saw limited combat action as an observer with the Army in New Georgia.

Shoup was assigned the task of planning the invasion. During the initial practice runs in the New Hebrides, the amphibious commander took ill and Shoup was assigned the task of leading the actual assault. Suddenly he was both the architect and executioner of the invasion of Tarawa. But Shoup had his doubts—about the amtracs that would carry his men to shore, about the tide, about the Japanese defenses, about the effectiveness of the naval bombardment. After thinking long and hard, he devised an elaborate plan to seize an offshore island near Betio and use it as an artillery base. Then for three days the Americans would pound Betio with bombers, naval guns, and artillery before the Marines landed. Meanwhile, the U.S. Army would come ashore at nearby Makin Island—last visited by Carlson's Raiders—and snatch it from the enemy. The Navy rejected the plan as too time consuming and the Marines were ordered to get in and out fast, because Nimitz did not want risk his vulnerable carriers.

The Japanese were busy too. After Carlson's Raiders assaulted Makin, high command was spooked enough to beef up all of their island defenses in the Central Pacific. Because Betio was so close to Makin, fortifications on the island were especially formidable. Rear Admiral Keiji Shibasaki and 2,600 Special Naval Landing Force troops were dispatched to defend Tarawa, along with 2,000 well-armed construction troops. As the American task force steamed toward Betio, the Japanese had 5,000 armed troops reinforcing an island that was smaller than the space occupied by a typical American shopping mall and its parking lots. They were hoping that the United States Navy would attack Tarawa. Admiral Shibasaki knew that all he had to do was hold out against an invasion for three days—the time it took for a rescue task force to steam from Japan. The Japanese had long wished for a "decisive sea battle" that would end the war. Now they hoped to engage the U.S. Navy near Tarawa long enough to stage just such a clash.

The main problem the Marines faced was a lack of workable landing craft. Tarawa was fringed by reefs that could rip the bottom out of a Higgins boat. Something better was needed. Converting unarmored amphibian tractors into reef-crawling, assault landing craft was the brainchild of Lieutenant Colonel Victor H. "Brute" Krulak, who had tested them earlier in the war. Shoup planned to use seventy-five of these converted vehicles from the Second Amphibian Tractor Battalion to hit the beaches at Betio. These tractors were mostly beat up crawlers left over from the assault on Guadalcanal. But when fitted with lightweight armor, a new exhaust and bilge pump system, machine guns and bolt-on steel plates to protect the driver in the cab, these tractors made serviceable LVTs—Landing Vehicle Tanks. The Marines called them Alligators. The conversion work had to be performed so rapidly that there were doubts the craft would be ready in time. At the last moment the Alligators arrived, and so did fifty of the new LVT-2 "Water Buffalo," which were faster and better armored. A company of "amtrackers" was sent from Samoa to operate the LVTs, but the men had barely became familiar with their new machines before they were loaded onto three huge Tank Landing Ships for the voyage to Tarawa.

The proposed three-day naval bombardment of Betio had been reduced to three hours—enough, the Navy insisted, to obliterate the Japanese defenses. But Lieutenant Colonel Shoup was concerned that his reinforcing elements might not be able to float over the reef in their Higgins boats. At low tide it was impossible, but at high tide—which would occur by midmorning—the water would rise enough to let the boats pass. Julian Smith expressed a fear that the Marines might be stranded on the reef and forced to wade ashore under heavy fire. But the Navy insisted that by the time of the amphibious landing, the enemy's defenses would be neutralized.

BLOODY TARAWA

When D day came early on the morning of November 20, 1943, the Japanese were taken completely by surprise. Admiral Shibasaki awakened that morning to find Betio surrounded by U.S. warships. He rallied his defenses and fired at the approaching vessels. Those shots were answered by a U.S. naval bombardment that lasted for three hours. The coastal defenses the Japanese had constructed by over the past year were obliterated in the first ten minutes. Unfortunately, the Navy neglected to use air burst shells. Japanese guns hidden in roofless trenches were untouched, because the battleships fired at zero elevation—level with the target. Many shells struck sandbag revetments or bounced off concrete pillboxes, causing little damage.

But things were not going well for the Japanese either. Rear Admiral Keiji Shibasaki realized that the Marines were approaching the reefs, the only waters around the island that were not yet mined; his overworked *rikusentai* had not completed the task. Shibasaki alerted high command that the assault had come, burned his sensitive materials, and shifted his forces from the south shore to the north shore. His men were forced to move through the merciless naval bombardment and many were slaughtered on open ground. It seemed as if the defenders were going to be overwhelmed—until things began to go terribly wrong for the Americans.

The guns of the battleships came nowhere near to obliterating the elaborate Japanese defenses, as promised. But they did a superb job of obliterating the U.S. Marines' communications system. The concussion from the battleship *Maryland*'s guns knocked the American radio net out of commission. Each time the guns fired, more landing craft lost their radios. Lieutenant Colonel Shoup found himself out of

▪ *Marine Corps Landing Craft*

When the Marines hit the beach, they made it there in a variety of specialized boats designed for amphibious operations. The evolution of these vehicles was slow. Two types of landing boats were tested in the Marine Corps winter exercises of 1924. The first was a version of the British "Beetle Boats" that had been used to make the amphibious landing at Gallipoli in the First World War. The second was the "Christie Tank," a heavier, armored track vehicle that proved unseaworthy. In the 1930s, the Marines unsuccessfully tried to adapt Atlantic fishing boats for use as landing craft.

Then they heard about the "Eureka," a specialized vessel designed and built by New Orleans boatbuilder Andrew Higgins. The boat was made for use by oil-drilling crews on the Mississippi, but the "Higgins boat" was ideal for use as a landing craft. It had a flat bottom, a propeller system protected by a tunnel, and it could run onto sand bars and beaches, reverse torque, and back away again.

Tests of the Higgins boat in 1941 went well. Then Major Ernest E. Linsert of the Marine Corps Equipment Board showed Andrew Higgins a photograph of a new type of landing boat that had been developed, ironically, by the Japanese. It looked much like the Higgins, but had a forward ramp that dropped to unload vehicles. Higgins quickly added the innovation to his own design, and the LCPR—Landing Craft, Personnel (Ramp)—was born.

When the war broke out, Higgins turned his attention to the development of an armored LCM—Landing Craft, Mechanized. The predecessor of the LCM had been developed in the 1930s as a nonmilitary vehicle to rescue hurricane victims in the Florida Everglades by Donald Roebling, grandson of the man who built the Brooklyn Bridge. The Marines turned his brainchild into the "Alligator," the first LVT—Landing Vehicle, Tracked. Add a gun turret and a little more armor and the result is the Buffalo. Both of these amtracs were used during the invasion of Tarawa.

Later developments included the LVT(A)—the Landing Vehicle, Tracked (Armored), which sported a turret-mounted 37mm gun, and the formidable LVT(A)-4, which had a 75mm howitzer mounted on its bow. A plethora of types followed: the LCI (Landing Craft, Infantry), the LCT (Landing Craft, Tank), the LCM (Landing Craft, Motorized), and several variations of the LCVP (Landing Craft, Vehicle and Personnel). Some attempts were made to turn existing vehicles like the Sherman tank amphibious. These conversions were generally unreliable in ocean surf but performed adequately when fording rivers or creeks.

One vehicle came courtesy of the United States Army. The DUKW—pronounced "Duck"—was basically a truck that could swim. The most popular was a 2.5-ton model that was used from 1944 through the end of the war. DUKWs were particularly effective in the landing on Tinian, where they ferried men and matériel ashore in good order.

The Marines also required vessels to get their amphibious craft to the site of the landing, and whole new class of ships were developed by the Navy for this purpose. Between 1942 and 1945, twenty-two LSDs—Landing Ships, Docks—were constructed. Each ship had a dock inside its stern and could carry as many as fourteen LCVPs, inside the hull. They provided on-the-spot repair facilities for LCTs, LCMs, LCVPs, and even PT boats. LSCs had a crew of about 240 sailors and mechanics and could cruise at fifteen knots. These vessels were 453 feet long and weighed in at 4,500 tons and were defended by a five-inch gun and a dozen antiaircraft cannons.

The LST—Landing Ships, Tank—were smaller, but could carry up to twenty tanks and land them right on the beach. These landings were not perfect and there was usually damage done to the LST. After about ten beachings the wear and tear rendered the LST unusable. With a maximum speed of twelve knots, these vessels crawled. Sailors joked that LST really meant "Large Slow Target." The crew of 100 men was armed with eight antiaircraft guns. The LSM—Landing Ship, Medium—was a smaller version of the LST. These came late in the war, and were the smallest oceangoing vessel capable of beach landings. At 200 feet, with a crew of sixty, the LSMs could ferry only a few tanks and LCMs, but had better seagoing qualities than the larger vessels. The LSM was perfect for smaller island assaults. Howitzers, mortars, and even rockets could be fired from inside its stern.

touch with his landing forces. He paced the deck of his transport ship, chomping on his cigar and cursing bitterly. Shoup would suffer from a total lack of communication with his tactical commanders ashore for the next thirty hours. Things soon got worse as the naval bombardment became as much of a danger to the Marines as it was to the Japanese. Shells bounced off concrete bunkers, creating ricochets that ripped through the thin armor of the approaching landing vehicles. The barrage created thick black smoke that obscured the island, making landings difficult. Two carrier aircraft strikes against the defenses accomplished little, and a United States Army Air Force bomber attack never even showed up—it was discovered later that they hadn't even received a request for their support, a snafu that cost countless lives.

Meanwhile, the *rikusentai* were wreaking holy hell on the landing vehicles with their versatile dual-purpose antiaircraft, antiship guns. These 75mm artillery pieces were crouching behind reinforced sandbag bunkers that were impervious to Navy shells, though vulnerable to air burst explosives. Fortunately for the Japanese, the Navy was not using air burst munitions, so these guns were still intact when the battleships withdrew. Now the Japanese fired their artillery at the landing crafts with deadly results. In the hours to come, each of these guns would have to be taken out by frontal assault—a slow and costly process. America's relative inexperience with amphibious landings was starting to show.

Suddenly, as the LVTs were moving slowly toward the beaches, the Navy ceased their bombardment. On board the flagship, "Red Mike" Edson and Julian Smith went ballistic, insisting that the boats were still twenty minutes from their targets and at their most vulnerable position. But Rear Admiral Harry Hill refused to fire, insisting that there was so much smoke he might hit the Marines on their way in, as had happened at Bougainville. During the unexpected lull in the bombardment, Shibasaki regrouped and replenished his troops. Finally, he spotted strange-looking LVTs approaching the shore. The Japanese had never seen their like, and reacted in panic when the lumbering vehicles climbed over the reef and crawled ashore, spitting machine gun fire at the retreating *rikusentai*. The Japanese officers finally rallied their men, who opened fire on the Alligators and Water Buffalo as they rolled out of the surf and charged their defenses.

Lieutenant Colonel Shoup managed to get the first three assault waves ashore relatively intact. Only eight of the eighty-seven LVTs had been sunk. In the first ten minutes after the Marines hit the beach, over 1,500 of them were ashore, most crouching behind the seawall on the north end of the island. As ordered, they held their position and waited for reinforcements. By midmorning the tide was supposed to rise enough to submerge the reef, enabling the Higgins boats ferrying the fourth and fifth waves to float over them. But something went horribly, tragically, inexplicably wrong.

"THE DAY GOD FORGOT THE CORPS"

When the fourth and fifth waves of Higgins boats arrived, the reef was still well above water level—the tide had not come in. The boats slammed into the coral and came to a grinding halt. Most boats were stuck 500 or 600 yards from the beach, and Japanese machine guns were already churning up the water around them. Once the Marines left the relative protection of the landing craft, they would face merciless and sustained enemy fire.

The Marines were confounded. Their intelligence indicated that the tide at Betio was a constant phenomenon, and the ocean should have risen more than enough to cover the reef. But the high tide never materialized that day or the next, and the Marines found their crowded boats stranded far from the beaches and vulnerable to enemy fire. The mystery of the failed tide would not be solved until 1987, when physicist Dr. Donald Olson discovered that the November 20, 1943, tide coincided with the moon's furthermost orbit from the earth—a phenomenon that creates an uncommonly low tide. The occurrence is rare—it happened only twice in 1943, but one of those two days just happened to be D day at Tarawa. Hundreds of Marines died trying to wade ashore across that barrier reef. The jagged, razor-sharp coral reef tore at their flesh, ripped holes in their fatigues, and even snagged their boots. In all, about one-fourth of the casualties at Betio occurred at the actual landing, prompting one Marine to blasphemously proclaim that D day on Tarawa was the day "God forgot the Corps."

Despite his fractured communications, Lieutenant Colonel Shoup sensed trouble and called for Plan B. The empty LVTs were to return to the island to transport the troops across the reef and onto the beach, then evacuate the wounded. But this time, when the thin-skinned LVTs appeared, they got a dose of heavy fire from the Japanese dual-purpose guns. The flimsy vehicles were blown apart or set ablaze while machine guns butchered the helpless Marines struggling to get in or out of them. Soon the blue water of the lagoon was red with American blood. The shattered hulks of Alligators and Buffalo littered the reef, the lagoon, and the beach—where they can still be seen today, more than a half century later. Around the shattered amtracs the blackened bodies of dead Marines bobbed in the water, their broken equipment scattered around them.

All along the beachhead the Marines were getting butchered. In the center of the assault, Lieutenant Colonel Herbert Amey was killed leading elements of his Second Battalion ashore. On the left the Marines managed to penetrate the seawall and seized their initial objectives—moving nearly halfway across the narrow island. But they were forced to pull back to the beach when U.S. Navy warplanes repeatedly strafed them by mistake. On the right, at Red Beach One, enemy fire was most intense. A battery of four Japanese dual-purpose guns chewed up the approaching LVTs. The slaughter was so complete that Major John Schoettel thought his command had been wiped out. "We have nothing left to land," he reported to Shoup.

But some of Schoettel's command *had* survived, to wade ashore far from their original objective. Major Mike Ryan made it to the beach with about half the men in his command. He established a permanent position on a piece of ground that would become known as Green Beach. Soon he attracted stunned stragglers from other shattered units who stumbled onto the island from blasted LVTs. These men would become "Ryan's Orphans" and would eventually turn the tide in the battle for Tarawa.

Sergeant William J. Bordelon

Shoup, raging and frustrated, finally started for shore himself. Soon after he arrived, he was crawling on his belly in the sand with the rest of his Marines. And, like many of them, he was bleeding—wounded in the left leg. During the long trip to shore, Shoup lost more than half of his regimental staff. When he established a command post near a bunker that was still occupied by the enemy, it was in waist-deep water. Shoup remained there, directing his forces, for the next two and a half days. Because of his stubborn stand, and his bullnecked, stocky frame, Lieutenant Colonel Shoup would forever after be known as "The Rock of Tarawa."

In the afternoon of that first day, Shoup ordered tanks ashore, but all but two of the big Shermans were obliterated by Japanese antitank guns before they could effectively enter the battle. The *rikusentai* fought like devils, refusing to give ground. Julian Smith was disturbed by the errant tide, and wondered if his division would survive D day. The issue was in doubt, and Smith admitted as much in a message to his superior officer. The fate of the Marines on Tarawa hung in the balance for the next day and a half. Only the courage and daring of a handful of hard-fighting Marines would turn the tide. Staff Sergeant William James Bordelon of San Antonio, Texas, was one of them. Bordelon enlisted right after Pearl Harbor and tried to get into the Navy, but was turned down because he had webbed toes. The Marine Corps accepted him and Bordelon was trained as a combat engineer.

On D day, Sergeant Bordelon was approaching Red Beach Two in an LVT carrying Captain Warren Morris, the twenty-five-year-old commander of Company F, and a flamethrower and demolitions platoon of the First Battalion, 18th Marines. Twenty yards from shore, the LVT was struck repeatedly by a Japanese dual-purpose gun. Foundering, the LVT burned until the munitions inside the vehicle detonated in a spectacular blast. Miraculously, Bordelon survived the explosion and found himself lying in the middle of the twisted wreckage. He crawled free and led four other survivors in salvaging what they could from the debris. Then they climbed out of the shattered vehicle and waded ashore. On the beach, Bordelon took command of his small detachment, gathered what explosives he could get from the other engineers, then eyed the enemy positions.

A series of concrete pillboxes blocked the Marines' advance, so Sergeant Bordelon mounted a one-man assault on them. He boldly approached each emplacement, firing at the gun port with a rifle he had taken from a dead Marine. When he got close,

Bordelon tossed one of his homemade dynamite bombs into the bunker. Each time he rose to make the throw a Japanese sniper shot him. But the stubborn Marine refused to fall.

After eliminating three pillboxes and getting shot three times, Bordelon waved off a Navy corpsman and covered five Marines who were going over the top. He found a rifle grenade and took out a fourth pillbox, when suddenly a Japanese grenade exploded in the midst of his companions. The blast tore the guts out of one Marine, killing him instantly. Moments later Bordelon spotted a wounded man struggling in the surf. He dived in and dragged the injured Marine to the safety of the seawall. When his engineers located more explosives, Bordelon made another dynamite bomb to take out a fifth enemy position. But when he rose to charge the emplacement, enemy machine gunners spotted the movement and shot him in the chest. Bordelon was killed instantly.

Sergeant William James Bordelon was posthumously awarded the Medal of Honor—the first of four Marines to receive the Medal of Honor at Tarawa and the only enlisted man to be so honored. His Medal of Honor was presented to Bordelon's mother and father by President Franklin Delano Roosevelt in a 1944 ceremony at Alamo Stadium in Texas. William James Bordelon was buried at the National Memorial Cemetery of the Pacific in Honolulu, Hawaii—but there is a postscript to his story. In 1995, on the fifty-second anniversary of the Tarawa Campaign, the citizens of San Antonio brought the body of their hero back home for reburial. Bordelon's casket, with his Medal of Honor displayed on the lid, lay in state for two days and nights inside the Alamo, surrounded by a Marine Corps honor guard before Bordelon was interred with honor.

By the afternoon of D day, Shoup recognized that victory rested with his artillery. But the Marines' big guns were still in Higgins boats, circling the island and waiting for a chance to come ashore. The pier the Japanese built on Tarawa had been set ablaze, and there was no other place to bring the artillery ashore. Lieutenant Colonel Presley Rixey solved the problem. He established a temporary harbor near the shattered pier. Over the next fifteen hours, his artillerymen would form a human chain, dragging the components of the dismantled guns out of boats, passing them hand to hand over the reef and onto the beach under withering fire.

When night fell, there were 3,500 Marines on Betio, with an additional 1,500 American troops floating dead in the water or sprawled on the sand. The survivors went to ground and waited for a Japanese counterattack. Though such a counterattack was part of Admiral Shibasaki's defense strategy, fate intervened and the attack never materialized because the admiral and almost his entire command staff was dead—killed by a volley fired from one of the U.S. Navy warships shelling Betio. This loss disrupted the defenders and prevented a Japanese counterattack on that first, critical night. When dawn came, the Marines were still clinging to their positions. Their hold was tenuous, however, and the issue was still in doubt.

Meanwhile, the First Battalion, Eight Marines, were seasick from spending the night bobbing up and down in the surf in their Higgins boat. Now they were the first unit to move ashore on D day plus one. The Marines hoped that the errant tide had finally come in and submerged the coral. That hope vanished when the bottom of their boat struck the reef; the tide had not varied at all in twenty-four hours. Nor had the enemy's stubborn resistance. As soon as the Higgins boat ran aground, the Japanese opened fire on it. Once again, the landing was bogged down and the Marine Corps' schedule shot to pieces. Only the bravery and initiative of individual Marines would bring victory.

Before the end of the first day of the invasion, Lieutenant William Deane Hawkins had made an impression on his troops. On D day, as his scout snipers approached the burning Japanese pier between Red Beach Two and Three, their LVT took heavy fire from the entrenched enemy. When the gunner of the amphibious vehicle had his chest blasted open by a machine-gun burst, Hawkins manned his weapon. With well-directed fire he cleaned out six Japanese machine-gun nests.

"I'll never forget the picture of him," said one of the officers in Hawkins's outfit. "Riding around with a million bullets a minute whistling by his ears, just shooting Japs. I never saw such a man in my life."

Hawkins was an unlikely hero. He was born on April 18, 1914, at Fort Scott, Kansas, and his parents moved to El Paso, Texas in 1919. There, a neighbor accidentally spilled a large pot of boiling water on him. Badly burned, with scar tissue covering over a third of his body, Hawkins also suffered severe muscle damage in his arm and leg. His mother refused a doctor's recommendation that he have surgery because, as the daughter of a physician, she knew the operation would leave her son a cripple. In time, and with constant massage treatment, the damaged muscles healed and Hawkins made a full recovery—though the scars never went away.

Hawkins became a collegiate athlete at the Texas College of Mines and spent summers working as a bellhop, ranch hand, and railroad handyman in order to care for his widowed mother. After earning his engineering degree, he took a well-paying job in Los Angeles. But the attack on Pearl Harbor enraged Hawkins, and he tried to enlist. Both the Army and Army Air Force rejected him because of his "disfigurement," so he enlisted in the Marine Corps on January 5, 1942. After basic, he attended sniper school and was sent to Guadalcanal.

During the battle for the Solomons, Hawkins so distinguished himself that he received a battlefield commission and was given his own sniper platoon to command. His men loved him and Hawkins took good care of them. They never used his first name, but referred to their commander as "Hawk." On D day, Hawkins and his men were instrumental in taking out the initial Japanese resistance on Betio pier. Though Hawkins was wounded twice in the shoulder, he admonished a corpsman tending his wounds not to tie his bandages too tight. "I'll have trouble shooting," he explained.

For three days, Hawkins and his men busied themselves taking out Japanese bunkers. On the third and final morning of the assault, armed only with hand grenades, Hawkins charged a pillbox and was shot in the shoulder for a third time. This wound was mortal—the Japanese bullet had severed an artery. Lieutenant Hawkins died in less than ten minutes, surrounded by the Marines who loved him.

"Boys," Hawkins told them, "I sure hate to leave you like this."

Hawkins's actions that day inspired the Marines in his unit. Lusting for vengeance, they rose en masse from their foxholes and charged the Japanese, eventually cutting Betio in two and dividing the enemy. Shoup would later credit Lieutenant

Hawkins with winning the campaign. William Deane Hawkins received a posthumous Medal of Honor for his gallantry. After Tarawa was captured, Julian Smith insisted that the American air base the Marines built there be christened Hawkins Field in his honor.

Meanwhile, unknown to Shoup and Smith because of the near-total lack of radio communications, Mike Ryan and his "Orphans" had broken through the main Japanese defensive line. Making the most of two Sherman tanks that had come their way—the only two tanks to survive the initial assault—Ryan swept south and eliminated an entire company of *rikusentai* who were manning a series of reinforced pillboxes. Now Green Beach—Ryan's Beach—was the one secure spot on Betio. Soon the Marines began to arrive there in force, many paddling to shore on rubber rafts—they would be forever remembered as the "Condom Attack Force."

First Lieutenant Alexander Bonnyman, Jr.

At 9:30 A.M., an American mortar shell struck an unmapped Japanese ammunition dump, destroying it along with an enemy bunker, constructed from coconut logs, that had been bedeviling the Marines since D day. Several Marines were wounded by coral shrapnel from the blast, but the Seabees moved quickly forward with bulldozers and buried the smoldering emplacement. Well-directed naval guns took out a second pillbox. Now only a single, sand-domed bunker remained in enemy hands. This bunker was the center of the Japanese defenses, a massive structure, bristling with guns and totally bombproof. The Marines had every reason to believe that Admiral Shibasaki and his high command were inside that bunker; they had no way of knowing the enemy commander and most of his staff were already dead.

A savage fight erupted on Red Beach Three when the Eighth Marines ran into this formidable emplacement. Soon the Marines were unable to edge forward without drawing fire and were preparing to withdraw to safer ground when an "old lieutenant" arrived to take command of their unit.

At thirty-three, First Lieutenant Alexander Bonnyman, Jr., was probably the oldest man on Betio. In fact, Bonnyman—called "Sandy" by his friends—should not have been there at all. He had a wife and three daughters and owned copper mines in New Mexico, a critical defense industry. By law, Bonnyman was triply exempt from the draft. But his desire to serve was so strong that he enlisted in the Marine Corps right after Pearl Harbor. Like William Deane Hawkins, Bonnyman fought with distinction at Guadalcanal and earned a battlefield commission for his courage and daring. On Tarawa, he was a combat engineer assigned to the division shore party, but since no supplies had yet arrived, he helped out where he could. When Bonnyman heard about the invincible Japanese sand bunker, he decided to take a look for himself. After studying the structure, which looked like a hill made out of sand with slit-like gun ports at the base, he devised a scheme to take it down.

Bonnyman assembled a team of a dozen flamethrowers and demolition experts supported by riflemen, and as they moved toward the bunker, the Japanese spotted them. So did the Marines on the beach, who watched in awe as Bonnyman and his party dodged Japanese fire and scrambled up the summit of the bunker, tossing explosive charges into every gun port they could find. Others poured diesel fuel down air shafts, followed by grenades. Suddenly several dozen *rikusentai* burst from the rear of the bunker and hurled grenades at the Americans. Then they charged, with samurai swords drawn. While two Marines continued to hurl explosive charges into the bunker's gun ports and air shafts, Bonnyman gunned down the oncoming Japanese with his rifle. One Japanese officer rushed past the lieutenant, toward the busy demolitionists. Bonnyman coolly shot him down. Another enemy soldier ran right up to Bonnyman's face, sword swinging. Bonnyman pumped bullets into the man until he dropped to the sand. When his clip was empty, Bonnyman reloaded and kept on firing. As more Japanese surged out of the bunker, he called for more explosives. Kneeling on top of the highest summit, Bonnyman was shot at repeatedly. Finally, the Marines saw him stumble. A moment later his lifeless body rolled down the slope of the bombproof bunker. Bonnyman had been struck in the head by a Japanese sniper.

More Marines surged forward, accompanied by a bulldozer that pushed sand into the gun ports. Then the Marines dropped more explosives down the air shaft. Finally, the bunker exploded. The sand dome seemed to rise, then collapse in on itself. Most of the Marines who assaulted the structure didn't even know the name of the lieutenant who had led them to victory, but as the story of Bonnyman's brave actions began to be told, the heroic lieutenant was awarded a posthumous Navy Cross. In time, and as events came into sharper focus, that award was upgraded to the Medal of Honor.

After dark on D day plus two, the Japanese hit the Marine Corps positions with dozens of sharp, nighttime attacks, culminating in a massive *banzai* charge by 700 screaming *rikusentai* riflemen, bayonets mounted. They were annihilated by artillery, mortar fire, and in ferocious hand-to-hand fighting with the tough, hard-bitten Marines. The Japanese were defeated that night—but had their attack occurred on the first night instead of the third, the U.S. Marines might well have been pushed into the sea.

When the sun came up on the twenty-third, the battle on the main island was all but over. On the morning of November 24, the final push began. Lieutenant Colonel Raymond Murray's Second Battalion, Sixth Marines, went after 200 stubborn *rikusentai* still occupying the outer atolls. For the next two days, the fighting was intense, but the Japanese were finally cornered on Buariki Island. The last attack of the campaign began at dawn and ended by nightfall, when the last *rikusentai* perished under the guns of the Marine Corps in a savage jungle engagement.

The battle for Tarawa was costly; 3,407 Marines were wounded, over 900 of them perished, and 88 Americans are still missing and unaccounted for today. One out of every three Marines wounded on Tarawa died, reflecting high command's inability to evacuate the wounded in the face of the tide that never rose high enough to allow the Higgins boats to reach land. The Japanese defenders died almost to a man—nearly 5,000 of them—and the campaign was so chaotic it would be over fifty years before the Marine Corps learned the whole truth about the enemy they faced. The fate of Vice Admiral Shibasaki, the Japanese commander many believed had died on the last day of the battle, inside the bombproof bunker, was a mystery until a Japanese survivor came forward in the 1980s and told the world the truth—that his commander had died two days before, on D day.

The last Marine to receive the Medal of Honor for action on Tarawa was Lieutenant Colonel David Monroe Shoup. The Rock of Tarawa, the reluctant architect of the successful invasion, was presented with his medal by then Secretary of the Navy James V. Forrestal. Shoup had succeeded against overwhelming bad luck. First, his radios were knocked out in the opening hours of combat, and for almost the entire battle he had to rely on runners to carry orders and deliver information from other commands. Then, as Shoup was moving to the beach, he was wounded by shrapnel. Though he pretended that the wound was minor, several times he almost went into shock. As the hours passed, his pain grew in intensity, but Shoup stubbornly fought on. Finally, there was the tide that never arrived. It seemed as if nature itself conspired against the Americans at Tarawa.

After a long stay in the hospital, Lieutenant Colonel Shoup returned to duty with the Second Marine Division as chief of staff. He remained with the division through the Marianas Campaign, then returned to the States for a staff position at Marine Corps headquarters. After the war, President Dwight D. Eisenhower nominated Colonel David Shoup to be the Marine Corps twenty-second commandant, and he began his first four-year term on January 1, 1960.

Almost immediately, Shoup became a lightning rod for controversy. Before the first two years of his tenure were up, he became openly critical of the American military buildup in Southeast Asia that would evolve into the Vietnam War. Even after he retired from the Corps in 1964, Shoup remained a vocal critic of America's involvement in Vietnam. He lost the friendship and respect of many Marines, but refused to be silenced. David Monroe Shoup, the hero of Tarawa, passed away on January 13, 1983, at the age of seventy-nine and is buried at Arlington National Cemetery.

In 1944, after some deliberation, President Franklin Delano Roosevelt authorized the release to the public of a documentary film shot by war correspondents on the bloody beaches at Tarawa. The film, *With the Marines at Tarawa*, became an overnight sensation. It was the most graphic, explicit document ever released during the war about the war. Featuring brutal, disturbing footage of actual combat—including scenes of the blackened bodies of what were once young American Marines floating dead in the surf—the documentary shocked the American public and delivered the message that the war was cruel and costly. The film, which included some footage of First Lieutenant Alexander Bonnyman's actual assault on the sand bunker, won an Academy Award in 1944. Americans were stunned by what they saw on the screen.

Enlistment in the Marine Corps dropped precipitously after the film was released, and did not rise again until late 1944. But the film ultimately had a positive effect. It changed the way Americans viewed the Marine Corps forever. After the public saw the grisly carnage with their own eyes, they began to think of the Marines fighting in the Pacific as a brotherhood of superhuman warriors undaunted by a mysterious, brutal, and savage enemy. After that, Americans watched in awe as the Marines ripped through the Marshall Islands, capturing one enemy stronghold after another in a matter of weeks or even days, pushing the Japanese closer and closer to their home islands.

KWAJALEIN

In early 1944, at the three-day battle for Kwajalein, four Marines earned the Medal of Honor in a brisk fight that culminated in an American victory. Capturing Kwajalein Atoll was the first step in the conquest of the Marshall Islands. The largest atoll in the Pacific, Kwajalein had a huge natural harbor that the Japanese never bothered to develop. It was dominated by two large landmasses—Roi and Namur—that were separated by a narrow sand and coral causeway. On Roi, the Japanese had constructed a large air base complete with facilities. On Namur they built a pier, living quarters for troops, and a supply depot for the Navy. Three other islands surrounded the Kwajalein Atoll. These islands were captured by the Americans on the night before D day and then heavily reinforced with artillery. They later served as fire-support bases to cover the main Marine assault on Roi and Namur.

The Marines hit the beaches at sunrise on February 1, 1944, and began to wrestle the island from several thousand Japanese defenders. The Navy stepped in to assist the landing. Under the command of Admiral Richard L. Conolly, who was determined to make up for the ineffective bombardment at Tarawa, the ships moved very close to the islands to deliver an effective punch. After the sustained bombardment—nearly three times as long as the pounding at Tarawa and twice as effective—the Marines came ashore in Alligators. The warships belonging to "Close-In Conolly"—a nickname the Marines lovingly bestowed on the U.S. Navy commander—obliterated most of the Japanese defenses. Follow-up air assaults were also effective.

Before the landings began, Underwater Demolition Teams (UDTs) were utilized in advance of the invasion to destroy some of the Japanese-built tank traps and minefields—formidable impediments to the landing boats. No longer would Marines cruise up and down the shore, searching for a suitable landing zone as they did at Tarawa. Now, using underwater demolition teams, prelanding reconnaissance of an entire island was possible. Teams went in without scuba gear and returned to report on the hazards the enemy had waiting for the Marines. UDTs were used with such effectiveness before the attack on Roi-Namur that they were dispatched in advance of every other amphibious assault in the Pacific theater.

The beaches of Roi-Namur were divided into segments—Red Beach One, Two, and Three on Roi, and Green Beach One, Two, and Three on Namur. At one o'clock in the afternoon, during the third wave of the assault on Namur, a Marine Corps engineer tossed a high-explosive satchel charge into what appeared to be an occupied bunker.

"Great God almighty! The whole damned island's blown up!" came a frantic call from an aerial observer seconds after a gigantic explosion shook the atoll. The force of the blast nearly swatted the observation plane out of the sky and blew men off their feet a half mile away from the roiling epicenter. The "bunker" turned out to be a massive storage facility for Imperial Japanese Navy torpedoes and bombs. The explosion killed 120 Marines—including the entire engineering unit—along with countless Japanese. The concussion was felt on the island of Roi and the mushroom cloud that rose over the devastation could be seen from miles out to sea. Navy spotters reported seeing human bodies swirling in the center of the fireball in the seconds after the blast. This accident of war slowed the initial American assault of Namur to a crawl. Fortunately, it also disoriented the Japanese defenders, and Kwajalein was captured in three days.

On the first day of the invasion, four Marines earned the Medal of Honor during the amphibious assault. All save one fought on the beach at Namur. The exception was twenty-two-year-old Private First Class Richard Beatty Anderson of Tacoma, Washington. Anderson hit the beach on Roi in the first wave and battled a determined enemy. The Japanese, who were outnumbered and outgunned, pulled back from the beach to a defensive line of pillboxes and emplacements where they made their last stand. By four o'clock in the afternoon, the fight had degenerated to a hundred individual skirmishes, pitting Marine attackers against the fierce Japanese *rikusentai*. During an assault on a pocket of determined defenders, Private Anderson was preparing to hurl a grenade at the enemy when it slipped out of his sweaty hands and dropped to the bottom of the foxhole. Realizing that the Marines around him were in danger, and he was responsible for their predicament, Anderson smothered the blast with his body and was killed.

On Namur, things were more evenly matched and the fighting was much more intense. The 24th Marines were pinned down on the beach by concrete bunkers bristling with machine guns. First Lieutenant John Vincent Power, a twenty-five-year-old officer from Worcester, Massachusetts, saw his platoon devastated by Japanese guns as they approached a pillbox. Rallying his men, Power tried to take out the emplacement, but they were driven back with heavy casualties. Realizing they could neither retreat nor advance until the enemy emplacement was neutralized, Power jumped to his feet and charged the bunker. He was shot in the stomach as soon as he emerged from cover. Clutching his belly with his left hand and firing his carbine with his right, the lieutenant raced forward, aiming into the gun ports of the enemy pillbox. He was struck two more times and died at the entrance to the bunker. It was left to his men to clean the emplacement out with rifles and grenades. Lieutenant Power's self-sacrifice earned him a posthumous Medal of Honor.

Private Richard Keith Sorenson was a Marine Corps machine gunner from Anoka, Minnesota. Born on August 8, 1924, he was one of the youngest men to assault Namur. During the first night, the Japanese staged a counterattack in force on a position occupied by Sorenson and five other Marines. A Japanese soldier hurled a grenade in the midst of the Americans, and without hesitation Sorenson threw his

Private Richard K. Sorenson   *Colonel Aquilla J. Dyess*

body over the explosive and smothered the blast. Miraculously, he survived—though he was severely wounded. Sorenson received his Medal of Honor at the Seattle Naval Hospital—the only one not awarded posthumously for this campaign. He was promoted to first lieutenant and stayed in the Corps.

The highest-ranking Marine to earn the Medal of Honor at Kwajalein was Lieutenant Colonel Aquilla James Dyess of Augusta, Georgia. Dyess was a decorated hero before he ever joined the Marine Corps. On July 13, 1928, nineteen-year-old Jimmy Dyess had just completed his freshman year at Clemson University and was vacationing on Sullivan's Island off the coast of South Carolina with his family. The strapping 190-pound, red-haired teenager spotted Mrs. Roscoe Holley struggling in the surf. Though a capable swimmer, the woman was being dragged out to sea by powerful waves. Two attempts to save her had already failed because the rescuers were not strong enough to fight the tide. There were no surfboats on the beach, and minutes before Dyess arrived, Barbara Muller, a young Charleston woman, swam out to Mrs. Holley in a third rescue attempt. Muller reached the woman, but was not strong enough to drag her back to shore.

An expert swimmer, Dyess quickly reached the women. The trio was now two hundred yards offshore and the tide was carrying them farther away by the minute. A crowd gathered on the beach to watch the drama unfold. After about ten minutes, the three swimmers appeared to be moving toward shore. The two exhausted women were floating over the crest of the waves while Jimmy dragged them slowly back to land. The trip took over a half hour, and when he came ashore, Jimmy's work wasn't over. He helped to revive Mrs. Holley, who had swallowed too much seawater.

When pursued by the press after the incident, Dyess was modest. "What else could a man do?" he asked a reporter, adding, "If there is any credit, it is due Miss Muller, the bravest girl I ever saw." Both Jimmy Dyess and Barbara Muller earned the Carnegie Medal for Heroism that day. The Carnegie Medal is awarded for heroic action or self-sacrifice during peacetime. Established by millionaire industrialist Andrew Carnegie, the honor had been awarded annually since 1904. Jimmy Dyess is the only individual to earn the Carnegie Medal for Heroism and the Medal of Honor.

Aquilla James Dyess was born on January 11, 1909, the third of four Dyess children and the second son. His family was old and distinguished Southern gentry. Though not wealthy, his father, Maurice, was the founder and president of a lumber company. From an early age, Jimmy was obsessed with all things military. During the First World War, recruits from Pennsylvania were trained in and around Augusta, and the Dyess family served Sunday dinners for many of them. These recruits regaled nine-year-old Jimmy with tales of military adventure.

When he was ten, Jimmy's older brother, Guyton, contracted typhoid fever and died quite suddenly. In his grief, Maurice Dyess told Jimmy that "the wrong son had died." This hurtful remark had a galvanizing effect on the young boy. Forever after, Jimmy Dyess would be driven to prove himself to his stern and demanding father. When he was old enough, he went off to military school and was active in the Boy Scouts of America. He excelled in athletics and was a collegiate football player at Clemson as well as an expert swimmer—it was between semesters that Jimmy earned the Carnegie Medal.

In 1934, when he was twenty-five, Jimmy met the woman he was to marry; she was literally the girl next door. Connor Cleckley was two years younger than Jimmy but far surpassed him in worldliness and sophistication. She had already traveled throughout Europe and had lived and studied in England before she agreed to become his wife. Jimmy was impressed by her beauty and intelligence. She was attracted to his flaming red hair, rugged frame, and positive attitude toward life. They had their only child, a daughter, in 1934.

Dyess spent much of his postgraduate days working for his father's lumber company, but his love of the military never wavered. He was a superlative cadet at Clemson and wore his uniform with pride. By the time he graduated in 1931, Jimmy Dyess was a nationally acclaimed marksman, a skill that would serve him well in the Marine Corps. In 1936, the Corps announced that they were establishing a reserve unit in Augusta. Jimmy joined immediately. He won a number of marksmanship medals in 1937 and 1938 and was a top-ranking expert in the Marine Corps Reserve.

In autumn 1940, Jimmy Dyess was called to active duty. Instead of being placed in an infantry unit, he was assigned to a barrage balloon detachment. He was still there when the Japanese attacked Pearl Harbor in December 1941. In May 1942, Jimmy Dyess was promoted to major, but he was still stuck in air defense—he was now executive officer of the Barrage Balloon School. In November 1942, Dyess was transferred to the Fourth Marine Division for the campaign in the Marshall Islands.

Months later he was named commander of the Fourth Division and instantly made a positive impression on his men by reorganizing the mess hall to make sure the food was palatable and nutritious.

The Marines of the Fourth Division were in good tactical shape as they approached Green Beach Two on D day afternoon. By the time Dyess and his Marines hit the beach at Namur, half the 3,500 Japanese defending the island were dead and Vice Admiral Yamada had been killed during the preinvasion bombardment. The beach was secure when Dyess's Alligator arrived and he debarked with the final elements of his command.

Ahead of Dyess a platoon of Marines had been pinned down. Corporal Frank Pokrop and his men were taking fire from three directions, and one Marine was wounded. His comrades refused to retreat without the injured man, and the Japanese fire was so merciless that they could not pull back without being cut to pieces anyway. Lieutenant Colonel Dyess organized a small rescue force and commandeered a half-track. They roared up to the front, disembarked, and were able to fight their way through Japanese lines and reach the trapped platoon. While several Marines led Pokrop and his men to safety, Lieutenant Colonel Dyess remained behind to provide covering fire. The rescue was barely completed before dark.

On the second day of fighting, Dyess found himself facing the last bastion of Japanese resistance. As he organized a final assault, a Japanese machine gunner opened up on his position. Dyess was struck in the head and died instantly. Moments after "Big Red" was killed, the final pillbox was silenced and Namur was in Marine Corps hands. For his bold leadership and for the rescue of the trapped Marines on the previous day, Lieutenant Colonel Aquilla James Dyess was awarded a posthumous Medal of Honor. He is buried in Westover Memorial Park and there is a tribute to him at the Heroes' Overlook at Riverwalk Augusta, where a flag flies over his marker.

Within three weeks after the campaign to capture Kwajalein, the Marines were at it again, this time at Eniwetok Atoll. It was during the assault on Engebi Island that Corporal Anthony Peter Damato of Shenandoah, Pennsylvania, earned the Medal of Honor. Damato, who was twenty-two, flung himself on a Japanese grenade hurled during a nighttime assault. He perished, but his self-sacrifice saved the lives of the men with him. The Medal of Honor was presented to Corporal Damato's mother in Pennsylvania on April 9, 1945.

The Marshall Islands—including Tarawa, Kwajalein, and Eniwetok Atoll—fell in short order. To the public, the Marines seemed unstoppable. Their performance after Guadalcanal and Tarawa dazzled the folks at home. The next stop would be the Marianas and the islands of Guam, Saipan, and Tinian, where the Marines hoped to extend their string of victories.

BATTLE FOR THE MARIANAS

The Japanese pulled back after their defeat in the Marshall Islands. Imperial General Headquarters, the Japanese equivalent to the American Joint Chiefs, established a fallback zone called the Absolute Defense Sphere. This zone—which encompassed the Marianas and the Philippines, including some former American territories—was the site of the Japanese military's last stand in the Pacific War. They would fight to defend this territory and would alter their tactics in an attempt to defeat the American forces arrayed against them.

Operation Forager called for the capture of Saipan, Tinian, and Guam, the latter a U.S. territory captured in the days after Pearl Harbor. Forager was meant to take the war to the enemy's doorstep with a thousand-mile leap into enemy territory. Lieutenant General Holland "Howlin' Mad" Smith would lead the 70,000 men of the "Northern Troops Landing Force," composed of Marines and elements of the United States Army, in the attack on Tinian and Saipan. Major General Roy Geiger commanded the 55,000 men of the "Southern Troops and Landing Force" in an attack on Guam.

Saipan was of great concern to the military planners. It was a seventy-two-square-mile island with fringing reefs, volcanic rock, mountains, cave-riddled cliffs, jungle, swamp, and a town where the Marines would have to fight house to house for the first time since Veracruz in 1914. Smith knew that Saipan would be costly. On the eve of the invasion, he told a reporters that "a week from now there would be a lot of dead Marines." Over 32,000 Imperial Army and Navy *rikusentai,* under the command of Lieutenant General Yoshitsuga Saito, were dug into hundreds of caves and were well equipped with massed artillery and even tanks. It was the largest enemy concentration the Americans faced so far in the Pacific theater.

D day came on June 15, 1944. Navy officers were puzzled by hundreds of tiny red flags that appeared on the reef just before the invasion. As the LVTs moved toward shore, they discovered why those flags were there. As the first amtracs touched the coral, the entire fringing reef exploded in a tremendous, rolling blast. LVTs were tossed into the air. Others had their bows shattered. Water swamped many. The Navy thought that the Japanese had mined the reef, but in reality the Americans faced a massive artillery salvo from every enemy artillery piece on Saipan, all firing in the same moment. This "time on target" salvo had been planned in advance. The red flags were artillery range markers.

Twenty LVTs were lost in this bombardment. Some were blasted to bits by direct hits. Others were swamped by geysers of water that erupted around the reef. A couple of these large, tracked vehicles were spun end over end, spilling men, weapons, and matériel into the surf. Hundreds more reached the shore. The new LVTs, sporting 75mm guns, were expected to clear the landing zone of enemy defenses. Instead they got bogged down in the shattered landscape on the beach and were decimated. Marines were forced to abandon the amtracs and scurry to cover among the rocks.

Lieutenant Colonel "Jim" Crowe was one of the first officers on the scene. A veteran of Tarawa, Crowe was wounded moving troops to fill a gap in the American lines. As he was being evacuated, he asked the stretcher bearers to stop at "Red Mike" Edson's position, where he turned over his command with an apology. Crowe would survive, but he never led men into battle again. By nightfall, 20,000 Marines were on the beach, and there were 700 casualties. The Americans had not penetrated far—most positions were less than a mile inland. Their grip on Saipan was tenuous.

Out of the darkness came the first Japanese counterattack. The Marines huddling in their foxholes heard the sound of engines, then forty Japanese tanks burst from the shadows and charged the American lines. The First Battalion, Sixth Marines, bore the brunt of the attack. These veterans of the final *banzai* assault on Tarawa annihilated the armor with mortars, artillery, rifle grenades, and bazookas. Two suicidal *banzai* charges followed, and both were beaten back with heavy casualties inflicted on the enemy. At dawn the Navy received shocking news. The Imperial Japanese Navy was on the way. The enemy was confident that the final, decisive naval battle was imminent. The naval and air battle that followed would become known as "The Great Marianas Turkey Shoot." The Allies decimated the Japanese fleet and swept the skies of enemy warplanes. Three Japanese carriers were sunk and 476 aircraft were shot out of the air. It was the enemy's worst defeat so far in the war and the Japanese were on the ropes.

On the second day of fighting, American tanks rolled ashore. With this force was Gunnery Sergeant Robert McCard of Company A, Fourth Tank Battalion. Leading a platoon of Shermans, McCard's tank rumbled forward into enemy territory. Almost immediately it was cut off from the main force and surrounded by Japanese infantry. McCard opened fire with his 75mm cannon and his turret-mounted machine gun in a futile attempt to push them back. He succeeded, but artillery began landing around his vehicle. The Sherman lurched and smoke filled the interior. The Japanese manning a battery of 75mm guns had crippled it.

"Take off!" the sergeant cried as smoke burned his eyes.

One by one the crew scurried out of the escape hatch, only to face Japanese infantrymen. As the enemy advanced on his crew, Sergeant McCard stayed on the turret, hurling grenades in an attempt to drive the Japanese away from his comrades. Bullets bounced off the Sherman's armor as Japanese machine gunners tried to pick McCard off. When the sergeant was wounded, he wavered for a moment, a stunned look on his face. Then McCard seemed to recover and returned fire with the .50-caliber machine gun mounted on the top hatch. He covered his crew's retreat, killing sixteen Japanese soldiers, before the rest swarmed over his tank and killed him.

Robert Howard McCard was only twenty-five years old when he died. Born in Syracuse, New York, he left behind a young wife named Lizette. On April 10, 1945, his widow was presented with Sergeant McCard's posthumous Medal of Honor—the first earned on Saipan.

During the assault on the rugged slopes of Mount Tapotchau, the 27th Division was hit by a nighttime tank attack. Private First Class Harold G. Epperson of Akron, Ohio, manned a machine gun and cut down the advancing infantry following the armor. One Japanese he assumed was dead rose and hurled a grenade into his position. Without hesitation, Epperson dived on the explosive and absorbed the brunt of the blast. Harold Glenn Epperson was weeks away from his twenty-first birthday when he was killed on Saipan. He received a posthumous Medal of Honor.

By the end of eight days of hard fighting, the Marines held the southern half of Saipan and had suffered 6,000 casualties. The Japanese lost over half their men— mostly squandered in *banzai* attacks. On the northern coast of Saipan, things were much worse. The U.S. Army troops became bogged down, and blame for this delay landed squarely on the shoulders of the Army commander, Major General Ralph

Smith. Holland Smith, the Marine commander, demanded that his timid Army counterpart be removed from command, launching the "Battle of the Smiths"—a public relations nightmare that overshadowed the victory on Saipan. In the end, Holland Smith prevailed and Ralph Smith was replaced, widening the rift between the Marines and the Army that had begun at Belleau Wood during World War I.

By the first of July, there was house-to-house fighting in the town of Garapan. It took two days for the Marines to secure the devastated city. The Japanese fought stubbornly, then retreated to their caves, where they prepared for their final stand. On July 5, 1944—twenty days into the invasion—all of the airfields on Saipan were in American hands. That night General Saito knelt outside his cave and committed ritual suicide. His final order was that his troops swarm over the Americans in a suicidal *banzai* charge. That charge came on the morning of July 6, when 4,000 enemy soldiers swarmed out of their caves in the largest *banzai* attack of the war. Hundreds of charging, sword-wielding Japanese descended on a thin line of Army defenders. The GIs put up a fight, but were overwhelmed at several key points. The Japanese then moved deep into American territory, descending on a Marine Corps artillery position in the rear. When the Marines spotted the enemy horde, they lowered their artillery pieces and fired into the massed attackers. Hundreds died, but the Japanese overwhelmed the artillerymen.

In brutal hand-to-hand combat the Marines were butchered before reinforcements arrived. When Marines brought up from the rear slammed into the enemy forces, the fighting swirled through every ravine, valley, and sugarcane field in the region. The fight lasted the entire day. When it was over the Japanese were wiped out, their corpses stacked two and three deep all over the battlefield. The savagery of the assault and the grisly aftermath shocked even the most hardened veteran.

During this final attack, Private First Class Harold Christ Agerholm, a nineteen-year-old Marine from Racine, Wisconsin, commandeered an ambulance and moved forty-five wounded men through the heaviest fighting to a field hospital in the rear, out of harm's way. Hours later, while aiding the wounded, he was killed by a Japanese sniper. For his courageous action Private Agerholm was awarded a posthumous Medal of Honor.

After the *banzai* attack, the Marines advanced on a tall cliff called Marpi Point, where an even more horrifying experience awaited them. The Japanese civilian population on Saipan had taken refuge on the cliff. Now, fearful of the American advance, they swarmed to the edge of the precipice. Most of the young men had died in the fighting, all that remained were the old and women and children of all ages. While the Marines watched helplessly, these civilians threw themselves and their children into the chasm. Some were forced over the edge by armed Japanese soldiers, but most died willingly. Hundreds of innocents perished.

On D day plus twenty-four, Saipan was declared secure. Over 3,000 Americans died and 13,000 had been wounded. Enemy dead were estimated at 33,000. The three-week battle for Saipan was the most difficult campaign yet, but the Marines had no time to rest. They had to prepare for the next step in the conquest of the Marianas, the invasions of Tinian and Guam.

DOUBLE FEATURE

Before the battle for Saipan was over, the aerial bombardment of Tinian had begun. When the invasion came, it was a masterpiece of intelligence, planning, and execution. All the elements fell into place—the Navy flattened enemy defenses, the beaches were mapped, and the Americans even obtained copies of the blueprints for the Japanese defenses on the island. Much of this fifty-square mile island was defended by high escarpments, but there was one natural beach. Instead of hitting that beach, which was mined and defended, the Marines landed at several strategic points on the northwest shore at breaks in the cliffs found by underwater reconnaissance teams.

At night the Japanese began to probe the American positions. There would be no *banzai* attack here. Colonel Keishi Ogata was a wise tactician and ordered his men to stalk the enemy. When the Japanese were sure of the disposition of the American lines, they struck. Mortar fire blanketed the Marines all along the front. Then the armor appeared, clanking out of the darkness, cannons roaring. Ogata had at his command hard-bitten veterans of Manchuria and an entire battalion of light tanks. They descended on the Americans like a tsunami, sweeping away everything in their path in the first few minutes of battle. But soon the Marines rallied and turned the tide.

By morning the Marines had driven the enemy back, and 2,000 of Ogata's elite were dead on the field. They lay among the burning hulks of shattered tanks. The Americans, using artillery, bazookas, and mortars, had decimated the Japanese armor. Colonel Ogata learned at great cost that the men he faced were no green recruits—these Americans were veterans of night fighting in the Marshall Islands and on Saipan. The Marines went toe-to-toe with Ogata's elite and took them down. Though the battle for Tinian continued until the last day in July, there was not much fight left in the Japanese after this disastrous night attack.

Two Marines earned the Medal of Honor, posthumously, in the battle for Tinian. Both threw their bodies over live grenades. Private Joseph William Ozbourn was twenty-three when he sacrificed his life on July 28. Born in Herrin, Illinois, he was trained as a BAR man. Robert Lee Wilson was also twenty-three, and also born in Illinois. He threw himself on a grenade on August 4, days after the island was declared secure. In a remote location, Wilson's platoon was ambushed by several Japanese stragglers. When a grenade was hurled at them, Wilson smothered the grenade, allowing his comrades to continue their mission. In all, less than 400 Marines were killed on Tinian and 2,000 were wounded. It was a comparatively cheap price to pay for some of the finest air bases in the Central Pacific. From Tinian, the new B-29 Superfortress could reach the Japanese mainland and bomb its cities to rubble.

Guam was attacked before Tinian was secure. Once an American territory, the island had a symbolic value above and beyond its strategic importance. There was a special sense of purpose felt by the Marines sent to recapture this former U.S. possession. Lying a hundred miles south of Saipan, Guam was shaped like a boot with Apra Harbor located at the heel. There were roughly twice as many defenders on

Guam than on Tinian—18,500 Japanese under the command of Lieutenant General Takeshi Takashina. Guam was much larger than Tinian, thirty miles long and five to eight miles wide. The Japanese knew the Americans were coming but bought themselves extra time to beef up their defenses when the Imperial Navy steamed into the Marianas. This action delayed the American invasion by thirty days, and the Marine landing force had to endure two months at sea in stifling, overcrowded transport ships under a broiling tropical sun.

Major General Roy Geiger commanded the American forces, made up of veterans of Eniwetok and Bougainville. Beginning in mid-July, the underwater demolition teams cleared the approaches to the beach, destroying over 900 log cribs and wire cages filled with coral. On one reef, the UDTs left a sign that said WELCOME MARINES! The enemy was concentrated in and around Apra Harbor and the island's two airfields. During the delay before the attack, the Japanese dug a huge system of trenches across the narrowest portion of the Orote Peninsula using 20,000 native citizens as forced labor. The Marines' task was to capture and hold the peninsula, then move inland.

Early on the morning of July 21, to the sound of "The Marine Corps Hymn" blasting over loudspeakers, the Marines—their bellies full from a hearty breakfast of steak and eggs—climbed into landing craft and headed for shore. A hundred yards from the beach the LVTs were hit with artillery and mortar fire, but by 8:30 A.M., they were all on the beach—and Americans were back on Guam after two and a half years of enemy occupation.

Chonito Cliff was a major obstacle to the Americans' advance. Surrounded by caves filled with Japanese soldiers, the 300-foot escarpment could neither be climbed nor encircled. It took a determined effort by Marine Corps flamethrower teams to neutralize the caves—usually by charging up to them and blasting fire through the gun ports. By noon the Marines had captured the cliff, but faced a tall ridge that was still heavily defended. The fight for "Banzai Ridge" would be costly. Weakened by tropical heat, long confinement on boats and a lack of water, Marines had to climb the hundred-foot cliff under merciless enemy fire. When those who survived made it to the top, they were immediately pinned down by machine-gun fire from another ridge just fifty yards away. Hitting the beach, taking the cliff, and climbing Banzai Ridge had already cost the Marines 500 dead. Now the sun was setting and the Americans dug in for the long night.

Under cover of darkness, the Japanese counterattacked in force. One Marine Corps rifle battalion was reduced to just four men. Demolition troops carrying explosive charges probed the American lines, infiltrating the perimeter at several points. They were spotted by the light of flares and gunned down by the Marines. Then Japanese tanks advanced and were promptly dispatched by artillery fire. Meanwhile, a Japanese counterattack attempted to recapture Chonito Cliff. Enemy troops came out of the darkness, hurling grenades and firing rifles. The Third Marines were defending the area, and this sudden attack tore them to pieces.

Private Luther Skaggs of Henderson, Kentucky, heard cries in the night, then something bounced through the jungle and landed near him. There was a blinding flash, a deafening explosion, and Skaggs felt a sharp jolt of agony—his leg had been shattered by a Japanese grenade. Feeling around in the dark, he improvised a tourniquet to stop the bleeding. Then he took command of his disorganized and leaderless mortar team. For the rest of the night, Skaggs hurled grenades and fired his rifle at the enemy, while his men manned the mortars. After eight hours of hard fighting, dawn came. Skaggs led his shattered platoon out of their foxholes to mop up the remaining Japanese. For assuming command of his unit, Private Skaggs earned the Medal of Honor. He survived the war to pass away in 1976.

In all, 800 Marines from the Third were killed or wounded in the first forty-eight hours of the battle. Enemy dead were estimated at around 600. But the Marines still held the beaches, the peninsula, the cliff, and the town. A few hours later the Marines captured the former U.S. Navy Yard at Piti, which made unloading critical supplies much easier.

Meanwhile, the Third Marines fought their way up Bundschu Ridge, a natural rock fortress that was defended by machine guns and mortars. The initial push was driven back, and in this failed assault a Marine from the Third—Private First Class Leonard Mason of Middlesboro, Kentucky—was killed in a solo attack on a pair of enemy machine-gun posts. He was shot repeatedly by the Japanese hiding behind the rocks, but circled the enemy position and wiped them out with his BAR before succumbing to his wounds. Private Mason received the Medal of Honor, posthumously.

On the second night the Japanese again attacked, and again they were slaughtered. Lieutenant Takashina knew his numbers were dwindling and planned a massive counterattack while he still had the strength to pull it off. He withdrew his men from Bundschu Ridge, leaving behind a skeleton force of suicidal defenders. The Marines advanced up the slopes as the Japanese consolidated their forces behind the ridge. On the night of July 25, the Japanese hit the Marines along a five-mile perimeter in the largest counterattack of the war. Thousands of *sake*-maddened enemy troops struck the overextended American lines. The First Battalion, 21st Marines, was the hardest hit. The Japanese slaughtered fifty men from B Company, then swarmed over the perimeter to hit American tanks in the rear. Many of the attackers were literally walking bombs. They carried high explosives and would hurl themselves into American foxholes and blow themselves and the Marines to smithereens. This Japanese assault pushed deep into American lines, and even reached a field hospital, where the walking wounded put up a stubborn defense.

That night, Captain Louis H. Wilson, Jr., of Brandon, Mississippi, was being treated for wounds at an aid station when he heard about the Japanese counterattack. He'd already had a hard day. That afternoon he was ordered to take his company up Fonte Hill, a steep incline that was staunchly defended. The advance was made across 300 yards of open terrain. As the Marines moved forward, they were peppered with machine-gun fire and pelted by mortar shells. Wilson's command was shattered, but he kept urging his men forward—shouting to be heard above mortar blasts.

Captain Wilson was a veteran of Bougainville, but on the first day of the invasion of Guam, he lost more men than he did at Bougainville after a month of hard fighting. As he charged Fonte Hill, he became enraged at the carnage and took the lead position. Still advancing on point, Wilson stopped several times to dispatch snipers with his carbine. When the Marines finally reached the summit, Wilson sent the wounded to the rear and established a defensive perimeter—all under relentless enemy fire. Captain Wilson was struck three times. Three times he was knocked to the ground, only to get up and resume his duties. Only after his men were firmly entrenched did Wilson report to the aid station established nearby. He was treated and ordered to rest, but after nightfall the *banzai* charge began. Wilson rose from his bunk and hurried up the hill to his Marines.

As drunken Japanese soldiers came charging up the slope, screaming "Marines, you die!" Wilson moved from platoon to platoon, fortifying each position and shifting troops to fill gaps left by casualties. At one point he spotted a wounded Marine in the open and charged across fifty yards of open ground to carry the man to safety.

The Japanese attacked Wilson's position seven times that night. Seven times they were beaten back. Twice the enemy was halted only a few yards from the perimeter. Once they made it into the American foxholes, where the Marines wrestled them to the ground and slaughtered them with rifles and bayonets. Captain Wilson used his rifle as a club to beat two attackers to death. In eight ferocious hours of fighting, F Company took over 50 percent casualties—but under the indomitable leadership of Captain Louis Wilson, they held the high ground.

At dawn his men began taking fire from enemy troops on an opposite hill. Leading a seventeen-man assault team, Captain Wilson charged up the second slope to the enemy emplacements. Machine guns cut thirteen of them down. The four survivors, including Captain Wilson, overran the Japanese position and slaughtered the defenders. By nine o'clock, the battle for Fonte Hill was over. Wilson was slightly injured in this final assault—his fourth wound in twenty-four hours. That afternoon he was forced to relinquish his command. The next day he was evacuated with the rest of the wounded.

Louis Wilson spent three months in a hospital before he returned to active duty. While serving at the Marine barracks in Washington, D.C., Wilson was summoned to the White House on October 5, 1945, where President Harry Truman hung the Medal of Honor around his bull neck. Wilson was promoted and later served a tour of duty with the First Marine Division in Korea. In 1975, he was named commandant of the Marine Corps. He served for four years and resigned in 1979 at the age of fifty-nine. Louis Hugh Wilson, now a retired general, returned to his native Mississippi, where he still lives today.

The Marines were stalled until July 26, when the Fourth Marines, supported by tanks, annihilated the weary and dispirited defenders. During this push, a Japanese sniper killed Lieutenant Colonel Samuel D. Puller—Lewis "Chesty" Puller's brother. For the next week, the Japanese slowed the American advance with pillboxes, booby traps, minefields, and well-planned ambushes. On August 4, one such ambush was thwarted by the heroic action of twenty-three-year-old Private First Class Frank P. Witek of Derby, Connecticut. When a Japanese surprise attack jumped his platoon, Witek rose from cover and killed eight enemy soldiers with his BAR before he was killed himself. Witek was the last man to earn the Medal of Honor at Guam. His award, like far too many others, was posthumous.

On August 10, Major General Roy Geiger declared Guam secure. But thousands of Japanese were still hiding on the island. They would conduct a guerrilla war for months until they starved to death or were killed. The island was rapidly converted into a naval base with two airfields for B-29 bombers. With American airpower within striking distance of the Japanese homeland, the end of the war was in sight. But the campaigns for the Marshalls and the Marianas had cost the Marines 27,000 casualties—more than the equivalent of an entire Marine Corps division. And the war wasn't over. For the Marines, some of the worst fighting was yet to come.

CHAPTER ELEVEN

ENDGAME:
PELELIU, IWO JIMA, OKINAWA

■

1944–1945

HALF of all the Marines who received the Medal of Honor in World War II earned it during the final campaigns of the Pacific War. The escalating violence at Peleliu, Iwo Jima, and Okinawa reflects a change in tactics that would mean trouble for the Americans. The Pacific War turned very ugly in 1944. The Japanese illusion of an Absolute Defense Sphere was shattered and the Home Islands were threatened from the air, by sea, and by land. The final, decisive sea battle the Japanese admirals thought would end the war was impossible to win without control of the sky. But the Zero had become obsolete, and the Japanese couldn't train pilots fast enough to stand up against the seasoned Americans.

In desperation, the Japanese turned to suicide warfare. *Kamikaze* attacks against American shipping began in October 1944. Hundreds of pilots wasted their lives in these futile attacks. By the end of the war, the Japanese were building *kamikaze*-operated torpedoes and rocket planes.

At Imperial General Headquarters, a new tactic was devised to slow the American juggernaut. No longer would the they resist the Marines on the beach. Instead, they would retreat inland at the first sign of an invasion and fight from the island's heavily fortified interior. This plan was a wise use of Japan's dwindling resources. Naval bombardment would leave the defenders untouched. Instead of squatting in pillboxes on the beach, absorbing punishment from American ships and planes, the Japanese would hide in heavily armed emplacements far from shore.

Ironically, while *kamikaze* pilots were being trained for air assaults, the Japanese Army scaled back the use of the *banzai* charge in favor of stinging counterattacks meant to force the Americans to fight a costly war of attrition. The elements of this new defensive strategy were implemented in mid-1944. Every Japanese-held island

▪ *Kamikaze—"Divine Wind"*

After the Battle of the Philippine Sea—"The Great Marianas Turkey Shoot"—it became obvious to the Japanese that American carrier-based aircraft now ruled the sky. Allied supply convoys were heavily defended as well, protected by American air cover and destroyer escort. The Japanese submarine force could not possibly stem the torrent of war matériel flowing to the front. Drastic measures were required to slow the American advance. Because aircraft were the best weapon to attack surface shipping, the Imperial Japanese Navy created the *kamikaze*—the "Divine Wind."

Japanese soldiers were ruthless and disciplined warriors willing to die for their homeland, and Japanese pilots were accustomed to making suicide attacks when there was no other alternative. It was easy for the military to take the next step and actually train suicide troops to carry out a single, fatal mission. The Japanese utilized obsolete or stripped-down aircraft for such operations, and these planes were filled with just enough fuel to complete the mission. The *kamikaze* pilots received only a week of flight training—sometimes their first solo flight was also their first mission.

On a typical *kamikaze* sortie, an old Zero or Val was stripped of all excess weight, including the guns, and packed with bombs or high explosives. The pilot was expected to lay his aircraft on the target. Such an attack was difficult to stop—even a damaged aircraft spinning out of control can strike a large target. Early kamikaze attacks were not effective, but in 1945, a mass attack of hundreds of *kamikaze* aircraft against a United States Navy fleet in the Lingayen Gulf was quite crippling. Many ships were hit and casualties among the crews were high. *Kamikaze* attacks continued until the end of the war and were used to defend Iwo Jima and Okinawa.

These suicide attacks stunned the U.S. Navy and sent a stab of fear through the frontline troops. No one had experienced anything like this before. An enemy with no regard for his own life was truly a dangerous foe, and though the *kamikaze* attacks were a sign of desperation, they were also a powerful indication that the Japanese would continue to fight to the bitter end.

began constructing inland defenses. The effectiveness of this tactic would soon be tested at a place called Peleliu.

The Marines invaded Peleliu because of a promise made by Admiral Chester Nimitz to General Douglas MacArthur at the outset of the war, in front of President Roosevelt. Though the war had altered drastically since that promise was made, Nimitz had to keep his word—MacArthur and the president expected no less, and General MacArthur wanted Peleliu. Capturing the Japanese air base on the island was an essential part of his plan to retake the Philippines. In the opinion of the Navy, Peleliu could have been bypassed and starved out. That's what they would have done too—if not for that promise made to MacArthur.

To Marines, Peleliu was already notorious as the scene of Major "Pete" Ellis's mysterious death in 1923. Ellis, who had sounded the alarm about Japanese expansion in the Pacific, was regarded as a visionary by the officers now waging war against them. Peleliu seemed to be a hard-luck place for Marines.

Ironically, the invasion of Peleliu was called Stalemate, and the title would prove apt. Major General Roy Geiger and his Third Amphibious Corps were assigned the unenviable task of taking the island—a steaming-hot tropical hell of coral cliffs, mangrove swamps, volcanic caves, and stinking jungle. The island's most impressive feature were the Umurbrogol Cliffs, a rugged spine of steep hills running north and south. These hills were riddled with limestone caverns connected by tunnels. To reinforce the island, the Japanese brought in mining engineers to expand the caverns and equip them with rolling steel doors and gun ports for machine guns and artillery. Some of these caverns were large enough to house a thousand men.

Geiger chose three veterans to lead the Marines on this operation: "Chesty" Puller commanded the First; Harold "Bucky" Harris had the Fifth; and Herman Hanneken took command of the Seventh. On the other side, Colonel Kunio Nakagawa controlled Peleliu. He commanded more than 10,000 Japanese troops, including his own regiment—experienced veterans of Manchuria. Nakagawa believed that Peleliu was the perfect place to implement the new defensive strategy and trained his men accordingly.

D day came on September 15, 1944. After a short U.S. Navy bombardment, which ended prematurely because of a "lack of suitable targets," the LVTs took to the seas. Far inland, the steel doors rolled open and Japanese artillery rained down on the approaching amtracs from the Umurbrogol Cliffs. From coral promontories, 47mm antiboat guns also fired salvo after salvo at the coming Americans. In the first hour, the Japanese destroyed sixty LVTs and DUKWs. Much of the fire came from an anti-tank gun positioned high on a cliff along the left flank known as "The Point." Many would die trying to silence the gun on that cliff.

The Point began as a tall, rugged coral cliff jutting higher than any hill around it. The Japanese blasted huge holes into its face and artillery was placed inside of them. Then the openings were sealed with concrete except for a small gun port. The Point was honeycombed with connecting caves packed with infantry and ammunition. Soldiers could emerge through secret trapdoors and put up an instant fight against the advancing Marines. The guns could lay fire on any of the three landing beaches. Taking the Point was the duty of Captain George Hunt and his King Company, and this struggle became an epic example of small-unit action. As they climbed into position, Hunt's men were already at a disadvantage. They had lost their machine guns on the trip to shore and Hunt had neither communications with his superiors nor the mortar section he had relied upon for fire support. But despite these impediments, a rifle platoon from King Company managed to eradicate the enemy guns arrayed at the Point, one position at a time. The job was costly and time-consuming, but King Company triumphed.

Taking the Point and keeping it were two different things. Colonel Nakagawa was desperate not to lose this strategic position and sent wave after wave of attackers to drive Hunt's men out. Over the next thirty hours, Hunt's company successfully beat back four counterattacks, and two nights of hand-to-hand combat failed to dislodge the Marines. When King Company was relieved, fewer than eighteen of them were still standing. The Point was secure at the cost of 157 American casualties. After the war, at the training base at Quantico, the Marine Corps constructed an exact duplicate of the Point and its weaponry to train young Marine lieutenants in the art of assaulting a fixed and heavily armed defensive position.

While the desperate contest for the Point was being fought high above the beaches, Colonel Hanneken's Seventh were overrunning the Japanese gun emplacements on the ground. The enemy had knocked out so many American LVTs that hundreds of Marines were forced to wade ashore from the reef. Many were cut down by machine guns. In the center, Harris's Fifth Marines faced an array of fortified pill-boxes and an afternoon tank attack that was defeated by artillery and air assaults. Lewis Kenneth Bausell, a corporal with the Fifth, led a squad of Marines against a pillbox that lay astride a vital point on the beach. Bausell was the first man to reach the emplacement and fired through the port while the rest of his squad encircled the position. Suddenly a Japanese grenade landed among the clustered Marines and Bausell threw his body over the explosive, saving his comrades. A twenty-year-old from Polaski, Virginia, Bausell died of his wounds three days later. He was the first Marine to earn the Medal of Honor on Peleliu.

When D day ended, the Marines occupied a beachhead two miles long and less than a mile deep—at some points they squatted within a few feet of the Japanese defenders. Casualties were higher than projected—200 dead and a thousand wounded. The heavy fighting lulled the Americans into thinking that once they got beyond the beaches, the Japanese would crack. No one knew that the enemy's tactics had changed and the fighting on the beaches was only the beginning of this arduous campaign. It would take ten weeks to secure Peleliu.

On the second day of fighting, the Marines captured the Japanese airfield and pushed through to the forest on the eastern shoreline. Other elements moved toward the Umurbrogol—which would forever after be known as "Bloody Nose Ridge." By noon the temperature was a blistering 115 degrees and Marines started to collapse from heat prostration. Their first water deliveries turned out to be contaminated with fuel oil. The Marines had a thirsty time of it on Peleliu. Puller began a series of fruit-less, frontal assaults on Bloody Nose Ridge as Colonel Nakagawa's concealed guns fired on the Americans. Though they gained a little ground, the Marines sustained horrendous casualties. Puller fought on despite his grief over the loss of his brother on Guam and the wounds from Guadalcanal that still pained him.

On the fourth day of Operation Stalemate, three more Marines earned the Medal of Honor. One of them was Private First Class Arthur Jackson, Jr. Born in Cleveland, Ohio, on October 18, 1924, he was just shy of twenty when he hit the beach at Peleliu. As a child, Jackson's family moved to Portland, Oregon, where he grew up. A high-school football player, he graduated in 1942 and was inducted into the Marine Corps shortly thereafter. A veteran of Cape Glouchester, Jackson saw his most intense action at Peleliu.

Early on the morning of September 18—D day plus three—Jackson was moving forward with his platoon when they were stopped by a Japanese pillbox. Concen-trated fire found some of his comrades as Jackson weighed his options. "I think I can get this pillbox," he told a comrade.

With covering fire and his own BAR blazing, the private charged. He reached the concrete emplacement unscathed and emptied his clip through the gun slit. More Marines came up behind him and one thrust an explosive charge into Jackson's hand. The private primed the explosive and tossed it through the gun port. Seconds later the pillbox and its occupants were blasted into oblivion. Private Jackson continued his one-man assault, destroying three more pillboxes in quick succession. Though his clothes were riddled with holes and his equipment was chipped and dented from enemy bullets, he was miraculously untouched. When he was out of targets, Jackson finally collapsed from exhaustion and the oppressive heat. In all, he had eliminated a dozen Japanese positions and killed over fifty enemy soldiers.

Jackson was wounded days later on Bloody Nose Ridge. He was evacuated but returned to action in time for Okinawa. He was wounded again during this final invasion of the war and was sent home. On October 5, 1945, President Harry Truman presented Private Arthur Jackson, Jr. with the Medal of Honor in a White House ceremony. The award came as a surprise to the humble Marine. "I'd heard . . . that I was going to be recommended for something," he told a reporter. "But I had forgotten about it."

On September 18, 1944, near Bloody Nose Ridge, twenty-one-year-old Private First Class Charles Howard Roan of Armstrong County, Texas, died saving his comrades when he threw himself on a Japanese grenade. He received a posthu-

Private Arthur J. Jackson. Jr.

mous Medal of Honor. First Lieutenant Robert Carlton Rouh of Lindenwold, New Jersey, also threw himself on a grenade that day, but survived. He was presented with the Medal of Honor by Harry Truman in a White House ceremony on June 15, 1945. Robert Rouh returned to his native New Jersey after the war, where he passed away December 8, 1977.

As Lieutenant Rouh received this honor, he stood beside another hero of Peleliu. It was D day plus four when Captain Everett Parker Pope of Milton, Massachusetts, led his company up the slope of Hill 100. Getting to the top of the hill took a full day of heavy fighting. But when he reached the summit, Pope discovered he wasn't on top of a hill at all—just on a crest that was part of a much larger hill, from which the Japanese fired down on his command. Pinned down, Pope and a few dozen Marines set up a perimeter the size of a tennis court. Then he radioed a message back to his commanders: "The line is flimsy as hell, and it is getting dark. We need grenades badly."

Before the night was over, Pope and his men would be out of grenades, ammunition, and nearly out of luck. They fought off one counterattack after another with knives, fists, rifle butts, thrown chunks of coral, and hurled ammo boxes. At dawn, Pope led nine wounded survivors off the summit. It was Chesty Puller who nominated Captain Pope for a Medal of Honor.

On September 24, Private First Class John Dury New of Mobile, Alabama, threw himself on a grenade and saved the lives of his comrades. The twenty-year-old Marine was awarded a posthumous Medal of Honor. On October 4, Private Wesley

Phelps of Neafus, Kentucky also threw himself on a grenade and was awarded a posthumous Medal of Honor.

The final Marine to earn the Medal of Honor on Peleliu was Richard Edward Kraus, a nineteen-year-old private from Chicago. Assigned to the Eighth Amphibious Tractor Battalion, Kraus was evacuating wounded when a Japanese grenade landed in the middle of his men. Kraus dived on the explosive, absorbing the blast and saving the lives of the wounded.

After six days of hard fighting, Chesty Puller was finally ordered to withdraw from Bloody Nose Ridge. He had lost 60 percent of his command in futile frontal assaults—the highest regimental losses in the history of the Corps. On September 21, Major General Roy S. Geiger ordered the First Marines to stand down and the Army's 81st Division was sent in to relieve them.

"Hey, are you guys the First Marines?" a correspondent asked the remnants of Puller's command as they withdrew from the ridge.

"Mister, there ain't no more First Marines," was the grim reply.

In the end, the Seventh and Eighth Marines with regiments of the Army encircled and overwhelmed Nakagawa's defenses on the Umurbrogol, but the battle raged for ten bloody weeks. Victory came only after the airfield was operational and Major Robert "Cowboy" Stout's VMF-114 arrived with Corsairs. The fighters provided close air support, dropping napalm on the Japanese and firing rockets into their cave emplacements. The Japanese were hunkered down so close to the airfield that the Corsair pilots never bothered to retract their landing gear; they took off, dropped their payload, strafed the enemy, and returned to base for rearming and refueling.

After weeks of relentless American attacks, Colonel Nakagawa sent a final message to his superiors: "Our sword is broken and we have run out of spears." Then he burned the regimental colors and committed ritual suicide.

Victory on Peleliu had cost the Marines 6,500 casualties. Another 3,000 GIs were lost. The final irony is that none of the airfields on Peleliu provided significant support for General MacArthur's Philippine Campaign. The effort it took to capture the island would have been entirely fruitless but for the fact that the lagoon at Ulithi Atoll became the assembly area for the invasions of Iwo Jima and Okinawa. The use of Ulithi as a safe harbor would have been impossible without the capture of Peleliu.

IWO JIMA

Peleliu was the costliest campaign in Marine Corps history. But it was nothing compared to the ferocity of the battle to come. In the next fight, the Americans would suffer almost as many casualties as the Japanese in the bloodiest fighting of the war—all to capture a black, stinking little piece of hell on earth called Iwo Jima.

The campaign was the largest Marine Corps amphibious assault of all time, but the objective was a desolate place with nothing on it. Iwo Jima was only five miles long, shaped like a pork chop, its beaches ankle-deep in fine volcanic ash. Noxious clouds hung over the broken lunar landscape. The rocky island had no harbor or fresh water. Its north end was about three miles wide; the center was high ground—called

Motoyama Plateau. The northern slope of this plateau was composed of cliffs and ridges that the Japanese had riddled with gun emplacements, camouflaged artillery sites, and miles of interconnected tunnels and caves. It was on this northern part of the island where the heaviest fighting would take place. On the southern end rose the steep cone of an extinct volcano called Mount Suribachi. The Japanese had built two airstrips on a flat plain near Iwo's center, Airfield Number One and Two. Airfield Number Three, on the northern end of the island, was still under construction when the invasion began.

The volcanic island gave off bursts of steam and was pervaded by a smell like rotten eggs. The name Iwo Jima literally means "Sulfur Isle." Nothing lived there but a few wading birds and lots of Japanese soldiers. The island was a vital link in the chain of conquests leading to the Japanese mainland. Less than 700 miles from Tokyo, an American air base on Iwo Jima would spell doom for the homeland. With a base two and a half hours' flying time from the capital, air raids would intensify. From Iwo Jima, B-29 Superfortress bombers could strike at the Japanese homeland accompanied by a shield of short-range fighter escorts—fighters that could land and refuel at Iwo Jima before accompanying the bombers to their target.

Lieutenant General Tadamichi Kuribayashi was assigned the suicidal task of defending Iwo Jima, which he identified as "the gateway to Japan." Indeed, Iwo Jima also held a symbolic importance to the samurai class. The island was considered part of the Prefecture of Tokyo, which made it Japanese soil in the eyes of high command. To lose Iwo Jima was to lose face. Before their new commander took over, the island was defended by 23,000 Japanese troops, 361 artillery pieces, and 22 tanks. Kuribayashi, a former cavalry officer and veteran of the Manchuria Campaign, shifted the main defenses away from the beach and created concentric rings of concentrated defenses at the interior of the island. He also established a command center on the highest hill at the northern end. Most importantly, he brought a new tactical vision to his command. Kuribayashi realized that he and his men were doomed—American airpower ruled the skies, the Japanese homeland was being pummeled by bombers, and the United States Navy had command of the seas. Once the invasion started, there was no hope of victory, of reinforcement, or of retreat. But the grim, potbellied, fifty-four-year-old officer, who once had an audience with the emperor himself, refused to go down without a fight. Before Iwo Jima, Kuribayashi had a mediocre military record. But he would prove to be a devilishly clever tactician who thwarted the American again and again in the battle for Iwo Jima.

Kuribayashi's tank commander, Lieutenant Colonel Takeichi Nishi, was as clever and as stubborn as his boss. He was also familiar with the American psyche. Nishi had spent time in the United States and won the Gold Medal for equestrian jumping at the 1932 Olympic Games in Los Angeles. Kuribayashi and Nishi saw eye to eye on the tactics they would employ to bleed the Americans. For the Marines, winning Iwo Jima became a slow and painful process because of the efforts of these brilliant leaders. Before the invasion, Kurabayashi transferred any officer who believed in the traditional, suicidal *banzai* charge. He wanted to defend Iwo Jima smartly, making the enemy pay for every inch of this forsaken chunk of rock.

REST AND RELAXATION

While the war was swirling around them, the Marines had been inactive since they came off Umurbrogol in mid-October of 1944. They had not fired a shot in anger for three months. Once hotly contested, frontline combat zones were now secure. Guadalcanal was an active U.S. air base. So was Bougainville. Guam was a Marine Corps training site, and on Kwajalein things were so dull the Marines had erected a sign:

HOTEL ATOLL
NO BEER ATOLL
NO WOMEN ATOLL
NUTHIN' ATOLL

Some of them began to complain that things were boring. But the unspoken truth was that the war would not stay quiet for long. The Japanese were fighting to protect their homeland and their way of life. Things were bound to get worse.

The Marines who invaded Iwo Jima were commanded by General Holland "Howlin's Mad" Smith. A lawyer from Alabama who was commissed in 1905, Smith had served in the Philippines, Panama, and the Dominican Republic. In 1917, he went to France, to fight at Aisne-Marne, St.-Mihiel, and the Meuse-Argonne Front. Smith began his combat career as a machine gunner; later he became a staff officer. As one of the visionaries behind the development of amphibious warfare, Smith was the ideal commander to take on Iwo Jima—he had already directed the assaults on Tarawa, Eniwetok, Saipan, Tinian, and Guam, sometimes personally taking charge of the battle on the front. The final assaults on Iwo Jima and Okinawa would mark the pinnacle of Smith's long and distinguished military career.

From the initial planning stage, things went badly. Smith wanted a ten-day preinvasion bombardment. He got three. Fortunately, the general had top officers on the ground, all decorated veterans of the First World War. Major General Graves Erskine of the Third Division won a Silver Star and two Purple Hearts in France. Major General Clifton Cates of the Fourth earned the Navy Cross, two Silver Stars, and two Purple Hearts with the American Expeditionary Forces. The Fifth Division's Major General Keller Rockey won the Navy Cross. These battle-hardened veterans would see their Marines through some of the heaviest fighting of the war.

D DAY, FEBRUARY 19, 1945

It was a Monday morning and the weather was beautiful. A cool, tranquil breeze pushed a few scattered clouds across the sky. As the sun rose, the 485 ships ferrying General Smith's Marines to Iwo Jima stretched beyond the limits of sight—the largest armada assembled so far in the war.

"You could see the coal-black strip of beach where our assault waves would land," wrote correspondent John F. Marquand, who stood on the deck of a battleship. "Above the beach went the gray terraces we had read about, mounting in gradual, uneven steps to the airstrip . . . To the north were the quarries . . . You could see caves to the south on Mount Suribachi."

At 6:30 A.M., Admiral Turner gave the command, and the Marines, riding 482 amtracs, began their approach to the beach. As the echo of the final, rolling barrage fired by Navy warships faded, the Marines landed to face a stubborn and determined enemy. When they debarked, the Marines waded through ankle-deep volcanic ash that all but immobilized their vehicles. As the first amtracs were landing, Hellcats strafed the beach to suppress the enemy's defenses. But the Japanese were untouched, hidden in underground bunkers waiting for the Marines to land before engaging them. The invasion plan was simple. Hit the beach. Establish a beachhead. Move inland and capture the Japanese airfields as fast as possible. Seize the high ground—in this case Mount Suribachi—then combine forces and push northward to the heart of the island and the multilayered enemy defenses. The U.S. planners were confident that Iwo Jima would fall in two weeks. Instead, it took over a month of hard fighting and almost 6,000 Marine Corps dead before this tiny island was secure.

At 8:39 A.M., the first Marines arrived ashore to flounder in the deep volcanic ash. They also faced an artificial, fifteen-foot rise in the terrain created by wind and tide and the Japanese defenders. This sand hill blocked their field of fire, but not the Japanese mortars that rained down on their heads. Machine guns and heavy rifle fire began hitting the Marine positions almost as soon as they landed, and their hastily dug foxholes filled with ash and silt as soon as they were dug. "Like digging a hole in a barrel of wheat," one Marine described it. In the first fifteen minutes, the beachhead became a killing field, and it was the Marines who were dying. All eight battalions landed on Iwo Jima in the first ninety minutes—all were bogged down on the shoreline and facing slow annihilation. Armor was sent ashore.

At 10:00 A.M., the first American tanks arrived. They moved onto the beach and into the middle of a Japanese minefield. Soon the beach was littered with burning tanks as the armored assault sputtered and died.

At noon, when the beaches were packed with American men and equipment, Kuribayashi signaled the attack. All over the island, hatches popped open and Japanese soldiers emerged to take up their firing positions. Cannon muzzles swung into action from hidden emplacements. Machine gunners aimed their weapons at the mass of humanity mired on the black sand beach between their guns and the ocean. When the Japanese opened fire, the results were devastating. It was the worst bombardment the Marine Corps had ever experienced. The cannon fire was merciless, but the worst casualties resulted from Japanese 320mm "spigot mortars," which sent 675-pound, high-explosive rounds the size of fifty-five-gallon drums high into the air and down on the Marines. These shells were visible to the Marines as they arched through they air and plunged onto their positions. There was nowhere to hide from these mortars, nor from the cannons and machine guns.

Corporal Tony Stein of Dayton, Ohio, was pinned down on the shore with A Company, 28th Marines. A thrill seeker, Stein relished another chance to see combat, even the vicious combat on Iwo Jima. During a lull in the shelling, he assaulted the

Corporal Tony Stein

formidable enemy defenses with an improvised, handheld machine gun he fabricated from the wing gun of a Navy fighter. Stein swept several enemy pillboxes clean, slaughtering twenty Japanese who manned them. His bold action would prove instrumental in moving the Marines off the beaches in those first critical hours.

Stein was born on September 30, 1921, of immigrant parents who settled in Ohio. A strikingly handsome youth, he was popular with the ladies. Though a bright student, Stein dropped out of high school during the Depression and helped support his family by serving with the Civilian Conservation Corps. Later he found work as a tool-and-die maker at the Delco Products plant in Dayton. Stein was always tough. In 1942, he became Ohio's Golden Gloves boxing champion. He tried to enlist in the Marine Corps after Pearl Harbor but was informed that he was involved in a trade that was vital to the war effort. When the government changed its mind, Stein happily enlisted in the Marine Corps. He was more than ready to fight.

Stein went overseas as a Marine Raider and saw action at Guadalcanal and Bougainville—where he became proficient at killing Japanese snipers. He soon had a reputation as a formidable hunter of hunters. "The snipers could hide everything but their eyes," Stein told a reporter. "I just waited 'til one raised his head and then I let fly with a burst before he could fire." He killed five enemy snipers in this manner, dropping one at his commanding officer's feet. After Bougainville, Stein was sent back to the States and promoted to corporal. He married on July 21, 1944, and after a three-day honeymoon returned to active duty in Hawaii.

It was while stationed on the Hawaiian Islands that Stein fashioned his "stinger"—a weapon made from a .30-caliber, air-cooled machine gun that could be fired from the hip. This one-of-a-kind weapon served him well on Iwo Jima. He fired it so much that he had to make eight trips back to the beachhead to retrieve ammunition. On each trip, Stein helped a wounded Marine make it onto the beach. Twice the stinger was shot from his hands. Twice Stein retrieved it and decimated any enemy soldier in his sights.

Near the end of the first day, Corporal Stein's commanding officer convinced him to seek medical attention. The young corporal had been wounded several times and was evacuated that night. He returned to Iwo Jima a few days later in order to fight alongside his comrades. Corporal Stein was killed by a Japanese sniper on March 1,

1945, while leading an assault on an occupied hill—the hunter had become the hunted. On the first anniversary of D day Stein's family was presented with his posthumous Medal of Honor—the first awarded for valor at Iwo Jima.

With B Company in the first wave, Sergeant Darrell S. Cole of Flat River, Missouri, led his machine-gun section up the sloping beach toward the airfield they were to capture. He obliterated two emplacements with grenades and a third with his machine gun. When he ran out of grenades, Cole went back for more. He wiped out another enemy strong point before he was killed by a Japanese grenade. Darrell Cole was twenty-four years old when he died. His Medal of Honor—like half of all Medals of Honor awarded for gallantry at Iwo Jima—was given posthumously.

In those first hours, casualties were horrendous and officers and NCOs were not immune to Japanese bullets. Near Stein and Cole's position on D day was the commander of B Company, 28th Marines, Captain Dwayne E. Mears. Mears attacked several enemy pillboxes armed only with a pistol until he was killed. To the right was the 27th Marines. With them on the first day of fighting was Gunnery Sergeant "Manila John" Basilone, the first enlisted Marine to receive the Medal of Honor in the Second World War. Basilone fought to the very end. "Come on, you bastards, we've gotta get these guns off the beach!" he cried before a mortar round laid him low.

On the beach with the 23rd Marines, Captain John J. Kalen, the commander of A Company, bled to death waiting to be evacuated. First Lieutenant William E. Worsham took command of A Company and was killed moments later. Then First Lieutenant Frank S. Doyoe, Jr., took over until he was wounded. Finally, First Lieutenant Arthur W. Zimmerman led the 23rd in the capture of one of the Japanese airfields. The battle for Iwo Jima was just hours old, but it had already cost the Corps some of its finest leaders.

In the early afternoon the Marines moved to capture Airfield Number One. No prisoners were taken in this action and few Marines had even laid eyes on the mass of concealed and entrenched enemy troops lying in wait for them. Though 30,000 Marines were ashore by dusk, and Mount Suribachi was surrounded and isolated, the first day's objectives had not been met. Over 500 Marines were dead and 2,000 more were wounded badly enough to require immediate evacuation. The shoreline was littered with smashed vehicles, overturned landing craft, shattered equipment, and the dead.

As darkness fell, the Marines went to ground expecting the usual *banzai* attack. But General Kuribayashi had learned the hard lessons of Guadalcanal, Tarawa, and Bougainville. Instead of senseless, costly frontal assaults, he was content to fire artillery at the Americans. At dawn there were still far too many Marines bogged down on or near the beaches. Most had moved inland only a hundred yards or so. Some waited on the foot of Mount Suribachi, but no one had climbed the summit of the volcano. As the Marines moved out of their positions for another day of fighting, four Marines of C Company, 26th Marines, were ambushed as they crept through a ravine. The Japanese fired from an adjoining trench and a firefight erupted.

Among these Marines was Private First Class Jacklyn Harold Lucas of Plymouth, North Carolina. It was February 20, D day plus one—and Jack Lucas's seventeenth birthday. Lucas was too young to be in the military but had forged his mother's signature on a consent form that stated that he was seventeen at the time of his enlistment in 1942. He was actually fifteen when he enlisted, but his strapping five-foot eight-inch frame fooled the draft board and he was accepted into the Marine Corps. Within a few months, the Corps was sorry they ever let this unruly recruit into their ranks. Jack got through basic without a hitch, but when he was assigned to a rear-echelon supply unit in Hawaii, he told his sergeant that he resented the job he was assigned, insisting that he had joined the Corps to fight Japanese not haul supplies. His pleas for a transfer fell on deaf ears and the underage Marine began to rebel. Lucas was sent to the brig numerous times for fighting, and was once sentenced to thirty days for being AWOL and punching out two MPs who tried to arrest him while he was in possession of a case of beer that didn't belong to him. A second sentence of thirty days' hard labor with only "bread and water" made Lucas wonder why he ever joined the Marines.

But Lucas was determined to participate in the war, no matter what. While ships were loading in Hawaii for the invasion of Iwo Jima, the young soldier—with the help of his cousin—sneaked aboard one of them. In the confusion he hid among the combat gear. His cousin brought him food until the ship was too far from port to turn around, then Lucas emerged and turned himself in to the ship's senior Marine Corps officer. Captain Robert H. Dunlap, commander of C Company, demanded to know why he had stowed away. The private told the captain that he signed up to fight Japanese and that's what he intended to do. Dunlap; a veteran of the Central Pacific Campaign, knew the real thing when he saw it and allowed Lucas to join C Company. Dunlap would go on to earn his own Medal of Honor at Iwo Jima.

Meanwhile, back at his old unit, Lucas was branded a deserter on January 10, 1945. Captain Dunlap, still aboard ship, pulled a few strings and had his record expunged. The brash young private hit the beach with the rest C Company on D day. Now the teenager was in the fight of his life. When he and the others were ambushed as they moved out of their shallow foxholes and through a narrow ravine, Lucas rose and shot one Japanese soldier in the forehead. "I saw blood spurt from his head as he stared at me."

Private Lucas was ready to fire again when his rifle jammed. Before he could clear it, a Japanese grenade landed among the Americans in the ravine. Lucas pounded the grenade into the volcanic ash with the butt of his rifle, but a second grenade tumbled to his feet. Lucas cried warning and dived on both of them. "The force of the explosions blew me up into the air and onto my back. Blood poured out of my mouth and I knew I was dying."

Jack Lucas *should* have died. On Iwo Jima, five other Marines received the Medal of Honor for throwing themselves on grenades—Corporal Charles Joseph Berry of Lorain, Ohio; Private First Class William Robert Caddy of Quincy, Massachusetts; Private George Phillips of Rich Hill, Missouri; Private James Dennis LaBelle of Columbia Heights, Minnesota; and Gunnery Sergeant William Gary Walsh of Roxbury, Massachusetts. All of those awards were posthumous. But, as one awestruck surgeon aboard the medical ship *Samaritan* stated, Jack Lucas was "too damned young and too damned tough to die."

After his comrades repelled the ambush, they returned to collect Lucas's dog tags. To their shock they found him sitting up, alive and conscious. Over the next two years, Lucas would endure twenty-two major operations to put him back together. Eight months into his recovery, he limped into the White House to receive his Medal of Honor from President Harry S. Truman—the youngest Marine in history to earn this award.

After his discharge, Lucas completed high school and tried to adapt to civilian life. His marriage was broadcast on national television in 1952 and that same year he enrolled in Duke University, where he received a degree in 1956. Unable to find a good job, Lucas accepted a commission in the United States Army but was discharged in 1956 with an uneven service record. In 1966, he started a home meat delivery service in California that made him rich. With his second wife, Erlene, Lucas moved to Maryland and established another meat

Private James D. LaBelle

delivery service. This business was even more prosperous than the first, and soon the Lucas family lived in a mansion, drove luxury cars, and bred racehorses. In 1973, Lucas discovered that his wife was swindling him. He threatened to divorce her and she reacted by hiring a hit man to kill him. Unfortunately, the "hit man" was a Maryland undercover cop, and Erlene Lucas was tried for attempted murder. Though Jack stood by his wife's side during the trial, they divorced a few years later.

In 1983, the IRS claimed Jacklyn Lucas owned hundreds of thousands of dollars in back taxes, fines, and interest. The federal government seized his home, his assets, and all of his property, including the $800-a-month disability check he received for injuries sustained while earning the Medal of Honor. Lucas was forced to move into a trailer with his eighteen-year-old son. A few weeks later he was arrested for trespassing on government property—his former home. He was trying to retrieve some of his property when he was caught.

In 1985, his trailer burned and Lucas moved into an abandoned, walk-in meat locker on a friend's property, where he slept on a Red Cross cot. He worked at odd jobs, and in 1985 pitched a tent on some property where he was to build a patio. A police raid found marijuana growing on the land and Lucas was arrested for possession of a controlled substance with intent to distribute. A judge dismissed all charges and the Veterans Administration intervened. Lucas's tax debt was forgiven and he was deluged with job offers. Today he lives in Hattiesburg, Mississippi—one of only two surviving Medal of Honor recipients from the battle for Iwo Jima.

With E Company, the 28th Marines, on that second day of fighting was Private

First Class Donald J. Ruhl from Columbus, Montana. A former farm boy and cattle wrangler, Ruhl landed in the ninth wave and remained hunkered down on the beach for much of the first day. At about five that afternoon, his unit was sent to mop up any Japanese emplacements that might have been bypassed in the headlong rush inland. At dusk they dug in near a large mound of sand that had been ignored by other units who passed through the area. The perimeter was quiet, but after chow a few Marines went forward to investigate the sand hill. As they approached, the muzzle of a three-inch fieldpiece popped out of a slit at the base of the mound and began firing at the Marines still on the beach.

A second group of Marines attacked the bunker with thermite grenades. When explosions began shaking the interior, a hatch popped open right in front of Ruhl. The young Marine dropped to one knee and emptied the magazine of his M-1 carbine into the eight Japanese soldiers who came charging out. Ammunition exhausted, Ruhl finished off a ninth enemy soldier with a bayonet. His sergeant was impressed. Ruhl had been a discipline problem who stubbornly refused to obey certain orders. He never wore a helmet, preferring the casual look of a baseball cap. Though not a braggart, Ruhl radiated a self-confidence that bothered his comrades.

On D day plus one, Ruhl dragged a wounded Marine to safety under heavy fire. But on D day plus three—February 21—his luck ran out. He was among the Marines who led the charge against a trench filled with Japanese soldiers. As he and Sergeant Henry Hanson were climbing a bunker, a Japanese soldier hurled a demolition charge.

"Look out, Hank!" Ruhl cried as he dived on the explosive and hugged it to his chest. The blast threw him backward, blowing a huge cavity in his chest. Donald Jack Ruhl was just twenty-one years old when he died. His Medal of Honor was presented to his parents on January 12, 1947.

RAISING THE FLAG

The single most recognizable image from the Pacific War is the photograph of five Marines raising the American flag on the summit of Mount Suribachi. This scene, captured by Associated Press photographer Joe Rosenthal, took place at 12:30 P.M. on Friday, February 23, 1945. Though the raising of a smaller flag preceded this event, the iconic photo of the five Marines planting the pole with the flag waving at its crest has come to symbolize American determination, military might, and nobility of spirit in the middle of the twentieth century.

This simple yet dramatic incident followed a horrendous four-day contest to secure the extinct volcano and the cliffs, tunnels, minefields, and booby-trapped landscape around it—a struggle so terrible its fury rivaled the horrors of the landing itself. The fight began on Wednesday morning when the 28th Marines and the Fifth Engineer Battalion set out to destroy the 165 concrete pillboxes that dominated the landscape around the mountain. There were over 200 caves in the area, filled with Japanese troops waiting to emerge from hiding and take on the Marines. While the battle for Suribachi raged on, the Third Division's 21st Marines came ashore. Their mission was to capture Airfield Number Two, which was not secure. Even the first Japanese airfield, which the Marines considered captured, was still being harassed by an active enemy presence along its battered perimeter. Iwo Jima was not like Guadalcanal. Warplanes would not land on these airstrips for many days.

Northeast of Airfield Number One a devout sergeant dubbed the Preacher by the men of his platoon was asking for their prayers. It was Friday morning, February 23, and these men were facing annihilation at the hands of several heavily defended pillboxes. "The Preacher" was Sergeant Ross Franklin Gray of A Company, 25th Marines. He had always been a religious man. Born in Marvel Valley, Alabama, he had been studying for the ministry when the war broke out. He joined the Marines out of a sense of duty, and though he never claimed any sort of conscientious-objector status, his commanders were sensitive to his religious devotion and he was assigned duties behind the lines. Ross read the Bible daily and conducted church services for his fellow Marines.

Things changed on Saipan when Gray's best friend was killed in action. After his initial shock wore off, he picked up a Browning automatic rifle and went to the front lines to kill Japanese. He became proficient in the arts of war and took command of his platoon on D day, Iwo Jima, when his lieutenant was killed. Now Sergeant Gray's unit was trapped between two enemies—a camouflaged pillbox thirty feet ahead of them and Japanese shock troops moving at their rear.

"Stay here and we're all dead," Gray hissed to his platoon as they were pinned down in a shallow ravine. Then he whispered, "Pray for me."

Sergeant Gray grabbed a satchel charge and took off. Dodging machine-gun fire and ignoring the mortars that were falling all around him, Gray zigzagged to the gun slit and hurled the charge inside. A muffled explosion blasted smoke and fire out of the slit and the pillbox was silent. Gray rushed back to the ravine, grabbed a second satchel charge, and destroyed another pillbox. For the next ten minutes, he made repeated attacks until six pillboxes were destroyed and twenty-five Japanese soldiers were dead. As his platoon began to advance once again, Sergeant Gray realized they had stumbled into a minefield. He single-handedly cleared a path through the mines and led his platoon to safety without sustaining a casualty. The Preacher would receive the Medal of Honor for his actions on this day.

Another veteran of Saipan was on the front this day. Captain Joseph J. McCarthy was commander of G Company, 25th Marines. A thirty-three-year-old former fireman from Chicago, McCarthy was a burly Irishman with a ruddy complexion and a pug nose. Though old for a combat commander, he earned the Silver Star on Saipan, where he captured a well-defended hill. A no-nonsense officer who didn't appreciate "malarkey or bullshit," McCarthy never smiled. But the men of G Company loved him.

It was late morning when G Company began taking casualties from a concealed enemy emplacement. McCarthy scanned the area and it took him fifteen minutes to locate several well-camouflaged pillboxes that were raking the advancing Marines with accurate fire. Between his men and the pillboxes were seventy-five yards of open ground. Grabbing a pack of grenades, McCarthy called out to an advance three-man flamethrower team—all old comrades from Saipan.

Captain Joseph J. McCarthy

"Let's get these bastards before they get us!"

Four men jumped to their feet and charged across the field like running backs on a football field. Weaving and dodging enemy bullets that kicked up black ash around their feet, the Marines reached the pillboxes and dived into the sand directly in front of the gun slits. McCarthy primed three grenades and tossed them through the opening. The force of the blast blew open a trapdoor behind the emplacement. Three enemy soldiers, blackened from the explosions, ran screaming out of it. McCarthy cut them down. Then the captain rolled up and over the pillbox and dived through the hatch, killing anyone who'd survived the grenade attack. McCarthy and his team finished off three more pillboxes in similar fashion. Captain Joseph Jeremiah McCarthy received the Medal of Honor on October 4, 1945, at a White House ceremony. Harry S. Truman, a former artillery officer in the First World War, told him that "there is nothing in the world I'd rather have than this decoration."

By late Friday afternoon, Captain Robert Hugo Dunlap's A Company was taking heavy casualties. Captain Dunlap—the officer who had allowed stowaway Jack Lucas to join his outfit before the invasion—had been on point since D day. His men had faced, crossed, and captured an area with little natural cover and ferocious interlocking fields of fire from hidden bunkers on the western slope of the Japanese airfield. Now they were blocked by a steep cliff studded with caves, all spitting well-coordinated machine gun and rifle fire. Suddenly artillery shells began to rain down on Dunlap's men. A Company had to advance or be annihilated.

"Cover me!" Dunlap cried. The twenty-six-year-old captain raced, zigzagging, across the open ground to the cliff's base. When he dived into the dirt, he found himself staring into the gun slit of a well-camouflaged emplacement filled with enemy soldiers. He spied a half-dozen machine guns, several mortar pits, and hordes of troops moving about inside of their concealed position. Dunlap raced back to his men and called for artillery.

After a short, fierce bombardment, Dunlap grabbed the field telephone and ran back to the caves to see how effective the shelling had been. At the base of the cliff he became pinned down. Dunlap held his position and called down artillery onto the Japanese for the next forty-eight hours. His lonely vigil was instrumental in clearing out the western beaches. Five days later he was wounded spearheading another attack. His hip shattered by a rifle bullet, he was evacuated and finished the war in a hospital on Saipan. Dunlap, who was born in Abingdon, Illinois, was aboard the medical ship *Samaritan* along with Private Jacklyn Lucas and hundreds of other casualties of Iwo Jima when he was told he would receive the Medal of Honor. After the war, he rose to the rank of major before retiring from the Marine Corps. He passed away on March 24, 2000.

Another officer fighting around Suribachi was Lieutenant Colonel Justice Marion Chambers. Known as "Jumpin' Joe" for his flamboyant style, Chambers "looked a bit like a buccaneer," says historian Robert Leckey, "with a cut-down bayonet knife dangling from his cartridge belt alongside a .38 revolver stuck in a special quick-draw holster." As if this wasn't enough, "Jumpin' Joe" also liked to carry a Colt .45 in a holster under his left armpit.

Lieutenant Colonel Justice M. Chambers

Chambers was a striking man—six feet, two inches tall, rawboned, hoarse-voiced and "tough as a fifty-cent steak." Born in Huntington, West Virginia, he never lost the slight Southern twang in his voice. Old for a combat officer—he actually celebrated his thirty-eighth birthday aboard ship on the journey to Iwo Jima—Chambers's comic-opera appearance struck the other officers as eccentric. But those who were familiar with him knew that Jumpin' Joe's personal arsenal was not for show; he used all of these weapons with proficiency as a raider under Red Mike Edson at Kwajalein, and later in the battle for Saipan. Now a respected battalion commander with a rousing combat reputation, Chambers was beloved by his men, who dubbed themselves "Chambers's Raiders" in his honor. The rest of the Marines had another name for Chambers's command— "The Ghouls," because of the ghostly antiflash burn cream they smeared on their faces in anticipation of the close demolition work they had to perform on Iwo Jima.

On D day, Chambers led his Third Battalion, 25th Marines, onto the northern beach and into the teeth of some of the heaviest enemy fire of the campaign. By late afternoon he pushed his men to ground above an enemy-occupied quarry, where the fight was furious. "You could have held up a cigarette and lit it on the stuff going by," Chambers said later. He lost 22 officers and 500 men taking the high ground, and was now down to 150 effective troops. Chambers's Raiders fought on, asking only to be resupplied and reinforced if possible.

In the middle of the second day, Chambers's Raiders were dispatched to capture "Charlie Dog," a heavily defended escarpment guarding the east-to-west runway of the second airstrip. Though it was late afternoon, Chambers decided to mount an

■ The "Buck Rogers" War

On March 4, 1945, the Marines who had been trying for two bloody weeks to capture Iwo Jima saw firsthand why they were fighting. A stricken B-29 dubbed *Dinah Might* and piloted by Lieutenant Raymond Malo made an emergency landing on the captured Japanese air base in the center of the island. The massive, gleaming silver bomber circled twice before making its final approach, casting a shadow over the whole island. It was the biggest warplane built during the Second World War, and the Marines had never seen anything like it.

Though Airstrip Number One was still unconverted, the bomber, which was shot up in a raid over Tokyo, managed a successful landing, halting less than thirty feet from the edge of the short, narrow runway. With its futuristic design, glass-encased, pressurized cockpit, radar-controlled gun turrets, and shining aluminum skin, the B-29 looked like something out of a science-fiction magazine. To the grimy Marines clinging to the volcanic rock by their dirty fingernails, this vision of the future was heartening. As soon as the mighty bomber rumbled to a halt, a cheer went up all over the island.

"That's why we are here!" said one ecstatic Marine.

American mechanics swarmed over the crippled B-29, and thirty minutes later the bomber lumbered into the afternoon sky and winged its way home to Saipan. Over the course of the next several weeks, thirty-six damaged B-29s made forced landings on Iwo Jima. Each of these dramatic visits was greeted with cheers and applause. It was as if these Marines had experienced their first glimpse of the future.

Other futuristic weapons made their debut in this campaign. Rocket-powered, self-propelled artillery shells were used for the first time on Iwo Jima. Though rockets were not new, mass artillery barrages by rocket-powered shells was an innovation. As the battle moved inland, rocket trucks and the "Buck Rogers" troops who manned them became a familiar sight to the American troops assaulting fortified caves and concrete pillboxes. These vehicles were fabricated from one-ton, four-by-four trucks modified to carry steel launching racks filled with thirty-six 4.5-inch high-explosive rockets. Though the range was short, these rocket trucks provided instant artillery support to the beleaguered frontline troops. They could be deployed fast and possessed a steep angle of fire that was ideal for Iwo Jima's rocky, jagged geography. A "ripple" of thirty-six rockets, fired from their racks in a matter of seconds, could demolish a target.

Though the trucks were effective, the Marines had mixed feeling about them. The secret of their deadly effectiveness was quick displacement. A rocket truck "fired and fled," leaving the ground troops behind to suffer the brunt of the enemy's response. During the campaign for Iwo Jima, rocket vehicles fired more than 30,000 missiles.

M-4 Sherman tanks were deployed during the battle for Iwo Jima. Though the better-armed German Tiger and Panther tanks outgunned the Sherman in the European theater, the durable M-4 was more than a match for the puny Japanese Type 97 "Te-Ke" tanks and their pathetic 37mm guns in the Pacific. In the fight for the second Japanese airfield on the island, the Shermans turned the tide of battle in a firefight against entrenched antitank guns. But no American tank was more appreciated by the Marines than the formidable "Zippo tanks" deployed for the first time on Iwo Jima. In 1944, British and American engineers codesigned the M-4 Sherman "Crocodile," a flame-throwing tank with a range of about seventy-five feet. Hauling a trailer filled with fuel, the Crocodile could clean out a fortified enemy emplacement in a matter of seconds. This variant on the traditional Sherman used the tank's main turret gun to direct the flames, but could also fire conventional tank shells when its flammable fuel was exhausted.

The Marines were expecting a delivery of these Crocodiles in time for Iwo Jima, but production problems delayed their arrival. Undeterred, Marine Corps engineers and U.S. Army chemical warfare experts field-modified their own version using eight M-4 Sherman tanks mounted with a look-alike tube in place of its main turret gun. This tube could spray napalm-thickened fuel at a range of 150 yards or more but could not fire conventional tank shells. Despite this limitation, the Zippo tanks proved their worth at Iwo Jima against the enemy's caves and concrete emplacements. When used in conjunction with infantry, they were unstoppable. They would burn out the enemy positions while the Marines on the ground protected the tank from suicidal demolitionists. Maintenance crews worked around the clock to keep these cranky, patchwork vehicles operational.

Another, less spectacular innovation proved crucial in saving lives during the battle for Iwo Jima. Military logistics had been improving throughout the war, and by 1945, there were few critical supply shortages, even on the most remote outposts. Improved logistics meant that in this campaign, casualties had a far better chance of survival than at any other time during the Pacific War. Field surgeons were employed on the front for the first time at Iwo Jima. Better logistics also meant that the first time whole blood—not plasma—was widely used. Donated stateside one day, flown into the theater of operation the next, then pumped into the arm of a desperately wounded soldier on the next, a reliable supply of whole blood was instrumental in saving lives.

After the first critical week, the most severely wounded Americans—some 2,500 of them—were promptly evacuated from Iwo Jima to Guam in transport aircraft, each flight staffed by a Navy nurse. These young angels of mercy ministered to shattered and dying Marines on a daily basis. The nurses administered drugs, performed triage, and held men's hands while admonishing them to "hold on for just a little longer." The casualty rate at Iwo Jima was astronomical—the ratio was 1.25 Marine casualties for every Japanese killed, the highest in the war. But this rate would have been far worse without a steady supply of blood and the heroic efforts of the brave field surgeons and Navy nurses who performed double duty under harrowing conditions.

---

attack and take the high ground before night fell. He called for a rocket-launching truck, hoping that a string of 4.5-inch missiles would keep the Japanese pinned down long enough for his battalion to take the escarpment in one sharp, deadly push. After the rocket salvo pelted the target, Chambers led his men forward. He had spearheaded every assault for two days and Charlie Dog was just another hill. But as they approached the enemy position, a burst of machine-gun fire cut Chambers down. A bullet had ripped through his shoulder, through his lung, and out his back. He had to be dragged to cover by his men. The angry officer ordered the docs to stuff some gauze in the wound and send him back to the front, but "Irish Mike" Kelecher, the regimental field surgeon, had other ideas.

Kelecher ordered Chambers off the island, but evacuation was a problem. A DUKW driver refused to make the run out to the hospital ship in the gathering darkness. Kelecher knew that Jumpin' Joe would be dead by morning without medical care. Instead of arguing with the driver, the field surgeon drew his pistol and pointed it at the man's head. The DUKW driver suddenly understood Kelecher's point of view and evacuated Chambers. Four days later Jumpin' Joe returned to Saipan, where a hospital bed and a long recuperation awaited him. Lieutenant Colonel Justice Marion Chambers received the Medal of Honor in a White House ceremony on November 1, 1950. He passed away on July 29, 1982.

Another West Virginia native was busy that day. Corporal Hershel Woodrow "Woody" Williams, a flamethrower operator, was in the fight of his life near the second airfield. Williams operated in a sector that was 1,000 yards wide and 200 yards deep, yet contained 800 enemy pillboxes! For hours he had blasted position after position, driving the Japanese back and exhausting the fuel in his flamethrower several times. The twenty-two-year-old Marine Corps reservist from Quiet Dell was a trained demolitions man and put a lot of faith in explosives. But before D day plus one was over, he would come to believe that there was not enough fire, fuel, or dynamite to silence all the enemy emplacements on that smelly little island. After destroying six pillboxes on his own, Williams looked up to find he was the last flamethrower operator from Charlie Company's original nine left alive.

"I might as well join them wherever they are," he muttered.

Corporal Williams checked the fuel and igniter, slung the heavy tanks over his back, and with four Marine riflemen for support continued to strike at the enemy. He approached a seventh pillbox and incinerated the occupants, only to be ambushed by a sniper from a concealed rifle pit. Williams dropped to one knee and bathed the sniper in flames. Four more Japanese emerged from the trench to be burned by Williams's fire-spitter.

"It was a major miracle that Williams lived, but he did," wrote battlefield historian Bill D. Ross. For his valor, Hershel Williams received the Medal of Honor from President Harry S. Truman on October 5, 1945. Today he resides in Ona, West Virginia, one of only two Medal of Honor recipients from this battle still living.

By the end of the second day, the Marines were starting to believe there was no island called Iwo Jima, just a hotly contended beachhead that stretched on into infinity. The harder they fought the worse things seemed to get. The Japanese had constructed concentric rings of defensive positions. Each time the Marines overran one line, they ran into another position right behind it. It was like peeling an onion—with each layer the stink got worse and the tears more plentiful. The familiar rhythm of break-in, break-out, break-through was not repeated on Iwo Jima. Holland Smith actually began to hope for a banzai charge. "We welcome a counterattack. That is generally when we break their backs."

But no counterattack came, and it was the Marines who were getting their backs broken. As they pressed northward, the Marines entered a heavily fortified area they would call "The Meat Grinder."

On D day plus three, February 21, a regiment of the Third Division struggled to capture the northern end of the island as concentrated fire chewed them up. Tanks that battered their way north were stopped by Japanese interlocking antitank guns or damaged by buried antitank mines, which detonated with such fury that they flipped one thirty-ton Sherman over on its side. The Marines couldn't advance or retreat.

On the twenty-third, Major General Schmidt ordered the 21st Marines forward. They were to push their way deep into the Japanese defenses "at all costs." The advance was to begin at 9:00 A.M. Lieutenant Colonel Wendell Duplantis led the assault and was promised tanks for support. Morning came but not the tanks. Duplantis was ordered to advance without armor. As the attack progressed, K Company broke through a line of pillboxes and dived into trenches swarming with Japanese. The fighting was fierce and hand to hand, with the Marines triumphant. Soon K Company was charging up the slope that led to the second airfield. They made it to the crest in time to be hammered by artillery—American artillery meant for the Japanese. They retreated until the shelling stopped. But when they advanced again, Japanese defenders, now reinforced, drove them back. I Company arrived on the scene and together the two Companies charged up the slope, taking fire from on exposed flanks as a brace of Japanese infantry appeared in front of them. The Marines fought back-to-back, in ankle-deep black sand, with knives, bayonets, gun butts, shovels, and their fists. In the end, the Americans were still standing among fifty Japanese dead. The Marines slogged up the slope and dug in, with orders to "hold at all cost."

Next morning, K and I Companies were reinforced as the Third Division flowed through the hole they had blasted in the Japanese perimeter. The Americans set their sights on Hill 199, a high piece of ground that overlooked Airfield Number Two. During the attack, Private Wilson Watson stood in plain view on top of a ridge in an effort to pin down an entire Japanese company with only a BAR. An Alabama native born in Colbert County, the private knocked out a pillbox and reached the top of the slope. Alone, Watson—who had celebrated his twenty-third birthday on the night before the invasion—now faced overwhelming odds as Japanese regulars surged forward to cut him down. He stood his ground until his ammunition was exhausted. When he finally came down from that ridge, Private Watson left sixty enemy dead behind him. He received the Medal of Honor in an October 5, 1945, White House ceremony that included many veterans of Iwo Jima. Wilson Douglas Watson married and moved to Arkansas after the war, and passed away in Russellville on December 19, 1994.

THE MEAT GRINDER

Unknowingly, the Marines had entered the most heavily fortified section of General Kuribayashi's defenses. By March 1, Airfield Number Two was in American hands, but there was still heavy fighting on the northeastern tip of the base. Southern Iwo Jima had been captured. The north now beckoned. The Hill—or Hill 382—was the highest ground on that end of the island. Beneath the Hill was an area called the Amphitheater. East of that was a place called Turkey Knob, where General Kuribayashi had established his command center. From the maze of crags, rocks, and outcroppings on the Hill, the Japanese had been observing the American advance since D day. The area was heavily defended. Tanks buried to their turrets guarded all approaches and antitank guns poked out of a hundred cave mouths. The region was also covered by Japanese artillery and antiaircraft guns, mortars and machine guns. The Hill, Amphitheater, and Turkey Knob were mutually supporting—artillery and mortar fire could be called down on all or any of them. This region, the Meat Grinder, could be captured only by storming all points at once to overwhelm the Japanese defenses.

Private First Class Douglas Thomas Jacobson was with the Marines when they first climbed the Hill. They made it to the top with ease, but the Japanese were only luring them in for the kill. Suddenly, murderous fire flew at them from all directions and the Marines went to ground. Born on Long Island, Jacobson was nineteen when he stormed ashore at Iwo Jima. He had quit high school in Port Washington to enlist in the Corps when he was seventeen and saw action on Tinian and Saipan. Now, as his platoon was pinned down by enemy fire, Jacobson grabbed a bazooka and a satchel of explosives from a fallen comrade and went into action.

First he destroyed a 20mm antiaircraft gun and wiped out its crew. Then he knocked out two machine-gun emplacements, two pillboxes, and seven rifle positions. After destroying an advancing Japanese Type 97 tank, Jacobson attacked more pillboxes. All the while the young Marine struggled with the heavy bazooka—a weapon meant to be loaded and fired by a team.

Major Douglas T. Jacobson

Jacobson came home to a hero's welcome, but discovered that receiving the nation's highest award for valor did not bring a smooth transition to civilian life. Because he had no high-school diploma, the jobs he was offered "turned out to be either $20-a-week office-boy jobs or being a salesman in order to wave the medal in a customer's face and dare him not to buy the product." Disillusioned, he reenlisted in the Marine Corps in April 1946 and graduated from officer candidate school after serving in China. In Vietnam, Jacobson saw duty aboard helicopters and rose to the rank of major. When he was preparing to retire, his commanding officer gave him some advice. "The old man," Jacobson reported, "told me I was among the few majors in the Marines who did not have a high-school diploma." After long studies, he passed a high-school equivalency exam.

After retiring, Jacobson lived in New Jersey and sold real estate. He moved to Florida in 1987. On the fiftieth anniversary of the battle for Iwo Jima, he joined then-President William Jefferson Clinton and other Medal of Honor recipients in ceremonies at the Marine Corps Memorial at Arlington Cemetery. Douglas Thomas Jacobson passed away on August 20, 2000, and is survived by his wife and three daughters.

For the next seven days—from February 25 to March 3, 1945—the Marines fought their way through the Meat Grinder. The fighting was so intense that on a single day medics used 400 pints of whole blood in an effort to keep the wounded alive. Casualties among these frontline doctors and corpsmen was also fierce.

The story of Sergeant William George Harrell is indicative of the savagery experienced by those who fought in the waning days of the campaign for Iwo Jima. Early on the evening of March 2, Harrell and his friend, Private First Class Andrew J. Carter, were dispatched to a remote outpost for surveillance duty. These two Texans had shared a foxhole since D day. Now they slogged through the rain to their forward position on a ridge that overlooked a deep ravine that was still enemy territory.

Harrell, of San Antonio, took first watch. Private Carter, who hailed from Paducah, took second watch. In the early hours of March 3, by the flickering light of a parachute flare, Carter spied movement and nudged Harrell with his foot. "They're coming out of the ravine," he whispered. Then Carter opened fire, cutting four enemy soldiers down.

Suddenly the gun jammed. Sand had fouled the chamber and the private could not clear it. "I'll get another rifle," he whispered, vanishing in the dark. Harrell watched helplessly as Japanese troops moved forward, surrounding his position. He lobbed grenades and shot at shadows—sometimes dropping an enemy soldier but mostly firing at phantoms. More Japanese were moving forward and Sergeant Harrell's company was in jeopardy. He kept firing his M-1 until the clip was empty. As he reloaded, a Japanese grenade landed in his foxhole. Harrell grabbed it with his left hand, but before he could hurl it away the missile exploded. Harrell was thrown backward. He tried to rise but his legs gave out—his left thigh was shattered and his left hand hung from the stump by a few bloody tendons.

Carter returned to find his friend struggling to reload his M-1 with his remaining hand. "I'm hit—bad," Harrell gasped.

Suddenly two Japanese soldiers sprang from the ravine. One was an officer waving a samurai sword; the other clutched a live grenade. When Carter's rifle misfired, he dived on the officer, driving his bayonet into the man's heart. The officer's sword came down—nearly severing Carter's right hand. Meanwhile, Harrell drew his .45 and shot the soldier in the head. Both men were now wounded, and Carter's rifle was out of commission. At that moment Japanese infiltrators hit the American perimeter. Mortars rained down all around Harrell's foxhole as flares sputtered in the night sky, illuminating the battle in a hellish, wavering half-light.

"I don't think I can make it," Harrell told his friend. "There's no sense in both of us dying. Go back to the CP and stay there."

"I'll be back with help," Carter promised. Clutching his bleeding wrist, he retreated, leaving Harrell at the bottom of the foxhole, bleeding profusely. Armed with only his .45, the sergeant prepared for his last stand. A Japanese soldier jumped into the trench, grenade in hand. A second was silhouetted in the sputtering light of the parachute flares. The first soldier rolled the grenade to Harrell's feet as the sergeant shot him dead. Harrell grabbed the grenade with his good hand and shoved it into the gut of the other Japanese. The blast tore the man's entrails out and shattered Sergeant Harrell's remaining hand. Gushing blood now from two stumps, Harrell collapsed. As the sun rose, the wounded sergeant was located by Private Carter and a team of stretcher bearers and evacuated. He had killed a dozen Japanese soldiers and halted a counterattack. Their comrades dubbed Harrell and Carter the "Two-Man Alamo" for their actions that night, and Private Carter received the Navy Cross for his courage. During the October 5, 1945, White House ceremony that honored so many, President Harry S. Truman was grim as he draped the Medal of Honor over Harrell's shoulders. For hands, the sergeant had two shiny steel hooks. "This medal is small tribute for what you have given for your country," Truman told Harrell.

William Harrell was determined to overcome his handicap. He learned to perform routine functions without hands and designed special prosthetics that allowed him to practice his marksmanship skills with his impressive collection of firearms. In 1946, he accepted a position with the Veterans Administration, rising to the chief of prosthetic appliance group. He married and fathered four children.

On August 9, 1964, Harrell shot and killed a neighbor and the man's wife with a Marine-issue M-1 carbine, then turned the weapon on himself. This incident resulted from a doomed love triangle.

BREAKTHROUGH

By March 4—the day the first B-29 made an emergency landing on Iwo Jima—the Marines had penetrated the core of Kuribayashi's defensive rings and were knocking on the commander's door. The general was calling Tokyo for help, though he knew full well it would never come.

The Marines had a new objective—Hill 362. This second summit was shorter than the "The Hill" but not much, and the fight to capture it would be just as bloody. The task fell to the Fifth Marines, and for three days of continuous combat they eradicated the enemy wherever they could find him, using every tool at their disposal. Devilish new ways were found to obliterate the enemy; Marines burned the Japanese out of their caves by rolling gasoline drums inside and shooting them aflame. Demolitionists hung from ropes and tossed explosives into cliffside caves. Sometimes Japanese infiltrators popped out of concealment long enough to cut those ropes and sent men plunging to their deaths. The Marines tossed grenades, satchel bombs, and dynamite into every crevice, hole, and outcropping.

As a last resort, rocket trucks smothered a range of targets with waves of high explosives. When the fury subsided, the infantry slogged forward to finish the job of clearing out the area. But no matter how hard a position was hit, there always seemed to be survivors. Even after Hill 362 was taken, the struggle for Iwo Jima was far from over. There were still pockets of resistance to be eradicated. The surviving Japanese defenders—about 4,000 of them—had been pushed to a ridge on the extreme end of Iwo Jima's rugged northern coast. Nishi Ridge extended from the central plateau to the sea. Along its length the Japanese had dug more tunnels and emplacements. They would have to be driven into the open and exterminated.

On March 8, Iwo Jima claimed the life of its second celebrity athlete. Back on February 27, the First Battalion lost Sergeant Fritz G. Truan, a world-famous rodeo cowboy who was killed while leading a charge up Hill 382. On March 8, Jack Lummus, a tall, slim former New York Giant from Ennis, Texas, was cut down in his prime. Lummus was a bona fide sports hero. Born on October 22, 1915, he was a twenty-nine-year-old first lieutenant when the invasion of Iwo Jima began. Before joining the Marine Corps, Lummus was all-American at Baylor University and his gridiron skills were so impressive he was tapped by the New York Giants to play professionally. Between college and his career in pro football, he played semiprofessional baseball with the Class D Sputters—a team from Wichita Falls, Texas—and had served a stint in the Army Air Corps.

Lummus had known that war was imminent and wanted to serve his country. But when he cracked up his plane upon landing after his first and only solo flight, he was mustered out of the Air Corps, so Jack Lummus headed north to join the Giants. Pearl Harbor changed everything. Jack quit the team and returned to Texas to enlist in the Marine Corps. He took basic at Camp Elliott in San Diego, where on December 17, 1943, he met Mary Hartman, the woman he intended to make his wife. Fate intervened and Lummus was sent to combat training at Camp Pendleton, then on to Hawaii with the Fifth Marines in preparation for the invasion of Iwo Jima.

On the morning of March 6, 1945, First Lieutenant Lummus was summoned to headquarters, where his commander placed him in charge of a leaderless rifle platoon with orders to move forward at all costs. Lummus's command was made up of demoralized young men who had fought on point for fifteen days straight. Their original commander had cracked under the strain and had been evacuated. It was up to Jack Lummus to motivate these confused, tired men and get them moving again.

Weaving his way through a shattered landscape of smashed tanks, overturned amtracs, and pockmarked rocks, Lummus arrived at the front and took charge. He decided that advancing in the face of hidden pillboxes and heavy machine-gun fire was impossible, so, on March 8, he contacted his commander and begged for armor support to help his unit secure an occupied section of Nishi Ridge. The

First Lieutenant Jack Lummus

Shermans arrived hours later, but the terrain was so rugged they could not get close enough to the enemy to make much of a difference. Lummus led his men on three separate assaults, taking out several enemy emplacements and capturing the ridge. Suddenly he and several Marines found themselves standing in the middle of a minefield.

"Watch where you step, Lieutenant," Harold Pedersen cautioned.

An explosion enveloped Lummus a moment later. When the smoke cleared, the lieutenant was still standing, though shakily—both of his feet had been blown off by the mine and he was balancing on two bloody stumps. His platoon surrounded him and laid him down on the rocks.

"Well, did we take the ridge?" Lummus asked.

"We got where you wanted us to go," someone replied.

Then Jack Lummus observed the stumps at the end of his legs and offered a wry smile. "I won't play any more football," he said.

Four members of his platoon carried Jack down from the high ground. The docs pumped the young lieutenant with pint after pint of blood in an effort to save his life. Later, Jack Lummus asked for a cup of coffee, took a deep swig, then closed his eyes for the last time. His fellow Marines laid him to rest in the Fifth Division Cemetery at the base of Suribachi. Jack Lummus never got the chance to marry his sweetheart. Instead, his mother was presented with his posthumous Medal of Honor on Memorial Day, 1946.

Fighting on March 9 resulted in more heavy casualties for the Fifth, including

Platoon Sergeant Joseph Rudolph Julian of Sturbridge, Massachusetts. Julian gave his life while attempting to capture a series of heavily defended Japanese positions to earn the Medal of Honor. On the fourteenth, Private Franklin Earl Sigler of Glen Ridge, New Jersey took command of his besieged rifle squad and led a charge to neutralize an enemy gun emplacement and personally annihilated the crew. Wounded himself, Sigler carried three of his injured comrades to safety, earning the Medal of Honor. Private Sigler stood with many other veterans of Iwo Jima at the White House ceremony on October 5, and received his award from the president.

Finally, on March 26—twenty-eight days after D day February 19, 1945—General Kuribayashi led the broken remnants of his command in their final assault against the Americans. Although Iwo Jima was officially declared secure at 6:00 P.M. on March 16, fighting on the island was still going on a week later. By March 24, the Japanese were pushed into an area that was fifty by fifty square yards. Marines sealed all the caves and surrounded an area called Bloody Gorge. They thought the battle was over.

On March 21, General Kuribayashi radioed his final message. "We have not eaten nor drunk for five days. But our fighting spirit is still running high. We are going to fight bravely to the last." During the early morning hours of March 26, Kuribayashi burned his regimental colors and led 500 soldiers in a final, suicidal assault. Many were officers, swords in hand. Most carried explosives—in shoulder bags, satchels, or taped to their bodies. Quietly, Kuribayashi's men slipped past the Marines guarding Bloody Gorge and moved along the western beach until they found the tents of the Army Air Corps' VII Fighter Command. These Americans were new to Iwo Jima, and not trained infantry fighters. The Japanese struck, exacting a fearful toll, stabbing and hacking many pilots and flight crews to death in their bunks and butchering the surprised and disorganized noncombat support troops.

The Japanese were slaughtering Americans at will until they attacked a nearby Marine unit. First Lieutenant Harry Martin of Bucyrus, Ohio, organized his African-American troops into a skirmish line and beat the enemy back. Explosions began going off all around the camp as the suicide bombers detonated their payloads. After hours of hand-to-hand fighting, the few pilots who survived joined the tattered remnants of a Seabee outfit and the black troops from the Fifth Marine Pioneer Battalion in a counterattack.

At dawn, 500 Japanese dead were scattered on the beach among over fifty Americans. Most of the enemy dead were so horribly ravaged that it comes as no surprise that General Kuribayashi's body was never found. Lieutenant Harry Martin received the Medal of Honor, posthumously, for hastily organizing the counterattack and leading his support troops against the last remnants of the enemy on Iwo Jima. He was the twenty-second and last Marine to receive the honor. Two African-American Marines from the 26th Depot Company—Private James M. Whitlock and Private James Davis—earned the Bronze Star in this final fight in the bloody campaign for Iwo Jima. Within two weeks U.S. Army Air Force P-51 Mustangs were taking off from the airfields on Iwo Jima to protect the B-29s on their way to bomb Tokyo.

The Battle of Iwo Jima was the costliest struggle in the history of the Marine Corps—5,885 Marines were killed and 17,000 were wounded. Many of the survivors—men like Sergeant Harrell—were handicapped for life. Another 2,648 Marines succumbed to "combat fatigue" and 738 Navy doctors and corpsmen were killed or wounded. Of the estimated 25,000 Japanese troops who defended Iwo Jima, fewer than 1,500 were captured. The rest preferred death to dishonor.

Admiral Chester A. Nimitz honored the Marines with words that were simple, honest, and heartfelt. These words are chiseled into the base of the Marine Corps Memorial at Arlington National Cemetery: "Uncommon valor was a common virtue . . ."

OKINAWA: THE LAST BATTLE

One more obstacle stood between the United States military and the Home Islands, a long, narrow strip of land off the coast of Japan called Okinawa. This skinny, irregularly shaped, sixty-mile-long plot was the largest island in the Ryukyu chain and lay less than 400 miles from Kyushu. Okinawa had a half dozen ports, good anchorage, multiple airfields, and 350-plus miles of shoreline—enough to support the massive buildup necessary to leap to Japan's main islands.

The Ryukyu Island chain had been ruled for centuries by the native Okinawans, a peaceful people of mixed Chinese, Malaysian, and Ainu blood, when the Japanese seized control in 1875 and swiftly relegated the original 500,000 inhabitants to the status of a conquered people. Most of Okinawa's natives and Japanese civilians lived on the populous southern end of the island. Okinawa was divided near the center by a narrow, two-mile stretch called the Ishikawa Isthmus. The towns and villages lay south of the isthmus. The northern end was wild, barren, and mountainous.

Okinawa is one of the most humid places on earth. Single-day rainfall could measure eleven inches in the wet season, and when the "plum rain" came, the lowlands turned into swamps and the roads became muddy bogs. The landscape was dotted with farms, hills, and red-tiled farmhouses resembling those found in China. The Okinawans grew vegetables, rice, sweet potatoes, and sugarcane. On hilltops, visitors often saw stone domes that served as shrines and family tombs for the native peoples. Some of these domes were transformed into armed strong points by the Japanese.

When the invasion of Okinawa was planned, the atomic bomb that would end the war was still a dream. No one realized at the start of the campaign that this invasion would be the final battle of the war. The Joint Chiefs thought of it as the single-most strategic stepping stone to their final goal—the invasion of the Home Islands. As England had served as a launching point for the invasion of Hitler's Fortress Europa, Okinawa would become the staging area for an invasion of the Japanese homeland.

The invasion was conceived as a joint Army/Marine Corps operation, and the amphibious assault would be the largest of the Pacific War. The Army's forces were led by Lieutenant General Simon Bolivar Buckner, who was given overall command of the 10th Army. The son of Confederate Lieutenant General Simon B. Buckner, Sr., Buckner attended VMI and West Point before being commissioned in the infantry in 1908. He would not perform brilliantly in the coming campaign, and was criticized by the Marines under his command for not making use of their amphibious capabilities. General Buckner was destined to die on Okinawa, the second-highest-ranking American Army officer killed in action during the war.

The Marines were led by Major General Roy Geiger, honored veteran of the victories at Guadalcanal, Guam, and Peleliu. He would once again coordinate artillery, airpower, and ground forces brilliantly, only to be frustrated by Buckner's timidity. For this operation, Geiger was given command over the oldest and newest divisions in the Marine Corps—the First and the Sixth Marines. Geiger gave over command of the First—his veteran Old Breed—to Major General Pedro del Valle, a Puerto Rican graduate of the Naval Academy and an artillery genius who had helped defend Guadalcanal. Major General Lemuel Shepherd led the brand-new Sixth Marine Division, which was formed from remnants of the Fourth, the 22nd, and the 29th.

Okinawa was defended by Lieutenant General Mitsuru Ushijima and his 32nd Army. General Ushijima's job was to delay the American advance long enough for the massive, carefully orchestrated *kamikaze* assaults to annihilate the invasion fleet. This talented and determined leader would come very close to accomplishing his mission, and so would those determined *kamikazes*. In the end, it would take eighty-two days and cost the United States 75,000 casualties to capture Okinawa—a grueling, unacceptable rate of 3,000 casualties a day. Most of these were sailors and naval aviators, who would suffer more than the infantry in this campaign.

Ushijima's strategy was simple. His 100,000 defenders—80,000 Japanese regulars and 20,000 native Okinawans forced into service—dug caves and tunnels, built concrete emplacements, and converted buildings and shrines into fortified strong points all through the southern end of the island. Ushijima took full advantage of Okinawa's unique geography. A series of cross-island ridges cut through the southern end of the island. These ridges were ideal for defense, and the Japanese dug caves, tunnels, and entrenched mortars in the reverse slopes. The work took seven long months. When it was done, Ushijima's line cut the upper two-thirds of Okinawa off from the rest of island. Though a few hundred native draftees were assigned the suicidal task of destroying shore facilities and harbors before the American invaders could capture them, most of Ushijima's forces were concentrated behind this defensive perimeter that stretched from Shuri and Shuri Castle—the city and citadel of the ancient Ryukuan kings—to the town of Naha, then across jungles and along ridges to the prized harbor of Nakagusuka Bay on the opposite coast. The Naha-Shuri-Yonabaru Line was probably the most heavily defended place in the world in 1945.

In a final act of desperation, the Imperial Navy committed the most magnificent seagoing weapon ever constructed, the battleship *Yamato*. Dispatched like the *kamikazes,* the *Yamato* carried fuel enough for a one-way voyage of destruction. The mighty vessel was sent out to fulfill the Japanese high command's dream of a decisive sea battle—a dream that was shattered once and for all on April 7, 1945, when hundreds of U.S. carrier-based aircraft and torpedo planes sank the *Yamato* off the coast of Okinawa.

On March 26, the first wave of *kamikaze* planes flew under the radar and attacked the American invasion fleet. Six ships were crashed that day, including Admiral Raymond A. Spruance's flagship, the U.S.S. *Indianapolis*. These deadly and determined *kamikaze* attacks came twice a day, at dawn and at dusk, for days on end. Hundreds of sailors and dozens of ships would be lost before Okinawa fell. But the Japanese put too much faith in their so-called Divine Wind assaults. Suicide bombers would not slow the American invasion for long, and desperate measures were taken to halt the *kamikaze* raids. At one point the Americans bombed the Japanese airfields on Okinawa for twelve hours straight—from 6:00 A.M. to 6:00 P.M.

Five days before L day—Iwo Jima's launch date was called D day, and because the Okinawa invasion was planned at the same time, the Joint Chiefs called the date for Okinawa's assault L day to avoid confusion—the U.S. Army invaded Keise Shima, an island five miles off the coast of Naha. When Keise Shima was secure, the Army set up twenty-four 155mm guns to fire on the Japanese defenses on the southern part of Okinawa. On April 1—Easter Sunday and April Fools' Day—the invasion of the main island began. The dawn was cool and clear, the weather perfect at seventy-five degrees. As the sun rose, 500 carrier-based planes strafed and napalmed the beaches, followed by a naval bombardment that proved ineffective—Ushijima's forces were deployed far from the effective range of the Navy guns.

When the first wave of Marines landed on the beach, there was almost no resistance. H hour came and went without a major clash. The amphibious landings went like clockwork. There was no fire from the Japanese shore batteries, and within the first hour 16,000 troops had come ashore. Okinawa was the only unopposed amphibious landing of the war. Corporal James L. Day, a rifle squad leader in the 22nd Marines, marveled at his good fortune. "I didn't hear a single shot all morning."

By dusk 60,000 Americans were on Okinawa and still virtually unopposed—the fight would come later. Meanwhile, assault troops stormed the western beaches and climbed the seawall to meet no resistance. Monday morning came and went without significant action, but by Monday night the fighting became more intense. The Fourth Marines killed 250 Japanese troops and advanced another 1,000 yards, while L Company of the 22nd engaged in a firefight for an occupied hill—a bitter clash that cost almost an entire platoon of Marines. But Okinawa still seemed like a walk in the park compared to Tarawa, Peleliu, and Iwo Jima.

It took almost a week for things to really heat up. On April 6 and 7, hundreds of *kamikaze* planes descended on the American task force, sinking six ships and damaging ten. On the seventh, the *Yamato* was sunk. More *kamikazes* struck on April 12, 13, 15, and 16.

Friday, the thirteenth of April, was unlucky indeed. Grim news reached the front that Franklin Delano Roosevelt, the president who guided the United States through the depths of the Great Depression and the horrors of World War II, had passed away. The men on Okinawa were deeply affected and held services on Sunday to honor their fallen commander.

Meanwhile, on the ground the Sixth Marine Division ran into a large enemy force that took their last stand in the mountains of the Motobu Peninsula on the East China Sea. The Americans faced the elite Kunigami Regiment led by Colonel Takesito Udo, who went to ground in a six-square-mile area around Mount Yaetake, near the town of Nago. The Japanese were concentrated in a complex of caves and reinforced positions in the middle of rugged terrain too rough for tanks. The Marines had to advance without armor just to get at the enemy, and they were chewed up as they came. It was mountain fighting at its worst, with an enemy that appeared and vanished at will—often before the Americans could react. The Marines assaulted the mountain from three sides, calling in naval bombardments and air strikes. But Udo and his men vowed to fight to the death, and over a thousand Marines from this brand-new division fell, with 200 dead.

During this fight, twenty-year-old squad leader Corporal Richard Earl Bush of Glascow, Kentucky, led his command through artillery fire toward a ridge on Mount Yaetake. When the corporal was wounded, he was dragged to cover behind rocks with the rest of the casualties. Suddenly a Japanese grenade landed at his feet, among the helpless Marines. Without regard to his own safety, Bush dragged the explosive to him and smothered it under his body. To his amazement and everyone else's, Corporal Bush survived the blast. Four other Marines received Medals of Honor for smothering enemy explosives during the Okinawa Campaign: Private First Class Harold Gonsalves of Alameda, California; Private First Class William Adelbert Foster of Cleveland, Ohio; Sergeant Elbert Luther Kinser of Greenville, Tennessee; and Corporal John Peter Fardy of Chicago, Illinois. Only Corporal Bush survived, to have the ribbon draped over his shoulder by Harry Truman in the October 5, 1945, White House ceremony that honored many veterans of the Pacific War. Bush's was the only Medal of Honor earned at the Battle of Mount Yaetake. The mountain did not fall to the Americans until April 16, when the last seventy-five Japanese soldiers were killed in an assault on the summit.

April 16 brought news of the first celebrity casualty in the battle for Okinawa. Beloved war correspondent Ernie Pyle, who covered the Second World War in Europe from the beginning of America's involvement, was killed during the assault on the island of Ie Shima, off Okinawa's coast. One of Pyle's last stories featured the journalist's impression of the Marines on Okinawa: "the Marines looked to me exactly like a company of soldiers in Europe. Yet that Marine Corps spirit still remained. I never did find out what perpetuated it . . . a marine still considered himself better than anybody else, even though nine-tenths of them didn't want to be soldiers at all." The island of Ie Shima did not fall to the Marines until April 21.

Meanwhile, the U.S. Army had slammed into Ushijima's main defensive line. Japanese artillery rained down on Buckner's men, and the general began demanding Marine Corps reinforcement. Buckner ordered the First Marine Division forward, snatching command away from Roy Geiger. For the next thirty days these Marines would batter themselves bloody against the Naha-Shuri-Yonabaru Line, suffering enormous casualties. The days on this perimeter were dirty, bloody, and stinking—the reek of unburied dead from both sides hovered over the battlefield. Some of the worst fighting took place after the Marines managed to capture a hill or a ridge. Before they could rest, Japanese regulars would pop out of hidden caves and appear among them, and the slaughter would began all over again. Every night Japanese infiltrators assaulted Marines in foxholes or on sentry duty. Americans were bayoneted, throats were cut, grenades were tossed among sleeping American soldiers, and heads were severed by sword-wielding Japanese officers.

General Ushijima made his first mistake when he staged a massive counterattack for May 3–4. The Japanese moved hundreds of men up both coasts by barge in an effort to flank the U.S. offensive. Meanwhile, 139 *kamikaze* planes assaulted the Navy task force in the sea. One of the enemy barges moving along the western coast was spotted by sharp-eyed observers. Over 700 enemy troops were annihilated before they even reached dry land. The assault force in a second barge made their scheduled landing on the western coast—only to be hunted down by the First Reconnaissance Company and their trusty war dogs. The east coast landing force managed to reach the Army's perimeter, but were cut down with over 400 dead. This disastrous counterattack cost the Japanese 6,000 casualties.

By May 5, the Marines were dug in along the Asa River—deep in Japanese territory. By May 7, the Marines were on the move. Their objective was General Ushijima's command center, hidden deep inside of Shuri Castle. With the Fifth Marines in the attack on Shuri Castle was Private First Class Albert E. Schwab, a twenty-four-year-old flamethrower operator from Tulsa, Oklahoma. During the heaviest fighting, Schwab's unit was pinned down by machine-gun fire emanating from a high ridge directly in front of them. Steep cliffs on either side of the machine-gun emplacement prevented a flanking move, so Schwab took his flamethrower up the summit in a bold frontal attack, burning out the Japanese. When a second machine gun opened up on the Marines, Schwab, despite low fuel and merciless enemy fire, continued to press his attack, burning out the second machine-gun nest before he was mortally wounded. A year later, on May 27, 1946, Rear Admiral Joseph J. Clark presented Private Schwab's posthumous Medal of Honor to his young son.

That same day—May 7, 1945—Private Dale Merlin Hansen of Wisner, Nebraska, single-handedly destroyed a Japanese pillbox with a bazooka round. When Japanese soldiers rose from cover and blasted the rocket gun out of his hand, Hansen grabbed a rifle and shot four of them to death. When the weapon jammed, he beat back two other assailants with its butt. Pumped with adrenaline, Private Hansen leapt into a Japanese trench, wiped out a mortar position, and killed eight more enemy soldiers. Hansen, who received a Medal of Honor for this action, was killed in combat four days later.

May 8 was VE day in Europe. Nazi Germany's "Thousand Year Reich" had been crushed once and for all. But for the Marines still fighting on Okinawa it was just another day. A cold rain fell most of that day, drenching the American troops struggling to make a breakthrough at the Naha-Shuri-Yonabaru Line at the banks of the Asa River.

On May 11, the Americans launched an offensive that began two weeks of bloody combat. Under fire and in darkness, engineers assembled a Bailey bridge over the Asa the night before. At 11:00 A.M., Sherman tanks rumbled across the span. The Marines surged forward, capturing the high ground over Okinawa's capital city of Naha, which was situated between the Asa and Asato Rivers. Marines entered the suburbs and crossed the center of town to the banks of the Asato, but their advance was stopped in its tracks on May 14. The defenses west of Wana and northeast of Naha were among the toughest the 10th Army faced so far. Not even the Marines could break through. Eighteen tanks were lost, and over 200 men were killed.

Meanwhile, the Sixth Marines came up against a complex of three high peaks they named Sugar Loaf Hill. From a front view, Sugar Loaf was a steep, rectangular mound that rose to a height of over fifty feet. It was surrounded by a flat, barren, 300-by-300-yard killing zone the Americans had to cross to gain the base of the promontory. To the right and behind the main hill was a lower ridge called the Horseshoe. To the left was a hill dubbed the Half-Moon. The enemy units on each peak were heavily armed, with mortars all through the Horseshoe, artillery in the Half-Moon, and machine guns bristling from the crest of Sugar Loaf. The 22nd Marines assaulted Sugar Loaf repeatedly, taking casualties each time they advanced. Each assault was driven back.

During one of these attempts, Corporal Louis James Hauge, Jr., went up against two Japanese machine gun emplacements that had pinned down his comrades, wiping both of them out with grenades before being killed himself. This twenty-year-old Marine Corps reservist from Ada, Minnesota, received a posthumous Medal of Honor for this doomed one-man assault.

Finally, on the afternoon of May 14, elements of the exhausted 22nd were ordered to take Sugar Loaf "at all cost." The 5:00 P.M. attack by 150 Marines was spearheaded by four Sherman tanks. Three of those tanks were knocked out by anti-tank guns almost immediately. Then the Japanese opened fire on the Marines as they charged across the barren ground. Only forty Marines made it to the base of Sugar Loaf, where they collapsed, exhausted and terrified. Mortars rained on them, and the Japanese tossed grenades at them from the summit of the hill. These Marines had just run through a ferocious gauntlet of fire and watched as two out of three of their comrades were cut down. Now dusk was settling in. The Americans knew that once the Japanese figured out they were at the base of the hill, they would descend in force and finish the them off.

During a lull in the shelling, the Marines heard the quiet voice of their commander, a twenty-eight-year-old executive officer and former attorney from Duluth, Minnesota, Major Henry Alexius Courtney, Jr.

"If we don't take the top of this hill tonight, the Japs will be down here to drive us away in the morning," he began. "The only way we can take it is to make a *banzai* charge of our own. I'm asking for volunteers."

Half his men volunteered on the spot. Out of the darkness, another twenty-six Marines arrived with ammunition and supplies. Major Courtney organized the fresh troops and his volunteers, and these forty-five Marines advanced while the rest remained behind. Courtney and his Marines climbed Sugar Loaf under cover of darkness, tossing grenades into caves and crevasses as they went. Merciless fire came from the Horseshoe and the Half-Moon, all directed at the Marines who ascended toward the peak. To attack Sugar Loaf meant taking fire from these supporting hills, and the Japanese spotted their enemies' silhouettes, even in darkness. But Courtney and his men kept going, losing Marines here and there as they climbed. At midnight, the battered assault force had made it about two-thirds of the way up to the summit. The men paused to rest, hugging the rocks to avoid enemy fire and their own mortar shells. Then Major Courtney heard the sound of voices—the Japanese had emerged from a secret cave and were assembling for a *banzai* attack right below the Marines' position.

"Take all the grenades you can carry," Courtney whispered. "When we get over the top, throw them and start digging in."

The Marines charged, hurling grenades. Explosions erupted among the clustered Japanese, blasting them off the promontory.

"Keep coming! There's a mess of them down there!" Those were Major Courtney's last words. A mortar blasted the boulder he was standing on and the officer was killed instantly. The Marines kept tossing grenades, slaughtering the Japanese and driving the survivors back into their holes. Then they huddled against the cliff as a cold rain came in from the East China Sea. At dawn, the beaten survivors of this assault staggered off the hill—there were only twenty of the original forty-five alive. For his valor, Major Henry A. Courtney, Jr., was awarded a posthumous Medal of Honor.

Another Marine would receive the Medal of Honor at the assault on Sugar Loaf. But James L. Day, a corporal with the Sixth Marine Division during the fight for Okinawa, would have to wait almost a half century to receive it. As a squad leader with the 22nd Marines, Day rallied his squad and the survivors from another unit and led them to a critical position forward of the front lines, near the base of Sugar Loaf. He and his men soon attracted intense mortar fire, then a ground attack by forty enemy soldiers. With his squad cut in half, Day fought on, hurling hand grenades and directing fire from a position without cover. The enemy was eventually driven back.

When Day found six Marines from another unit, he reassembled his squad and let them in, repelling three nighttime attacks. During the engagement, Day's squad heard Courtney's Marines fighting atop Sugar Loaf in the darkness. Five of his men were killed in the last assault, and Day heard the cries from a sixth—one of his Marines was wounded and calling for help. Day went after the man, brought him back, then went out to rescue more injured Americans.

In all, Corporal Day retrieved four Marines from the battlefield, then manned a light machine gun and drove off another night attack. A grenade landed near him, and Day was blasted backward. His machine gun was destroyed and he suffered white phosphorus burns on his hands, arms, and face along with fragmentation wounds. Tenaciously he fought on, reorganizing his defenses in time to drive off the fifth attack of that night.

"We could hear them climbing up the rocks," Day told historian Colonel Joseph H. Alexander. "We had plenty of grenades and the darkness behind us. Those who survived the grenades would be silhouetted as they climbed over the ledge and we'd shoot 'em."

At dawn, the Japanese conducted numerous swarming attacks against Day and his men. During a lull in the fighting, the Marines counted the dead; seventy Japanese soldiers lay around their position. On the third morning, Day repulsed a final enemy assault by killing twelve Japanese at close range. That afternoon, he and the remnants of his command were relieved.

Day remained in the Marine Corps after the war and rose through the ranks. He commanded combat troops in Korea and Vietnam and held commands in Japan, San Diego, Washington, and at Camp Pendleton. Forty years after the battle, General Day returned to Okinawa as the commander of all Marines Corps forces on the island. General Day's thirty-one decorations included three Silver Stars, a Bronze Star, six Purple Hearts, and two Navy Commendations. After retiring from the Marines, he became chancellor of the National University campus in Palm Springs, California, and a partner in a construction company. But General Day's life took a strange new turn in 1980. A retired Marine veteran of the war found faded carbon copies of James Day's Medal of Honor recommendation among his personal memorabilia. The man checked into the situation and discovered that the original paperwork for Day's award had been lost in the chaos after the battle. It took an additional eighteen years for the paperwork to reach the appropriate officials. Finally, on January 20, 1998, President William Jefferson Clinton presented retired Marine Corps General James L. Day with the Medal of Honor in a White House ceremony. Nine months later, on October 28, 1998, General Day died at Cathedral City, California, after suffering a massive heart attack. He was seventy-four.

A statue of James L. Day is on display aboard the U.S.S. *Yorktown* at Patriot's Point Naval and Maritime Museum in Mount Pleasant, South Carolina. It was donated by the Sixth Marine Division Association, which is made up of veterans of that distinguished unit.

More assaults were mounted against the Japanese fortifications atop Sugar Loaf, the Horseshoe, and the Half-Moon. The fighting continued until May 18, when U.S. Marines finally secured the summit. While the fight raged at Sugar Loaf, another battle was being fought by the First Marine Division at a place called Wana Draw. Casualties were horrendous, and as the division report later read: "Gains were measured by yards won, lost, then won again." Wana Draw was another fortified position, with steep cliffs dotted by heavily armed cave openings overlooking a deep valley with a twisted stream running along its bottom. The Japanese had camouflaged spotters all along the Draw to direct fire against the advancing Marines. The Americans lost 500 men in the first five days of the battle. Wana Draw finally fell to Marines, tanks, and napalm.

Even after Sugar Loaf and Wana Draw were captured, the battle for Okinawa dragged on. One reason for the delay was Army General Simon Bolivar Buckner's unimaginative frontal assaults, which played right into the hands of Ushijima's campaign of attrition. The Marines urged Buckner to open a second front by executing a "left-hook" amphibious landing—circling around Japanese concentrations and attacking them from the rear. The Marines even volunteered to perform the operation by themselves. Buckner refused. Meanwhile, *kamikaze* attacks continued to strike at the Fifth Fleet, until Admiral Nimitz complained, "I'm losing a ship and a half a day out here." Still, the campaign dragged on, and it was getting dangerously close to Okinawa's rainy season.

Then the so-called plum rains arrived, bogging the 10th Army down in mud, choking supply columns, and slowing the offensive from a crawl to a stumble. It rained for two solid weeks, halting all military operations. Time was on the enemy's side. Ceaseless *kamikaze* attacks had worn down American pilots and damaged many ships. In the skies over Okinawa, the Americans had already lost 800 planes. The Japanese lost 7,830—many of them suicide bombers that never made their targets, thanks to the fighters. But this fierce air battle could not continue for much longer. Something had to be done to break the stalemate before Nimitz lost his fleet.

For many weeks, Buckner's leadership was not openly challenged. Neither the Army nor the Marine Corps wanted another "Smith vs. Smith" controversy. But it was feared that the Army's slow, overcautious tactics and Buckner's refusal to use further Marine Corps amphibious assaults might lead to disaster.

On May 24, the rains ceased. During the first clear night in two weeks, while a bright full moon shone in the sky, Japanese twin-engine Sally bombers appeared over captured Yontan and Kadena Airfields. The antiaircraft on the ground was primed and ready, and when they opened fire, eleven enemy planes were slapped out of the air in plain sight of the entire base. The rest turned and fled—all but one crippled Sally.

The wounded bomber crash-landed on its belly and skidded to a halt on one of Yontan's strips. Fourteen Japanese paratroopers died in the crash, but eight survivors poured out of the burning wreckage and rushed the parked aircraft with explosives. These men fought furiously, destroying eight aircraft and damaging many others. They blew up a fuel dump—destroying 70,000 gallons of gasoline—and killed all the Americans they could find. The determined suicide troopers butchered two Marines and wounded eighteen others before they were hunted down and exterminated. It was a desperate act, but one that demonstrated to the Americans that the Japanese fighting spirit was not yet extinguished.

On May 29, the Marines literally walked into Shuri Castle. Though the citadel was technically located in the Army's zone of operations, they sensed a lull in the fighting around the shattered ruin and decided to investigate. Marine Corps General Pedro del Valle, a native of North Carolina, gave permission for elements of Fifth to move forward. They discovered that the bulk of Ushijima's forces had retreated, during the bad weather, to take positions on a line of fortified ridges along the southern edge of the island for a final stand.

Soon a flag appeared above the ruins of Shuri—the stars and bars of the Confederate battle flag, which General del Valle had provided. This incident led to some friction between Buckner and del Valle. Buckner was already angry that the Marines had seized a major prize out from under his men; that Rebel flag was the last straw. General del Valle felt that Buckner, of all people, should enjoy the gesture. Buckner didn't, and ordered the Stars and Stripes to be raised in its place. But remnants of the Japanese defenders took aim at the flagstaff, so the Confederate flag flew above Shuri Castle for two days before it was removed.

Buckner continued his slow, cautious advance, peppering each area with tons of artillery before moving his men forward. By the time the Americans reached the Kiyamu Peninsula—the southernmost five miles stretch of Okinawa—General Ushijima and his men were dug in and waiting for them. Ushijima holed up on Hill 89, just eleven miles south of Shuri. It would take three more weeks of bloody fighting to ferret him out.

While the 10th Army and the First Marine Division hunted Ushijima, the Sixth Marines attacked the Oroku Peninsula. The Marines began an amphibious assault on June 4. Fortunately, the Japanese did not defend the beaches, but remained hidden in the central highlands.

A Divine Wind of a different kind struck the U.S. fleet off Okinawa when a typhoon decimated the region on June 5. Damage was inflicted on four battleships, eight carriers, seven cruisers, and eleven destroyers. Dozens of support ships were also crippled and there were many casualties. The few remaining Japanese defenders on Okinawa must have been heartened by this violent act of nature directed against their enemy. But when the typhoon passed, so did the rain, and the American advanced again.

The Marines on Oroku met heavier resistance. The enemy was dug into hills, so the Marines encircled them and began to close in. The 29th Marines were in a tough spot. Many of their frontline troops were replacements, which lowered the level of combat effectiveness. One of these recruits was Private Robert Miller McTureous, Jr., of Altoona, Florida. He was only with his unit for a week when he spotted stretcher bearers hit by enemy machine-gun fire as they evacuated the wounded. Small and wiry, McTureous had tremendous fighting spirit. Filling his shirt with grenades, the twenty-one-year-old Marine charged the Japanese guns in a furious one-man attack. He threw grenades into caves, clearing them out. He returned to his unit for more grenades, then went out again. Finally, McTureous was wounded in the stomach. He crawled over 200 yards in heavy fire, back to his squad. He was evacuated with the wounded and died on June 11, 1945, aboard the hospital ship U.S.S. *Relief*. Private Robert M. McTureous, Jr., was awarded a posthumous Medal of Honor. His is the last action of the war to earn this distinction.

By June 9, the Japanese on Oroku were pressed into a corner. On the tenth, the survivors tried to break out of their trap. Many were killed and fifty-six were taken prisoner. By the fourteenth, resistance on Oroku was over. But the Japanese were still fighting at a place called Kunishi Ridge. A furious two-day and two-night battle failed to neutralize that position. The ridge was not taken until June 16, and the cost was high for the Marines.

On June 18, Lieutenant General Simon Bolivar Buckner moved up to the front to watch the Marine advance. A Japanese shell exploded nearby, and a piece of coral ripped into his chest. The wound proved to be mortal—Buckner died just three days before the Battle for Okinawa ended. That end came at 1:05 P.M. on June 21, 1945, when Lieutenant General Roy S. Geiger declared Okinawa secure. The next day General Ushijima committed ritual suicide on a lonely cliff overlooking the sea. During the mopping-up, the Americans estimated that 102,000 Japanese soldiers perished in the doomed defense of Okinawa, along with another 40,000 Okinawans and perhaps 150,000 civilians. Though 7,000 Japanese troops surrendered, thousands of soldiers and civilians committed suicide rather than face capture.

The U.S. 10th Army suffered 7,613 killed and missing and over 31,000 wounded. The Marines and their medical personnel lost over 20,000 casualties—of which 3,561 were combat deaths. But the United States Navy suffered the most. Over 10,000 sailors, aviators, and officers were killed or wounded in *kamikaze* attacks. There also were over 25,000 nonbattle casualties—"shell shock" was the term used at that time to describe the neuropsychiatric cases. This horrendous, across-the-board casualty rate was a major factor in President Harry S. Truman's decision to drop the atomic bomb on Japan. He and the Joint Chiefs knew that an invasion of the Home Islands would be even bloodier than Okinawa.

THE FIRE OF THE SUN

On August 6, a B-29 dubbed *Enola Gay* took off from North Field on Tinian. At 8:15 A.M., the single bomb the Superfortress dropped on the target detonated over the Japanese city of Hiroshima—the first nuclear weapon used in anger. The second would follow on August 9, dropped on Nagasaki, a town where many of the survivors of the Hiroshima blast fled after the destruction of their city. On August 10, the Japanese government sued for peace. After three days of negotiations, Emperor Hirohito surrendered. At 6:15 A.M. the next morning, Admiral Nimitz ordered all hostilities against Japan to cease. The invasion of the Home Islands, which so many had anticipated with dread, would not occur.

On Sunday, September 2, 1945, aboard the battleship *Missouri,* moored in Tokyo Bay, in front of the thirty-one-starred flag that Commodore Perry had carried into that bay in 1853, the formal surrender ceremonies were conducted. Lieutenant General Roy Geiger represented the Marine Corps. General Holland Smith was left out of the ceremonies—Admiral Nimitz never forgave him for the Smith-vs.-Smith controversy at Saipan. The Marines finally landed in Japan in late August. But instead of storming the beach in a bloody amphibious assault, a small provisional detachment—with U.S. sailors and a group of Royal Marines—walked ashore at Yokosuka to seize the harbor. The bloodiest and costliest conflict in human history was over.

During World War II, the Marine Corps reached an unbelievable size—nearly half a million men wore the uniform. Almost 20,000 women joined the Corps as well, to serve as stenographers, motor pool mechanics, parachute riggers, and cryptologists. The Corps sustained 92,000 combat casualties during the war, with the dead numbering 20,000. Some 70 percent of the members of the other armed services were sent overseas during the war, and 90 percent of all Marines. And though the Marine Corps constituted less than 5 percent of the Americans who served in the armed forces during the Second World War, they suffered over 10 percent of the nation's casualties.

PART FOUR

COLD WAR IN KOREA

■

1950–1953

". . . the Marine Corps is the Navy's police force and as long as I am President that is what it will remain. They have a propaganda machine that is almost equal to Stalin."

—President Harry S. Truman, in response to a congressman's
suggestion that the commandant of the Corps have a seat with
the Joint Chiefs of Staff, September 1950

■

"It is my conviction that the successful assault on Inchon could have been accomplished only by the United States Marine Corps."

—Rear Admiral James Doyle,
Commander of Amphibious Group One, Inchon

■

"We're not retreating. We're simply attacking in another direction."

—Major General Oliver P. Smith
to reporters at Hagaru-ri, December 1950

CHAPTER TWELVE

KOREA

■

1950–1953

B Y the end of the Second World War, the political situation in Asia had changed drastically. The Japanese were a conquered people and the United States and the Soviet Union emerged as the major players in the region. The Dutch, British, and French abandoned many of their Pacific colonies in the postwar chaos, while the United States increased its presence. In 1946, America's sphere of influence extended to the Philippines, Hawaii, Okinawa, and the Korean Peninsula. American political and economic interests began to clash with the Soviet Union's, and with the rise of the People's Republic of China, future conflict was inevitable. That conflict erupted on the Korean Peninsula in 1950.

Korea was a divided nation. During the war it was occupied by the Japanese. In 1945, the United States proposed the Thirty-eighth Parallel as the temporary line for dividing the Korean Peninsula into sectors in which the Russian and American forces would accept the surrender of the Japanese. The Soviet Union already had a military presence inside Korea, so this severing of north and south was an expedient way to limit further Communist expansion. But the plan backfired in 1948 when the Soviets halted elections in the sectors they controlled, an act that led to the creation of two Koreas—one democratic, the other totalitarian. The Thirty-eighth Parallel became a line of demarcation between freedom and Communist domination.

When the U.S. Congress decided that keeping 50,000 troops based in Korea was too expensive, the State Department began urging South Korea to stand on its own. In a few years the South Koreans created an impressive military, and when the U.S. withdrew its forces in June 1949, only 500 American military advisers remained in the country. When the Communists invaded the south the following year, there were fewer than ten divisions in the Pacific—two of them Marine Corps.

President Truman, who disliked Syngman Rhee's "extreme-right-wing attitude," refused to provide weapons to South Korea—a terrible mistake with dire consequences. Though Rhee was an autocratic strongman, he was much preferable to the Communist regime in the north. But the precarious situation on the Korean Peninsula might have stabilized if not for a political blunder by U.S. Secretary of State Dean Acheson. On January 12, 1950, Acheson gave a speech at the National Press Club in Washington, D.C., in which he described America's strategic frontier in Asia as a "defensive perimeter [that] runs along the Aleutians to Japan and then goes to the Ryukyus." Acheson inexplicably left out the Korean Peninsula and Formosa. Peking and Moscow parsed Acheson's words, and five months later—on Sunday, June 25, 1950—eight North Korean divisions spearheaded by Russian-built T-34 tanks invaded the Republic of Korea. In response to this aggression the United Nations met in emergency session and passed a resolution to defend South Korea. Truman ordered ammunition and supplies to be shipped to South Korea, but it was too late for them to do much good. South Korea's Army was disintegrating in the face of the swift, Soviet-inspired invasion, and General Douglas MacArthur's meager forces in South Korea—mostly disorganized units rushed to the front—were threatened with a disastrous, Dunkirk-like evacuation if they were not reinforced.

President Truman gave MacArthur permission to unleash his army—but only south of the Thirty-eighth Parallel. But the U.N. resolution and Truman's swift, decisive actions caught military leaders off guard. The U.S. military was unprepared to fight a war in Korea. Both Congress and the administration had pressured the military to downsize after the war, and were now paying the price. After VE day, the Marine Corps had shrunk from half-million men to fewer than 72,000. When the Korean War broke out, President Truman was lucky he *had* a Marine Corps to deploy, because Truman himself had led the charge to eliminate the Corps altogether.

In the years after the Second World War, the Marine Corps grappled with four problems—the pressure to demobilize; desegregation; the evolution of atomic weapons; and the desire by ex–Army officers like Truman, Dwight D. Eisenhower, and Omar Bradley to see the Corps absorbed—"unified" was their euphemism—or abolished. The bloody sacrifices and the stirring victories of the Pacific War were forgotten. Truman's secretary of defense, Louis Johnson, was openly contemptuous of the Corps and wasn't afraid to demonstrate that contempt. In 1950, Johnson ordered that the traditional celebration of the Corps' birthday on November 10 be banned at all Marine and Navy bases.

But one man stood in Truman's way. General Alexander Vandegrift, the postwar commandant of the Marine Corps, resisted unification, insisting that those who believed atomic weapons would transform the battlefield were placing too much emphasis on technology and not enough on manpower and common sense. Vandegrift outmaneuvered his foes and prevailed as he did on Guadalcanal—and like Guadalcanal there were some high-profile casualties in this struggle. One of them was "Red Mike" Edson, a hero of Guadalcanal, who resigned his commission when ordered not to make public statements in favor of a separate Corps.

Desegregation was a long time coming, but the implementation of this controversial policy during the 1940s and 1950s was not without its problems. The Marine

Corps began to implement desegregation slowly—first by desegregating the on-base athletic teams, then the clubs, then the training areas and units, and finally all facilities. Though they made great progress, it was not until the end of the Korean conflict that full integration became a reality. In 1950, there were 1,502 black enlisted men on active duty in the Marine Corps. By the beginning of 1953, that number had increased ten times, with nineteen African-American officers and 14,468 enlisted men in the Corps. Though no black Marine received the Medal of Honor in Korea, African-Americans in the Corps earned the Distinguished Flying Cross, the Bronze Star, and the Silver Star.

The advent of atomic warfare also threatened the existence of the Marine Corps. With the blasts at Hiroshima and Nagasaki, a decade of amphibious warfare tactics and doctrine—developed in combat and paid for in blood—were rendered obsolete. Strategists asked why anyone would storm a beachhead when a single bomb could annihilate the entire island? The invasion of Inchon would demonstrate the folly of such thinking. At Inchon the Marines proved that no matter how big a bang one can make, there will always be a place for amphibious operations in modern warfare.

THE WAR BEGINS

The attack on the Republic of Korea began at 4:00 A.M. on a Sunday. The North Korean People's Army—NKPA—attacked across the Thirty-eighth Parallel with a tank battalion and 90,000 troops. They rushed into the south through a drizzling rain, leading with an artillery barrage and launching the infantry attack with blasts from their bugles. The North Koreans overwhelmed the South Korean frontline units. Because it was a weekend, many South Korean troops were on leave or in staging areas forty or fifty miles from the front, too far away to do much good in those critical first hours.

The NKPA moved down the Uijongbu Corridor, a main travel artery that led from north to south and into the heart of Seoul, the ROK capital. By 8:30 A.M., the desperate ROK forces were calling Seoul for reinforcements. There were none to be had. By nightfall the ROK had retreated to the town of Uijongbu. If the invasion was not stopped, Seoul would be overrun. The South Koreans put all they had in the defense of Uijongbu, but it wasn't enough. On June 26, the city fell and the NKPA moved to capture Seoul.

On Tuesday, June 27, the South Korean government abandoned their capital and moved to Taejon ninety miles south, and military headquarters were moved to Suwon. By midnight the NKPA was bombing the suburbs of Seoul and refugees were fleeing south across the Han River bridges. Bringing up the rear were thousands of disorganized and retreating ROK units threatened with total annihilation. At 2:15 A.M., a frightened demolition team set off the charges under the Han River bridges. The explosions killed thousands of refugees and cut off over 40,000 ROK troops and their vital equipment from their comrades in the south. These troops were butchered to a man, their weapons captured and used by the Communists. The ROK Army, which had been touted by *Time* magazine as the best military force outside the United

States, was routed in three days. By the time the United Nations entered the war, the South Korean military commanders could not account for two-thirds of their forces.

Quick flights from Japan hustled U.S. troops to the front. By July 5, a thin line of United States Army defenders were dug into the hillsides along the Suwon to Osan road. In the driving rain, Americans engaged the enemy for the first time. T-34 tanks overran many U.S. positions in the first few minutes, but the Army rallied and reinforced. For the next seven hours the fight raged. The poorly armed and outnumbered Americans were no match for the disciplined NKPA troops, and the U.S. Army was pushed back almost as easily as the South Koreans had been. American soldiers abandoned their weapons and equipment and even their wounded.

Over the next three weeks U.S. ground and air forces, along with reorganized elements of the Republic of Korea's military, fought the NKPA to a standstill. Everything inside the so-called Pusan Perimeter was eventually secured. But holding on to these fragile positions would do nothing to drive the Communists back across the Thirty-eighth Parallel. It would take a bold plan devised by General Douglas MacArthur to defeat the enemy. To implement this plan, MacArthur would need help from the Marines Corps.

General MacArthur wanted to land a U.S. division at the port of Inchon—right in the middle of enemy-held territory. This bold amphibious landing would flank the NKPA troops now operating in the south, blocking their retreat and crushing them "between a hammer and anvil." General Vandegrift vowed to provide enough Marines to accomplish the mission, and from the end of July into early August, Marine reserve units began reporting for active duty at Camp Pendleton.

Marines were already fighting in Korea, at places like the Chinju-Masan Corridor. They faced the enemy at Hill 308, at the village of Changchon, and at the battle for Naktong. These Marine units, composed of veterans of the Second World War and young recruits, stood firm against the NKPA and fought to solidify the Pusan Perimeter before their reinforcements arrived from the States. Marine Corps aviators flew hundreds of ground support missions in Corsairs—the "bent-wing widow-makers" were still in service after their heyday in the Second World War.

The first elements of the Marine Corps brigade came ashore at Pusan on August 2. These Marines streamed out of their troop ships and hustled to the outer edges of the Pusan Perimeter, where they were needed to reinforce the Army's tenuous defenses. But the symbolic beginning of the Marine Corps' ground war came on August 7, 1950—eight years to the day after the invasion of Guadalcanal—when the Fifth Marines marched through blistering 112-degree heat to Hill 342 to relieve a beleaguered Army unit.

INCHON

MacArthur's Inchon strategy seemed risky. None of the Joint Chiefs placed much faith in the plan except General MacArthur and the Marine Corps. Yet Inchon would prove to be the most strategically important amphibious landing of the twentieth cen-

■ *Hand-Me-Down War*

The Korean War was waged with equipment left over from World War II—the result of the downsizing and cutbacks in the U.S. military. But using "outmoded" and "obsolete" conventional weapons in Korea may also have been a shrewd political calculation. Five years before North Korea invaded the South, two atomic bombs had been detonated over Japanese cities. In the years following the war, the human race learned the horrifying effects of those weapons. By the Korean War, the world's number-one fear was of a new world war waged with nuclear weapons. Humanity breathed a sigh of relief when they realized that conventional warfare was still an option in an international crisis like the Korean conflict.

The enemy had no choice but to fight with secondhand weapons. It was all they had. It would be decades before the Chinese tested their first nuclear bomb and longer for the North Koreans to develop such weapons. Though no one was equipped for war on the Korean Peninsula, the Republic of Korea was the most poorly armed combatant of them all. Truman was opposed to arming Syngman Rhee's "right-wing" government, so when the North Koreans struck, the south crumbled. Small arms, hand grenades, machine guns, and satchel charges weren't much defense against T-34 tanks and massed attacks by shock troops. The NKPA even employed a division of mobile infantry that used motorcycles with armed sidecars to outmaneuver and outflank the South Koreans.

The United States Marines went to Korea with the same secondhand small arms the Army carried—the M-1 Garand, the .30-caliber carbine, the .45-caliber pistol, and the Browning automatic rifle. For more firepower, the Americans used the .30-caliber, M-1919 light machine gun; the water-cooled, tripod mounted M-1717 A-1 heavy machine gun, and the formidable .50-caliber MG M2HB machine gun—which was usually mounted in the back of jeeps, half-tracks, and tanks.

The mortar was used effectively in Korea. Most rifle companies carried the 60mm into battle. Weapons companies lugged the heavier 81mm mortars. The 4.2-inch mortars were quite deadly, but too large to carry and had to be mounted on a vehicle. Mortars are capable of throwing high explosives into the air at steep angles, to fall almost vertically onto the enemy. Mortar shells can reach into trenches, foxholes, valleys, and emplacements. Because mortars could be fired at steep angles and deployed and withdrawn rapidly, they were impervious to direct fire. Unfortunately, mortar rounds tended to misfire in the sub-zero temperatures of Korea's winters. It took two men, working closely, to clear a mortar. One man tipped the mortar tube and dumped the dud into the other man's cupped hand. A mistake could be fatal. This process was hazardous and unnerving and almost always occurred in the heat of battle.

The most common antitank weapon was the M9AI 2.36-inch rocket launcher—better known as the bazooka. Developed in World War II, the bazooka did not fare well against heavily armored German tanks, though the 2.36-inch shell was able to penetrate the armor of a Russian-made T-34. The bazooka man had to hit the right spot, however, or the rocket would bounce off of sloped armor or detonate harmlessly against the thick plate on the T-34's front hull. Bazookas required a two-man team to operate and were cumbersome. The weapon was shoulder-fired, which meant that the loader had to beware of the back blast. That blast also revealed the bazooka team's position, which was inconvenient in a fight. Far more effective—and far less portable—were the various types of recoilless rifles used by the Army.

Handheld explosives included satchel bombs and the grenade. Five types of grenades were used in Korea, but the most popular were the fourteen-ounce, Mark IIIA-I fragmentation grenade, the cardboard concussion grenades, and the M-15 white phosphorus grenade. Fragmentation grenades were activated by pulling a pin, which started a four-second time fuse. A grenade was thrown from a distance of thirty-five yards or less. When it detonated, the explosive core blasted steel shrapnel from its thick metal casing in a circular killing radius of ten yards. These fragments were dangerous up to fifty yards, which meant the attacker was also at risk.

Tanks were at a premium in Korea. At the outset, there were no American tank battalions in the Far East. The M-26 Pershing tank, an upgrade of the Patton tank with a new engine and a larger 90mm gun, gradually made it onto the battlefield by the closing months of 1950. The old M4A3 Sherman IV, an upgrade of the outmoded Second World War model, became the principal battle tank of the Korean War. Mounted with a new high-velocity 76.2mm gun, the Sherman was still outgunned. But because it was high and narrow instead of wide and squat—and much lighter than the Pattons and Pershings—the Sherman could maneuver on the confined, muddy Korean roads better than more modern tanks. When the British joined the U.N. forces, they brought the formidable Centurion III main battle tank, which could stand up to anything the Chinese threw against it.

Two battlefield innovations led to an evolution in medical care. The large-scale presence of the helicopter resulted in the prompt evacuation of casualties. The wounded in Korea had a better chance of surviving than in any previous war. The helicopter, along with the evolution of the Mobile Army Surgical Hospitals helped save American lives in Korea.

The first Marine mass helicopter resupply mission took place on September 13, 1951, when Marine Helicopter Transport Squadron 161 successfully executed Operation Windmill 1. Eight days later, on September 21, that same squadron landed 224 Marines and nearly 18,000 pounds of cargo and supplies on an isolated hilltop at the Punchbowl. This second operation would have taken fifteen days without helicopters. With helicopters it took just forty-eight hours. These operations were the brainchild of Major General Gerald C. Thomas, and proved helicopter's logistical value in combat. Thomas's vision would change the nature of the modern battlefield—though not in Korea. All-out helicopter warfare would not come about until the Vietnam conflict a decade and a half later.

There was nothing new about the weapons the North Koreans carried into battle, either. Many enemy troops began the war carrying U.S. arms and equipment captured from the ROKs in the first month of fighting. The Communist Chinese were armed with many U.S.-manufactured weapons, supplied to the Nationalist Chinese during the Second World War and captured from them during the Communist uprising. The Chinese and North Koreans also carried rifles and machine guns taken from the Japanese in World War II, including the 8mm Type 100 submachine gun and the 6.5mm Type 8 rifle. It was quite a surprise for some Marine Corps veterans of the Pacific Campaign who found themselves facing these all-too-familiar weapons yet again.

Though the use of captured arms was common, the bulk of Chinese and North Korean weapons were produced by the Soviet Union. Russian weapons are perfect for "proletariat" armies. They are user-friendly, easy to operate, and difficult to damage. Even soldiers with limited exposure to technology can be trained to operate Soviet equipment effectively.

The Russian 7.62 carbine, a bolt-action rifle that first saw action in 1944, was used primarily by the Chinese Communist forces, though these troops preferred the Shpagin PPSh41 submachine gun—the infamous "burp gun" designed by George Shpagin to meet the desperate need of the Soviet people in the bitter war against Nazi aggression. Communist forces generally disdained marksmanship skills in favor of massed firepower. The burp gun wasn't very accurate, but it threw a lot of rounds into the air. Cheap to manufacture and simple to operate, the Soviet submachine gun was the best weapon of its type designed in the Second World War—despite the fact that it was inaccurate except at close range. The Communists believed that if their soldiers shot enough times, they were bound to hit something important sooner or later.

The Tokarev semiautomatic 7.62mm was the Russian version of the BAR, though much less effective. It was neither very prevalent nor popular. Russian-made machine guns were more effective. Sensibly, they were all 7.62mm, including the wheel-mounted Goryunov heavy machine gun used by both the CCF and the NKPA.

The Communist forces had no effective bazooka-type weapon, though the 14.5mm PTRD-1941 antitank rifle was close. This weapon was long and unwieldy and difficult to use. It was also ineffective against heavy armor, but could damage lightly armored half tracks and vehicles like jeeps and supply trucks. The Americans called them "elephant" or "buffalo" rifles, and they were mostly used for antipersonnel purposes such as long-range sniping.

Mortars were used effectively by the CCF and the NKPA. Cheap and easy to manufacture, simple to transport, and quite user friendly, Russian-made mortars came in several sizes—the 120mm, the 82mm, and the 61mm. Though Russian-made hand grenades predominated, many North Korean and Chinese units also hurled World-War-II-era Japanese grenades at the Americans, including the old-fashioned potato-masher variety.

The thirty-five-ton, T-34 was the main battle tank of the Communist forces in Korea. The last of them was manufactured in the late 1940s and by 1950 they were obsolete. Nevertheless, the NKPA used them quite effectively to spearhead their initial incursion into the south. With a top speed of thirty-five miles per hour, the T-34 was lighter than the American tanks and thus better suited to the rugged Korean landscape and rudimentary roads. Though the T-34 dominated the battlefield in the first months of the war, they were overwhelmed by American armor and airpower in the later stages of the conflict. And hard-fighting Marines like Walter Monegan took out a few Korean tanks too.

A large number of the front troops—in the Marine Corps especially—were left over from the Second World War. But in this case, such holdovers were an advantage. Marine Corps officers and NCOs had already fought the Japanese to a standstill and their experience was invalu-able in turning the tide of the Korean conflict. When the First Marine Division was dispatched to Korea, it was a patchwork assembly of personnel, weapons, and equip-ment thrown together and shipped out with haste and little planning. Despite its dubious ancestry, the First performed magnificently in that first bitter year of fighting. So it was that the United States entered the war with the most for-midable weapon of any participant—the Marine Corps.

tury, a dramatic assault that had an immediate impact on the war. With this decisive attack, the Marines reversed the tide of the Korean War.

Inchon had a population of 250,000 in 1950 and was the size of Omaha. It was one of the most important ports in South Korea, which was surprising considering the difficulties encountered when navigating its waters. The tides around Inchon vary wildly. Deep draft vessels could negotiate the passage only a few days out of every month and the shores were dominated by shoals and mudflats. Accessing the city was difficult; the approach from the Yellow Sea required twelve miles of precision navi-gation through Flying Fish Channel. More daunting to the Marines was the fact that Inchon's harbor was defended by Wolmi-Do Island, which was crawling with NKPA soldiers and would have to be captured at least twelve hours in advance of the Marine landing at Inchon—it was the only time the tides were right. While Wolmi-Do was being secured, the rest of the invasion fleet would wait in plain sight for the tide to return. There would be no element of surprise here.

Because of the vagaries of Inchon's freakish tides, the fifteenth was the only day a landing could be made in the entire month of September. But launching the inva-sion so soon meant that one of the three Marine Corps combat elements—the Sev-enth—wouldn't arrive from the States in time to participate. It also meant that the Fifth Marines, who had been fighting hard on the Pusan Perimeter, would jump from the frying pan into the fire when they moved from the front lines to invasion mode in a fortnight. Once the Marines came ashore, they would be forced to change tactics again. Within the first hours of D day, they would move from the beachhead into the towns and cities. Fighting from street to street in an occupied city was hard and costly, and the Marines' first objective was Seoul. The Communists were expected to put up a fierce resistance to retain their enemy's capital.

While Marines were risking their lives to stem the tide of the North Korean advance, President Harry S. Truman made derogatory public statements about the Marine Corps. In a letter to a congressman, he stated that the Marine Corps was noth-ing more than "the Navy's police force" whose past glories were the result of a "pub-lic relations machine equal to Stalin's." His rash words did not endear this commander in chief to the Marines, and in defiance, many frontline Leathernecks painted "Horrible Harry's Police Force" in bold letters on their jeeps and tanks.

The 260-ship invasion force of "Operation Chromite" departed Japan on Septem-ber 8, about the same time as the five-day naval preinvasion bombardment of Inchon began. Navy ships and Marine Corps Corsairs dropped bombs and napalm on the hills of Wolmi-Do, burning off vegetation and revealing cave mouths and camouflaged NKPA positions. At 6:30 A.M., the Marines stormed ashore on the beaches at Wolmi-Do. In two hours they had secured the island. Fourteen Marines were wounded, none seriously. The Marines dug in and waited for high tide to return, bringing the rest of the invasion force in with it. At 2:30 P.M., the bombardment of Inchon's harbor began. Soon the waterfront was ablaze. Follow-up air support pumped thousands of rockets into NKPA emplacements, adding to the smoke, the fire, and the noise. Late in the afternoon the high tide returned and Higgins boats and LVTs began to approach the shore. Inchon looked ghostly in the smoky haze and fading light as the Marines closed on their landing sites at Red and Blue Beach.

Though the Inchon invasion was launched on the fly, the landings went surprisingly well. There was the usual chaos—several LVTs got mired in the mudflats, the Navy hit some Marine Corps units with friendly fire, and several groups landed at the wrong beaches. By the time the sun set, the initial landings had been accomplished despite enemy resistance and the minimal experience these Marines had with amphibious warfare. Chesty Puller's First Marines landed at Blue Beach, an industrial area three miles to the southwest of Red Beach. They were supposed to link up with the Fifth. Lieutenant Ray Murray's Fifth Marines landed on Red Beach. They were to use scaling ladders to climb a high seawall that blocked the shore, link up with the Marines who captured Wolmi-Do, then enter the city to join Puller's boys.

There was minimal resistance at Blue Beach, but the Fifth faced stubborn resistance. When Murray's Leathernecks came ashore, they ran into a wall of heavy fire. As the first wave placed ladders and began to scale the seawall, they were cut down by machine guns. Many were hit as they made it to the top of the ladder, when they were most vulnerable. Only a few Marines got over the wall alive and fewer continued their advance in the face of merciless fire from enemy pillboxes.

Lieutenant Baldomero Lopez, a twenty-five-year-old Hispanic-American Annapolis graduate from Tampa, Florida, led the Third Rifle Platoon over the seawall and forward against fortified North Korean defensive positions. His platoon's main objective was Cemetery Hill, one of three high points around Seoul that were all priority targets. As casualties mounted, Lopez spied the culprit—an NKPA bunker armed with a machine gun had the range on his Marines. Calling for covering fire, he crawled forward until he was within throwing range of the pillbox, then he primed a grenade and rose from cover to hurl it inside the bunker. Instantly, he was struck in the arm and shoulder by machine gun fire. Lieutenant Lopez lost his grip on the grenade as he was thrown back. Though wounded, he searched for the grenade, but seconds went by and his injured arm refused to function. Shouting a warning, Lopez smothered the blast with his body.

Baldomero Lopez was awarded the first Medal of Honor in the Cold War era and the first for action in Korea. His award was posthumous. Eleven Marines would receive a posthumous Medal of Honor for smothering grenades and saving their comrades during the Korean War: Private First Class William Bernard Baugh of McKinney, Kentucky; Corporal Jack Arden Davenport of Kansas City, Missouri; Corporal Duane Edgar Dewey of Grand Rapids, Michigan; Private First Class Fernando Luis

Private Edward Gomez

Private Herbert A. Littleton

Garcia of Utuado, Puerto Rico; Private First Class Edward Gomez of Omaha, Nebraska; Private First Class Herbert A. Littleton from Mena, Arkansas; Private First Class Whitt Lloyd Moreland of Waco, Texas; Second Lieutenant Robert Dale Reem of Lancaster, Pennsylvania; Private First Class Robert Ernest Simanek from Detroit, Michigan; and Second Lieutenant Sherrod Emerson Skinner, Jr., of Hartford, Connecticut.

Staff Sergeant Robert Sidney Kennemore of Greenville, South Carolina, received a Medal of Honor after he miraculously survived an exploding grenade he had smothered with his body. Private Hector Albert Cafferata, Jr., of New York City was wounded while tossing a grenade away from his fellow Marines at the risk of his own life and received the Medal of Honor. Corporal David Bernard Champagne of Waterville, Maine, and Staff Sergeant Lewis George Watkins of Seneca, South Carolina, both perished while attempting to hurl explosives away from their comrades.

By nightfall 13,000 Marines were ashore. Despite resistance, casualties had been light—fewer than 200 wounded and only 22 killed. In the darkness, the Marines dug in. On Saturday morning, September 16—D day plus one—they began to move at dawn. Within three hours they had secured the streets of Inchon and were ready to advance. The Fifth Marines marched toward Kimpo Airfield, sixteen miles away. The First went up the highway to Yongdungpo, an industrial suburb across the Han River from Seoul.

By Saturday night the Second Battalion, First Marines, had reached the hamlet of

Staff Sergeant Robert S. Kennemore

Sosa-ri, where they dug in for the night. At dawn on Monday morning the North Koreans launched a massive counterattack to push the Americans back into the Yellow Sea. This attack began at Sosa-ri.

TANK KILLER

Private First Class Walter Carleton Monegan was a teenage husband with a pregnant wife when he landed with the Marines at Inchon. Born in Melrose, Massachusetts, Monegan had lied about his age and enlisted in the Army in November 1947. When the Army discovered that he was only sixteen, they discharged him. Months later Monegan convinced his parents to sign his Marine Corps enlistment papers and he reported to Parris Island for boot camp in March 1948. As a private, he got a first taste overseas duty when he was stationed at Tsingtao. But the Communist takeover of mainland China forced his company to withdraw with the rest of the U.S. forces, and Monegan ended up completing his first enlistment at Camp Pendleton. It was there that he met and married. Ready to settle down in Seattle with his pregnant wife, Elizabeth, Monegan reenlisted when America went to war.

Monegan came ashore at Inchon with F Company of the Second Battalion. At dawn on the morning of September 17, just outside of Sosa-ri, the first elements of the Korean counterattack rumbled into position. The Marines heard the clank of approaching T-34 tanks from the road ahead of their position. From out of the morning fog, six Russian-built tanks roared into view. The lead tanks were covered with sandbags and camouflage nets, but the tanks behind them had NKPA infantrymen clinging to their hulls and turrets. Monegan and Private First Class Robert F. Perkins moved out of their foxholes and cautiously approached the enemy tanks.

Though he'd earned an expert's badge at Pendleton for his talent with a bazooka, Monegan had never used the weapon in combat. Now, from a roadside ditch, he aimed the six-foot metal tube at the T-24 closest to his position, but still over a hundred yards away. Crouching behind him, Perkins slipped the 3.5-inch rocket into the launcher. Then Perkins tapped his helmet—the signal that the bazooka was "hot"—and Monegan drew a bead on the first tank. The clank of the metal treads battered their ears and the ground began to quake under their feet, but the young private patiently waited to fire. When the T-34 had lumbered to within forty yards of him, Monegan squeezed the trigger. The tank exploded with a roar and skewed sideways.

Engulfed in flames, the shattered vehicle blocked the road. The other T-34s ground to a halt behind it.

As Perkins was loading another round, a North Korean cavalry officer popped out of the hatch on the damaged tank to escape the flames. Monegan shot the man down with his M-1. Without pause, he then dropped the carbine, raised the bazooka, and took out a second T-34. The NKPA infantry began jumping off the tanks to seek cover. Monegan got off two more bazooka rounds before American Pershing tanks arrived and finished off the rest of the armored column, its 90mm antitank rounds turning the T-34s into funeral pyres for the crews. Over 200 NKPA regulars were killed and six enemy tanks smashed in less than fifteen minutes.

For two days Monegan's company moved up the road toward Yongdungpo, fighting every step of the way. On Sep-

Private Walter C. Monegan

tember 20, they dug in along a hillside 300 yards from the highway, just three miles from the outskirts of Yongdungpo. At 1:00 A.M., they heard the sound of approaching armor. Tanks were assembling in the darkness for an assault on the Marines' positions. Pershing tanks moved forward in response, but the column got mired in mud. If the NKPA attacked, the Marines would have to face them without armor support. That attack came at 4:00 A.M., led by four T-34s, a half-track, and a ten-ton truck filled with ammo. A Marine from D Company hurled a grenade into the munitions truck, and the blast alerted everyone that the enemy had arrived.

Monegan grabbed his bazooka and raced across 300 yards of open ground along with Corporal William Creek, who lugged a pack stuffed with bazooka rounds. Perkins, Monegan's regular loader, grabbed more ammo from the supply company and followed his comrades. Monegan took up position on the crest of a hill—clearly visible because the fire from the truck illuminated the battlefield. When he fired, the rocket sputtered out, missing the lead T-34 by ten yards.

"We gotta get closer," Monegan shouted. Then he spied a water tower a hundred yards away. He and Corporal Creek darted across open ground without being spotted. Perkins joined them a few moments later. The flickering glow from the burning truck still illuminated the battlefield. Monegan crawled under the tower and aimed at the enemy tank directly behind the shattered truck.

With a bright flash the projectile struck the tank at the base of its turret and the T-34 burst into flame. Then NKPA infantrymen responded to the bazooka flash by peppering the area around the three Marines with machine-gun and rifle fire. Chunks of wood from the water tank's support struts splintered and pierced exposed flesh. When the staccato fire died away Perkins slammed another projectile into the bazooka and Monegan emerged from cover, aimed, and fired. Another T-34 erupted in smoke and fire. Now only two tanks remained, and one of them was backing up in a desperate effort to escape. "Hurry up and load me!" Monegan cried.

Perkins slid a fresh round into place and slapped his helmet. Monegan stepped out of the shadows of the water tower just as a burst of enemy fire came his way. He ignored the enemy bullets and aimed, but before he could fire another burst from an automatic weapon stitched its way up Monegan's chest, killing him instantly. Moments later the Marines of D Company poured out of their foxholes and overwhelmed the last tank. In the red glow from the burning armor, Perkins and Creek carefully moved Monegan's corpse under the water tower. His remains were brought down at first light. Private Walter Carleton Monegan, F Company's "Killer of Tanks," received a posthumous Medal of Honor, presented to his widow and infant son at a solemn ceremony at the Pentagon on February 8, 1952.

LIEUTENANT HENRY A. COMMISKEY

While Walter Monegan faced down North Korean tanks outside of Yongdongpo, the Marines of A and C Companies were fighting for their lives on Hill 118 three miles away. When these Marines first took possession of 118 after a savage fight, they were unaware that nearby Hill 80 and Hill 85 were also occupied. After repulsing the North Koreans in a night attack, the Marines were ordered to clear a village at the base of Hill 85. They began at dawn, and by noon the hamlet was secure—then the Marines were ordered to climb up Hill 85. But they were being watched as they ascended the slope with Lieutenant Henry A. Commiskey's platoon in the lead.

Commiskey was from a long line of fighting men. His father fought in the First and Second World Wars, his older brother was on Guadalcanal with the Marine Raiders, and his other brother was somewhere in Korea with the 187th Airborne. Commiskey followed the family tradition and entered service. Like his older brother, Henry was all Marine. Born in Hattiesburg, Mississippi, and raised a Catholic, he attended the local parochial school and was an altar boy. While in high school he got a summer job with the Illinois Central Railroad. In January 1944, Henry Commiskey enlisted in the Marine Corps and celebrated his eighteenth birthday aboard a transport ship bound for Iwo Jima—where he earned a Purple Heart.

After the war, Commiskey served in Hawaii and occupied Japan before being selected for drill instructor school. His selection to Officer Candidate School quickly followed and Commiskey was commissioned in September 1949. He was on his way to a new assignment at Quantico when the Korean War erupted and he volunteered for frontline service. Now the husky, twenty-three-year-old second lieutenant found himself leading a platoon up Hill 85 after twenty grueling hours of continuous fighting.

Just short of the summit all hell broke loose. A fusillade of enemy gunfire was followed by the sound of agonized screams as the platoon began dropping all around

Commiskey. The shooting came from three sides, but Commiskey spotted the key to the enemy's firepower—a machine-gun nest on the crest, manned by five NKPA troopers. Scrambling to his feet, he cut loose with his Browning automatic rifle, sending the enemy diving behind the shelter of their emplacement. When their machine gun fell silent, Commiskey launched a solo attack.

"Cover me!" he cried, tossing the BAR to another Marine.

He drew his .45 automatic pistol and ran forward, head down. Commiskey continued the charge even after the North Koreans spotted him and opened fire. As bullets whizzed past his head, he covered forty yards in record time, firing his pistol at the machine gun crew. One North Korean clutched his chest and slumped over the gun as Commiskey leapt into the middle of the enemy position. He fired four shots in quick succession. His first finished off the wounded Korean, the rest killed three others. He trained his pistol on the final Korean soldier, who faced him from the opposite side of the trench. But when he squeezed the trigger, nothing happened—Commiskey was out of ammunition. The North Korean lunged at him and the two wrestled at the bottom of the trench, trading punches.

Commiskey overpowered the enemy soldier and rolled on top of him just as a Marine popped his head over the edge of the machine-gun emplacement. "Gimme your pistol!" Commiskey barked.

With one hand Commiskey held the North Korean down while he aimed the other Marine's pistol at the man's head and fired. Pumped with adrenaline, Commiskey searched for another target. He spotted a second machine-gun nest and charged it too. Jumping onto the lip of the trench, Commiskey fired down at the Koreans with the borrowed .45, killing two and driving the others from cover, where they were cut down. Inspired by their lieutenant's valor, the rest of Commiskey's platoon captured the hill, killing fifty NKPA regulars. Commiskey was unscathed despite his near-suicidal solo attacks. His luck ran out a week later, though, when he was wounded in house-to-house fighting in Seoul. Though he recovered enough to return to his old command, frostbite finally laid him low and he was evacuated for good.

For his solo assault on two emplacements, Lieutenant Henry Alfred Commiskey, Sr., received the Medal of Honor in a White House ceremony. He returned to active duty in the Marine Corps as an aviator and volunteered for Vietnam. During a routine physical, doctors discovered a brain tumor and the growth proved to be malignant. After a long bout with cancer, Henry Commiskey passed away on August 16, 1971. He was forty-four. Commiskey was cremated, his ashes scattered over the Gulf of Mexico.

After the capture of Hill 85, American artillery shelled Yongdongpo in an effort to break up the North Korean counterattack and clear the city. After repeated assaults and fierce street fighting, Yongdongpo fell to the First Marines on September 22, 1950. Meanwhile the Fifth Marines had captured Kimpo Airfield on September 18 and were advancing to the Han River, where they boarded landing craft and crossed under heavy fire on September 20. After two more days of fighting, the Marines were across the Han and advancing on Seoul. Within three miles of Seoul's main train station, they clashed with the elite 25th NKPA Brigade along a line of low hills west of the capital.

Fighting was heavy inside Seoul too. It was urban warfare at its worst—a bitter, costly, point-blank fight in which every corner, every house, every barricade had to be neutralized before the Marines could push on to the next block and the next objective. When they got to the new neighborhood, the same cycle began all over again. The stalemate was broken on September 24 when the Marines captured Hill 66—the heart of the North Korean defenses. On the twenty-fifth, the entire North Korean perimeter collapsed and the enemy was on the run. Half of Seoul was swiftly secured, though enemy snipers controlled much of the other half. The four days of house-to-house fighting that followed resulted in the heaviest casualties of the war. Hundreds fell in an effort to push 12,000 North Koreans out of the capital. In twelve days the Marines had landed on Inchon, fought their way to Seoul, and recaptured the city. The cost was high—2,500 American casualties and 421 dead—but much of South Korea had been liberated.

On the afternoon of September 26, in the heart of Seoul, Private First Class Eugene A. Obregon of Los Angeles, California, saw a fellow Marine lying wounded in the street. The man's howls bounced off the walls and he was so horribly wounded he could not even crawl to safety. Obregon burst into the open and began to drag the wounded man to cover. He was nearly there when North Korean machine-gun fire ripped through him. The nineteen-year-old was killed and received a posthumous Medal of Honor for this act of selfless courage.

It was not until September 29 that the fighting ended in Seoul. At noon General Douglas MacArthur escorted Republic of Korea President Syngman Rhee into the National Assembly Hall, restoring the free government of South Korea to its seat of power. Overwhelmed with gratitude, the old man spoke in English. "How can I ever explain to you my own undying gratitude and that of the Korean people?"

It looked as if the Korean War was over. Even the Marines began to speak about going home by Christmas. That night, as Marines dug in on Hill 132 just outside of Seoul, the men of Company C anticipated an end to this short, bloody conflict. In the center of the camp exhausted Marines drifted off to sleep, protected by a ring of machine-gun nests. At one far-flung listening post, Private First Class Stanley Reuben Christianson heard movement and woke his partner, Private First Class Al Walsh. It soon became apparent that NKPA regulars were closing on their position.

"You warn the others. I'll hold them off," Christianson told Walsh. But Walsh hesitated, reluctant to leave his friend.

"Go!" his friend insisted. "I'll be okay." Walsh crawled out of the foxhole to warn the rest of the company. Minutes later Christianson opened up with a machine gun. More than a dozen North Koreans were slaughtered in his initial burst. Meanwhile, Walsh reported to his company commander, then rushed back with reinforcements to rescue his friend.

Private First Class Stanley Reubin Christianson, a twenty-five-year-old recruit from Mindoro, Wisconsin, was found dead, slumped over his machine gun. More than fifty NKPA corpses surrounded his foxhole and the machine gun was empty. Christianson's sacrifice attack kept the enemy from butchering his company. For his valor, a posthumous Medal of Honor was presented to his parents on August 30, 1951.

A battle for Naktong took place near the ruined town. This time it was the North

Koreans who streamed out of the hills in full retreat, their units broken by a swift and determined American attack. As the remnants of the once-proud NKPA retreated across Naktong Bridge, it was *their* equipment that lay abandoned on the battlefield. It was *their* troops who left wounded behind. It was *their* army that had been defeated and demoralized by a superior force. Now, with Seoul secure and the Marines ensconced at Uijongbu and Suwon, General MacArthur's "anvil" was in place. It was time for the "hammer" to crush the invaders once and for all.

ACROSS THE THIRTY-EIGHTH PARALLEL

On October 1, 1950, General Douglas MacArthur issued surrender terms to the North Korean commander. The last remnant of the once-formidable invasion force had been pushed to within five miles of the Thirty-eighth Parallel. Most were positioned in an assembly area in North Korea called the Iron Triangle. Only 30,000 of the original 90,000-man force remained. The rest had been captured or annihilated. In the face of the determined American advance, many North Korean military units had all but ceased to exist. Now, as summer waned and the weather grew colder, U.N. forces and ROK regulars moved into the rugged mountains of South Korea, where thousands of NKPA troops were still holed up.

Though his invasion had been thwarted and his army smashed, North Korean Premier Kim Il Sung made no formal reply to the United Nations' demands for a cease-fire. He rejected their surrender terms in a fiery radio speech to the North Korean people. Despite suffering over 25,000 casualties, the Communists would not surrender. The only way to end the war was to invade North Korea and end the threat of aggression once and for all.

By October 9, American and South Korean units had crossed the Thirty-eighth Parallel and began their march on the North Korean capital of Pyongyang. The allies advanced north of Kaesong to the Kumch'on Pocket, where heavy fighting dragged on for five days. When it was over the road to Pyongyang was wide open. This phase of the Korean Campaign was a mirror image of the North Korean invasion three months before—with the U.N. forces advancing quickly through North Korean territory, ready to envelope and capture their capital just as the North Koreans had captured Seoul. The U.S. Army's Fifth and Seventh Cavalry Regiments moved so quickly that, at 10:00 A.M., October 20, the North Korean capital was declared secure. Fighting was still heavy in the hills, but the U.N. force advanced toward the Yalu River with minimal resistance.

The military objectives in Korea had changed. No longer content to restore the previous borders, MacArthur wanted to liberate *all* of Korea, despite an implied threat from the Communist Chinese that they might enter the conflict on the side of the North Koreans if the Thirty-eighth Parallel was crossed. General MacArthur, in his first and only meeting with President Harry S. Truman, insisted that the Chinese threat was "probably in a category of diplomatic blackmail" and that the chance of intervention was "very little." The first American armies crossed the Thirty-eighth Parallel on October 9.

Sergeant James I. Poynter

On October 13, four Chinese battalions of the Fourth Field Army moved south, across the Yalu River. They advanced a under cover of darkness and went undetected until they clashed with ROK forced at Onjong on October 26. Over the next two days the Chinese Communist forces chewed up the ROK army. The American high command refused to accept the notion that the Chinese were in the war, but when Chinese forces at Usan annihilated the U.S. Army's First Cavalry Regiment on October 30, they could deny reality no longer.

The Marines had been inactive since the battle for Seoul. Now MacArthur wanted the First Marine Division to make an amphibious landing at Wonsan. But Wonsan Harbor was mined and the landings were delayed a few days while those explosives could be cleared. As a result, the Marines didn't came ashore until October 26—Bob Hope's USO show actually beat them into the city. Meanwhile, the Seventh Infantry Division landed at Iwon, a hundred miles north of Wonsan and much closer to the railhead at Hamhung, the port of Hungnam, and Yudam-ni—all American objectives.

The road to Yudam-ni—which the Marines had chosen as their Main Supply Route—was narrow and winding, with a towering cliff on one side and a sheer drop of hundreds of feet on the other. The most difficult part of this route was an eight-mile stretch of road that reached from Funchilin Pass to Koto-ri and on to Hagaru-ri eleven miles away. It was there that the road forked, with one branch running north to the Chosin Reservoir and the other running west and north through the Toktong Pass to Yudam-ni. On October 31, the Seventh Marines marched from Hamhung to Sudong thirty miles away to relieve an ROK force. The Marines suspected that the Chinese were ensconced in the hills south of Sudong, but had no proof. At dusk they dug in at a bridge south of Sudong. The First Battalion occupied high ground, the Second Battalion rested on the slope, and the Third protected the regiment's rear. On the bitterly cold night of November 2, these Marines clashed with the Communist Chinese for the first time.

At 11:00 P.M. on the night of November 1, two Chinese battalions attacked and enveloped the Marines. By 1:00 A.M., November 2, the Marines were reeling under a full-scale assault on both their flanks. The Chinese did not attack from the valley. Instead, they assaulted the Americans from the ridgelines above the Main Supply Route, attacking Marine positions with grenades and submachine guns. At one point a T-34 tank appeared and wiped out an American antitank crew before vanishing in the darkness. Company A's First and Second Platoons were forced to pull back. Sergeant James I. Poynter of Bloomington, Illinois, was critically wounded when the Chinese surrounded his squad. As the enemy charged out of the night, Poynter bayoneted several Chinese soldiers. When he spied the enemy setting up machine guns ahead of him, Poynter gathered grenades from fallen Americans and charged the nests himself, killing two machine-gun crews and blasting a third before he was mortally wounded. Sergeant Poynter's assault gave his beleaguered squad time to reorganize and defend itself, and the forty-three-year-old squad leader received a posthumous Medal of Honor, presented to his widow on September 4, 1952.

Corporal Lee H. Phillips

As Poynter was fighting his last battle, twenty-three-year-old Corporal Lee H. Phillips—born in Stockbridge, Georgia, but raised in Ben Hill—was retreating with the rest of his unit. They had been thrown off Hill 698, just west of the Main Supply Route, by a surprise night attack. After regrouping at the bottom of the hill, the survivors of Company E, Second Battalion, Seventh Marines, charged back up that hill five times in failed attempts to recapture their former position. During their sixth try, Phillips led his squad forward with bayonets fixed. When mortars began to rain down on them, the corporal raced through the barrage into the teeth of small-arms and machine gun fire. With only five Marines from his unit still standing, Phillips arrived at the crest to crawl forward through a gauntlet of enemy corpses. With his squad down to three men, Phillips charged a machine gun, blasting it clear with grenades. This final emplacement was so difficult to reach that the corporal had to climb a rocky cliff with one hand while tossing grenades with the other.

A Chinese counterattack reduced Phillips's forces to two, but the pair held on until the hill was reinforced. Corporal Phillips came away from this engagement unscathed, only to be declared missing in action three weeks later on November 27, 1950, in another engagement with the Chinese Communists. For his courageous actions on Hill 698, Corporal Lee Hugh Phillips received the Medal of Honor.

In fighting near Sudong, Staff Sergeant Archie Van Winkle, a Marine reservist from Seattle, Washington, was fighting harder than ever before. As wave after wave of Chinese soldiers attacked his position, Van Winkle led his Third Platoon, Company B, in a bold counterattack through withering fire in an attempt to halt the enemy advance toward the main Marine positions.

Staff Sergeant Archie Van Winkle

Archie Van Winkle had been attending college at the University of Washington when he was called to active duty in Korea. A former dive-bomber pilot who fought in the Solomon Islands during World War II, Van Winkle found himself assigned to the infantry in this new war. He was among the Marines who scaled the seawall at Inchon and fought house to house in the streets of Seoul. Husky and dark-haired, Van Winkle was born in Juneau, Alaska, on March 17, 1925. His family moved south so he could attend high school at Darrington, Washington. He enrolled at the University of Washington after graduation but dropped out to enlist in the Marines in December 1942. After the Second World War, Van Winkle left the Corps and returned to the University of Washington. His studies were once again interrupted by the outbreak of the Korean conflict.

On the night of November 2, Van Winkle's platoon was placed on the edge of the Marines' perimeter and were the first to face the Chinese assault. Shortly after 11:00 P.M. the platoon's forward position fell silent while the sergeant spoke to them over a sound phone. A moment later all hell broke loose as his men came under direct and sustained fire from three sides.

"Let's get out of here," he shouted to the four men remaining from his platoon. As they moved backward up a hill, a flare burst above them, illuminating the battlefield with a harsh, flickering glare.

"Don't move!" Van Winkle cried as he flung himself to the ground. When he looked up, the Marines were gone and the enemy had surrounded him. "Everywhere I looked there was a Chinaman," he said.

Van Winkle didn't even have to aim his .30-caliber machine gun—just pulling the trigger guaranteed a kill. When his ammo was gone, he used his rifle like a club, smashing Chinese until his weapon broke. After scattering the Chinese, Van Winkle gathered up as many Marines as he could find and led them in a counterattack. As they slammed into the Chinese, a bullet shattered Van Winkle's left elbow. The impact spun him to the ground. Undaunted, he rose and continued the assault, which ultimately broke the back of the Chinese advance. In a lull in the fighting, Van Winkle saw that a Marine manning a machine gun was down and surrounded by Chinese. He surged through the enemy to the wounded man's side. Taking over the machine gun, he mowed down Chinese troops until a grenade blew a hole in his shoulder and another bullet struck him in the back. Still, Van Winkle fought on, alternately firing an M-1 and a pistol when the machine gun's ammo was spent.

Finally, a Chinese grenade flew out of the darkness and struck him in the chest. It was an old potato masher, with a sputtering fuse. There was a bright flash, then pain. Dazed, Van Winkle found himself on the ground. He rose and staggered forward, but could not seem to catch his breath; the blast had broken every rib on his left side. He ordered the Marines to press on, then collapsed in their midst. While he lay unconscious and bleeding, the Chinese overran the Marines' position and then were overrun themselves in an American counterattack that came at 4:00 A.M. When the medics found Van Winkle at dawn, he was surrounded by Chinese dead. The sergeant woke up at an evacuation hospital and spent the next six months in recovering from his wounds. He was discharged from active duty in July 1951 and returned to college, with high hopes of finishing school this time. When friends in the Corps called him in January 1952 to inform him he was to receive the Medal of Honor, he thought he was the victim of a hoax. Even a follow-up telegram from the Pentagon was ignored.

Sergeant Van Winkle finally accepted his Medal of Honor on February 6, 1952—the only native of Alaska to receive this award. He returned to active duty as a second lieutenant and remained in the Marine Corps until 1974, retiring as a full colonel. He worked for the California Department of Corrections and built a fifty-five-foot boat, which he planned to sail around Alaska after he retired. On May 26, 1986, Archie Van Winkle was found dead aboard on his boat, which was moored in the harbor at Ketchikan. He had suffered a massive heart attack. Van Winkle was cremated and his ashes were scattered at sea.

Over the next two nights, the Marines beat back repeated attacks around Sudong. Several American units were overrun, but most held their ground in the face of overwhelming odds. The fighting cost the Marines 60 dead and 300 wounded. The enemy lost an estimated 800 dead before they were finally driven out of the region on November 6. The Marines continued to advance along the Chosin Reservoir's southern shore, toward Yudam-ni.

After the battle for Sudong-ni, the CCF seemed to melt away. The lull gave the Marines a chance to celebrate the 175th anniversary of the Corps on November 10—and to hell with Secretary of Defense Louis Johnson's decree to the contrary! The undeclared cease-fire lasted three weeks, during which General MacArthur made preparations for an all-out, after-Thanksgiving push to capture North Korea. The Truman Administration reluctantly went along with the scheme, and the "race to the Yalu" began. Unfortunately for General MacArthur, the Communists had made plans of their own.

"FROZEN CHOSIN"

Chosin was the Japanese name for the reservoir beyond the Funchilin Pass. Since the Marines were using Japanese maps in the Korean campaign, they called it that too. The Korean name is Changjin, but since "Chosin" rhymes with "frozen," the Japanese name seemed more appropriate to the men who fought and froze there during the brutal North Korean winter of 1950.

As Thanksgiving approached the Marines moved up the Main Supply Route in their cross-country march to link up with the Eighth Army eighty miles away. The Fifth and Seventh Marines were dispatched west of the reservoir, with an Army regimental combat team marching up the east coast of the Chosin and very close to the Manchurian border. Suddenly a winter storm blew in from Siberia and temperatures plummeted. Everything the Marines had froze solid—carbines, artillery, mortar shells, and the water in their canteens, along with their ears, noses, fingers, and toes. Cold-weather clothes were doled out, but there was not enough to go around. Medics carried vials of morphine in their mouths to keep them from freezing solid. Still the Marines pushed on, crossing the Toktong Pass on November 24 and arriving in Yudam-ni.

On November 25, the Chinese crossed the Manchurian border in force and all but annihilated the Army regiment on the west coast of the Chosin Reservoir. Scattered elements of the Army staggered toward the Marine Corps positions in the days following the invasion. Unlike the violent and abrupt clashes at Sudong, this attack was part of an all out offensive. The Communists were in it for real, and 15,000 Marines were stuck deep in North Korea with inadequate clothing, dwindling supplies, and no armor. Long-range patrols fanned out around Yudam-ni. One patrol of A Company, Seventh Marines—with First Lieutenant Frank N. Mitchell's platoon on point—were approaching the village of Hansan-ni along a narrow, snow-covered ridgeline. When they were most exposed at the top of the ridge, they were hit at close range by sustained enemy fire.

Marines fell, wounded or dead, and Lieutenant Mitchell was hit. Bleeding, the officer grabbed a BAR from a dying Marine and returned fire. When the ammunition was exhausted, Mitchell tossed the BAR aside and took up his bayonet. In brutal hand-to-hand combat, the lieutenant and the surviving Marines of his platoon repulsed the attack. Fighting around the village continued and Mitchell retreated— only to return leading a team of litter bearers to rescue the wounded. As the casualties were withdrawn, Lieutenant Mitchell covered their retreat. When last seen by his fellow Marines, he was firing away at the oncoming Chinese soldiers.

For his courage that night, First Lieutenant Frank Nicias Mitchell of Indian Gap, Texas, received the Medal of Honor. It was presented to his wife, Beverly, and his daughter, Barbara. The body of the twenty-nine-year-old was never recovered and Mitchell is still listed as missing-in-action.

After swarming across the Manchurian border, Red Chinese General Sung Shin-lun—commanding 120,000 troops of the Ninth Army Group—headed straight for the United States Marines. The Americans were strung out in a thin line along forty miles of bad roads; their Main Supply Route had become a trap and General Shin-lun, one of China's greatest military leaders, was ready to spring it shut and trap the Marines.

On the night of November 27, in a blinding winter storm and in temperatures of twenty below zero, tens of thousands of Chinese soldiers descended on the Marines from their staging area in the Taeback Mountains. Green flares burst in the sky and the sound of bugles filled the night as screaming Chinese troops rushed into the teeth of American guns. Though many outposts were overrun by the crushing human wave of Red Chinese regulars, the Marines fought back at several strategic positions, forcing the enemy to withdraw.

At Yudam-ni, the Marines counterattacked at dawn on the twenty-eighth. Their goal was Hill 1282. After a murderous hand-to-hand fight, they reached the summit by midmorning—in time to annihilate a Chinese company advancing up the opposite slope. But the situation was critical. Enemy troops were massing for an attack on the Main Supply Route, and the Chinese occupied Hill 1403. From there they could command the road and enfilade the entire valley. At another point along Northwest Ridge, E and F Companies of the Fifth Marines still held out. Though their position was surrounded by 500 Chinese dead, more enemy troops were on the way.

C and F Companies, Seventh Marines, were also under siege. C Company was trapped on Hill 1419, F Company was stuck on Fox Hill. Both units were threatened with destruction if they were not rescued. On the twenty-eighth, A Company fought a five-hour running battle with the Chinese in an effort to rescue C Company. They made it to within a mile of Hill 1419 but were stopped cold by a superior force. B Company, led by Lieutenant Colonel Raymond G. Davis, got close enough to the enemy to call in an air strike and mortar fire, which routed the Chinese. But in the next few days the Chinese would threaten Hagaru-ri, cut the Main Supply Route at a dozen places, and come close to annihilating the U.S. Army elements trapped along the shores of Chosin Reservoir. Even worse, Toktong Pass—the only means of retreat for the trapped regiments—was threatened. If the pass was captured, there would be no escape for the Americans. In the face of these sudden Chinese attacks, Marine Corps units all along the Main Supply Road and those trapped near Chosin Reservoir were in disarray. As the Chinese continued to pour across the Manchurian border, only one thing was certain—MacArthur's "race to the Yalu River" was over.

FOUR HEROES OF TOKTONG PASS

The battle on Fox Hill began at 2:30 A.M., November 28, when the Chinese hit Company F, composed mostly of Marine reservists assigned the task of guarding Toktong Pass. F Company was commanded by Captain William Earl Barber, who had been in charge for less than a week before he received orders to climb Fox and secure the pass. A native of Denhart, Kentucky, Barber played baseball and basketball at Morehead State Teachers' College before joining the Marine Corps in March 1940. After basic training at Parris Island, he volunteered to attend airborne training and become a paramarine. Though he never used his parachute training in actual combat—no Marine ever did—Barber saw action on Iwo Jima, where he earned the Silver Star and a Purple Heart.

Barber had led his company up Fox Hill at 9:00 P.M. A full moon illuminated the clear, crisp night as the Marines scraped foxholes into the frozen ground, established machine-gun positions, and ranged their mortars. As F Company settled into their sleeping bags at midnight, they could not know that they were encircled and trapped—cut off by a large force that had moved down from another hill and severed

Captain William E. Barber

the Main Supply Route, the Americans' only avenue of retreat. At 2:30 A.M., a Marine at an outpost on the outer perimeter heard a strange sound, like footsteps crushing popcorn. It was the sound of Chinese boots crunching through the ice-crusted snow. A company of Chinese regulars were approaching the Americans from less than a hundred yards away. The shooting started instantly. In the initial exchange fifteen of the thirty-five Marines manning that remote outpost were killed, another nine wounded. The survivors rose from cover to meet the enemy that closed on them with bayonets. Three more Americans died, and the eight survivors withdrew to their main position.

Captain Barber spotted a column of Chinese regulars as they broke from cover and charged his command post, tossing grenades and firing burp guns as the came. Barber rallied his staff of clerks, radiomen, and technicians and they repulsed the attack, sustaining a few casualties. At F Company's right flank was twenty-one-year-old Private Hector Cafferata, a tough youth from Montville, New Jersey. He was sleeping in his bedroll when he heard shooting. Before he glimpsed the enemy, bullets ripped through the Marines on either side of him. Suddenly Cafferata was the only man from his squad still standing. He fired into the human wave that charged his position.

When his carbine was empty, Cafferata dived into a foxhole. He began tossing grenades while a wounded Marine reloaded his rifle. Then he rose and began firing, shooting methodically and utilizing the marksmanship skills drilled into him by the Marine Corps. Cafferata killed eight Chinese with the eight rounds before dropping to the ground to reload. Suddenly a grenade landed in the foxhole. Cafferata scooped it up and tossed it back. The missile detonated, blasting six more enemy troops. Two more grenades landed beside him. He tossed away the first, but the second grenade exploded as it left his hand. Cafferata's finger was blown off and shrapnel tore through his arm. He fought on, defending his position. Later that night, Private Cafferata would be wounded in the arm a second time.

At dawn the Chinese pulled back, fearful that Corsairs would swoop down on them, dropping napalm. Captain Barber called for just such a strike, then collected the wounded. One of them was Private Cafferata. A corpsman noticed that the private's feet were swollen and blue.

"Where's your boots?" the medic asked. Only then did Cafferata realize he'd fought through bitter cold and ankle-deep snow in his bare feet.

With daylight came an airdrop of badly needed supplies. His commanders suggested Barber relinquish his position, but the captain refused. He knew that if he abandoned Toktong Pass, the Marines at Yudam-ni and beyond would be cut off with no hope of escape. He also knew that his dwindling force could not retreat carrying fifty wounded men—leaving Marines behind was not an option. So as darkness fell, Captain Barber and F Company waited for another attack. It came at 2:00 A.M., prefaced by a mortar barrage. The artillery was ineffective, and when the Chinese attacked, F Company butchered the first wave. But the second wave came in screaming and broke through the American perimeter. Captain Barber rushed into the breach, rallying his Marines. When the flank was secure, the center threatened to cave, so Barber rushed forward again, only to be wounded in the leg. Barber stuffed a

Private Hector A. Cafferata, Jr.

handkerchief into the hole. The frigid air froze the blood and sealed the wound. The rising sun revealed 200 enemy dead around the Marines' perimeter. Barber lost another five killed and thirty wounded. He worried that a third night of fighting would finish his company for good. It was November 30—Captain Barber's thirty-first birthday. He was certain it would be his last.

The Chinese returned at midnight, charging up the hill to the sound of bugles. They didn't even try to surprise the Americans. F Company unleashed their mortars, dropping a curtain of smoke, fire, hot shrapnel, and sudden death on the advancing enemy. From his original 240 Marines, Barber had fewer than 90 left. He placed them in a thin line along his perimeter, then organized an assault squad to stick by his side. When the Chinese broke through, Barber led this squad forward to reinforce the weakened position. They did this several times, usually arriving just in time to throw the Chinese back. Finally, as Barber moved to plug another gap, he was shot in the leg again. This time the captain went down and didn't get up. His wound was so severe that he could not stand, so a stretcher was brought up and he was loaded onto it. As medics worked on him, Barber still shouted commands to his harried Marines. At dawn Fox Hill was still in American hands—but barely.

While F Company battled to hold Toktong Pass, the American evacuation of Yudam-ni began. Part of the organized retreat included the rescue of Barber's company, but no one knew when help would arrive.

As the breakout from Yudam-ni began, the Chinese unleashed mortar and small-arms fire on the Americans. The CCF were ensconced in the surrounding hills and

Staff Sergeant William G. Windrich   *Lieutenant Colonel Raymond G. Davis*

fired on the retreating Marines from either side of the Main Supply Route. A company was dispatched to capture each hill. The Marines on the left took their objective and silenced the mortars with relative ease, but the Marines on the right found themselves facing stiff resistance. I Company, Third Battalion, Fifth Marines, was cut to pieces by crossfire from high ground. Before the men could deploy, the Chinese attacked. The Marines pushed them back, only to face a mortar barrage. For ten minutes mortar shells blasted rock and snow and men. Then the barrage lifted and the Chinese attacked again.

Twenty-nine-year-old Staff Sergeant William G. Windrich led a squad forward to plug a gap in the line. They slammed into a determined Chinese charge. Seven of Windrich's eleven men fell wounded in the first moments, and an enemy grenade detonated near the sergeant, wounding him in the head. Despite suffering from intense pain, Windrich raced back to the command post to gather volunteers to help him evacuate the wounded. Leading the volunteers forward, Windrich was shot in the legs by Chinese snipers. Unable to move, the sergeant provided cover fire as the casualties were evacuated. For over an hour the East Chicago native poured withering fire on the enemy, keeping them at bay. Twice he refused aid, directing the corpsmen to tend others. At last Sergeant Windrich succumbed to loss of blood. He died slumped over his rifle. His widow and young daughter received his posthumous Medal of Honor.

While the Marines fought to clear the Main Supply Route, Lieutenant Colonel Raymond G. Davis pushed his First Battalion, Seventh Marines, on a cross-country march to rescue Barber and C Company. In a single day—December 1—Davis stripped his men down to "fighting trim." Realizing that the march would be hard and his unit would be fighting the whole way, Davis had his Marines jettison all heavy weapons except for two mortars and six .30-caliber machine guns. Each Marine carried one mortar round in addition to his personal ammunition, and the heavy machine guns were hoisted onto stretchers and carried into action. All personal gear with the exception of sleeping bags was loaded onto trucks, and four meals of rations were doled out to each Marine. After culling the sick and weak, Davis was in command of the toughest Marine Corps outfit in Korea.

Born in Fitzgerald, Georgia, in 1915, the forty-five-year-old Davis had joined the Corps in 1938 after graduating high school in Atlanta and attending the Georgia School of Technology, where he earned a degree in chemical engineering. By 1942, Davis was commanding an antiaircraft battery at Guadalcanal. As a major, he led the First Battalion, First Marines, First Marine Division, onto the beachhead at Peleliu. His exceptional bravery in the face of a *banzai* charge earned Major Davis a Navy Cross.

His first objective on this march was a peak on the east side of the Main Supply Route dubbed "Turkey Hill" because the Marines had enjoyed a hot Thanksgiving dinner on its crest. Turkey Hill fell to the Marines without incident, and at 9:00 P.M. Davis decided to press on to Fox Hill despite the darkness and bitter cold. Following a star in the eastern sky, his battalion entered an area swarming with enemy troops. As they slogged through knee-deep snow across a barren meadow, Chinese snipers began picking them off. Davis deployed his mortars and divided his battalion into two assault columns. Soon mortar shells were dropping among the Chinese. As each Marine walked past the mortar, he dropped the single shell he carried down the tube. Then the Marines charged a hill occupied by hundreds of enemy troops. Their attack was so swift it caught many Chinese in their sleep. They were butchered where they lay.

At 2:00 A.M. they clashed with another force, which was quickly annihilated. At 3:00 A.M. Davis ordered his exhausted battalion to dig in and get some rest. That same night Barber and F Company waited for an attack that never came. They could not know that the enemy was now concentrating on the rescue force, satisfied that Barber's surrounded unit wasn't leaving anytime soon. While his men slept, Davis reconnoitered the ground ahead, refusing to rest until he rescued Barber's unit. But the strain of command was taking its toll on the major. While issuing orders, Davis would stop talking in midsentence, forgetting just what he was going to say. He had not slept in over thirty-six hours.

When Davis got his men moving again, they marched through a thousand yards of hilly ground without being fired upon. The lull in the fighting ended when B Company was hit by a large Chinese force. Luckily, Major Davis was close to Barber and the two officers were talking over the radio. Barber directed an air strike against the Chinese who attacked Davis's battalion. The planes arrived and the Chinese scattered. At 11:25 A.M., the first of Davis's Marines reached Barber's perimeter. Reinforced and resupplied, they waited for relief. At noon on December 3, the Marines moving down Toktong Pass from Yudam-ni joined with Barber and Davis's shattered units. Over the next twenty-four hours, the bulk of the Yudam-ni garrison arrived in

Hagaru-ri. The crisis had passed and Captain Barber was evacuated with the wounded on December 5. He remained hospitalized until March of 1951. Then he was transferred to San Diego, where he served as a recruitment officer. He received a promotion to major and was summoned to the White House on August 26, 1952, and presented with the Medal of Honor. As a colonel, Barber retired from the Marine Corps in 1970 to accept a job in the aerospace industry.

After the rescue, Davis was promoted. But when Lieutenant Colonel Davis was informed he had been recommended for a Medal of Honor, he objected. He didn't think he deserved one and said so. Then a fire at First Marine Division headquarters destroyed his citation papers and all the documents pertaining to the action. Only intervention by Marine Corps General Victor Krulak resurrected the paperwork and Davis received the Medal of Honor on November 26, 1952. In 1988, Raymond Davis received another honor—President Ronald Reagan tapped him to head the National Korean War Veterans Memorial Commission.

As 1950 came to a close, the First and Seventh Marine Regiments were camped at Hagaru-ri and threatened by a hundred thousand Chinese Communists determined to destroy them. To escape they would have to fight their way out. No one was going home this Christmas.

BREAKOUT AT CHOSIN

With two Marine Corps regiments trapped in North Korea and the MSR blocked at a dozen places, the United States Army Corps commander, General Edward Almond, urged Marine Corps General Oliver P. Smith to abandon his equipment and his dead at Hagaru-ri and evacuate North Korea by airplane. Smith wouldn't have it. "We'll fight our way out as Marines," he insisted, "bringing all our weapons and equipment and gear with us."

Smith was confident he could get his Marines out without an air evacuation that looked more like a rout. But a sudden push by the Chinese threw the Americans off East Hill, which overlooked the valley and the town. From East Hill the Chinese could fire artillery into the middle of the Marine base in Hagaru-ri. Something had to be done. On November 29, Major Reginald Myers of Boise, Idaho, assembled a rag-tag unit of 250 Army, Marine, and ROK soldiers and attacked East Hill. The peak was now occupied by 4,000 Communist troops armed with machine guns, mortars, and small arms, and artillery was on the way.

Myers had been a Marine for ten years before he got the orders to attack East Hill from Lieutenant Colonel Thomas Ridge, his CO. Myers graduated high school in Salt Lake City, then attended the University of Idaho. With a degree in mechanical engineering and a ROTC commission, he transferred to the Marine Corps in September 1941 and spent most of the Second World War aboard various ships as a seagoing Marine. Myers was promoted and transferred to the First Marine Division. He fought at Okinawa and was part of the occupation forces in northern China. He earned two Bronze Stars for street fighting in Seoul.

Myers led his small force through darkness, a steady snowfall, and twenty-below-zero temperatures to a position at the base of East Hill, where they found some of the original defenders. Myers organized his ragtag force of 300 into something resembling a skirmish line. Ice and snow made the advance up the steep hill difficult and it took an hour to make it to the first ledge. From there they could see the enemy position beyond several gaps in the rocks. At Myers's command they charged.

Major Reginald R. Myers

The Americans advanced, dodging bullets, mortar bursts, and snipers. Many fell in the initial charge and more were hit as they moved through the gaps. As the sun rose, the Marines were silhouetted in the glare. When Myers's team made it to the crest, there were fewer than eighty men left. Grenades rained down from the heights and more Marines died in the bloodstained snow. Reluctantly, Myers ordered a retreat. Their bold counterattack in the face of superior odds had failed to dislodge the enemy, but bought some time for the Americans to reorganize their own emplacements in the valley below. At 9:30 A.M. Corsairs dived out of the overcast sky and burned East Hill with napalm, then the Marines advanced again. Each time the Americans neared the summit, they were thrown back. Reinforcements arrived, but usually in twos and threes. As night fell, Myers doubted his exhausted force could survive a Chinese counterattack. He decided to hold, but believed it was a suicidal gesture. He could not know that relief was on the way.

Colonel "Chesty" Puller assembled a 900-man force to fight their way to Hagaru-ri, climb East Hill, and attack in force. It was a mixed unit—250 were British, from the 41st Royal Marine Commandos under Lieutenant Colonel Donald Drysdale. Behind them were the U.S. Marines, Company G, the Third Rifle Company, under Captain Carl L. Sitter. Sitter was born in Syracuse, Missouri, on December 2, 1921, and enlisted in the Corps in June 1940 after completing high school in Pueblo, Colorado. He served in Iceland, then moved on to the Pacific, where he fought at Eniwetok and was wounded on February 20, 1944. He recovered and was sent to Guam, where he was wounded a second time.

The move to Hagaru-ri was slow and bloody. Fourteen Marines fell in the first hour. Sitter counterattacked, butchering forty Chinese regulars. But now it was noon and Sitter's command had not yet advanced two miles. Drysdale and Sitter decided to load their men onto trucks and literally crash through the Chinese, running a gauntlet of enemy emplacements as fast as they could. They advanced three miles in two hours using this method—better than before, but still slow. Time and time again the

Captain Carl L. Sitter

Chinese would stop the column. Then Sitter's Marines would pile out of the trucks, charge the enemy, then return to the truck for the ride to the next engagement. Soon "Task Force Drysdale" was stretched out over five miles, with trucks shattered by enemy fire delaying the advance. Mortars rained down on them. Machine gun fire riddled Sitter's jeep and killed his driver. Still they fought on, until Captain Sitter could see the lights of Hagaru-ri shimmering in the distance. At 9:00 P.M.—twelve hours after his men began the eleven-mile trek to Hagaru-ri—the battered remnants of Captain Sitter's command limped into town. Of his original 270-man detachment, fewer than 160 were alive. Lieutenant Colonel Drysdale arrived an hour later with less than half of his 250-man commando unit. They still had a job to do. Myers was on East Hill, waiting for reinforcements. Sitter let his men sleep, then roused them at dawn, divided his company into two assault elements, with a third in reserve. Then they advanced up the hill until they linked with Myers's command.

Fighting every step of the way, Company G blasted their way up the slope in the face of heavy fire. Halfway to the summit, Captain Sitter came to the same realization that Myers had come to two days before—to advance in the teeth of the entrenched enemy was suicide. He pulled back and dug in. It was five o'clock in the afternoon and the Marines commanded two-thirds of East Hill. For three hours all was quiet. Then the Marines heard the bugles. Green flares lit the sky as the Chinese poured down from the crest of the hill. The Americans responded with mortars and machine guns—exacting a terrible toll. Still the enemy came, in wave after wave, threatening to overrun the Americans. As Sitter called for artillery support, a mortar shell erupted close by and shrapnel ripped through his chest and face.

As the enemy raced through a break in the defenses, a Chinese soldier leapt out of the darkness and tossed a grenade at Sitter, who was wounded again. At 3:00 A.M. the Chinese pulled back, only to attack again at four. As the sun rose on December 5, Captain Sitter and Major Myers were relieved by elements of the Fifth Marines recently arrived from Yudam-ni. Only ninety-six men survived. By December 9, the Fifth Marines had cleared the enemy from East Hill in a battle that raged many hours. Securing East Hill opened the back door and the first Americans began to move out of Hagaru-ri next morning. In time, 10,000 troops and 1,000 vehicles would pour through the town on their way south, to safety. Both Myers and Sitter survived the march south. For their remarkable leadership in the face of superior odds, the two

Marines received the Medal of Honor in a double ceremony at the White House on October 29, 1951. Major Myers survived the war to rise to the rank of colonel. Captain Sitter remained in the Corps until 1970, when he retired a colonel. For Carl Sitter retirement meant starting a string of new careers. When he passed away on April 8, 2000, he was a seventy-seven-year-old divinity student at Union Theological Seminary.

On December 9, the advance elements of the First Marine Division linked up with the Army's Third Infantry Division on the Main Supply Route. For the next three days they moved south, bringing out the wounded and dead and even some prisoners. Along with the Americans, over 100,000 Korean refugees moved along the MSR, desperate to escape the Communists. Frostbite, enemy fire, exhaustion, sickness, and malnutrition took their toll, but the Marines pressed on until their retreat from North Korea began to resemble a victory.

"We're not retreating," Major General Oliver Smith insisted. "We're simply attacking in another direction."

The Americans and the refugees reached the port of Hugnam, where they boarded hundreds of ships even as United Nations aircraft bombed the Chinese surrounding the city. When the last ship sailed on Christmas Eve, Army and Marine demolition teams leveled the harbor and destroyed their abandoned equipment and supplies. They left Hugnam a smoldering ruin.

The Marines had suffered 4,400 casualties in the Chosin breakout, including 730 dead. There were uncounted thousands of painful and debilitating frostbite cases. Men lost ears, fingers, toes, hands, feet, and even limbs. The North Koreans and their Chinese allies once again controlled North Korea and would soon move to recapture Seoul. The formidable public relations machine that Truman compared to Stalin's must have taken the Christmas holidays off, because the U.S. media was not kind to the Marine Corps following their retreat: "America's worst military licking since Pearl Harbor," said *Newsweek*. "The worst defeat the United States ever suffered," *Time* magazine proclaimed. General Douglas MacArthur tried to put a more positive spin on events. "This was undoubtedly one of the most successful strategic retreats in history," he said. "Comparable with and markedly similar to Wellington's great Peninsula withdrawal."

THE SEESAW WAR

After securing the Pusan Perimeter and the successful landing at Inchon, after their hard-fought victory in Seoul and their advance north, the Marines found themselves out of the war for the next few months. Many rested in Masan, far from the front, where they watched with frustration as a Communist offensive launched on New Year's Eve broke through the U.N.'s lines and recaptured much of the territory the Marines had fought so hard to retake. Again there was an ignominious retreat from Seoul before the city fell. The gains of the first six months of the war were erased overnight.

In February 1951, Puller's First Marines were deployed to a line of hills north of

Hoengsong as part of an operation called Killer. They crossed the Sum River with a bridge they concocted from timber and telephone wire, then occupied a position north of Hoengsong. Operation Killer was followed by Ripper, which began in March, and Rugged in April. These thrusts were meant to push back the Chinese, but each of them suffered setbacks. It rained constantly. The roads were muddy, the streams flooded. Though the Chinese retreated before the advancing Marines, there were clashes—mostly in the hills. On April 4, the Seventh Marines was among the Eighth Army units to re-cross the thirty-eighth Parallel. The Marines were probing an area called The Iron Triangle, where the Chinese were massing for another offensive.

On April 11, President Truman fired General MacArthur. Their mutual animosity had been growing for some time and the general was blamed for dismantling a cease-fire arranged by Truman back on March 24. MacArthur never trusted the Chinese or their diplomatic overtures, and the "peace talks" in Kaesong proved him right. Unfortunately, the general made some public statements that the commander in chief found insubordinate, including the suggestion that Nationalist Chinese troops be used against the North Koreans and their Communist Chinese allies. Such a move, in Truman's eyes, would have provoked World War III, so MacArthur was given the boot.

When Douglas MacArthur was relieved of his command, the Marines lost their greatest ally. The new commander of the Eighth Army, Lieutenant General Matthew B. Ridgeway, was not inclined to indulge the Marine Corps and quickly relegated the Marines in Korea to the status of "just another division." With that loss of status came a loss of Marine Corps close air support. All requests for air strikes now had to be made through the Air Force high command, which absorbed Marine Corps squadron operations. The move was supposed to streamline command structure, but proved to be a disastrous policy for the Marines, who depended on their "flying artillery" in a catfight. Before the change Marines waited fifteen or twenty minutes for air support to arrive. But with the Fifth Air Force in charge of the skies, the Marines waited up to an hour and a half for air strikes—if they came at all.

With public opinion turning against the war, U.S. military strategy grew increasingly conservative. No more bold strikes like the Inchon landings loomed on the horizon. Instead, the United Nations forces were content to push the NKPA back across the thirty-eighth Parallel while sustaining as few casualties as possible. In the weeks ahead, Seoul would be recaptured by the United States Army and the thirty-eighth Parallel would be crossed at a half dozen places. But soon the Korean conflict bogged down until it resembled the stagnant situation in France during the First World War. This long outpost war would be fought unit by unit, day after day, across the same bloodstained ground—a seesaw war where one side was up while the other was down, but neither could gain a significant edge or defeat the other. Under the restrictive rules of engagement, no victory was possible. The best result would be a truce or an armistice. More Marines became casualties in this fifteen-month stalemate than in the all-out fighting of the first months.

As the U.N. forces fought the Communists to a standstill a political solution was sought. Jacob Malik, the Soviet Union's delegate to the U.N., proposed talks in mid-March 1951. A few days later the Chinese agreed and talks were scheduled to begin in Kaesong. Meanwhile, more men died.

On the night of April 22, as the Eighth Army advanced toward the Iron Triangle, the Chinese struck back: 250,000 Chinese regulars crossed a forty-mile frontier in what became their spring offensive. The Republic of Korea's Sixth Division crumbled and Marine Corps units were rushed to the front by truck to plug a large gap through which the enemy was advancing. Fighting was heavy along the perimeter, but the left flank—where the First Battalion, Seventh Marines, was posted—faced the stiffest resistance. In a furious, three-hour battle the Chinese broke through, only to be halted as reserves from Lieutenant Colonel Robley E. West's First Battalion, First Marines, shored up the shattered defenses. With dawn came an air strike—the Marine Corps aviators were still working closely with the Leathernecks at this point—and the Marines used the bombing as an oppor-

Sergeant Harold E. Wilson

tunity to fall back to a position near the Hwachon Reservoir.

At 8:00 P.M., April 23, the Chinese attacked Captain Wray's C Company, First Marines, as they occupied a piece of high ground called Horseshoe Ridge. The charge was concentrated and relentless as wave after wave of Chinese troops assaulted the entrenched Marines for four hours. At the center of this desperate fight, on the crest of Hill 902, was a twenty-nine-year-old technical sergeant named Harold E. Wilson. Wilson was from Birmingham, Alabama, and had worked at a steel mill before joining the Marine Corps in 1942. He spent twenty-two months on Midway Island during the Pacific War, was sent home after VJ day, pumped gas, worked in a railyard, and was recalled to duty for Korea. Now, as his position was close to being overrun, Sergeant Wilson led his platoon in the fight of their lives. Wounded repeatedly, with his right arm and left leg injured, he was unable to hold a rifle, so he resupplied his men with ammunition taken from the dead. At 2:00 A.M., a mortar round exploded at Sergeant Wilson's feet. He was knocked to the ground but rose again. Dazed and suffering from a concussion, Wilson fought on, refusing medical aid. He lived up to his nickname "Speedy," limping from foxhole to foxhole, hauling weapons and ammunition and directing fire. At dawn, with the help of Marine and Army reinforcements, the final assault was repulsed.

Only after Sergeant Wilson accounted for every one of the men in his platoon did he walk to the aid station. On April 30, while Wilson was in an evacuation hospital, he heard the news that the Chinese offensive had been stopped and the enemy suffered over 70,000 casualties. For his valor that night and the following day, Harold

Edward Wilson received the Medal of Honor in a White House ceremony. Wilson remained in the Corps, served in Vietnam, and retired as a chief warrant officer in 1972. As a civilian, Wilson worked as a benefits counselor for the Veterans Administration. He was a modest man, and few who knew him were familiar with his illustrious past. One former Marine and fellow member of the Marine Corps League knew Wilson for six months before he found out his comrade had received the Medal of Honor. Harold Wilson—the sergeant his men called "Speedy"—passed away in April 1998 at the age of seventy-six.

After the Communists' spring offensive petered out, the combatants faced one another along a rugged, heavily armed frontier. Few advances were made by either side, but during one push across the rugged terrain leading to Hill 1316, a bloody engagement erupted. The area was studded with enemy pillboxes and defensive positions. As Lieutenant Colonel Robley West's First Battalion experienced some of the hardest fighting of the campaign, nineteen-year-old fire-team leader Corporal Charles G. Abrell of Terre Haute, Indiana, was wounded three times before he made a solo attack on an armed bunker. Bursting into the enemy emplacement, Abrell was shot several more times. Clutching a live grenade to his chest, he dived among the enemy, killing the gun crew and himself. Charles Gene Abrell received a posthumous Medal of Honor, presented to his mother by Dan A. Kimball, secretary of the navy, on September 4, 1952.

The seesaw war continued until the Communist delegates walked out of the truce talks in Kaesong on August 22, 1951. The talks had been a humiliating disaster from the start. The Communists seemed more interesting in embarrassing the United Nations delegates than in negotiating a mutually agreeable truce. On the first day, when the delegates were helicoptered into Kaesong, they were driven to the site of the talks in captured U.S. Army jeeps festooned with white flags. The Chinese attitude at the table was condescending and arrogant and their demands unrealistic. They cared not a whit for their own losses, only in making the international community squirm. Despite the dubious nature of the discussions, the United Nations felt compelled to pressure the Chinese and North Koreans back to the negotiating table, so the war heated up again. What followed the breakdown of peace talks was the final Marine Corps mobile assault of the Korean War.

On August 27, the Seventh Marines and a detachment of Korean Marine Corps were ordered into battle. Composed of new replacements, with a smattering of Chosin veterans, the Seventh moved through driving rain to attack several strong points at Yoke Ridge. A four-day battle ensued on Hills 924, 602, and 1026. As the Marines moved deeper into the Korean highlands, their supply line was increasingly strained, while the enemy seemed to have more matériel than ever. The Communists were well armed with artillery, mortars, and machine guns. On September 11, after a six-day delay to move up ammunition and supplies, the Seventh Marines resumed their offensive, moving to seize Hills 673 and 749—the first stop in the capture of Kanmubong Ridge. Heavy fire from mortars and machine guns halted the ascent of Hill 680, and the Marines were twice driven back. The Third Platoon, I Company, led by thirty-four-year-old Second Lieutenant George H. Ramer of Meyersdale, Pennsylvania, nearly made it to the summit. Despite wounds, and the loss of many of his men, Ramer wiped out a North Korean bunker. When the enemy counterattacked, the Marines were swept off the crest. Lieutenant Ramer covered their retreat until he was killed.

Across the valley, the First Battalion assaulted Hill 673. Sergeant Frederick W. Mausert III of Cambridge, New York, rescued two wounded Marines under intense enemy fire. Though wounded in the head, he led his men on a bayonet charge against a bunker and wiped out the gun crew. Still advancing, Mausert attacked another bunker and destroyed another machine gun nest before he fell in a hail of bullets. He was twenty-four years old.

Two days later, on September 14, a Chinese counterattack was launched to drive the Second Battalion off Hill 749. The Marines were depleted from days of fighting, but they still managed to repulse wave after wave of attackers. As

Corporal Joseph Vittori

casualties mounted on both sides, Corporal Joseph Vittori, a twenty-two-year-old BAR man from F Company, led a three-man counterattack. Leaping from one foxhole to the next in order to lay concentrated fire on the enemy, Vittori reached a machine gun just as its gunner was struck down. Manning the gun himself, the Beverly, Massachusetts, native massacred a human wave that charged his perimeter. During this all-night engagement, Corporal Vittori made repeated trips through heavy artillery to bring up ammunition. When a shell detonated near him, the young corporal was mortally wounded. Next morning, the Marines on Hill 749 were reinforced and swept the area of enemy troops. The four-day battle for that hill cost the Marines 90 men, with over 700 wounded. Ramer, Mausert, and Vittori received Medals of Honor—posthumously.

On September 20, 1951, the Marine Corps offensive was called off because of the high casualty rate and because it had failed to push back the enemy. Both sides settled in for what was to become known as the "outpost war"—twenty-two months of static conflict punctuated by short, furious bouts of vicious localized combat.

THE LONG OUTPOST WAR

When the war stagnated, the Marines occupied a 13-mile section of the 125-mile front, stretching from the circular valley called the Punchbowl eastward to the I Republic of Korea Corps, which guarded the coast. On October 25, 1951, negotia-

Corporal David B. Champagne   **Private John D. Kelly**

tions for a truce were resumed, this time at a town just south of the thirty-eighth Parallel called Panmunjom. By November 27, a temporary cease-fire was agreed upon, but the lull in the fighting did not last long. By January 1952, the Marine Corps division was fighting a sustained trench war, with snipers firing at them by day and attacks by night. The Marines received some better equipment, including lightweight thermal boots and armored vests. But what they needed was a better war.

At the end of March, the Marine division was shifted to the extreme western portion of Korea, replacing the First ROK Division at the Imjin River, a vital crossing point for any attack against Seoul. The Marines occupied a thirty-two-mile stretch of the so-called Jamestown Line. The landscape was composed of coastal lowlands, with hills and valleys to the northeast. The Marine Corps sector of operation started on the Kimpo Peninsula in the west, crossed the Han River and ran along the Imjin. The Corps line ended at the Samichon River. Across the thirty-eighth Parallel the Marines faced the 65th and 63rd Chinese Armies, not the NKPA. The Marines would stay here for the rest of the war.

Spring brought no increase in violence, though the Marines and the Chinese pounded each other with artillery barrages by day and probed each other's lines at night. Then, on the night of April 15, the Chinese assaulted Outpost 3, a high hill occupied by a platoon from E Company, Fifth Marines. Corporal Duane E. Dewey of Grand Rapids, Michigan, smothered a grenade that landed in his position. Dewey was lucky and survived to receive a Medal of Honor from the new president, former Army General Dwight D. Eisenhower.

By the end of that month the Marine front had been extended farther, and the defensive lines were replaced with fortified forward outposts and remote listening posts. May brought a new commander of the Korean forces when Army General Mark W. Clark replaced General Ridgeway. Clark began a war of attrition, sending U.N. aircraft over North Korea and China to bomb hydroelectric plants and industrial targets. The strike against the Suiho plant on the shore of the Yalu knocked out electricity in much of North Korea for two weeks. The air war was heating up.

On the ground the Marines sent daily patrols to scour the no-man's-land between the two dug-in armies. On May 28, the First Battalion was dispatched to seize Hill 104 and Tumae-ri Ridge. C Company, on the left flank, became embroiled in a hand-to-hand fight with Chinese regulars and Second Lieutenant John J. Donahue led a platoon from A Company in taking the ridge by bayonet point. Two Marines received posthumous Medals of Honor for this action—Corporal David B. Champagne, an aspiring actor from Wakefield, Rhode Island, died trying to toss a Chinese grenade back at the enemy; Private First Class John D. Kelly, who was raised in Homestead, Pennsylvania, a steel town outside of Pittsburgh, joined the hand-to-hand fighting with the rest of his comrades during the assault on Tumae-ri Ridge. Kelly personally wiped out a Chinese emplacement and killed two machine gunners, then attacked a bunker that was decimating his unit. Kelly was wounded in this second assault, but managed to silence the machine gun, killing three more enemy soldiers. Then he was mortally wounded trying to destroy a third bunker. His Medal of Honor was presented to his mother by Vice President Richard M. Nixon.

In June, the Chinese staged an attack on Outpost Yoke, killing nine Marines and overrunning the position. Artillery and a brisk counterattack drove the Chinese back across the border. On July 2, G Company, Seventh Marines were surprised by a Chinese battalion near Outpost Yoke. Many Marines were wounded in the first exchange of fire. Staff Sergeant William E. Shuck, Jr., led his machine-gun team and a rifle squad up the hill and was wounded himself. Resistance was too heavy for his meager forces, and the sergeant was ordered to withdraw. Shuck made sure all the wounded and the dead were evacuated, but was struck by a sniper bullet as the last of the Marines pulled back bearing the final casualty. Shuck and four other Marines were killed in this uneven clash, and Shuck, a native of Cumberland, Maryland, received a posthumous Medal of Honor for covering the retreat. The award was presented to his widow by Vice President Richard M. Nixon at the Marine Corps barracks in Washington. Outpost Yoke remained hotly contested throughout the month of July. C Company recaptured the position, but was driven back with horrendous casualties by a Chinese artillery bombardment.

The next engagement was the infamous Battle of Bunker Hill, or Hill 122, which began on August 9 when a Chinese assault forced a squad of Marines from E Company, the First, off 122 and onto Hill 58A. Because Hill 122 was close to the Main Supply Route, it had enough strategic value to call for a counterattack. Over the next four days, Hill 122 was captured and lost a half-dozen times—with heavy casualties on both sides. The struggle for Bunker Hill lasted throughout August and became the subject of debate among the Joint Chiefs and the general staff. With Marine casualties at 50 dead and 313 wounded, the entire operation was roundly criticized.

Private Fernando L. Garcia

Three outposts fell to the Chinese in short order during the month of August. These were provisional outposts manned only in daylight. The enemy captured them during nighttime probes while the Marines pulled back to their own lines. On August 17, when the Marines moved forward at dawn to reoccupy Outpost Irene, they found the Chinese waiting for them. In the ensuing firefight the Marines were outgunned and outmanned and withdrew. It was during this aborted mission that Private First Class Robert E. Simnanek threw himself over a grenade. The Detroit, Michigan, native survived to receive a Medal of Honor from President Dwight D. Eisenhower.

On September 5, during another Chinese night assault on Bunker Hill, a United States Navy corpsman and two Marines earned Medals of Honor. Private First Class Fernando L. Garcia of San Juan, Puerto Rico, threw himself on a grenade to save his sergeant's life. His award was posthumous. Corpsman Edward C. Benfold of Staten Island, New York, moved forward to check on the condition of two Marines wounded and lying in a shell crater. As he climbed down, the Chinese tossed two grenades into the pit. Benfold snatched them up, charged the enemy, and thrust the grenades into the bellies of two Chinese soldiers. The explosion killed the Chinese and mortally wounded Benfold. His Medal of Honor was presented to his son. Private First Class Alford L. McLaughlin was a machine gunner from Leeds, Alabama, who was wounded in the initial Chinese assault. Firing two machine-guns from his hip until his hands were blistered, he defended his position in plain sight of the enemy. Wave after wave came at him and McLaughlin cut them all down—killing an estimated 150 Chinese soldiers and wounding 50. He kept up the hail of bullets until his machine-gun barrels overheated and glowed faintly in the darkness. Rushing between two machine guns mounted on tripods, McLaughlin fooled the Chinese into thinking there were more Marines defending the position than there actually were. His aggressive tactics kept the enemy at bay until 2:00 A.M., when a mortar shell exploded at his side. McLaughlin was thrown to the ground. When he rose again, he was bleeding from a score of shrapnel wounds. Battling on, he cradled the remaining machine-gun in his arms and continued to fire. When the gun got too hot to handle, he wrapped his coat around it and continued to shoot until his hands were burned through the thick cloth. The clash lasted all night.

The corpsmen found McLaughlin at dawn. He was bleeding, and his hands and forearms were burned to the bone by the heat of the guns. He was sent to Japan and a special burn unit. From there he went home and spent an additional year in a stateside hospital. As a newly promoted corporal, Alford McLaughlin stood before President Dwight D. Eisenhower on October 27, 1953, to accept his Medal of Honor. McLaughlin was the only Marine Corps Medal of Honor recipient to survive that bloody nighttime assault. He remained a Marine, rising through the ranks to become a master sergeant. Alford McLaughlin retired in 1972 and passed away on January 14, 1977.

On October 2, 1952, a Chinese night attack overran Outpost Seattle and Outpost Warsaw on the eastern end of the division line. At Warsaw, Private Jack William Kelso of Madera, California, was surprised inside his bunker when a Chinese grenade landed at his feet. Without thinking, the eighteen-year-old picked it up and hurled it back at the enemy. Then, as his comrades escaped from the now-burning bunker, Private Kelso covered them until he was mortally wounded. Kelso's posthumous Medal of Honor was presented to his parents by Vice President Richard M. Nixon. Outpost Warsaw was promptly recaptured, but three separate counterattacks failed to secure Outpost Seattle. A fourth attempt four days later also failed to recapture Seattle. Twenty-five Marines perished in these failed assaults.

That night, the Chinese struck back against five Marine Corps outposts. Outpost Detroit was overrun, with the loss of almost two squads. East of this fight, the enemy overwhelmed Outpost Frisco, where Staff Sergeant Lewis George Watkins of Seneca, South Carolina, led a counterattack. Though wounded, Watkins managed to grab a BAR from a fallen Marine and silenced a machine-gun emplacement that had pinned down the Americans. When a grenade was tossed into his position, Watkins threw himself over it and died in the blast. His posthumous Medal of Honor was presented to his parents. Outpost Frisco was abandoned.

A major attack was mounted against the Marines at a vulnerable position known as the Hook. The Hook was a vital strategic position that overlooked the Samichon Valley and the road to Seoul. The position was protected by two outposts—Warsaw, 600 yards to the east, and Ronson, 300 yards to the west. Colonel Thomas C. Moore's Seventh Marines defended the Hook and a six-mile front around it. The force was overextended, with only one company in reserve—a ripe target for Chinese aggression. The assault began with two days and nights of continuous shelling along the perimeter, but mostly directed at the Hook itself. Then, at 6:00 P.M. on October 26, Outpost Ronson was assaulted. It fell in less than thirty minutes, with all the Marines defending it killed. By 7:00 P.M., Warsaw was attacked and its defenders were fighting hand to hand against superior numbers. By 7:38, the Chinese had reached the Marine trenches along the main line of resistance. They quickly overran the Americans and advanced along both sides of the ridge.

The reserve company was sent in, and shortly after midnight the Chinese launched a diversionary attack against Outpost Reno two miles away. This time it was the enemy who was surprised when an ambush patrol behind Reno sent them packing. A second assault came at 4:00 A.M. and was also repulsed. The Hook still held, though the Chinese controlled more than a mile of the Marines' main defensive perimeter. When daylight came, a counterattack took place. The Marines were met by a barrage of enemy fire. Second Lieutenant George Herman O'Brien, Jr., of Fort

Second Lieutenant George H. O'Brien

Worth, Texas, leapt from the safety of his trench and hustled across barren ground to charge up an enemy-occupied hill. He raced forward, zigzagging through heavy fire until he was shot through the arm and thrown to the ground. Rising again, O'Brien urged his men forward, then assisted a wounded Marine to safety. Returning to the fight, the Texan killed three Chinese. When grenades exploded near him, O'Brien was knocked down. He would be blown from his feet twice more by enemy grenades, but continued the fight for four hours. For this action, Lieutenant O'Brien received the Medal of Honor.

Second Lieutenant Sherrod E. Skinner, Jr., also earned the Medal of Honor—posthumously—in this engagement. Skinner directed his men to feign death as the Chinese overran their position. To make sure the Americans were dead, the enemy tossed a grenade among them. Skinner rolled over on the explosive and shielded two other Marines from injury. At daylight warplanes dropped napalm on the Chinese. It took seventy-two planes flying close support and a counterattack by the 11th Marines, A Company—along with a tank battalion—to recapture the outposts.

As winter descended on the Korean Peninsula—the third harsh winter of this increasingly unpopular war—President-Elect Dwight D. Eisenhower kept a campaign promise and visited the frontline troops in Korea. Peace negotiations were stalled, with the Communists demanding the repatriation of all North Korean and Chinese prisoners. The United Nations balked at the demand—over 60,000 Koreans and Chinese did not want to return to their homeland and the international body was loath to force them to return. In January, Eisenhower was sworn in as president. On March 5, 1953, Josef Stalin, the dictator of the Soviet Union who had led his troubled nation through the horrors of the Second World War, died of natural causes. The players on the international stage had suddenly changed, and the stalled negotiations went forward. By February, the war began to heat up too.

In February 1953, small-unit engagements against enemy strongpoints in no-man's-land had intensified. The Fifth Marines had a new commander—Colonel Lewis W. Walt, who earned two Navy Crosses in the Second World War. Walt was a hawkish commander and his Fifth Marines became the aggressors in clashes against Hills 31 and 31A. Just north of infamous Bunker Hill was Hill 101—Ungok, to the Koreans. A massive granite peak, Ungok was held by several companies of crack Chinese infantry. Though it was too strong to capture, Walt believed that a raiding party might be able to snatch a few prisoners and prove to the enemy that the Marines were still in the war. With Third Platoon, A Company, on this assault against Ungok was twenty-three-year-old Second Lieutenant Raymond G. Murphy of Pueblo, Colorado, a former high school athlete whose football skills had won him a scholarship to Adams State College in Alamosa. He graduated with a degree in physical education and looked for an opening as a coach. But facing the draft, Murphy opted to join the Marine Corps and was placed in a special program to train new officers—the attrition rate in Korea was so high that the Corps had a shortage of qualified graduates of the officers' basic course at Quantico. Though originally assigned to Camp Pendleton, Murphy was quickly hustled off to Korea in June 1952.

Second Lieutenant Sherrod E. Skinner, Jr.

He assumed command of the Third Platoon—the same unit that the posthumous Medal of Honor recipient Baldomero Lopez had led ashore at Inchon. Murphy was careful not to put his men in harm's way unnecessarily and took every precaution to see that there were few casualties in his unit. In one engagement—in which several of his men were seriously wounded—he evacuated them through the so-called neutral peace zone, a violation of the rules of engagement. Murphy thought he might be court-martialed for this offense but didn't care. His wounded men survived; they might not have made it if he hadn't moved them through forbidden territory. To Murphy's surprise, he was awarded the Silver Star.

When word of the Ungok operation came, Murphy was upset. He was scheduled to rotate out of Korea on the last day of January 1953. Instead, he voluntarily extended his tour of duty so he could go up against Ungok with the men of his old platoon. When the assault began, Murphy's unit was assigned the job of evacuation and reserve. At first light the Marines advanced, and in a few minutes Lieutenant Murphy could hear the sound of battle raging on the granite cliff that loomed above his position. Within the first hour casualties began coming down the hill in a steady stream. When the fighting lasted for over an hour, Murphy sensed something was wrong—the Marines on Ungok should have secured their prisoners and returned by now. The young lieutenant decided to go forward and see for himself what was happening. After a short climb, Murphy found himself in hell.

The Chinese resistance on Ungok was much more formidable than anyone had expected. In the first few minutes of the Marine assault, most of the officers and NCOs had fallen. Chaos resulted as the leaderless Marines sought cover and all but abandoned their original mission objectives. Realizing that the Marines were doomed unless they reorganized, Lieutenant Murphy set about restoring a semblance of command structure and staged a withdrawal. He attacked several key enemy points, leading the charge at the head of his own platoon. As the Chinese reeled from this unexpected counterattack, Murphy began to send the original assault team to the rear, carrying their wounded. Several times he exposed himself to enemy fire to rescue wounded Marines and drag them to safety. Then Murphy was wounded himself, when a mortar blasted him off his feet. Bleeding from wounds to his left side, he made many trips across open ground to aid casualties, and pushed the wounded to the rear.

As the column of dazed Marines moved down the slope, an enemy strong point opened fire on them. Enraged, Murphy stalked these enemy soldiers, cornered them in a rocky cul-de-sac, and gunned them down without mercy. When the order came to withdraw completely, he directed the retreat and covered his men with a BAR from a fallen Marine. The lieutenant repulsed a determined Chinese advance against his retreating forces. Near the Main Line of Resistance, artillery rained down on the Marines and Murphy was wounded again—this time in the right hand.

Though this attack was a disaster, Lieutenant Murphy prevented the operation from becoming a massacre. His injuries forced his evacuation, and Murphy became a patient at the Naval Hospital at Mare Island, California. On April 12, 1953, he was released from active duty and enrolled in graduate school in Massachusetts. While attending classes Murphy received word that he would receive the Medal of Honor. "It didn't seem to me I'd done anything to warrant this high honor," said the surprised former Marine. President Eisenhower disagreed and draped the ribbon over Murphy's shoulders on October 27, 1953. After pursuing several careers, Raymond Murphy joined the Veterans Administration, where he works to help veterans today, just as he aided the wounded on Ungok a half century ago.

The end of March brought the heaviest fighting yet in the Marine Corps sectors of western Korea. The four-day battle for Outposts Carson, Reno, and Vegas was violent and costly, with over a thousand Marine Corps casualties. This clash was part of a general Chinese attack all across the front. The enemy feared another U.N. offensive and hoped to combat it with an offensive of their own. The attacks began on March 23 when the Chinese overran Old Baldy, a U.S. Army–held strongpoint northeast of the "Nevada Cities" outposts. Reno, Vegas, and Carson were all located on high ground ten miles east of Panmunjom. Reno was in the middle and closest to enemy lines, Carson was to the west, and Vegas was on the highest ground. Each outpost was manned by forty or fifty Marines.

At 7:00 P.M. on March 26 the Chinese began a mortar attack on Carson. At 7:10, 4,000 Chinese regulars converged on the Nevada outposts from three directions while another group made diversionary probes at Outposts Berlin and East Berlin. By sheer weight of numbers the Chinese drove the Marines out of Reno and overran Vegas. But the men at Outpost Carson held, repulsing the enemy with knives, fists, and gun butts. Reinforcements were rushed forward, but suffered heavy casualties in the face of the enemy advance. At midnight, contact with Vegas was lost and the reinforcing Marines were fighting for their lives against repeated Chinese assaults. By

3:00 A.M., the advancing Marines were within 200 yards of Vegas and discovered that the position was in enemy hands. They were ordered to withdraw.

In the morning air support pounded the enemy-held positions. It was decided to attempt a recapture of Vegas but to abandon Reno to the enemy. When the Fifth Marines set out for the outpost, Chinese artillery pushed them back with many casualties. Three platoons made it to Vegas and seized part of the hill in a ninety-minute battle, but were eventually repulsed. During this engagement Corpsman William K. Charette of Ludington, Michigan, became the only corpsman to be awarded the Medal of Honor in Korea who lived to receive it.

Before midnight of the second day, Captain Ralph F. Estey's F Company, Seventh Marines, withstood three enemy attacks and established a perimeter defense at the base in Vegas. The Marines made three assaults on the summit but were thrown back each time. During the third assault, F Company reached an area only fifteen yards from the enemy trench line and battled the Chinese in a thirty-minute clash. Sergeant Daniel P. Matthews of Van Nuys, California, spotted a corpsman trying to evacuate a wounded Marine exposed to machine-gun fire. He traced the fire to enemy gunners on the peak. Slowly and carefully, Matthews worked his way to the gun emplacement and leapt into it. Although wounded, he killed two Chinese soldiers and chased another one away before succumbing to his injuries. The twenty-two-year-old sergeant was awarded a posthumous Medal of Honor for this action. By midday F Company was nearly decimated, with only forty effective troops left after six determined enemy assaults. E Company, the Fifth, moved forward and relieved them and attacked the summit themselves at 1:00 P.M. The fight lasted just six minutes. When it was over, Vegas was in Marine hands.

Fifteen minutes later the Chinese counterattacked. Artillery pounded the Marines and did not slacken for almost an hour. Then the Chinese infantry advanced against the entrenched Marines. With armor and more reinforcements pouring into the area, the Americans held on after a ten-hour fight. That night, the Chinese attacked again and were defeated. In the morning it began to rain, but a halfhearted Chinese attack came at sunset on the twenty-ninth. Marine Corps artillery decimated the enemy, and after a failed early-morning offensive on March 30, the Chinese gave up. Marine casualties were over a thousand, with 116 killed and a hundred missing—it was later learned that of the missing, nineteen had been taken prisoner. The enemy suffered twice as many casualties with the Chinese 358th Regiment so completely decimated that it was no longer effective.

On March 28, the Communists announced that they were prepared to discuss the return of sick and wounded prisoners. After a six-month stalemate, both sides began to talk again on April 6 at Panmunjom. More political infighting caused delays and no agreement emerged in the first few months of talks. On the front, the battle raged.

On July 19, the Chinese mounted several successful assaults against Outposts Berlin and East Berlin. Fifty Marines were killed and both outposts were overrun. At Outposts Esther and Dagmar on July 25, the Marines drove back an enemy attack but lost a dozen men. Many of these mass assaults were as sudden and overwhelming as the banzai attacks of the previous war, and far more effective. Fighting continued around the former Nevada Cities outposts and around Hill 119, where, on July 25, a determined Chinese assault pressed the Marines hard. Staff Sergeant Ambrosio Guillen, a former drill instructor, was in command of a reaction team near the front. Guillen's platoon had a tough assignment. If the enemy weakened any position along the perimeter, they were to hustle forward and reinforce it. As the fighting intensified, Sergeant Guillen advanced through a mortar barrage to reinforce a distant position. When they arrived at the beleaguered outpost, it was almost 10:00 P.M. In the darkness Guillen deployed his team just as the enemy struck. Their timely arrival helped to halt a determined Chinese advance and the fighting was fierce, if short-lived. Just when it looked like the attacks were over, the Chinese charged out of the night in the largest assault yet mounted. They hit with such ferocity that they broke through the line at several key points. Chinese soldiers were swarming into the American trenches, to grapple hand to hand with the hard-pressed Marines.

Sergeant Guillen reorganized his men and led them in a classic infantry advance through the trenches. Guillen's men cleared the Chinese from bunkers and strong points, and the enemy began to scramble out of the trenches in a desperate effort to escape the relentless Marine assault. Silhouetted by the night sky, they were gunned down too. In a savage, fifteen-minute engagement, Guillen's platoon had cleared the Communists out of the trenches and driven them off. Sergeant Guillen was wounded in the attack but refused aid, urging his Marines to press the enemy instead. Sporadic attacks continued for another two hours. When daylight came, Sergeant Guillen was evacuated. But the wiry Colorado native had lost too much blood and died before reaching the MASH unit.

Sergeant Ambrosio Guillen was buried at Fort Bliss National Cemetery in Fort Bliss, Texas. Guillen, who entered service in El Paso, became a legend in the state of Texas, which honored their transplanted hero from La Junta, Colorado. Guillen's Medal of Honor was given posthumously—the last awarded for action in the Korean War. Thirty-six hours after Ambrosio Guillen fell, a political agreement ended the conflict.

On July 26, as the armistice approached, the Chinese made an concerted effort to kick the Marines off Hill 119. This time the Americans held and the Chinese were forced to pull back, leaving their dead behind. The endgame had been costly. In July, the Marines suffered 1,611 casualties. Though the Chinese had absorbed over 72,000 casualties, they gained ground along the front in localized fighting at several key strategic locations.

On Monday morning, July 27, 1953, the armistice agreement was signed and the war in Korea was over. The battle had raged for three years one month and two days and ended in a draw. The borders were roughly the same as they had been before the shooting started. The difference was that many people who were alive in the spring of 1950 were dead by summer 1953. President Truman's doctrine of containment dictated that the United States could not make a major military commitment to the struggle against communism, and the United Nations had demonstrated only a half-hearted determination to battle Communist aggression. Both the U.N.'s and Truman's insistence on a limited war restricted the number of military options and denied total victory to either side. The best the West could hope to attain was the status quo.

Meanwhile, the Red Chinese demonstrated their willingness to absorb horrendous casualties for an opportunity to strut upon the world political stage and advance the cause of communism. Those costs were staggering. Though no accurate figures have ever been produced by China or North Korea, estimates are that they lost a combined total in excess of two million men in arms, with perhaps another million civilian casualties. The U.N. command suffered 88,000 killed—one in four of the dead were American. Total casualties for the United Nations—killed, wounded, and missing— were 996,937. Of these, 850,000 were Republic of Korea. These are sobering statistics for what was supposed to be a "limited war."

THE LESSONS OF KOREA

Despite the victories in the first few months of the war, the American military performed below par in the Korean conflict. Most of these early triumphs can be attributed to the Marine Corps—the landing at Inchon, the liberation of Seoul, the push to the north were all successful Marine Corps operations and shining examples of the success of their tactics and doctrine. It was only after the Chinese entered the war and the goals of the U.N. changed that the Marines stumbled.

Even after the disaster at Chosin, the Marines demonstrated their courage and tenacity during the subsequent breakout and the torturous withdrawal. After the world had given them up for dead, the Marines marched out, heads held high, with their equipment intact and carrying their dead. But when the Corps lost General MacArthur, they lost their independence. Stripped of the air support they took for granted and stuck holding their positions at far-flung outposts instead of advancing, the Marines began to lose their edge. Once the Korean War bogged down, there was no opportunity for them to exercise the greatest assets—mobility, amphibious assaults, and bold small-unit operations. For the Marines, trench warfare was a no-win situation.

United Nations political and military leaders were not clear or united on their goals and objectives, which led to friction and sometimes chaos. Political leaders placed many unreasonable strictures on military operations, and these rules of engagement also prevented effective action against an enemy who ignored such niceties. Once negotiations between the U.N. and the Chinese began, the Korean Campaign became a war of geographical borders, propaganda ploys, and public relations events—not a true struggle of arms and men. The sad reality is that the Communists usually won these public relations wars—hence Harry Truman's remark about Stalin's "propaganda machine."

There was no denying that the enemy had fought bravely and effectively in the Korean conflict. Like the Japanese in World War II, the Chinese and North Koreans excelled in night fighting. They were also skilled at camouflage and in the construction of durable defensive bunkers and emplacements. The enemy also traveled light—much more lightly than American troops. Their fast burp-gun assaults achieved great victories against the overburdened American soldiers. This mobility combined with night fighting skills gave the enemy the distinct advantage of surprise in the darkness. Often the American troops were unaware they were under siege until the enemy was within grenade-throwing range.

Despite the U.N. command's highly touted mastery of the air, their interdiction program failed miserably. Bombing failed to prevent the enemy from building up its troops and artillery strength, and airpower was unable to stop enemy supplies from reaching the front. When trucks and railheads and bridges were bombed, the enemy resorted to boats, horses, and even camels to move weapons and ammunition to the front. Interdiction against such guerrilla tactics is virtually impossible, a fact that the American military would relearn in Vietnam.

PART FIVE

THE MARINES IN VIETNAM

◼

1965–1970

"War is an ugly thing, but not the ugliest of things. The decayed and degraded state of moral and patriotic feeling which thinks that nothing is worth war is much worse. The person who has nothing for which he is willing to fight, nothing which is more important than his own personal safety, is a miserable creature and has no chance of being free unless made and kept so by the exertions of better men than himself."

> —John Stuart Mill, 1868

◼

"One thing about Vietnam is that there is no front line. Everything's a 360 degree perimeter."

> —Captain Robert J. Modrzejewski, Medal of Honor recipient, Operation Hastings, 1966

◼

"We have been too often disappointed by the optimism of the American leaders, both in Vietnam and Washington, to have faith any longer in the silver linings they find in the darkest clouds."

> —Walter Cronkite, *CBS Reports*, 1968

CHAPTER THIRTEEN

VIETNAM

▦

1965–1972

T HE United States lurched into the Vietnam War through a series of diplomatic missteps and political blunders that began in the Truman Administration and continued through the presidencies of Dwight D. Eisenhower, John F. Kennedy, and Lyndon Baines Johnson. After World War II, the farms, factories, and rubber plantations of Laos, Cambodia, and Vietnam were important to France's economic recovery. When Communist insurgents threatened stability in Southeast Asia, Truman agreed to provide financial and military aid to the French colonies.

But when a formidable force of French legionnaires and paratroopers were defeated by Communist insurgents at Dien Bien Phu in 1954, the French left the region. Without a stabilizing colonial presence, Vietnam was facing the same north/south political divide as Korea. To halt further expansion, President Dwight D. Eisenhower unleashed the Central Intelligence Agency and dispatched a few dozen military advisers to Vietnam to undermine the Communists.

For President John F. Kennedy, Vietnam was redemption, a golden opportunity to atone for the diplomatic blunders like the disastrous Bay of Pigs invasion. It was Kennedy who began military escalation by sending Green Beret "advisers" to South Vietnam in order to wage a "counterinsurgency war" against the Communists.

But it was Lyndon Johnson who fully committed the United States to war. In August 1964, he secured from Congress a functional declaration of war called the Tonkin Gulf Resolution. Armed with this dubious piece of legislation, LBJ began large-scale bombing of the north in February and March of 1965. When he dispatched 3,500 Marines to Vietnam on March 8, he began a cycle of escalation that would lead to over a half-million American men in uniform conducting a war in Asia with no clear objective, no obvious beginning, and seemingly without end.

FIRST TO FIGHT—AGAIN

When Brigadier General Frederick J. Karch led the Third Battalion, Ninth Marines, ashore on the morning of March 8, 1965, they were greeted by pretty South Vietnamese "flower maidens" who draped garlands of red and yellow blossoms around their necks. It was a deceptively peaceful beginning to one of America's cruelest wars.

To President Johnson, it made perfect sense to send the Marines in first. They were America's expeditionary force, and Vietnam was their kind of war. The Marines had waged similar wars in Nicaragua, the Philippines, Haiti, and elsewhere. And at first glance, Vietnam looked easy. Storm the beach, battle some nasty guerrillas, kill as many of the wrong people as possible while protecting the good ones, take some political heat on the home front, and be with the family by Christmas.

But the North Vietnamese were not the typical bandits and brigands the Marine Corps was used to. These guerrillas were funded, armed, and trained by the Soviet Union and fueled by a political ideology and nationalistic fervor not seen in Asia since the Korean conflict. These Vietnamese Communists had small arms and grenades, rockets and artillery, antiaircraft missiles and even fighter planes—many flown by Russian advisers. It would take more than five years—and nearly 15,000 Marine casualties—before the Corps spent Christmas at home.

The first U.S. Marine to arrive in Vietnam was Lieutenant Colonel Victor Croizat, who came just six months after the fall of Dien Bien Phu. Croizat was there to train a small unit that would form the nucleus of the Vietnam Marine regiment. He taught these Asian Marines the basics, along with the new strategy of counterinsurgency—a concept vital to U.S. Marine Corps strategy. While the Army trained soldiers to fight a full-scale land war against the Soviet Union in Europe, the Marines prepared to fight Communist surrogates like the North Koreans, the Syrians, Dominican rebels, etc. Many of these foes would be insurgents—armed rebels battling established authority with the goal of overthrowing the government. These rebels had to be countered by the tactic of "counterinsurgency," in which the government sets out to disrupt and quell such an uprising.

British counterinsurgency expert Robert Thompson drew on the experience he gained in defeating Communist rebels in Malaysia to set down the basic tenets of counterinsurgency. According to Thompson, successful counterinsurgency begins the establishment of a stable democratic government that works within the law and the development of a coherent plan to defeat the rebels. But the key to defeating the insurgents is winning the support of the populace. If these tenets had been followed in Vietnam, the outcome might have been different.

Though the Third Battalion, Ninth Marines, were the first American ground forces to deploy in South Vietnam, more than 100,000 American troops would follow. Marine Corps F4B Phantom jet fighter-bombers arrived in Da Nang in April. A few days later Marines boarded landing craft and moved up the Perfume River to the ancient city of Hue. Again, they were greeted by a cheering populace. On May 6, Brigadier General Marion Carl led his Third Amphibious Brigade ashore at a place called Chu Lai. A sandy plain surrounded by high hills, the region was named by Marine Corps commander Brigadier General Victor H. Krulak—"Chu Lai" were the Mandarin characters for "Krulak." By the end of June 1965, there were over 16,500 Marines in South Vietnam.

U.S. Army General William Westmoreland assigned the Marines to the I Corps Tactical Zone. "Eye-Corps" consisted of the five northernmost provinces of South Vietnam, stretching from the Laotian border in the west to the South China Sea in the east. The 265-mile zone included a spur of the Annamite Mountains at Sa Huynh and most of the DMZ—demilitarized zone. The zone was about seventy miles deep and ran along the seventeenth Parallel separating the Communist north from the democratic south and included the cities of Hue, Da Nang, and Quang Tri. About 25,000 ARVN troops also occupied the region. The South Vietnamese government controlled the cities and the Communist insurgents—the Viet Cong—controlled the countryside. Two and a half million Vietnamese people lived in the Eye-Corps zone of control, and no one really knew which side most of them were on.

On May 30, the Viet Cong ambushed a battalion of ARVN regulars near Ba Gia. Only three American advisers and 66 of the 400 ARVN troops survived the slaughter, and by the end of the first week in June, the Marines had suffered 200 casualties and 30 dead. The new commandant of the Marine Corps, Wallace M. Greene, Jr., hurled the gauntlet when he visited Da Nang a month later. Greene declared his Marines were in Vietnam to "kill Viet Cong." On July 1, at about 1:30 A.M., a strong force of Viet Cong infiltrated Da Nang airfield and destroyed three warplanes. Three Marines were wounded and an Air Force airman was killed. The attack was repulsed and the Marines expanded their area of operation to include the area around the airfield. This new patrol area was densely populated, with clusters of farming villages and hamlets.

On July 12, eleven days after the demolition attack, a Marine reconnaissance patrol that had entered the new expanded area of operations south of Da Nang was ambushed by the Viet Cong. On point was an eighteen-year-old junior officer from Spokane, Washington. First Lieutenant Frank Stanley Reasoner was leading an eighteen-man patrol from Company A, the Third Reconnaissance Battalion, when they came under heavy fire from small arms and automatic weapons. They were about twenty kilometers from the air base and were struck by a force estimated at around a hundred guerrillas.

In the first seconds First Lieutenant Reasoner was wounded and the other five men on point went to ground. Instantly, the Viet Cong surrounded and isolated the point men from the rest of the patrol. When his radioman was wounded, Reasoner moved forward to render aid and provide covering fire so his men could withdraw. The determined patrol leader killed two Viet Cong who emerged from cover and silenced a machine gun that was chewing up the Marines. But before he could reach the wounded radioman, Reasoner was struck again. Arriving at the radioman's side through a hail of machine gun fire, Reasoner was mortally wounded and died on the spot.

First Lieutenant Frank Reasoner became the first Marine to earn the Medal of Honor in Vietnam. Secretary of the Navy Paul H. Nitze presented the posthumous award to Reasoner's family in a ceremony at the Pentagon.

OPERATION STARLIGHT—AUGUST 18–24, 1965

The Marines' first offensive was Operation Starlight. Three battalions led by Colonel Oscar F. Peatross moved into position on the night of August 17 and were in place by dawn of the eighteenth. Marine intelligence had learned that the First Viet Cong Regiment was assembling in the Van Tuong Peninsula for an all-out assault on Chu Lai. To thwart them the Marines mounted a surprise attack of their own that began on August 18. The campaign quickly came to resemble a battle in the jungles of the South Pacific from two decades before. The Cong stubbornly resisted the American incursion and occupied caves, spider holes, and fortified villages in an effort to halt the Marine advance. Barbed wire, mines, punji spears and other booby-traps were placed in the Americans' path. Colonel Peatross wanted to strike the enemy from the west and drive them into the sea. In one section his plan worked. There the Viet Cong attempted to board sampans and escape only to be slaughtered by the guns of a U.S. Navy destroyer. But in other areas of the jungle the fight degenerated into localized brawls with small units from both sides trading blows.

The Viet Cong had several recoilless rifles in place and they used them to destroy two Marine Corps tanks. The Viet Cong were dug in, with the Marines assaulting their fixed positions as they did against the Japanese in World War II. Every enemy emplacement neutralized was paid for with sweat and blood. Mortars and machine guns shredded the Americans. In response, the Marines called down close air support, naval bombardments, and artillery on Viet Cong positions. On the very first day of this brutal campaign, two Marines earned the Medal of Honor. Corporal Robert E. O'Malley of I Company, Third Marines, led his squad against a strongly entrenched and heavily armed Viet Cong force. The twenty-two-year-old corporal, who hailed from the Irish-American enclave of Woodside, Queens, splashed through a rice paddy, jumped into a trench, and killed eight Viet Cong with his rifle and with grenades. When O'Malley learned that a nearby unit was pinned down and threatened with annihilation, he led his squad to lend a hand. Wounded three times, O'Malley provided covering fire while helicopter evacuated the wounded. For his courage, Corporal Robert Emmett O'Malley was presented with the Medal of Honor in a ceremony at the Federal Building in Austin, Texas. It was President Lyndon Baines Johnson who draped the ribbon over the young Marine's shoulders.

That same day, nineteen-year-old Lance Corporal Joe Calvin Paul of Williamsburg, Kentucky, was killed when he placed himself between five wounded Marines and the Viet Cong. Firing to divert the enemy's attention long enough for the injured to be evacuated, Paul was mortally wounded in a fierce exchange. Though bleeding, the lance corporal returned fire until he collapsed. Lance Corporal Joe C. Paul's posthumous Medal of Honor was presented to his family at the Marine Corps barracks in Washington, D.C.

Operation Starlight continued for six days. Though the Viet Cong fought back effectively, Marine Corps firepower overwhelmed them. By August 24,600 Viet Cong had been killed. The American forces lost forty-five, but with odds of fourteen to one the clear winner was the United States Marine Corps. Never again would the Viet

Cong fight toe-to-toe with the Marines—they would save that honor for the better-armed and better-trained regulars of the Communist People's Army of North Vietnam, the NVA. But even as the Viet Cong were dealt a stunning defeat, a new enemy reared its ugly head—an enemy back in America, in the living rooms of every American home.

Though media reports about Starlight were generally favorable, CBS television widely reported a series of Marine Corps "atrocities" stemming from a single piece of footage shot during the operation. Some Marines of the First Battalion, Ninth Marines, were filmed setting fire to Vietnamese huts with a cigarette lighter. Taken out of context, Morley Safer's report of the incident seemed to confirm the American public's worst fears about this unsettling new war. This television report was followed by a story in the Chicago *Daily News* that erroneously stated that Marines "have killed or wounded Vietnamese civilians." Journalist Keyes Beech—displaying a profound ignorance of American history—called Vietnam "the dirtiest war we Americans ever had to fight." The unfortunate result of these inaccurate reports was to stigmatize the brave men who served in Vietnam.

Operation Starlight's success was a morale booster for the Marines and inspired high command to act more aggressively. Starlight was followed in September by a three-day campaign called Operation Piranha, which was moderately successful but overshadowed by a stunning, high-profile raid against the Marine base at China Beach—an eight-mile stretch of shore along the South China Sea east of Da Nang. Marines and Seabees had constructed a hospital and a helicopter base at China Beach in the belief that the area was secure. But on October 27, a force of fifty Viet Cong raiders armed with bangalore torpedoes and satchel charges attacked China Beach by sea, destroying nineteen helicopters and damaging thirty-five others. The attackers all but leveled the new hospital, killing three and wounding ninety. The Viet Cong were exterminated, but the fires from burning choppers and exploding munitions were visible all over Quang Nam Province.

This unexpected assault illustrated the need for more American troops, but Lyndon Johnson infuriated the Marine Corps commanders by refusing to call up reserves and face the political consequences. In response to this slow, incremental approach to mobilization, the Marines emptied Camp Pendleton, transplanting the entire First Marine Division to Vietnam. The Fifth Marines was also activated—for the first time since VJ day twenty years before. Still the Marines were stretched thin, and Eye-Corps became a much more dangerous place as the conflict escalated.

On November 10, United States and Vietnamese Marine units participated in their first combined amphibious operation. It was the middle of the monsoon rain season and conditions were bad. But the Marines landed successfully at Tam Ky and swept the area. They met no resistance because the Viet Cong were elsewhere. That same night the First Viet Cong Regiment—the same unit the Marines had whipped in Operation Starlight—captured the district capital of Hiep Duc in Que Son Valley with a surprise night attack. The town was twenty-five miles west of the Marines in Tam Ky, and American and South Vietnamese Marines boarded choppers and flew to the rescue. When the Marines dropped out of the rain-swept skies, the Viet Cong melted into the countryside—one stinging defeat at the hands of the Leathernecks was enough for them. Though Hiep Duc was quickly recaptured, it was later abandoned for lack of manpower to defend the town.

As the monsoon rains fell at a rate of an inch or more a day, the Viet Cong continued their shadow war—striking at weak positions and isolated units, but careful to avoid a pitched battle against the Americans. During this time, the Marines engaged in "Golden Fleece"—hazardous night patrols to protect the rice harvest the farmers depended upon for survival. The pacification program, intended to protect settlements from Viet Cong terrorism, also began at this time, with initially mixed results. Later this program resulted in the formation of Combined Action Platoon, or CAP, operations, which were very successful.

By Thanksgiving, it was apparent that the Viet Cong were moving into Que Son in large numbers. Operation Harvest Moon, which began on December 9, was meant to drive the enemy out of this strategic valley. Two Marine battalions were airlifted into the region and high-level B-52 bombers made four air strikes in support of these troops as they moved into position. Monsoon rains hampered ground operations. The soil was so saturated that soldiers constantly walked through standing water. Over fifty Marines had to be evacuated because of "immersion foot"—a problem not faced in such magnitude since trench fighting in the First World War.

During a temporary break in the weather on December 18, Lieutenant Colonel Leon N. Utter's Second Battalion, Seventh Marines, was withdrawing from the Que Son Valley. G Company took point, with F Company following. Behind G and F was H Company, composed of headquarters and service staff. As the Marine column moved along a narrow, muddy road that snaked its way through an area of flooded rice paddies, they were being stalked by the enemy. G Company had just moved through the village of Ky Phu when they were ambushed by a large, well-concealed Viet Cong force. From his position in the rear with H Company, Lieutenant Colonel Utter ordered G Company to deploy to the south of the road as F Company rushed forward to support them.

No sooner were those orders issued than a Viet Cong mortar barrage hit H Company, where Lieutenant Colonel Utter was still trying to coordinate his forces. Two Viet Cong companies moved out of cover in a bold move to isolate and destroy Utter's unit. Lieutenant Colonel Utter radioed F Company and ordered them to make an about-face and return to the aid of his headquarters staff—it was clear by now that the initial attack on G Company at point was just a diversion. Utter's staff fought their way into the village of Ky Phu and found some cover, but were now completely isolated from the rest of the column. The Viet Cong attacked them from the rear and at both flanks. The company commander and radioman were killed and the rest of the Marines were facing annihilation.

First Lieutenant Harvey Curtiss Barnum—"Barney"—was an artillery forward observer on temporary duty from his post in Hawaii. He discovered his vocation in high school when representatives from all the branches of the military visited the school to find eager young recruits. With the junior and senior boys assembled in the auditorium, each recruiter stood on stage and made his pitch. The Air Force officer was first and was greeted with catcalls and whistles. The Army and Navy recruiters

▪ *Atrocities in the Vietnam War*

Atrocities were common during the Vietnam War. Because the Viet Cong practice of seeking refuge in the guise of innocent civilians frustrated and angered American troops, enemy activity sometimes led to reprisals against the general population. Most American atrocities occurred because of misdirected aggression in response to guerrilla attacks. Small units patrolled the countryside in pursuit of the elusive enemy, who left mines, booby traps, or punji pits in their wake. When Americans were killed or maimed by these terror weapons, they sometimes lashed out at the next Vietnamese they encountered—which was not always a Viet Cong or even a sympathizer. The general atmosphere of mistrust toward Vietnamese civilians was fueled by the guerrillas, who lurked among the people and struck when Americans were at their most vulnerable.

There are well-documented instances in which U.S. troops used Vietnamese civilians or livestock for target practice and incidents of rape. Harsh interrogation involving physical intimidation of prisoners was routine. This hostility is understandable. The Viet Cong were not a legitimate political entity; they were terrorists who utilized terror tactics to achieve their political ends. And it should be remembered that American prisoners of the Viet Cong were routinely tortured and executed—their mutilated bodies left along jungle trails for other Americans to find. Sometimes American POWs were subjected to public humiliation at the hands of angry villagers.

Lieutenant Commander John S. McCain—now Senator John McCain of Arizona—was severely injured when he ejected from his stricken warplane. His captors denied McCain medical care for four days, until they discovered he was the son of an admiral and provided a doctor. "I tell the story to make this point," wrote McCain in the *Washington Post*. "The North Vietnamese just would not give medical treatment to someone who was badly injured—they weren't going to waste their time."

The deplorable treatment of American airmen imprisoned in the "Hanoi Hilton" is now widely known, but was hardly reported by Western media outlets at the time.

Sometimes routine ground operations by American troops or their South Vietnamese allies degenerated into a massacre. In 1967, after three days of fighting and sustaining many casualties, Marines entered the village of Thuy Bo and, by their own account, shot everyone they could find. On the night of February 7, 1970, a five-man team from B Company, Seventh Marines, entered Son Trang after days of heavy fighting in Quang Nam Province. Led by Lance Corporal Randall D. Herrod, a recent transfer and a Silver Star nominee, they killed five women and a dozen small children. But the most infamous atrocity of the war was committed by three companies of the Americal Division at My Lai. Between 100 and 400 Vietnamese civilians—mostly women, children, and the elderly—were massacred.

The U.S. media reported every atrocity they could uncover as long as such crimes were perpetrated by Americans or their allies. Far less reported were the atrocities committed by the Viet Cong and their allies in the Army of the People's Republic of North Vietnam. Yet it was the Communists who regarded brutality against the civilian population as a legitimate means of waging war—mass executions, torture, and intimidation were not only condoned but encouraged as a matter of policy.

William Tuohy, a journalist in Vietnam, wrote an article about enemy atrocities for the November 28, 1965, edition of the *New York Times Magazine*. "U.S. soldiers and civilians captured by the Vietcong have been dragged through villages like prisoners in the Roman wars, jeered at, laughed at, spit upon, kept in solitary confinement, and executed," Tuohy wrote. "Sometimes their bodies have been mutilated."

According to Tuohy, the young wife of a South Vietnamese officer headquartered at Saigon returned home to her native village for a visit. "She was seized by the V.C., disemboweled and her body hung on a fence post as a warning." Tuohy concluded that "The catalogue of Vietcong atrocities is long and sickeningly repetitious."

In Saigon and other urban areas, bombs were placed to kill and maim off-duty American soldiers and innocent civilians. Viet Cong terror attacks routinely targeted hospitals, schools, and community centers. Bars, restaurants, sports stadiums, police stations, and market areas were also scenes of terrorist attacks by guerrillas mingling with the general population.

During the 1968 Tet Offensive, the Viet Cong murdered 150,000 unarmed civilians in the urban areas they controlled, however briefly. These victims included prominent intellectuals, professionals, and the wives and families of South Vietnamese officials, policemen, and soldiers. Some were tortured before they were killed, others were maimed and tortured before being rescued or released. In the rural areas it was much worse—there the enemy was a constant presence.

The Viet Cong ruled the countryside, especially at night. When roving bands of these black-clad predators moved through a village, it was routine for them to round up the town's leaders, members of the local constabulary, doctors, schoolteachers, and small-business owners and murder them on the spot. Their intention was to disrupt social stability and send a message to those who cooperated, even tacitly, with the South Vietnamese government or its allies. Town leaders who resisted Communist ideology were assassinated in their homes when purging an entire community of "political undesirables" was impossible. Over 6,000 such leaders were assassinated during the period of U.S. involvement in the war. Western missionaries and Roman Catholic priests and nuns were also routinely butchered.

The Marines took the physical security of the rural population quite seriously. In 1965, a tactic called the Combined Action Platoon evolved. A handpicked, extensively trained Marine rifle squad with a corpsman attached would move into a village and train the local militia skills and tactics. The senior American authority in these villages was usually a twenty-one-year-old Marine Corps NCO. Many voluntarily extended their tours of duty to continue to train and minister to their "charges." Gradually these units gained the confidence of the community and began to establish villages that were secure against Viet Cong incursion by day and by night.

William Tuohy cut to the heart of the problem Americans faced in Vietnam. "Despite the U.S. attempt to make the struggle more conventional, it is still basically a guerrilla war . . . It is also a civil war, inevitably unleashing violent passions. It is also a war fought by Asian standards, without even lip service to the niceties of warfare prescribed by Western convention."

got the same treatment. Then the Marine Corps recruiter, a hard-nosed gunnery sergeant, rose and glared at the assembly. "There's no one here worthy of being a United States Marine," he declared. "I'm horrified that the faculty would let students carry on like this. There isn't anybody here I want in my Marine Corps."

When the sergeant sat down, several eager students gathered around his table. One of them was the senior-class president Harvey Barnum, Jr. He enlisted while still a senior. After graduation, as a student at St. Anselm College in Manchester, New Hampshire, he joined the Platoon Leadership Class. From there he became an active duty Marine. Now, just seven years after enlisting, Harvey Barnum was in the fight of his life.

When the company commander was killed, Barnum strapped on a radio and assumed command of the besieged company. Rallying the dazed Marines, he reorganized his defenses and formed a tight perimeter around the village. He placed the wounded in the center of the circle and pushed back several determined Viet Cong assaults. With the help of several UH-1E Huey gunships, Barnum destroyed a key enemy position on his flank and called for a medevac. Exposed to enemy fire, he directed the helicopters onto the LZ—landing zone. Under a constant barrage First Lieutenant Barnum oversaw the loading and evacuation of his wounded Marines. When the helicopters lifted off a few tense minutes later, he resumed command of his beleaguered forces. The Marines pushed back at the enemy with concentrated and coordinated fire. After a hard, four-hour firefight, Barnum led the Marines of H Company to a position of safety. They left over a hundred Viet Cong dead on the field, while suffering 11 killed and 70 wounded in this fierce, bloody clash.

"Barney" Barnum received the Medal of Honor for the exceptional calm and courage he exhibited during this action. He subsequently rose to the rank of colonel.

After retiring, Colonel Barnum served as the principal director, drug enforcement policy, office of the Secretary of Defense, and later as the corporate and community affairs adviser for ARLTEC, Inc. He returned to Vietnam in 1995 to walk the same ground he fought over thirty years before. Colonel Barnum now serves as the president of the Congressional Medal of Honor Society and resides in Reston, Virginia.

Harvest Moon was the last Marines Corps operation conducted in 1965. By the end of this first year, the Marines had suffered 454 killed and 2,100 wounded. They had conducted six battalion-size operations and learned some hard lessons about their enemy and the tactics that both succeeded and failed on the battlefield. Unfortunately the Marine Corps policy of rotating combat troops out of the field after thirteen months meant that those lessons would have to be relearned by a new crop of replacements.

1966

Over 38,000 Marines were in South Vietnam by January 1966. Things were quiet through the Christmas holidays and the Vietnamese celebration of Tet in mid-January. LBJ even halted the bombing of the north in a failed effort to promote peace talks. The Vietnam "conflict" was starting to look like a real war and the Marines had the slang to prove it. Soldiers became "grunts" from the noise they made hoisting ninety-pound packs onto their backs. Vietnam became "The 'Nam." It's countryside the "boonies." Going on patrol was called "humping the boonies." The Viet Cong guerrillas were casually known as "Charlie," but the trained, uniformed NVA regulars were more formally addressed as "Mr. Charles." The first priority of the average "grunt" was personal survival. They all wanted to make it "back to the real world riki-tik"—get home as fast as possible.

After the three-day Tet holiday, a new offensive was mounted. Meanwhile, the First Marine Division was entering the war in a whole new way. In an effort to establish government control of the rural villages and hamlets, an innovative new tactic dubbed "County Fair" was tried. Combined units of South Vietnamese troops and U.S. Marines would seal off a town, move the people to another location, and search homes and barns for hidden Viet Cong, weapons, and contraband. Meanwhile, the people would be treated to a party. Kitchens were set up and food was served. The villagers were issued identity cards that were checked in an effort to ferret out Viet Cong lurking among the populace. At the party the villagers were offered free medical care while they enjoyed entertainment in the form of pro-government music, plays, and puppet shows. County Fair was surprisingly effective—so effective that General William Westmoreland adopted the program for use in the U.S. Army's area of operations, though he changed the name to Hamlet Festival.

In February and March, things heated up. There was hard fighting near Quang Ngai and A Shau, a town near the Laotian border where Communist guerrillas wiped out a Special Forces camp on March 9. But the most dangerous situation to confront the U.S. forces was political. On March 10, Prime Minister Nguyen Cao Ky of South Vietnam fired his I Corps commander and political rival General Nguyen Chanh Thi.

▪ *Weapons of the Vietnam War*

The United States military began the Vietnam War with equipment ranging from World War I weapons like the Colt. 45 to those added to America's arsenal during the war in Korea. Until replaced by the M-16, the M-14, the 7.62mm was the standard rifle used by the military in Vietnam. It weighed eleven pounds with a full magazine and was a favorite of the Marine Corps. "The M-14 was a very reliable weapon," says Captain Robert Modrzejewski. "It was a rifle that you could drop in the mud . . . you could drop the magazine, the bullets could get dirty and yet the weapon would still fire."

The M-16 arrived on the front in 1965, at the Ia Drang Valley of Vietnam, and had a less impressive operational history. Designed by former Marine Eugene Stoner for the Army, early models tended to jam with lethal consequences for the soldiers who relied on them. In May 1967, one disgusted Marine wrote home about the problem: "Believe it or not, you know what killed most of us? Our own rifle . . . Practically every one of our dead was found with his rifle torn down next to him where he had been trying to fix it. There was a newspaper woman . . . photographing all this . . ." That journalist was Catherine Leroy and the pictures were published in *Paris-Match* magazine. The photographs caused a political firestorm at home, and the problem with the M-16 was repaired in less than six months.

The M-16 was designed to give the infantryman fire superiority over the enemy. With a maximum rate of fire of 650 to 700 rounds per minute and a magazine of nineteen shells, it assured that the U.S. soldier was better armed than his enemy. To sustain fire superiority, the men in squad took turns firing and reloading, thereby keeping a steady stream of lead flying at the enemy. The M-16 was easy to maintain: it split in two for cleaning and the entire bolt and firing pin group came out for quick access.

The M-203, 40mm grenade launcher—a combination of the M-16A1 automatic rifle and an M-203 grenade launcher—was universally used. The XM-177E2, known as the Colt Commando, is a shortened version of the M-16 with a telescoping stock. Though popular with special operations units, it saw limited use among line troops.

Some things never change and two of them are the dependability of the Colt Model 1911 A1 pistol and the admiration it engendered among those who relied on it. "Naturally I think it is the finest hand weapon that the armed forces could carry," says Captain John McGinty III, who owes his life to the Colt. 45. "I slept with that weapon . . . And when I had to use it, it fired every round, never missed." This holdover from the First World War was carried by most officers in Vietnam.

The Browning .50-caliber machine gun was still in use, and the M-60, 7.62mm general-purpose machine gun was used as both a light machine gun and as protective armament on helicopters and vehicles. Antitank weapons included the M-72 light antitank weapon, or LAW, and the M-20 3.5-inch rocket launcher, called the "Super-bazooka."

Both the Viet Cong and the ARVN carried the ubiquitous AK-47, 7.62-caliber assault rifle. Shorter and heavier than the M-16, the AK-47 had a lower rate of fire and less muzzle velocity. Variants include the Chicom Type 56, manufactured by the Chinese and featuring a folding metal stock instead of the heavier wooden stock of the Soviet-made version. Among the Viet Cong, the Simonov 7.62mm self-loading rifle, or SKS, was used. With a ten-round magazine, the SKS could fire thirty to thirty-five rounds per minute. Like the M-14 it was very reliable. The standard infantry-support weapon for the North Vietnamese was the RPD 7.62mm general-purpose machine gun. The RPD had a drum magazine that could quickly be changed by an experienced loader and could fire 150 rounds per minute.

The most profound change in tactics during the Vietnam War was caused by the proliferation of the helicopter on the battlefield. In many ways, Vietnam was the first helicopter war. Amphibious landings and landing craft were replaced by helicopter insertions and extractions. During the Korean War, the wounded were evacuated from the battlefield by helicopters. Innovations in helicopter design made troop movement—including the transport of heavy weapons, ammunition, and supplies—feasible. Entire combat companies were flown in on a dozen or more helicopters, leaving their base and arriving on the battlefield in less than an hour. This kind of mobility had never existed before air cavalry was born.

For the Marine Corps, the change made sense; the helicopter was faster than a boat and could deliver men and matériel inland, on the top of a mountain, or in any open area close to the enemy. If things went wrong, reinforcements were only minutes away. If these went *really* wrong, a quick extraction was always an option. The most ubiquitous chopper of the Vietnam War was the Bell UH-1H

Iroquois, known today as the Huey. The first prototype flew in August 1961, and variants of this fine helicopter are still operational today. Only a few helicopters have two blades, and this design oddity gave the Huey its distinctive "swooshing" sound. No other helicopter sounds quite like the Huey. Armed with machine guns and rocket launchers, they became formidable gunships. But primarily the UH-1H was used to move troops.

The Bell AH-1 Cobra gunship was also used in Vietnam. With four weapons stations mounted under its stubby wings and a chin turret featuring a 7.62mm machine gun, the Cobra has a two-man crew, composed of a pilot and weapons officer. Variants include TOW missile launchers, night-vision equipment, a three-barrel M197 cannon, and helmet display systems. Today the Cobra has been replaced by the McDonnell Douglas AH-64 Apache attack helicopter, which was used so effectively in the Persian Gulf War.

One of the oddest innovations of the Vietnam air war was the AC-130E "Spectre" gunship. A lethal variant of the lumbering C-130 transport, the Spectre was used to patrol the Ho Chi Minh Trail and provide support for friendly bases. Its main task was to destroy Vietnamese supply con-voys, which it accomplished quite efficiently. The Spectre gunship was armed with two 40mm Gatling guns, a 40mm Bofors antiaircraft gun, four 7.62mm miniguns, and even a M105-A1 light howitzer! The crew consisted of a pilot, copilot, flight engineer, navigator, and radar operator, a fire control officer, a right scanner, an illuminator operator, and three or four gunners. The illuminator operator was not only in charge of the searchlight mounted in the rear of the cargo area, but was also responsible for firing flares, watching for enemy antiaircraft, and dropping smoke bombs to designate targets for follow-up air strikes.

While there was no chemical warfare in Vietnam, Agent Orange was used to defoliate the jungle and rob the Viet Cong of their cover. The United States military sprayed millions of gallons of this toxic substance onto the Vietnamese jungle. A mixture of several herbicides, Agent Orange contains dioxin—a highly toxic poison and proven carcinogen. Agent Orange had a deleterious effect on the people of Vietnam, and on the American troops assigned to disperse it or who conducted combat operations in areas where the substance had been used. Many veterans of the Vietnam War still suffer the effects of Agent Orange exposure.

This move sparked a crisis that swept through South Vietnam. There were student demonstrations and mass strikes in the capital of Saigon and the cities of Da Nang, Hue, and Hoi were torn by riots. American property and personnel were attacked and cars were burned in the streets. Even the Buddhists joined in the orgy of anti-Americanism that was gripping the South. As the crisis mounted, Prime Minister Ky declared Da Nang a hostile city and sent in ARVN troops to quell the unrest. The Marine Corps base at Da Nang suffered artillery attacks. It seemed as if South Vietnam was about to self-destruct, and the violence continued even after President Thieu announced new elections for the fall. Soon the Marines were facing angry military elements of their supposed allies in hostile confrontations like the incident at the Tourane River Bridge.

This strategically important bridge lay east of the Marine base at Da Nang. During a tense period of civil unrest, South Vietnamese Army engineers wired it with explosives and threatened to blow it up if the Marines attempted a crossing. Lieutenant General Lewis Walt confronted an angry Vietnamese officer in the middle of the span while a pair of bold Marines sneaked under the bridge to defuse the explosives. The Vietnamese officer refused to pull back his troops and repeatedly threatened to blow the bridge if the Americans did not withdraw.

The confrontation continued until an American gave Walt a thumbs-up, indicating that the explosives had been defused. General Walt told the Vietnamese officer that he had five minutes to clear the explosives and pull out. When time ran out Walt led his officers onto the bridge. The officer ordered the bridge destroyed, but when the plunger was pushed nothing happened. The Vietnamese withdrew and the Marines took charge of the bridge and the area around it. Though Lieutenant General Walt had quite literally defused a tense situation, it was clear that the first tenet of a successful counterinsurgency war was being violated—there was no stable, democratic government left in South Vietnam for the Americans to defend.

The Third Marine Division continued to push south from Da Nang, broadening their area of control through a series of "search and clear" missions. Marine Corps units would cordon off an area and enter it to eradicate the Viet Cong trapped inside. They pushed the guerrillas back as far south as An Hoa by early June. The next offensive, Operation Kansas, began on the afternoon of June 13 when a thirteen-man recon team was helicoptered onto Nui Loc Son, a mountain in the Que Son Valley. Over the next twenty-four hours, six more recon teams, each between a dozen and twenty men in strength, took positions around the valley. They were there to report enemy activity and call artillery or air strikes against Viet Cong clusters.

The team south of Hiep Duc found the enemy on the first day and the enemy found them the next morning. They had to be extracted. On Nui Vu hill—Hill 488— east of the valley, an eighteen-man team commanded by Staff Sergeant Jimmie L. Howard called in numerous artillery strikes against the enemy massing in the valley. Sergeant Howard—a tall, blunt, crew-cutted former Marine football player and coach from San Diego—was born in Burlington, Iowa. Before arriving in Vietnam, he received the Silver Star and three Purple Hearts for action in Korea.

In Vietnam, Howard's unit was handed a hazardous mission and he knew it. Fortunately, the sergeant had been around the block and knew a how to outfox the enemy. He waited until an American helicopter or scout plane was within earshot before calling in artillery, figuring that the NVA would think the aircraft was responsible for the attack. The canny sergeant's scheme worked for a while, but soon the NVA figured that there must be American spotters in the region and began a search to root them out. At 11:30 P.M. on the night of June 15—the unit's third night in the "boonies"—a battalion-size force of NVA regulars gathered at the bottom of Nui Vu hill. Sergeant Howard heard the commotion and called for an artillery strike. He and his men hunkered down and listened as big guns hammered the base of the hill, scattering the North Vietnamese. The next two hours passed quietly, until Lance Corporal Ricardo Binns, one of the sentries, spotted a shadowy figure moving up the hill. Before he could shout a warning, a cluster of grenades fell among the Marines and the enemy charged.

Lance Corporal John T. Adams of Portland, Oregon, emptied his M-16 at the horde. Then, using his rifle as a club, he beat two more Cong to death before he was mortally wounded. Corporal Jerrald R. Thompson of Palmer, California, was mortally wounded by a grenade, but killed two NVA regulars with his knife before he succumbed.

Firing their weapons on full automatic, the enemy encircled the entrenched Marines. Bright flashes lit the night and tracers whizzed through the darkness as the Marines fought back. Despite being outnumbered, Howard's Marines eventually pushed the Communists off the hill. As the NVA retreated, they shouted threats and insults in broken English. Cries of "American dogs," "Marines, you die," and "We come back soon!" were heard. During the lull, Howard called for an evacuation. The helicopters were dispatched, but were spotted by enemy searchlights and attacked by antiaircraft batteries as they made their approach. The choppers were forced to pull back—Sergeant Howard and his men were on their own until daybreak. Though artillery support and helicopter gunships attacked the NVA several times that the night, the enemy still managed to mount three more assaults against the isolated recon team.

By 3:30 A.M., Howard was down to twelve men—a third of his command had been killed—and was temporarily paralyzed below the waist by a shrapnel wound. Half the Marines still standing had been wounded and their ammunition was running low. They squeezed off single shots and soon ran out of grenades. The final NVA assault that came near dawn was repulsed with thrown rocks, gun butts, and shots from captured AK-47 rifles.

At dawn the helicopters landed at the base of the promontory and a relief column fought its way up the slope to rescue the survivors. The Marines continued to press the NVA after Howard's men were evacuated, and secured the area by midafternoon. The NVA left forty-two dead and Howard lost a third of his command. Two Marines were killed in the relief effort.

Staff Sergeant Howard's recon team became the most decorated unit of the Vietnam War. Fifteen members of this group received the Silver Star and two—Lance Corporal Ricardo Binns and Corpsman Billie D. Holmes—were awarded the Navy Cross. Sergeant Howard received the Medal of Honor, presented to the tenacious thirty-five-year-old NCO by President Lyndon Johnson at a White House ceremony. In the years after the war, Jimmie Howard rose to the rank of first sergeant. He passed away in San Diego, California, on November 12, 1993.

Operation Kansas ended on June 22 without further contact with the enemy. But up north, NVA units crossed the DMZ to support the Viet Cong guerrillas. The Marines responded by creating Task Force Delta, a five-battalion-strength strike force commanded by Brigadier General Lowell E. English. Task Force Delta soon conducted their first campaign—dubbed Operation Hastings—which commenced near Cam Lo on July 13, 1966.

On July 18, 130 men from K Company were choppered into an area near the DMZ to block a Viet Cong supply trail. The Marines piled into four Hueys and flew to the combat zone. Things seemed to go wrong from the start. The LZ was too small to allow the four helicopters to land simultaneously, so K Company came down in two waves. The first pair of choppers touched down and the Marines dispersed without incident. But when the second pair of helicopters attempted to land, their rotors collided and both Hueys went down. "The aircraft I was on hit too hard," Staff Sergeant John I. McGinty III of Boston, Massachusetts, recalls. "One of my troops saved my life. He held on to my belt and suspenders. The aircraft went up in the air and settled back down and we all piled out."

As night fell, K Company moved toward an enemy strong point in total darkness. Though the position had been abandoned, there were signs that the enemy had recently occupied the area. Holes were dug. There were empty ammunition boxes

Captain John I. McGinty, III

Captain Robert J. Modrzejewski

and even mess kits, and remains of a meal were scattered about. The Viet Cong were very close. "These foxholes that were dug hadn't been more than maybe 24 hours old and dug in a very hasty manner," recalls Captain Robert J. Modrzejewski of Milwaukee, Wisconsin. "It looked like there were probably two or three hundred of them. We figured we were going to be in for some difficult times."

Captain Modrzejewski was correct. On the first day, K Company suffered a few harassment attacks, but nothing they couldn't handle. The trouble came on the second day, when the enemy presence in the region more than doubled. By nightfall the men of K Company had sought shelter in the holes dug by their enemy. As the Viet Cong advanced on their position, the Marines began to return fire that seemed to come from every direction. It was clear that they were surrounded. Soon the Americans began to run out of ammunition in the face of repeated attacks. Captain Modrzejewski ordered his men to conserve bullets. Sergeant McGinty began to break down bandoliers, filling helmets with loose rounds. Under heavy fire, K Company's platoon leaders crawled throughout the perimeter, visiting each two-man foxhole and issuing M-14 rifle ammunition from their helmets. The assaults continued for three days, with enemy fire intensifying each night, until, on July 18, Captain Modrzejewski realized his Marines were surrounded by a regiment-size enemy force.

With no hope of evacuation, McGinty told the wounded to "eat it and continue to fire." As the enemy drew closer, Modrzejewski had no choice but to call down artillery on his own position; the enemy was so close there was no other option. The Marines hunkered deep into their foxholes as the artillery shells ripped up the ground around them. The noise was deafening and splinters of wood and blasted vegetation rained down on the American positions. The fighting intensified after the artillery strike ended.

"It reminded me of pictures I'd seen of World War I in the trenches, with solid light from gunfire over your head," McGinty remembers.

On July 18, support arrived in the shape new battalions and more ammunition. K Company was ordered to evacuate, which meant that they had to quick-march back to the bad-luck LZ where they had first arrived four days before. But as K Company prepared to move out of their foxholes in the middle of the night, the enemy responded with their most effective attack so far. "This is when all the North Vietnamese started coming out of the hills," Modrzejewski remembers. "They were kind of running in between John [McGinty]'s platoon."

As the rest of K Company withdrew, McGinty and thirty-two Marines were ordered to remain behind and cover their retreat. They held off a determined enemy assault for four hours, until they were surrounded and isolated again. When part of his platoon was cut off from the rest, Sergeant McGinty charged through the enemy, blasting them with his rifle until he reached the trapped men. He found twenty Marines down—all of them wounded—and the only corpsman dead. He reloaded weapons for the injured and redirected their fire. Though wounded himself, McGinty kept on fighting. Suddenly there was a lull in the battle. Then McGinty spotted movement in the darkness ahead of him. "One of my troops said 'Here comes some more Marines,'" recalls McGinty. "But I looked and they weren't Marines . . ."

Moving toward McGinty's position were five North Vietnamese, their mushroom-shaped helmets silhouetted against the night sky. Their AK-47s were raised and ready. McGinty drew his pistol and fired. "The training took over," McGinty remembers. "I squeezed the trigger and fired twenty rounds to get those people . . . Were it not for the Colt .45, I would be dead." But McGinty was alive— with five NVA regulars lying dead at his feet. "I don't remember shooting them. I don't remember a face," says Sergeant McGinty of the short, fierce engagement.

Now the North Vietnamese were closing in again, and this time it was Sergeant McGinty who called down artillery and air strikes on his own position. "I called in air strikes . . . Closer than normal," McGinty states. "Some of that steel and iron, I'm sure, caused casualties on our side." Luckily the strikes decimated the Vietnamese, who retreated in disarray. A few hours later McGinty's platoon was relieved.

Captain Robert Joseph Modrzejewski III and Staff Sergeant John James McGinty stood side by side when they received their Medals of Honor from Lyndon Johnson in a White House ceremony on March 12, 1968. Both had been wounded during Operation Hastings, and later in the war Sergeant McGinty lost sight in his right eye from a combat injury.

"I don't think anyone goes into combat with the intention of receiving a Medal of Honor," Modrzejewski has said. "All that's gonna get you is a pine box."

When asked if he was happy to receive the Medal of Honor, McGinty shakes his head. "It was just bloody bad luck to be there, that's all. I didn't do anything that any other Marine sergeant wouldn't do in that same spot."

Operation Hastings continued. On July 24, in another clash with the North Viet-

Captain Howard V. Lee

namese on a remote jungle trail near the DMZ, I Company of the Fifth Marines was ambushed, with its platoon on point hit the hardest. Lance Corporal Richard A. Pittman of San Joaquin, California, was with the Second Platoon in the column when he heard the sound of fighting. Dropping his rifle, Pittman grabbed a machine gun and belts of ammunition and rushed forward. While moving up the trail he came under fire from a hidden sniper. He raised the machine gun and fired a burst into the jungle. A lucky shot silenced the sniper, but two automatic weapons barked back at him. Pittman spotted his attackers, raised the machine gun, and cut them down.

Advancing again, Corporal Pittman covered fifty yards in record time. He found the point men lying dead or wounded on the trail and heard cries for help. But before he could render aid, he was attacked by a force of forty Vietnamese. He braced himself in the middle of the trail, placing his body and his weapon between the wounded and the enemy as he raked the jungle with machine-gun fire. When his gun jammed, Pittman picked up an AK-47 from a dead Vietnamese and used it until it was empty. Then he grabbed a pistol from a fallen Marine and continued to fire until the enemy fled into the bush. Tossing a final grenade their way, Corporal Pittman returned to his unit to get help for his wounded comrades. For his courage in the face of superior numbers, Lance Corporal Richard Allen Pittman was presented with the Medal of Honor by Lyndon Johnson in a ceremony held at the Inner Courtyard—known as the Hall of Heroes—at the Pentagon.

Operation Hastings ended on August 3, but the fighting continued without pause. Less than a week later, on August 8, just four miles south of the DMZ, a reconnaissance patrol flushed out a sizable enemy force. A platoon of E Company, Fourth Marines, were helicoptered in but found no trace of Mister Charles. As the choppers returned to ferry out the Marines, the North Vietnamese surrounded the landing zone. They waited patiently until most of the units were flown out. Then, in the gathering darkness, they struck at the Marines still waiting to be evacuated.

Two Hueys were damaged, stranding twenty-one Marines and four pilots at the besieged landing zone. New York City–born Captain Howard Vincent Lee heard the frantic calls of his trapped Marines over the radio net and acted. The thirty-three-year-old officer grabbed seven Marines and all the ammunition they could carry. Then they boarded two light choppers and flew to the battlefield. Lee landed and took command just as a large enemy force made a determined assault on the perimeter. In the first moments of this clash, shrapnel from a grenade wounded Captain Lee in the torso and eye, but he remained in command and fighting throughout the rest of the night. Another chopper appeared, this one loaded with ammo. It landed with the intention of evacuating out the wounded, but it was damaged and its crew grabbed weapons from the wounded and joined the firefight. With fewer than twenty Marines still standing, Lee fought off intermittent attacks that continued throughout the night. At dawn a large helicopter force arrived and Lee and his Marines were rescued. Captain Howard Vincent Lee received the Medal of Honor from Lyndon Baines Johnson in a White House ceremony on October 25, 1967.

Fighting continued along Route 9 and around the DMZ for the rest of the year. Another operation, conducted by the Third Marine Division under the general title Prairie began on August 3. The goal was to stop the People's Army of Vietnam's 324B Division from crossing the DMZ and invading Quang Tri Province. Operation Prairie was successful, but casualties were quite high—200 Marines were killed and 1,000 wounded. Faced with overwhelming numbers, the North Vietnamese retreated north, regrouped, and moved south again when the U.S. operation ended.

The South Vietnamese conducted their first constitutional election on September 11, 1966. After the elections, the South Vietnamese went through the motions of drawing up a new constitution. When the presidential election was held a year later, the ticket of Thieu and Prime Minister Ky predictably won, and the two strongmen immediately set about jailing their political rivals. Critics in the United States were outraged. What kind of government were the young men of America being asked to fight and perhaps die for?

By now there were 60,000 Marines in South Vietnam. They had killed 7,000 North Vietnamese with losses of 1,700 dead and 9,000 wounded. The big picture was more frightening. The United States had 400,000 troops in Vietnam, at a cost of $2 *billion* a month. Beyond that exorbitant price, Congress and the Johnson Administration also doled out funds to shore up the corrupt government of South Vietnam. In a 1967 visit to Australia, our allies in Vietnam, President Johnson promised the American and Australian people that victory was near. "I believe there is a light at the end of what has been a long and lonely tunnel," he stated. At that time no one could even imagine how long and lonely that tunnel would prove to be.

1967

In the first weeks of 1967, the Marines took part in various "clear and secure" operations to block infiltration and supply routes leading toward the city of Hue. They also had a rare opportunity to utilize their amphibious training. On January 5, the First Battalion, Ninth Marines, landed sixty-two miles south of Saigon to join with two Vietnamese Marine battalions to form the Special Landing Force. Operation Deckhouse V introduced U.S. troops to the war in "The Delta." During the remainder of 1967, the Special Landing Force would make twenty more landings, all of them in the I Corps area.

As the Tet holiday drew to a close, the Marines launched Operation Stone. In

Private James Anderson, Jr.

February, the Marines were given permission to fire artillery into the DMZ. In response rockets came down on Da Nang airfield, damaging seventeen aircraft and killing thirty-two civilians. Eleven American servicemen were killed including one Marine. The war was escalating and so was the body count.

On February 28, in the dense jungles near Cam Lo, the Second Platoon of F Company, Second Battalion, Third Marine Division, was rushing to rescue a besieged reconnaissance patrol when they came under heavy and sustained fire. On point was Private First Class James Anderson, Jr., of Compton, California, who found himself bunched with several other Marines in a position less than twenty yards from the enemy. Suddenly a grenade landed among them. Private Anderson found the grenade, closed his fist around it, and clutched the explosive to his chest as he curled into a fetal position. He was killed instantly. This twenty-year-old hero became the first African-American Marine to receive the Medal of Honor.

In all, five African-American Marines received the Medal of Honor for shielding their fellow Marines from harm. Along with Private Anderson, they were Private First Class Oscar P. Austin of Phoenix, Arizona; Sergeant Rodney M. Davis of Macon, Georgia; Private First Class Robert H. Jenkins, Jr., of Interlachen, Florida; and Private First Class Ralph H. Johnson of Charleston, South Carolina. Fifteen other Marines received posthumous Medals of Honor for sacrificing their lives to shield their comrades from harm by explosives and shrapnel: Lance Corporal Richard Allen Anderson of Washington, D.C.; Lance Corporal Jedh Colby Barker of Franklin, New Hampshire; Private First Class Daniel Dean Bruce of Michigan City, Indiana; Private First Class Bruce Wayne Carter; Lance Corporal Thomas Albert Creek of Joplin, Missouri; Lance Corporal Emilio Albert de la Garza of East Chicago, Indiana; Corporal William Thomas Perkins, Jr., a combat photographer from Rochester, New York; Private First Class Douglas Eugene Dickey of Greenville, Ohio; Sergeant Paul Hellstrom Foster of San Mateo, California; Lance Corporal James Donnie Howe of Six Mile, South Carolina; Private First Class Jimmy Wayne Phipps of Santa Monica, California; Lance Corporal Roy Mitchell Wheat of Moselle, Mississippi; Dewayne Thomas Williams of Brown City, Michigan; Private First Class Alfred Mac Wilson of Olney, Illinois (who entered service in Abilene, Texas); and Lance Corporal Kenneth Lee Worley of Farmington, New Mexico.

Gunnery Sergeant Allan Jay Kellogg, Jr., of Bridgeport, Connecticut, thrust a grenade into the mud and threw his body on top of it to save the other Marines in his platoon. Though the explosive detonated under him, Kellogg miraculously survived. He received the Medal of Honor from President Richard Nixon in a White House ceremony on October 15, 1973. On February 23, 1969, near Da Nang, Private First Class Oscar Palmer Austin of Nacogdoches, Texas, and Phoenix, Arizona, thrust himself in front of a bullet meant for another Marine. He was awarded a posthumous Medal of Honor. Private First Class Ronald Leroy Coker of Alliance, Nebraska, sacrificed his life rescuing a wounded comrade, placing his body in front of shots meant for the injured man. Private Coker managed to drag the fallen Marine to safety before he succumbed to his wounds.

On March 20, 1967, the Special Landing Force went ashore four miles south of the DMZ to assist with Operation Prairie III. On March 24, Sergeant Walter Keith Singleton from Memphis, Tennessee, was part of an ammunition-and-supply column from A Company, Ninth Marines, that was ambushed by a superior force. The Marines—mostly raw recruits in their first combat mission—panicked under fire and began shooting indiscriminately, resulting in friendly-fire casualties. Singleton carried the wounded to a place of safety. When the twenty-two-year old sergeant discovered that an area of brush—called a "hedgerow" in the official citation—was where the heaviest volume of fire originated, he grabbed a machine gun and entered the thicket, killing eight Viet Cong and scattering the rest. He was mortally wounded, but this action so surprised the enemy that they eventually withdrew. Sergeant Singleton received a posthumous Medal of Honor.

Six days later I Company, Third Battalion, Ninth Marines, was attacked while establishing night ambush sites. Several Americans were killed by a North Vietnamese Company supported by heavy machine guns and mortars. Second Lieutenant John Paul Bobo of Niagara Falls, New York, organized a hasty defense of the perimeter. He moved from position to position, urging his men to fight back and directing their fire. Lieutenant Bobo recovered a rocket launcher and established a new launcher team, which immediately laid fire onto enemy machine-gun positions.

When an exploding mortar round severed Lieutenant Bobo's right leg below the knee, he refused evacuation and placed himself in a firing position. With a web belt wrapped around his stump as a tourniquet and his leg jammed into the dirt to contain the bleeding, Bobo sent devastating fire into the North Vietnamese positions. His courageous stand enabled the Marines to repulse the initial attack.

Wounded again—this time mortally—Lieutenant Bobo continued to rake the enemy until his men could reach a place of safety. The twenty-four-year-old second lieutenant, who had celebrated his birthday just five weeks before his death, received a posthumous Medal of Honor for his heroism.

In April, the Marines participated in Operation Union, which began in the Viet Cong–controlled Que Son Valley. Though brief, Operation Union I and II—April 21 to June 5—were the bloodiest Marine Corps clashes in Vietnam to date. On April 21 near Bihn Son, elements of F Company, First Marines, clashed with an entrenched enemy. Eighteen-year-old Private First Class Gary Wayne Martini of Lexington, Virginia, charged across an open rice paddy with other members of his platoon. The

Marines got within thirty feet of the enemy before they were stopped by grenades and automatic weapons and small-arms fire. Fourteen Marines died. Eighteen were wounded and the survivors of Martini's platoon were pinned down behind a low paddy dike, unable to advance or retreat. Martini crawled over the dike and, moving on his belly under intense fire, got close enough to hurl grenades into the North Vietnamese position.

When he returned to the paddy dike, Martini spotted wounded Marines who were lying exposed to enemy small-arms fire. One Marine had already been cut down as he tried to rescue the wounded, but this did not deter Private Martini. Without regard for his own safety, he raced from cover and dragged one wounded man behind cover—and was wounded in the process. Spurning aid, Martini braved enemy fire a second time and was mortally wounded. Despite his injuries, he pushed a second wounded Marine to cover before succumbing. Private First Class Gary Wayne Martini "unhesitatingly yielded his life to save two of his comrades and insure the safety of his platoon." His posthumous award was presented to his family in a ceremony at the Marine Corps barracks in Washington, D.C.

Two additional Marine battalions were airlifted into the valley to reinforce this action. By mid-May, 110 Marines had been killed and almost 500 had been wounded in Operation Union I. Enemy casualties were estimated to be around 900. Operation Union II began in Quang Tin Province in May and quickly degenerated into an eleven-day brawl with a stubborn and entrenched enemy. After artillery and air strikes, the fighting became bunker to bunker, with Marines rooting out the Cong in the brutal style of the island-hopping campaign against the Japanese.

Captain James Albert Graham of Wilkinsburg, Pennsylvania, led F Company, Second Battalion, Fifth Marines, across an open rice paddy in the face of a mortar bombardment and small-arms fire. When two concealed machine guns pinned down his platoon, Graham rounded up his headquarters staff and charged the enemy emplacement. The furious attack routed the enemy, who left their machine guns and dead behind. Graham killed fifteen in this clash.

As his men and the trapped platoon withdrew, Captain Graham stayed with a Marine who was too seriously wounded to be moved. As he covered his unit's retreat, he sent a final radio message that he was being attacked by a force of twenty-five North Vietnamese. Graham, a twenty-seven-year-old company commander, gave his life for his men. His posthumous Medal of Honor was given to his family on October 29, 1968.

When Union I and II ended on June 5, 1,566 enemy dead had been counted. The Marines lost 220 killed and 700 wounded. During June and July, the enemy continued to build their forces around Khe Sanh. Fighting erupted on July 2 when B and C Companies, Ninth Marines, were attacked. More battalions were flown into the region and the fighting persisted until July 14, with 159 Marines killed. The North Vietnamese suffered over a thousand dead, and two were captured and interrogated.

On August 19, near Quang Ngai on the northern coast of the Republic of Vietnam, twenty-seven-year-old helicopter pilot Captain Stephen Wesley Pless of Atlanta, Georgia, his copilot Captain Rupert E. Fairfield, and two weapons officers—

Gunnery Sergeant Leroy N. Poulson and Lance Corporal John G. Phelps—participated in a daring airborne rescue. At the controls of a helicopter gunship festooned with rocket launchers and machine guns—but lacking a cargo hold for passengers—Pless heard by radio that a U.S. Army Huey was down on a remote beach and its crew was under attack. Over the scene, Pless saw four Americans being beaten and stabbed by more than thirty Viet Cong who had streamed out of the jungle and attacked the stricken GIs. At first Pless tried to scare the Cong off by diving low and whizzing over their heads. Then he fired his machine guns and a battery of rockets into the jungle, scattering the enemy.

Captain Pless saw a wounded American on the ground wave at him. Convinced that the Viet Cong would return before a rescue chopper arrived, he landed just as the enemy began to fire from inside the tree line. A wounded American stumbled forward and Sergeant Poulson ran out under intense fire to rescue him as well as two other Americans. Captain Fairfield climbed out of the copilot seat to help drag the injured to the chopper while Lance Corporal Phelps kept up a steady stream of machine-gun fire to cover their movements. When the Viet Cong finally rushed the helicopter, Phelps cut them down. The three wounded men were loaded aboard the idling helicopter. Under increasing fire, Pless took off. A United States Army Cobra gunship arrived to cover their evacuation, but Captain Pless had so overloaded his gunship that he had trouble getting off the ground. His chopper shot out over the water, striking the waves four times before becoming airborne. For his courage and initiative, Captain Stephen Wesley Pless was awarded the Medal of Honor in a White House ceremony. Two years later, on July 20, 1969, Captain Pless lost his life in a tragic accident. He was twenty-nine years old.

In August and September, the Vietnamese used artillery and rocket attacks to disrupt Marine Corps strong points, airfields, and ammunition dumps at Dong Ha, Phu Bbai, and Da Nang. On September 4, Navy Chaplain Vincent R. Capodanno of Staten Island, New York, was killed rendering last rites to the dying on the battlefield. In this same engagement Sergeant Lawrence D. Peters of Johnson City, New York, was killed leading his squad against a superior force. During the attack, Peters stood in full view of the enemy in an effort to force them to reveal their firing positions. His tactic was successful, but Sergeant Peters—who had celebrated his twenty-first birthday just a few days before—was mortally wounded. Both Sergeant Peters and Chaplain Capodanno received posthumous Medals of Honor.

In the final weeks of 1967, more United States Army units moved into I Corps. Four days before Christmas, the First Platoon of D Company, Seventh Marines, fought an all-night battle with a battalion of North Vietnamese regulars at the mouth of Happy Valley near Phouc Ninh. The fighting was furious and at close range. Second Lieutenant Michael Neil led his platoon in the fierce engagement and received a Navy Cross. Corporal Larry Eugene Smedley, one of Lieutenant Neil's squad leaders, spotted the North Vietnamese advancing through the valley toward a concentration of U.S. Marines. After radioing the coordinates, Smedley maneuvered his squad to ambush the enemy. The Marines attacked, only to be flanked by North Vietnamese machine-gun fire. The eighteen-year-old corporal was blown off his feet by a Viet

Cong rifle grenade, got to his feet, and charged the North Vietnamese machine guns. Wounded a second time, Smedley silenced the guns before he was shot in the chest and killed.

Born in Front Royal, Virginia, Larry Eugene Smedley entered service in Orlando, Florida, where his family relocated when he was a child. On June 20, 1969, the Smedley family accepted their son's posthumous Medal of Honor from President Richard M. Nixon.

As 1967 came to a close, 77,679 Marines were serving with twenty-one battalions in the I Corps area of operation. The United States Army had fifteen battalions in the field, some of them in the southern end of I Corps. There were also three battalions of South Korean Marines and thirty-one ARVN battalions. In 1967, the Marines had killed nearly 18,000 enemy soldiers, and suffered 3,452 dead and 26,000 wounded. With nearly 5,500 dead overall, the Vietnam War was rivaling World War II in the number of Marine Corps casualties.

In 1968, U.S. intelligence noted a buildup of North Vietnamese troops along the DMZ. General William Westmoreland, commander in chief of U.S. Forces in South Vietnam, expected an attack on Khe Sanh and began shifting his forces northward, away from the cities. Facing the enemy along the DMZ was the Third Marine Division, strung out in a fragile line in the northernmost area of I Corps. Early in 1968, General Westmoreland sent reinforcements into the area, including units of the First Marines Division, the First Air Cavalry Division, and the Second Brigade of the 101st Airborne. There were now a quarter of a million U.S. servicemen inside I Corps. Of the Corps' total strength of 300,000, more than 80,000—more than one in four—were stationed in South Vietnam. By the time the Tet holidays rolled around, the stage was set. Soon the most intense, knock-down-drag-out fight of the war would take place.

THE TET OFFENSIVE

Tet Nguyen Day is the celebration of the Vietnamese New Year. Tet is both a secular and religious holiday and the date changes from year to year. Though it is called Tet Nguyen Day, the actual celebration lasts three days. The Vietnamese believe that gods live in their homes, track their deeds, and protect their families. Before the Tet holidays they make offerings so that their gods will look favorably upon them. The holiday's traditional trappings include fireworks, candles, and good cheer; it is said that everyone must remain happy during Tet to ward off bad luck in the upcoming year.

In 1968, a national cease-fire was declared for the Tet holidays, which ran from January 27 through February 3. But the truce was broken on the second and third day when the North Vietnamese bombarded Da Nang and Chu Lai with rockets. These attacks, though devastating, were merely probes; the real offensive came on January 30 and 31 when thousands of North Vietnamese troops launched ground attacks against all five provincial capitals and thirty other cities in South Vietnam, including Hue and Da Nang in the I Corps area of operations. In all, 60,000 North Vietnamese troops and Viet Cong guerrillas participated in the surprise Tet Offensive.

Communist infiltrators entered the major cities with the holiday crowds, then changed into their uniforms and gathered at rally points to strike at strategic targets like government buildings, police stations, and power stations. The attacks stunned the American high command, which had been fixated on Khe Sanh and the enemy buildup in the region for many months. General Westmoreland and his staff were so certain that the enemy attack would come at Khe Sanh that they even convinced President Lyndon Baines Johnson, who had a scale model of the Khe Sanh Marine Corps base constructed in the War Room. But though the fighting had been heavy around Khe Sanh since mid-January, the enemy activity was a classic feint—the real target of North Vietnamese aggression were the cities, which fell like dominoes under their determined onslaught.

Fortunately for the Americans, the attacks were not well coordinated. Several North Vietnamese units actually launched their assault twenty-four hours early—they were working from the traditional lunar calendar instead of the Communist-imposed new calendar. As soon as these initial attacks occurred, the cease-fire was canceled and many South Vietnamese and American units were put on high alert. Otherwise the enemy offensive might have been even more devastating. As it was, by the end of January the NVA had taken control of Hue. With brutal efficiency they rounded up and executed political prisoners—including doctors, educators, government bureaucrats, and the families of officers and enlisted men fighting with the ARVN. Many Westerners, including U.S. government workers and foreign diplomats, civilians, and missionaries, were also attacked.

In the capital city of Saigon, the infiltrators staged a rocket attack on the United States embassy. They held the compound for six hours, killing several Marine Corps and U.S. Army personnel. Other Viet Cong units attacked the Presidential Palace and Tan Son Nhut Airport. But enemy success was not universal; the Communists were repelled at Tam Ky, Quang Ngai, and at Quang Tri city—where they were repulsed by the First Air Cavalry Division.

At Cam Lo on the night of February 2, the enemy smashed through the town's defenses and attacked the district headquarters compound with rockets, mortars, recoilless rifles, small arms, and machine guns. On duty that night was a young Marine corporal from Glendale, California, Larry Leonard Maxam. At twenty—he had just celebrated his birthday on January 9—Maxam had many responsibilities. One of them was keeping his men at their positions at the perimeter of a compound that was rapidly being overrun. As his men hunkered down under the merciless assault, Maxam noticed that the North Vietnamese were massing near his position on the wire. It was obvious that they were preparing an attack on a weakened section of his perimeter. Corporal Maxam turned over his command to another fire-team leader, then proceeded to the besieged area to drive the enemy off. The North Vietnamese spotted the tall Marine as he raced across open ground toward a machine-gun emplacement that had already been overrun. Several grenades detonated near Corporal Maxam and he was nearly knocked off his feet. Bleeding from shrapnel wounds, Maxam reached the machine gun and fired on the enemy, cutting them down as they charged the wire.

Corporal Maxam's position suffered a direct hit by a North Vietnamese rocket-propelled rifle grenade, but the explosive failed to silence the corporal's gun. Though Maxam was blasted backward and shrapnel wounds peppered his face and shattered his right eye, he shook off the pain and kept on fighting. Partially blinded and weakened by loss of blood, he lay down on his belly in the dirt but continued to inflict heavy fire on the North Vietnamese. Unfortunately, Corporal Maxam was trapped in a remote location and could neither retreat nor expect reinforcements to get through the intense fire and rescue him. But the knowledge that he was probably doomed didn't deter him, and the volleys from Maxam's machine gun never wavered. Eventually the North Vietnamese pulled back behind the wire, leaving their dead behind. For over ninety minutes Corporal Maxam held the North Vietnamese off, through grenade attacks, a hail of small-arms fire, and several blasts from an Soviet-made recoilless rifle. Though he finally succumbed to his injuries, Corporal Maxam single-handedly defended half of the beleaguered perimeter. His posthumous Medal of Honor was received by his family in a White House ceremony on October 22, 1968.

Back at Hue, the American high command demonstrated a decided reluctance to bombard the once-peaceful and still-revered city. That reticence ended when the ARVN commander in the city asked for Marine Corps help in recapturing Hue. The fight began almost immediately and was house to house, much as it had been for the Marines battling in Seoul, Korea, eighteen years before.

Five days into their battle for Hue, the Marines of A Company, First Battalion, First Marine Division, had advanced steadily despite vicious and sustained street fighting. They had secured street after street, overcoming the obstacles the North Vietnamese threw up at each intersection. When the street was secure, the Marines moved through buildings, neutralizing enemy troops who stayed to fight. On February 4, 1968, after five days of urban warfare, the Third Platoon of A Company was stopped in their tracks near the intersection of Tran Cao Van Street and Ly Thuong Kiet Street, at the location of a stone structure that housed the Jeanne d'Arc girls' high school.

Sergeant Alfredo "Freddy" Gonzalez, a Mexican-American from San Antonio, Texas, had demonstrated superb leadership skills in the first days of street fighting. Only twenty-one, the sergeant had taken command of his platoon days before when its original leader was wounded and evacuated. Now, as he eyed the school, he tried to figure a way to dislodge the North Vietnamese snipers who lurked inside.

Gonzalez led his platoon inside one of the school structures, where they quickly cleared the first floor of snipers. Then, after grabbing a bundle of light antitank weapons, Gonzalez crept up to the second floor and took position in a window opposite the rest of the school compound. From there he proceeded to blast the enemy in the opposite building with rockets fired across the central courtyard. One after the other, Sergeant Gonzalez blasted snipers out of windows and cleared a large portion of the occupied structure. In desperation, the North Vietnamese brought up a rocket-propelled gun and fired it through the window Gonzalez occupied, killing him instantly. Vice-President Spiro T. Agnew presented Sergeant Alfredo Gonzalez's posthumous Medal of Honor to his family in October 1969.

It was not until February 6 that the Marines recaptured Hue's hospital, jail, and the provincial headquarters. Resistance south of the Perfume River was stamped out on February 9. Then the Marines crossed the river and helped the ARVN units retake the old city. It took until February 22 to drive the North Vietnamese completely out of Hue and two more days before the city was declared secure. The fighting finally ended near the Citadel at the center of the old city.

Eventually, nearly all of the cities taken by the North Vietnamese were recaptured with huge losses to the enemy. In response to the surprise attack, General William Westmoreland asked that an additional 200,000 troops be deployed in Vietnam. His request shocked the Johnson Administration and led to a political firestorm in Washington.

But despite the surprise of their attack, at the Tet Offensive the Communists had gone head-to-head with the United States military for the first time, and were defeated. Once the shock of the attack wore off, American units rallied and pushed the enemy out of the urban areas. Never again would the North Vietnamese mount an organized offensive. Instead, they would melt into the countryside and continue their guerrilla war of attrition against the people of South Vietnam. But the political damage had already been done. The American press went wild, questioning the ability of the United States military to defeat the enemy. Had this American victory occurred earlier in the war, things might have been different. Though the Communists lost one-third of their assault force—over 15,000 men—they also caused tremendous destruction all over the south and had murdered 165,000 civilians. It appeared to the world that the Americans were losing the war—it was a myth, but a pervasive one. All the people at home saw—thanks to a journalistic community that was hostile to military involvement in Southeast Asia—were more dead Americans, more shattered cities, more bombs, more mobilization, and no light at all at the end of the tunnel. On March 1, 1968 Clark Clifford replaced Robert S. McNamara as secretary of defense. On March 22, President Johnson also relieved General Westmoreland of his command. Army General Creighton W. Abrams, Jr., replaced him. The war in Vietnam was causing casualties at the top of the pecking order. Even President Johnson sat uneasily in the Oval Office.

KHE SANH

The seventy-seven-day siege known as the Second Battle of Khe Sanh was another Dien Bien Phu waiting to happen, or so the North Vietnamese thought. A large concentration of Marines trapped in a compound and surrounded by an enemy poised to overrun them seemed to be a target ripe for plucking. But it was 1968, not 1954, and with the debut of helicopters, no base, no matter how remote or isolated, was as vulnerable as the French had been at Dien Bien Phu. This fact was established months before, when the Communists cut the only road to Khe Sanh. After the loss of Route 9, the outpost was supplied and reinforced exclusively and efficiently by helicopter.

General Westmoreland wanted the Marines at Khe Sanh to block enemy infiltration from Laos. By mid-January 1968, there were 6,000 Marines concentrated in and around the village—half of them housed inside the main compound. Khe Sanh and its inhabitants would pay dearly when the fighting commenced. On January 20, as the North Vietnamese were planning the Tet Offensive, two Third Battalion companies attacked a North Vietnamese force that had dug in near Khe Sanh. On the twenty-first, the North Vietnamese retaliated, bombarding the base with high-explosive artillery rounds. The Marine Corps ammunition depot was struck and destroyed—an explosion heard around the world, as American and European journalists covered the story on the nightly news telecasts, complete with graphic footage of the burning ruins. Reinforcements were rushed into the area and a thousand refugees from the village of Khe Sanh were evacuated. Three thousand others were refused entry to the Marine Corps compound and made their way to Route 9 in an effort to reach safety. Less than half of them would live to see Dong Ha.

After several attacks by North Vietnamese regulars, air strikes were launched. B-52s carpet-bombed targets around Khe Sanh every three hours, and fighter-bombers flew over 300 sorties daily. At times air strikes placed bombs within a thousand yards of the American compound. Sniper duels were common, and daily exchanges of fire sometimes reached critical intensity. At times the fighting was hand to hand. On March 6, the Communists began to withdraw their troops from Khe Sanh. They had lost thousands of casualties and failed to overrun the compound. Though much of the activity around the village was the result of a ploy to turn America's attention away from the cities, the North Vietnamese wanted to capture Khe Sanh—why pay such a high price otherwise?

Over 200 Marines were killed in the Second Battle of Khe Sanh and 1,600 were wounded. Communist casualties numbered over 10,000—some estimate those losses at closer to 15,000—most falling victim to the deadly B-52 bombing raids. At Khe Sanh the U.S. forces in Vietnam achieved their most decisive victory of the war. If the Communists had intended to inflict another Dien Bien Phu–type defeat on the West, they had failed, and paid dearly in the bargain.

When the monsoon season ended, the Americans launched a triple spring offensive—the relief of Khe Sanh, an attack in the A Shau Valley, and an incursion into the DMZ. The operations at Khe Sanh and A Shau were both successful, but the campaign in the DMZ did not go according to plan. On April 29, the ARVN tackled a North Vietnamese regiment just seven kilometers outside of Dong Ha. This action began a three-day battle that raged through the village of Dong Huan to the hamlet of Bac Vong and along the banks of the Cua Viet River. On May 1, three companies of Marines attacked a fortified village called Dai Do, which lay to the west of the main fighting. It was to be a two-pronged attack—H Company was to approach Dai Do via Dong Huan while F Company was to advance directly to Dai Do across an expanse of open ground, and were promised a smoke screen to cover their movements. Before H Company entered Dong Huan, a pair of F-4 Phantoms unleashed 500 pound bombs and napalm canisters on the village to disrupt the defenders and allow the Marines to move into the area undetected. But as H Company approached Dong Huan through thick jungle vegetation—where the visibility was often less that five feet—the crack of AK-47s interrupted the stillness. The ambush killed some Marines and scattered the rest.

Popping out of spider holes and hidden in tangles of jungle vines, the Communists chewed up the Marine detachment. Soon the fighting was hand to hand, with men from H Company tossing grenades into spider holes and grappling with NVA regulars. The Marines finally reached Dong Huan after hours of intense fighting. They gazed across wide-open rice paddies at their next objective—the fortified town of Dai Do, which was ringed by enemy strong points and bunkers. F Company was ready to move. But as they approached Dai Do, they were greeted by small-arms fire, so an artillery attack was called down on the village. When it ended, the Marines advanced, gaining a tenuous foothold on the edge of the enemy-held town.

G Company was dispatched to reinforce F Company, but did not arrive until May 1. Commanded by Winslow, Arizona–born Captain Jay R. Vargas, a thirty-one-year-old career officer, G Company was ordered to advance across a vast expanse of open rice paddy, facing enemy mortar, rocket, and artillery fire. After a thirty-minute napalm bombardment by Marine Corps Phantoms and Skyhawks, G Company—supported by two tanks—began their advance. They made it two-thirds of the way before the NVA opened fire on them. Marines were cut down by a North Vietnamese 12.7mm machine gun that decimated their ranks. Despite the intense fire, about half of G Company gained a foothold in a copse of trees and moved parallel to the enemy lines, neutralizing hot spots, rooting out spider holes, and cutting down snipers who lurked in huts, trees, and hedgerows. The Marines had almost reached the far side of Dai Do when the NVA staged a counterattack. Hundreds of North Vietnamese regulars poured into the town, and Captain Vargas was ordered to withdraw.

But it was too late. The North Vietnamese were so close that the fighting was hand to hand. Troops slammed into one another like clashing medieval knights. Finally, Vargas and forty-five Marines took cover in a drainage ditch on the outskirts of the village. Artillery was called for in an effort to push the North Vietnamese back. Soon explosives began to come down perilously close to Vargas's men. Captain Vargas, now wounded, established a defensive perimeter at the edge of the village, along the deep drainage ditch. Eventually their return fire and the artillery bombardment drove the Communists off, and Vargas and his men settled in for the night.

G Company fought off numerous night assaults while twenty-eight-year-old Captain James E. Livingston of Towns, Georgia, led E Company through several miles of fierce enemy fire to relieve Vargas's unit. At dawn on May 2, Livingston ordered his Marines to fix bayonets as they began their advance on Dai Do. The entrenched Vietnamese waited until the Marines had crossed most of no-man's-land before cutting loose. When they did, the results were devastating. Livingston's Marines would have been slaughtered to a man if not for some quick thinking by Captain Vargas.

Witnessing the advance, he ordered his men to fire into the Vietnamese from their own positions along the drainage ditch. Suddenly flanked, the North Vietnamese withdrew long enough for Livingston's Marines to reach Vargas's unit. Together the two commands dug in at the northwestern edge of Dai Do and waited for reinforcements. Unbelievably, they were ordered forward to attack another fortified village. Despite their doubts, Captain Vargas and Captain Livingston obeyed their orders, but the Marines were repulsed by a superior enemy. Wounded three times and crippled from his final injury, Livingston continued to direct his troops as they withdrew through Dai Do to link up with an American relief column dispatched to evacuate them.

Captain James Everett Livingston and Captain Jay R. Vargas both received the Medal of Honor on May 17, 1970, for this action. It was presented to them by President Richard M. Nixon in a White House ceremony. Vargas and Livingston remained in the Marine Corps after Vietnam. Vargas attained the rank of colonel before his retirement. Major General James E. Livingston is still on active duty today.

Marines continued several operations in 1968. On May 17, during the execution of Operation Allen Brook, I Company, Third Battalion, First Marine Division, was approaching a dry riverbed when they came under sustained fire. Several Marines were killed outright. Though the enemy was well concealed, Private First Class Robert Charles Burke of Monticello, Illinois, spied a piece of jungle where much of the enemy fire originated. The eighteen-year-old machine gunner grabbed his weapon and proceeded to launch a one-man assault on the enemy position.

From the edge of a steep riverbank Burke leveled fire on the Vietnamese, driving them back and allowing other American units to move forward and retrieve the wounded. He spotted a North Vietnamese machine-gun nest and wiped it out, killing three. Then Burke moved from position to position along the dry riverbed, neutralizing enemy strong points and rooting the Vietnamese out into the open, to be gunned down by other Marines. When his machine gun jammed, Burke picked up a rifle from a dead soldier and continued to fire, killing two more Communists as they closed in on him. When a fellow Marine cleared the jam, Burke took up his machine gun again and moved toward a dense thicket. He saturated the area until he was mortally wounded. His solo assault saved his unit and helped them to secure the area. Vice-President Spiro T. Agnew presented Burke's posthumous Medal of Honor to his family on December 16, 1971.

In November, Richard M. Nixon was elected president on the promise that he would end the war. Outgoing President Johnson announced the cessation of all air, naval, and artillery bombardment of North Vietnam. The Communists responded with a pledge to attend the peace talks in Paris and to withdraw their troops from South Vietnam. This truce was short-lived; on November 5, the Communists accused the United States of conducting reconnaissance flights over their territory and hostilities resumed.

As 1968 drew to a close, the Marines launched Operation Meade River. On December 8, twenty-nine-year-old Gunnery Sergeant Karl Gorman Taylor, Sr., of Laurel, Maryland, earned a posthumous Medal of Honor for silencing a machine gun that was tearing his unit apart. He saved the lives of several Marines at the cost of his own and his award was presented to his family by Richard M. Nixon on October 15, 1973.

By the end of 1968, 62,000 enemy soldiers were killed in the Marine Corps zone of operation in a twelve-month period. The Marines sustained a total of 4,618 dead and 30,000 wounded. Marine Corps strength in Vietnam peaked in December, with 85,500 Marines fighting in-country. Defeated during the Tet Offensive and bloodied at Hue, the Viet Cong and their North Vietnamese allies were reeling in the face of American firepower. Some of their units had been completely decimated and the Viet

Cong especially had suffered severe casualties. But the Communists were not defeated, and the war in Vietnam was far from over.

1969

Richard Nixon assumed the office of president in January and immediately began his "Vietnamization" program. Nixon wanted to strengthen the ARVN while scaling back U.S. operations and eventually withdrawing all American troops from Vietnam. On June 8, he made good on his word, announcing that the first 25,000 United States troops would be withdrawn from South Vietnam by the end of August. Though doomed to failure, Nixon's Vietnamization program was a bold political move—the troop withdrawals appeased the antiwar protesters and the "doves" in Congress, while the buildup of the South with more arms and matériel appealed to those "hawks" who believed that the Vietnamese people should not be abandoned. But despite this highly publicized withdrawal—which amounted to less than one-twentieth of the U.S. forces stationed Vietnam—the war continued.

On January 13, the largest Special Landing Force amphibious operation of the Vietnam War took place. Enemy resistance was so light around their objective at Chu Lai that the landing amounted to little more than an exercise. Things were different in the mountains of Quang Tri Province, where Operation Dewey Canyon began on January 22. Colonel John Barrow's Ninth Marines moved into the area and were supplied by helicopter—a risky proposition during monsoon season. Bad weather could come up at any time, grounding Marine Corps resupply helicopters and rendering evacuation impossible. Though Marine air groups flew 1,617 sorties, Barrow's Ninth Marines experienced one hairy ten-day period without any resupply at all.

By February 18, the fighting was intense. After a clash with the NVA on February 22, First Lieutenant Wesley Lee Fox of Herndon, Virginia, sent twenty men out to fill canteens at a creek. Within minutes of reaching the banks, the detail came under machine-gun and small-arms fire. Fox recalled the detail and sent his First Platoon into action against the enemy. They advanced through thick jungle for a short distance, only to run into a reinforced NVA company dug into a network of interconnected bunkers. Fox kept the pressure on, pushing the platoon forward against heavy fire. An enemy mortar round decimated the command group. Everyone except First Lieutenant Lee R. Herron was killed or wounded, so Herron assumed command of the Second Platoon. Fox and First Platoon continued to advance, fighting hand to hand as they entered the network of bunkers.

First Lieutenant Fox personally destroyed several strong points. Though wounded twice, he fought until the bitter end, driving the NVA from their position. This clash was the last action of Operation Dewey Canyon and earned Fox a Medal of Honor. First Lieutenant Herron, who was killed in this engagement, received a posthumous Navy Cross.

Three days after Operation Dewey Canyon ended, in an engagement in Quang Tri Province, the NVA ambushed H Company. Two Marines on a flanking patrol were killed and five wounded in the first seconds of the ambush. Corporal William David Morgan, a twenty-two-year-old Marine from Pittsburgh, Pennsylvania, charged the enemy, then dived into a jungle thicket to draw enemy fire. Though Morgan was killed, his action enabled others to evacuate the wounded and wipe out the enemy. For his brave self-sacrifice, Corporal Morgan received a posthumous Medal of Honor, presented by President Richard Nixon to his family.

Lance Corporal Thomas F. Noonan of Brooklyn, New York, sacrificed his life during Operation Dewey Canyon in an attempt to save a wounded Marine. Noonan, a fire-team leader, managed to get the man to safety before he was mortally wounded. His family received his posthumous Medal of Honor from President Nixon in the East Ballroom of the White House.

Lance Corporal William Raymond Prom, also of Pittsburgh, was killed during Operation Taylor Common when he assumed position behind a machine gun and made a stand in the open against a superior force. His action allowed others to evacuate wounded Marines, regroup, and overrun the enemy. His Medal of Honor was presented posthumously to his family by Vice-President Spiro T. Agnew on April 20, 1970.

Twenty-one-year-old Lance Corporal Lester William Weber of Aurora, Illinois, received a Medal of Honor for actions near Bo Ban on February 23. As a machine-gun squad leader with the Second Platoon, M Company, Seventh Marines, Weber was sent forward to help another unit under fire. As the platoon moved into an area of tall grass, they were attacked by small arms and machine guns. Corporal Weber plunged into the waving grasses, killed one NVA regular, and forced eleven others to retreat. A second North Vietnamese soldier appeared out of the swishing grass, and Weber grappled with the man, killing him in a brutal, hand-to-hand duel.

When Corporal Weber spied two NVA firing on his platoon from behind the cover of a dike, he dived into their position, wrestling two North Vietnamese to the ground and killing them with their own weapons. As he rushed to attack another NVA position, Corporal Weber was mortally wounded. His Medal of Honor was awarded posthumously.

In August, the Marines moved into the Que Son Valley and joined units of the U.S. Army in a fight against NVA regulars near the town of Hiep Duc. On the morning of the twenty-sixth, the men of K Company, Third Battalion, Seventh Marines, came under fire as they were moving to link up with the Army's 31st Infantry. During the engagement, Mexican-born Lance Corporal José Francisco Jimenez, a fire-team leader, plunged into an enemy position in a jungle thicket. Killing several NVA who stood in his way, Corporal Jimenez took over an enemy machine gun and began pumping lead into the ranks of the enemy. The twenty-three-year-old Marine from Mexico City drew fire from other enemy machine guns but refused to abandon his position. Jimenez personally destroyed two emplacements before he was killed. His Medal of Honor was awarded posthumously, presented to his family by Richard Nixon in a somber White House ceremony.

Marine combat in the first half of 1969 was less intense than during the two previous years, and among the first 25,000 troops to be withdrawn were 8,388 Marines. The slow pullout had begun, but Marine Corps operations would continue into 1970.

EXIT THE MARINES

The Marines fought several engagements along the DMZ in the autumn of 1969, and the final Special Landing Force operation of the war began on September 7, when they landed near Hoi An. The Third and Fourth Marines were pulled out in the second wave of troop withdrawals in mid-December. On April 15, another batch of Marines—nearly 13,000—were shipped home. The war was winding down, but it was not over yet.

The first major action of 1970 was a January 6 NVA night attack on Fire Support Base Ross in the Que Son Valley. Through heavy rain enemy sappers penetrated the perimeter behind an artillery barrage. Forty NVA were killed or captured, and thirteen Marines died pushing the enemy back.

The CAP program—or Marine Combined Action Platoon—was one of the success stories of the war. Marines took the pacification of their area of responsibility seriously, and understood that they would have to win the support of the local populace to deny the North Vietnamese and their Viet Cong allies local support and bases of operations. Based on their earlier experiences in Central America and the Caribbean, the Marines formed the first CAP units in the fall of 1965. In a typical CAP operation, a Marine rifle squad and a Navy corpsman along with a platoon of ARVN would be assigned to a particular village. The Marines got to know the people, helped them build schools and public works, and taught the young and able-bodied the art of self-defense. It was a very effective way to win the hearts and minds of the people and pacify an area.

Jean Sauvageot, an Army officer sent to observe the Marine Corps CAP program in action, was impressed with what he saw. "There was absolutely no comparison between CAP and what most Army units were doing . . . if CAP killed fifteen enemy soldiers, they usually had fifteen weapons to show for it. At the same time, Army units were killing fifteen or five or fifty enemies and might not have a single weapon to show when the fighting stopped." Sauvageot ended his report with a startling conclusion. The Army units "were killing noncombatants and claiming them as dead enemy soldiers."

In the hamlets with CAP operations, villagers learned how to fight their own battles against the Viet Cong, to protect their prominent citizens, conduct aggressive patrols of their own, and resist Communist incursion into their region. The last CAP unit was withdrawn in the spring of 1971.

One Marine who participated in these Combined Action Platoon operations earned a Medal of Honor. In the dark, early-morning hours of May 8, 1970, a CAP unit in Quang Nai Province was ambushed by a vastly superior force. Wounded in the initial exchange, eighteen-year-old Lance Corporal Miguel Keith from San Antonio, Texas, advanced across fire-swept terrain to deliver a hail of machine-gun fire against the approaching North Vietnamese. As five NVA flanked the main American force and moved to attack the command post, Corporal Keith intercepted them, firing from the hip as he advanced. Three North Vietnamese were cut down. The others fled. One of the retreating NVA tossed a grenade over his shoulder. When it exploded, the blast knocked Corporal Keith to the ground. Bleeding from a score of wounds, the young corporal rose, secured his machine gun, and charged a cluster of twenty-five or more NVA regulars massing to attack. Four North Vietnamese died where they stood, the rest dispersed. A parting shot mortally wounded Corporal Keith. Lance Corporal Miguel Keith was the final Marine to receive the Medal of Honor in the Vietnam War. The posthumous award was presented to his family in a White House ceremony presided over by Vice-President Spiro T. Agnew.

By 1970, Army units outnumbered the Marines operating in I Corps. In July and August, the Marines attacked enemy bases around Da Nang, and on August 31, the Marines made one last trip into the Que Son Valley during Operation Imperial Lake. This would be the last Marine Corps offensive of the Vietnam War. The Seventh Marines left Vietnam in the autumn, followed by the Fifth Marines in February 1971. Only a few Marine Corps air units and several hundred advisers remained in Southeast Asia after 1971, and all Marine ground missions ceased on May 7. The last Marine ground troops sailed for home on June 25.

For the Leathernecks, the long ordeal in Vietnam was finally over.

During the Vietnam conflict, 730,000 men and women served in the Marine Corps—130,000 more than served in all of World War II. Although there were still 70,000 American soldiers in Vietnam after the Marines departed, most ground action was left to the ARVN. After a flurry of furious bombing—which included Hanoi for the first time in the war—an agreement was reached at the Paris peace talks on January 28, 1973. By the end of March 1973, there were no U.S. troops left in Southeast Asia. It had been the longest and least successful war in United States history.

After the peace agreement was signed, twenty-six Marines were among the hundreds of American prisoners of war to be repatriated. Only after they returned did the terrible stories of their captivity emerge. One Marine, Captain Donald Gilbert Cook, distinguished himself and demonstrated extreme courage as a prisoner of the Communists.

A military adviser in Vietnam, Cook was captured on the last day of 1964 when he was ambushed in Phuoc Tuy Province. The thirty-year-old, Brooklyn-born Marine quickly established himself as the senior prisoner—which earned him harsher treatment and more severe beatings. During his four years of captivity, Cook always put the interests of his comrades ahead his own. He took on the assigned tasks of the sick and injured, increasing his own burden while alleviating the burden of others. He provided leadership and served as an inspiration to the other prisoners of war. Cook refused to cooperate in any way with his sadistic masters, and finally died of malnutrition, mistreatment, and malaria on December 8, 1967. On May 16, 1980, President Jimmy Carter presented a posthumous Medal of Honor to Cook's widow.

FINAL SPASMS

After the United States pulled out of Vietnam, the end came quickly. Almost twenty-one years to the day after the French defeat at Dien Bien Phu and three years after the last combat Marine was withdrawn, South Vietnam fell to the Communists.

There would be no divided nation as there was on the Korean Peninsula. Vietnam became a Communist country. Over $5 billion of weapons and equipment left behind to help the ARVN defeat their foe was not enough.

Two Marines were killed in action in the final days before the fall of South Vietnam. Lance Corporal Darwin J. Judge and Corporal Charles McMahon, Jr.—both security guards at the United States embassy in Saigon—were killed in a rocket attack on Tan Son Nhut Airport as the South Vietnamese capital was being bombarded prior to invasion. Two other Marines died that same day in a helicopter accident while evacuating.

The Marines were called upon to perform one more mission in Vietnam. It was their helicopters and personnel that evacuated the refugees trapped in Saigon from the roof of the American embassy. The entire world witnessed this humiliating withdrawal, broadcast into living rooms by media mavens who could not seem to contain their glee—they had been proven right. All along, Western journalists had insisted that the war in Vietnam was unwinnable. They set out to prove it by helping the Communists emerge victorious in the propaganda war—a war waged on our television sets, on the editorial pages of newspapers, and by antiwar activists on the streets and campuses all over the United States. The Vietnam War divided America as it had not been divided since the Civil War. Half the country saw America's vital interests threatened; the other half saw the war as futile and immoral. There was no common ground between these two opinions and the nation tore itself apart.

In Vietnam, the Marines were practicing the kind of warfare they had learned in the Philippines, in the Caribbean, in Haiti, and in Central America. But it was a different world now. The "bandits" in Vietnam weren't a bunch of ill-trained and poorly organized guerrilla fighters—they were highly trained and highly motivated Communist insurgents drilled in terrorist tactics and armed by a hostile foreign power. It was a proxy war—the United States and the Soviet Union going at it through their Third World surrogates. In truth, Vietnam was two wars, one a guerrilla war fought with counterinsurgency tactics, the other a full-fledged ground war against a well-equipped and organized army.

The Marines had been the first to fight in Vietnam. It was probably the ugliest war they were ever asked to wage, a war against civilians as well as armies. In Vietnam, Marines killed and maimed civilians, tortured prisoners, and burned homes. They also provided protection and medical care to the Vietnamese people and built schools and public works and civic projects in their areas of control. The mistakes in Vietnam were made by the politicians back home. The American troops were asked to support a government that—though supposedly an ally—was just as corrupt, untrustworthy, and brutal as the enemy they fought.

Vietnam was a war the Marines could not win.

CHAPTER FOURTEEN

THE FEW, THE PROUD

∎

W E are pulling our heads out of the jungle and getting back into the amphibious business," Commandant General Robert Cushman announced in 1972, two years after the last Marine left Vietnam. The Marines had taken on a role they were not suited for and became a second land army, while at the same time eschewing the amphibious skills that made the Corps special. It was time for the Marines to again establish themselves as the world's premier amphibious force. This much-needed change was ushered in by two strong-willed commandants—Louis Wilson and Robert Barrow—who were determined to return the Corps to its traditional roots. The shake-up began in the mid-1970s as draftees were culled from the ranks and the Marine Corps returned to the tough, stringent recruiting standards of the past. The Marine Corps pushed for an all-volunteer force that stressed discipline and honor over selfishness and permissiveness, a change that set it apart from mainstream American culture and the indulgent social climate of the time.

Though no Marine received the Medal of Honor for action after the Vietnam War, the Marine Corps has not been idle. In the 1970s and 1980s, they responded to critical situations all over the globe. Their first post-Vietnam mission came in the Middle East, when Marines were dispatched to Lebanon during the October War of 1973. Marines also participated in the ill-fated mission to rescue Americans captured aboard the *Mayaguez* and held hostage by the Cambodian government. A joint services operation, this raid was a disaster that cost more than fifty Americans their lives. History would repeat itself seven years later with Operation Eagle—the calamitous, failed operation meant to free the American hostages held in Teheran. Both of these raids were doomed in part because they was micromanaged by politicians and career diplomats.

To counter this negative trend, the Corps added new weapons and vehicles to its arsenal while developing new special operations training programs to respond to crises involving hostage rescue, embassy evacuation, and terrorist threats. But political interference continued. Too often Marines were forced to operate under restrictive rules of engagement that prevented them from utilizing their formidable fighting skills. Such was the case on October 23, 1983, when a suicidal terrorist drove a truck packed with explosives into the lobby of the four-story structure that housed the First Battalion, Eighth Marines, in Lebanon. The blast killed 241 of the 300 Marines sleeping inside—more casualties than the siege of Khe Sanh or the invasion of Eniwetok. After this attack, American forces withdrew from Lebanon.

Things went better when the Marines were dispatched to the island of Grenada where American medical students were threatened by a newly installed Marxist government. The Marines made multiple amphibious landings, moved inland, rescued the hostages, and engaged hard-core Cuban regulars in a fierce battle from which the Leathernecks emerged victorious. Grenada was the first decisive victory by an American force since Vietnam, though the American people were slow to notice. Grenada was followed by the joint services operation in Panama to capture Panamanian dictator Manuel Noriega, a fugitive from American justice. The successful outcome of this operation added to the Marine Corps' luster in the 1980s, though the scars from the Vietnam War were far from healed.

On the day after Christmas 1991, the Cold War against communism ended when the Soviet Union dissolved and its military disintegrated. For fifty years the Marine Corps had faced the Soviet threat—usually through proxy enemies such as the North Koreans and the North Vietnamese. Marines had killed, bled, and died battling Soviet surrogates in Southeast Asia and on the Korean Peninsula. Suddenly, without a shot being fired at a Russian soldier, the prolonged, undeclared Cold War was over. Not so the mission of the Marine Corps. On August 2, 1990, Iraqi dictator Saddam Hussein—once an ally of the United States—sent his formidable army across the border to seize the sovereign nation of Kuwait and one-fourth of the oil fields in the world. Within hours, Saddam's Republican Guard was in control of Kuwait while a large Iraqi tank force was poised to enter Saudi Arabia. President George Bush, supported by British Prime Minister Margaret Thatcher, formed a thirty-seven-nation coalition to drive the Iraqis out of Kuwait. Once again, it was the United States Marine Corps who led the charge. While a Marine Corps expeditionary brigade deployed to America's East Coast to conduct a traditional amphibious operation, two battalions marched into transport aircraft and flew directly into the combat zone, landing in Saudi Arabia to form an instant bulwark against further Iraqi aggression. Other U.S. forces arrived days and weeks later—on the Marines' coattails.

By the end of the buildup and the commencement of hostilities, Operation Desert Storm became the largest single combat operation in the history of the Marine Corps. Ninety-two thousand Leathernecks, men and women, took part under the command of Marine Lieutenant General Walter Boomer. This time the military entered the fray with the assurance that their commander in chief would not micromanage the campaign. In the words of Joint Chiefs chairman, Army General Colin Powell, President Bush's job was to "set a clear political objective, provide sufficient forces to do the job, then keep out of the way."

When the order was given to begin air attacks, Marine Corps aviators and heli-copter pilots went into action alongside pilots from the other services. On February 24, 1992, the ground war to liberate Kuwait began. Once again, the Marines led the way when the First Marine Division surged across a heavily fortified Iraqi defensive perimeter dubbed the Berm. Many military experts deemed this line impenetrable and discussed ways in which the Marines could circumvent it. But when the shooting started, the Marines advanced right through the center of the Berm—wiping out land mines, concrete barriers, and tank traps. They did it with artillery, tanks, bulldozers, and thousands of grunts charging through the enemy's defenses.

After the Berm was breached, Marine air support worked flawlessly, with Harri-ers stacked up in the skies overhead waiting to swoop down in response to a "quick-fire" call from any Marine Corps unit that found itself in trouble. Though the weather was bad and the smoke from burning oil wells made visibility worse, Marine aviators performed miracles—losing only four of their numbers to Iraqi shoulder-fired anti-aircraft missiles during the four-day battle.

In the face of the Marine Corps ground assault, the Iraqi defenses crumbled. By nightfall of that first day, every Marine Corps objective had been met and surpassed and over 16,000 Iraqi prisoners had been captured—at a cost of only three Marines killed and seventeen wounded. "I can't say enough about the two Marine divisions," Army General Norman Schwarzkopf stated in a press conference. "If I used words like brilliant, it would really be an under-description of the absolutely superb job that they did in breaching the so-called impenetrable barrier."

On the second day of fighting, an Iraqi tank column moved to block the Marines. In what later became known as "The Reveille Counterattack," the First Battalion, Eighth Marines, intercepted the Iraqis and left thirty-nine of their armored vehicles and tanks burning in the desert. Meanwhile, units of the First Marine Division met Iraqi armor as it emerged from the Burquan Oil Field, resulting in the largest Marine tank battle in history. By the end of the third day of the ground war, the Iraqis inside of Kuwait had been crushed. As the enemy retreated along the highway to Basra, Marine aircraft exacted a terrible toll. Thousands of Iraqis died in the carnage along "The Highway to Hell," while thousands more abandoned their vehicles and fled across the burning sands to escape the rampaging American warplanes.

In Kuwait City, after the Kuwaiti and Arab forces had liberated the main urban area, a Marine Corps recon team moved to the United States embassy and found the flag still flying. They hauled it down and replaced it with a larger Stars and Stripes—a flag that had last flown over Vietnam. With this simple act the Marines healed the wounds left by the divisive Vietnam conflict once and for all.

When President George Bush declared a cease-fire exactly 100 hours after the start of the ground war, Saddam Hussein's forces had been decimated. During Oper-ation Desert Storm, the Marines lost only five killed and fifty injured. They had destroyed 1,040 Iraqi tanks, 608 armored personnel carriers, 432 artillery pieces, and at least 5 missile sites. The Marines themselves eliminated 1,500 Iraqi troops and captured 20,000 prisoners of war. Over the course of this war, five Marine Corps avi-ators had been captured. After a short period of imprisonment, they were released.

For the first time since the Second World War, the American people greeted their returning veterans with cheers and accolades instead of indifference and disdain. Units of all the military services, along with their proud commanders, marched triumphantly through the streets of Washington, D.C., and were honored with a ticker-tape parade down Wall Street. The specter of the defeat in Vietnam had finally been banished from the American psyche.

Since Desert Storm, Marines have been deployed to fight famine in Somalia and restore order in Haiti. More trouble spots await. One thing that all Marines can be sure of—at some point they will be asked to leave their homes and families and sail off to a faraway hot spot. Once there, they will be expected to fight and perhaps to die for their country. This they will do, to the best of their abilities and without complaint, upholding the finest traditions of honor, courage, and resourcefulness that began in the Marine Corps before our nation was born.

To all of the Marines that have gone before and to Marines who have yet been born, we honor their sacrifices with the poignant lyrics to "Taps":

Day is done,
Gone the sun,
From the lakes from the hills from the sky,
All is well, safely rest, God is nigh.

Fading light,
Dims the sight,
And a star gems the sky gleaming bright,
From afar, drawing nigh, falls the night.

Thanks and praise,
For our days,
'Neath the sun, 'neath the stars, 'neath the sky,
As we go, this we know, God is nigh.

INDEX

■

Page numbers in italics indicate photographs.